W9-BYO-506

Rick Steves'

ITALY
2004

AUSTRIA

San Candido

• Cortina

Klagenfurt

Tarvisio

DOLOMITES

• Calalzo

Bled

Lake Bohinj

Lake Bled

Brnik Airport ✈

FRIULI

• Udine

Ljubljana ✈

SLOVENIA

• Palmanova

Aquileia ■

I Postojna Caves •

Postojna Caves

• Asolo

• Treviso

VENETO

Grado • Lipica

Skocjan Caves ■

Trieste

Piran •

Marco Polo ✈

Padua

Venice

Pazin

Rijeka •

• Chioggia

ISTRIA

KRK

Po

Ferrara

CRES

RAB

Pula •

BOSNIA & HERZ.

CROATIA

Ravenna

Zadar •

Rimini

Pesaro

DUGI OTOK

SAN MARINO

San Leo •

Rubicon

Urbino

Falconara

Sibenik •

Split ✈

Trogir •

Sansepolcro •

LE MARCHE

Ancona

BRAC

Arezzo

• Gubbio

Macerata

HVAR

• Cortona

L. Trasimeno

Assisi

Monte- pulciano •

Perugia

• Spello

to Dubrovnik, Croatia

• Pienza

Deruta

Chiusi •

Bevagna •

Montefalco •

UMBRIA

Ascoli Piceno •

Orvieto •

Todi •

Spoleto •

Pitigliano •

Bagnoregio & Civita •

Mt. Gran Sasso

to Patras, Greece

Lago di Bolsena

• Viterbo

Terni

Rieti •

Pescara

Tarquinia •

Orte •

Tiber

• L'Aquila

ABRUZZO

Chieti •

• Termoli

LATIO

Cerveteri •

Tivoli •

Hadrian's Villa •

ABRUZZO NAT'L PARK

GARGANO PENINSULA

VATICAN CITY

Rome

Fiumicino ✈

Ostia Antica •

Ciampino ✈

Isernia •

MOLISE

Manfredonia

Campobasso •

Foggia •

Anzio •

Latina •

Montecassino ■

PUGLIA

Formia •

Caserta •

CAMPANIA

BASI

Tyrrhenian Sea

PONZA

Naples • Mt. Vesuvius

Herculaneum • Pompeii •

Potenza •

ISCHIA

Positano •

Sorrento •

Amalfi •

CAPRI

AMALFI COAST

Paestum •

to Sicily

Adriatic Sea

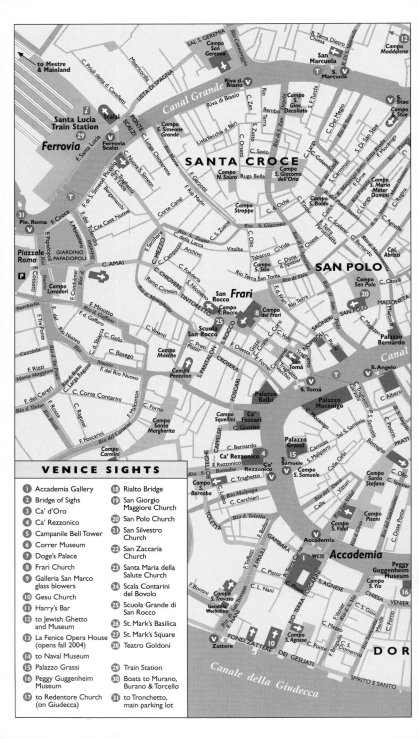

VENICE SIGHTS

1. Accademia Gallery
2. Bridge of Sighs
3. Ca' d'Oro
4. Ca' Rezzonico
5. Campanile Bell Tower
6. Correr Museum
7. Doge's Palace
8. Frari Church
9. Galleria San Marco glass blowers
10. Gesu Church
11. Harry's Bar
12. to Jewish Ghetto and Museum
13. La Fenice Opera House (opens fall 2004)
14. to Naval Museum
15. Palazzo Grassi
16. Peggy Guggenheim Museum
17. to Redentore Church (on Giudecca)
18. Rialto Bridge
19. San Giorgio Maggiore Church
20. San Polo Church
21. San Silvestro Church
22. San Zaccaria Church
23. Santa Maria della Salute Church
24. Scala Contarini del Bovolo
25. Scuola Grande di San Rocco
26. St. Mark's Basilica
27. St. Mark's Square
28. Teatro Goldoni
29. Train Station
30. Boats to Murano, Burano & Torcello
31. to Tronchetto, main parking lot

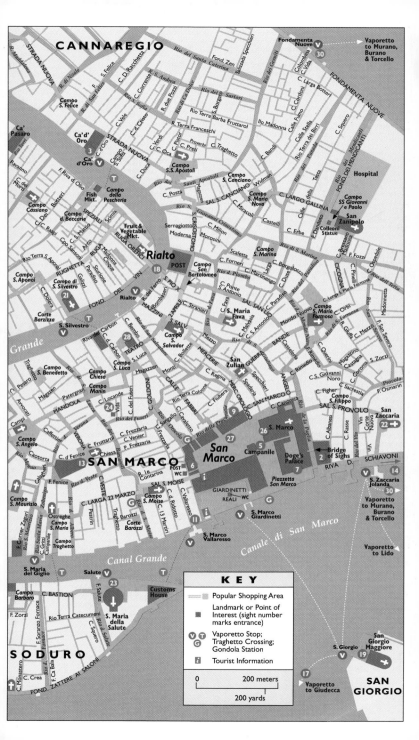

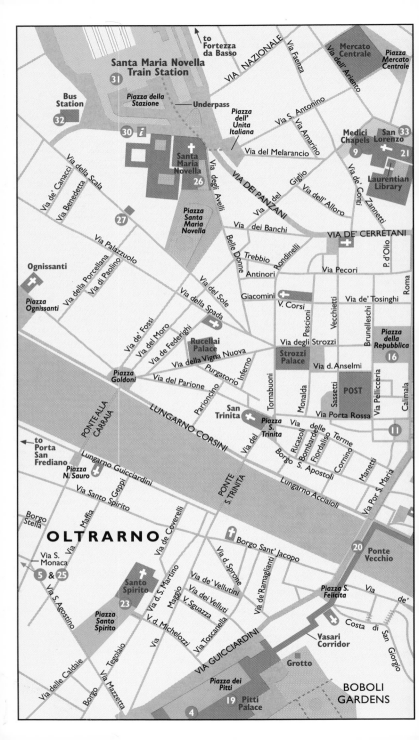

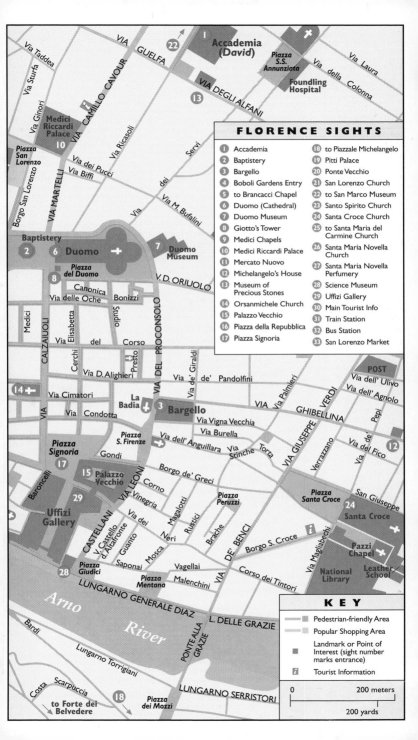

FLORENCE SIGHTS

1. Accademia
2. Baptistery
3. Bargello
4. Boboli Gardens Entry
5. to Brancacci Chapel
6. Duomo (Cathedral)
7. Duomo Museum
8. Giotto's Tower
9. Medici Chapels
10. Medici Riccardi Palace
11. Mercato Nuovo
12. Michelangelo's House
13. Museum of Precious Stones
14. Orsanmichele Church
15. Palazzo Vecchio
16. Piazza della Repubblica
17. Piazza Signoria

18. to Piazzale Michelangelo
19. Pitti Palace
20. Ponte Vecchio
21. San Lorenzo Church
22. to San Marco Museum
23. Santo Spirito Church
24. Santa Croce Church
25. to Santa Maria del Carmine Church
26. Santa Maria Novella Church
27. Santa Maria Novella Perfumery
28. Science Museum
29. Uffizi Gallery
30. Main Tourist Info
31. Train Station
32. Bus Station
33. San Lorenzo Market

KEY

- Pedestrian-friendly Area
- Popular Shopping Area
- Landmark or Point of Interest (sight number marks entrance)
- 𝒊 Tourist Information

0   200 meters

200 yards

TUSCANY

═A24═	Freeway	S68	Major Road
───	Major Rail Line	✈	Airport
Siena	Recommended location*		
Livorno	Just passing through**		
■	Ruin, Museum, other Point of Interest		

* Cities with names in black are of touristic interest.
Many shown in Tuscany are covered in this book.

** Cities with names in gray are of no touristic interest.

Marco Polo ✈
Mestre
Venice
Padua
Chioggia
VENETO
Po

Adriatic
Sea

Parma
Modena
Reggio Emilia
A13
EMILIA
ROMAGNA
Bologna
A14
Imola
ITALY
Faenza
E45
Ravenna
Cesena
Rimini
APUAN ALPS
A15
CINQUE TERRE
La Spezia
SAN MARINO
Rubicon
San Leo
S423
Porto-venere
Carrara
Massa
Montecatini
Pistoia
Vespucci ✈
Fiesole
Urbino
S36
LE MARCHE
Lucca
A12
A11
Vinci
Florence
Sansepolcro
Viareggio
Pisa
Empoli
Arno
U.S. Cemetery ■
Galileo ✈
Poggibonsi
CHIANTI
Gubbio
Livorno
S1
San Gimignano
S222
A1
Arezzo
E45
UMBRIA
Volterra
Monte-riggioni
Siena
Teron-tola
Cortona
S68
Cecina
S73
L. Trasimeno
Perugia
Assisi
TUSCANY
Monte Oliveto Maggiore
Monte-pulciano
Deruta
San Galgano ■
Montalcino
Pienza
S146
Chiusi
Bevagna
VIA AURELIA
Piombino
S2
A1
Todi
to Corsica and Sardinia
ELBA **Portoferraio**
Grosseto
Orvieto
Baschi
CAPRAIA
Pitigliano
Lago di Bolsena
Bagnoregio & Civita
MAREMMA
Viterbo
Orte
Tiber
MONTE ARGENTARIO
S1
Tarquinia
S2
VIA CASSIA
GIGLIO
LAZIO
Civitavecchia
Cerveteri
A12
Roma
VATICAN CITY
Leonardo da Vinci ✈
Ostia Antica
Ciampino
Mediterranean Sea
to Sardinia

N

0 km	50 km
0 miles	50 miles

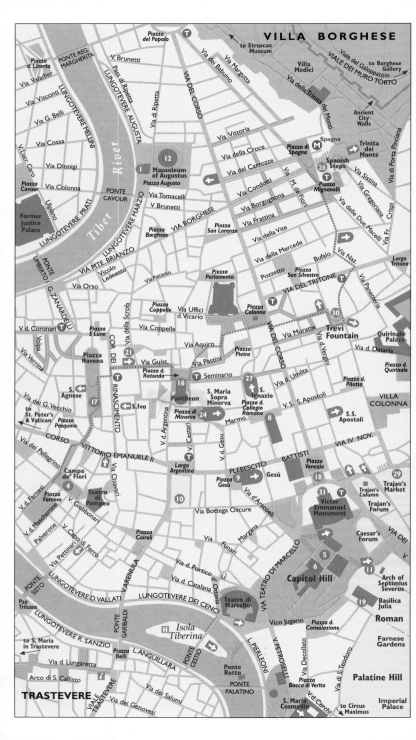

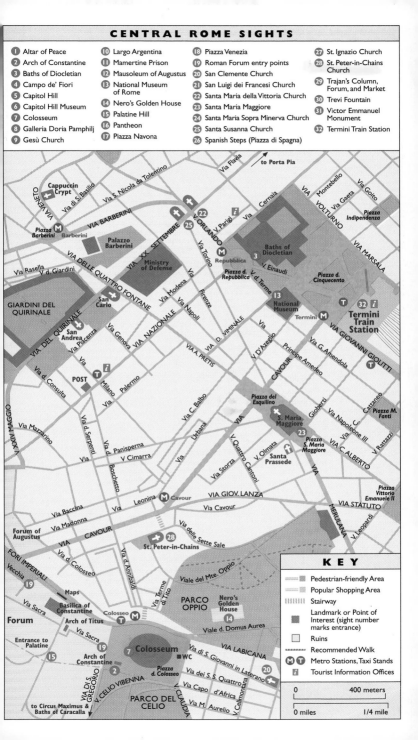

CENTRAL ROME SIGHTS

1. Altar of Peace
2. Arch of Constantine
3. Baths of Diocletian
4. Campo de' Fiori
5. Capitol Hill
6. Capitol Hill Museum
7. Colosseum
8. Galleria Doria Pamphilj
9. Gesù Church
10. Largo Argentina
11. Mamertine Prison
12. Mausoleum of Augustus
13. National Museum of Rome
14. Nero's Golden House
15. Palatine Hill
16. Pantheon
17. Piazza Navona
18. Piazza Venezia
19. Roman Forum entry points
20. San Clemente Church
21. San Luigi dei Francesi Church
22. Santa Maria della Vittoria Church
23. Santa Maria Maggiore
24. Santa Maria Sopra Minerva Church
25. Santa Susanna Church
26. Spanish Steps (Piazza di Spagna)
27. St. Ignazio Church
28. St. Peter-in-Chains Church
29. Trajan's Column, Forum, and Market
30. Trevi Fountain
31. Victor Emmanuel Monument
32. Termini Train Station

KEY

- Pedestrian-friendly Area
- Popular Shopping Area
- Stairway
- Landmark or Point of Interest (sight number marks entrance)
- Ruins
- Recommended Walk
- Ⓜ Ⓣ Metro Stations, Taxi Stands
- 𝒊 Tourist Information Offices

0   400 meters

0 miles   1/4 mile

Rick Steves'
ITALY
2004

by Rick Steves

AVALON
TRAVEL

For a complete list of Rick Steves' guidebooks, see page 12.

Avalon Travel Publishing
1400 65th Street, Suite 250
Emeryville, CA 94608
Avalon Travel Publishing is a division of Avalon Publishing Group, Inc.

Printed in the USA by Worzalla. First printing November 2003.
Distributed by Publishers Group West.

ISBN 1-56691-533-3
ISSN 1084-4422

For the latest on Rick's lectures, guidebooks, tours, and public television series, contact Europe Through the Back Door, Box 2009, Edmonds, WA 98020, 425/771-8303, fax 425/771-0833, www.ricksteves.com, or e-mail: rick@ricksteves.com.

Europe Through the Back Door Managing Editor: Risa Laib
Europe Through the Back Door Editors: Cameron Hewitt, Jill Hodges
Avalon Travel Publishing Series Manager: Laura Mazer
Research Assistance: Heidi Sewell, Sarah Murdoch
Production Coordinator: Jacob Goolkasian
Cover Design: Kari Gim, Laura Mazer
Interior Design: Jane Musser, Laura Mazer, Amber Pirker
Maps & Graphics: David C. Hoerlein, Rhonda Pelikan, Zoey Platt, Mike Morgenfeld
Front Cover Photos: House facade in Tuscany © Russel Mountford,
Jernazza harbor © Dominic Bonuccelli
Front Matter Color Photos: p. i, Tuscan vineyards © Mary Liz Austin; p. iv, Trevi
Fountain, Rome © Richard T. Nowitz; p. xii, Val d'Orcia hills © Terry Donnelly
Avalon Travel Publishing Graphics Coordinator: Justin Marler

CONTENTS

INTRODUCTION 1

ITALY 38

Venice 40

Sights Near Venice 94
> Padua 94 • Vicenza 105 • Verona 112 •
> Ravenna 122

The Dolomites 129

Lake Como 145

Milan 162
> Stresa 194

The Cinque Terre 201
> Vernazza 207 • Riomaggiore 209 •
> Manarola 223 • Corniglia 226 •
> Monterosso al Mare 228

Riviera Sights near Cinque Terre 236
> Levanto 236 • Sestri Levante 240 •
> Santa Margherita Ligure 242

Florence 254

Sights Near Florence 295
> Pisa 295 • Lucca 304

Siena 313

Assisi 333

Hill Towns of Central Italy 352
> San Gimignano 355 • Volterra 359 •
> Montalcino 361 • Montepulciano 363 •
> Pienza 365 • Cortona 367• Urbino 371•
> Orvieto 378 • Civita di Bagnoregio 387•
> More Hill Towns and Sights 393

Rome 397

Naples and the Amalfi Coast 482
> Naples 483 • Sorrento 498 • The Amalfi
> Coast 509 • Positano 511 • Amalfi and
> Atrani 515 • Capri 516 • Pompeii,
> Herculaneum, and Vesuvius 519 •
> Paestum 526

HISTORY 532

APPENDIX 543

INDEX 553

Top Destinations in Italy

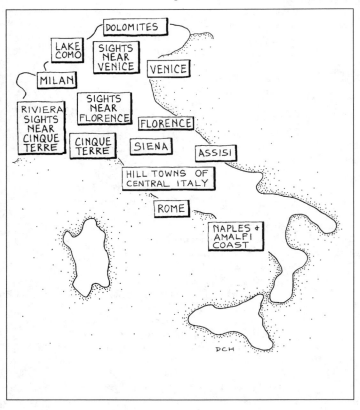

INTRODUCTION

This book breaks Italy into its top big-city, small-town, and rural destinations. It then gives you all the information and opinions necessary to wring the maximum value out of your limited time and money in each of these destinations.

If you plan a month or less in Italy and have a normal appetite for information, this lean and mean little book is all you need. If you're a travel info fiend (like me), you'll find this book sorts through all the superlatives and provides a handy rack upon which to hang your supplemental information.

Italy is my favorite country. Experiencing its culture, people, and natural wonders economically and hassle-free has been my goal for over 25 years of traveling, researching, and tour guiding. With this book, I pass on to you the lessons I've learned, updated (in mid-2003) for 2004.

Rick Steves' Italy is a tour guide in your pocket, offering a comfortable mix of big cities and cozy towns, from brutal but *bello* Rome to *tranquillo*, traffic-free Riviera villages. It covers the predictable biggies and adds a healthy dose of "Back Door" intimacy. Along with marveling at Michelangelo's masterpieces, you'll enjoy a *bruschetta* snack as a village boy rubs fresh garlic on your toast. I've been selective, including only the top sights. For example, after visiting many hill towns, I recommend just the best.

The best is, of course, only my opinion. But after more than two busy decades of travel writing, lecturing, and tour guiding, I've developed a sixth sense for what travelers enjoy.

This Information Is Accurate and Up-to-Date

This book is updated every year. Most publishers of guidebooks that cover a country from top to bottom can afford an update only every two or three years, and rarely is the research done in person. Since this book is selective, I'm able to personally update it each summer. Even with an annual update, things change. But if you're traveling with the current edition of this book, I guarantee you're using the most up-to-date information available in print. For the latest, see www.ricksteves.com/update. Also at my Web site, check my Graffiti Wall (select "Rick Steves' Guidebooks," then "Italy") for a huge, valuable list of reports and experiences—good and bad—from fellow travelers.

Use this year's edition. People who try to save a few bucks by traveling with an old book are not smart. They learn the seriousness of their mistake...in Italy. Your trip costs about $10 per waking hour. Your time is valuable. This guidebook saves lots of time.

Planning Your Trip

This book is organized by destinations. Each destination is a mini-vacation on its own, filled with exciting sights and comfortable, good-value places to stay. In the following chapters, you'll find:

Planning Your Time, a suggested schedule with thoughts on how best to use your limited time.

Orientation, including tourist information, city transportation, and an easy-to-read map designed to make the text clear and your arrival smooth.

Sights with ratings: ▲▲▲—Don't miss; ▲▲—Try hard to see; ▲—Worthwhile if you can make it; no rating—Worth knowing about.

Sleeping and **Eating,** with addresses and phone numbers of my favorite hotels and restaurants.

Transportation Connections to nearby destinations by train, and route tips for drivers.

The **appendix** is a traveler's tool kit, with telephone tips, a climate chart, events calendar, and survival phrases.

Browse through this book, choose your favorite destinations, and link them up. Then have a great trip! You'll travel like a temporary local, getting the absolute most out of every mile, minute, and dollar. You won't waste time on mediocre sights because, unlike other guidebook authors, I cover only the best. Since your major financial pitfalls are lousy, expensive hotels, I've worked hard to assemble the best accommodations values for each stop. And as you travel the route that I know and love, I'm happy you'll be meeting some of my favorite Italian people.

Trip Costs

Six components make up your trip cost: airfare, surface transportation, room and board, sightseeing/entertainment, shopping/miscellany, and gelato.

Airfare: Don't try to sort through the mess. Find and use a good travel agent. A basic round-trip U.S.A.-to-Milan (or Rome) flight should cost $700 to $1,000, depending on where you fly from and when (cheapest in winter). Always consider saving time and money in Europe by flying "open jaw" (into one city and out of another).

Surface Transportation: For a three-week whirlwind trip to all my recommended destinations, allow $300 per person for public transportation (train and buses) or $500 per person (based on 2 people sharing a car) for a three-week car rental, tolls, gas, and insurance. Car rental is cheapest if arranged from the United States. Some train passes are available only outside of Europe. You might save money by getting an Italian railpass or buying tickets as you go (see "Transportation," page 15).

Room and Board: You can thrive in Italy on $90 a day for room and board. This $90/day budget allows $10 for lunch, $20 for dinner, and $60 for lodging (based on 2 people splitting the cost of an $120 double room that includes breakfast). If you've got more money, I've listed great ways to spend it. And students and tightwads can enjoy Italy for as little as $50 a day ($20 for a bed, $30 for meals and snacks). But budget sleeping and eating require the skills covered later in this chapter (and in more depth in my book *Rick Steves' Europe Through the Back Door*).

Sightseeing and Entertainment: In big cities, figure about $5 to $8 per major sight (museums, Colosseum), $3 for minor ones (climbing church towers), and $25 to $30 per person for splurge experiences (such as tours and gondola rides). An overall average of $15 a day works for most. Don't skimp here. After all, this category directly powers most of the experiences that all of the other expenses are designed to make possible.

Shopping and Miscellany: Figure $1 per postcard, coffee, and soft drink and $2 per gelato. Shopping can vary in cost from nearly nothing to a small fortune. Good budget travelers find that this category has little to do with assembling a trip full of lifelong and wonderful memories.

Exchange Rate
I've priced things throughout this book in euros.

```
1 euro (€) = about $1.10
```

Just like the dollar, the euro is broken down into 100 cents. You'll find coins ranging from 1 cent to 2 euros, and bills from 5 euros to 500 euros. To roughly convert prices in euros to dollars, add 10 percent to Italian prices: €20 is about $22, €45 is about $50, and so on.

Prices, Times, and Discounts
The opening hours and telephone numbers listed in this book are accurate as of mid-2003—but once you pin Italy down, it wiggles. At each major destination, ask the local tourist information office for a current list of the city's sights, hours, and prices. Any guidebook on Italy starts to yellow even before it's printed.

In Italy—and in this book—you'll use the 24-hour clock. It's the same through 12:00 noon, then keep going—13:00, 14:00, and so on. For anything over 12, subtract 12 and add p.m. (14:00 is 2:00 p.m.).

Don't expect discounts on sights in Italy if you're a youth or senior. Discounts are generally available only to people who are members of the European Union and "reciprocating countries," meaning countries that offer discounts to European youth and seniors—which the U.S. doesn't.

When to Go

Italy's best travel months are May, June, September, and October. November and April usually have pleasant weather, with generally none of the sweat and stress of the tourist season. Off-season, expect shorter hours, more lunchtime breaks, and fewer activities.

Peak season offers the longest hours and the most exciting slate of activities—but terrible crowds and, at times, suffocating heat. During peak times, many resort-area hotels maximize business by requiring that guests take half-pension, which means buying dinner in their restaurants. August, the local holiday month, isn't as bad as many make it out to be, but big cities tend to be quiet (with discounted hotel prices), and beach and mountain resorts are jammed (with higher hotel prices). If you anticipate crowds, arrive early in the day or call hotels in advance (call from one hotel to the next; your fluent-in-Italian receptionist can help you).

Summer temperatures range from the 70s and 80s in Milan to the high 80s and 90s in Rome. Air-conditioning, when available, usually doesn't kick in until June 1 and shuts off September 30. Most mid-range hotels come with air-conditioning—a worthwhile splurge in the summer. Spring and fall can be cold, and many hotels do not turn on their heat until October 1. In the winter, it often drops to the 40s in Milan and the 50s in Rome. (See climate chart in the appendix.)

Sightseeing Priorities

Depending on the length of your trip, here are my recommended priorities:

4 days:	Florence, Venice
6 days, add:	Rome
8 days, add:	Cinque Terre
10 days, add:	Civita and Siena
14 days, add:	Sorrento, Naples, Pompeii, Amalfi, Paestum
18 days, add:	Milan, Lake Como, Varenna, Assisi
21 days, add:	Dolomites, Verona, Ravenna

(This includes everything on the "Italy's Best Three-Week Trip" map on page 7.)

Considering that you're likely to go both broke and crazy driving in Italian cities, and how handy and affordable Italy's trains and buses are, I'd do most of Italy by public transportation. If you want to drive, consider doing the big, intense stuff (Rome, Naples area, Milan, Florence, and Venice) by train or bus and renting a car for the hill towns of Tuscany and Umbria and for the Dolomites. A car is a worthless headache on the Riviera and in the Lake Como area.

Red Tape and Business Hours
You need a passport but no visa or shots to travel in Italy.

Business Hours: Traditionally, Italy uses the siesta plan. People usually work from about 8:00 to 13:00 and from 15:30 to 19:00, Monday through Saturday. Nowadays, however, many businesses have adopted the government's new recommended 8:00 to 14:00 workday. In tourist areas, shops are open longer.

Watt's up? If you're bringing electrical gear, you'll need a two-prong adapter plug (sold cheap at travel stores like mine, www.ricksteves.com) and a converter. Travel appliances often have convenient, built-in converters; look for a voltage switch marked 120 (U.S.) and 240 (Europe).

Banking
You'll want to spend local hard cash. The fastest way to get it is by using plastic: your ATM, credit, or debit card at a cash machine (Bancomat). To withdraw cash, you'll need to use your PIN code (numbers only, no letters) with your bank card. Before you go, verify with your bank that your card will work and alert them that you'll be making withdrawals in Europe; otherwise, the bank may not approve transactions if it perceives unusual spending patterns.

Cards with Visa and MasterCard logos are more commonly accepted than American Express. Bring two cards in case one is demagnetized, eaten by a machine, or rejected by a temperamental ATM. (If your card is rejected, try again, and request a smaller amount; some cash machines won't let you take out more than about €150—don't take it personally. If the card still doesn't work, try a different bank's machine.) Just as at home, credit or debit cards work easily at larger hotels, restaurants, and shops, but smaller businesses prefer payment in hard cash.

If you bring traveler's checks, use them only as a backup. Even if issued in euros, travelers' checks are not spendable like cash. Regular banks have the best rates for cashing traveler's checks. For a large exchange, it pays to compare rates and fees (Bank of Sicily consistently has good rates). Banking hours are generally 8:30 to 13:30 and 15:30 to 16:30 Monday through Friday, but can vary wildly. Banks are slow; simple transactions can take 15 to 30 minutes. Post offices (also slow) and train stations (probably faster) usually change money if you can't get to a bank.

Use a money belt. Thieves target tourists. A money belt (order online at www.ricksteves.com or call 425/771-8303 for my free newsletter/catalog) provides peace of mind and allows you to carry lots of cash safely.

Don't be petty about taking out money. You'll pay fees (and waste

ITALY'S BEST THREE-WEEK TRIP (BY CAR)

Day	Plan	Sleep in
1	Arrive in Milan	Milan
2	Milan to Lake Como	Varenna
3	Lake Como	Varenna
4	To Dolomites via Verona (pick up car in Varenna)	Castelrotto
5	Dolomites	Castelrotto
6	To Venice	Venice
7	Venice	Venice
8	To Florence	Florence
9	Florence	Florence
10	To Cinque Terre	Vernazza
11	Cinque Terre	Vernazza
12	To Siena	Siena
13	Siena	Siena
14	To Orvieto	Orvieto
15	Orvieto	Orvieto
16	To Sorrento via Pompeii	Sorrento
17	Sorrento	Sorrento
18	To Paestum	Sorrento
19	To Rome, drop car	Rome
20	Rome	Rome
21	Rome	Rome
22	Rome, fly home	

Modifications for train travelers: This trip is designed to be done by car, but works fine by rail with a few modifications. An Italy Rail Card (8 days in 1 month) can work well—pay out of pocket for short runs, such as Milan to Varenna, or the hops between villages in the Cinque Terre. Consider basing yourself in Bolzano in the Dolomites. From Venice, go directly to the Cinque Terre, then do Florence and Siena. A car is efficient in the hill towns of Tuscany and Umbria, but a headache elsewhere. Sorrento is a good home base for Naples and the Amalfi Coast. Skip Paestum unless you love Greek ruins. To save Venice for last, start in Milan, seeing everything but Venice on the way south, then sleeping through everything you've already seen by catching the night train from Naples or Rome to Venice. This saves you a day and gives you an early arrival in Venice.

Italy's Best Three-Week Trip

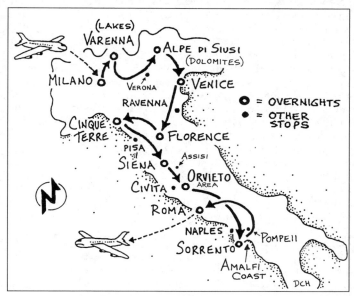

valuable sightseeing time) each time you have to return to an ATM or bank. Withdraw a week's worth of money, get big bills, stuff them in your money belt, and travel!

VAT Refunds and Customs Regulations

VAT Refunds for Shoppers: Wrapped into the purchase price of your Italian souvenirs is a Value Added Tax (VAT) that's generally about 16.7 percent. If you purchase more than €155 worth of goods at a store that participates in the VAT refund scheme, you're entitled to get most of that tax back. Personally, I've never felt that VAT refunds are worth the hassle, but if you do, here's the scoop.

If you're lucky, the merchant will subtract the tax when you make your purchase (this is more likely to occur if the store ships the goods to your home). Otherwise, you'll need to do this:

Get the paperwork. Have the merchant completely fill out the necessary refund document, called a "cheque." You'll have to present your passport at the store.

Have your cheque(s) stamped at the border at your last stop in the European Union by the customs agent who deals with VAT refunds. It's best to keep your purchases in your carry-on for viewing, but if they're too large or dangerous (such as knives) to carry on, then track down the proper customs agent to inspect them before you check your bag. You're not supposed to use your purchased goods before you leave. If you show up at customs wearing your new shoes, officials might look the other way—or deny you a refund.

To collect your refund, you'll need to return your stamped documents to the retailer or its representative. Many merchants work with a service, such as Global Refund or Cashback, which have offices at major airports, ports, or border crossings. These services, which extract a 4 percent fee, can refund your money immediately in your currency of choice or credit your card (within two billing cycles). If you have to deal directly with the retailer, mail the store your stamped documents and then wait. It could take months.

Customs Regulations: You can take home $800 in souvenirs per person duty-free. The next $1,000 is taxed at a flat 3 percent. After that, you pay the individual item's duty rate. You can also bring in duty-free a liter of alcohol (slightly more than a standard-sized bottle of wine), a carton of cigarettes, and up to 100 cigars. To check customs rules and duty rates, visit www.customs.gov.

Language Barrier

Many Italians in larger towns and the tourist trade speak at least some English. Still, you'll get more smiles and results by using at least the Italian pleasantries. In smaller, nontouristy towns, Italian is the norm. See the "Survival Phrases" near the end of this book (excerpted from *Rick Steves' Italian Phrase Book*).

Note that Italian is pronounced much like English, with a few exceptions, such as: *c* followed by *e* or *i* is pronounced *ch* (to ask, *"Per centro?"*—"To the center?"—you say, pehr CHEHN-troh). In Italian, *ch* is pronounced like the hard *c* in Pinocchio (*chiesa*—church—is pronounced kee-AY-zah). Give it your best shot. Italians appreciate your efforts.

Travel Smart

Many people travel through Italy thinking it's a chaotic mess. They feel any attempt at efficient travel is futile. This is dead wrong—and expensive. Italy, which seems as orderly as spilled spaghetti, actually functions quite well. Only those who understand this and travel smart can enjoy Italy on a budget.

Your trip to Italy is like a complex play—easier to follow and really appreciate on a second viewing. While no one does the same trip twice to gain that advantage, reading this book in its entirety before your trip accomplishes much the same thing.

Reread entire chapters as you travel, and visit local tourist information offices. Upon arrival in a new town, lay the groundwork for a smooth departure; write down the schedule for the train or bus you'll take when you depart. Buy a phone card (or mobile phone) and use it for reservations, reconfirmations, and double-checking hours. Use taxis in the big cities, bring along a water bottle, and linger in the shade. Connect with the cultures. Set up your own quest for the best gelato, sculpture, cheesy souvenir, or whatever. Enjoy the friendliness of the local people. Ask questions. Most locals are eager to point you in their idea of the right direction. Keep a notepad in your pocket for organizing your thoughts. Those who expect to travel smart, do.

Sundays have the same pros and cons as they do for travelers in the United States. Sightseeing attractions are generally open but have shorter hours, shops and banks are closed, and minor transportation connections are more frustrating (e.g., no bus service to or from Civita). City traffic is light. Rowdy evenings are rare on Sundays. Saturdays are virtually weekdays with earlier closing hours. Hotels in tourist areas are often booked up on Easter weekend, in August, and on Fridays and Saturdays year-round. Religious holidays and train strikes can catch you by surprise anywhere in Italy.

Plan ahead for banking, laundry, post-office chores, and picnics. Mix intense and relaxed periods. Every trip (and every traveler) needs at least a few slack days. Pace yourself. Assume you will return. Drink your water *con gas.*

Tourist Information

During your trip, your first stop in each town should be the tourist office (abbreviated "TI" in this book, and "i," "*turismo,*" and "APT" in Italy). While Italian TIs are about half as helpful as those in other countries, their information is twice as important. Prepare. Have a list of questions and a proposed plan to double-check. If you're arriving late, telephone ahead (and try to get a map for your next destination from a TI in the town you're departing from).

Be wary of the travel agencies or special information services that masquerade as TIs but serve fancy hotels and tour companies. They are crooks and liars selling things you don't need.

While the TI is eager to book you a room, use its room-finding service only as a last resort. Across Europe, room-finding services are charging commissions from hotels, taking fees from travelers, and blacklisting establishments that buck their materialistic rules. They are unable to give hard opinions on the relative value of one place over another. The accommodations stakes are too high to go potluck through the TI. You'll do better going direct with the listings in this book.

Italian Tourist Offices in the United States

Before your trip, contact the nearest Italian TI, briefly describe your trip, and request information. You'll get the general packet and, if you ask for specifics (individual city maps, a calendar of festivals, good hikes around Lake Como, info on wine-tasting in Umbria, and so on), an impressive

TIPS ON SIGHTSEEING IN ITALY

• Churches offer some amazing art (usually free), a cool respite from heat, and a welcome seat. A modest dress code (no bare shoulders or shorts for anyone) is enforced at larger churches, such as Venice's St. Mark's and the Vatican's St. Peter's. Some churches have coin-operated audioboxes that describe the art and history. A deposit in the coin box near a piece of art often illuminates the art (and presents a better photo opportunity). Whenever possible, let there be light.

• Reservations are advisable for some of the more famous museums (Florence: Uffizi and Accademia) and mandatory at others (Milan: Da Vinci's *Last Supper*, Padua: Scrovegni Chapel, Rome: Borghese Gallery and Nero's Golden House). The process is simple for English-speakers and generally free or nearly free.

• Hours listed anywhere can vary. On holidays, expect shorter hours or closures. In summer, some sights are open late, allowing easy viewing without crowds. Ask the local TI for a current listing of museum hours. You can confirm sightseeing plans each morning with a quick telephone call asking, "Are you open today?" (*"Aperto oggi?"*; ah-PER-toh OH-jee) and "What time do you close?" (*"A che ora chiuso?"*; ah kay OH-rah kee-OO-zoh). I've included telephone numbers for this purpose.

amount of help. If you have a specific problem, they're a good source of sympathy.

Contact the office nearest you...

In New York: 630 Fifth Ave. #1565, New York, NY 10111, tel. 212/245-5618, brochure hotline tel. 212/245-4822, fax 212/586-9249, enitny@italiantourism.com.

In Illinois: 500 N. Michigan Ave. #2240, Chicago, IL 60611, tel. 312/644-0996, brochure hotline tel. 312/644-0990, fax 312/644-3019, enitch@italiantourism.com.

In California: 12400 Wilshire Blvd. #550, Los Angeles, CA 90025, tel. 310/820-1898, brochure hotline tel. 310/820-0098, fax 310/820-6357, enitla@italiantourism.com.

Web sites: www.italiantourism.com (Italian Tourist Board in the United States), www.museionline.it (museums in Italy, in English), and www.fs-on-line.com (Italian rail schedules).

- Art historians and Italians refer to the great Florentine centuries by dropping a thousand years. The *Trecento* (300s), *Quattrocento* (400s), and *Cinquecento* (500s) were the 1300s, 1400s, and 1500s.

- In Italian museums, art is dated with *sec* for *secolo* (century, often indicated with Roman numerals), A.C. (for Avanti Cristo, or B.C.), and D.C. (for Dopo Cristo, or A.D.). O.K.?

- Audioguides are becoming increasingly common at museums. These small portable devices give you information in English on what you're seeing. After you dial a number that appears next to a particular work of art, you listen to the spiel (cutting it short if you want). Though the information can be dry, it's usually worthwhile (about €4; extra for 2 sets of headphones).

- About half the visitors at Italian museums are English (not Italian) speakers. If a museum lacks audioguides and the only English you encounter explains how to pay, politely ask if there are plans to include English descriptions of the art. Think of it as a service to those who follow.

- In museums, rooms can begin closing about 30 to 60 minutes before actual closing time. Don't save the best for last.

- WCs at museums are usually free and clean.

Rick Steves' Books, Videos, and DVDs

Rick Steves' Europe Through the Back Door 2004 gives you budget-travel skills, such as minimizing jet lag, packing light, planning your itinerary, traveling by car or train, finding rooms, changing money, avoiding rip-offs, buying mobile phones, hurdling the language barrier, staying healthy, taking great photographs, using a bidet, and much more. The book also includes chapters on 38 of my favorite "Back Doors," six of which are in Italy.

Rick Steves' Country Guides, an annually-updated series that covers Europe, offer you the latest on the top sights and destinations, with tips on how to make your trip efficient and fun. You'll learn the best places to stay, eat, enjoy, and explore.

My **City and Regional Guides**, freshly updated every year, focus on Europe's most compelling destinations. Along with specifics on sights, restaurants, hotels, and nightlife, you'll get self-guided, illustrated tours of the outstanding museums and most characteristic neighborhoods.

New for 2004, Rick Steves' *Easy Access Europe*, written for travelers with limited mobility, covers London, Paris, Bruges, Amsterdam, and the Rhine River.

Rick Steves' Europe 101: History and Art for the Traveler (with Gene Openshaw) gives you the story of Europe's people, history, and art. Written for smart people who were sleeping in their history and art classes before they knew they were going to Europe, *101* really helps resurrect the rubble.

Rick Steves' Mona Winks: Self-Guided Tours of Europe's Top Museums (with Gene Openshaw) gives you easy-to-follow, self-guided tours of Europe's top 25 museums and cultural sites. Nearly half of the book is devoted to Italy, with tours of Rome (Colosseum, Forum, Pantheon, National Museum of Rome, Borghese Gallery, Vatican Museum, and St. Peter's Basilica), Venice (St. Mark's, Doge's Palace,

RICK STEVES' GUIDEBOOKS

Country Guides
Rick Steves' Best of Europe
Rick Steves' Best of Eastern Europe
Rick Steves' France
Rick Steves' Germany, Austria & Switzerland
Rick Steves' Great Britain
Rick Steves' Ireland
Rick Steves' Italy
Rick Steves' Scandinavia
Rick Steves' Spain & Portugal

City and Regional Guides*
Rick Steves' Amsterdam, Bruges & Brussels
Rick Steves' Florence & Tuscany
Rick Steves' London
Rick Steves' Paris
Rick Steves' Provence & the French Riviera
Rick Steves' Rome
Rick Steves' Venice
Rick Steves' Easy Access Europe
    (with a focus on London, Paris, Bruges, Amsterdam, and the Rhine)

*All of Rick's city guides are co-authored by Gene Openshaw

(Avalon Travel Publishing)

and Accademia Gallery), and Florence (Uffizi Gallery, Bargello, Michelangelo's *David*, and a Renaissance walk through the town center). If you want to enjoy the great sights and museums of Italy, *Mona* will be a valued friend.

In Italy, a phrase book is as fun as it is necessary. My *Rick Steves' Italian Phrase Book* will help you meet the people and stretch your budget. It's written by a monoglot who, for more than 25 years, has fumbled through Italy struggling with all the other phrase books. Use this fun and practical communication aid to make accurate hotel reservations over the telephone, ask for a free taste of cantaloupe-flavored gelato at the *gelatería*, have the man in the deli make you a sandwich, and tell your cabbie that if he doesn't slow down, you'll throw up.

My latest television series, *Rick Steves' Europe*, features five new shows on Italy: Venice, Veneto (sights near Venice), Florence, Siena/Assisi, and the Cinque Terre. Between the new series and the earlier *Travels in Europe* series (more than 80 shows total), I've hosted and written 15 half-hour shows on Italy. These air throughout the United States on public television stations. Each episode is also available on an information-packed home video (order online at www.ricksteves.com or call 425/771-8303 for my free newsletter/catalog).

Rick Steves' Postcards from Europe, my autobiographical book, packs more than 25 years of travel anecdotes and insights into the ultimate 2,000-mile European adventure. Through my guidebooks, I share my favorite European discoveries with you. *Postcards* introduces you to my favorite European friends. Half of *Postcards* is set in Italy: Venice, Florence, Rome, and the Cinque Terre.

All of my books are published by Avalon Travel Publishing (www.travelmatters.com).

Other Guidebooks

Especially if you'll be traveling beyond my recommended destinations, you may want some supplemental information. When you consider the improvements they'll make in your $3,000 vacation, $30 for extra maps and books is money well spent. Especially for several people traveling by car, the weight and expense are negligible. One budget tip can save the price of an extra guidebook.

Lonely Planet's *Italy* is thorough, well-researched, and packed with good maps and hotel recommendations for low- to moderate-budget travelers, but it's not updated annually. Use it only with a one- or two-year-old copyright. The hip *Rough Guide to Italy* (British researchers, more insightful) and the highly opinionated *Let's Go: Italy* (by Harvard students, better hotel listings) are great for students and vagabonds. If you're a low-budget train traveler interested in the youth and nightlife scene (which I have basically ignored), get *Let's Go: Italy*. The Italy section in the bigger *Let's Go: Europe* is sparse.

Cultural and Sightseeing Guides: The colorful Eyewitness series is popular with travelers (editions include Italy, Florence/Tuscany, Venice, Rome, and Sicily). They are fun for their great, easy-to-grasp graphics and photos, and just right for people who want only factoids. But the Eyewitness written content is relatively skimpy, and the books weigh a ton. I buy them in Italy (no more expensive than in the United States) or simply borrow them for a minute from other travelers at certain sights to make sure I'm aware of that place's highlights. The tall, green Michelin guides to Italy and Rome have minimal information on room and board, but include great maps for drivers and lots of solid encyclopedic coverage of sights, customs, and culture (sold in English in Italy). The Cadogan guides to various parts of Italy offer an insightful look at the rich and confusing local culture. Those heading for Florence or Rome should read Irving Stone's *The Agony and the Ecstasy* for a great—if romanticized—rundown on Michelangelo, the Medici family, and the turbulent times of the Renaissance.

Maps
The black-and-white maps in this book, drawn by Dave Hoerlein, are concise and simple. Dave, who is well-traveled in Italy, designed the maps to help you locate recommended places and the tourist offices, where you can pick up more in-depth maps of the city or region (cheap or free).

For a map of Italy, consider my Rick Steves' Italy Planning Map—geared to travelers' needs—with sightseeing destinations listed prominently. On the back of the Italy map, you'll find city maps of Rome, Venice, and Florence. For an all-Europe trip, consider my Rick Steves' Europe Planning Map (see www.ricksteves.com).

Train travelers can do fine with a simple rail map (such as the one that comes with your railpass) and city maps from the TI as they travel. But drivers shouldn't skimp on maps. Excellent maps are available throughout Italy at bookstores, newsstands, and gas stations. Get a good 1:200,000 map to get the most out of your miles; study the key to get the most sightseeing value out of your map.

Tours of Italy
Travel agents can tell you about all the mainstream tours of Italy, but they won't tell you about mine. At Europe Through the Back Door, we offer one-week getaways to **Rome**, to **Venice**, and to **Florence** (departures Jan–Dec, 24 people max).

Our longer Italy tours come with a great guide, most meals, all your group sightseeing, small groups (of 28), and a big, roomy bus. The 17-day **Best of Italy** tour features all of the biggies and my favorite "back doors" (April–Oct). The 15-day **Village Italy** adventure laces together intimate towns (May–Oct). The 14-day **Best of South Italy** tour savors the Amalfi Coast before exploring Naples and Sicily (April–Oct). For more information, call 425/771-8303 or visit www.ricksteves.com.

Transportation

By Car or Train?

Each mode of transportation has pros and cons. Public transportation is one of the few bargains in Italy. Trains and buses are inexpensive and good. City-to-city travel is faster, easier, and cheaper by train than by car. Trains give you the convenience and economy of doing long stretches overnight. By train, I arrive relaxed and well-rested—not so by car.

Parking, gas (about $4 per gallon), and tolls are expensive in Italy. But drivers enjoy more control, especially in the countryside. Cars carry your luggage for you, generally from door to door—especially important for heavy packers (such as chronic shoppers and families traveling with children). And groups know that the more people you pack into a car or minibus, the cheaper it gets per person.

Trains

To travel by train cheaply in Italy, you can simply buy tickets as you go, though train station lines can be long and the fast-train supplement charges are confusing. You'll save some hassle but not money by buying the Italian State Railway's **Italy Flexi Rail Card** (also called *TrenItalia Pass*, see chart on page 18). Although the Rail Card covers most supplements, it doesn't cover reservations (purchased separately, optional for most trains—€4, required for Eurostar Italia—€8–11). Buying supplements on the train (instead of before you board) comes with a nasty penalty.

Newsstands sell up-to-date regional and all-Italy **timetables** (€4, ask for the *orario ferroviario*). On the Web, check http://bahn.hafas.de/english.html or www.fs-on-line.com.

You'll encounter several **types of trains** in Italy. Along with the various milk-run trains, there are the slow IR (Interregional) and *diretto* trains, the medium *espresso*, the fast IC (InterCity), and the Eurostar Italia bullet train (abbreviated "ES," a.k.a. the T.A.V., which stands for *Treno Alta Velocita*). Compared to fast InterCity trains, the speedier Eurostar Italia shaves a little time off typical trips (15–45 min faster between Venice and Florence, 30–60 min on Florence–Rome trip, and 10–20 min on Rome–Naples journey) but requires a reservation before boarding (€8–11 with railpass; this train may not be worth the effort and expense). If you're buying tickets as you go, fast trains are affordable (e.g., a second-class Rome-to-Venice Eurostar ticket costs about $50 with reservation at any ticket window or machine).

Avoid big-city train station ticket lines whenever you can. At travel agencies, such as CIT or American Express, you can make reservations, buy tickets, and reserve a *cuccetta* (overnight berth). The cost is the same

DECIPHERING ITALIAN TRAIN SCHEDULES

At the station, look for the big yellow posters labeled *Partenze*—Departures (ignore the white posters, which show arrivals).

Schedules are listed chronologically, hour by hour, showing the trains leaving the station throughout the day. The first column *(Ora)* lists the time of departure. The next column *(Treno)* shows the type of train. The third column *(Classi Servizi)* lists the services available (first- and second-class cars, dining car, couchettes, etc.) and, more important, whether you need reservations (usually denoted by an *R* in a box). The next column lists the destination of the train *(Principali Fermate Destinazioni)*, often showing intermediate stops, followed by the final destination, with arrival times listed throughout in parentheses. Note that *your* final destination may be listed in fine print as an intermediate destination. If you're going from Milan to Florence, scan the schedule and you'll notice that virtually all trains that terminate in Rome stop in Florence en route. Travelers who read the fine print end up with a greater choice of trains. The next column *(Servizi Diretti e Annotazioni)* has pertinent notes about the train, such as "also stops in..." *(ferma anche a...)*, "doesn't stop in..." *(non ferma a...)*, "stops in every station" *(ferma in tutte le stazioni)*, and so on. The last column lists the track *(Binario)* the train departs from. Confirm the *binario* with an additional source: a ticket seller, the electronic board listing immediate departures, TV monitors on the platform, or the railway officials who are usually standing by the train unless you really need them.

For any odd symbols on the poster, look at the key at the end. Some of the phrasing can be deciphered easily, such as *servizio periodico* (periodical service—doesn't always run). For the trickier ones, ask a local or railway official or simply take a different train.

or minimally higher (about €2), the lines and language barrier are smaller, and you'll save time.

First-class tickets cost 50 percent more than **second-class**. While second-class cars go as fast as their first-class neighbors, Italy is one country where I would consider the splurge of first class. The easiest way to upgrade a second-class ticket once on board a crowded train is to nurse a drink in the snack car.

Some travelers can get a discount on already-cheap point-to-point tickets purchased in Italy. **Youth** and **seniors** can buy €25 discount cards

Italy by Rail: Cost and Distance

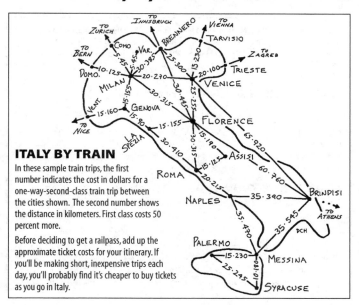

ITALY BY TRAIN

In these sample train trips, the first number indicates the cost in dollars for a one-way-second-class train trip between the cities shown. The second number shows the distance in kilometers. First class costs 50 percent more.

Before deciding to get a railpass, add up the approximate ticket costs for your itinerary. If you'll be making short, inexpensive trips each day, you'll probably find it's cheaper to buy tickets as you go in Italy.

at any train station, then save 20 percent on second-class or first-class tickets for one year. If you're under 26, ask for a Carta Verde. If you're 60 or over, request a Carta d'Argento. The **Tariffa Famiglia** discount allows one child (aged 4–11) to travel for free with two or more adults when they buy first- or second-class point-to-point tickets in Italy (no card needed).

Before boarding the train, you must **validate** (stamp) your train documents in the machine near the platform. This includes whatever you need to take a particular trip, which can be as simple as a single ticket, but can also involve a supplement, seat reservation, or *cuccetta* reservation. You don't need to stamp Eurailpasses or Italy Rail Cards. If you forget to stamp your ticket, go right away to the train conductor—before he comes to you—or you'll pay a fine.

Trains can fill up, even in first class; if a popular train route originates at your departure point (e.g., you're catching the Milan-to-Venice train in Milan), arrive a minimum of 15 minutes before the departure time to snare a seat. If you anticipate a crowd, you can get a firm seat reservation in advance for about €4. Some major stations have train composition posters on the platforms showing where first- and second-class cars are located when the trains arrive (letters on the poster correspond to letters posted over the platform).

Railpasses

Prices listed are for 2004. My free *Rick Steves' Guide to European Railpasses* has the details. To get the railpass guide or an order form, call us at 425/771-8303 or visit www.ricksteves.com/rail. TrenItalia passes are also sold in Italy at travel agencies and major train stations.

ITALY FLEXI RAIL CARD (TrenItalia Pass)

	1st Class Individual	1st Class Saver	2nd Class Individual	2nd Class Saver	2nd Class Youth
Any 4 days in 1 month	$239	$203	$191	$163	$160
Extra rail days (max 6)	$24	$20	$19	$16	$16

Kids 4-11: half adult or saver price, under 4: free. Saver price per person for two or more. Youthpasses are for travelers under age 26 only.

ITALY RAIL & DRIVE PASS

Any 4 days of rail travel + 2 days of Hertz car rental in 1 month.

Car Category	1st Class	2nd Class	Extra car day
Economy	$251	$195	$41
Compact	265	215	61
Intermediate	273	222	67
Small Automatic	289	222	67

Rail & Drive prices are approximate per person, two traveling together. Solo travelers pay about 20% more. For more info, call your travel agent or Rail Europe at 800/438-7245.

FRANCE 'N ITALY PASS

	1st Class Individual	1st Class Saver	2nd Class Individual	2nd Class Saver	2nd Class Youth
Any 4 days in 2 months	$279	$239	$239	$209	$199
Extra rail days (max 6)	28	25	25	22	21

Kids 4-11: half adult or saver price, under 4: free. Youthpasses are for travelers under age 26 only. Saver prices are per person for two or more.

Be aware of your route. Many daytime connections from Paris to Italy pass through Switzerland (an add'l $40 2nd class or $60 1st class if not covered by your pass). Night trains, and routes via Nice, Torino, or Modane are okay.

EURAIL SELECTPASSES

This pass covers travel in three adjacent countries. For details and our five-country option, visit www.ricksteves.com/rail or see *Rick Steves' Guide to European Railpasses.*

	1st Class Selectpass	1st Class Saverpass	2nd Class Youthpass
5 days in 2 months	$356	$304	$249
6 days in 2 months	394	336	276
8 days in 2 months	470	400	329
10 days in 2 months	542	460	379

Saverpass: price is per person for two or more traveling together at all times.
Youthpasses: Under age 26 only. Kids 4-11 pay half adult fare; under 4: free.

Italy's Public Transportation

Italian trains are famous for their thieves. Never leave a bag unattended. I've noticed that police now ride the trains, and things seem more controlled. Still, for an **overnight** trip, I'd feel safe only in a *cuccetta* (a berth in a special sleeping car with an attendant who keeps track of who comes and goes while you sleep—approximately €13 in a 6-bed compartment, €18 in a less-cramped 4-bed compartment).

Many stations have **baggage storage** *(deposito bagagli)* where you can safely leave your bag for €3 per 12-hour period (payable when you pick up the bag, double-check closing hours). Since the terrorist attacks of September 11, 2001, no stations have lockers.

Strikes are common. Strikes generally last a day, and train employees will simply say, "*Sciopero*" (strike). But in actuality, sporadic trains, following no particular schedule, lumber down the tracks during most strikes.

Multi-Country Railpasses: For travel exclusively in Italy, a 17-country **Eurailpass** is a bad value. If you're branching out beyond Italy, the **Eurail Selectpass** allows you to tailor a pass to your trip, provided you're traveling in three, four, or five adjacent countries directly connected by rail or ferry. For instance, with a three-country pass allowing 10 days of train travel within a two-month period ($542 in 2003), you could choose France–Italy–Greece or Germany–Austria–Italy. A **France and Italy Pass** combines just those two countries and covers night trains to and from Paris via Switzerland (but if your route crosses Switzerland by day, you'll pay extra—so the Selectpass is a better choice).

Car Rental

Research car rental before you go. It's cheaper to arrange for car rentals through your travel agent while still in the United States. Rent by the week with unlimited mileage. If you need a car for three or more weeks, it's cheaper to lease; you'll save money on insurance and taxes. Explore your drop-off options (south of Rome can be a problem).

For peace of mind, I purchase collision damage waiver (CDW) insurance, which covers the value of the car (sometimes entirely, but more often with a small deductible) in case of an accident. CDW costs from $10 to $25 a day, depending on the car and the company. Figure roughly $150 per week. A few "gold" credit cards include CDW coverage if you pay for the rental with the card; quiz your credit-card company on the worst-case scenario.

Theft insurance (different from CDW insurance) is mandatory when you're renting a car for use in Italy. The insurance usually costs about $10 to $15 a day, payable when you pick up the car.

A rail-and-drive pass (such as a EurailDrive, Selectpass Drive, or Italy Rail and Drive) can be put to thoughtful use. Certain areas are great by car, such as the Dolomites and the hill towns of Tuscany and Umbria, while most of Italy is best by train.

Standard European Road Signs

 AND LEARN THESE
ROAD SIGNS

Speed Limit
(km/hr)

Yield

No Passing

End of
No Passing
Zone

One Way

Intersection

Main
Road

Freeway

Danger

No Entry

No Entry
for Cars

All Vehicles
Prohibited

Parking

No Parking

Customs

Peace

Driving

Driving in Italy is frightening—a video game for keeps, and you only get one quarter. All you need is a U.S. driver's license and a car. According to everybody but the Italian police, international driver's permits are not necessary. The police fine you if they can't read your license.

Autostradas: Italy's freeway system is as good as our interstate system, but you'll pay about a dollar for every 10 minutes of use. (I paid €20 for the four-hour drive from Bolzano to Pisa.) While I favor the autostradas because I feel they're safer, cheaper (saving time and gas), and less nerve-racking than smaller roads, savvy local drivers know which toll-free "super-stradas" are actually faster and more direct than the autostrada (e.g., Florence to Pisa). For more information, visit www.autostrade.it.

Driving in Italy: Distance and Time

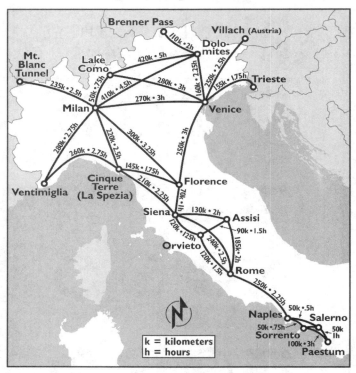

Gas: Most cars take unleaded gas (*senza piombo*, from green pumps, available everywhere). Autostrada rest stops are self-service stations open daily without a siesta break. Small-town stations are usually cheaper and offer full service but shorter hours. Many 24-hour-a-day stations are entirely automated, with machines that trade gas for paper money.

Metric: A liter is about a quart, four to a gallon; a kilometer is about six-tenths of a mile. Figure kilometers to miles by cutting them in half and adding back 10 percent of the original (120 km: 60 + 12 = 72 miles, 300 km: 150 + 30 = 180 miles).

Parking: White lines generally mean parking is free. Blue lines mean you'll have to pay—usually €0.75 to €1 per hour. If there's no meter, there is probably a roving attendant who will take your money. Study the signs. Many free zones are cleared out (by car owners or tow trucks) one day a week for street cleaning. Often the free zones have a 30- or 60-minute time limit. *Zona disco* has nothing to do with dancing. Italian cars have a time disk (a cardboard clock), which you set at your arrival time and lay on the dashboard so the attendant knows how long you've been parked. This is a fine system that all drivers should take advantage of. (If your rental car doesn't come with a *zona disco*, pick one up at a tobacco shop or just write your arrival time on a piece of paper and place it on the dashboard.) Garages are safe, save time, and help you avoid the stress of parking tickets. Take the parking voucher with you to pay the cashier before you leave.

Theft: Cars are routinely vandalized and stolen. Try to make your car look locally-owned by hiding the "tourist-owned" rental company decals and putting a local newspaper in your back window.

Telephones, Mail, and E-mail

Smart travelers use the telephone every day, especially in Italy, to check opening hours, confirm hotel reservations, and phone home.

Phone Cards: There are two kinds of phone cards—those that you insert into the phone instead of coins, and long-distance scratch-off PIN cards that can be used from virtually any phone (you dial a toll-free number and enter your PIN code). The Italian Telecom phone system sells both kinds.

Insertable phone cards are sold in varying denominations at tobacco shops, post offices, and machines near phone booths (many phone booths indicate where the nearest phone card sales outlet is located). Rip off the perforated corner to "activate" the card before you insert it into the phone.

PIN cards are usually the least expensive way to call back to the United States (about 10 min/$1). They're sold at small newsstands and hole-in-the-wall long-distance phone shops (Telecom brand also sold at tobacco shops and post offices). Since you don't insert these cards into a phone, you can use them from most phones, including the one in your hotel room (if it's set on pulse, switch it to tone). Because there are so many brand names, ask for an international telephone card *(carta telefonica prepagato internazionale,* KAR-tah teh-leh-FOHN-ee-kah pray-pah-GAH-toh in-ter-naht-zee-oh-NAH-lay); specify that you want a card for making calls to America or Canada to avoid getting the PIN cards that are only good within particular regions in Italy. After you buy a card, scratch off and reveal your Personal Identification Number, dial the toll-free access number, punch in your PIN, and talk. If the PIN doesn't work on one phone, try another phone. Get a low denomination in case the card is a dud.

The orange SIP public telephones are everywhere and take cards or coins. About a quarter of the phones are broken (which could explain why so many Italians carry mobile phones). The rest of the phones work reluctantly. Dial slowly and deliberately, as if the phone doesn't understand numbers very well. Often a recorded message in Italian will break in, brusquely informing you that the phone number does not exist *(non-esistente),* even if you're dialing your own home phone number. Dial again with an increasing show of confidence, in an attempt to convince the phone of your number's existence. If you fail, try a different phone. Repeat as needed.

When spelling out your name on the phone, you'll find that some letters are pronounced differently in Italian: *a* is pronounced "ah," *i* is pronounced "ee," and *e* is pronounced "ay." To avoid confusion, say "*a*, Acqua," "*e*, Empoli," and "*i*, Italia" to clear up that problem. If you plan to access your voice mail from Italy, be advised that you can't always dial extensions or secret codes once you connect (you're on vacation—relax).

Dialing within Italy: Italy has a direct-dial phone system (no area codes). To call anywhere within Italy, just dial the number. For example, the number of one of my recommended Florence hotels is 055-293-451. To call it from the Florence train station, dial 055-293-451. If you call it from Venice, it's the same: 055-293-451.

Italian phone numbers vary in length; a hotel can have, say, a 10-digit phone number and an 11-digit fax number.

Italy's toll-free numbers start with 800 (like U.S. 800 numbers, though in Italy you don't dial a "1" first). In Italy, you can dial these 800 numbers—called *freephone* or *numero verde* (green number)—free from any phone without using a phone card or coins.

Dialing International Calls: When calling internationally, dial the international access code (00 if you're calling from Europe, 011 from the U.S. or Canada), the country code of the country you're calling (39 for Italy; see appendix for list of other countries), and the local number. To call the Florence hotel (mentioned above) from the United States, dial 011 (the U.S. international access code), 39 (Italy's country code), then 055-293-451. To call my office from Italy, I dial 00 (Europe's international access code), 1 (the U.S. country code), 425 (Edmonds' area code), and 771-8303. European time is six/nine hours ahead of the east/west coasts of the United States.

Hotel-room phones are reasonable for calls within Italy (the faint beeps stand for €0.10 phone units) but a terrible rip-off for calls to the United States (unless you use a PIN card or your hotel allows toll-free access to your calling card service—see below).

Calling Card Services: Since direct-dialing rates have dropped, calling cards (offered by AT&T, MCI, and Sprint) are no longer the good value they used to be. In fact, they are a rip-off. You'll likely pay $3 for the first minute with a $4 connection fee; if you get an answering machine, it'll cost you $7 to say "Sorry I missed you." Simply dialing direct (even from your hotel room) is generally a much better deal.

Mobile Phones: Many travelers now buy cheap mobile phones in Europe to make both local and international calls. (Typical American mobile phones don't work in Europe, and those that do, have horrendous per-minute costs.) For about $75 you can get a phone with $20 *(non-esistente)*, even if you're dialing your own home phone number. Dial again with an increasing show of confidence, in an attempt to convince the phone of your number's existence. If you fail, try a different phone. Repeat as needed.

When spelling out your name on the phone, you'll find that some letters are pronounced differently in Italian: *a* is pronounced "ah," *i* is pronounced "ee," and *e* is pronounced "ay." To avoid confusion, say "*a*, Acqua," "*e*, Empoli," and "*i*, Italia" to clear up that problem. If you plan to access your voice mail from Italy, be advised that you can't always dial extensions or secret codes once you connect (you're on vacation—relax).

Dialing within Italy: Italy has a direct-dial phone system (no area codes). To call anywhere within Italy, just dial the number. For example, the number of one of my recommended Florence hotels is 055-293-451. To call it from the Florence train station, dial 055-293-451. If you call it from Venice, it's the same: 055-293-451.

Italian phone numbers vary in length; a hotel can have, say, a 10-digit phone number and an 11-digit fax number.

Italy's toll-free numbers start with 800 (like U.S. 800 numbers, though in Italy you don't dial a "1" first). In Italy, you can dial these 800 numbers—called *freephone* or *numero verde* (green number)—free from any phone without using a phone card or coins.

Dialing International Calls: When calling internationally, dial the international access code (00 if you're calling from Europe, 011 from the U.S. or Canada), the country code of the country you're calling (39 for Italy; see appendix for list of other countries), and the local number. To call the Florence hotel (mentioned above) from the United States, dial 011 (the U.S. international access code), 39 (Italy's country code), then 055-293-451. To call my office from Italy, I dial 00 (Europe's international access code), 1 (the U.S. country code), 425 (Edmonds' area code), and 771-8303. European time is six/nine hours ahead of the east/west coasts of the United States.

Hotel-room phones are reasonable for calls within Italy (the faint beeps stand for €0.10 phone units) but a terrible rip-off for calls to the United States (unless you use a PIN card or your hotel allows toll-free access to your calling card service—see below).

Calling Card Services: Since direct-dialing rates have dropped, calling cards (offered by AT&T, MCI, and Sprint) are no longer the good value they used to be. In fact, they are a rip-off. You'll likely pay $3 for the first minute with a $4 connection fee; if you get an answering machine, it'll cost you $7 to say "Sorry I missed you." Simply dialing direct (even from your hotel room) is generally a much better deal.

Mobile Phones: Many travelers now buy cheap mobile phones in Europe to make both local and international calls. (Typical American mobile phones don't work in Europe, and those that do, have horrendous per-minute costs.) For about $75 you can get a phone with $20 worth of calls that will work in the country where you purchased it. (You can buy more time at newsstands or mobile phone shops.) For about $100 you can get a phone that will work in most countries once you pick up the necessary chip per country. If you're interested, stop by any European shop that sells mobile phones (you'll see prominent store window displays). Depending on your trip and budget, ask for a phone that works only in that country or one that can be used throughout Europe. If you're on a budget, skip mobile phones and use PIN cards instead.

Mail: Mail service is miserable throughout Italy. Postcards get last priority. To arrange for mail delivery, reserve a few hotels along your route in advance and give their addresses to friends, or use American Express mail services (free to AmEx cardholders and for a minimal fee to anyone else). Allow 14 days for U.S.-to-Italy mail delivery, but don't count on it. Federal Express makes pricey two-day deliveries. Phoning is so easy that I've completely dispensed with mail stops. If possible, mail nothing precious from Italy.

E-mail: More and more hotels have e-mail addresses and Web sites (included in this book). I've listed some Internet cafés, but your hotelier or TI can steer you to the nearest Internet access point.

In cities, when you see a cluster of orange public phones in a room off a busy street, you might see several computers in the batch. With these, you can use your phone card to access the Internet. You won't be comfortable (no seat), and you'll get cut off if your phone card runs out of time, but this can be a handy, quick way to check your e-mail.

Sleeping

For hassle-free efficiency, I favor hotels and restaurants handy to sight-seeing activities. Rather than list hotels scattered throughout a city, I describe two or three favorite neighborhoods and recommend the best accommodations values in each, from $20 bunks to plush $300 doubles with all the comforts.

Sleeping in Italy is expensive. Cheap big-city hotels can be depressing. Tourist information services cannot give opinions on quality. A major feature of this book is its extensive listing of good-value rooms. I like places that are clean, small, central, quiet at night, traditional, inexpensive, and friendly, with firm beds—and those not listed in other guidebooks. (In Italy, for me, 6 out of 9 attributes means a keeper.)

Hotels

Double rooms listed in this book will range from about $50 (very simple, toilet and shower down the hall) to $300 (maximum plumbing and more), with most clustering around $80–100 (with private bathrooms). Prices are higher in big cities and heavily touristed cities, and lower off the beaten path. Three or four people can economize by requesting larger rooms. Solo travelers find that the cost of a *camera singola* is often only

25 percent less than a *camera doppia*. Most listed hotels have rooms for anywhere from one to five people. If there's room for an extra cot, they'll cram it in for you.

The Italian word for "hotel" is *hotel*, and in smaller, nontouristy towns, *albergo*. A few places have kept the old titles, *locanda* or *pensione*, indicating that they offer budget beds.

You normally get close to what you pay for. Prices are fairly standard. Shopping around earns you a better location and more character, but rarely a cheaper price.

However, prices at nearly any hotel can get soft if you do any of the following: arrive direct (without using a pricey middleman like the TI), offer to pay cash, stay at least three nights, or visit off-season. Breakfasts are legally optional (though some hotels insist they're not). Initial prices quoted often include breakfast and a private bathroom. Offer to skip breakfast for a better price.

You'll save $10 to $20 if you ask for a room without a shower and just use the shower down the hall. Generally, rooms with a bath or shower also have a toilet and a bidet (which Italians use for quick sponge baths). Tubs usually come with a frustrating "telephone shower" (hand-held nozzle). If a shower has no curtain, the entire bathroom showers with you. The cord that dangles over the tub or shower is not a clothes-line. You pull it when you've fallen and can't get up.

Double beds are called *matrimoniale*, even though hotels aren't interested in your marital status. Twins are *due letti singoli*.

When you check in, the receptionist will ask for your passport and keep it for a couple of hours. Hotels are required to register each guest with the police. Relax. Americans are notorious for making this chore more difficult than it needs to be.

Rooms are safe. Still, zip cameras and keep money out of sight. More pillows and blankets are usually in the closet or available on request. In Italy, towels and linen aren't always replaced every day. Hang your towel up to dry.

Many hotel rooms have a TV and phone. Rooms in fancier hotels usually come with a tiny safe, a small stocked fridge (called a *frigo* bar, FREE-goh bar; if it's noisy at night, unplug it), and air-conditioning (sometimes you pay an extra per-day charge for this, and it may only be turned on during the heat of the day—around 10:00–24:00). Conveniently, many business-class hotels drop their prices in July and August, just when the air-conditioned comfort they offer is most important.

Most hotel rooms with air conditioners come with a control stick (like a TV remote) that generally has the same symbols and features: fan icon (click to toggle through wind power, from light to gale); louver icon (choose steady airflow or waves); snowflake and sunshine icons (cold air or heat, depending on season); clock ("O" setting: run x hours before

SLEEP CODE

To help you sort easily through these listings, I've divided the rooms into three categories based on the price for a standard double room with bath:

$$$ **Higher Priced:** Most rooms more than €180.
$$ **Moderately Priced:** Most rooms between €130–180.
$ **Lower Priced:** Most rooms under €130.

To pack maximum information into minimum space, I use this code to describe accommodations in this book. When there is a range of prices in one category, that means the price fluctuates with the season, size of room, or length of stay. Prices listed are per room, not per person.

S = Single room (or price for one person in a double).
D = Double or Twin room. "Double beds" are often two twins sheeted together and are usually big enough for nonromantic couples.
T = Triple (generally a double bed with a single).
Q = Quad (usually two double beds).
b = Private bathroom with toilet and shower or tub.
s = Private shower or tub only (the toilet is down the hall).
no CC = Doesn't accept credit cards; pay in local cash.
SE = Speaks English. This code is used only when it seems predictable that you'll encounter English-speaking staff.
NSE = Does not speak English. Used only when it's unlikely you'll encounter English-speaking staff.

According to this code, a couple staying at a "Db-€85, SE" hotel would pay a total of 85 euros (about $95) for a double room with a private bathroom. The staff speaks English. The hotel accepts credit cards or Italian cash in payment; you can assume a hotel takes credit cards unless you see "no CC" in the listing.

---

turning off; "I" setting: wait x hours to start); and the temperature control (20° or 21° Celsius is comfortable).

The hotel breakfast, while convenient, is often a bad value—€8 for a roll, jelly, and usually unlimited *caffè latte*. You can sometimes request cheese or salami (about €2.50 extra). I enjoy taking breakfast at the corner café. It's OK to supplement what you order with a few picnic goodies.

You can usually save time by paying your bill the evening before you leave instead of paying in the busy morning, when the reception desk is crowded with tourists wanting to pay up, ask questions, or check in.

Hotels near Airports: If you have an early-morning flight, I'd suggest staying in the center of town and getting to the airport via bus, train, or taxi. But if you really want a hotel near an airport for the first or last night of your trip, try www.worldairportguide.com.

Private Rooms and Apartments

In small towns, there are often few hotels to choose from, but an abundance of *affitta camere*, or rental rooms. This can be anything from a cozy B&B with your own Tuscan grandmother to a set of keys and a basic bed. The local TI can give you a list of possibilities. These rooms are generally a good budget option, but since they vary in quality, shop around to find the best value. Apartment rentals, a great value for families or couples traveling together, are also listed at the TI and are very common in small towns. Apartments generally offer a couple of bedrooms, a sitting area, and a teensy *cucinetta*, usually stocked with dishes and flatware. Once you have the keys, you will probably be on your own.

Agritourism

Agriturismo (or agricultural tourism) began in the 1980s as a way to encourage farmers to remain on their land, produce food, and offer accommodation to tourists. A peaceful home base for exploring the region, these rural Italian B&Bs are ideal for couples or families traveling by car.

It's wise to book several months in advance for high season (May–Sept). Weeklong stays are preferred in July and August, but shorter stays are possible off-season. To sleep cheaper, avoid peak season. A Tuscan farmhouse that rents for as much as $1,900 a week in summer can go for as little as $600 in late fall. In the winter, you might be charged extra for heat, so confirm the price ahead of time. Payment policies vary, but generally a 25 percent deposit is required (lost if you cancel), and the balance is due one month before arrival.

As the name implies, agriturismos are in the countryside, although some are located within a mile of town. Most are family-run, and can vary wildly in quality. Some properties are simple and rustic, while others are downright luxurious, offering amenities such as swimming pools and riding stables. The rooms are usually clean and comfortable. Breakfast is often included, and *mezzo pensione* (half-pension, which in this case means a home-cooked dinner) may be built into the price whether you want it or not. Kitchenettes are often available to cook up your own feast. Make sure you know how to operate the appliances. To maximize your time, ask the owner for suggestions on local restaurants, sights, and activities.

I've listed some agriturismos in this book, but there are thousands. Be aware that agricultural tourism is organized "*alla Italiana*," which means, among other things, a lack of a single governing body. Local TIs can give you a list of farms in their area. Also visit www.agriturist.it or www.agriturismoitaly.it (among dozens of Web sites). If you'd prefer to use an agency, consider Farm Holidays in Tuscany. They book rooms and apartments at 300 farms in Tuscany, Umbria, and elsewhere in Italy (Mon–Fri 9:00–13:00 & 15:00–18:00, Via Manin 20, Grosseto, tel. 0564-417-418, www.it-farmholidays.it, Andrea Mazzanti).

Making Reservations

It's possible to travel at any time of year without reservations, but, given the high stakes and the quality of the gems I've found for this book, I'd recommend making reservations. You can call long in advance from home or grab rooms a few days to a week in advance as you travel. If you like more spontaneity (or if you're traveling off-season), you might make a habit of calling between 9:00 and 10:00 on the day you plan to arrive, when the hotel clerk knows who'll be checking out and just which rooms will be available. I've taken great pains to list telephone numbers with long distance instructions (see "Telephones," page 23; also see the appendix). Use the telephone and convenient telephone cards. Most hotels listed are accustomed to English-only speakers. (If you have difficulty, ask the fluent receptionist at your current hotel to call for you.) A hotel receptionist will usually trust you and hold a room until 16:00 without a deposit, though some will ask for a credit-card number.

If you know where you want to stay each day (and you don't need or want flexibility), reserve your rooms a month or two in advance. To reserve from home, e-mail, phone, or fax your request. Phone and fax costs are reasonable, e-mail is a steal, and simple English is usually fine. To fax, use the handy form in the appendix (online at www.ricksteves.com/reservation). If you don't get an answer to your fax request, consider that a "no." (Many little places get 20 faxes a day after they're full, and they can't afford to respond.)

A two-night stay in August would be "2 nights, 16/8/04 to 18/8/04" (Europeans write the date in this order—day/month/year—and hotel jargon uses your day of departure).

If you receive a response from the hotel stating its rates and room availability, it's not a confirmation. You must confirm that you indeed want a room at the given rate. One night's deposit is generally required. A credit card is often accepted as a deposit (though you may need to send a signed traveler's check or, rarely, a bank draft in the local currency). To make things easier on yourself and the hotel, be sure you really intend to stay at the hotel on the dates you requested. These family-run businesses lose money if they turn away customers while holding a room for someone who doesn't show up. Understandably, some hotels bill no-shows for one night. *If you must cancel, give at least two days' notice.* Long distance is cheap and easy from public phone booths. Don't let these people down—I promised you'd call and cancel if for some reason you won't show up.

Reconfirm your reservations a few days in advance for safety, and let them know about what time you'll arrive. Don't needlessly confirm rooms through the tourist office; they'll take a commission.

Eating Italian

The Italians are masters of the art of fine living. That means eating...long and well. Lengthy, multi-course lunches and dinners and endless hours sitting in outdoor cafés are the norm. Americans eat on their way to an evening event and complain if the check is slow in coming. For Italians, the meal is an end in itself, and only rude waiters rush you. When you want the bill, mime-scribble on your raised palm or ask for it: "*Il conto?*" You may have to ask for it more than once. To save time, ask for the check when you receive the last item you order.

Even those of us who liked dorm food will find that the local cafés, cuisine, and wines become a highlight of our Italian adventure. Trust me, this is sightseeing for your palate, and even if the rest of you is sleeping in cheap hotels, your taste buds will relish an occasional first-class splurge. You can eat well without going broke. But be careful; you're just as likely to blow a small fortune on a disappointing meal as you are to dine wonderfully for €20.

Restaurants

When restaurant-hunting, choose places filled with locals, not the place with the big neon signs boasting, "We speak English and accept credit cards." Restaurants parked on famous squares generally serve bad food at high prices to tourists. Locals eat better in lower-rent locales. Family-run places operate without hired help and can offer cheaper meals. The word *osteria* (normally a simple, local-style restaurant) makes me salivate.

For unexciting but basic values, look for a *menu turistico* (also called *menu del giorno*—*menu* of the day), a three- or four-course, set-price meal (price includes service charge, no need to tip). Galloping gourmets order à la carte with the help of a menu translator. (The *Marling Italian Menu Master* is excellent. *Rick Steves' Italian Phrase Book* has enough phrases for intermediate eaters.) Some restaurants have self-serve antipasti buffets, offering a variety of cooked appetizers spread out like a salad bar (pay per plate, not weight; usually costs around €6–8); a plate of antipasti combined with a pasta dish makes a healthy, affordable, interesting meal.

A full meal consists of an appetizer (antipasto, €2.50–5), a first course (*primo piatto,* pasta or soup, €4–7), and a second course (*secondo piatto,* expensive meat and fish dishes, €5–10). Vegetables *(contorni, verdure)* may come with the *secondo* course or cost extra (€3) as a side dish.

Seafood and steak are sometimes sold by weight (if you see "100 g" or "*l'etto*" by the price on the menu, you'll pay that price *per* 100 grams—about a quarter pound; sometimes also abbreviated *s.q.*, or "according to quantity"). Tourists without good language skills are commonly shell-shocked by the bill when ordering dishes sold by the weight. Some special dishes come in large quantities meant for two people; the shorthand way of showing this on a menu is "X2" (meaning "times two").

TIPS ON TIPPING

Tipping in Italy isn't as automatic and generous as it is in the United States, but for special service, tips are appreciated, if not expected. As in the United States, the proper amount depends on your resources, tipping philosophy, and the circumstance, but some general guidelines apply.

Restaurants: Tipping is an issue only at restaurants that have waiters and waitresses. If you order your food at a counter, don't tip. (Many Italians don't ever tip.)

At restaurants with table service, menus list if there is a *pane e coperto* charge (bread and cover charge, usually €2 per person) and if service is included (*servizio incluso*, generally 15 percent). If the service is included, there's no need to tip beyond that, but if you like to tip and you're pleased with the service, throw in €1 to €2 euros per person.

If service is not included *(servizio non incluso),* you could tip about 10 percent by rounding up or leaving the change from your bill. Leave the tip on the table or hand it to your server. It's best to tip in cash even if you pay with your credit card. Otherwise the tip may never reach your waiter.

Taxis: To tip the cabbie, round up. For a typical ride, round up to the next euro on the fare (to pay a €13 fare, give €14); for a long ride, to the nearest 10 (for a €75 fare, give €80). If the cabbie hauls your bags and zips you to the airport to help you catch your flight, you might want to toss in a little more. But if you feel like you're being driven in circles or otherwise ripped off, skip the tip.

Special services: It's thoughtful to tip a couple of euros to someone who shows you a special sight and who is paid in no other way (such as the man who shows you an Etruscan tomb in his backyard). Tour guides at public sites often hold out their hands for tips after they give their spiel; if I've already paid for the tour, I don't tip extra, though some tourists do give a euro or two, particularly for a job well done. I don't tip at hotels, but if you do, give the porter a euro for carrying bags and leave a couple of euros in your room at the end of your stay for the maid if the room was kept clean. In general, if someone in the service industry does a super job for you, a tip of a couple of euros is appropriate...but not required.

When in doubt, ask. If you're not sure whether (or how much) to tip for a service, ask your hotelier or the TI; they'll fill you in on how it's done on their turf.

Restaurants normally pad the bill with a cover charge (*pane e coperto,* around €2) and a service charge (*servizio,* 15 percent); see "Tips on Tipping," page 31.

As you will see, the euros add up in a hurry. Light and budget eaters get by with a *primo piatto* each and a shared antipasto. Italians admit that *secondi* are the least interesting aspect of the local cuisine. My standard ordering procedure is to mix *antipasti* and *primi piatti* family-style with my dinner partners (skipping *secondi*) to keep the prices down and the experience up. When done well (e.g., under-ordering since courses are often bigger than necessary), we eat well in better places for less than the cost of a tourist *menu* in a cheap place.

Delis, Cafeterias, Pizza Shops, and Tavola Calda (Hot Table) Bars

Italy offers many cheap alternatives to restaurants. Stop by a *rosticceria* for great cooked deli food; a self-service cafeteria (called "free flow" in Italian) that feeds you without the add-ons; a *tavola calda* bar for an assortment of veggies or first courses; or a Pizza Rustica shop for stand-up or take-out pizza.

Pizza is cheap and everywhere. Key pizza vocabulary: *capricciosa* (generally ham, mushrooms, and artichokes), *funghi* (mushrooms), *margherita* (tomato sauce and mozzarella), *marinara* (tomato sauce, oregano, garlic, no cheese), *quattro formaggi* (4 different cheeses), and *quattro stagioni* (different toppings on each of the 4 quarters—for those who can't choose just 1 menu item). If you ask for *peperoni* on your pizza,

EATING WITH THE SEASONS

Italian cooks love to serve you fresh produce and seafood at its tastiest. If you must have porcini mushrooms outside of October and November, they'll be frozen. To get the freshest veggies at a fine restaurant, request *"Un piatto di verdure della stagione, per favore."* (A plate of seasonal vegetables, please.)

Here are some examples of what's fresh when:

April–May:	Calamari, squid, green beans, artichokes, and zucchini flowers
April, May, Sept, Oct:	Black truffles
May–June:	Mussels, asparagus, zucchini, cantaloupe, and strawberries
May–Aug:	Eggplant
Oct–Nov:	Mushrooms and white truffles
Fresh year-round:	Clams, meats, and cheese

you'll get green or red peppers, not sausage. Kids like spicy *diavola* (closest thing in Italy to American "pepperoni") or the simple, bland *margherita* (tomato and cheese). At Pizza Rustica take-out shops, slices are sold by weight (100 grams, or *un etto*, is a hot, cheap snack; 200 grams, or *due etti*, makes a light meal).

For a fast, cheap, and healthy lunch, find a *tavola calda* bar with a buffet spread of meat and vegetables and ask for a mixed plate of vegetables with a hunk of mozzarella *(piatto misto di verdure con mozzarella)*. Don't be limited by what you can see. If you'd like a salad with a slice of cantaloupe and a hunk of cheese, they'll whip that up for you in a snap. Belly up to the bar and, with a pointed finger and key words in the chart in this chapter, you can get a fine mixed plate of vegetables. If something's a mystery, ask for *un assaggio* (a little taste).

Italian Bars/Cafés

Italian "bars" are not taverns, but cafés. These local hangouts serve coffee, mini-pizzas, sandwiches, and cartons of milk from the cooler. Many dish up plates of fried cheese and vegetables from under the glass counter, ready to reheat. This is my budget choice, the Italian equivalent of English pub grub.

For quick meals, bars usually have trays of cheap, ready-made sandwiches *(panini* or *tramezzini)*—some kinds are delightful grilled *(riscaldato)*. To save time for sightseeing and room for dinner, my favorite lunch is a ham and cheese *panini* at a bar (called *tost*, grilled twice to get really hot). To get food "to go," say, *"Da portar via"* (for the road). All bars have a WC *(toilette, bagno)* in the back, and the public is entitled to use it.

Bars serve great drinks—hot, cold, sweet, or alcoholic. Chilled bottled water *(naturale* or *frizzante)* is sold cheap to go.

Coffee: If you ask for *"un caffè,"* you'll get espresso. Cappuccino is served to locals before noon and tourists any time of day. (To an Italian, cappuccino is a breakfast drink and a travesty after anything with tomatoes.) Italians like it only warm. To get it hot, request *"Molto caldo"* (very hot) or *"Più caldo, per favore"* (hotter, please; pew KAHL-doh, pehr fah-VOH-ray).

Experiment with a few of the options...
- *caffè macchiato* (mah-kee-AH-toh): espresso with only a splash of milk
- *caffè latte*: coffee with lots of hot milk, no foam
- *caffè Americano*: espresso diluted with hot water
- *caffè corretto*: espresso with a shot of liquor, usually *grappa* (but Sambuca is good, too)
- *caffè freddo*: sweet and iced espresso
- *cappuccino freddo*: iced cappuccino
- *caffè hag*: instant decaf (any coffee drink is available decaffeinated; ask for it *decaffeinato*: day-kah-fay-een-AH-toh)

Beer: Beer on tap is *"alla spina."* Get it *piccola* (11 oz), *media* (17 oz), or *grande* (34 oz, or 1 liter).

Wine: To order a glass (*bicchiere;* bee-kee-AY-ray) of red *(rosso)* or white *(bianco)* wine, say, *"Un bicchiere di vino rosso/bianco."* *Corposo* means full-bodied. House wine often comes in a quarter-liter carafe (8.5 oz, *un quarto*), half-liter pitcher (17 oz, *un mezzo*), or one-liter pitcher (34 oz, *un litro*). Trendy wines with small production (such as Brunello di Montalcino) are good but overpriced. There are better values on wines with greater production and less demand (such as Frescobaldi Montisodi).

Prices: You'll notice a two-tiered price system. Drinking a cup of coffee while standing at the bar is cheaper than drinking it at a table. If you're on a budget, don't sit without first checking out the financial consequences. Ask "Same price if I sit or stand?" by saying, *"Costa uguale al tavolo o al banco?"* (KOH-stah oo-GWAH-lay ahl TAH-voh-loh oh ahl BAHN-koh).

If the bar isn't busy, you'll often just order and pay when you leave. Otherwise: 1) decide what you want; 2) find out the price by

ORDERING FOOD AT TAVOLA CALDAS

"Heated, please."	*"Scaldare, per favore."*	skahl-DAH-ray pehr fah-VOH-ray
"A taste, please."	*"Un assaggio, per favore."*	oon ah-SAH-joh pehr fah-VOH-ray
plate of	*piatto misto*	pee-AH-toh MEES-toh
mixed veggies	*di verdure*	dee vehr-DOO-ray
artichoke	*carciofi*	kar-CHOH-fee
asparagus	*asparagi*	ah-SPAH-rah-jee
beans	*fagioli*	fah-JOH-lee
green beans	*fagiolini*	fah-joh-LEE-nee
broccoli	*broccoli*	BROK-oh-lee
canteloupe	*melone*	may-LOH-nay
carrots	*carote*	kah-ROT-ay
ham	*prosciutto*	proh-SHOO-toh
mushrooms	*funghi*	FOONG-ghee
potatoes	*patate*	pah-TAH-tay
rice	*riso*	REE-zoh
spinach	*spinaci*	speen-AH-chee
tomatoes	*pomodori*	poh-moh-DOH-ree
zucchini	*zucchine*	zoo-KEE-nay
breadsticks	*grissini*	gree-SEE-nee

Excerpted from *Rick Steves' Italian Phrase Book*

checking the price list on the wall or the prices posted near the food, or by asking the barman; 3) pay the cashier; and 4) give the receipt to the barman (whose clean fingers handle no dirty euros) and tell him what you want.

Picnics

In Italy, picnicking saves lots of euros and is a great way to sample local specialties. In the process of assembling your meal, you get to deal with the Italians in the market scene. On days you choose to picnic, gather supplies early. You'll probably visit several small stores or market stalls to put together a complete meal, and many close around noon. While it's fun to visit the small specialty shops, a local *alimentari* is your one-stop corner grocery store (most will slice and stuff your sandwich for you if you buy the ingredients there). A *supermercato* gives you more efficiency with less color for less cost.

Juice-lovers can get a liter of O.J. for the price of a Coke or coffee. Look for "100% *succo*" (juice) on the label. Hang onto the half-liter mineral-water bottles (sold everywhere for about €0.50). Buy juice in cheap liter boxes, drink some, and store the extra in your water bottle. (I drink tap water—*acqua del rubinetto*.)

Picnics can be an adventure in high cuisine. Be daring. Try the fresh mozzarella, *presto* pesto, shriveled olives, and any UFOs the locals are excited about. Shopkeepers are generally happy to sell small quantities of produce. A typical picnic for two might be fresh rolls, 100 grams of cheese, 100 grams of meat, two tomatoes, three carrots, two apples, yogurt, and a liter box of juice. Total cost—about €10.

Culture Shock—Accepting Italy as a Package Deal

We travel all the way to Italy to enjoy differences—to become temporary locals. You'll experience frustrations. Certain truths that we find "God-given" or "self-evident," like cold beer, ice in drinks, bottomless cups of coffee, hot showers, and bigger being better, are suddenly not so true. One of the benefits of travel is the eye-opening realization that there are logical, civil, and even better alternatives. A willingness to go local ensures that you'll enjoy a full dose of Italian hospitality.

If there is a negative aspect to the image Italians have of Americans, it is that we are big, loud, aggressive, impolite, rich, and a bit naive. While Italians, flabbergasted by our Yankee excesses, say in disbelief, "*Mi sono cadute le braccia!*" ("I throw my arms down!"), they nearly always afford us individual travelers all the warmth we deserve.

Send Me a Postcard, Drop Me a Line

If you enjoy a successful trip with the help of this book and would like to share your discoveries, please fill out and send the survey at the end of this book to me at Europe Through the Back Door, Box 2009, Edmonds,

:rsonally read and value all feedback. Thanks in
a lot.

t travel information on Italy, tap into my Web site at
www.ricksteves.com. To check on any updates for this book, visit www
.ricksteves.com/update. My e-mail address is rick@ricksteves.com.
Anyone is welcome to a free issue of my *Back Door* quarterly newsletter.

Judging from all the positive feedback and happy postcards I receive
from travelers who have used this book, it's safe to assume you'll enjoy a
great, affordable vacation—with the finesse of an independent, experienced traveler. Thanks, and *buon viaggio!*

BACK DOOR TRAVEL PHILOSOPHY

From *Rick Steves' Europe Through the Back Door*

Travel is intensified living—maximum thrills per minute and one of the last great sources of legal adventure. Travel is freedom. It's recess, and we need it.

Experiencing the real Europe requires catching it by surprise, going casual..."through the Back Door."

Affording travel is a matter of priorities. (Make do with the old car.) You can travel—simply, safely, and comfortably—anywhere in Europe for $90 a day plus transportation costs. In many ways, spending more money only builds a thicker wall between you and what you came to see. Europe is a cultural carnival, and, time after time, you'll find that its best acts are free and the best seats are the cheap ones.

A tight budget forces you to travel close to the ground, meeting and communicating with the people, not relying on service with a purchased smile. Never sacrifice sleep, nutrition, safety, or cleanliness in the name of budget. Simply enjoy the local-style alternatives to expensive hotels and restaurants.

Extroverts have more fun. If your trip is low on magic moments, kick yourself and make things happen. If you don't enjoy a place, maybe you don't know enough about it. Seek the truth. Recognize tourist traps. Give a culture the benefit of your open mind. See things as different but not better or worse. Any culture has much to share.

Of course, travel, like the world, is a series of hills and valleys. Be fanatically positive and militantly optimistic. If something's not to your liking, change your liking. Travel is addictive. It can make you a happier American, as well as a citizen of the world. Our Earth is home to six billion equally important people. It's humbling to travel and find that people don't envy Americans. They like us, but, with all due respect, they wouldn't trade passports.

Globe-trotting destroys ethnocentricity. It helps you understand and appreciate different cultures. Travel changes people. It broadens perspectives and teaches new ways to measure quality of life. Many travelers toss aside their hometown blinders. Their prized souvenirs are the strands of different cultures they decide to knit into their own character. The world is a cultural yarn shop. And Back Door travelers are weaving the ultimate tapestry. Come on, join in!

ITALY

(Italia)

- 120,000 square miles (a little larger than Arizona)
- 60 million people (500 people per square mile)
- 800 miles long, 100 miles wide
- 1 euro (€) = about $1.10.

Bella Italia! It has Europe's richest, craziest culture. If you take it on its own terms, Italy is a cultural keelhauling that actually feels good.

Some people, often with considerable effort, manage to hate it. Italy bubbles with emotion, corruption, stray hairs, inflation, traffic jams, body odor, strikes, rallies, holidays, crowded squalor, and irate ranters shaking their fists at each other one minute and walking arm in arm the next. Have a talk with yourself before you cross the border. Promise yourself to relax and soak in it; it's a glorious mud puddle.

There are two Italys: The north is industrial, aggressive, and "time is money" in its outlook. The south is crowded, poor, relaxed, farm-oriented, and traditional. Families here are very strong and usually live in the same house for many generations. Loyalties are to family, city, region, soccer team, and country—in that order.

Economically, Italy has had its problems, but somehow things have always worked out. Today, Italy is the Western world's seventh-largest industrial power. Its people earn more per capita than the British. Italy is the world's leading wine producer. It is sixth in cheese and wool output. Tourism is big business. Cronyism, which complicates my work, is an integral part of the economy.

Italy, home of the Vatican, is Catholic, but the dominant religion is life—motor scooters, soccer, fashion, girl-watching, boy-watching, good coffee, good wine, and *la dolce far niente* ("the sweetness of doing nothing"). The Italian character shows itself on the streets in the skilled maniac drivers and the classy dressers who star in the ritual evening stroll, or *passeggiata*.

The language is fun. Be melodramatic and talk with your hands. Hear the melody; get into the flow. Italians are outgoing. They want to communicate, and they try harder than any other Europeans. Play with them.

Italy, a land of extremes, is also the most thief-ridden country you'll visit. Tourists suffer virtually no violent crime—but there are plenty of petty purse-snatchings, pickpocketings, and shortchangings. Wear your money belt! The scruffy-looking women and children loitering around the major museums aren't there for the art.

Take advantage of the cheap, colorful, and dry-but-informative city guidebooks sold on the streets. Use the information telephones you'll find in most historic buildings. Just set the dial on English, pop in your coins, and listen. The narration is often accompanied by a brief slide show.

Some important Italian churches require modest dress: No shorts or bare shoulders on men, women, and sometimes even children. With a little imagination (except at the ultrastrict Vatican's St. Peter's), those caught by surprise can improvise something—a jacket for your knees and maps for your shoulders. I wear a super-lightweight pair of long pants for my hot and muggy big-city Italian sightseeing.

While no longer a cheap country, Italy is still a hit with shoppers. Glassware (Venice), gold, silver, leather, prints (Florence), and high fashion (Rome and Milan) are good souvenirs, but do some price research at home so you'll recognize the good values.

La dolce far niente is a big part of Italy. Zero in on the fine points. Don't dwell on the problems. Accept Italy as Italy. Savor your cappuccino, dangle your feet over a canal (if it smells, breathe through your mouth), and imagine what it was like centuries ago. Ramble through the rabble and rubble of Rome and mentally resurrect those ancient stones. Look into the famous sculpted eyes of Michelangelo's *David* and understand Renaissance man's assertion of himself. Sit silently on a hilltop rooftop. Get chummy with the winds of the past. Write a poem over a glass of local wine in a sun-splashed, wave-dashed Riviera village. If you fall off your moral horse, call it a cultural experience. Italy is for romantics.

VENICE

(Venezia)

Soak all day in this puddle of elegant decay. Venice is Europe's best-preserved big city. This car-free urban wonderland of a hundred islands—laced together by 400 bridges and 2,000 alleys—survives on the artificial respirator of tourism.

Born in a lagoon 1,500 years ago as a refuge from barbarians, Venice is overloaded with tourists and is slowly sinking (unrelated facts). In the Middle Ages, the Venetians, becoming Europe's clever middlemen for East-West trade, created a great trading empire. By smuggling in the bones of St. Mark (San Marco, A.D. 828), Venice gained religious importance as well. With the discovery of America and new trading routes to the Orient, Venetian power ebbed. But as Venice fell, her appetite for decadence grew. Through the 17th and 18th centuries, Venice partied on the wealth accumulated through earlier centuries as a trading power.

Today, Venice is home to about 65,000 people in its old city, down from a peak population of nearly 200,000. While there are about 500,000 in greater Venice (counting the mainland, not counting tourists), the old town has a small-town feel. Locals seem to know everyone. To see small-town Venice away from the touristic flak, escape the Rialto–San Marco tourist zone and savor the town early and late without the hordes of vacationers day-tripping in from cruise ships and nearby beach resorts. A 10-minute walk from the madness puts you in an idyllic Venice few tourists see.

Planning Your Time

Venice is worth at least a day on even the speediest tour. Hyperefficient train travelers take the night train in and/or out. Sleep in the old center to experience Venice at its best: early and late. For a one-day visit, cruise the Grand Canal, do the major sights on St. Mark's Square (the square itself, Doge's Palace, and St. Mark's Basilica), see the Church of the Frari (Chiesa dei Frari) for art, and wander the backstreets on a pub crawl

Venice Overview

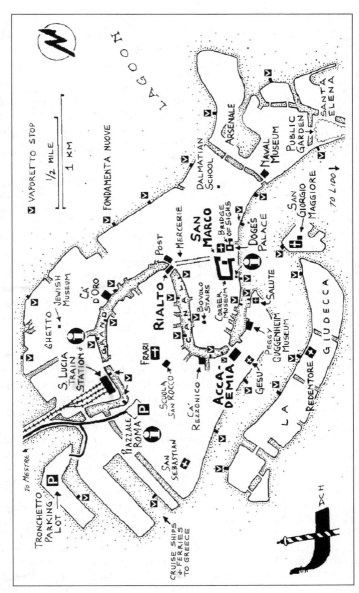

LAGOON

☒ VAPORETTO STOP

½ MILE

1 KM

FONDAMENTA NUOVE

SANTA ELENA

ARSENALE

DALMATIAN SCHOOL

NAVAL MUSEUM

PUBLIC GARDEN

MERCERIE

SAN MARCO

BRIDGE OF SIGHS

DOGE'S PALACE

SAN GIORGIO MAGGIORE

TO LIDO

POST

RIALTO

CANAL

BOVOLO STAIRS

CORRER MUSEUM

SALUTE

JEWISH MUSEUM

CA' D'ORO

GHETTO

GRAND

S. LUCIA TRAIN STATION

FRARI

SCUOLA SAN ROCCO

CA' REZZONICO

ACCA-DEMIA

GESU

PEGGY GUGGENHEIM MUSEUM

LA

GIUDECCA

IL REDENTORE

PIAZZALE ROMA

SAN SEBASTIAN

TO MESTRE

TRONCHETTO PARKING LOT

CRUISE SHIPS & FERRIES TO GREECE

ACH

(described in "Eating," page 85). Venice's greatest sight is the city itself. Make time to simply wander. While doable in a day, Venice is worth two. It's a medieval cookie jar, and nobody's looking.

ORIENTATION

The island city of Venice is shaped like a fish. Its major thoroughfares are canals. The Grand Canal winds through the middle of the fish, starting at the mouth where all the people and food enter, passing under the Rialto Bridge, and ending at St. Mark's Square (Piazza San Marco). Park your 21st-century perspective at the mouth and let Venice swallow you whole.

Venice is a car-less kaleidoscope of people, bridges, and odorless canals. The city has no real streets, and addresses are hopelessly confusing. There are six districts: San Marco (most touristy), Castello (behind San Marco), Cannaregio (from the train station to the Rialto), San Polo (other side of the Rialto), Santa Croce, and Dorsoduro. Each district has about 6,000 address numbers.

To find your way, navigate by landmarks, not streets. Many street corners have a sign pointing you to (per) the nearest major landmark, such as San Marco, Accademia, Rialto, and Ferrovia (train station). Obedient visitors stick to the main thoroughfares as directed by these signs and miss the charm of backstreet Venice.

Tourist Information

There are three main TIs: at the train station (daily 8:00–18:30, crowded and surly); at St. Mark's Square (Mon–Sat 9:00–15:30, closed Sun; with your back to St. Mark's Basilica, it's in far left corner of square); and near St. Mark's Square vaporetto boat stop on the lagoon (daily 10:00–18:00, sells vaporetto tickets, rents audioguides at €3.65/hr for self-guided walking tours). Smaller offices are at Piazzale Roma and the airport (daily 9:30–19:30). For a quick question, save time by phoning 041-522-5150 or 041-541-5887. The TI's offical Web site is www.turismovenezia.it.

At any TI, pick up a free city map and the free *Leo* bimonthly magazine, which comes with an insert, *Leo Bussola*, listing museum hours, exhibitions, and musical events (in Italian and English). Confirm your sightseeing plans. Ask for the fine brochures outlining three offbeat Venice walks. The free periodical entertainment guide *Un' Ospite di Venezia* (a monthly listing of events, nightlife, museum hours, train and vaporetto schedules, emergency telephone numbers, and so on) is available at the TI or fancy hotel reception desks (www.aguestinvenice.com).

Maps: The cheap Venice map on sale at postcard racks has much more detail than the TI's free map, but the "Illustrated Venice Map" by Magnetic North is by far the best ever (€6, listing nearly every shop, hotel, and restaurant). Also consider the little guidebook (sold alongside the postcards), which comes with a city map and explanations of the major sights.

Arrival in Venice

A two-mile-long causeway (with highway and train lines) connects Venice to the mainland. Mestre, Venice's sprawling mainland industrial base, has fewer crowds, cheaper hotels, and plenty of parking lots, but no charm. Don't stop here, unless you're parking your car in a lot. Trains regularly connect Mestre with Venice's Santa Lucia station (6/hr, 5 min). Don't leave your train at Venezia-Mestre—the next stop is Venezia Santa Lucia (end of the line for Venice).

By Train: Venice's **Santa Lucia train station** plops you right into the old town on the Grand Canal, an easy vaporetto ride or fascinating 40-minute walk to St. Mark's Square. Upon arrival, skip the station's crowded TI because the two TIs at St. Mark's Square are better, and it's not worth a long wait for a minimal map (buy a good one from a newsstand with no wait; see "Maps," above). Confirm your departure plan (stop by train info desk or just study the *partenze*—departure—posters on walls). The train station can be crowded with long lines to buy train tickets, supplements, and *couchette* reservations. You can take care of these tasks at downtown travel agencies (see "Services," page 46). The cost is the same, the lines and language barrier are smaller, and you'll save time.

Consider storing unnecessary heavy bags, even though lines for the **baggage check** may be very long (platform 14, €3/12 hrs, €5.20/24 hrs, daily 6:00–24:00; there are no lockers).

Then walk straight out of the station to the canal. The dock for **vaporetti** #1 and #82 is on your left (for downtown Venice; most recommended hotels; and Grand Canal Cruise of Venice—see page 51); the dock for #51 and #52 is on your right (for some recommended hotels). Buy a €5 ticket (or €10.50 all-day pass) at the ticket window and hop on a boat after confirming that it's heading downtown (direction: Rialto or San Marco). Some boats only go as far as Rialto *(solo Rialto)*, so check with the conductor.

By Car: The freeway ends at Venice in a parking lot on the edge of the island. Follow the green lights directing you to a parking lot with space, probably Tronchetto (across the causeway and on the right), which has a huge, multistoried garage (€18/day, tel. 041-520-7555). From there, you'll find travel agencies masquerading as TIs and vaporetto docks for the boat connection (#82) to the town center. Don't let taxi boatmen con you out of the relatively cheap €5 vaporetto ride. Parking in Mestre is easy and cheap (open-air lots €4/day, €5/day garage across from Mestre train station, easy shuttle-train connections to Venice's Santa Lucia Station—6/hr, 5 min). There are also huge and economical lots in Verona, Padua, and Vicenza.

By Plane: Venice's sleek, modern Marco Polo Airport on the mainland, six miles north of the city, has a brand-new wood-beam-and-glass terminal, with a TI, cash machines, car-rental agencies, a few shops and eateries, and easy connections by bus and speedboat to the city center. Airport info: tel. 041-260-611, flight info: tel. 041-260-9240.

Romantics can jet to St. Mark's Square by Alilaguna **speedboat** (easiest transportation to historical center, €10, 2/hr, 70 min, runs 6:15–24:00 from airport; 6:00–22:50 from St. Mark's Square, generally departing airport 10 min after the hour, www.alilaguna.com). A **water taxi** zips you directly to your hotel in 30 minutes for €80. **Buses** connect the airport and the Piazzale Roma vaporetto stop: Catch either the blue ATVO shuttle bus (€3, 2/hr, 20 min, 5:30–20:40 to airport, 8:30–23:30 from airport, www.atvo.it) or the cheaper orange ACTV bus #5 (€1, 2/hr, 20–40 min, 4:40–1:00).

Passes for Venice

To help control (and confuse?) its flood of visitors, Venice now offers cards and passes that cover some museums and/or transportation. For most visitors, the simple Museum Card (the combo Doge's Palace/Correr Museum ticket) or Museum Pass will do.

The **Museum Card** covers the museums of St. Mark's Square: Doge's Palace, Correr Museum, and the two museums accessed from within the Correr—the National Archaeological Museum and the Monumental Rooms of Marciana National Library (€11, called "*Museum Card per i Musei di Piazza San Marco*," valid for 3 months; purchase it at the Correr Museum, then use your card at the Doge's Palace to bypass the long line).

The pricier **Museum Pass** includes the St. Mark's Square museums listed above, plus Ca' Rezzonico (Museum of 18th-Century Venice), Mocenigo Palace museum (textiles and costumes), Casa Goldoni (home of the Italian playwright), and museums on the islands—Murano's Glass Museum and Burano's Lace Museum (€15.50, valid for 3 months).

Venice also (pointlessly) offers two other Museum Cards: €8 for the museums of the 18th century (called "*Museum Card per area del Settecento*"; the museums are Ca' Rezzonico, Casa Goldoni, and Palazzo Mocenigo) and €6 for the island museums (called "*Museum Card per i musei delle isole*," covering Murano's Glass Museum and Burano's Lace Museum).

No cards or passes cover these top attractions: The sights within St. Mark's Basilica, the Campanile, Accademia, Peggy Guggenheim Museum, Scuola Grande di San Rocco, and the Frari Church.

Venice Cards: Personally, I'd skip these, but here's the information. These cards include Venice's public transportation, public toilets, and, if you get the "orange" version, some sights.

DAILY REMINDER

Sunday: The Church of San Giorgio Maggiore (on an island near St. Mark's Square) hosts a Gregorian Mass at 11:00. The Rialto open-air market consists mainly of souvenir stalls today (fish and produce sections closed). These sights are open only in the afternoon: Frari Church (13:00–18:00, closed Sun in Aug) and St. Mark's Basilica (14:00–17:00). It's a bad day for a pub crawl, as most pubs are closed.

Monday: All sights are open except for the Rialto fish market, Dalmatian School, the skippable Palazzo Mocenigo (textiles), and Torcello Museum (on Torcello island). The Accademia and Ca d'Oro (House of Gold) close at 14:00. Don't side-trip to Verona or Vicenza today; most sights are closed.

Tuesday: All sights are open except the Peggy Guggenheim Museum, Ca' Rezzonico (Museum of 18th-Century Venice), and the Lace Museum (on Burano island).

Wednesday: All sights are open except the Glass Museum (on Murano island).

Thursday/Friday: All sights are open.

Saturday: All sights are open (Peggy Guggenheim Museum until 22:00 April–Oct) except the Jewish Museum.

The **Blue Venice Card** covers all your vaporetto rides—plus entry to public toilets: 1 day–€11, 3 days–€23, 7 days–€41; cheaper for "Juniors" under 30. (If all you want is a vaporetto pass, you can get a 24-hour pass for €10.50 at any vaporetto dock; described under "Getting around Venice," page 48.)

The **Orange Venice Card**, which also includes transportation and toilets, gets you into the museums covered by the Museum Pass. It's like getting a Blue Venice Card and a Museum Pass (1 day–€26, 3 days–€43, and 7 days–€58; cheaper for "Juniors" under 30).

"Rolling Venice" Youth Discount Pass: This worthwhile €2.60 pass gives those under 26 discounts on sights and transportation, plus information on cheap eating and sleeping. It is sold at major vaporetto kiosks (tel. 041-271-4747, press 2 for English).

Helpful Hints

Venice is expensive for locals as well as tourists. The demand is huge, supply is limited, and running a business is costly. Things just cost more here; everything must be shipped in and hand-trucked to its destination. Perhaps the best way to enjoy Venice is to just succumb to its charms and blow a lot of money.

Get Lost: Accept the fact that Venice was a tourist town 400 years ago. It was, is, and always will be crowded. While 80 percent of Venice is, in fact, not touristy, 80 percent of the tourists never notice. Hit the backstreets.

Venice is the ideal town to explore on foot. Walk and walk to the far reaches of the town. Don't worry about getting lost. Get as lost as possible. Keep reminding yourself, "I'm on an island, and I can't get off." When it comes time to find your way, just follow the directional arrows on building corners or simply ask a local, "*Dov'è San Marco?*" ("Where is St. Mark's?") People in the tourist business (that's most Venetians) speak some English. If they don't, listen politely, watching where their hands point, say "*Grazie,*" and head off in that direction. If you're lost, pop into a hotel and ask for their business card—it comes with a map and a prominent "you are here."

Take Breaks: Venice's endless pavement, crowds, and tight spaces are hard on the tourist. Schedule breaks in your sightseeing. Grab a cool place to sit down, relax, and recoup—meditate on a pew in an uncrowded church or buy a cappuccino and a fruit cup in a café.

Etiquette: Walk on the right and don't loiter on bridges. Picnicking is technically forbidden (keep a low profile). Dress modestly. Men should keep their shirts on. When visiting St. Mark's Basilica or other major churches, men, women, and even children should cover their knees and shoulders (or risk being turned away).

Pigeon Poop: If bombed by a pigeon, resist the initial response to wipe it off immediately—it'll just smear into your hair. Wait until it dries and flake it off cleanly.

Public Toilets: There are handy public WCs near St. Mark's Square and the Accademia Bridge (see maps on pages iv–v and 50). You'll find public pay toilets near most major landmarks. Use free toilets—in a museum you're visiting or a café you're eating in—when you can.

Water: Venetians pride themselves on having pure, safe, and tasty tap water piped in from the foothills of the Alps; you can actually see the mountains from Venice bell towers on crisp, clear winter days.

Lingo: *Campo* means square, *calle* is street, *fondamenta* is the road running along a canal, and *rio* is a small canal.

Services

Money: ATMs are plentiful and the easiest way to go. Bank rates vary. The American Express change desk is just off St. Mark's Square (see "Travel Agencies," below). Non-bank exchange bureaus, such as Exacto, will cost you $10 more than a bank for a $200 exchange.

Travel Agencies: If you need to get train tickets, pay supplements, make reservations, or arrange a *couchette*, avoid the time-consuming trip to the crowded train station by using a downtown travel agency. While American Express charges railpass holders a €5 service fee for reservations, the other agencies do basically everything the train station does for the same price with no fee. All can give advice on cheap flights. Remember, you'll get a far better price if you're able to book at least a week in advance. Consider booking flights for later in your trip while you're here (and remember that in Europe, you don't have to buy a round-trip ticket to get the best price).

Kele & Teo Viaggi e Turismo is good and handy (accepts credit cards for train tickets only, Mon–Fri 8:30–19:00, Sat 9:00–12:00, closed Sun, at Ponte dei Bareteri on the Mercerie midway between Rialto and St. Mark's Square, tel. 041-520-8722, incoming@keleteo.com).

American Express books flights, sells train tickets, and makes train reservations (travel agency: Mon–Fri 9:00–17:30, closed Sat–Sun; about 2 blocks off St. Mark's Square at 1471 San Marco, en route to Accademia, tel. 041-520-0844).

Rip-offs, Theft, and Help: While pickpockets work the crowded main streets, docks, and vaporetti (wear your money belt and carry your daybag in front), the dark, late-night streets of Venice are safe. A service called Venezia No Problem tries to help tourists who've been mistreated by any Venetian business (toll-free tel. 800-355-920, for complaints only, not for information).

Church Services: The **San Zulian Church** (the only church in Venice that you can actually walk around) offers a Mass in English at 9:30 on Sunday (May–Sept, 2 blocks toward Rialto off St. Mark's Square). Gregorians would enjoy the sung Gregorian Mass on Sundays at 11:00 (plus Mon–Sat at 8:00) at the Church of **San Giorgio Maggiore** (on island of San Giorgio Maggiore, visible from Doge's Palace, see "Venice Lagoon," page 66). Call 041-522-7827 to confirm times.

Laundry: I list several below, but your hotelier can direct you to one near your hotel.

A modern self-serve *lavanderia* is near St. Mark's Square on Ruga Giuffa at #4826 (€11 per load, daily 9:00–22:00, next to Hotel al Piave, see "Sleeping," page 71; tel. 041-241-1223, Massimo).

At either of the following full-service laundries, you can get a nine-pound load washed and dried for €16—confirm price carefully. Drop it off in the morning and pick it up that afternoon. (Call to be sure they're open.) Don't expect to get your clothes back ironed, folded, or even entirely dry. **Lavanderia Gabriella** is near St. Mark's Square (Mon–Fri 8:00–12:30, closed Sat–Sun, 985 Rio Terra Colonne, from San Zulian Church go over Ponte dei Ferali, then take first right down Calle dei Armeni, tel. 041-522-1758). **Lavanderia S.S. Apostoli** is close to the Rialto Bridge on the St. Mark's side (Mon–Fri 9:00–12:00 & 15:30–19:00, closed Sat–Sun, just off Campo S.S. Apostoli on Salizada del Pistor, tel. 041-522-6650).

Post Office: A large post office is just outside the far end of St. Mark's Square (farthest from the basilica, Mon–Sat 8:10–18:00, closed

S.... shorter hours off-season). A branch is near the Rialto Bridge (on St. Mark's side, Mon–Fri 8:10–13:30, Sat 8:10–12:30, closed Sun).

Internet Access: The **Net House** has dozens of terminals and is open 24 hours most days (on Campo San Stefano, just north of Accademia Bridge, photocopy of your passport required before you start surfing, not cheap as Internet cafés go). **Rialtonet** is near the Rialto fish market (daily 9:30–24:00, San Polo 278, tel. 041-241-3862).

Haircuts: I've been getting my hair cut at Coiffeur Benito for 15 years. Benito has been keeping local men and women trim for 25 years. He's an artist—actually a "hair sculptor"—and a cut here is a fun diversion from the tourist grind (€19.50 for women, €16.50 for men, Tue–Sat 8:30–13:00 & 15:30–19:30, closed Sun–Mon, behind San Zulian Church near St. Mark's Square, Calle S. Zulian Gia del Strazzanol 592A, tel. 041-528-6221).

Getting around Venice

By Vaporetto: The public transit system is a fleet of motorized bus-boats called vaporetti. They work like city buses except that they never get a flat, the stops are docks, and if you get off between stops, you may drown.

For most travelers, only two lines matter: #1 is the slow boat, taking 45 minutes to make every stop along the entire length of the Grand Canal; #82 is the fast boat that zips down the Grand Canal in 25 minutes, stopping mainly at Tronchetto (car park), Piazzale Roma (bus station), Ferrovia (train station), Rialto Bridge, San Tomà (Frari Church), the Accademia Bridge, and St. Mark's Square (specifically, the San Marco/Vallaresso dock). Some #82 boats go only as far as Rialto ("*solo Rialto*")—confirm with the conductor before boarding.

Since boats going both directions often share the same dock, check the direction (e.g., San Marco, Piazzale Roma). Buy a €5 ticket ideally before boarding (at the booth at the dock) or from a conductor on board (before you sit down or you risk being fined). Tickets for non-Grand Canal rides cost €3.50. The €5 Grand Canal tickets are good for 90 minutes. To avoid a fine, be sure your ticket is stamped with a time before boarding. Some tickets come stamped but to be safe, I stick mine into a time-stamping yellow machine before boarding.

A 24-hour pass (€10.50) saves money after two trips. The cheaper "Laguna Tour" covers only stops on the Grand Canal and Murano, Burano, and Torcello (€8.50, valid for 12 hrs). Also consider the 72-hour (€22) pass. It's fun to be able to hop on and off spontaneously. Technically, luggage costs the same as dogs—€3.50—but I've never been charged. Riding free? There's a 1-in-10 chance a conductor will fine you €23.

For vaporetto fun, take the Grand Canal Cruise (see page 51); avoid rush hour, when boats are packed heading to St. Mark's Square early in the day and packed heading to the train station late in the day. If you like joyriding on vaporetti, ride a boat around the city and out into the lagoon and back. Ask for the circular route—*circulare* (cheer-koo-LAH-ray). It's usually the #51 or #52, leaving from the San Zaccaria vaporetto stop (near the Doge's Palace) and from all the stops along the perimeter of Venice.

By *Traghetto*: Only three bridges cross the Grand Canal, but *traghetti* (gondolas) shuttle locals and in-the-know tourists across the Grand Canal at several handy locations (see map on page 52; routes also marked on pricier maps sold in Venice). Take advantage of these time-savers. They can also save money. For instance, while most tourists take the €5 vaporetto to connect St. Mark's with La Salute Church, a €0.40 *traghetto* does the job just as well. Most people stand while riding. *Traghetti* generally run from 6:00 until 20:00, sometimes until 23:00.

By Water Taxi: Venetian taxis, like speedboat limos, hang out at most busy points along the Grand Canal. Prices, which average €40 (about €80 to the airport), are a bit soft. Negotiate and settle before stepping in. For travelers with lots of luggage or small groups who can split the cost, taxi rides can be a worthwhile and time-saving convenience—and skipping across the lagoon in a classic wooden motorboat is a cool indulgence.

By Gondola: To hire a gondolier for your own private cruise, see "Gondola Rides," page 68.

TOURS

Walking Tours

Audioguide Tours—At the Campanile bell tower and the TI (on the lagoon side of St. Mark's Square), you can rent audioguides for self-guided walking tours of Venice (2 hrs-€5, 24 hrs-€10, just punch the number of what you'd like described—exteriors only). The commentary is boring and—if you're reading this book—unnecessary.

Venice Walks and Tours—This company offers a selection of historic and entertaining walks, including the basic St. Mark's Square introduction, Cannaregio and the Jewish Ghetto, San Polo and Dorsoduro, Ghosts and Legends, Casanova, and secret gardens (€20 per person, cheaper for returnees and students, €5 off if you say "Rick sent me," small groups, English language only, 2 hours each, rain or shine, also day trips into the mainland, www.venicewalksandtours.com, tel. 041-520-8616, mobile 340-050-2444, Monica and Jonathan).

Classic Venice Bars Tour—Debonair local guide Alessandro Schezzini is a connoisseur of Venetian *bacaros*—classic old bars serving traditional *cicchetti* (local munchies). He offers evening tours that involve stopping and sampling a snack and a glass of wine at three of these (Sat and Wed April–Sept at 18:00, other evenings by request and with demand, meet at top of Rialto). The fee—about €30 per person—includes wine, *cicchetti*, and a great insight into this local tradition (tel. & fax

Sights in Venice

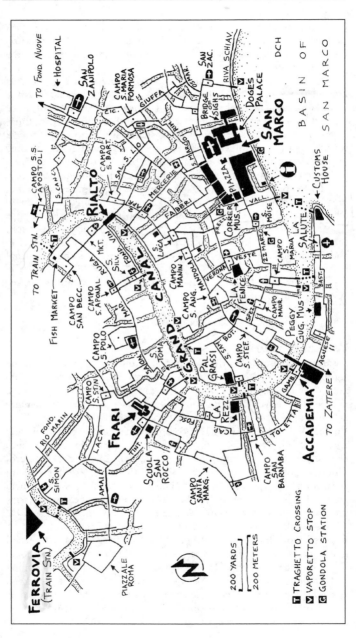

041-534-5367, mobile 335-530-9024, venische@tiscalinet.it). He also does Ghost Tours for spooky evening fun (€20, 90 min).

Venicescapes—Michael Broderick's private theme tours of Venice are intellectually demanding and beyond the attention span of most mortal tourists, but for the curious with stamina, he can be enthralling. Michael's challenge: To help visitors gain a more solid understanding of Venice. For a description of his various itineraries, see www.venicescapes.org (book well in advance, 4–6 hour tour: €275 for 2, €50 per person after that, plus admissions and transportation, tel. 041-520-6361, info @venicescapes.org).

Local Guides—Licensed guides are carefully trained and love explaining Venice to visitors. The following companies and guides give excellent tours to individuals, families, and small groups. If you organize a small group from your hotel at breakfast to split the cost (€65/hour with 2-hour minimum), the fee becomes quite reasonable. **Walks Inside Venice** is a group of three women enthusiastic about their teaching (Roberta Curiel, tel. 041-524-1706, mobile 347-253-0560, www .walksinsidevenice.com, info@walksinsidevenice.com). **Venice With A Guide** is a co-op of 10 equally good guides (see www.venicewith-aguide.com). **Elisabetta Morelli** is also reliable (tel. 041-526-7816, mobile 328-753-5220, bettamorelli@inwind.it).

Alessandro Schezzini (while not a licensed guide and therefore unable to take you into actual sights) does a great job getting you beyond the clichés and into off-beat Venice (€90, 2.5 hrs, listed above in "Classic Venice Bars Tour").

Grand Canal Cruise

For a ▲▲▲ joyride, introduce yourself to Venice by boat. Cruise the Canal Grande from Tronchetto (car park) or Ferrovia (Santa Lucia train station) all the way to San Marco. You can ride boat #1 (slow and ideal, 45 min) or #82 (too fast to comfortably follow this tour, 25 min). When catching either boat, confirm that you're on a "San Marco via Rialto" boat (some boats finish at the Rialto Bridge and others take a non-scenic outside route). The conductor announces "Solo Rialto!" for boats going only as far as Rialto. You do not want boats heading for Piazzale Roma.

If you can't snag a front seat, lurk nearby and take one when it becomes available or find an outside seat in the stern. This ride has the best light and fewest crowds early or late. Twilight is magic. After dark, chandeliers light up the building interiors. While Venice is a barrage on the senses that hardly needs a narration, these notes give the cruise a little meaning and help orient you to this great city. Some city maps (on sale at postcard racks) have a handy Grand Canal map on the back.

Overview: The Grand Canal is Venice's "Main Street." At over two miles long, nearly 150 feet wide, and nearly 15 feet deep, it's the biggest canal with the most impressive palaces. The canal is the remnant of a

Venice's Grand Canal

GHETTO

CANNAREGIO CANAL

SCALZI BRIDGE

SAN MARCUOLA

CASINO

FADED FRESCOES

TRAIN STATION

RIVA DI BIASIO

S. STAE

CA' D'ORO

CA' D'ORO

TO TRONCHETTO

FERROVIA

TURKISH FOUNDATION

TRAGHETTO

POST

S. SIMON

FISH + PRODUCE MARKET

PIAZZALE ROMA

CAPTAIN-GENERAL'S PALACE

SAN SILV.

RIALTO BRIDGE

MERCHANTS' PALACES

RIALTO

SAN MARCO

FIRE STATION

S. TOMÁ

SANT' ANGELO

TWO PALACES

CA' FOSCARI

PALAZZO GRASSI

CA' REZZONICO →

CA' REZZONICO

SAN SAMUELE

FANCY HOTELS

HARRYS BAR

SAN ZACCARIA

ACCADEMIA

S. MARIA D. GIGLIO

SAN MARCO VALLARESSO

200 YARDS

200 METERS

ACCADEMIA GALLERY + BRIDGE

SALUTE

LA SALUTE

CUSTOMS HOUSE

PEGGY GUGGENHEIM MUSEUM

TO SAN GIORGIO MAGGIORE

T TRAGHETTO CROSSING

V VAPORETTO STOP

DCH

TO GIUDECCA

river that once spilled from the mainland into the Adriatic. The sediment it carried formed a delta that was eventually swallowed up by the sea, becoming a lagoon.

Venice is a city of **palaces**, dating from the days when Venice was the world's richest city. The most lavish formed a grand chorus line along the Grand Canal. Once painted in reds and blues, with black-and-white borders and gold-leaf trim, they made Venice a city of dazzling color. This cruise is the only way to really appreciate the palaces, approaching them at water level, where their main entrance were located. Today, strict laws prohibit any changes in these buildings, so while landowners gnash their teeth, we can enjoy Europe's best-preserved medieval city—slowly rotting.

Start at the **train station** or **Tronchetto** car park. We'll orient by the vaporetto stops.

Venice's main thoroughfare is busy with all kinds of **boats:** taxis, police boats, garbage boats, ambulances, construction cranes, and even brown-and-white UPS boats. Venice's sleek, black, graceful **gondolas** are a symbol of the city. While used gondolas cost around €10,000, new ones run up to €65,000 apiece. Today, with over 400 gondoliers joyriding amid the churning vaporetti, there's a lot of congestion on the Grand Canal. Watch your vaporetto driver curse the better-paid gondoliers.

Ferrovia: The **Santa Lucia train station** (on the left bank of the canal), one of the few modern buildings in town, was built in 1954. It's been the gateway into Venice since 1860, when the first station was built. "F.S." stands for "Ferrovie dello Stato," the Italian state railway system. The **bridge** at the station is the first of only three that cross the Canal Grande.

Opposite the train station, atop the green dome of **San Simeone Piccolo** church, Saint Simon waves *ciao* to whoever enters or leaves the "old" city.

Riva di Biasio: Just past the Riva di Biasio stop, look left down the broad **Cannaregio Canal**. The twin pale-pink six-story "skyscrapers" are a reminder of how densely populated the world's original **ghetto** was. Set aside as the local Jewish quarter in 1516, the area (located behind the San Marcuola stop) became extremely crowded. This urban island developed into one of the most closely knit business and cultural quarters of all the Jewish communities in Italy, and gave us our word ghetto (from the copper foundry located here). For more information, visit the Jewish Museum in this neighborhood (listed under "Cannaregio District," page 65).

San Marcuola: The gray **Turkish Exchange** (right side, opposite the vaporetto stop), is considered the oldest house in Venice. Its horseshoe arches and roofline of triangles-and-dingleballs is Byzantine. Turkish traders in turbans docked here, unloaded their goods into the warehouse on the bottom story, then went upstairs for a home-style meal and a place to sleep. Venice in the 1500s was very cosmopolitan, welcoming every people of religion and ethnicity, so long as they carried cash.

Venice's **Casino** (left-hand side) is housed in the palace where German composer Richard *(The Ring)* Wagner died in 1883. See his distinct, strong-jawed profile in the white plaque on the brick wall. In the 1700s, Venice was Europe's Vegas, with casinos and prostitutes everywhere. Today, this elegant Casino welcomes men in ties and ladies in dresses.

San Stae: Opposite the San Stae stop, look for the **faded frescoes** (left bank, on lower story). Imagine the facades of the Grand Canal at their finest. As colorful as the city is today, it's still only a sepia-toned snapshot of a Technicolor era.

Ca' d'Oro: The lacy **Ca' d'Oro**, or "House of Gold," (left bank, next to the vaporetto stop) is the best example of "Venetian Gothic" on the canal. Its three stories offer different variations on balcony design, topped with a spiny white roofline. Venetian Gothic mixes traditional Gothic (pointed arches and round medallions stamped with a four-leaf clover) with Byzantine styles (tall, narrow arches atop thin columns), filled in with Islamic frills. Like all the palaces, this was originally painted and gilded to make it even more glorious than it is now. Today the Ca' d'Oro is a museum but, other than temporary exhibits, there's little to see inside.

Farther along, on the right, the outdoor arcade of the **fish and produce market** bustles with people in the morning but is quiet the rest of the day. This is a great scene to wander through—even though new European hygiene standards recently required a less-colorful remodeling job. Find the *traghetto* gondola ferrying shoppers—standing like Washington crossing the Delaware—back and forth.

The huge **post office** (left side, just before the Rialto Bridge), with *servizio postale* boats moored at its blue posts, was once the German Exchange, the trading center for German metal merchants. Rising above the post office, you can see in the distance the golden angel of the Campanile bell tower at St. Mark's Square, where this tour will end.

As the canal bends, we pass beneath the impressive Rialto Bridge. Singing gondoliers love the acoustics here: "*O sole mio...*"

Rialto: A major landmark of Venice, the **Rialto Bridge** is lined with shops and tourists. Constructed in 1588, it's the third bridge built on this spot. With a span of 160 feet and foundations stretching 650 feet on either side, the Rialto was an impressive engineering feat in its day. Earlier Rialto Bridges could open to let in big ships, but not this one. When this new bridge was completed, much of the Grand Canal was closed to shipping and became a canal of palaces. Locals call the summit of this bridge the "icebox of Venice" for its cool breeze. Tourists call it a great place to kiss.

Rialto, a separate town in the early days of Venice, has always been the commercial district, while San Marco was the religious and governmental center. Today, a winding street called the Mercerie connects the two, providing travelers with human traffic jams and a mesmerizing gauntlet of shopping temptations. The restaurants that line the canal feature great views, midrange prices, and low quality.

San Silvestro: On the left side, opposite the vaporetto stop, **two palaces stand side by side**, with stories the same height, creating the effect of one long balcony.

We now enter a long stretch of important **merchants' palaces**, each with proud and different facades. Since ships couldn't navigate beyond the Rialto Bridge (to reach the section of the Grand Canal you just came from), the biggest palaces—with the major shipping needs—lie ahead. Many feature the Roman country villa design of twin towers flanking a huge set of central windows. These were showrooms designed to let in maximum sunlight.

Just after the San Silvestro stop, you'll see (on the right) the palace of a 15th-century **"captain general of the sea."** The Venetian equivalents of five-star admirals were honored with twin obelisks decorating their palaces. This palace flies three flags: those of Italy (green-white-red), the

European Union (blue with ring of stars), and Venice (the lion).

Sant' Angelo: Notice how many buildings have a foundation of waterproof white stone *(pietra d'Istria)* upon which the bricks sit high and dry. Many canal-level floors are abandoned; the rising water level takes its toll. The **posts**—historically painted with the gaily-colored equivalent of family coats of arms—don't rot under water. But the wood at the waterline does rot.

Take a deep whiff of Venice. What's all this nonsense about stinky canals? All I smell is my shirt. By the way, how's your captain? Smooth dockings? To get to know him, stand up in the bow and block his view.

San Tomà: After the San Tomà stop, look down the side canal (on the right, before the bridge) to see the traffic light, the **fire station**, and the fireboats ready to go.

We now prepare to round the corner and double back toward St. Mark's. The impressive **Ca' Foscari** (right side) dominates the bend in the canal. Its four stories get increasingly ornate as they rise from the water—from simple Gothic arches at water level, to Gothic with a point, to Venetian Gothic arches topped with four-leaf clovers, to still more medallions and laciness that look almost Moorish. Wow.

Ca' Rezzonico: The grand, heavy, white **Ca' Rezzonico**, directly at the stop of the same name, houses the Museum of 18th-Century Venice. Across the canal is the cleaner and leaner **Palazzo Grassi**, which often showcases special exhibitions.

These days, when buildings are being renovated, huge murals with images of the building mask the ugly scaffolding. Corporations hide the scaffolding for the goodwill—and the publicity.

Accademia: The wooden **Accademia Bridge** crosses the Grand Canal and leads to the **Accademia Gallery** (right side), filled with the best Venetian paintings. The bridge was put up in 1932 as a temporary one. Locals liked it, so it stayed. Cruising under the bridge, you'll get a classic view of the domed La Salute Church ahead.

The low white building among greenery (on the right, between the bridge and the church) is the **Peggy Guggenheim Museum**. The American heiress "retired" here, sprucing up the palace that had been abandoned in mid-construction; the locals call it the "palazzo non finito." Peggy willed the city her fine collection of modern art (described under "Dorsoduro District," page 63).

Salute: A crown-shaped dome supported by scrolls stands atop **La Salute Church**. This Church of Saint Mary of Good Health was built to coax God into delivering Venice from the devastating plague of 1630 (which eventually killed about a third of the city's population).

Across the canal (left side), several **fancy hotels** have painted facades that hint at the canal's former glory.

As the Grand Canal opens up into the lagoon, the last building on the right with the golden ball is the 16th-century **Customs House**

VENICE AT A GLANCE

▲▲▲**St. Mark's Square** Venice's grand main square. **Hours:** Always open.

▲▲▲**St. Mark's Basilica** Cathedral with mosaics, saint's bones, treasury, museum, and viewpoint of square. **Hours:** Mon–Sat 9:45–17:00, Sun 14:00–17:00, some areas close at 16:30 in winter.

▲▲▲**Doge's Palace** Art-splashed palace of former rulers, with prison accessed through Bridge of Sighs. **Hours:** April–Oct daily 9:00–19:00, Nov–March daily 9:00–17:00, last entry 90 min before closing.

▲▲**Correr Museum** Venetian history and art. **Hours:** April–Oct daily 9:00–19:00, Nov–March 9:00–17:00.

▲▲**Frari Church** Franciscan church featuring Renaissance masters. **Hours:** Mon–Sat 9:00–18:00, Sun 13:00–18:00, closed Sun in Aug.

▲▲**Scuola Grande di San Rocco** Tintoretto's "Sistine Chapel." **Hours:** Daily 9:00–17:30, Nov-March 10:00–16:00.

▲▲**Accademia** Venice's top art museum. **Hours:** Mon 8:15–14:00, Tue–Sun 8:15–19:15, shorter hours off-season.

▲▲**Peggy Guggenheim Museum** Popular collection of 20th-century art. **Hours:** Wed–Mon 10:00–18:00, Sat until 22:00 April-Oct, closed Tue.

▲**Campanile** Dramatic bell tower with elevator to top. **Hours:** Daily June–Sept 9:00–21:00, Oct–May 9:00–19:00.

▲**Ca' Rezzonico** Posh Grand Canal palazzo with 18th-century Venetian art. **Hours:** April–Oct Wed–Mon 10:00–18:00, Nov–March 10:00-17:00, closed Tue.

San Giorgio Maggiore Island across the lagoon featuring church with worth-the-trip bell tower view. **Hours:** Daily 9:30–12:30 & 14:00–18:30, closed for sightseeing during Mass on Sun.

La Salute Church Striking church dedicated to the Virgin Mary. **Hours:** Daily 9:00–12:00 & 15:00–18:00.

Jewish Ghetto Neighborhood and Jewish Museum. **Hours:** Museum: June–Sept Sun–Fri 10:00–19:00, Oct–May Sun–Fri 10:00–17:30, closed Sat.

Dalmatian School Exquisite Renaissance meeting house. **Hours:** Tue–Sat 9:30–12:30 & 15:30–18:30, Sun 9:30–12:30, closed Mon.

Santa Elena 100-year-old neighborhood with few tourists. **Hours:** Always open.

(Dogana da Mar, not open to the public). Its two bronze Atlases hold a statue of Fortune riding the ball. Arriving ships stopped here to pay their tolls.

As you prepare to disembark at the San Marco/Vallaresso stop, look from left to right out over the lagoon. On the left, a wide harborfront walk leads past the town's most elegant hotels to the green area in the distance. This is the public garden, the largest of Venice's few parks, which hosts the Biennale art show. Farther in the distance is the **Lido**, the island with Venice's beach. It's tempting, with sand and casinos, but its car traffic breaks into the medieval charm of Venice.

The ghostly white church that seems to float is the architect Palladio's **San Giorgio Maggiore**. It's just a vaporetto ride away (#82 from the "San Zaccaria Jolanda" stop, just past the Bridge of Sighs; see "Venice Lagoon," page 66). Across the lagoon (to your right) is a residential island called **Giudecca**.

San Marco/Vallaresso: Get off at the San Marco/Vallaresso stop. Directly ahead is **Harry's Bar**. Hemingway drank here when it was a characteristic no-name *osteria* and the gondoliers' hangout. Today, of course, it's the overpriced hangout of well-dressed Americans who don't mind paying triple for their Bellinis (peach juice with Prosecco wine) to make the scene. St. Mark's Square is just around the corner.

SIGHTS

St. Mark's Square

For information on Venice's Museum Card and Museum Pass, see page 44.

▲▲▲**St. Mark's Square (Piazza San Marco)**—Surrounded by splashy and historic buildings, Piazza San Marco is filled with music, lovers, pigeons, and tourists by day and is your private rendezvous with the Middle Ages late at night. Europe's greatest dance floor is the romantic place to be. St. Mark's Square is about the first place in Venice to flood (you might see stacked wooden benches; when the square floods, these are put end to end to make elevated sidewalks).

With your back to the church, survey one of Europe's great urban spaces, and the only square in Venice to merit the title "Piazza." Nearly two football fields long, it's surrounded by the offices of the republic. On the right are the "old offices" (16th-century Renaissance). On the left are the "new offices" (17th-century Baroque). Napoleon, after enclosing the square with the more simple and austere neoclassical wing across the far end, called this "the most beautiful drawing room in Europe."

The clock tower, a Renaissance tower built in 1496, marks the entry to the Mercerie, the main shopping drag, which connects St. Mark's Square with the Rialto. From the piazza, you can see the bronze men (Moors) swing their huge clappers at the top of each hour. In the 17th

St. Mark's Square

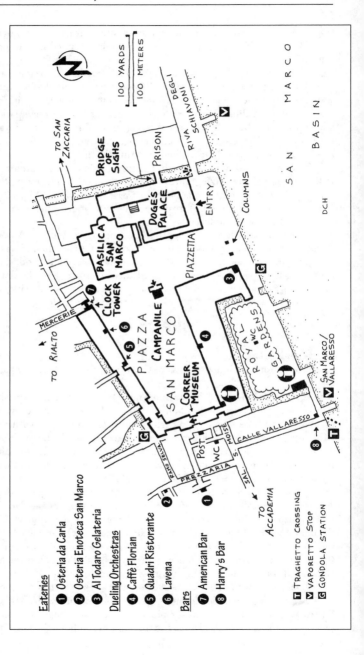

Eateries
1 Osteria da Carla
2 Osteria Enoteca San Marco
3 Al Todaro Gelateria

Dueling Orchestras
4 Caffè Florian
5 Quadri Ristorante
6 Lavena

Bars
7 American Bar
8 Harry's Bar

T TRAGHETTO CROSSING
V VAPORETTO STOP
G GONDOLA STATION

century, one of them knocked an unsuspecting worker off the top and to his death—probably the first-ever killing by a robot. Notice the world's first "digital" clock on the tower facing the square (with dramatic flips every 5 minutes).

For a slow and pricey evening thrill, invest €6.20 (plus €4 if the orchestra plays) in a beer or coffee at one of the elegant cafés with the dueling orchestras (see Caffè Florian, described in "Nightlife in Venice," page 70.) If you're going to sit and savor the scene, it's worth the splurge. If all you have is €1, buy a bag of pigeon feed and become popular in a flurry. To get everything airborne, toss your sweater in the air.

Venice's best TI is in the far left corner of the square (Mon–Sat 9:00–15:30, closed Sun; a €0.50 WC is nearby, located a few steps beyond St. Mark's Square en route to the American Express office and the Accademia—see *Albergo Diorno* sign marked on pavement, open daily 9:00–20:00). The other TI is on the lagoon (daily 9:00–18:00, walk toward the water by the Doge's Palace, go right; pay WCs nearby open daily 9:00–19:00).

▲▲St. Mark's Basilica—Built in the 11th century to replace an earlier church, the basilica has a distinctly Eastern-style of architecture to under-score Venice's connection with Byzantium (thus protecting it from the ambition of Charlemagne and his Holy Roman Empire). It's decorated with booty from returning sea captains—a kind of architectural Venetian trophy chest.

Since about A.D. 830, the saint's bones have been housed on this site. The mosaic above the door at the far left of the church shows two guys carrying Mark's coffin into the church. Mark looks pretty grumpy after the long voyage from Egypt.

To enter the church, modest dress is required even of kids (no shorts or bare shoulders). In peak season, there can be long lines of people wait-ing to get into the church. People who ignore the dress code hold up the line while they plead fruitlessly with—or put on extra clothes under the watchful eyes of—the dress code police.

The church has 43,000 square feet of Byzantine mosaics, the best and oldest of which are in the atrium (turn right as you enter and stop under the last dome—this may be roped off, but dome is still visible). Facing the church, gape up (it's OK, no pigeons), and read clockwise the story of Adam and Eve that rings the bottom of the dome. Now, facing the piazza, look domeward for the story of Noah, the ark, and the flood (two by two, the wicked being drowned, Noah sending out the dove, a happy rainbow, and a sacrifice of thanks).

Step inside the church (the stairs on the right lead to the bronze horses—save these for later). The interior glows mysteriously with gold mosaics and colored marble. Notice the marble floor richly decorated in mosaics. As in many Venetian buildings, because the best foundation pilings were made around the perimeter, the floor rolls. As you shuffle

FLOODS AND A DYING CITY

Venice floods about 60 times a year—normally in March and November—when the wind blowing from the south (Egypt) and high barometric pressure on the lower Adriatic Sea are most likely to combine to push water up to this top end of the sea. (The lunar tide in the Mediterranean is miniscule.)

Floods start in St. Mark's Square. The entry of the church is nearly the lowest spot in town. (You might see stacked wooden benches; when the square floods, these are placed end to end to make elevated sidewalks). The measuring devices at the base of the outside of the Campanile bell tower (near the exit, facing St. Mark's Square) show the current sea level *(livello marea)*. When the water level rises one meter, a warning siren sounds. It repeats if a serious flood is imminent. Find the mark showing the high-water level from the terrible floods of 1966 (waist-level, on right).

In 1965, Venice's population was over 150,000. Since the flood of 1966 the population has been shrinking. Today the population is about 65,000...and geriatric. Sad, yes, but imagine raising a family here: The fragile nature of the city means piles of regulations (no biking, and so on), and costs are high—even though the government is now subsidizing rents to keep people from moving out. You can easily get glass and tourist trinkets, but it's hard to find groceries. And floods and the humidity make house maintenance an expensive pain.

under the central dome, look up for the Ascension (free, Mon–Sat 9:30–17:00, Sun 14:00–17:00, no photos, tel. 041-522-5205). See the schedule board in the atrium, listing free English guided tours (schedules vary but May–Oct generally Wed and Thu at 11:00). The church is particularly beautiful when lit (unpredictable schedule but worth trying to see, often weekdays 11:30–12:30, Sat–Sun all day). During peak times, the line can be very long.

In the **Galleria and Museum** upstairs, you can see an up-close mosaic exhibition, a fine view of the church interior, a view of the square from the balcony with bronze horses, and (inside, in their own room) the newly restored original horses. These well-traveled horses, made during the days of Alexander the Great (4th century B.C.), were taken to Rome by Nero, to Constantinople/Istanbul by Constantine, to Venice by crusaders, to Paris by Napoleon, back "home" to Venice when Napoleon fell, and finally indoors and out of the acidic air (€1.60, daily 9:45–17:00, 9:45–16:30 in winter, enter from atrium either before or after you tour church).

San Marco's **treasury** (with included and informative audioguide free for the asking) and **altarpiece** (€2 each, daily 9:45–17:00, 9:45–16:30 in winter) give you the best chance outside of Istanbul or Ravenna to see the glories of Byzantium. Venetian crusaders looted the Christian city of Constantinople and brought home piles of lavish loot (until the advent of TV evangelism, perhaps the lowest point in Christian history). Much of this plunder is stored in the treasury *(tesoro)* of San Marco. As you view these treasures, remember that most were made around A.D. 500, while western Europe was still rutting in the mud. Beneath the high altar lies the body of St. Mark ("Marxus") and the Pala d'Oro, a golden altarpiece made with 80 Byzantine enamels (A.D. 1000–1300). Each shows a religious scene set in gold and precious stones. Both of these sights are interesting and historic, but neither is as much fun as two bags of pigeon feed.

▲▲▲**Doge's Palace (Palazzo Ducale)**—The seat of the Venetian government and home of its ruling duke, or doge, this was the most powerful half-acre in Europe for 400 years.

The Doge's Palace was built to show off the power and wealth of the republic and remind all visitors that Venice was number one. In typical Venetian Gothic style, the bottom has pointy arches, and the top has an Eastern or Islamic flavor. Its columns sat on pedestals, but in the thousand years since they were erected, the palace has settled into the mud, and the bases have vanished.

Enjoy the newly restored facades from the courtyard. Notice a grand staircase (with nearly naked Moses and Paul Newman at the top). Even the most powerful visitors climbed this to meet the doge. This was the beginning of an architectural power trip. The doge, the elected-for-life duke or leader of this "dictatorship of the aristocracy," lived with his family on the first floor near the halls of power. From his living quarters (once lavish, now sparsely furnished), you'll follow the one-way route through the public rooms of the top floor, finishing with the Bridge of Sighs and the prison. The place is wallpapered with masterpieces by Veronese and Tintoretto. Don't worry much about the great art. Enjoy the building.

In room 12, the Senate Room, the 200 senators met, debated, and passed laws. From the center of the ceiling, Tintoretto's *Triumph of Venice* shows the city in all her glory. Lady Venice, in heaven with the Greek gods, stands high above the lesser nations, who swirl respectfully at her feet with gifts.

The Armory—a dazzling display originally assembled to intimidate potential adversaries—shows remnants of the military might that the empire employed to keep the East-West trade lines open (and the local economy booming). Squint out the window at the far end for a fine view of Palladio's San Giorgio Maggiore Church and the *lido* (cars, casinos, crowded beaches) in the distance.

The giant Hall of the Grand Council (180 feet long, capacity 2,000) is where the entire nobility met to elect the senate and doge. Ringing the room are portraits of 76 doges (in chronological order). One, a doge who opposed the will of the Grand Council, is blacked out. Behind the doge's throne, you can't miss Tintoretto's monsterpiece, *Paradise*. At 1,700 square feet, this is the world's largest oil painting. Christ and Mary are surrounded by a heavenly host of 500 saints. Its message to electors who met here: Make wise decisions and you'll ultimately join that holy crowd.

Walking over the Bridge of Sighs, you'll enter the prisons. In the privacy of his own home, a doge could sentence, torture, and jail his opponents secretly. As you walk back over the bridge, squeeze your arm through the marble lattice window and wave to the gang of tourists gawking at you.

Cost: €11 (combo-ticket includes admission to the Correr Museum). If the line is very long at the Doge's Palace, buy your ticket at the Correr Museum across the square. With that, you can go directly through the Doge's Palace turnstile without waiting in the long line.

Hours: April–Oct daily 9:00–19:00, Nov–March daily 9:00–17:00, last entry 90 minutes before closing.

TIPS ON SIGHTSEEING IN VENICE

Crowd Control: Crowds can be a serious problem only at the Accademia (to minimize crowds, go early or late); St. Mark's Basilica (try going early or late); Campanile bell tower (go late—it's open until 21:00 in the summer); and the Doge's Palace. For the Doge's Palace, you have three options for avoiding the ticket-sales line: Buy your Museum Card or Museum Pass at the Correr Museum (then step right up to the Doge's Palace turnstile, skipping the long line); visit the Doge's Palace at 17:00 (if it's April–Oct) when lines disappear; or book a "Secret Itineraries" tour (see page 63).

Hours: The Accademia is open earlier (daily at 8:15) and closes later (19:15 Tue–Sun) than most sights in Venice. Some sights close earlier off-season (e.g., Doge's Palace; Correr Museum; the Campanile bell tower; and St. Mark's Museum, Treasury, and Golden Altarpiece).

Churches: Modest dress is recommended at churches and required at St. Mark's Basilica—no bare shoulders, shorts, or short skirts. Some churches are closed to sightseers on Sunday morning (e.g., St. Mark's Basilica and Frari Church) and many are closed from roughly 12:00 to 15:00 Monday through Saturday (e.g., La Salute and San Giorgio Maggiore).

Tours: Consider the €5.50 audioguide or the "Secret Itineraries Tour," which takes you into palace rooms otherwise not open to the public (€12.50, at 10:00 and 11:30 in English, 75 min; to make reservation for tour, call 041-291-5911 or 041-520-9070 several days in advance). While the tour skips the main halls inside, it finishes inside the palace and you're welcome to visit the halls on your own.

▲▲**Correr Museum (Museo Civico Correr)**—The city history museum is now included (whether you like it or not) with the admission to the Doge's Palace. In the Napoleon Wing, you'll see fine neoclassical sculpture by Canova. Then peruse armor, banners, and paintings re-creating festive days of the Venetian republic. The top floor lays out a good overview of Venetian art, including several paintings by the Bellini family. And just before the cafeteria is a room filled with traditional games. There are English descriptions and great Piazza San Marco views throughout (€11 on the combo-ticket that includes the Doge's Palace, April–Oct daily 9:00–19:00, Nov–March 9:00–17:00, last entry 70 min before closing, enter at far end of square directly opposite church, tel. 041-240-5211 or 041-522-4951).

▲**Campanile (Campanile di San Marco)**—This dramatic bell tower replaced a shorter lighthouse, once part of the original fortress/palace that guarded the entry of the Grand Canal. The lighthouse crumbled into a pile of bricks in 1902, a thousand years after it was built. Ride the elevator 300 feet to the top of the reconstructed bell tower for the best view in Venice. For an ear-shattering experience, be on top when the bells ring (€6, June–Sept daily 9:00–21:00, Oct–May 9:00–19:00). The golden angel at its top always faces into the wind. Beat the crowds and enjoy crisp morning air at 9:00.

Dorsoduro District

▲▲**Accademia (Galleria dell' Accademia)**—Venice's top art museum, packed with highlights of the Venetian Renaissance, features paintings by the Bellini family, Titian, Tintoretto, Veronese, Tiepolo, Giorgione, Testosterone, and Canaletto. It's just over the wooden Accademia Bridge. Expect long lines in the late morning because they allow only 300 visitors in at a time; visit early or late to miss crowds (€6.50 entry, Mon 8:15–14:00, Tue–Sun 8:15–19:15, shorter hours off-season, ticket window closes 45 min early, no photos allowed, tel. 041-522-2247). The dull audioguides (€4, €6 with 2 earphones, or €6 for a Palm Pilot) don't let you fast-forward to works you want to hear about; you have to listen to the whole spiel for each room.

At the Accademia Bridge, there's a decent pizzeria canalside (Pizzeria Accademia Foscarini; see "Eating," page 82); a public WC under it; and usually a classic shell game being played on top (study the system as partners in the crowd win big money, inspiring suckers to lose the same). Nearby sights include the Peggy Guggenheim Museum and La Salute Church.

▲▲**Peggy Guggenheim Museum**—This popular collection of far-out art, housed in the American heiress' former retirement palazzo, offers one of Europe's best reviews of the art of the first half of the 20th century. Stroll through styles represented by artists whom Peggy knew personally—cubism (Picasso, Braque), surrealism (Dalí, Ernst), futurism (Boccione), American abstract expressionism (Pollock), and a sprinkling of Klee, Calder, and Chagall (€8, Wed–Mon 10:00–18:00, plus Sat 10:00–22:00 April–Oct, closed Tue, audioguide-€4, guidebook-€18, free and mandatory baggage check, pricey café, photos allowed only in garden and terrace—a fine and relaxing perch overlooking Grand Canal, near Accademia, tel. 041-240-5411). The place is run (cheaply) by American interns working on art history degrees.

La Salute Church (Santa Maria delle Salute)—This impressive church with a crown-shaped dome was built and dedicated to the Virgin Mary by grateful survivors of the 1630 plague (free, daily 9:00–12:00 & 15:00–18:00, tel. 041-522-5558 to confirm). It's a 10-minute walk from Accademia Bridge, or vaporetto ride (stop: Salute), or inexpensive *traghetto* crossing from near St. Mark's Square—catch it on the lagoon next to the TI and Harry's Bar.

▲**Ca' Rezzonico (Museum of 18th-Century Venice)**—This grand Grand Canal palazzo offers the best look in town at the life of Venice's rich and famous in the 1700s. Wander under ceilings by Tiepolo, among furnishings from that most decadent century, enjoying views of the canal and paintings by Guardi, Canaletto, and Longhi (€6.70, April–Oct Wed–Mon 10:00–18:00, Nov–March 10:00-17:00, closed Tue, ticket office closes 1 hour early, audioguide-€5.50, located at Ca' Rezzonico vaporetto stop, tel. 041-241-0100).

San Polo District

▲▲**Frari Church (Chiesa dei Frari)**—My favorite art experience in Venice is seeing art *in situ*—the setting for which it was designed—and my favorite example is the Chiesa dei Frari. The Franciscan "church of the friars" and the art that decorates it are warmed by the spirit of St. Francis. It features the work of three great Renaissance masters: Donatello, Bellini, and Titian, each showing worshipers the glory of God in human terms.

In Donatello's wood carving of St. John the Baptist (just to the right of the high altar), the prophet of the desert—dressed in animal skins and almost anorexic from his diet of bugs 'n' honey—announces the coming of the Messiah. Donatello was a Florentine working at the dawn of the Renaissance.

Bellini's *Madonna and the Saints* painting (in the chapel farther to the right) came later, done by a Venetian in a more Venetian style—soft focus without Donatello's harsh realism. While Renaissance humanism demanded Madonnas and saints that were accessible and human, Bellini places them in a physical setting so beautiful it creates its own mood of serene holiness. The genius of Bellini, perhaps the greatest Venetian painter, is obvious in the pristine clarity, rich colors (notice Mary's clothing), believable depth, and reassuring calm of this three-paneled altarpiece. It's so good to see a painting in its natural setting.

Finally, glowing red and gold like a stained-glass window over the high altar, Titian's *Assumption* sets the tone of exuberant beauty found in the otherwise sparse church. Titian the Venetian—a student of Bellini—painted steadily for 60 years...you'll see a lot of his art. As stunned apostles look up past the swirl of arms and legs, the complex composition of this painting draws you right to the radiant face of the once dying, now triumphant Mary as she joins God in heaven.

Be comfortable discreetly freeloading off passing tours. For many, these three pieces of art make a visit to the Accademia Gallery unnecessary (or they may whet your appetite for more). Before leaving, check out the neoclassical, pyramid-shaped tomb of Canova and (opposite that) the grandiose tomb of Titian. Compare the carved marble Assumption behind Titian's tombstone portrait with the painted original above the high altar.

Cost and Hours: €2, Mon–Sat 9:00–18:00, Sun 13:00–18:00, closed Sun in Aug, last entry 15 min before closing, audioguides-€1.60/person or €2.60/double set (tel. 041-523-4864). Modest dress is recommended.

▲▲**Scuola Grande di San Rocco**—Sometimes called "Tintoretto's Sistine Chapel," this lavish meeting hall (next to the Frari Church) has some 50 large, colorful Tintoretto paintings plastered to the walls and ceilings. The best paintings are upstairs, especially the *Crucifixion* in the smaller room. View the neck-breaking splendor with one of the mirrors (*specchio*) available at the entrance (€5.50, includes free and informative audioguide, daily April–Oct 9:00–17:30, Nov–March 10:00–16:00, or see a concert here and enjoy the art as an evening bonus—see "Nightlife," page 70).

Cannaregio District

Jewish Ghetto—The word "ghetto" is Venetian for foundry, and was inherited by Venice's Jewish community when it was confined to the site of Venice's former copper foundries in 1516. Notice how an island—dominated by the Campo del Ghetto Nuovo square and connected with the rest of Venice by only two bridges—would be easy to isolate. While little survives from that time, in its day the square was densely populated, lined with proto-skyscrapers seven to nine stories high.

This original ghetto becomes most interesting after touring the **Jewish Museum** (€3, June–Sept Sun–Fri 10:00–19:00, Oct–May Sun–Fri 10:00–17:30, closed Sat, Campo di Ghetto Nuovo, tel. 041-715-359). The synagogues are open only by tour (€8, hourly 10:30–16:30, later in summer, in English, contact museum).

Castello District

Dalmatian School (Scuola Dalmata dei San Giorgio)—This "school" (which means "meeting place") is a reminder that Venice was Europe's most cosmopolitan place in its heyday. It was here that the Dalmatians (from the present-day region of Croatia) worshiped in their own way, held neighborhood meetings, and worked to preserve their culture. The chapel on the ground floor happens to have the most exquisite Renaissance interior in Venice, with a cycle painted by Carpaccio ringing the room (€3, Tue–Sat 9:30–12:30 & 15:30–18:30, Sun 9:30–12:30, closed Mon; between St. Mark's Square and Arsenale, on Calle dei Furlani, 3 blocks southeast of Campo San Lorenzo; tel. 041-522-8828).

Santa Elena—For a pleasant peek into a completely non-touristy, residential side of Venice, walk or catch vaporetto #1 or #82 from St. Mark's Square to the neighborhood of Santa Elena (at the fish's tail). This 100-year-old suburb lives as if there were no tourism. You'll find a kid-friendly park, a few lazy restaurants, and beautiful sunsets over San Marco.

Venice Lagoon

The island of Venice sits in a lagoon—a calm section of the Adriatic protected from wind and waves by the neutral breakwater of the *lido*. Four interesting islands hide out in the lagoon.

San Giorgio Maggiore is the dreamy island you can see from the waterfront by St. Mark's Square. The striking church, designed by Palladio, features art by Tintoretto and a bell tower with oh-wow views of Venice (free entry to church, daily 9:30–12:30 & 14:00–18:30, closed Sun to sightseers during Mass, Gregorian Mass sung on Sun at 11:00, Mon–Sat at 8:00; €3 for bell tower lift, stops 30 min before church's closing time). To reach the island from St. Mark's Square, take the five-minute vaporetto ride on #82 from the San Zaccaria Jolanda stop, just past the Bridge of Sighs, closest to the big statue. (Note: This is not the same vaporetto stop as San Marco/Vallaresso.)

The islands of **Murano, Burano,** and **Torcello** are reached easily, cheaply, and slowly by vaporetto. Pick up a free map of the islands from any TI. Depart from San Zaccaria dock nearest the Bridge of Sighs and Doge's Palace. **Vaporetto line #12** connects all three islands, or take #41 to Murano (get off at the Murano Colonna stop), then #12 to the other islands. If you plan to visit even two of these islands, get a 24-hour €10.50 vaporetto pass or a 12-hour €8.50 "Laguna Tour" pass for convenience. **Speedboat tours** (3–5 hrs) of these three lagoon destinations leave twice a day from the dock past the Doge's Palace near the Cipriani Hotel shuttle dock—look for the signs and booth (€20, usually at 9:30 and 14:30; Nov–March 14:30 only, tel. 041-523-8835); the tours are speedy indeed, stopping for roughly 35 minutes at each island.

Venice Lagoon

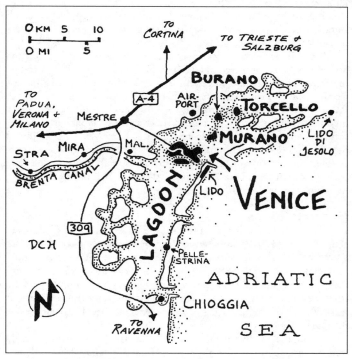

Murano, famous for its glass factories, has the Glass Museum, which displays the very best of 700 years of Venetian glassmaking and exhibits of ancient and modern glass art (Museo Vetrario, €4, covered by €15.50 Museum Pass, Thu–Tue 10:00–17:00, Nov–March 10:00–16:00, last entry 30 min before closing, closed Wed, tel. 041-739-586). You'll be tempted by salesmen offering free speedboat shuttles from St. Mark's Square to Murano. If you're interested in glass, it's handy. You must watch the 20-minute glassmaking show, but then you're free to buy or escape and see the rest of the island. Numerous glass factories (*fabbrica* or *fornace*) offer demonstrations all over the island—check one out. When you're ready to go, head to the Faro vaporetto stop and take the #12 to either Burano or Torcello or the #41 back to San Zaccaria.

Burano, famous for its lace, is a sleepy island with a sleepy community—village Venice without the glitz. Lace fans enjoy the Lace Museum (Scuola di Merletti, €4, covered by €15.50 Museum Pass, Wed–Mon 10:00–17:00, Nov–March 10:00–16:00, closed Tue, tel.

041-730-034). The park next to Burano's only vaporetto dock is perfect for a waterfront picnic. While the main drag leading from the vaporetto stop into town is packed with tourists and lined with shops (some sell Burano's locally-produced white wine), simply wander to the far, peaceful side of the island.

Torcello is the least-developed island (pop. 20), with little for the tourist to see except the church (a 10-min walk from the dock), claiming to be the oldest in Venice. It's impressive for its mosaics, but not worth a look on a short visit unless you really love mosaics and can't make it to Ravenna. The complex consists of the church itself, the bell tower (behind the church, climb a ramped stairway for great lagoon views), a sacristy, and a small museum (facing the church, in 2 separate buildings) that displays Roman sculpture and medieval sculpture and manuscripts. A €5.20 combination ticket gets you into all the sights (most open daily 10:30–17:30, museum closed Mon, tel. 041-730-761; pay WC between museum's two buildings).

Gondola Rides

A rip-off for some, this is a traditional must for romantics. Gondoliers charge about €62 for a 50-minute ride during the day; from 20:00 on, figure on €77–105 (for *musica*—singer and accordionist—it's an additional €88 during day, €98 after 20:00). You can divide the cost—and the romance—among up to six people per boat. Note that only two seats (the ones in back) are next to each other. If you want to haggle, you'll find softer prices on back lanes where single gondoliers hang out than at the bigger departure points.

Though they cost nearly double after dark, gondolas are triply romantic and relaxing under the moon. Glide through nighttime Venice with your head on someone's shoulder. Follow the moon as it sails past otherwise unseen buildings. Silhouettes gaze down from bridges while window glitter spills onto the black water. You're anonymous in the city of masks as the rhythmic thrust of your striped-shirted gondolier turns old crows into songbirds. This is extremely relaxing. Since you might get a narration plus conversation with your gondolier, talk with several and choose one you like who speaks English well. Women, beware...while gondoliers can be extremely charming, local women say anyone who falls for one of these Romeos "has slices of ham over her eyes."

For cheap gondola thrills during the day, stick to the €0.40 one-minute ferry ride on a Grand Canal *traghetto*. At night, vaporettos are nearly empty, and it's a great time to cruise the Grand Canal on the slow boat #1. Or hang out on a bridge along the gondola route and wave at—or drop leftover pigeon feed on—romantics.

Festivals

Venice's most famous festival is **Carnevale**, the celebration Americans call Mardi Gras (Feb 14–24 in 2004; www.carnivalofvenice.com). Carnevale, which means "farewell to meat," originated centuries ago as a wild two-month-long party leading up to the austerity of Lent. In Carnevale's heyday—the 1600s and 1700s—you could do pretty much anything with anybody from any social class if you were wearing a mask. These days it's a tamer 10-day celebration, culminating in a huge dance lit with fireworks on St. Mark's Square. Sporting masks and costumes, Venetians from kids to businessmen join in the fun. Drawing the biggest crowds of the year, Carnevale has nearly been a victim of its own success, driving away many Venetians (who skip out on the craziness to go ski in the Dolomites).

Other typically Venetian festival days filling the city's hotels with visitors and its canals with decked-out boats are: **Feast of the Ascension Day** (mid-May), **Feast and Regatta of the Redeemer** (parade and fireworks, July 17–18, 2004), and the **Historical Regatta** (old-time boats and pageantry, first weekend in September). Smaller regattas include the **Murano Regatta** (early July) and the **Burano Regatta** (in September).

Venice's patron saint, **St. Mark**, is commemorated every April 25. Venetian men celebrate the day by presenting roses to the women in their lives (mothers, wives, and lovers).

Every November 21 is the **Feast of Our Lady of Good Health**. On this local "Thanksgiving," a bridge is built over the Grand Canal so the city can pile into the Salute Church and remember how Venice survived the gruesome plague of 1630. On this day, Venetians eat smoked lamb from Dalmatia (which was the cargo of the first ship admitted when the plague lifted).

Every odd year, the city hosts the **Venice Biennale International Art Exhibition**, a world-class contemporary fair spread over the sprawling Castello Gardens (generally March–Nov, vaporetto stop: Giardini/Biennale, www.labiennale.org).

Venice is always busy with special musical and artistic events. The free monthly *Un Ospite de Venezia* lists all the latest in English (free at TI or from fancy hotels). For a comprehensive list of festivals, contact the Italian tourist information office in the United States (see pages 9–10) and visit www.whatsonwhen.com, www.festivals.com, and www.hostetler.net.

SHOPPING

Shoppers like Murano glass, Burano lace (fun lace umbrellas for little girls), Carnevale masks (fine shops and local artisans all over town), art reproductions (posters, postcards, and books), prints of Venice scenes, traditional stationery (pens and marbled paper products of all kinds), calendars with Venice scenes, silk ties, scarves, and plenty of goofy knickknacks (Titian mousepads, gondolier T-shirts, and little plastic gondolas).

If you're buying a substantial amount from nearly any shop, bargain. It's accepted and almost expected. Offer less and offer to pay cash; merchants are very conscious of the bite taken by credit-card companies.

Popular **Venetian glass** is available in many forms: vases, tea sets, decanters, glasses, jewelry, lamps, mod sculptures (such as solid-glass aquariums), and on and on. Shops will ship it home for you (snap a photo of it before it's packed up). For a cheap, packable souvenir, consider the glass-bead necklaces sold at vendors' stalls throughout Venice.

If you're serious about glass, visit the small shops on **Murano Island**. Murano's glass-blowing demonstrations are fun; you'll usually see a vase and a "leetle 'orse" made from molten glass.

Various companies offer glass-blowing demos for tour groups around St. Mark's Square. **Galleria San Marco**, a tour-group staple, offers great demos just off St. Mark's Square every few minutes. They have agreed to let individual travelers flashing this book sneak in with tour groups to see the show (and sales pitch). And, if you buy anything, show this book and they'll take 20 percent off the listed price. The gallery faces the square behind the orchestra nearest the church; at #139, go through the shop and climb the stairs (daily 9:30–12:30 & 13:30–17:00, manager Walter Brunello, tel. 041-271-8650).

Along Venice's many shopping streets, you'll notice fly-by-night vendors selling knockoffs of famous-maker handbags (Louis Vuitton, Gucci, etc.). These vendors are willing to bargain. I bought a genuine $1,000 Rolex for $10. Buyer beware.

NIGHTLIFE

Venice is quiet at night, as tour groups are back in the cheaper hotels of Mestre on the mainland, and the masses of day-trippers return to their beach resorts. **Gondolas** can cost nearly double, but are worth the extra expense. Vaporettos are uncrowded, and it's a great time to cruise the Grand Canal on slow boat #1.

Take your pick of traditional Vivaldi **concerts** in churches throughout town. Homegrown Vivaldi is as trendy here as Strauss in Vienna and Mozart in Salzburg. In fact, you'll find frilly young Vivaldis all over town hawking concert tickets. The TI has a list of this week's Baroque concerts (tickets from €18, shows start at 21:00 and generally last 90 min). There's music most nights at Scuola San Teodoro (east side of Rialto Bridge) and San Vitale Church (north end of Accademia Bridge), among others. If you see a concert at Scuola di San Rocco (tickets €15–30), you can enjoy the art (which you're likely to pay €5.50 for during the day) for free during the intermission. Another unique music experience is a Rondo Veneziano concert—classically inspired music with a modern electronic sound. The general rule of thumb: musicians in wigs and tights offer better spectacle, and musicians in black-and-white suits are better performers. Consider the venue carefully. For the latest on church concerts, see www.musicinvenice.com or call 041-962-9999.

On St. Mark's Square, the dueling **café orchestras** entertain at Caffè Florian (listed below), Quadri Ristorante, and Lavena (see map on page 58). Every night, enthusiastic musicians play the same songs, creating the same irresistible magic. Hang out for free behind the tables (which allows you to easily move on to the next orchestra when the musicians take a break) or spring for a seat and enjoy a fun and gorgeously set concert. If you sit a while, it can be €10.20 well spent (€6.20 drink plus a one-time €4 fee for entertainment). Dancing on the square is free (and encouraged).

Caffè Florian, on St. Mark's Square, is the most famous Venetian café and one of the first places in Europe to serve coffee. It has been a popular spot for a discreet rendezvous in Venice since 1720. Today, it's most famous for its outdoor seating and orchestra, but do walk inside through the richly decorated, 18th-century rooms where Casanova, Lord Byron, Charles Dickens, and Woody Allen have all paid too much for a drink (reasonable prices at bar in back, tel. 041-520-5641). A cheaper late-night spot is the stand-up **American Bar**, under the clock tower on St. Mark's Square.

You're not a tourist, you're a living part of a soft Venetian night...an alley cat with money. Streetlamp halos, live music, floodlit history, and a ceiling of stars make St. Mark's magic at midnight. In the misty light, the moon has a golden hue. Shine with the old lanterns on the gondola piers where the sloppy Grand Canal splashes at the Doge's Palace...reminiscing. Comfort the small statues of the four frightened Byzantine emperors where the Doge's Palace hits the basilica. Cuddle history.

SLEEPING

Hotels in Venice are usually booked up on Carnevale (Feb 14–24 in 2004), Easter (April 11 in 2004), April 25, May 1, in August, Nov 1, and on Fridays and Saturdays year-round.

Reserve a room as soon as you know when you'll be in town. Book direct—not through any tourist agency. Most places take a credit card number for a deposit. If everything's full, don't despair. Call a day or two in advance and fill in a cancellation. If you arrive on an overnight train, your room may not be ready. Drop your bag at the hotel and dive right into Venice.

I've listed prices for peak season: April, May, June, September, and October. Prices can get soft in July, August, and winter. Hotels sometimes give discounts if you stay at least three nights and/or pay cash. If on a budget, ask for a cheaper room or a discount. Always ask.

Virtually all of these hotels are central. See the map on page 73 for hotel locations. I've listed rooms mainly in two neighborhoods: in the

SLEEP CODE

(€1 = about $1.10, country code: 33)
Sleep Code: **S** = Single, **D** = Double/Twin, **T** = Triple, **Q** = Quad, **b** = bathroom, **s** = shower only, **no CC** = Credit Cards not accepted, **SE** = Speaks English, **NSE** = No English. Breakfast is included and credit cards are accepted unless otherwise noted. Air-conditioning, when available, is usually only turned on in summer.

To help you sort easily through these listings, I've divided the rooms into three categories based on the price for a standard double room with bath:

$$$ **Higher Priced**—Most rooms €180 or more.
$$ **Moderately Priced**—Most rooms between €130-180
$ **Lower Priced**—Most rooms €130 or less.

Rialto–San Marco action and in a quiet Dorsoduro area behind the Accademia Gallery. If a hotel has a Web site, check it. Hotel Web sites are particularly valuable for Venice, because they often come with a map that at least gives you the illusion you can easily find the place.

Between St. Mark's Square and Campo Santa Maria di Formosa

$$ **Hotel al Piave**, with 27 fine, air-conditioned rooms above a bright and classy lobby, is fresh, modern, and comfortable (Db-€145, Tb-€190, family suites-€250 for 4, €280 for 5–6, prices good through 2004 with this book, accepts CC but gives discount for cash; take vaporetto to Rialto, find your way to Campo Santa Maria Formosa and it's straight down Ruga Giuffa to #4838/40, Castello; tel. 041-528-5174, fax 041-523-8512, www.hotelalpiave.com, hotel.alpiave@iol.it, Mirella, Paolo, and Ilaria SE, faithful Molly NSE).

$$ **Locanda Correr** is a tight and tiny five-room place buried in the old center and up a long stairway. Newly-opened and proudly-run by Roberto, it features open-beamed ceilings and Venetian-style furnishings along with air-conditioning and modern comforts (Db-€135 with cash and this book promised through 2004, from Campo San Filippo e Giacomo, walk north up Calle Drio la Chiesa, take first left onto Calle del Figher and it's hiding just past the well-signed Hotel Castello, Castello 4370, tel. 041-277-7847, fax 041-277-5939, www.locandacorrer.it, info@locandacorrer.com).

$$ **Locanda Casa Querini** has 11 plush rooms on a quiet square tucked away behind St. Mark's (Db-€140 with cash and this book through 2004, €10 more during festivals, air-con, exactly halfway

Near St. Mark's Square Hotels

1 Hotel Riva
2 Hotel al Piave
3 Locanda Casa Querini & Locanda Correr
4 Hotel Campiello
5 Albergo Paganelli
6 Albergo Doni
7 Hotel Fontana
8 Corte Campana
9 Hotel Astoria
10 Locanda Gambero
11 Hotel Bel Sito
12 Alloggi alla Scala

between San Zaccaria vaporetto stop and Campo Santa Maria Formosa at Campo San Giovanni in Oleo 4388, Castello, tel. 041-241-1294, fax 041-241-4231, www.locandaquerini.com, casaquerini @hotmail.com, Silvia).

$ **Hotel Riva**, with gleaming marble hallways and bright modern rooms, is romantically situated on a canal along the gondola serenade route. You could actually dunk your breakfast rolls in the canal (but don't). Sandro may hold a corner *(angolo)* room if you ask, and there are also a few rooms overlooking the canal. Confirm prices and reconfirm reservations, as readers have had trouble with both (32 rooms, Sb-€88,

2 D with adjacent showers-€95, Db-€120, Tb-€170, Qb-€210, €10 extra for view; Ponte dell' Angelo—also spelled Anzolo, Castello 5310; tel. 041-522-7034, fax 041-528-5551). Face St. Mark's Basilica, walk behind it on the left along Calle de la Canonica, take the first left (at blue "Pauly & C" mosaic in street), continue straight, go over the bridge, and angle right to the hotel.

$ **Corte Campana** rents four comfy, quiet rooms just behind St. Mark's Square (Db-€80–130, Tb-€105–150, Qb-€140–180; facing St. Mark's Basilica, take Calle Canonica—to the far left of the church—turn left before canal on Calle dell' Anzolo, take first right on Calle del Remedio, cross the bridge and follow signs to Locanda Remedio and enter little courtyard to your right, go up three flights of steps and ring bell at Calle del Remedio 4410, Castello; tel. 041-523-3603, mobile 389-272-6500, www.cortecampana.com, info@cortecampana.com, enthusiastic Riccardo SE).

On or near the Waterfront, East of St. Mark's Square

These places, about one canal down from the Bridge of Sighs, on or just off the Riva degli Schiavoni waterfront promenade, rub drainpipes with Venice's most palatial five-star hotels. The first two, while a bit pricey because of their location, are professional and comfortable. Ride the vaporetto to San Zaccaria (#51 from train station, #82 from Tronchetto car park).

$$ **Hotel Campiello**, a lacy and bright little 16-room, air-conditioned place, was once part of a 19th-century convent. It's ideally located 50 yards off the waterfront (Sb-€110–120, Db-€120–180, 8 percent discount with cash, cancellation fee; elevator; behind Hotel Savoia, up Calle del Vin off the waterfront street—Riva degli Schiavoni 4647, San Zaccaria; tel. 041-520-5764, fax 041-520-5798, www.hcampiello.it, campiello@hcampiello.it; family-run for 4 generations, sisters Monica and Nicoletta, and Thomas).

$$ **Albergo Paganelli** is right on the waterfront—on Riva degli Schiavoni—and has a few incredible view rooms (S-€100, Sb-€125, Db-€150–181, Db with view-€200, 5 percent discount with cash, prices often soft; request *con vista* for view, air-con; at San Zaccaria vaporetto stop, Riva degli Schiavoni 4182, Castello; tel. 041-522-4324, fax 041-523-9267, www.hotelpaganelli.com, hotelpag@tin.it). With spacious rooms, carved and gilded headboards, and chandeliers, this elegant place is a good value. Seven of their 22 rooms are in a less interesting but equally comfortable *dipendenza* (annex), a block off the canal.

$$ **Hotel Fontana** is a two-star, family-run place with 14 rooms and lots of stairs on a touristy square two bridges behind St. Mark's Square (Sb-€55–110, Db-€90–170 depending on season and length of stay, 10 percent discount with cash, see Web site for off-season deals;

air-con, family rooms, quieter rooms on canal side, piazza views can be noisy, 2 rooms have terraces; vaporetto #51 to San Zaccaria, find Calle de le Rasse—to left of Hotel Danieli—take it, turn right at end, continue to first square, Campo San Provolo 4701, Castello; tel. 041-522-0579, fax 041-523-1040, www.hotelfontana.it, htlcasa@gpnet.it).

$ **Albergo Doni** is a dark, hardwood, clean, and quiet place—a bit of a time-warp—with 13 dim but classy rooms run by a likable smart aleck named Gina (D-€90, Db-€115, T-€120, Tb-€153, secure telephone reservations with CC but must pay in cash; ceiling fans; Riva degli Schiavoni, Calle del Vin 4656, San Zaccaria N.; tel. & fax 041-522-4267, www.albergodoni.it, albergodoni@libero.it, Nicolo, Tessa, and Gina SE). Leave Riva degli Schiavoni on Calle del Vin and go 100 yards with a left jog.

North of St. Mark's Square

$$ **Locanda Gambero**, with 26 rooms, is a comfortable and very central three-star hotel run by Sandro (Sb-€50–130, Db-€90–190, Tb-€150–240, Internet access, air-con, 5 percent discount for payment in cash; from Rialto vaporetto dock walk away from the Rialto bridge, cross one bridge, take first left down skinny Calle le Bembo/Calle del Fabbri; or from St. Mark's Square go through Sotoportego dei Dai then down Calle dei Fabbri to #4687; tel. 041-522-4384, fax 041-520-0431, www.locandaalgambero.com, hotelgambero@tin.it, cheery Gianni covers the night shift, all SE). Gambero runs the pleasant, Art Deco–style La Bistrot on the corner, which serves old-time Venetian cuisine.

$$ **Hotel Astoria** has 24 simple rooms tucked away a few blocks off St. Mark's Square (S-€80–90, Sb-€100, Db-€125, cheaper off-season; some air-con suites available; 2 blocks from San Zulian Church at Calle Fiubera 951; from Rialto vaporetto #1 dock, go straight inland on Calle le Bembo, which becomes Calle dei Fabbri, turn left on Calle Fiubera; tel. 041-522-5381, fax 041-528-8981, www.hotelastoriavenezia.it, info @hotelastoriavenezia.it, Giorgia and Giovanni SE).

West of St. Mark's Square

$$$ **Hotel Bel Sito**, friendly for a three-star hotel, has Old World character and a picturesque location—facing a church on a small square between St. Mark's Square and the Accademia. With solid wood furniture, its 38 rooms feel elegant. Those on the back side are more charming (Sb-€100–130, Db-€170–200, air-con, elevator, some rooms with canal or church views; vaporetto #1 to Santa Maria del Giglio stop, take narrow alley to square, hotel at far end to your right, Santa Maria del Giglio 2517, San Marco, tel. 041-522-3365, fax 041-520-4083, belsito@iol.it).

$ **Alloggi alla Scala**, a seven-room place run by Signora Andreina della Fiorentina, is homey, central, and hidden away on a quiet square that features a famous spiral stairway called Scala Contarini del Bovolo (small Db-€80, big Db-€90, extra bed-€26, breakfast-€9, reserve by CC, 6 percent discount for payment in cash; Campo Manin 4306, San Marco; tel. 041-521-0629, fax 041-522-6451, daughter Emma SE). To find the hotel from Campo Manin, follow signs to (on statue's left) "Scala Contarini del Bovolo."

Near the Rialto Bridge

The first three hotels are on the west side of the Rialto Bridge (away from St. Mark's Square) and the last three are on the east side of the bridge (on St. Mark's side). Vaporetto #82 quickly connects the Rialto with both the train station and the Tronchetto car park.

On West Side of Rialto Bridge

$$$ **Hotel Locanda Ovidius**, with an elegant Grand Canal view terrace, a breakfast room with a wood-beamed ceiling, and nine bright, comfortable rooms, is on the Grand Canal (Sb-€77–190, Db-€130–230, Db with view-€185–280, check Web site for special offers, air-con, Calle del Sturion 677a, tel. 041-523-7970, fax 041-520-4101, www.hotelovidius .com, info@hotelovidius.com).

$$$ **Locanda Sturion**, with air-conditioning and all the modern comforts, is pricey because it overlooks the Grand Canal (Db-€150–200, Tb-€180–230, family deals, canal-view rooms cost €25 extra; piles of stairs; 100 yards from Rialto Bridge, opposite vaporetto dock, Calle Sturion 679, San Polo, Rialto; tel. 041-523-6243, fax 041-522-8378, www.locandasturion.com, info@locandasturion.com, SE).

$ **Albergo Guerrato**, overlooking a handy and colorful produce market two minutes from the Rialto action, is run by friendly, creative, and hardworking Roberto and Piero. Giorgio takes the night shift. Their 800-year-old building is Old World simple, airy, and wonderfully characteristic (D-€85, Db-€110, big top floor Db-€130, T-€105, Tb-€135, Qb-€155, prices promised through 2004 with this book in hand, cash only; walk over the Rialto away from St. Mark's Square, go straight about 3 blocks, turn right on Calle drio la Scimia—not simply Scimia, the block before—and you'll see the hotel sign, Calle drio la Scimia 240a; tel. 041-522-7131 or 041-528-5927, fax 041-241-1408, hguerrat@tin.it, SE). My tour groups book this place for 50 nights each year. Sorry. Call to determine availability before you fax (otherwise, they won't return the fax). They rent family apartments in the old center (great for groups of 4–8) for around €55 per person.

On East Side of Rialto Bridge

$$$ **Hotel Giorgione**, a four-star hotel in a 15th-century palace on a quiet lane, is super-professional, with plush public spaces, pool tables, Internet access, a garden terrace, and 76 spacious, over-the-top rooms with all the comforts (Sb-€90–173, Db-€130–265, pricier superior rooms and suites

Near the Rialto Bridge Hotels

⊢ ☑ TRAGHETTO CROSSING
⌐ Ⓣ VAPORETTO STOP

TO GHETTO, TRAIN STN, ❼
& TRONCHETTO

200 YARDS

200 METERS

CA D'ORO
STRADA NUOVA
S.S. APOSTOLI
FISH MKT.
HOSP.
MKT.
LARGA
CAMPO S. GIOVANNI & PAOLO
ERBE
RIALTO
POST
MARCELLO
S. BART.
SAL. SAN LIO
S. MARIA FORMOSA
CAMPO S.M. FORMOSA
RUGA VECCHIA
CARBON
CAMPO S. LUCA
MERCERE
BANDE
FABBRI
GIUFFA
CAMPO MANIN
CANAL
TO SAN MARCO

❶ Locanda Sturion & Hotel Locanda Ovidius

❷ Albergo Guerrato

❸ Locanda Novo Venezia

❹ Hotel Giorgione

❺ Locanda la Corte

❻ Foresteria della Chiesa Valdese

❼ To Hotel San Geremia

available, extra bed-€60, 10 percent discount with Web reservations, elevator, air-con, 200 yards off Campo S.S. Apostoli on Salizada del Pistor, #4587, tel. 041-522-5810, fax 041-523-9092, www.hotelgiorgione.com, giorgione@hotelgiorgione.com).

$$ **Locanda la Corte**, a three-star hotel, has 18 attractive, high-ceilinged, wood-beamed rooms—done in pastels—bordering a small, quiet courtyard (Sb-€90–120, standard Db-€120–150, superior Db-€140–170, suites available, air-con; vaporetto #52 from train station to Fondamente Nove, exit boat to your left, follow waterfront, turn right after second bridge to get to S.S. Giovanni e Paolo square, and facing Rosa Salva bar, take street to left—Calle Bressana, hotel is a short block away at #6317 bridge; Castello, tel. 041-241-1300, fax 041-241-5982, www.locandalacorte.it, info@locandalacorte.it).

$ **Locanda Novo Venezia**, a charming eight-room place in a 15th-century palazzo run by industrious Claudio and Ivan, is just off a super square—Campo dei S.S. Apostoli, north of the Rialto Bridge (Db-€130 with this book, family deals for up to 6 in a room; air-con; from Campo dei S.S. Apostoli head down Salizada del Pistor, take first right on Calle dei Preti to #4529, Cannaregio; tel. 041-241-1496, fax 041-241-5989, www.locandanovo.it, locandanovo@tin.it).

Near the Accademia Bridge

When you step over the Accademia Bridge, the commotion of touristy Venice is replaced by a sleepy village laced with canals. This quiet area, next to the best painting gallery in town, is a 15-minute walk from St. Mark's Square and the Rialto. The fast vaporetto #82 connects the Accademia Bridge with both the train station (15 min) and St. Mark's Square (5 min).

On South Side of Accademia Bridge

$$$ **Hotel Belle Arti** is a good bet if you want to be in the old center without the tourist hordes. With a grand entry and all the American hotel comforts, it's a big, 67-room, modern, three-star place sitting on a former schoolyard (Sb-€114–150, Db-€145–210, Tb-€186–255, ask for the "Rick Steves" discount, then get 5 percent more off for cash; plush public areas, air-con, elevator; 100 yards behind Accademia art museum—facing museum, take left, then forced right, Via Dorsoduro 912; tel. 041-522-6230, fax 041-528-0043, www.hotelbellearti.com, info@hotelbellearti.com, SE).

$$ **Pensione Accademia** fills the 17th-century Villa Maravege. While its 27 comfortable and air-conditioned rooms are nothing extraordinary, you'll feel aristocratic gliding through its grand public spaces and lounging in its breezy garden (Sb-€83–123, standard Db-€160–180, bigger "superior" Db-€180–230, family deals; facing Accademia art museum, take first right, cross first bridge, go right, Dorsoduro 1058; tel. 041-523-7846, fax 041-523-9152, www.pensioneaccademia.it, info@pensioneaccademia.it).

$$ **Hotel Galleria** has nine tight, velvety rooms, most with views of the Grand Canal. Some rooms are quite narrow; ask for a larger room (S-€66–90, D-€90–97, Db-€110–145, big canal-view rooms #8 and #10 Db-from €135, includes scant breakfast in room; fans; near Accademia art museum, and next to recommended Foscarini pizzeria, Dorsoduro 878a; tel. 041-523-2489, tel. & fax 041-520-4172, www.hotelgalleria.it, galleria@tin.it).

$$ **Hotel Agli Alboretti** is a cozy, family-run, 24-room place in a quiet neighborhood a block behind the Accademia art museum. With red carpeting and wood-beamed ceilings, it feels elegant (Sb-€104, Db-€180, Tb-€210, Qb-€240; air-con; 100 yards from the Accademia

Near the Accademia Bridge Hotels

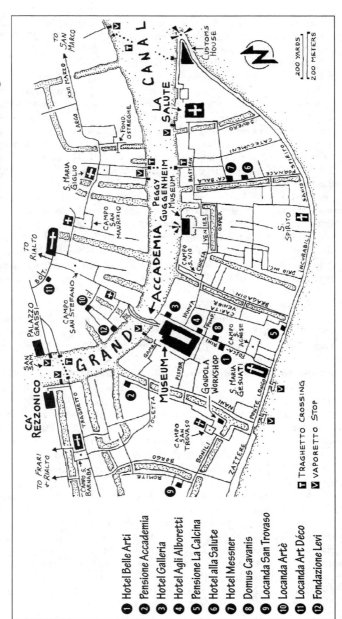

1 Hotel Belle Arti
2 Pensione Accademia
3 Hotel Galleria
4 Hotel Agli Alboretti
5 Pensione La Calcina
6 Hotel alla Salute
7 Hotel Messner
8 Domus Cavanis
9 Locanda San Trovaso
10 Locanda Artè
11 Locanda Art Déco
12 Fondazione Levi

vaporetto stop on Rio Terra a Foscarini at Accademia 884—facing Accademia art museum, go left, then forced right; tel. 041-523-0058, fax 041-521-0158, www.aglialboretti.com, alborett@gpnet.it, SE).

$$ Pensione La Calcina, the home of English writer John Ruskin in 1876, comes with all the three-star comforts in a professional yet intimate package. Its 29 rooms are squeaky clean, with good wood furniture, hardwood floors, and a peaceful canalside setting facing Giudecca island (S-€75, Sb-€96, Sb with view-€110, Db-€130–145, Db with view-€160–185, prices vary with room size and season; air-con, rooftop terrace, killer sundeck on canal and canalside buffet-breakfast terrace; Dorsoduro 780, at south end of Rio di San Vio; tel. 041-520-6466, fax 041-522-7045, www.lacalcina.com, la.calcina@libero.it). They also rent apartments nearby (max 2 people, €140–240, air-con). From the Tronchetto car park or station, catch vaporetto #51 or #82 to Zattere (at vaporetto stop, exit right and walk along canal to hotel). Guests get a fine dinner at their La Piscina restaurant discounted to €20.

$$ Hotel alla Salute, a basic retreat buried deep in Dorsoduro, is ideal for those wanting a quiet Venice residence (Db-€140, cash discount, plans air-con for 2004, facing the canal Rio delle Fornace near La Salute church, tel. 041-523-5404, fax 041-522-2271, www.hotelsalute .com, info@hotelsalute.com).

$$ Hotel Messner, a sprawling place popular with groups, rents 40 nondescript rooms in a peaceful canal-side neighborhood near La Salute Church. While remote, it has cheap and handy *traghetto* access to St. Mark's Square (Sb-€90–110, Db with air-con-€120–150, Db without air-con in simpler annex-€100–120, Tb-€145–180, Qb-€160–200, peaceful garden, midway between lagoon and Grand Canal on Rio delle Fornace canal, tel. 041-522-7443, fax 041-522-7266, www.hotelmessner .it, messnerinfo@tin.it).

$ Domus Cavanis, across the street from—and owned by—Hotel Belle Arti, is a big, practical, stark place with a garden, renting 30 quiet, simple, and spacious rooms (Db-€103, Tb-€150, family rooms, includes breakfast at Hotel Belle Arti, air-con, elevator, Dorsoduro 895, tel. 041-528-7374, fax 041-522-8505, www.hotelbellearti.com, info @hotelbellearti.com).

$ Locanda San Trovaso is sparkling new, with seven classy, spacious rooms and a peaceful location on a small canal (Sb-€90, Db-€115–130, Tb-€145; breakfast in your room, fans, small roof terrace; Dorsoduro 1351, take vaporetto #82 from Tronchetto or #51 from Piazzale Roma or train station, get off at Zattere, exit left, turn right at tiny Calle Trevisan, cross bridge, cross adjacent bridge, take immediate right, then first left; tel. 041-277-1146, fax 041-277-7190, www.locandasantrovaso.com, s.trovaso@tin.it, Mark and his son Alessandro SE).

On North Side of Accademia Bridge

$ **Locanda Artè** has eight homey rooms with high ceilings, old-style Venetian furnishings, air-conditioning, and thoughtful touches (Db-€90–120, 10 percent cash discount, family room sleeps up to 6, just north of Accademia Bridge, 100 yards west of Campo San Stefano on Calle de Frutariol, San Marco 2900, tel. 041-520-0882, fax 041-277-8395, www.locandaarte.com, info@locandaarte.com, Alberto SE).

$ **Locanda Art Déco** is a charming place run by accommodating and equally charming Judith. While the art deco theme is pretty scant, a wrought-iron staircase leads from her inviting lobby to seven thoughtfully decorated rooms. Confirm that your booking is for this hotel (Db-€100–160, min 3 nights on weekends, 10 percent discount with this book and cash, 2 family rooms, air-con, just north of the Accademia Bridge off Campo Santo Stefano at 2966 Calle delle Botteghe, tel. 041-277-0558, fax 041-270-2891, www.locandaartdeco .com, info@locandaartdeco.com).

$ **Fondazione Levi**, a dorm run by a foundation that promotes research on Venetian music, offers 21 quiet, institutional yet comfortable and spacious rooms (Sb-€70, Db-€105, Tb-€120, Qb-€140, twin beds only, elevator; 80 yards from base of Accademia Bridge on St. Mark's side—from Accademia vaporetto stop, cross Accademia Bridge, take immediate left—, cross the bridge Ponte Giustinian, go down Calle Giustinian directly to the Fondazione, buzz the "Foresteria" door to the right, San Vidal 2893; tel. 041-786-711, fax 041-786-766, foresterialevi @libero.it, SE).

Near the Train Station

$$ **Hotel San Geremia**, a three-minute walk from the station, offers 20 clean and simple rooms at decent prices near a self-service laundry, Internet café, and the Ferrovia vaporetto stop. Head left outside the station and follow Lista di Spagna to Campo San Geremia #290/A (small Db-€75, Db-€110–145, the higher price is for weekends, tel. 041-716-245, fax 041-524-2342, sangeremia@yahoo.it, Claudio SE).

Cheap Dormitory Accommodations

$ **Foresteria della Chiesa Valdese**, warmly run by the Methodist church, offers 33 beds in dorms and doubles, halfway between St. Mark's Square and the Rialto Bridge. This run-down but charming old place has elegant ceiling paintings (dorm bed-€22, D-€56, Db-€74, family apartment-€155 for 5, must check in and out when office is open: 9:00–13:00 & 18:00–20:00, from Campo Santa Maria Formosa, walk past Bar all' Orologio to end of Calle Lunga and cross bridge, Castello 5170, reservation by phone only, tel. & fax 041-528-6797, fax 041-241-6238, foresteriavenezia@diaconiavaldese.org).

$ Venice's **youth hostel** on Giudecca Island is crowded and inexpensive (€16 beds with sheets and breakfast in 10- to 16-bed rooms, membership required, office open daily 7:00–9:30 & 13:30–23:00, catch vaporetto #82 from station to Zittele, tel. 041-523-8211). The budget cafeteria welcomes non-hostelers (nightly 17:00–23:30).

EATING

While touristy restaurants are the scourge of Venice, and most restaurateurs believe you can't survive in Venice without catering to tourists, there are plenty of places that are still popular with locals and respect the tourists who happen in. First trick: Walk away from triple-language menus. Second trick: Order the daily special. Third trick: Most seafood dishes are the local catch-of-the-day.

For romantic—and usually pricey—meals along the water, see "Eating with a Romantic Canalside Setting," page 90. For dessert, it's gelato (see end of this chapter).

Between Campo Santi Apostoli and Campo S.S. Giovanni e Paolo

For locations, see map on page 83.

Trattoria da Bepi is a classy family-run place where mama scours the market for just the best ingredients and son, Loris, takes good care of the hungry clientele (€30 meals; Fri–Wed 19:00–22:00, closed Thu; near Rialto, half a block north of Campo Santi Apostoli on Calle Pistor; tel. 041-528-5031).

Antiche Cantine Ardenghi de Lucia e Michael is a leap of local faith and an excellent splurge. Effervescent Michael and his wife, Lucia, proudly cook Venetian for a handful of people each night by reservation only. You must call first. You pay €50 per person and trust them to wine, dine, and serenade you with Venetian class. (The €50 price—promised for 2004—includes absolutely everything...including a "reasonable" amount of wine.) The evening can be quiet or raucous depending on who and how many are eating. While Michael's menu is very heavy on crustaceans, he promises to complement the seafood with plenty of veggies and fruit as well (but *only* if you request this—be forceful with your needs—when you reserve). Find #6369. There's no sign, the door's locked, and the place looks closed. But knock, say the password *(La Repubblica Serenissima)*, and you'll be admitted. From Campo S.S. Giovanni e Paolo, pass the church-like hospital (notice the illusions painted on its facade), go over the bridge to the left, and take the first right on Calle della Testa to #6369 (you must reserve the day before, Tue–Sat 20:00–24:00, closed Sun–Mon, tel. 041-523-7691, mobile 389-523-7691).

Venice Restaurants

1. Trattoria da Bepi
2. Antiche Cantine Ardenghi
3. Osteria da Alberto
4. Osteria ai Promessi Sposi
5. Osteria al Bomba
6. Osteria di Santa Marina
7. Osteria il Milion
8. Devil's Forest Pub & Bora Bora Pizzeria
9. Cantina do Mori
10. Antica Osteria Ruga Rialto
11. Bancogiro (Osteria da Andrea)
12. To Pane Vino e San Daniele
13. Osteria al Diavolo e l'Aquasanta & Tratt. alla Madonna
14. Antica Trattoria ai Tosi
15. Osteria Alla Botte
16. Rosticceria San Bartolomeo
17. Pasticceria Ponte delle Paste
18. Osteria al Portego
19. Enoteca al Volto
20. Bar all' Orologio
21. Cip Ciap Pizza
22. Trattoria agli Artisti
23. Pizzeria Spizzico
24. La Boutique del Gelato
25. Michielangelo Gelato
26. Zanzibar Gelato

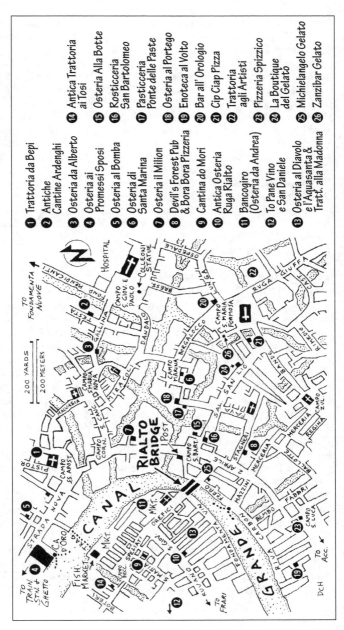

The following colorful *osterias* are good for *cicchetti* (munchies), wine-tasting, or a simple, rustic, sit-down meal surrounded by a boisterous local ambience:

Osteria da Alberto serves *cicchetti* (18:15–19:30) and great €20 dinners (Mon–Sat 19:30–23:00, closed Sun; midway between Campo Santi Apostoli and Campo S.S. Giovanni e Paolo, next to Ponte de la Panada on Calle Larga Giacinto Gallina; tel. 041-523-8153).

Osteria ai Promessi Sposi does *cicchetti* with gusto—the best selection I found—and offers a little garden for sit-down meals. The ambience is Venetian shipwreck (Thu–Tue 9:00–23:00, closed Wed, a block off Campo S.S. Apostoli and a block inland from Strada Nova at Calle dell' Oca, tel. 041-522-8609).

Osteria al Bomba is run attentively by Sr. Filippi and his two sons. Ask for the menu and stand or sit at the very long table. The place is less ye olde and has a fun list of Bollicine—the local champagne (Tue–Sun from 18:00, closed Mon, near Campo SS Apostoli a block off the Strada Nuova on Calle Oca, tel. 041-520-5175). You'll find more pubs nearby, in the side streets opposite Campo St. Sofia across Strada Nova.

East of the Rialto Bridge, near Campo San Bartolomeo

Osteria di Santa Marina is a dressy new place rapidly gaining fame for its mission to reinvent traditional dishes with a creative twist. They serve only the finest seasonal produce (fun-if-pricey menu with €14 pastas and €20 *secondi*, Mon–Sat 12:30–14:30 & 19:30–23:00, closed Sun, eat indoors or outdoors on pleasant little square, midway between Rialto and Campo Santa Maria Formosa on Campo Marina, tel. 041-528-5239).

Osteria il Milion, with bow-tied waiters and dressy candle-lit tables indoors and out, is quietly situated next to Marco Polo's home. It serves traditional Italian meals for around €25 (Thu–Tue 12:00–15:00 & 18:30–23:00, closed Wed; near Rialto, head north from Campo San Bartolomeo, over one bridge, take first right off San Giovanni Grisostomo, at #5841; tel. 041-522-9302).

The **Devil's Forest Pub**, an air-conditioned bit of England tucked away a block from the crowds, is—strangely—more Venetian these days than the *tipico* places. Locals come here for good English and Irish beer on tap, big salads (€7.50, lunch only), hot bar snacks, and an easygoing ambience (daily 8:00–24:00, meals 12:00–15:30, bar snacks all the time, closed Sun in Aug, no cover or service charge, fine prices, backgammon and chess boards available-€2.50, a block off Campo San Bartolomeo on Calle dei Stagneri, tel. 041-520-0623). Across the street, **Bora Bora Pizzeria** serves pizza and salads from an entertaining menu (Thu–Tue 12:00–15:00 & 19:15–22:30, closed Wed, tel. 041-523-6583).

The Stand-Up Progressive Venetian Pub-Crawl Dinner

My favorite Venetian dinner is a pub crawl. A *giro di ombra* (pub crawl) is a tradition unique to Venice—ideal in a city with no cars. (*Ombra*—slang for a glass of wine—means shade, from the old days when a portable wine bar scooted with the shadow of the Campanile bell tower across St. Mark's Square.)

Venice's residential back streets hide plenty of characteristic bars (*baccaros*) with countless trays of interesting toothpick munchies *(cicchetti)* and blackboards listing which wines are uncorked and served by the glass. This is a great way to mingle and have fun with the Venetians.

Cicchetti **bars** have a social stand-up zone and a cozy gaggle of tables where you can generally sit down with your *cicchetti* or order from a simple menu. Food generally costs the same price whether you stand or sit.

I've listed plenty of pubs in walking order for a quick or extended crawl below. If you've crawled enough, most of these bars make a fine one-stop, sit-down dinner.

Try fried mozzarella cheese, gorgonzola, calamari, artichoke hearts, and anything ugly on a toothpick. Meat and fish *(pesce*; PESH-shay)* munchies can be expensive; veggies *(verdure)* are cheap, around €3 for a meal-sized plate. In many places, there's a set price per food item (e.g., €1.50). To get a plate of assorted appetizers for €8 (or more, depending on how hungry you are), ask for: *"Un piatto classico di cicchetti misti da €8"*(oon pee-AH-toh KLAH-see-koh dee cheh-KET-tee MEE-stee da OH-toh ay-OO-roh). Bread sticks *(grissini)* are free for the asking.

Drink the house wines. A small glass of house red or white wine *(ombra rosso* or *ombra bianco)* or a small beer *(birrino)* costs about €1. The house keg wine is cheap—€1 per glass, around €4 per liter. *Vin bon*, Venetian for fine wine, may run you from €1.50 to €6 per little glass. *Corposo* means full-bodied. A good last drink is *fragolino*, the local sweet wine—*bianco* or *rosso*. It often comes with a little cookie *(biscotti)* for dipping.

Bars don't stay open very late, and the *cicchetti* selection is best early, so start your evening by 18:00. Most bars are closed on Sunday.

Cicchetterie and Light Meals West of the Rialto Bridge

Cantina do Mori is famous with locals (since 1462) and savvy travelers (since 1982) as a classy place for fine wine and *francobollo* (a spicy selection of 20 tiny mayo-soaked sandwiches nicknamed "stamps"). Choose from the featured wines. Order carefully or they'll rip you off. From Rialto Bridge, walk 200 yards down Ruga degli Orefici away from St. Mark's Square—then ask a local for directions (Mon–Sat 17:00–20:30, closed Sun, arrive early before the *cicchetti* are gone, stand-up only, San Polo 429, tel. 041-522-5401).

Antica Osteria Ruga Rialto, "the Ruga," is a local fixture where Marco serves great bar snacks and wine to his devoted clientele (daily

11:00–14:30 & 19:00–24:00, easy to find, just past Chinese Restaurant on Ruga Vecchia S Giovanni).

Bancogiro (Osteria da Andrea), a simple bar behind the Rialto market, has stark yet powerfully atmospheric outdoor seating overlooking the Grand Canal. Peruse their wine list and basic menu at the bar (strong local cheeses are a forte), order, and grab a table—worth the reasonable cover charge (Tue–Sat 10:30–15:00 & 18:30–22:00, closed Sun—Mon; less than 200 yards from Rialto Bridge on Campo San Giacometto, San Polo 122; tel. 041-523-2061).

Pane Vino e San Daniele means bread, wine and the very best ham. While its tables are rustic, the jazz and decor give the bar a trendy feel. They offer free little bruschetti, a rich cheese plate, refreshing and substantial *spritzes*, fine trios of explosive little ham sandwiches, a helpful menu and a blackboard of great wine by the glass (Tue–Sun 10:30–16:00 & 18:00–24:00, closed Mon, from Rialto it's a quarter of the way to the train station on Calle dei Boteri 1544—worth the walk, mobile 380-410-8446).

Osteria al Diavolo e l'Aquasanta, three blocks west of the Rialto, serves good—if pricey—pasta and makes a handy lunch stop for sightseers (Mon 12:00–15:00, Wed–Sun 12:00–15:00 & 19:00–23:00, closed Tue; hiding on a quiet street just off Rua Vecchia S. Giovanni, on Calle della Madonna; tel. 041-277-0307). While they list *cicchetti* and wine by the glass on the wall, I'd come here for a light meal rather than tapas.

Trattoria alla Madonna, also on Calle della Madonna, serves Venetian fare informally at lunch—on long tables—and formally at dinner, with private tables and a more varied menu (tel. 041-522-3824).

Antica Trattoria ai Tosi, a small, classy place near the Rialto fish market, offers simple €15, two-course *menus* for *turisticos*—the seafood one is great. Add wine/water and you'll get out for about €20–25 per person. With its pleasant stay-awhile atmosphere, it's good for a quiet, romantic dinner (closed Mon, near Sora al Ponte, Rialto San Polo 1586, tel. 041-524-1086).

Cicchetterie and Light Meals East of the Rialto Bridge, near Campo San Bartolomeo

Osteria "Alla Botte" Cicchetteria is an atmospheric place packed with a young, local, bohemian-jazz clientele. It's good for a *cicchetti* snack with wine at the bar (see the posted, enticing selection of wines by the glass) or for a light meal in the small back room (Fri–Tue 10:00–15:00 & 18:00–23:00, closed Thu and Sun, 2 short blocks off Campo San Bartolomeo in the corner behind the statue—down Calle de la Bissa, notice the "day after" photo showing a debris-covered Venice after the notorious 1989 Pink Floyd open-air concert, tel. 041-520-9775).

If the statue on the Campo San Bartolomeo walked backward 20 yards, turned left, and went under a passageway, he'd hit **Rosticceria San Bartolomeo**. This cheap—if confusing—self-service restaurant has a likeably surly staff (good €6–7 pasta, great fried *mozzarella al prosciutto* for €1.40, delightful fruit salad, and €2 glasses of wine, prices listed on wall behind counter, no cover or service charge, daily 9:30–21:30, tel. 041-522-3569). Take out, grab a table, or munch at the bar.

From Rosticceria San Bartolomeo, continue over a bridge to Campo San Lio. Here, turn left, passing Hotel Canada and following Calle Carminati straight about 50 yards over another bridge. On the right is the pastry shop *(pasticceria)* and straight ahead is Osteria Al Portego (at #6015). Both are listed below:

Pasticceria Ponte delle Paste is a feminine and pastel *salon de tè*, popular for its pastries and aperitifs. Italians love taking 15-minute breaks to sip a *spritz* aperitif with friends after a long day's work, before heading home. Ask sprightly Monica for a *spritz al bitter* (white wine, *amaro*, and soda water, €1.50; or choose from the menu on the wall) and munch some of the free goodies at the bar around 18:00 (daily 7:00–20:30, Ponte delle Paste).

Osteria al Portego is a friendly, local-style bar serving great *cicchetti* and good meals (Mon–Fri 9:00–22:00, closed Sat–Sun, tel. 041-522-9038). The *cicchetti* here can make a great meal, but you should also consider sitting down for an actual dinner. They have a fine menu.

Enoteca al Volto offers a vast assortment of Italian wines by the glass and comes with a commitment to good *cicchetti* (the best selection of munchies is 17:00–20:00, closed Sun; from Rialto vaporetto stop walk along the canal away from the bridge, take last left before road ends, on Calle Cavalli; tel. 041-522-8945, Andrea).

On or near Campo Santa Maria di Formosa

Campo Santa Maria Formosa is just plain atmospheric (as most squares with a Socialist Party office seem to be). For a balmy outdoor meal, have a pizza with wine on the square. **Bar all' Orologio** has a good setting and friendly service but mediocre "freezer" pizza (they're happy to let you split a pizza, Mon–Sat 6:00–23:00, closed Sun and in winter at 18:00). To have a great pizza picnic on the square, cross the bridge behind the canal-side *gelateria* and grab a slice to go from **Cip Ciap Pizza** (Wed–Mon 9:00–21:00, closed Tue; facing *gelateria*, take bridge to the right, Calle del Mondo Novo).

Trattoria agli Artisti is efficient and friendly, with good food, especially the spaghetti *frutti di mare* (dinner from 18:00, closed Wed, half block off square down Ruga Giuffa, tel. 041-277-0029).

Pub-crawlers get a salad course at the fruit-and-vegetable stand next to the water fountain (Mon–Sat, closes about 19:30 and on Sun). The **Zanzibar** *gelateria* on the canal at Campo Santa Maria Formosa seems to wish the tourists would go away…but is very well-situated (open 8:00–24:00).

Near the Accademia Bridge

For location, see map on page 89.

Restaurant/Pizzeria Accademia Foscarini, next to the Accademia Bridge and Galleria, offers decent €7–8 pizzas in a great canalside setting (Wed–Mon 7:00–22:00 in summer, until 21:00 in winter, closed Tue, Dorsoduro 878C, tel. 041-522-7281).

Enoteca Cantine del Vino Gia Schiavi—much loved for its *cicchetti*—is a good place for a glass of wine and appetizers (Mon–Sat 8:00–14:30 & 15:30–20:00, closed Sun; 100 yards from Accademia Gallery on San Trovaso canal—facing Accademia, take a right and then a forced left at canal to the second bridge—S. Trovaso 992; tel. 041-523-0034). You're welcome to enjoy your wine and finger-food while sitting on the bridge.

Ai Gondolieri is considered one of the best restaurants for meat— not fish—in Venice. Its sauces are heavy and prices are high, but carnivores love it (Wed–Mon 12:00–13:00 & 19:00–22:00, closed Tue and for lunch July–Aug, reservations smart, Dorsoduro 366 San Vio, behind Peggy Guggenheim Museum on west end of Rio delle Torreselle, tel. 041-528-6396).

Cantinone Storico, also in this neighborhood, and Ristorante da Raffaele (on St. Mark's side of Accademia Bridge) is described below under "Eating with a Romantic Canalside Setting."

Vino Vino is a small, simple place that seats about 25 (pasta-€5, *secondi*-€9–125, open long hours, closed Tue; between Accademia Bridge and St. Mark's Square, just south of La Fenice on Ponte delle Veste, 2007/A; tel. 041-241-7688).

Near Campo San Barnaba

A number of less-touristed restaurants cluster around this small square. From the Accademia, head northwest, following the curve of the Grand Canal. In five minutes, you'll spill out onto Campo San Barnaba (and the nearby Campo Santa Margherita). Follow the straight and narrow path (Calle Lunga di San Barnaba) west of the square for more restaurants.

Casin dei Nobili has a diverse, reasonably-priced menu in an informal setting (closed Mon, a half-block south of Campo San Barnaba, tel. 041-241-1841). The name means pleasure-palace (Casino) of the nobles.

Ai Quattro Ferri is a trattoria-style noisy, bustling place for catch-of-the-day seafood, with excellent grilled fish, but very few non-seafood items (closed Sun, just off the square on Calle Lunga di San Barnaba, tel. 041-520-6978).

La Furattola is more upscale, with an extensive seafood menu (closed Thu, farther west on Calle Lunga di San Barnaba, tel. 041-520-8594).

Avogaria is a hip, modern, goateed-waiter wine bar and restaurant. You can have a full meal, or just sit at the tiny bar and drink a glass of Soave Classico while you build a meal of appetizers and delicious

Near the Accademia Bridge Restaurants

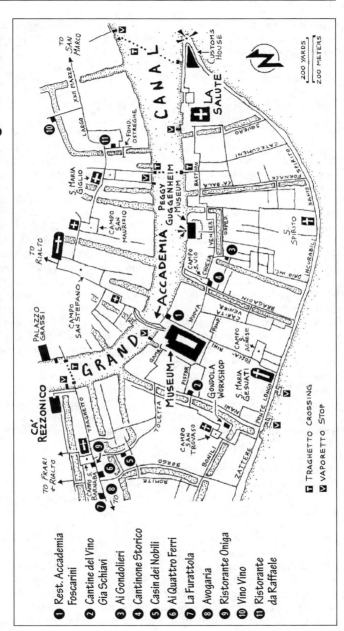

1 Rest. Accademia
  Foscarini
2 Cantine del Vino
  Gia Schiavi
3 Ai Gondolieri
4 Cantinone Storico
5 Casin dei Nobili
6 Ai Quattro Ferri
7 La Furattola
8 Avogaria
9 Ristorante Oniga
10 Vino Vino
11 Ristorante
   da Raffaele

🔲 TRAGHETTO CROSSING
🔽 VAPORETTO STOP

desserts. The small outside terrace was made for warm evenings (closed Mon; several hundred yards west of Campo San Barnaba on Calle Lunga San Barnaba, near San Sebastian church; tel. 041-296-0491).

Ristorante Oniga, right on Campo San Barnaba, is a wine bar/restaurant (closed Tue, tel. 041-522-4410).

Eating with a Romantic Canalside Setting

Of course, if you want a canal view, it comes with lower quality or a higher price. But the memory is sometimes most important.

Ristorante da Raffaele is *the* place for classy food on a quiet canal. It's filled with top-end tourists sent by the fancy hotels. The place was a haunt of the avant-garde a few generations ago. Today it's on a main gondolier thoroughfare—in fact, many guests arrive or depart by gondola. Make a reservation if you want a canalside table (you do). While the multilingual menu is designed for the tourists, locals stick with the daily specials (expensive—plan on €60, Fri–Wed 18:30–22:30, closed Thu, exactly halfway between Piazza San Marco and the Accademia Bridge at Ponte delle Ostreghe, tel. 041-523-2317). Before leaving, wander around inside to see the owner's intriguing old weapons collection.

Ristorante Cantinone Storico sits on a peaceful canal in Dorsoduro between the Accademia Bridge and the Peggy Guggenheim Museum. It's dressy, specializes in fish, has six or eight tables on the canal, and is worth the splurge (Mon–Sat 12:30–14:30 & 19:30–21:30, closed Sun, reservations wise, on the canal Rio de S. Vio, tel. 041-523-9577).

Rialto Bridge Tourist Traps: Locals are embarrassed by the lousy food and aggressive "service" of the string of joints dominating the best romantic Grand Canal real estate in town. Still, if you want to linger over dinner with a view of the most famous bridge and the romantic song of gondoliers oaring by (and don't mind eating with other tourists), this can be enjoyable. Don't trust the waiter's recommendations for special meals. Just get a simple pizza or pasta and a drink, and you'll savor the ambience without being ripped off.

Near St. Mark's Square

For the location of these restaurants, see the map on page 58.

Osteria da Carla, two blocks west of St. Mark's Square, is a fun and very local hole-in-the-wall where the food is good and the price is right (€8–12 dishes). They have hearty tuna salads and a daily pasta special along with traditional antipasti, polenta, and decent wine by the glass (see blackboard). Seafood-lovers might try their "triple fish and polenta" plate (sardine, squid and cod, €10). While you can eat outside, table #3 comes with a flushing soundtrack (Mon–Sat 8:00–22:00, closed Sun; from American Express head toward St. Mark's Square, first left down Frezzeria, first left again through "Contarina" tunnel, at Sotoportego e Corte Contarina, sign over door says "Pietro Panizzolo"—it's historic and can't be removed; tel. 041-523-7855, Michela SE).

Osteria Enoteca San Marco offers beautifully-presented "creative new Italian" cuisine with a mod ambience in a classic medieval shell. They proudly offer fine wine by the glass (€20 meals, Mon–Sat 12:30–3:00 & 19:30–23:00, closed Sun, a long block west of St. Mark's Square at #1610 Frezzeria, tel. 041-528-5242, Carlo and his hard-working staff SE).

Near the Train Station
For fast, cheap food near the station, consider **Brek**, a popular self-service cafeteria (after serving breakfast, it's open 11:30–22:00; with back to station, facing canal, go left on Rio Terra—it becomes Lista di Spagna in 2 short blocks, Lista di Spagna 124; tel. 041-244-0158).

Eating Elsewhere in Venice
Ristorante Aqua Pazza (literally, "crazy water") provides good pizza in a wonderful setting on Campo San Angelo (check out the leaning tower over your shoulder) midway between the Rialto, Accademia, and St. Mark's. The owner is from Naples and he delights locals with Amalfi/Naples cuisine. That means perhaps the best—and most expensive—pizza in Venice (Tue–Sun 12:00–15:00 & 19:00–23:00, closed Mon, Campo S. Angelo 3809, tel. 041-277-0688).

Osteria al Bacco, far beyond the crowds in a rustic Venetian setting, is worth the hike for its local cuisine (€35 for 3 courses and wine; Tue–Sun 19:00–22:00, closed Mon; reservations recommended; halfway between train station and northernmost tip of Venice, Fondamenta Cappuccine, Cannaregio 3054; tel. 041-717-493).

Osteria la Zucca is a hardworking, homey place on the Rio del Megio canal away from the crowds. You'll get good, typical Venetian cuisine at a moderate price (€20 meals, Mon–Sat 12:30–14:30 & 19:00–22:30, closed Sun; mostly indoors, reserve for canal windows, a few outdoor tables with one on the canal; midway between train station and Rialto Bridge at San Giacomo dell'Orio, Calle Larga, Santa Croce 1762; tel. 041-524-1570). A short block away is the square called San Giacomo dell'Orio—a breezy scene with trees, families at play, and a couple of simple trattorias offering basic food and classic non-touristy outdoor seating.

Cheap Meals
A key to cheap eating in Venice is **bar snacks**, especially stand-up mini-meals in out-of-the-way bars. Order by pointing. *Panini* (sandwiches) are sold fast and cheap at bars everywhere. Basic reliable ham-and-cheese sandwiches (white bread, crusts trimmed) come toasted—simply ask for "toast"; these make a great supplement to Venice's skimpy hotel breakfasts.

For budget eating, I like small *cicchetti* **bars** (see "Pub-Crawl Dinner," page 85); for speed, value, and ambience, you can get a filling plate of local appetizers at nearly any of the bars.

Pizzerias are cheap and easy—try for a sidewalk table at a scenic location. If you want a fast-food pizza place, try **Spizzico** on Campo San Luca (roughly between St. Mark's Square and the Rialto Bridge).

The **produce market** that sprawls for a few blocks just past the Rialto Bridge is a great place to assemble a picnic (best 8:00–13:00, closed Sun). The adjacent fish market is wonderfully slimy. Side lanes in this area are speckled with fine little hole-in-the-wall munchie bars, bakeries, and cheese shops.

Gelato

La Boutique del Gelato is considered the best *gelateria* in Venice (daily 10:00–20:30, closed Dec–Jan; 2 blocks off Campo Santa Maria di Formosa on corner of Salizada San Lio and Calle Paradiso, next to Hotel Bruno, #5727—just look for the crowd).

Late-Night Gelato: At the Rialto, try **Michielangelo**, just off Campo San Bartolomeo, on the St. Mark's side of the Rialto Bridge on Salizada Pio X (Thu–Tue 10:00–22:00, closed Wed). At St. Mark's Square, the **Al Todaro** *gelateria* opposite the Doge's Palace is open late (daily 8:00–22:00, closes at 20:00 and on Mon in winter).

TRANSPORTATION CONNECTIONS

See rail map on next page.

By train to: Padua (1/hr, 30 min), **Vicenza** (1/hr, 1 hr), **Verona** (1/hr, 90 min), **Ravenna** (1/hr, 3–4 hrs, transfer in Ferrara or Bologna), **Florence** (7/day, 3 hrs), **Dolomites** (8/day to Bolzano, about hourly, 4 hrs with 1 transfer; catch bus from Bolzano into mountains), **Milan** (1/hr, 3–4 hrs), **Monterosso/La Spezia/Cinque Terre** (2/day, 6 hrs, departs Venice at 10:00 and 15:00), **Rome** (7/day, 5 hrs, slower overnight), **Naples** (change in Rome, plus 2–3 hrs), **Brindisi** (3/day, 11 hrs, change in Bologna), **Bern** (3/day, change in Milan, 8 hrs), **Munich** (2/day, 8 hrs), **Paris** (4/day, 11 hrs), and **Vienna** (4/day, 9 hrs). Train and *couchette* reservations (about €18) are easily made at a downtown travel agency.

Rail Lines between Venice and Milan

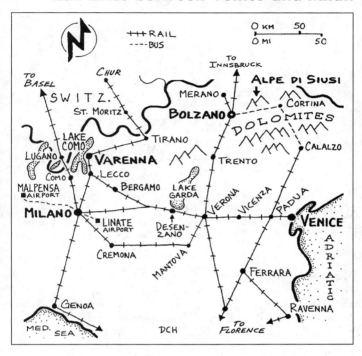

SIGHTS NEAR VENICE:
PADUA, VICENZA, VERONA, AND RAVENNA

While Venice is just one of many towns in the Italian region of Veneto (VEN-eh-toh), few venture off the lagoon. Four important towns and possible side trips, in addition to the lakes and the Dolomites, make zipping directly from Venice to Milan (or Florence) a route strewn with temptation.

Planning Your Time

The towns of Padua, Vicenza, Verona, and Ravenna are all, for various reasons, good stops. Each town gives the visitor a low-key slice of Italy that complements the urbanity of Venice, Florence, and Rome.

Visiting Verona, Padua, and Vicenza couldn't be easier: All are 30 minutes apart on the Venice–Milan line (hrly, 3 hrs). Spending a day town-hopping between Venice and Milan—with 3-hour stops at Padua, Vicenza, and Verona—is exciting and efficient. Trains run frequently enough to allow flexibility and little wasted time. Of the towns discussed below, only Ravenna (2.5 hours from Padua or Florence) is not on the main Venice–Milan train line.

If you're Padua-bound, note that you need to reserve ahead to see the Scrovegni Chapel (see page 100). Most sights in Verona and Vicenza are closed on Monday.

Padua (Padova)

Living under Venetian rule for four centuries seemed only to sharpen Padua's independent spirit. Nicknamed "the brain of Veneto," Padua has a prestigious university (founded 1222) that was home to Galileo, Copernicus, Dante, and Petrarch. The old town, even when packed with modern-day students, is a colonnaded time-tunnel experience.

Sights Near Venice

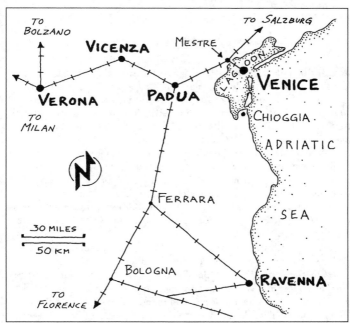

And Padua's museums and churches hold their own in Italy's artistic big league.

Arrival in Padua: Enter the station lobby. To get oriented, turn around and face the exit. At your right is a small office, marked Bus Tickets, which sells exactly that (€0.85, also available at the *tabacchi* shop at the far right and at newsstands). An ATM is just outside to your right under the colonnade as you exit. Pick up a map and list of sights at the TI (also to the right, past the ATM, Mon–Sat 9:30–18:30, Sun 9:30–12:30, tel. 049-875-2077, www.turismopadova.it). Beyond the TI is a post office (Mon–Fri 8:30–14:00, Sat 8:30–13:00, closed Sun).

Day-trippers: The baggage check window is to the far right as you face the exit (€4, daily 6:00–23:00). If you have reservations for the Scrovegni Chapel, that will dictate the order of your sightseeing. But if you don't plan on seeing the chapel, here's an efficient plan: Take the bus from the station to the Basilica of St. Anthony, then walk through the old town, sightseeing your way back to the station (buy your €0.85 bus ticket at the Bus Ticket office in the station lobby or at a *tabacchi* shop; from platform/*corsia* 3 catch bus #8, #12, or #18 to Via Luca Belludi, next to Piazza del Santo and the Basilica of St. Anthony). A taxi into town costs about €5. (If you have any train business, such as reservations, note that a CIT travel agency is on the square in front of the station; Mon–Fri 9:00–18:00, Sat 9:30–12:30, closed Sun.)

SIGHTS

▲▲Basilica of St. Anthony—Friar Anthony of Padua, "Christ's perfect follower and a tireless preacher of the Gospel," spent his last two years here. Within a year of his 1231 death, he was made a saint, and construction had begun on the impressive Romanesque Gothic church that would be his final resting place. For nearly 800 years, his remains (and the church) have attracted pilgrims to Padua.

Nod to St. Anthony (looking down from the facade) and enter the basilica. As you step inside, you're leaving Italy and entering Vatican territory. Gaze past the crowds and through the incense haze at Donatello's glorious crucifix rising from the altar, and realize that this is one of the most important pilgrimage sites in Christendom. Over three million people a year visit (daily in summer 6:30–20:00, winter 6:30–19:00, modest dress code enforced).

Along with the crucifix, Donatello's bronze statues—Mary with Padua's six favorite saints—grace the high altar.

On the left, pilgrims file slowly by the chapel containing **St. Anthony's tomb**. This Renaissance masterpiece from 1500 is circled by nine marble reliefs showing scenes and miracles from the life of the saint. The pilgrims believe Anthony is their protector—a confidant and intercessor of the poor. And they believe he works miracles. Votives placed here by the faithful ask for help or give thanks for miracles they believe he's performed. By putting their hand on his tomb while saying a silent prayer, pilgrims show devotion to Anthony and feel the saint's presence.

Next on the pilgrim route is the **Chapel of the Reliquaries** (behind the altar). Join the pilgrims as they shuffle past the relics of St. Anthony (stacked three high in the middle case surrounded by lavish gifts to the church). These are St. Anthony's vocal chords (in glass ball at bottom—discovered intact when his remains were examined in 1981), "uncorrupted tongue" (the speckled triangle above that—discovered when the remains were examined in 1263), and his toothy jaw (on top). These relics—considered miraculously preserved—befit the saint who couldn't stop teaching, preaching, and praying. In front of the relics is Anthony's tunic (from 1231, found when the tomb was opened in 1982).

Check out the dome. This chapel is a 17th-century addition to the church, built in a heavily stuccoed Baroque style unusual in this corner of Italy so enamored by the reserved neoclassicism of Palladio.

The information desk just inside the cloisters (daily 8:30–13:00 & 14:00–18:30) is very helpful, with an abundance of St. Anthony–related handouts. Pick up a free map of the complex from the desk. Wander

Padua

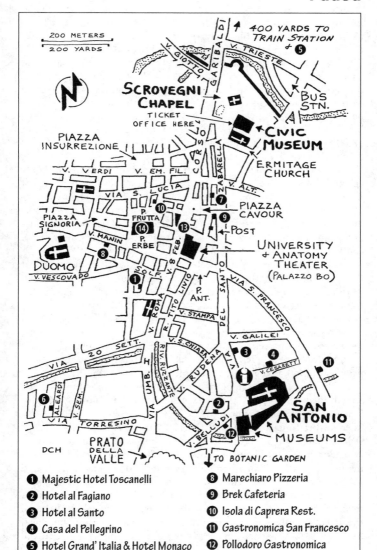

200 METERS
200 YARDS

400 YARDS TO
TRAIN STATION
➍ ➎

V. GIOTTO
GARIBALDI
V. TRIESTE

SCROVEGNI
CHAPEL
TICKET
OFFICE HERE

BUS
STN.

CIVIC
MUSEUM

PIAZZA
INSURREZIONE

CORSO
ZABARELLA
V. ALT.

ERMITAGE
CHURCH

V. VERDI

V. EM. FIL.

VIA S. LUCIA

PIAZZA
CAVOUR

P.
FRUTTA

➓

➒

PIAZZA
SIGNORIA

⓮

⓭

POST

V. MANIN

P.
ERBE

UNIVERSITY
& ANATOMY
THEATER
(PALAZZO BO)

➑

DUOMO

V. VESCOVADO

➊

V. 8 FEB.

V. SOLF.

V. TITO LIVIO

P.
ANT.

DEL SANTO

VIA S. FRANCESCO

V. ROMA

V. STAMPA

V. GALILEI

VIA 20 SETT.

V. S. CHIARA

RIV. RUZZANTE

RUDENA

➌

➍

V. CESARETT.

➒

VIA

V. ALEARDI

V. SEM.

➏

VIA UMB.

TORRESINO

➋

⓬

SAN
ANTONIO

MUSEUMS

DCH

PRATO
DELLA
VALLE

TO BOTANIC GARDEN

BELLUDI

➊ Majestic Hotel Toscanelli
➋ Hotel al Fagiano
➌ Hotel al Santo
➍ Casa del Pellegrino
➎ Hotel Grand' Italia & Hotel Monaco
➏ Ostello Città di Padova
➐ La Cova Ristorante

➑ Marechiaro Pizzeria
➒ Brek Cafeteria
➓ Isola di Caprera Rest.
⓫ Gastronomica San Francesco
⓬ Pollodoro Gastronomica
⓭ Caffè Pedrocchi & TI
⓮ Palazzo della Ragione

around the various cloisters. Picnic tables invite pilgrims and tourists to enjoy eating within the solitude of one of the cloisters (it's covered and suitable even when rainy, WCs in same cloister). In the far end, a fascinating little museum is filled with votives and folk art recounting miracles attributed to Anthony (follow signs to Museo Antoniano).

Outside, on Piazza del Santo, stands Donatello's much-admired equestrian statue of the Venetian mercenary General Gattamelata. Even military commanders—such as this powerful Venetian—wanted to be close to St. Anthony. This statue is famous as the first of this size cast out of bronze since ancient Roman times. On the square, you'll find a handy **TI** (April–Nov Mon–Sat 9:30–13:00 & 15:00–19:00, closes at 18:00 Sun) and a couple of friendly cafés. A 10-minute stroll up Via del Santo takes you back into the center.

Palazzo della Ragione—This grand 13th-century palazzo commonly called *il Salone* (great hall) once held the medieval law courts. The first floor consists of a huge hall—265 feet by 90 feet—adorned with a series of over 300 15th-century frescoes depicting the signs of the zodiac, labors of the month, symbols representing characteristics of people born under each sign, and finally, figures of saints to legitimize the power of the courts in the eyes of the church.

The hall is topped with a keel-shaped roof, which helps to support the structure without the use of columns—quite an architectural feat in its time, considering the building's dimensions. The curious stone in the right-hand corner just inside the entry is the "Stone of Shame," which was the seat of debtors being punished during the Middle Ages. Instead of being sentenced to death or prison, debtors sat upon this stone, renounced their possessions, and denounced themselves publicly before being exiled from the city. Locals thank St. Anthony for this more compassionate alternative for the bankrupt.

The palace is free, but often houses temporary exhibitions for a fee. You'll likely have to pay the admission to get a peek of the interior (entrance on west side of building).

▲▲**Market Squares: Piazza Erbe and Piazza Frutta**—The stately Palazzo della Ragione (described above) provides a quintessentially Italian backdrop for Padua's almost exotic-feeling market. Each morning (except Sunday) the surrounding squares—Piazza delle Erbe and Piazza della Frutta—are a fragrant and tempting commotion of local produce. This market has been renowned for centuries as having the region's freshest and greatest selection of herbs, fruits, and vegetables. Beneath the Palazzo della Ragione (in the covered stalls), various butchers, *salumerie* (delicatessens), cheese shops, bakeries, and fishmongers sell their goods.

On the Piazza delle Erbe side (by the fountain), notice the neoclassical wing of the city hall with its historical panels—depicting the unification of Italy in 1866 and the aerial bombardment of Padua by the

Austrians in World War I (town map marks where each bomb hit—not very destructive in those days). Another map trumpets the glorious Italian empire Mussolini put together in the 1930s (with vast and important holdings, from Albania to Libya to Ethiopia and Somalia).

Make a point to explore this scene. Students gather here each evening, spilling out of colorful bars and cafés—drinks in hand—into the square. Their drink of choice is a *spritz,* an aperitif with Campari and Cynar (two bitter, alcoholic liqueurs), white wine, and sparkling water, garnished with an olive and a blood-orange wedge. **Bar Nazionale** offers outdoor seating for a ringside view of the action (at #41 under staircase of Palazzo della Ragione in Piazza delle Erbe). **Bar degli Spritz** is the students' hangout (at #36 near the middle of the palazzo at the passage-way). Get your *spritz* and join the young people out on the piazza (remember to return your glass when finished). This is a classic oppor-tunity to enjoy a real discussion with smart, English-speaking students who see tourists not as pests but as interesting people from far away. For an instant conversation starter, ask about the current political situation in Italy, the cultural differences between the north and the south...or what they think of America's president.

Caffè Pedrocchi—This café was built in the mid-1800s to provide a congress and convention center for the town and a place for the acade-mic populace to gather. This neoclassical people's palace symbolized progress—nationalism, industrial revolution, freedom of speech, and modern thinking. Nicknamed "the café with no doors," it was famously open 24/7, offering an inviting space in which people could gather and share ideas—political, social...whatever.

Wandering through here, you can imagine the heady days leading up to Italian unification in the mid-1800s. Austria was testy about this issue—flying the Italian colors could get you in hot water. But the cafe's three main rooms are like the flag: decorated red, white, and green. The green room (*Sala Verde*) has always been open to the non-paying public. Anyone—pensioner, poor student, penniless anarchist—is welcome to sit here and read the paper or chat. In the white room (*Sala Bianca*), a bullet hole in the wall is marked by a memorial. This is where students plotted an uprising against the Austrians in 1848, and where one of the insurgents was killed.

The café is just off Piazza delle Erbe (near Piazza Cavour, at inter-section of Oberdan and VIII Febbraio; daily 9:00–21:00, until 24:00 Thu–Sat; access to the most-decorated rooms upstairs-€3, Tue–Sun 9:30–12:30 & 15:30–18:30, closed Mon; tel. 049-820-5007).

University of Padua—This prestigious university is just across the street from Caffè Pedrocchi. Founded in 1222, it's one of the first, greatest, and most progressive universities in Europe. Back when the Church con-trolled university curricula, a group of professors broke away and created this liberal school, independent of Catholic constraints and accessible to people of all faiths. A haven for free thinking, it attracted intellectuals from all over Europe. The great astronomer Copernicus made some of his most important discoveries here. And Galileo—notorious for disagreeing with the Church's views on science—called his 18 years on the faculty here the best of his life. Students gather in ancient courtyards, surrounded by memories of illustrious alumni—including the first woman ever to receive a university degree (in 1678).

The 16th-century courtyard is generally open and free. In the good old days, only nobles taught and studied here. This courtyard (and much of the rest of the school) is wallpapered with some 3,000 coats of arms left by alums. The frieze is decorated with symbols representing the various faculties. The times of the daily tours are posted in this courtyard (€3, generally 3/day—Mon, Wed, and Fri at 15:15, 16:15, and 17:15 or Tue, Thu, and Sat at 9:15, 10:15, and 11:15, tel. 049-827-3047).

The tour takes you to venerable lecture halls and Europe's first great **anatomy theater**. The fragile wooden theater survives, and visitors get a quick cadaver's-eye view. In the 1500s, dissection was a dicey issue. The church allowed the University of Padua limited dissection. To get the most teaching mileage out of each one, up to 250 students would pack this standing-room-only theater to watch professors pick apart human organs. According to legend, they did more dissecting than allowed—and always had an animal corpse on hand if a Church official checked and a quick switch was necessary.

University Botanical Gardens (Orto Botanico)—Green thumbs will appreciate the oldest university botanical garden in Europe, founded in 1545 to cultivate medicinal plants. Your admission includes a good plan and history. Kids love the carnivores—both fly-trap and super-sticky. Across from the bug-eaters is a line of plants introduced to Europe by this institution around 1600 (€4, April–Oct daily 9:00–13:00 & 15:00–18:00, Nov–March Mon–Sat 9:00–13:00, closed Sun, entrance 150 yards south of St. Anthony's Basilica).

▲▲Scrovegni Chapel (Cappella degli Scrovegni)—The newly-restored and absolutely exquisite private chapel of the Scrovegni family, decorated by the most complete and best-preserved cycle of frescoes by Giotto, offers one of Europe's great art experiences. As only 25 people at a time are allowed into this fragile space, visitors must reserve in advance and go through a high-tech dehumidifying ritual.

Cost, Hours, Reservations: The chapel is open daily 9:00–22:00 in summer, until 19:00 off-season (people are allowed in every 15 min at :00, :15, :30, and :45 past the hour). To reserve a 15-minute visit, call 049-201-0020 (ticket office open Mon–Fri 9:00–19:00, Sat 9:00–13:00, closed Sun) or book online at www.cappelladegliscrovegni.it. The cost is €11, payable only by credit card (tickets reduced to €7.50 for visits after 19:00). As the chapel often books up, it's wise to reserve well in advance. While the telephone reservation service can't book same-day visits, they can tell you if it's slow and you might be able to drop by and find a spot open immediately or (more likely) in the evening. No photos are allowed in the chapel.

The Experience: You're advised to arrive one hour before your appointed time to exchange your booking receipt for a ticket at the ticket office in the Civic Museum (30 min early if you have a 9:00 visit). While waiting, you can visit the Civic Museum and the new Multimedia Center inside the museum (both described below and covered by the Scrovegni ticket, good for entry all day).

Report to the actual chapel 10 minutes before your time slot (100 yards from the ticket desk, outside and well-signed). Once admitted, you'll wait in the "compensation room" for 15 minutes to establish humidity levels friendly to the frescoes before continuing into the chapel. Your enforced wait passes quickly as you watch a fascinating and very helpful presentation about the frescoes (English subtitles). The rhythm is very strict—15 minutes in the humidity room followed by exactly 15 minutes in the chapel.

The Background: The Scrovegni family—local Rockefellers—built their family palace and chapel on the sacred and ancient grounds of the Roman town (you'll see Roman ruins scattered around outside the chapel today). The palace was destroyed in 1824, leaving the chapel standing alone (with no windows on the side that once abutted the palace).

The chapel was built out of guilt. Reginaldo degli Scrovegni charged sky-high interest rates at a time when this practice of "usury" was forbidden by the Church. He even caught the attention of Dante, who awarded him a place in hell in his *Inferno*. When Reginaldo died, the church denied him a Christian burial. His son Enrico tried to buy forgiveness for his dad's sins by building this superb chapel. To decorate the chapel, Enrico hired the top artistic gun of his day: Giotto.

Painted by Giotto and his assistants from 1303 to 1305, and considered by many to be the first piece of modern art, this work makes it clear: Europe was breaking out of the Middle Ages. In a sign of the Renaissance to come, Giotto placed real people in real scenes. These frescoes were radical for their use of 3-D, lively colors, light sources, emotion, and humanism. You're in a Giotto time capsule, looking back at an artist ahead of his day. It's safe to say this is the best of Giotto. The artist was in his mid-thirties at the time, and this is considered his most mature work. (Since it was painted in chronological order and he was continually improving, art historians note that the last scenes are his finest).

The Theological Plan of the Scrovegni Chapel: The frescoes decorate the Chapel in a cohesive cycle. The starry, starry sky features Mary and Jesus with four prophets from the Old Testament and four prophets from the New Testament.

The walls tell a story chronologically in three tiers, spiraling down and clockwise from the top.

Top level: The lives of Joachim and Anne (parents of Mary) and scenes from Mary's life.

Middle level: Jesus' birth and life.

Bottom level: The Passion of Jesus (the story of the days leading up to his crucifixion).

Note the unprecedented explosion of emotion surrounding the crucifixion scene and the deposition (to the right—taking Christ off the cross), with the flock of distraught angels and actual tears pouring down the faces of the mourners. Giotto's use of color to show light and shadow on the robes in these scenes was groundbreaking.

The west end (where the public entered) shows the Last Judgment, with the saved having a good day (on the left) and a fiery river of hopelessness sweeping the damned away (on the right). Those who had had run-ins with the law in their mortal lives would recognize many of the tortures Giotto featured in this hell. In the middle (on the "saved" side), Enrico Scrovegni (without much humility, given the size he had himself portrayed) gives this chapel to God in return for forgiveness for his family's sinful money-lending.

The arch by the altar features God telling the Archangel Gabriel of his mission to inform Mary she'll give birth to the Messiah. Below that, Gabriel breaks the news to the Virgin. The two tiny empty scenes (flanking the altar in the arch, with the empty wrought-iron candelabra) show Giotto's way-ahead-of-his-time mastery of depth. Note the fine old 14th- and 15th-century wooden seats. While the public sat back in the nave, the Scrovegnis sat up front (their private entrance was where you entered today).

The frescoes around the altar—painted after the others (and not by Giotto)—are not up to Giotto's standards (flat, no real emotions, lousy proportions) and not considered artistically important. But the altar statues—by the great sculptor Giovanni Pisano, a friend of Giotto's—are top-notch. From the tomb behind the altar, the figure of Enrico Scrovegni looks out at all of you.

Civic Museum (Musei Civici Eremitani)—Next to the Scrovegni Chapel, this museum—once an Augustinian hermits' monastery—displays pre-Roman, Roman, and Etruscan archaeological finds, buckets of rare coins, and 13th- to 18th-century paintings by Titian, Tintoretto, Giorgione, Tiepolo, Veronese, and other Veneto artists. The highlight is an exquisite Giotto crucifix that once hung in the Scrovegni chapel. Near the crucifix is a statue of Enrico degli Scrovegni looking as though he's wondering how to save his father's soul.

The museum's latest addition is the **Multimedia Center,** offering a virtual chapel visit with explanations of the individual panels, Giotto's fresco technique, close-ups of the art, and a description of the restoration (included with €11 Scrovegni Chapel ticket, daily 9:00–19:00 in summer, until 18:00 off-season, Piazza Eremitani, tel. 049-820-4551).

The Church of the Eremitani (Chiesa degli Eremitani)—This church, next door to the Civic Museum, is worth a peek. Its 14th-century wooden ceiling is shaped like the hull of a ship (similar to the ceiling of Palazzo della Ragione downtown). Just inside the door are two fine Venetian Gothic crypts. To the left of the high altar are photos of the church after its 1944 destruction by Allied bombs. To the right of the altar is a chapel with the scant remains of a once-brilliant cycle frescoed by Mantegna. Flip the switch (back wall facing the chapel) to illuminate slides of the chapel before the WWII bombs fell.

SLEEPING

Many travelers make Padua a low-stress, low-price home base for touring Venice. I'd rather flip-flop it—sleeping in Venice and side-tripping to Padua, 30 minutes away by train.

In the Center
$$$ **Majestic Hotel Toscanelli** is a big, fancy hotel with 32 pleasant air-conditioned rooms, a touch of charm, and a relatively quiet location on a side street (Sb-€96–116, Db-€140–165, 10 percent discount with this book, superior rooms and suites available at extra cost, includes wonderful breakfast; Via dell' Arco 2, several blocks south of Piazza delle Erbe; tel. 049-663-244, fax 049-876-0025, www.toscanelli.com/realtour, majestic@toscanelli.com). It's buried deep in what was the ghetto, two blocks off Piazza Erbe (head up Via Fabbri and take the first left, then turn right onto Via dell' Arco).

SLEEP CODE

(€1 = about $1.10, country code: 33)
Sleep Code: **S** = Single, **D** = Double/Twin, **T** = Triple, **Q** = Quad, **b** = bathroom, **s** = shower only, **no CC** = Credit Cards not accepted.
    To help you easily sort through these listings, I've divided the rooms into three categories, based on the price for a standard double room with bath:

$$$ **Higher Priced**—Most rooms €140 or more.
  $$ **Moderately Priced**—Most rooms between €100-140.
    $ **Lower Priced**—Most rooms €100 or less.

Near St. Anthony's Basilica

$ Hotel al Fagiano has 30 bright and cheery air-conditioned rooms on a side street just off Piazza del Santo (Sb-€54, Db-€75, Tb-€85, breakfast €3–6 extra, Via Locatelli 45, tel. & fax 049-875-0073, www.alfagiano.it, info@alfagiano.it).

$ Hotel al Santo offers 16 quiet and comfortable rooms a few steps from St. Anthony's (Sb-€52, Db-€90, Tb-€130, Qb-€145, includes breakfast, air-con, double-paned windows, tel. 049-875-2131, fax 049-878-8076, www.alsanto.it, alsanto@alsanto.it).

$ Casa del Pellegrino, with 160 spotless, cheap, institutional rooms, is home to the pilgrims who come to pay homage to St. Anthony in the basilica, which is right next door (S-€37, Sb-€51, D-€48, Db-€63, T-€59, Tb-€70, air-con extra, ask for room off the street, breakfast-€6, elevator, Via Cesarotti 21, tel. 049-823-9711, fax 049-823-9780, info@casadelpellegrino.it).

Near the Train Station

$$$ Hotel Grand'Italia comes with elegant four-star comfort, convenience, and prices. Housed in a palace, the hotel has 61 comfortable rooms, and the breakfast room is bright and inviting (Db-€155–200 depending on season and size, includes breakfast; elevator, air-con; Corso del Popolo 81, right outside train station; tel. 049-876-1111, fax 049-875-0850, www.hotelgranditalia.it, booking@hotelgranditalia.it).

$$ Hotel Monaco, a three-star hotel a few doors away from the Grand'Italia, is plain in comparison—with 57 darkly-decorated rooms—but much cheaper (Db-€95–112, includes breakfast; elevator, air-con, traffic noise; Piazzale Stazione 3—as you exit station, it's to your right and across the street; tel. 049-664-344, fax 049-664-669, www.hotelmonacopadova.it, info@hotelmonacopadova.it).

Hostel

$ Ostello Città di Padova is a well-run hostel with 6- and 8-bed rooms (€14 beds with sheets and breakfast, 4-person family rooms-€54, non-members pay €2.60/night extra, Internet and laundry available, reception open 7:15–9:30 & 16:00–23:00 with lockout in between, 23:00 curfew, bus #12, or #18 from station, Via Aleardi 30, tel. 049-875-2219).

EATING

The university population means cheap, good food in central *osterie*, *trattorie*, and take-out joints. There are generally vendors' stands selling calamari-type munchies to the student gang hanging out on Piazzas della Erbe and Frutta. All of my listings are centrally located in the historic core.

La Cova Ristorante/Pizzeria, at Piazza Cavour, offers a pleasing range of pizza and pasta. If you sit in the *ristorante* rather than the pizzeria, you're expected to have multiple courses (Wed–Mon 12:00–15:30 & 18:00–24:00, closed Tue; just off Piazza Cavour, Via P.F. Calvi 20; tel. 049-654-312).

Marechiaro Pizzeria/Trattoria is another good bet, just off Piazza delle Erbe (Tue–Sun 12:00–14:30 & 18:00–23:30, closed Mon, Via D. Manin 37, tel. 049-875-8489).

Brek, tucked into a corner of Piazza Cavour 20, is a mod and easy self-service *ristorante* (daily 11:30–15:00 & 19:30–22:00, tel. 049-875-3788).

To dine rather than eat, consider **Isola di Caprera** for traditional Veneto cuisine (€21 *menu* or €37 seafood *menu*, cheaper à la carte options; Mon–Sat 12:00–15:00 & 19:30–22:30, closed Sun; air-con; Via Marsilio da Padova 11-15, half-block north of eastern edge of Piazza della Frutta; to reserve call 049-664-282 or 049-876-0244).

Take-out: **Gastronomica San Francesco** serves up all kinds of homemade finger food, lasagna, roast meats, and vegetables by the *etto*, or 100 grams. A half-kilo (about a pound) of lasagna and some vegetables make a light, portable lunch for two, perfect for a picnic in the nearby cloisters of St. Anthony's. They'll set you up with to-go containers, plastic silverware, and napkins (Fri–Wed 10:00–13:30 & 17:00–20:00, closed Thu, Via San Francesco 214). **Pollodoro La Gastronomica,** another take-out deli near the basilica, sells roasted chicken and makes sandwiches (Wed–Sat and Mon 8:30–14:00 & 17:00–20:00, Sun 8:30–14:00, closed Tue; 100 yards from basilica, Via Belludi 34—with your back to the church entrance, it's under the arches on the left).

Gelato: Locals flock to **Gelateria K2** for top-quality, made-on-location gelato (long and happy hours, near Piazza Erbe at Via Roma 63).

TRANSPORTATION CONNECTIONS

By train to: Venice (2/hr, 20 min), **Vicenza** (3/hr, 20 min), **Milan** (hrly leaving at :28 past the hour, 2.5 hrs), **Verona** (2/hr, 1 hr).

Vicenza

To many architects, Vicenza is a pilgrimage site. Entire streets look like the back of a nickel. This is the city of Palladio, the 16th-century Renaissance architect who gave us the Palladian style that is so influential in countless British country homes. For the casual visitor, a quick stop offers plenty of Palladio (1508–1580)—the last great artist of the Renaissance. Note that Vicenza's major sights are closed on Monday.

Tourist Information: The main TI is at Piazza Matteotti 12 (daily 9:00–13:00 & 14:00–18:00, tel. 0444-320-854, www.vicenzae.org). Pick up a map and, if staying the night, an entertainment guide (in Italian but *teatro* and *concerto* are easy enough to understand). Architect fans will appreciate the free *Vicenza Città del Palladio* brochure in English. Guided **tours** of Vicenza may be offered in English in 2004; ask at the TI.

Arrival in Vicenza: From the train station, it's a five-minute **walk** up wide Viale Roma to the bottom of Corso Palladio. Or it's a short **bus** ride to Piazza Matteotti and the top of Corso Palladio. For a day trip, consider catching the bus to Piazza Matteotti and doing your sightseeing on the way back to the station: From the station, catch bus #1, #2, or #5 (€0.95, tickets sold at *tabacchi* shop in station, stop is immediately to your left as you exit the station). Validate your ticket in the machine near the back of the bus. Get off at Piazza Matteotti, a skinny, park-like square in front of a white neoclassical building. A **taxi** to Piazza Matteotti costs about €6.

You can store luggage at the train station (baggage check-€3.90, daily 9:00–13:00 & 15:00–19:00, to the far right as you face the ticket booths).

Launderette: The self-service Euro Lavanderia Fai da Te is near the TI and a couple of blocks from Piazza Matteotti (daily 7:30–22:30, with your back to TI, turn left around corner, cross bridge, take right middle fork to Contrà XX Settembre 27, go under the arches on left).

Market Days: Vicenza hosts a Tuesday market (7:00–13:00) on Piazza dei Signori and a larger Thursday market that also spills into Piazza Duomo, Piazza del Castello, and Viale Roma (7:00–13:00).

SIGHTS

Most of Vicenza's sights are covered by a Biglietto Unico ticket (€7, good for 3 days, sold only at the Olympic Theater). In addition to the theater, this combo-ticket includes the Pinacoteca (paintings in Palazzo Chiericati on Piazza Matteotti) and the Santa Corona Archaeological and Natural History Museum (next to the Church of Santa Corona). The pricier €11 combo-ticket gets you into every sight in Vicenza except for exhibits in the Basilica Palladiana.

▲▲**Olympic Theater (Teatro Olimpico)**—Palladio's last work is one of his greatest. It was commissioned by the Olympic Academy, a society of Vicenzan scholars and intellectuals (including Palladio), for the purpose of staging performances and intellectual debates. Begun in 1580, shortly before Palladio died, the theater was actually completed by a fellow architect, Scamozzi.

Modeled after the theaters of antiquity, this is a wood-and-stucco festival of classical columns, statues, and an oh-wow stage bursting with perspective tricks. Behind the stage, framed by a triumphal arch, five

Vicenza

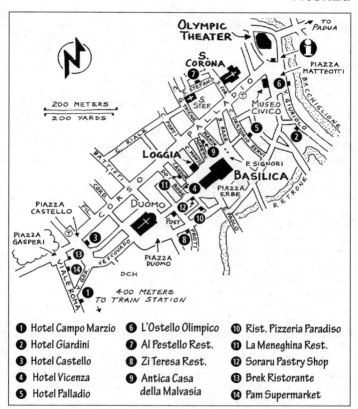

1 Hotel Campo Marzio	**6** L'Ostello Olimpico
2 Hotel Giardini	**7** Al Pestello Rest.
3 Hotel Castello	**8** Zi Teresa Rest.
4 Hotel Vicenza	**9** Antica Casa
5 Hotel Palladio	della Malvasia

10 Rist. Pizzeria Paradiso
11 La Meneghina Rest.
12 Soraru Pastry Shop
13 Brek Ristorante
14 Pam Supermarket

streets recede at different angles. The streets, depicting the idealized form of the city of Thebes, were created for the gala opening of *Oedipus Rex*, the first play ever performed in the theater and now a tradition for every season.

Many of the statues in niches on the stage are modeled after the people who funded the work—junior members are portrayed as soldiers of antiquity and senior members as senators. The panels at the top show the labors of Hercules, in keeping with the classical antiquity theme that was all the rage in the 16th century. In contrast to the stunning stage, the audience's wooden benches are simple and crude (€7 Biglietto Unico, Tue–Sun 9:00–17:00, July–Aug until 19:00, last entry 15 min before closing, closed Mon, hours can vary, entrance to the left of TI, tel. 0444-222-800, www.olimpico.vicenza.it, WC just past the ticket booth on the right).

Performances: One of the oldest indoor theaters in Europe and considered one of the world's best, it's still used for performances from April through June (jazz and classical) and from September through October (Shakespeare and Greek tragedies, shows start at 21:00; for details see TI's Web site, www.vicenzae.org, or e-mail scsculturaespettacolo@interfree.it).

▲**Church of Santa Corona (Church of the Holy Crown)**—A block away from the Olympic Theater, this church was built in the 13th century to house a thorn from the crown of thorns given to the Bishop of Vicenza by the French king Louis IX (free, Mon 15:00–18:00, Tue–Sun 8:30–12:00 & 15:00–18:00). It has Giovanni Bellini's fine *Baptism of Christ* (c. 1500, put in a coin for light, to the left of the altar). Study the incredible inlaid marble and mother-of-pearl work on the high altar (1670) and the inlaid wood complementing that in the stalls of the choir (1485).

Archaeological and Natural History Museum—Next door to the Church of Santa Corona, the ground floor of this humble museum features Roman antiquities (mosaics, statues, and swords) and a barbarian warrior skeleton complete with sword and helmet. Prehistoric scraps are upstairs, and there are a few English description sheets near exhibit entryways throughout (€7 Biglietto Unico, Tue–Sun 9:00–17:00, closed Mon, tel. 0444-320-440, WC on second floor at end of prehistoric hall).

Strolling Corso Palladio—From the Olympic Theater or Church of Santa Corona, stroll down Vicenza's main drag, Corso Andrea Palladio, and see why they call Vicenza "Venezia on terra firma." A steady string of Renaissance palaces and Palladian architecture is peopled by Vicenzans (considered by their neighbors to be as uppity as most of their colonnades) and punctuated by upper-class *gelaterias*.

After a few blocks, you'll see the commanding **Basilica Palladiana** (this was not a church, but a meeting place for local big shots). With its 270-foot-tall, 13th-century tower, the basilica dominates the Piazza dei Signori, the town center since Roman times. It was young Palladio's proposal to redo Vicenza's dilapidated Gothic palace of justice in the neo-Greek style that established him as Vicenza's favorite architect. The rest of Palladio's career was a one-man construction boom. Opposite the basilica, the brick-columned **Loggia del Capitaniato**— home of the Venetian governor and one of Palladio's last works—gives you an easy chance to compare early Palladio (the basilica) with late Palladio (the loggia).

The basilica is open to tourists only during exhibitions (which are frequent); see the TI's Web site for details on what's coming up. Even without a ticket, climb the 15th-century stairs. After a few steps, you'll see the lion's mouth (representing the long arm of the Venetian Republic); centuries ago, people used to sneak notes into the mouth, anonymously reporting neighbors suspected of carrying communicable diseases such as the plague. You can walk around the arcaded upper floor (has WC in back), which contains the entrance to the huge basilica. The basilica's roof, shaped like an upside-down keel, has a nautical feel, augmented by the porthole windows. Set in the wall in front, the winged lion (symbol of St. Mark and Venice) laid the course for this little town in the 15th century.

Outside on the Piazza dei Signori, note the two tall **15th-century columns** topped by Jesus and the winged lion. When Venice took over Vicenza in the early 1400s, these columns were added—à la St. Mark's Square—to give the city a Venetian feel.

Finish your Corso Palladio stroll at Piazzale Gasperi (where the Pam supermarket is a handy place to grab a picnic for the train ride), dip into the park called Giardino Salvi (for one last Palladio loggia), and then walk five minutes down Viale Roma back to the station. Trains leave about every hour for Milan/Verona and Venice (less than an hour away).

Villa la Rotonda—Thomas Jefferson's Monticello was inspired by Palladio's Rotonda (a.k.a. Villa Almerico Capra). Started by Palladio in 1566, it was finished by his pupil, Scamozzi. The white, gently domed building, with grand colonnaded entries, seems to have popped out of the grassy slope. Palladio, who designed a number of country villas, had a knack for using the setting for dramatic effect. This private—but sometimes tourable—residence is on the edge of Vicenza (€3 for grounds, mid-March–mid-Nov Tue–Sun 10:00–12:00 & 15:00–18:00, closed Mon; €6 for interior—open only Wed 10:00–12:00 & 15:00–18:00; everything closed mid-Nov–mid-March, Via Rotonda 29, tel. 0444-321-793). To get to the villa from Vicenza's train station, hop a bus (#8, 2/hr, stop is to the left of the station as you're facing it on Viale Venezia) or take a taxi (about €5.50). For a quick round-trip any time of day, you can zip out by cab (5 min from train station) to see the building sitting regally atop its hill, and then ride the same cab back.

Villa Valmarana Ai Nani—The 17th-century "Villa of the Dwarfs" is just up the street from Villa Rotonda, convenient if you want to see a villa interior, but you're not in Vicenza on a Wednesday. This elegant neoclassical estate features panoramic views and 18th-century murals by Tiepolo.

The villa's name comes from the local legend of an ancient manor house owned by a nobleman whose daughter was born a dwarf. Her father surrounded her with dwarf servants so she wouldn't realize she was small. One day as she was looking out the window, she saw a handsome prince ride by on his horse. Realizing she was a dwarf, she killed herself in anguish. Her servants—so saddened by her death that they turned to stone—now line the wall of the villa like petrified sentries.

The rooms in the main house include frescoes with scenes from the Trojan War, classical myths, and Italian lyrical poems. The frescoes in the guest house *(foresteria)* are nearly all by Tiepolo's son, Giandomenico, whose themes highlight 18th-century gentrified culture—the idealized tranquility of peasants, the exotic fashion and styles of the Chinese from a Western perspective, and scenes from Carnevale.

Both houses are furnished with period pieces and have good English descriptions. Pick up a free Villa Valmarana English brochure from the TI if you plan to visit (€6, 10:00–12:00 & 15:00–18:00, closed Mon, and Tue and Fri mornings, from Villa Rotonda head a few steps downhill, then up the slope on Stradella Valmarana about 200 yards, tel. 0444-321-803).

SLEEPING

(€1 = about $1.10, country code: 39)

$$$ **Hotel Campo Marzio**, a four-star, American-style, pricey place, faces a park on the main drag a few minutes' walk in front of the station (Db-€143–207 depending on season and size of room—"superior" means bigger, includes breakfast, easy parking, air-con, elevator, free bike, Viale Roma 21, tel. 0444-545-700, fax 0444-320-495, www.hotelcampomarzio .com, info@hotelcampomarzio.com).

$$ **Hotel Giardini,** with three stars and 17 sleek rooms, has splashy pastel colors and a refreshing feel (Sb-€88, Db-€119, these prices with this book only, includes breakfast, elevator, air-con, on busy street but has double-paned windows, within a block of Piazza Matteotti/Olympic Theater on Via Giuriolo 10, tel. & fax 0444-326-458, www.hotelgiardini .com, info@hotelgiardini.com).

$$ **Hotel Castello**, on Piazza Castello, has 18 dim, quiet rooms (Sb-€82–103, Db-€103–134, includes breakfast; air-con; Contrà Piazza del Castello 24, down alley to the right of Ristorante agli Schioppi, 5-min walk from station; tel. 0444-323-585, fax 0444-323-583, www.hotel-castello.net, mail@hotelcastello.net).

$ **Hotel Vicenza** is ideally located on a quiet street just off Piazza dei Signori in an 18th-century theater. Its 34 peaceful rooms, some with small balconies, have a worn, Old World feel (D-€50, Db-€65, elevator, no breakfast, Stradella dei Nodari, tel. & fax 0444-321-512).

$ **Hotel Palladio** is a last resort, rundown but sleepable (25 rooms, S-€36, Sb-€52, D-€55, Db-€65, Tb-€103, includes minimal breakfast; fans available, ask for quieter room as long as it's not garret-like #35; a block off Piazza dei Signori, left of the church, right to Via Oratorio dei Servi 25; tel. 0444-321-072, fax 0444-547-328, hotelpalladio@libero.it).

$ *Hostel:* **L'Ostello Olimpico,** just a few years old, has a great location on Piazza Matteotti (80 beds, €14.50 beds in 4–6 bed rooms, €15.50 beds in family room, €18 beds in doubles, closes from 9:30–15:15 and at 23:30, no breakfast, Internet access, laundry nearby on Contrà XX Settembre 27, best to reserve several weeks in advance by fax or e-mail, tel. 0444-540-222, fax 0444-547-762, ostello.vicenza@tin.it).

EATING

The local specialty is marinated cod, called *baccalà alla Vicentina*.

Al Pestello serves typical *cucina Vicentina* a block from the Church of Santa Corona (Mon–Sat 12:30–14:30 & 19:30–22:30, closed Sun, Santo Stefano 3, tel. 0444-323-721).

Locals like the romantic **Zi Teresa** for its moderately priced traditional cuisine and pizzas (Thu–Tue 11:45–14:30 & 18:30–23:00, closed Wed; a couple blocks southwest of Piazza dei Signori, Contrà S. Antonio 1, at intersection with Contrà Proti; tel. 0444-321-411).

Antica Casa della Malvasia is an atmospheric, cavernous trattoria serving up affordable regional favorites and homemade pastas (daily 12:00–15:30 & 19:00–24:00; Contrà delle Morette 5, just off Piazza dei Signori on a little alley between Loggia del Capitaniato and St. Mark Lion column; tel. 0444-543-704).

Ristorante Pizzeria Paradiso offers dozens of inexpensive pizza/pasta options and indoor/outdoor seating on a narrow square south of Piazza dei Signori and Piazza Erbe (Tue–Sun 12:00–14:30 & 18:30–22:30, closed Mon, Via Pescherie Vecchie 5, tel. 0444-322-320).

A cheap, self-service **Brek Ristorante** is just off Piazza del Castello, in the shadow of the arch where Corso Palladio meets Viale Roma (Tue–Sun 11:30–15:00 & 18:30–22:00, closed Mon eve, Corso Palladio 10, tel. 0444-327-829). A few steps from that same arch is the **Pam supermarket**, perfect for picnics (daily 8:00–20:00, Wed only until 13:00, closed Sun, follow the curve of the road just outside the city wall).

Pastry: **La Meneghina** is an atmospheric pastry shop (daily 8:00–1:00, full meals from 12:00–14:30 & 19:00–23:00, closed Mon off-season; on Contrà Cavour 18, a short street between Piazza dei Signori and Corso Palladio, tel. 0444-323-305). Nearby, on Piazza dei Signori, the tiny **Soraru** pastry shop has lots of sidewalk tables within tickling distance of the Palladio statue (Thu–Tue 8:30–13:00 & 15:30–20:00, closed Wed; next to basilica, at far end of square from the two tall columns, tel. 0444-320-915).

TRANSPORTATION CONNECTIONS

By train to: Venice (2/hr, 1 hr), **Padua** (3/hr, 20 min), **Ravenna** (hrly, 3–4 hrs, depending on train, with changes in Padua and Ferrara), **Verona** (2/hr, 40 min).

Verona

Romeo and Juliet made Verona a household word. Alas, a visit here has nothing to do with those two star-crossed lovers. You can pay to visit the house falsely claiming to be Juliet's, with an almost believable balcony (and a courtyard swarming with tour groups), take part in the tradition of rubbing the breast of Juliet's statue to ensure finding a lover (or picking up the sweat of someone who can't), and even make a pilgrimage to what isn't "La Tomba di Giulietta." Despite the fiction, the town has been an important crossroads for 2,000 years and is therefore packed with genuine history. R and J fans will take some solace in the fact that two real feuding families, the Montecchi and the Capellis, were the models for Shakespeare's Montagues and Capulets. And, if R and J had existed and were alive today, they would recognize much of their "hometown."

Verona's main attractions are its wealth of Roman ruins; the remnants of its 13th- and 14th-century political and cultural boom; its 21st-century, quiet, pedestrian-only ambience; and a world-class opera festival each July and August (schedule at www.arena.it). After Venice's festival of tourism, Veneto's second city (in population and in artistic importance) is a cool and welcome sip of pure Italy, where dumpsters are painted by schoolchildren as class projects. If you like Italy but don't need great sights, this town is a joy.

Ask a Veronese to tell you about Papa del Gnoccho (NYO-ko). Every year someone from the San Zeno neighborhood is elected Papa del Gnoccho. On the Friday before Mardi Gras, he's dressed like a king. But instead of a scepter, he holds a huge fork piercing a *gnoccho* (potato dumpling). Lots of people wear costumes, including little kids who dress as gnocchi. The focal point is the Church of San Zeno; the origin is in medieval times. About 500 years ago, at a time when the Veronese were nearly starving, the prince handed out gnocchi to everyone. Even now it's customary for the Veronese to eat gnocchi on Friday during Lent.

ORIENTATION

The most enjoyable core of Verona is along Via Mazzini between Piazza Bra and Piazza Erbe, Verona's market square since Roman times. Head straight for Piazza Bra—and stroll. All sights of importance are located within an easy walk through the old town, which is defined by a bend in the river. For a good day trip, see the Arena and take the self-guided "Introductory Old Town Walk," outlined on page 117.

Tourist Information: Verona's TI offices are at the station (Mon–Sat 9:00–19:00, Sun 9:00–15:00, tel. 045-800-0861, www.tourism.verona.it) and at Piazza Bra (Mon–Sat 9:00–19:00, Sun 9:00–15:00, facing the large yellow-white building, TI is across street to your right, tel. 045-

806-8680, public WC on Piazza Bra). Pick up the free city map that includes a list of sights, opening hours, and walking tours. Many sights are closed on Monday and are free on the first Sunday of every month. If you're staying the night, ask for the free *Agenda di Verona*, the monthly entertainment guide (it's in Italian, but *concerto di musica classica* is darn close to English).

The **Verona Card** covers bus transportation and most of Verona's sights (€8/day or €12/3 days, sold at sights covered by the card).

Verona's historic **churches**—San Zeno, San Lorenzo, Sant' Anastasia, San Fermo, and the Duomo—charge admission (covered by Verona Card or €2 apiece, €5 for a combo-ticket sold at the churches, hours roughly Mon–Sat 9:00–18:00, Sun 13:00–18:00, off-season daily 10:00–13:00 & 15:30–16:00, tel. 045-592-813, no photos allowed, no touring during Mass, modest dress expected).

Arrival in Verona

If you arrive at Verona's airport, catch a shuttle bus to the train station (€4.20, buy tickets on board, daily 6:00–23:00, every 20 min).

Arriving by train, get off at Verona's Porta Nuova station. The station is modern, but so cluttered with shops it can be hard to get oriented. As you come out of the underground passage from the tracks, an ATM machine is to your right, and pay toilets and phones to your left. In the lobby, with your back to the tracks, you'll find the baggage check to your far left (€3/12 hrs/bag), and, if you search hard, you'll see the TI (tel. 045-800-861, Mon–Sat 9:00–19:00, closed Sun), and train information desk tucked inside an office labeled "Centro Accoglienza e Informazioni." To the right of the TI is another ATM.

The 15-minute walk from the station (on busy streets) to Piazza Bra is boring; take the **bus.** Buses leave from directly in front of the station. You need to buy a ticket before boarding (€0.93, or €3.10 for an all-day ticket good until midnight, from *tabacchi* shop inside station or at white bus kiosk outside at Platform A). Bus information will likely be posted in English on the window of the bus kiosk. Or ask, "*Che numero per centro?*" (kay NOO-may-roh pehr CHEN-troh). You'll probably have a choice of orange bus #11, #12, or #13, leaving from Platform A. Validate your ticket on the bus by stamping it in the machine in the middle of the bus (good for 60 min). Buses stop on Piazza Bra, the square with the can't-miss-it Roman Arena. The TI is just a few steps beyond the bus stop. Buses return to the station from the bus stop just outside the city wall (on the right), where Corso Porta Nuova hits Piazza Bra.

Taxis pick up only at taxi stands (at Piazza Bra and train station) and cost about €5.50 for a ride between the train station and Piazza Bra.

Helpful Hints

Opera: In July and August, Verona's opera festival brings crowds and higher hotel prices (tickets €19.50–154, book tickets either online at www.arena.it or by calling tel. 045-800-5151).

Internet Access: Try Internet Train on Via Roma 17a, a couple of blocks off Piazza Bra toward Castelvecchio (Mon–Fri 11:00–22:00, Sat–Sun 14:00–20:00, tel. 045-801-3394), or Internetfast.it (Mon–Fri 10:00–22:00, Sat 10:00–20:00, Sun 15:00–19:00, Via Oberdan 16/B, just off Porta Borsari toward Piazza Bra, tel. 045-803-3212).

Post Office: The post office is on Via Cattaneo 23E (Mon–Sat 8:30–18:30, closed Sun, from Piazza Bra take Via Roma and turn right on Via Cattaneo).

Laundry: Mr. Lava Lava self-service laundry is near Ponte Nuovo (daily 9:00–23:00, last wash at 22:00, €3/wash load, €2 dry, soap vendor and change machine available, follow Via Carducci and turn right onto Via Interrato 36).

Bike Rental: El Pedalo Scaligero rents city, mountain, and tandem bikes in Piazza Bra near Via Roma (mid-April–mid-Sept only, from €3.50/hr and €12/day, ID required, mobile 333-536-7770, vespucci92@hotmail.com).

Walking Tours: Juliet & Co. offers 90-minute tours in English (€10/person, admission fees not included, April–Sept daily at 17:30, meet in front of equestrian statue on Piazza Bra, tel. 045-810-3173, www.julietandco.com).

Private Guides: For private guides, consider knowledgeable and enthusiastic Marina Menegoi (€95/hour, 2-hr min for 1–30 people, itinerary varies according to your preference, tel. 045-801-2174 and mobile 328-958-1108, milanit@libero.it) or the Verona guide association (tel. 045-869-8601).

SIGHTS

Arena—This elliptical 466-by-400-foot amphitheater is the third-largest in the Roman world. Dating from the first century A.D., it looks great in its pink marble. Over the centuries, crowds of up to 25,000 spectators have cheered Roman gladiator battles, medieval executions, and modern plays (including the popular opera festival that takes advantage of the famous acoustics every July and August). Climb to the top for a fine city view (€3.10, Tue–Sun 8:30–19:15, Mon 13:45–19:15, closes at 15:00 during opera season, hours can vary so check TI, last entry 45 min before closing, info boxes and WC near entry, located on Piazza Bra).

House of Juliet—This bogus house is a block off Piazza Erbe (detour right to Via Cappello 23). The tiny, admittedly romantic courtyard is a spectacle in itself, with Japanese posing from the balcony, Nebraskans polishing Juliet's bronze breast, and amorous graffiti everywhere. The info boxes (€0.50 for 2) offer a good history. ("While no documentation

Verona

- ❶ Bus to Station
- ❷ Bus from Station
- ❸ Hotel Aurora
- ❹ Hotel Europa
- ❺ Hotel Bologna
- ❻ Hotel Giulietta e Romeo
- ❼ Hotel Torcolo
- ❽ Locanda Catullo
- ❾ To Hostel
- ❿ Osteria al Duca
- ⓫ Osteria Giulietta e Romeo
- ⓬ Ristorante Greppia & Bottega del Vino
- ⓭ Ristorante Sant' Eufemio
- ⓮ Oreste Dal Zovo
- ⓯ Brek Cafeteria
- ⓰ Pizzeria Salvatore
- ⓱ VeronAntica Rest.

has been discovered to prove the truth of the legend, no documentation has disproved it either.") The "museum" exhibits art inspired by the love story and costumes and the bed from Franco Zeffirelli's *Romeo and Juliet*, certainly not worth the €3.10 entry fee (Tue–Sun 9:00–19:00, closed Mon, tel. 045-803-4303).

▲**Piazza Erbe**—This square is a photographer's delight, with pastel buildings corralling the fountains, pigeons, and people that have come together here since Roman times, when this was a forum.

In recent years, there has been an ongoing battle between market stall owners who have earned their living from the tourists, and the community, which wants the square left free to enjoy it as the open "living space" it was meant to be. The debate continues—stop by to see if the recently-banned stall owners have bought their way back onto the square. Whether a lovely, open square or a lively market square, it's a pleasure.

Notice the Venetian Lion hovering above the square, reminding locals since 1405 of their conquerors. During medieval times, the stone canopy in the center held the scales where merchants measured the weight of things they bought and sold, such as silk, wool, even wood. The fountain has bubbled here for 2,000 years. Its statue, originally Roman, had lost its head and arms. After a sculptor added a new head and arms—voilà—the statue became Verona's Madonna. She holds a small banner that reads: "I want justice and I bring peace."

▲▲**Evening** *Passeggiata*—For me, the highlight of Verona is the *passeggiata* (stroll)—especially in the evening—from the elegant cafés of Piazza Bra through the old town on Via Mazzini (one of Europe's many "first pedestrian-only streets") to the colorful Piazza Erbe.

Roman Theater (Teatro Romano)—Dating from the first century A.D., this ancient theater was discovered in the 19th century and restored. To reach the worthwhile museum, high up in the building above the theater, you can take the stairs or the elevator (to find the elevator, start at the stage and walk up the middle set of stairs, then continue straight on the path through the bushes).

The museum displays Roman artifacts (mosaic floors, busts, and clay and bronze votive figures), a model of the theater and a small Jesuit chapel. There are helpful English information sheets in virtually every room (€2.60, free first Sun of month, Tue–Sun 8:30–19:30, Mon 13:30–19:30, last entry 45 min before closing, across the river near Ponte Pietra, tel. 045-800-0360, WC to the right of the theater entrance after the ticket booth). Every summer, the theater stages Shakespeare plays—only a little more difficult to understand in Italian than in Old English.

Giardino Giusti—If you'd enjoy a Renaissance garden with manicured box hedges and towering cypress trees, you could find this worth the walk and fee (€5; daily 8:00–20:00, 8:00–19:00 off-season; cross river at Ponte Nuovo, continue 5 blocks up Via Carducci, then turn left to Via Giardino Giusti 2).

Introductory Old Town Walk

This walk will take you from Piazza Erbe to the major sights and end at Piazza Bra. Allow an hour (including tower climb and dawdling but not detours).

From the center of Piazza Erbe, head toward the river on Via della Costa. The street is marked by an arch with a whale's rib suspended from it. When you pass through the arch, don't worry. The whale's rib has hung there a thousand years. According to legend, it will fall when someone who's never lied walks under it.

The street soon opens up to a square, **Piazza dei Signori**, which has a white statue of Dante center-stage. The pensive Dante seems to wonder why the tourists choose Juliet over him. Dante—expelled from Florence for political reasons—was granted asylum in Verona by the Scaligeri family. With the whale's rib behind you, you're facing the brick, crenellated, 13th-century Scaligeri residence. Behind Dante is the yellowish 15th-century Venetian Renaissance-style Portico of the Counsel. In front of Dante—and to his right (follow the white "WC" signs) is the 12th-century Romanesque **Palazzo della Ragione**.

Enter the courtyard. The impressive staircase—which goes nowhere—is the only surviving Renaissance staircase in Verona. For a grand city view, you can climb to the top of the 13th-century **Torre dei Lamberti** (€1.50 for stairs, €2.10 elevator, Tue–Sun 8:00–19:30, Mon 13:30–19:30). The elevator saves you 245 steps—but you'll need to climb about 45 more to get to the first view platform. It's not worth continuing up the endless spiral stairs to the second view platform.

Exit the courtyard the way you entered and turn right, continuing down the whale-rib street. Within a block you'll find the strange and very **Gothic tombs** of the Scaligeri family, who were to Verona what the Medici family were to Florence. Notice the dogs' heads near the top of the tombs. On the first tomb, the dogs peer over a shield displaying a ladder. The story goes that the Scaligeri family got rich making ladders, but money can't buy culture. When Marco Polo returned from Asia boasting of the wealthy Kublai Khan, the Scaligeris wanted to be associated with this powerful Khan by name. But misunderstanding "Khan" as "Cane" (dog), one Scaligeri changed his name to Can Grande (big dog) and another to Can Signori (lead dog).

Continue straight for one long block and turn left on San Pietro Martire (you'll need to step into the street to check the road sign). After one block, you'll reach Verona's largest church, the brick **Church of Sant' Anastasia**. It was built from the late 13th century through the 15th century, but the builders ran out of steam, and the facade was never finished. You can enter the church for €2 (or pay €5 for a combo-ticket that includes other churches, including the Duomo, which we'll stop at later; ask for English brochure, Mon–Sat 9:00–18:00, Sun

13:00–18:00, off-season daily 10:00–13:00 & 15:30–16:00), or just peek in over the screen to get a sense of its size. The highlights of the interior are the grimacing hunchbacks holding basins of holy water on their backs (near entrance at base of columns) and Pisanello's frag-mented fresco of *St. George and the Princess* (above chapel to right of altar). The story of the church is available in English from the screen at the entry/exit.

Back to the walking tour. Face the church, then go right and walk along the length of it. Take a left on Via Sottoriva. In a block, you'll reach a small riverfront park that usually has a few modern-day Romeos and Juliets gazing at each other rather than the view. Get up on the side-walk right next to the river. You'll see the red-and-white bridge, **Ponte Pietra**. The white stones are from the original Roman bridge that stood here. After the bridge was bombed in World War II, the Veronese fished the marble chunks out of the river to rebuild it.

You'll also see, across the river and built into the hillside, the **Roman Theater** (description in "Sights," page 116). Way above the the-ater is the fortress, Castello San Pietro. We'll be heading toward the Roman bridge. This is your chance to break away, cross the bridge, and visit the Roman Theater; or climb the stairs to the left of the theater for a city view; or take the little road Scalone Castello S. Pietro and climb to the top of the hill to the Castello for an expansive view.

Me? I'm simply passing the bridge on the way to the next church. Leave the riverfront park and take the street to the right, Via Ponte Pietra, toward the bridge. One block before you reach the bridge (bridge entry clearly marked by an arch in a tower), turn left on Via Cappelletta. After two long blocks, turn right on Via Duomo (the corner is marked by a little church). Straight ahead you'll see the striped **Duomo**. One of Verona's historic churches, it costs €2 to enter (€5 combo-ticket; English descriptions given at the entrance, Mon–Sat 9:30–18:00, Sun 13:00–18:00, off-season daily 10:00–13:00 & 15:30–16:00). Started in the 12th century, it was built over a period of centuries, showing with its bright interior the tremendous leaps made in architecture. (OK, so the white paint helps.)

The highlights are Titian's *Assumption* and the ruins of an older church. To find the Titian, stand at the very back of the church, facing the altar; the painting is to your left. Mary calmly rides a cloud—direc-tion up—to the shock and bewilderment of the crowd below.

To find the ruins of the older church, walk up toward the altar to the last wooden door on the left. If the door's not open, ask someone for help. Inside are the 10th-century foundations of the Church of St. Elena, turned intriguingly into a modern-day chapel.

Leave the church, returning down Via Duomo. Continue straight ahead on Via Duomo until you reach the Church of Sant' Anastasia. With your back to this church, walk down Corso S. Anastasia.

In five minutes (at a brisk pace), you'll reach the ghostly white **Porta Borsari**, stretching across the road. This sturdy first-century Roman gate was one of the original entrances to this ancient town.

Continue straight (the name of the street changes to Corso Cavour). In a little park next to the castle is a first-century Roman triumphal arch, **Arco dei Gavi.** After being destroyed by French revolutionary troops in 1796, it was rebuilt at this location in the 1900s.

Castelvecchio, the medieval castle next to the arch, is now a sprawling art museum displaying Christian statuary, some weaponry, and fine 15th- to 17th-century paintings with good English descriptions throughout (€3.10, free first Sun of month unless there are special exhibits, Mon 13:30–19:30, Tue–Sun 8:30–19:30, last entrance 45 min before closing, audioguide-€3.62 or €5.16 for two, WC 3 rooms past the ticket booth). If you visit the castle, you'll pass outdoors between the museum's buildings; look for the skinny stairway leading up to the ancient wall overlooking the river. Climb up. It's a dead end but offers a great opportunity to shoot arrows at medieval invaders.

From the castle, you have several options. For a city view, you can walk out upon the grand bridge that leads from the castle over the river. Or head to Piazza Bra for a rest at a sidewalk café—Brek's is cheap (the castle's drawbridge points the way to Via Roma, taking you to Piazza Bra).

Or: A few blocks from the castle following the river away from town is the 12th-century **Basilica of San Zeno Maggiore.** This offers not only a great example of Italian Romanesque but also Mantegna's *San Zeno Triptych* (sit on the right-side pews for the best view of Mantegna's perspective) and a set of 48 paneled 11th-century bronze doors that are nicknamed "the poor man's Bible." Pretend you're an illiterate medieval peasant and do some reading. Facing the altar on the far right, you can see frescoes painted on top of other frescoes and graffiti from the 1300s (€2, €5 combo-ticket, March–Oct Mon–Sat 8:30–18:00, Sun 13:00–18:00, off-season daily 10:00–13:00 & 15:30–16:00)

SLEEPING

(€1 = about $1.10, country code: 39)

Prices soar in July and August (during opera season) and any time of year for a trade fair or holiday. Hotel Aurora and Hotel Torcolo are my favorites for their family-run feeling.

Near Piazza Erbe

$$ **Hotel Aurora,** just off Piazza Erbe, has friendly family management, a terrace overlooking the piazza, and 19 fresh and air-conditioned rooms (S-€70, Sb-€116, Db-€130, Tb-€158, includes good buffet breakfast, lower prices off-season, reserve with traveler's check or personal check

for deposit, elevator, church bells ring the hour early, Piazza Erbe, tel. 045-594-717, fax 045-801-0860, www.hotelaurora.biz, info@hotelaurora .biz, SE). Their two quads (each with 2 rooms, a double bed, 2 twins, and bathroom; €220/night) are better for families than couples because the bedrooms aren't private.

Near Piazza Bra

Several fine places are in the quiet streets just off Piazza Bra, within 200 yards of the bus stop and well-marked with yellow signs.

$$$ **Hotel Europa** offers sleek, modern comfort. Nearly half of its 46 rooms are smoke-free, a rarity in Italy (Db-€130 but €160 July–Aug, in off-season mention this book when you reserve and they can offer a reduced rate, includes breakfast, air-con, elevator, Via Roma 8, tel. 045-594-744, fax 045-800-1852, www.veronahoteleuropa.com, hoteleuropavr @tiscali.it, SE).

$$$ **Hotel Bologna,** within a half block of the Arena, has 30 bright, classy, and well-maintained rooms; attractive public areas; and an attached restaurant (Sb-€96–115, Db-€117–172, Tb-€148–218, includes breakfast, air-con, Piazzetta Scalette Rubiani 3, tel. 045-800-6830, fax 045-801-0602, www.hotelbologna.vr.it, hotelbologna@tin.it).

$$$ **Hotel Giulietta e Romeo**, just behind the Arena, is on a quiet side street. Its 30 decent rooms are decorated in dark colors, but on the plus side, they have non-smoking rooms (on first floor) and don't take tour groups (Sb-€75–110, Db-€115–175, includes breakfast, air-con, elevator, free Internet access in lobby, bike rental-€5/half-day, laundry-€7.50, garage-€17/day, Vicolo Tre Marchetti 3, tel. 045-800-3554, fax 045-801-0862, www.giuliettaeromeo.com, info@giuliettaeromeo.com).

$ **Hotel Torcolo** provides 19 comfortable, lovingly maintained rooms (many non-smoking) in a good location near Piazza Bra (Sb-€48–73, Db-€82–104, breakfast-€7–10.30, prices vary with season; air-con, fridge in room, elevator, garage-€8–11/day; Vicolo Listone 3, with your back to the gardens and the Arena over your right shoulder, head down the alley to the right of #16 on Piazza Bra; tel. 045-800-7512, fax 045-800-4058, www.hoteltorcolo.it, hoteltorcolo@virgilio.it, well-run by Silvia and Diana, SE).

Between Piazza Bra and Piazza Erbe

$ **Locanda Catullo** is an inexpensive, quiet, and quirky place deeper in the old town, with 21 good basic rooms up three flights of stairs (S-€42, D-€57, Db-€68, Qb-€129, no breakfast; left off Via Mazzini onto Via Catullo, down an alley between 1D and 3A at Via Valerio Catullo 1; tel. 045-800-2786, fax 045-596-987, locandacatullo@tiscali.it, SE a leettle).

Hostel

$ **Villa Francescatti** is a good hostel (€12.50 beds with breakfast, 8- to

10-bed rooms, some family rooms, €7.50 dinners, launderette, 23:30 cur-
few; bus #73 from station during the day or #90 at night and Sun, over
the river beyond Ponte Nuovo at Salita Fontana del Ferro 15; tel. 045-
590-360, fax 045-800-9127). During busy times, hostel members get
priority over nonmembers.

EATING

Near Piazza Erbe: **Osteria al Duca** has an affordable two-course menu
(€14) and lots more options. For dessert, try the chocolate salami.
Family-run with a lively atmosphere, it's popular—go early (Mon–Sat
12:00–14:15 & 18:45–22:30, closed Sun, Via Arche Scaligere 2, half
block from Scaligeri Tombs, tel. 045-594-474). Its sister restaurant,
Osteria Giulietta e Romeo, serves up the same menu a block away with
fewer crowds (Mon–Sat 12:15–14:30 & 19:00–22:30, closed Sun, Corso
Sant' Anastasia 27, tel. 045-800-9177).

More good choices include **Ristorante Greppia** (Tue–Sun
12:00–14:30 & 19:00–22:30, closed Mon, Vicolo Samaritana 3, tel. 045-
800-4577) and the pricier **Bottega del Vino** (Wed–Mon 12:00–15:00 &
19:00–24:00, closed Tue, Via Scudo di Francia 3, tel. 045-800-4535).
To find these, head from Piazza Erbe up Via Mazzini—they're within a
couple of blocks.

Ristorante Sant' Eufemio, just off Porta Borsari, specializes in fish
and puts out a great antipasto buffet with lots of vegetarian choices
(Mon–Sat 12:00–14:30 & 19:00–1:00, closed Sun, tel. 045-800-6865).
It's on Corte S. Gio in Foro, an alley directly across from Porta Borsari
27—go through the gate at the end of the alley.

For a fun, local wine/grappa bar (no formal food but an abundance
of fun and hearty bar snacks), try **Oreste Dal Zovo**, run by Oreste and
his wife Beverly from Chicago (March–Dec 8:00–20:00, no chairs, just
a couple of benches; it's on the alley—Vicolo San Marco in Foro 7—off
Porta Borsari, just a block from Piazza Erbe; tel. 045-803-4369).

On Piazza Bra: For fast food with a great view of Verona's main
square, consider the self-service **Brek** (daily 11:30–15:00 & 18:30–22:00,
indoor/outdoor seating, cheap salad plates, Piazza Bra 20, tel. 045-800-
4561). **Enoteca Cangrande** serves great wine (such as the local *passito
bianco*) and delicious seasonal specialties thoughtfully paired with wines
suggested by enologist owner Flavio and friendly, knowledgeable Marco
(Tue–Sun 11:00–14:00 & 17:00–1:00, closed Mon; Via dietro Liston
19/D, one block off Piazza Bra and Via Roma; tel. 045-595-022).

Near Ponte Nuovo: **Pizzeria Salvatore**, just across the Ponte Nuovo
bridge (and to the left), serves good pizza and calzone on funky, modern
art tables (Tue–Sat 12:00–14:30 & 19:00–23:00, Sun 19:00–23:00,
closed Mon, Piazza San Tomasso 6, tel. 045-803-0366).

VeronAntica is family-run, offering fine dining at reasonable prices.

Dinners start with sparkling wine, savory bruschetta, and warm rolls served up by gracious owner Davide. Specialties include homemade pastas and regional dishes prepared according to what's in season (Wed–Mon 12:00–15:00 & 19:15–22:45, closed Tue, Via Sottoriva 10/A, tel. 045-800-4124).

TRANSPORTATION CONNECTIONS

By train to: Florence (5/day, 3 hrs, more with transfer in Bologna; note that all Rome-bound trains stop in Florence—listed as Fireenza on train schedules), **Bologna** (nearly hrly, 2 hrs), **Milan** (hrly, 90 min), **Rome** (4/day, 4–6 hrs, more with transfer in Bologna), **Bolzano** (hrly, 90 min, note that Brennero-bound trains stop in Bolzano).

Parking in Verona: Drivers will find lots of free parking at the stadium, and cheap long-term parking near the train station and city walls and across the river from San Zeno and Castelvecchio. The most central lot is behind the Arena on Piazza Cittadella (guarded, €1/hr). Street parking costs €0.77 for two hours (buy ticket at *tabacchi* shop to put on dashboard, spaces marked with blue lines). The town center is closed to regular traffic.

Ravenna

Ravenna is on the tourist map for one reason: Its 1,500-year-old churches, decorated with best-in-the-West Byzantine mosaics. Known in Roman times as Classe, the city was an imperial port for the large naval fleet. Briefly a capital of eastern Rome during its fall, Ravenna was taken by the barbarians. Then, in A.D. 540, the Byzantine emperor Justinian turned Ravenna into the westernmost pillar of the Byzantine empire. A pinnacle of civilization in that age, Ravenna was a light in Europe's Dark Ages. Two hundred years later, the Lombards booted out the Byzantines, and Ravenna melted into the backwaters of medieval Italy, staying out of historical sight for a thousand years.

Today the local economy booms with a big chemical industry, the discovery of offshore gas deposits, and the construction of a new ship canal. The bustling town center is Italy's most bicycle-friendly (bike paths are in the middle of pedestrian streets, subtly indicated by white brick paving). Locals go about their business, while busloads of tourists slip quietly in and out of town for the best look at the glories of Byzantium this side of Istanbul.

Ravenna's only a 90-minute detour from the main Venice–Florence train line and worth the effort for those interested in old mosaics. While its sights don't merit an overnight stop, many find that the peaceful charm of this untouristy and classy town makes it a pleasant surprise in their Italian wandering.

ORIENTATION

Central Ravenna is quiet, with a pedestrian-friendly core and more bikes than cars. On a quick visit to Ravenna, I'd see the Basilica di San Vitale and its adjacent Mausoleum of Galla Placidia, the Basilica of Sant' Apollinare Nuovo, the covered market, and Piazza del Popolo.

Tourist Information: The TI is a 15-minute walk (or a 5-minute pedal) from the train station (Mon–Sat 8:30–19:00, Sun 10:00–16:00, Via Salara 8, tel. 0544-35404, www.turismo.ravenna.it, iatravenna @comune.ra.it). For directions to the TI, see the section "Orientation Walk," below.

Combo-Tickets: Many top sights can only be seen by purchasing a combo-ticket (called *biglietto cumulativo* or Visit Card, €8.50, sold at the sights). It includes admission to the Basilica of San Vitale, Mausoleum of Galla Placidia, Sant' Apollinare Nuovo, Spirito Santo, Battistero Neoniano, and Cappella Arcivescoville. There are no individual admissions to these sights.

A different combo-ticket (€5) covers admissions to the National Museum and Mausoleum of Teodorico. You can pay an extra €1.50 to include the Sant' Apollinare in Classe. Unlike the other combo-ticket mentioned above, you can buy individual admissions to the sights: National Museum-€4 (Tue–Sun 8:30–19:30, off-season until 19:00, closed Mon); Mausoleum of Teodorico-€2 (daily 8:30–18:00); and Sant' Apollinare in Classe-€2 (Mon–Sat 8:30–19:30; Sun 13:00–19:00, closes off-season at 17:00). Most sights close early in the off-season winter months; pick up a schedule from the TI when you arrive.

Helpful Hints

Local Guide: For a private guide, consider Claudia Frassineti (€85/half-day, mobile 335-613-2996, www.abacoguide.it).

Bike Rental: Yellow community bikes are available free from the TI (passport required); the bikes are parked at the TI and other locations around town. Or rent bikes from the Coop San Vitale on Piazza Farini (on the left just as you exit train station, Mon–Sat 6:15–20:00, closed Sun, €1.03/hour, €7.75/day, ID required, tel. 0544-37031).

Parking: You can park for free in the lot on north end of town just west of Via di Roma, or for €3 during the day and free from 20:00–8:00 at Largo Giustiniano just north of San Vitale.

SIGHTS

Orientation Walk—A visit to Ravenna can be as short as a three-hour

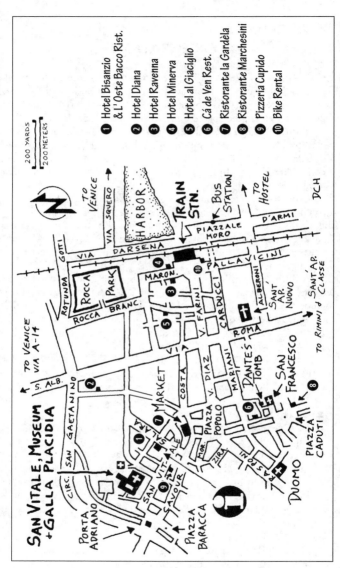

Ravenna

1 Hotel Bisanzio & L'Oste Bacco Rist.
2 Hotel Diana
3 Hotel Ravenna
4 Hotel Minerva
5 Hotel al Giaciglio
6 Cá de Ven Rest.
7 Ristorante la Gardèla
8 Ristorante Marchesini
9 Pizzeria Cupido
10 Bike Rental

loop from the train station. From the station, walk straight down Viale Farini to Piazza del Popolo. This square was built around 1500, during a 60-year period when the city was ruled by Venice. Under the Venetian architecture, the people of Ravenna gather here as they have for centuries.

Most sights are within a few minutes' walk of Piazza del Populo. A right on Via IV Novembre takes you a block to the colorful covered market (Mercato Coperto, Mon–Sat 7:00–14:00, closed Sun, good for picnic fixings). The TI is a block away (head up Via Cavour and take the first right onto Via Salara 8). Ravenna's two most important sights, Basilica di San Vitale and the Mausoleum of Galla Placidia, are two blocks from Piazza del Popolo (head down San Vitale). On the other side of Piazza del Popolo is the Basilica of Sant' Apollinare Nuovo, also worth a look. From there, it's about a 10-minute walk back to the station.

▲▲Basilica di San Vitale—Imagine...it's A.D. 540. The city of Rome had been looted, the land was crawling with barbarians, and the infrastructure of Rome's thousand-year empire was crumbling fast. Into this chaotic world came the emperor of the East, Justinian, bringing order and stability, briefly reassembling the empire, and making Ravenna a beacon of civilization. His church of San Vitale—standing as a sanctuary of order in the midst of that chaos—is covered with lavish mosaics: gold and glass chips the size of your fingernail. It's impressive enough to see a 1,400-year-old church. But to see one decorated in brilliant mosaics, still managing to convey the intended feeling that "this peace and stability was brought to you by your emperor and God," is rare indeed.

In a medieval frame of mind, study the scene: High above the altar, God is in heaven, portrayed as Christ sitting on a celestial orb. He oversees his glorious creation, symbolized by the four rivers. And running the show on earth is Justinian (left side), sporting both a halo and a crown to show he's leader of the church and the state. Here, Justinian brings together the military leaders and the church leaders, all united by the straight line of eyes. The bald bishop of Ravenna—the only person who was actually here—is portrayed most realistically.

Facing the emperor (from the right side) is his wife, Theodora, and her entourage. Decked out in jewels and pearls, the former dancer who became Justinian's mistress and then empress carries a chalice to consecrate the new church.

The walls and ceilings sparkle with colorful Bible scenes told with a sixth-century exuberance. This was a time of transition, and many consider the mosaics of Ravenna both the last ancient Roman and the first medieval European works of art. For instance, you'll see a beardless Christ (as he was depicted by ancient Romans) next to a bearded Christ, his standard medieval portrayal.

The church's octagonal design—clearly Eastern—inspired the construction of the Hagia Sofia, built 10 years later in Constantinople. Charlemagne traveled here in about A.D. 800. He was so impressed that when he returned to his capital, Aix le Chapelle (present-day Aachen in Germany), he built what many consider the first great stone building in northern Europe—modeled after this church (€8.50 for combo-ticket, see above, daily 9:00–19:00, off-season until 16:30, tel. 0544-219-938).

▲▲**Mausoleum of Galla Placidia**—Just across the courtyard (and included in San Vitale admission) is this tiny, humble-looking mausoleum, with the oldest—and to many, the best—mosaics in Ravenna. The Mausoleum of Galla Placidia (plah-CHEE-dee-ah) is reputed to be the burial place of this daughter, sister, and mother of emperors, who died in A.D. 450. The little light that sneaks through the thin alabaster panels brings a glow and a twinkle to the early Christian symbolism that fills the little room. Opposite the door is St. Lawrence martyred on a fiery grill. He's legendary for mocking his executors, reportedly saying something like "I'm done on this side, you can turn me over now." He was famous as an example of the strength of the feisty early Christians. The four gospels clearly labeled on the bookshelf were the source of this strength as they were persecuted by the Romans. The dome is filled with stars. Along with Mark's lion, Luke's ox, and John's eagle, the golden cross rises from the east bringing life to all. Doves drink from fountains, symbolic of souls finding nourishment in the word of God. Cover the light of the door with your hand to see the standard Roman portrayal of Christ—beardless and as the Good Shepherd. Jesus, dressed in gold and purple like a Roman emperor, is king of paradise—receiving faithful (represented by lambs). The Eastern influence is apparent in the carpet-like decorative patterns (€8.50 for combo-ticket, daily 9:00–19:00, off-season until 16:30, reservations necessary March–June 15, call 0544-219-938 to book ahead).

▲▲**Basilica of Sant' Apollinare Nuovo**—This austere sixth-century church, with a typical early-Christian basilica floor plan, has two huge and wonderfully preserved side panels. One is a procession of haloed virgins, each bringing gifts to the Madonna and the Christ Child. Opposite, Christ is on his throne with four angels, awaiting a solemn procession of 26 martyrs. Ignoring the Baroque altar from a thousand years later, we can clearly see the rectangular Roman hall of justice or basilica plan—which was adopted by churches and used throughout the Middle Ages (€8.50 for combo-ticket, daily 9:00–19:00, off-season until 16:30, on Via di Roma, tel. 0544-219-938). The Self-service S. Apollinare Nuovo is a cheap, air-conditioned and efficient place for lunch right on the church grounds (daily 11:30–14:30, tel. 0544-35679).

▲**Church of Sant' Apollinare in Classe**—Featuring great Byzantine art, this church is a favorite among mosaic pilgrims (€2, or €6.50 combo-ticket with National Museum and Mausoleum of Teodorico, Mon–Sat 8:30–19:30, Sun 13:00–19:00, closes off-season at 17:00, last entry 30 min before closing, closed May 1, tel. 0544-473-661). It's two miles out of town. Catch bus #4 across the street from the train station (on the corner by the park) or #44 from Piazza Caduti (with your back to the tobacco shop, stop is on the corner; 3/hr, 15 min, reduced service Sun, €0.75, buy bus tickets from any tobacco shop). As you leave Sant' Apollinare, the return bus stop is 100 yards up the road to the right.

Other Sights—The **Basilica San Francesco** is worth a look for its simple interior and flooded, mosaic-covered crypt below the main altar (daily 7:30–12:15 & 14:30–19:00). Nearby in Via Dante Alighieri, the **Tomb of Dante** is the true site of his remains. After being exiled from Florence for his political beliefs, Dante lived out the rest of his life in Ravenna. The Florentines forgave Dante posthumously and wanted to bring their famous poet's bones home to rest. To protect his relics from theft by the Florentines, Ravenna hid his bones in the neighboring Basilica of San Francesco in 1519. They lay forgotten in the church for three centuries until they were rediscovered and replaced in his tomb in 1865. The Dante memorial—often mistaken for a tomb—in Florence's Santa Croce Church is empty (daily 9:00–19:00, off-season daily 9:00–12:00 & 15:00–17:00).

Overrated Sight—The nearby beach town of Rimini is a crowded mess.

SLEEPING

(€1 = about $1.10, country code: 39)

$$$ **Hotel Bisanzio** is a business-class splurge in the city center (Sb-€98, Db-€124, larger Db-€154; from Piazza del Popolo take Via IV Novembre to the Mercato, turn left onto Via Cavour and take the first right, Via Salara 30; tel. 0544-217-111, fax 0544-32539, www.bisanziohotel.com, info@bizanziohotel.com).

$ **Hotel Diana,** with 33 bright and tasteful rooms, is a classy, peaceful haven. Though a bit outside the town center, it's still an easy walk from San Vitale (Sb-€57, Db-€83, superior and deluxe rooms available, free Internet in lobby, free parking nearby, Via G. Rossi 47, tel. 0544-39164, fax 0544-30001, www.hoteldiana.ra.it, info@hoteldiana.ra.it).

$ **Hotel Ravenna,** with spanking clean rooms and double-paned windows, is across from the train station (S-€40, Sb-€45, D-€55, Db-€68, Viale Maroncelli 12, tel. 0544-212-204, fax 0544-212-077, hotelravenna@ravennablu.it, SE).

$ **Hotel Minerva,** just to the right of the train station as you exit, has 18 newly renovated rooms (Sb-€55, Db-€90, no breakfast, elevator, aircon, nearby laundry service and Internet access, Viale Maroncelli 1, tel. & fax 0544-213-711, www.minerva-hotel.com, hotel.minerva@libero.it).

$ **Hotel al Giaciglio,** also near the station, is a last resort (S-€33, D-€42, Db-€51, Via R. Brancaleone 42, tel. & fax 0544-39403, mmambo @racine.ra.it, SE).

$ *Hostel:* **Ostello Dante,** a 15-minute walk from the station, has Internet access with phone card, laundry service, free community bikes, and bike rentals (140 beds, €13/bed in 4–6 bed rooms, family rooms €14/person, €2.50/night extra for nonmembers, includes breakfast, 10:00–17:00 lockout, 23:00 curfew, Via Nicolodi 12, can reserve by fax or e-mail, tel. & fax 0544-421-164, www.geocities.com/hostel_ravenna, hostelravenna@hotmail.com, SE). From the station, follow signs for Ostello Dante or catch bus #1 or #70 from the station.

EATING

The atmospheric **Ristorante-Enoteca Cá de Ven**—or House of Wine—fills a 16th-century warehouse with locals enjoying quality wine and traditional cuisine. *Piadina* (peeah-DEE-nah) dominates the menu. An unleavened bread that kids are raised on here, it's served with cheese and prosciutto. Try their dessert specialty—*torta di marzipan*—made exclusively for them by a local bakery. This decadent almond and cocoa brownie is best eaten with sweet red wine (Tue–Sat 11:00–14:00 & 17:30–22:15, Sun 17:30–22:15, closed Mon; Via C. Ricci 24, 2-min walk from Piazza del Popolo on Via Cairoli which turns into Via C. Ricci; tel. 0544-30163).

Locals like **Ristorante la Gardèla,** which offers reasonables prices and cuisine specialities from Italy's mountainous Emilia Romagna region, such as *cappelletti in brodo*, a light, meat-stuffed pasta served in broth (Fri–Wed 12:00–14:30 & 19:00–22:00, closed Thu, from Piazza del Popolo follow Via IV Novembre past Piazza della Costa to corner of Via Ponte Marino 3, tel. 0544-217-147). **L'Oste Bacco** is run by the same owners with the same menu (homemade pastas from €5.50–7.50, Wed–Mon 12:15–14:30 & 19:15–22:30, closed Tue, just north of TI at Via Salara 20, tel. 0544-35363).

Ristorante Marchesini has a classy, self-serve menu that includes some delicious salads and homemade pastas (Mon–Sat 12:00–14:30, Sat 19:30–22:30, closed Sun; Via Mazzini 6, 5-min walk from Piazza del Popolo, on corner of Piazza Caduti, ride elevator to first floor; tel. 0544-212-309).

Free Flow Bizantino, inside the covered market, is another self-serve (Mon–Fri open for lunch only, 11:45–14:30). Or assemble a picnic at the market and enjoy your feast in the shady gardens of the **Rocca Brancaleone** fortress (5-min walk from station, following Via Maroncelli until you see the walls, closes at 20:00 off-season).

For a cheap and traditional lunch or snack, try a *piadina* or *cresciolo* (calzone-like) sandwich from **Pizzeria Cupido** just up Via Cavour, past the covered market. These tasty sandwiches come stuffed with a variety of meats, cheeses, and vegetables for €3–4.50. Try one filled with *squacquerone*, a soft regional cream cheese (Tue–Sun 8:00–20:00, closed Mon; Via Cavour 43, through the archway; tel. 0544-37529).

TRANSPORTATION CONNECTIONS

By train to: Venice (3 hrs with transfer in Ferrara: Ravenna to Ferrara, every 2 hrs, 1 hr; Ferrara to Venice, hrly, 90 min), **Florence** (4 hrs with transfer in Bologna: Ravenna to Bologna, 8/day, 90 min; Bologna to Florence, hrly, 90 min).

THE DOLOMITES

(Dolomiti)

Italy's dramatic limestone rooftop, the Dolomites, offers some of the best mountain thrills in Europe. Bolzano is the gateway to the Dolomites, and Castelrotto is a good home base for your exploration of Alpe di Siusi, Europe's largest alpine meadow.

The sunny Dolomites are well-developed, and the region's famous valleys and towns suffer from après-ski fever. The cost for the comfort of reliably good weather is a drained-reservoir feeling. Lovers of the Alps may miss the lushness that comes with the unpredictable weather farther north. But the bold limestone pillars, flecked with snow over green meadows under a blue sky, offer a worthwhile mountain experience.

A hard-fought history has left the region bicultural, with an emphasis on the German. Locals speak German first, and some wish they were still part of Austria. In the Middle Ages, as part of the Holy Roman Empire, the region faced north. Later, it was firmly in the Austrian Hapsburg realm. By losing World War I, Austria's South Tirol became Italy's Alto Adige. Mussolini did what he could to Italianize the region, including giving each town an Italian name. But even in the last decade, local secessionist groups have agitated violently for more autonomy.

The government has wooed locals with economic breaks that make it one of Italy's richest areas (as local prices attest), and today all signs and literature in the province of Alto Adige/Süd Tirol are in both languages. Many include a third language, Ladin, the ancient Latin-type language still spoken in a few traditional areas. (I have listed both the Italian and German, so the confusion caused by this guidebook will match that caused by your travels.)

In spite of all the glamorous ski resorts and busy construction cranes, the local color survives in a warm, blue-aproned, ruddy-faced, long-white-bearded way. There's yogurt and yodeling for breakfast. Culturally as much as geographically, the area is reminiscent of Austria. The Austrian Tirol is named for a village that is now part of Italy.

The Dolomites

Planning Your Time

Train travelers should side-trip in from Bolzano (90 min north of
Verona). To get a feel for the alpine culture, spend a night in
Castelrotto. With two nights in Castelrotto, you can actually get out
and hike. Tenderfeet ride the bus, catch a chairlift, and stroll. For mountain thrills, do a six-hour hike. And for a thrill that won't soon fade
away, spend a night in a mountain hut. This means two nights in
Castelrotto straddling a night in a hut.

Car hikers with a day can drive the three-hour loop from Bolzano
or Castelrotto (Val Gardena–Sella Pass–Val di Fassa) and ride one of

the lifts to the top for a ridge walk. Connecting Bolzano and Venice by the Great Dolomite Road takes two hours longer than the autostrada but is far more scenic (see below).

Hiking season is mid-June through mid-October. The region is packed, booming, and blooming from mid-July through mid-September. Spring is dead, with no lifts running, huts closed, and the most exciting trails still under snow. Many hotels and restaurants close in April and November. Ski season (Dec–Easter) is busiest of all.

Helpful Hints

Study Ahead: The South Tirol's Web site is www.suedtirol.com.

Sleeping: Most towns offer hotels, which charge about €34–36 per person, and private homes, which offer beds for as low as €16 but are often a long walk from the town centers. Beds nearly always come with a hearty breakfast. Those traveling in peak season or staying for only one night pay more. Local TIs can always find budget travelers a bed in a private home *(Zimmer)*. Drivers on a tight budget should pick remote *Zimmers*. Most mountain huts offer reasonable doubles, cheap dorm (lager) beds, and inexpensive meals. Call any hut to secure a spot before hiking there (most huts open mid-June–Sept only).

Eating: In local restaurants, there is no cover charge. A Jausenstation is a place that serves cheap, hearty, and traditional mountain-style food to hikers.

Bolzano (Bozen)

Willkommen to the Italian Tirol! If it weren't so sunny, you could be in Innsbruck. This enjoyable old town of 100,000 is the most convenient gateway to the Dolomites, especially if you're relying on public transportation. It's just the place to take a Tirolean stroll. Everything mentioned in Bolzano is a 10-minute walk from Piazza Walther.

The medieval heart of town is a couple of blocks northwest of Piazza Walther. Follow your favorite Italian and head down the arcaded Via dei Portici to Piazza Erbe, with its ancient and still-thriving open-air produce market (wash your produce in the handy drinking fountain in the middle of the market).

Tourist Information: To get to the TI and downtown from the train station, veer left up the tree-lined Viale Stazione (Bahnhofsallee), walk past the bus station (on your left) two blocks to Piazza Walther, where you'll see the helpful TI on your right (Mon–Thu 9:00–12:30 & 15:00–17:30, Fri 9:00–14:00, closed Sat–Sun, tel. 0471-307-000, www.bolzano-bozen.it). Pick up the city map (includes a walking tour).

The excellent Dolomites Information Center is one block west of Piazza Walther down Via Posta across from the post office (Mon–Fri 9:00–12:00 & 14:00–17:00, Parrocchia 11, tel. 0471-999-955).

Internet Access: Try Café Meraner on Via Bottai/Bindergasse (Mon–Sat 7:00–19:15, closed Sun, 2 computers) or AthesiaBuch bookstore at Lauben/Portici 41 (free but €5 deposit required, 2 computers, 30 min max, terminals 2 floors down from street level, Mon–Fri 9:00–12:20 & 14:30–19:00, closed Sat eve and Sun, second entrance on Silbergasse/Via Argentieri, tel. 0471-927-111).

SIGHTS

▲▲**South Tirol Museum of Archaeology (Museo Archeologico dell'Alto Adige)**—This excellent museum features the original Ice Man. "Oetzi the Ice Man" was discovered high in the mountains near Bolzano by some German hikers in 1991. Initially thinking it was the corpse of a lost hiker, officials chopped him out of the glacier (damaging his left side). But upon discovering his older-than Bronze Age hatchet, they realized what they had found—a 5,500-year-old, nearly perfectly preserved man with clothing and gear in excellent condition for his age. With Oetzi as the centerpiece, the museum takes you on an intriguing journey through time, recounting the evolution of man from the Paleolithic era to the Roman and finally the Middle Ages in vivid detail with informative displays and models, video demonstrations of the extraction of Oetzi and his personal effects, a great audioguide, and interactive computers. You'll see a convincing reconstruction of Oetzi, and yes, you actually get to see the man himself lying peacefully inside a specially built freezer (€8, audioguide-€2, Tue–Sun 10:00–18:00, Thu until 20:00, last entry 60 min before closing, closed Mon, mandatory and free bag check if you have a camera, WCs on ground floor near elevator and on 4th floor, near the river at Via Museo 43, tel. 0471-320-100, www.iceman.it).

Domenican Church (Chiesa dei Domenicani)—If you're an art-lover who won't make it to Padua to see Giotto's Scrovegni Chapel, drop by this 13th-century church to see its Chapel of St. John/San Giovanni (chapel near altar to the right), frescoed by the Giotto School. It lacks the high quality and that divine "Smurf" blue of the Scrovegni Chapel, but it gives you a sense of Giotto's vision (free, Mon–Sat 9:30–17:30, closed Sun, also see peaceful cloisters to right of Piazza Domenicani, church entrance at #19).

Cable Car to Oberbozen—Of the three different cable cars that can whisk you out of Bolzano, the most popular is the Ritten lift to the touristy town of Oberbozen. From Bolzano train station, walk about five blocks down Via Renon to reach the Rittner Sielbahn cable car (3/hr in summer, hrly off-season, tel. 0471-999-955 for cable car info

Bolzano

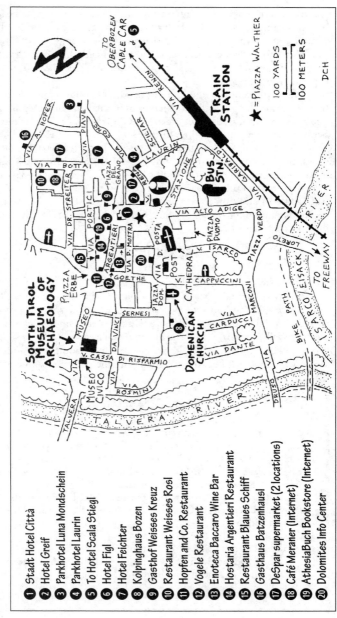

★ = PIAZZA WALTHER

TO OBERBOZEN CABLE CAR

TRAIN STATION

BUS STN.

100 YARDS
100 METERS

DCH

SOUTH TIROL MUSEUM OF ARCHAEOLOGY

MUSEO CIVICO

DOMENICAN CHURCH

CATHEDRAL

TALVERA RIVER

ISARCO / EISACK RIVER

BIKE PATH

TO FREEWAY

1 Stadt Hotel Città
2 Hotel Greif
3 Parkhotel Luna Mondschein
4 Parkhotel Laurin
5 To Hotel Scala Stiegl
6 Hotel Figl
7 Hotel Feichter
8 Kolpinghaus Bozen
9 Gasthof Weisses Kreuz
10 Restaurant Weisses Rosl
11 Hopfen and Co. Restaurant
12 Vogele Restaurant
13 Enoteca Baccaro Wine Bar
14 Hostaria Argentieri Restaurant
15 Restaurant Blaues Schiff
16 Gasthaus Batzenhausl
17 DeSpar supermarket (2 locations)
18 Café Meraner (Internet)
19 AthesiaBuch Bookstore (Internet)
20 Dolomites Info Center

and trail conditions). More interesting than Oberbozen are the nearby "earth pyramids," a 20-minute walk from the cable car station. The pyramids are Bryce-like pinnacles rising out of the ridge. A little train runs along the ridge, connecting Oberbozen nearly hourly with other villages. Both the cable car and train cost €2.50 apiece (€3.50 round-trip) and run year-round.

Many are tempted to wimp out on the Dolomites and see them from a distance by hiking from Oberbozen to the Pemmern chairlift (€7 one-way including Rittner funicular, €8.60 round-trip), riding to Schwarzseespitze, and walking 45 more minutes to the Rittner Horn. You'll be atop a 7,000-foot peak with distant but often hazy Dolomite views. It's not worth the trouble. (But if you're determined to do it and it's outside of summer, call the nearby Collalbo TI at tel. 0471-356-100 to make sure the trails are clear of snow.)

Markets—In addition to the produce market on Piazza Erbe (daily except Sat afternoon and all day Sun), a market is held Saturday morning on Piazza della Pace.

SLEEPING

All of the listed hotels are in the city center.

$$$ **Stadt Hotel Città** is ideally situated on Piazza Walther. The hotel's café spills out onto the piazza, offering a prime spot for people-watching. While the hotel is expensive for singles, it's a fine value for doubles, especially if you plan to spend an afternoon in their Wellness Center (open 16:00–22:00)—Turkish bath, massage by appointment, Finnish sauna, whirlpool—all free to hotel guests and the perfect way to unwind

SLEEP CODE

(€1 = about $1.10, country code: 39)
Sleep Code: **S** = Single, **D** = Double/Twin, **T** = Triple, **Q** = Quad, **b** = bathroom, **s** = shower only, **no CC** = Credit Cards not accepted, **SE** = Speaks English, **NSE** = No English. You can assume credit cards are accepted unless otherwise noted.

To help you sort easily through these listings, I've divided the rooms into three categories based on the price for a standard double room with bath:

$$$ **Higher Priced**—Most rooms €100 or more.
$$ **Moderately Priced**—Most rooms between €60-100.
$ **Lower Priced**—Most rooms €60 or less.

after a day of hiking or skiing in the Dolomites (Sb-€85–96, Db-€113–155, Tb-€138–185, superior rooms and family apartments available, includes breakfast, air-con, elevator, Piazza Walther 1, tel. 0471-975-221, fax 0471-976-688, www.hotelcitta.info, info@hotelcitta.info).

$$$ **Hotel Greif** is also right on Piazza Walther. When you walk into any of their 33 rooms, designed by artists, you feel like you're in a modern art installation. It's not cozy, but it is striking (5 types of rooms: comfort/superior/deluxe/junior suite/suite—priciest, Sb-€126–180, Db-€158–225, suites €260–300, includes buffet breakfast, most rooms non-smoking, air-con, computers, expensive laundry, parking-€16/day, Piazza Walther, entrance on Via della Rena, tel. 0471-318-000, fax 0471-318-148, www.greif.it, info@greif.it, SE).

$$$ **Parkhotel Luna Mondschen** is an elegant, well-maintained hotel in a park setting offering 76 posh rooms a five-minute walk from Piazza Walter (Sb-€83, Db-€127, buffet breakfast-€10, parking-€12, Internet access, tel. 0471-975-642, fax 0471-975-577, www.hotel-luna.it, info@hotel-luna.it).

$$$ **Parkhotel Laurin** is probably *the* most affordable, Old World luxury hotel. With 100 tastefully decorated rooms, the historic hotel sports marble bathrooms, a classy dining room and terrace, frescoes throughout the grand lobby depicting the legend of King Laurin, a swimming pool, extensive garden, and attentive staff (Db-€158, suites available but with rooms like this who needs one, breakfast-€15, parking-€13, Via Laurin 4, tel. 0471-311-000, fax 0471-311-148, www.laurin.it, info@laurin.it).

$$$ **Scala Stiegl** has a traditional feel with modern touches. It's convenient to the station, Rittner lift, and Piazza Walter and has a garden with a swimming pool (May–Sept only), and four free bikes to loan (Sb-€65-80, Db-€105–130, garden views cost more, includes breakfast, Internet available, parking-€8, Via Brennero 11, tel. 0471-976-222, fax 0471-981-141, www.scalahot.com, info@scalahot.com).

$$$ **Hotel Figl**, warmly run by Anton and Helga Mayr, has 23 comfortable rooms and an attached café on a pedestrian square a block from Piazza Walther (Sb-€78, Db-€105, junior suite-€105–115, extra bed €10–30, apartment available, breakfast extra, air-con, elevator, Kornplatz 9, tel. 0471-978-412, fax 0471-978-413, www.figl.net, info@figl.net, SE).

$$ **Hotel Feichter** is a bright, cheery lodging with a characteristic Alpine feel and 30 rooms overlooking the rooftops of Bolzano (Sb-€54, Db-€83, Tb-€98, includes breakfast, from Rathaus Platz head toward Piazza Walther on Weintraubengasse/Via Grappoli to #15, tel. 0471-978-768, fax 0471-974-803, www.paginegialle.it/feichter, hotel.feichter@dnet.it, SE).

$$ **Kolpinghaus Bozen,** modern, clean, and church-run, has 40 rooms with twin beds and all the comforts. It makes one feel thankful

(Sb-€52, Db-€76, Tb-€114, includes breakfast, confusing elevator, Internet access with phone card, 4 blocks from Piazza Walther, near Piazza Domenicani at Spitalgasse 3, tel. 0471-308-400, fax 0471-973-917, www.kolping.it/bz, kolping@tin.it, SE). The lineup in front of the building at lunchtime consists mainly of workers waiting for the institutional cafeteria to open up (€9.50 meals, open to public, Mon–Fri 11:45–14:00 & 18:30–19:30).

$ **Gasthof Weisses Kreuz**, with 15 basic rooms, is a great value, but it's usually booked up (S-€29, D-€48, Db-€58, Tb-€75, includes breakfast, 1 block off Piazza Walther in old town at Kornplatz 3, tel. 0471-977-552, fax 0471-972-273, weisseskreuzbz@yahoo.it, NSE).

EATING

All listings are in the downtown core. Many places offer a smaller, light menu outside of regular serving hours. Most are closed on Sunday; a few Sunday options are listed below.

Weisses Rosl offers affordable Italian, German, and veggie options in a pub-like setting (8:00–24:00, closed Sat eve and all Sun, Bindergasse/Via Bottai 6, 2 blocks north of Piazza Municipio, tel. 0471-973-267).

The next three places cluster at the southern edge of Piazza Erbe. **Hopfen and Co.** offers delicious meals (Mon–Sat 9:30–24:00, closed Sun, Obstmarkt/Piazza Erbe 17, tel. 0471-300-788). **Vogele**, a half block south, serves German/Italian cuisine and has a rare non-smoking floor upstairs, bigger than it initially looks (Mon–Sat 9:00–24:00, closed Sun, Via Goethe Strasse 3, tel. 0471-973-938). **Enoteca Baccaro**, a wine bar a half block east, is an intriguing spot for a glass of wine and bar snacks amid locals (in winter Mon–Sat 9:00–21:00, in summer Mon-Fri 9:00-21:00, Sat 9:00-15:00, closed Sun, located on alley off Silbergasse/Via Argentieri 17, tel. 0471-971-421).

Hostaria Argentieri, pricier than the rest, serves Italian and German cuisine plus seafood in a classy setting a block away from Kornplatz/Piazza del Grano (Mon–Sat 12:00–14:30 & 19:00–22:30, closed Sun, Via Argentieri 14, tel. 0471-981-718).

On Sundays, when nearly all restaurants are closed, try the cheap **Restaurant Blaues Schiff** (daily 11:30–15:00 & 18:00–23:00, Lauben 57, tel. 0471-979-099) or **Gasthaus Batzenhausl** (daily 12:00–14:00 & 19:00–24:00, Via Andreas Hofer Strasse 30, tel. 0471-050-956).

Picnic: Assemble the ingredients at the **Piazza Erbe** market; dine in a superb setting in Piazza Walther or in the park along the Talvera River. A **DeSpar supermarket** is on Via della Rena near Piazza Walther (Mon–Fri 8:30–19:30, Sat 8:00–18:00, closed Sun; from Piazza Walther, facing TI, take street to the left for 2 blocks, supermarket's at bottom of stairs on your left) and another Despar is up Bindergasse/Via Bottai about a block from the Rathuas Platz/Piazza Municipale

(Mon–Fri 8:00–19:15, Sat 8:00–13:00, closed Sun).

TRANSPORTATION CONNECTIONS

By train to: Milan (hrly with a change in Verona, 3.5 hrs), **Verona** (hrly, 90 min), **Trento** (hrly, 40 min), **Venice** and **Florence** (via Verona, 3–4 hrs), **Innsbruck** (about hrly, 2.5 hrs).

   By bus to: Castelrotto (2/hr, 50 min, leaves Bolzano at :10 and :40 virtually every hour from Bolzano's bus station 1 block west of train station; buy one-way ticket for €3.25—round-trip not available—from station ticket window or driver, reduced price of €3 for return trip—show original ticket to get discount); get off in the village of **Siusi** and take Seiser Alm Bahn the funicular if you are heading directly to Alpe di Siusi (€10 round-trip to Compatsch, daily 8:00–19:00, 12 min).

Castelrotto (Kastelruth)

Castelrotto (population 6,000, altitude 3,475 feet), the ideal home base for exploring the Alpe di Siusi, has more village character than any other town I know of in the region. Friday morning is the farmers' market (June–Oct), and a crafts market fills the town square most Thursday mornings. It's touristy but not a full-blown resort—it's full of real people. Pop into the church to hear the choir practice or be on the town square weekdays at 14:45 when the moms gather their kindergartners, chat, and then head home or stop by the playground on Plattenstrasse. On Fridays, the bells peal at 15:00, commemorating Christ's sacrifice. On Sundays, townspeople and farmers attend church and linger to visit. Against a backdrop of mountains, Castelrotto conveys the powerful message that simple pleasures are enough. The folk-singing group Kastelruther Spatzen has an avid following in town, produces "more CDs than Michael Jackson" (a local told me proudly), and holds a concert here every October.

   Castelrotto's medieval tournament of games on horseback—usually held in late spring—features teams of riders dressed in old-time costumes competing in contests.

   The **TI** is on the main square (Mon–Sat 8:30–12:30 & 13:30–18:00, Sun 9:00–12:00, tel. 0471-706-333, www.kastelruth.com). The bus parking lot has a little building with an ATM, WC, and phones; take the stairs to the right of this building to get to the main square. Another cash machine is to the left of the TI.

   For a scenic viewpoint, take a short walk uphill from the TI (facing TI, take road under arch to the right, then follow signs to Kalvarienberg/Calvario). Footpaths take you past several little chapels,

Castelrotto

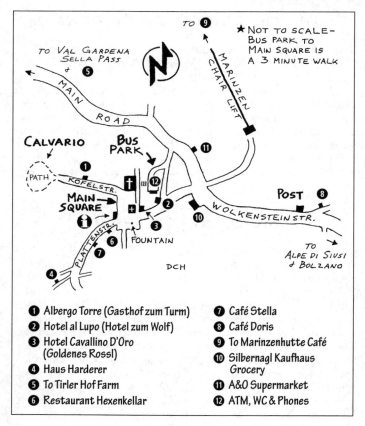

TO ⑨

★ NOT TO SCALE-
BUS PARK TO
MAIN SQUARE IS
A 3 MINUTE WALK

TO VAL GARDENA
SELLA PASS
& ⑤

MARINZEN CHAIR LIFT

MAIN ROAD

CALVARIO

BUS PARK

⑪

PATH

① KOFELSTR.

⑫

MAIN SQUARE

②

POST ⑧

⑩

WOLKENSTEIN STR.

③

PLATTENSTR.

⑥ FOUNTAIN

⑦

TO
ALPE DI SIUSI
& BOLZANO

④

DCH

① Albergo Torre (Gasthof zum Turm)
② Hotel al Lupo (Hotel zum Wolf)
③ Hotel Cavallino D'Oro (Goldenes Rossl)
④ Haus Harderer
⑤ To Tirler Hof Farm
⑥ Restaurant Hexenkellar
⑦ Café Stella
⑧ Café Doris
⑨ To Marinzenhutte Café
⑩ Silbernagl Kaufhaus Grocery
⑪ A&O Supermarket
⑫ ATM, WC & Phones

each depicting a scene from Christ's passion (with the Roman soldiers looking decidedly German), culminating in the crucifixion.

SLEEPING

(€1 = about $1.10, country code: 39)

$$$ **Albergo Torre** (in German, **Gasthof zum Turm**) is comfortable, clean, and traditional, with great beds and modern bathrooms (Db-€50–120, Tb-€69–155, prices vary with season and amenities, includes breakfast, €4 extra for 1-night stays, closed April and Nov, elevator, behind TI at Kofelgasse 8, tel. 0471-706-349, fax 0471-707-268, www.zumturm.com, info@zumturm.com, Gabi and Günther SE). If

you're driving, go right through the traffic-free town center (very likely with a police escort). Under the bell tower, enter the white arch to the right of the TI and park (free for guests) in the lot opposite the front door.

$$ Hotel zum Wolf (in Italian, **Al Lupo**) is pure Tirolean, with all the comforts (Sb-€35–50, Db-€56–85, prices vary with season and view, includes breakfast, non-smoking rooms, CNN in rooms, closed April–mid-May and Nov–mid-Dec, a block below main square at Wolkensteinstrasse 5, tel. 0471-706-332, fax 0471-707-030, www .hotelwolf.it, info@hotelwolf.it, Arno SE).

$$ Hotel Cavallino D'Oro (in German, **Goldenes Rössl**), on the main square, has plenty of Tirolean character and is run by friendly and helpful Stefan. Every room is different, and locals frequent the bar. If you love antiques by candlelight (or have only credit cards), this 600-year-old hotel is the best in town (Sb-€53–70, Db-€83–98 depending on season, discount for 3-night stay, no elevator, Krausplatz 1, tel. 0471-706-337, fax 0471-707-172, www.cavallino.it, cavallino@cavallino.it, SE). Stefan converted his 500-year-old wine cellar into a spa and sauna, complete with heated tile seats, solarium (tanning), and tropical plants.

$ Haus Harderer, below Hotel Kastelruth (take the middle road where it forks), rents three rooms (Ss-€26, Ds-€52, includes breakfast, no CC, min 2-night stay in summer) and a fine apartment for longer stays (€82–85/day, sleeps 4–6, no breakfast, no CC, Plattenstrasse 20, tel. 0471-706-702, run by Inge—SE, plus Oswald, Heinz—SE, Ida, and Mimme the cat). As you enter the driveway, the Harderer house is the one to the right with the Zimmer sign.

$ Tirler Hof, the storybook Jaider family farm, has 50 cows, one friendly *Hund,* four Old World–comfy guest rooms, and a great mountain view (D-€42, includes breakfast, practical only for drivers, it's the first farm a half-mile outside of town on the right on road to St. Michael, Paniderstrasse 44, tel. 0471-706-017, jaider.klaus @rolmail.net, Paola SE). The ground-floor double has a private bath. The top-floor rooms share a bathroom and a great balcony. Take a stroll before breakfast.

EATING

The hotels' restaurants are good. Consider **Cavallino D'Oro** (on one side of hotel is the *ristorante,* on the other side is the bar—each side gets the same menu; Wed–Mon 12:00–14:00 & 18:00–2:00, closed Tue) or the less expensive **Albergo Torre** (Thu–Tue 12:00–14:00 & 18:00–21:00, closed Wed, April, and Nov).

The **Hexenkellar**, or the "Witch Cellar," dishes up affordable German and Italian cooking (Mon–Sat 17:00–22:00, closed Sun, a half block from TI on Plattenstrasse—facing TI, go left through arch).

For strudel, locals like the simple **Stella** (Tue–Sun 7:30–19:00, closed Mon, on Plattenstrasse; facing TI, go left through arch) and **Café Doris** (Wed–Mon 12:30–23:00, closed Tue, on main road at Wolkenstein 29, tel. 0471-706-340); both have terraces. Even better, for strudel *mit* view, take the little Marinzen cable car up the mountain to the **Marinzenhutte** café (May–Oct daily 9:00–17:00, tel. 0471-707-158, has animal park for kids). The lift runs from the end of May through October (€4.50 one-way, €6.50 return, from the town square head downhill toward Wolkensteinstrasse, cross the road and continue straight another 200 yards to the lift). You can hike down from Marinzen or return on the lift.

Castelrotto has two groceries: **Silbernagl Kaufhaus** (Mon–Sat 8:00–12:00 & 15:00–19:00, closed Sat afternoons off-season and Sun, on Wolkensteinstrasse) and the smaller **A&O Supermarket,** two blocks away, also on the main drag (Mon–Sat 8:00–12:00 & 15:00–18:30, closed Sun, off-season closed Sat afternoon as well, Via Panider).

TRANSPORTATION CONNECTIONS

To Alpe di Siusi: From Castelrotto, take a bus to the village of Siusi (2/hr, June–mid-Oct, discounted return tickets), where you catch the Seiser Alm Bahn funicular to Compatsch (€10 round-trip, 12 min, runs 8:00–19:00); from Compatsch, you can take hikes, rent bikes or horses, or hop the shuttle bus to Saltria, where you'll find more hiking trails. Off-season, four buses run daily in both directions between Castelrotto and Siusi. Guests at some Castelrotto hotels may be able to ride free on buses in summer—ask.

By bus to: Bolzano (€3.25, reduced price of €3 for return trip, 2/hr, 50 min, runs 6:30–19:00), **Vigo di Fassa** and **Canazei** (late June–mid-Sept only, 4/day, 2 hrs), and **Ortisei/St. Ulrich** and **St. Cristina** (summer only, 4/day, 1 hr). Get bus schedules at the TI, or call toll-free tel. 800-846-047 or 0471-706-633 (English-speaking help).

Alpe di Siusi (Seiser Alm)

Europe's largest high alpine meadow, Alpe di Siusi, separates two of the most famous Dolomite ski-resort valleys. Measuring eight by 20 miles and soaring up to 6,500 feet high, Alpe di Siusi is dotted by farm huts and wildflowers (mid-June–July), surrounded by dramatic—if distant—Dolomite peaks and cliffs, and much appreciated by hordes of walkers.

The Sasso Lungo (Langkofel) mountains at the head of the meadow provide a storybook Dolomite backdrop, while the spooky

Alpe di Siusi

NOTE: THIS 3-D VIEW LOOKS SOUTHEAST & IS NOT TO SCALE. ELEVATIONS IN METERS

SELLA 3152
SASSOLUNGO 3181
MARMOLADA 3342
SELLA PASS
WILLIAMS 2100
ZALLINGER 2054
TIERSER-ALPI 2441
BOLZANO 2450
FLORIAN
MOLIGNON 2060
SALTRIA 1675
A L P E D I S I U S I
PANORAMA 2014
SPITZBÜHL 1979
MT. PEZ 2563
SCHLERN
ARNIKA 2061
PUFLATSCH
COMPATSCH 1830
A.V.S.
SALTNER SCHWAIGE 1830
TO VAL GARDENA & SELLA PASS
CASTELROTTO KASTELRUTH 1060
SIUSI/SEIS 1002
TO BOLZANO & AUTOSTRADA
TO PONTE GARDENA & S-12

★ = PENSION SEELAUS

DCH

KEY:
- • = TOWN
- — = ROAD
- ↦ = LIFT
- ····· = TRAIL
- ▲ = MTN. HUT (HUTTE/RIFUGIO)

1 Compatsch Hike
2 Panorama Hike
3 Zallinger Hutte Hike
4 Schlern Summit Hike
5 Sasso Lungo Loop Hike

Schlern peak stands boldly staring into the haze of the peninsula. The Schlern, looking like a devilish *Winged Victory,* gave ancient peoples enough willies to spawn legends of supernatural forces. The Schlern witch, today's tourist brochure mascot, was the cause of many a broom-riding medieval townswoman's fiery death.

The Alpe di Siusi is my recommended one-stop look at the Dolomites because of Castelrotto's charm as a home base, its easy accessibility for those with and without cars, its variety of walks and hikes, and its quintessentially Dolomite mountain views.

A natural preserve, Alpe di Siusi is closed to cars unless you are staying in one of the area hotels (show your reservation confirmation for proof). A car park is located just 200 yards outside Siusi on the road from Bolzano.

A new funicular runs hikers and skiers from Suisi to Compatsch; from there, buses shuttle visitors to and from key points along the tiny road all the way to Saltria at the foot of the postcard-dramatic Sasso peaks (Sasso Lungo, 10,433 feet). Meadow walks, for flower-lovers and strollers, are pretty—or maybe pretty boring. Chairlifts are springboards for more dramatic and demanding hikes.

Trails are well-marked, and the brightly painted numbers are keyed into local maps. The Kompass Bolzano map #54 covers everything in this chapter (scale 1:50,000, €4.10). The Wanderkarte map of Alpe di Siusi (produced by Tabacco) offers more detail and focuses on just Alpe di Siusi (scale 1:25,000, €2.60).

Compatsch is the tourist village (6,135 feet), served by Alm Bahn funicular from Siusi or by car if you are staying at a hotel in Alpe di Siusi. It has a TI (Mon–Sat 9:00–17:00, Sun 9:00–12:00; off-season Mon–Sat 9:00–13:00, closed Sun; free WCs behind TI, tel. 0471-727-904), grocery store (open mid-June–mid-Oct), mountain bike rentals (€6.75/1 hr, €17.50/4 hrs), an ATM, parking (€3.50/day), hotels, restaurants, shops, and so on. Trocker rents horses and provides guides (€13/1 hr, €23/2 hrs, €32/3 hrs, April–Oct, 100 yards, next to Compatsch TI, or at barn above Piccolo Hotel down the road from Compatsch, tel. 0471-727-807, NSE).

Sleeping near the Park Entrance: $ Pension Seelaus, a 10-minute walk downhill from Compatsch, is a cozy, friendly, family-run place with a Germanic feel and down comforters. Its Wellness Center has a sauna, hydromassage, and mini-pool (Sb-€53–88, Db-€106–176, prices vary with season and type of room, includes buffet breakfast and hearty dinner, Via Compatsch 8, tel. 0471-727-954, fax 0471-727-835, www.hotelseelaus.it, info@hotelseelaus.it, Roberto SE).

Hikes in the Alpe di Siusi

Easy meadow walks abound, giving tenderfeet classic Dolomite views from baby-stroller trails. Experienced hikers should consider the tougher and more exciting treks. Before attempting a hike, call or stop by the local TI to confirm your understanding of the time and skills required. Many lifts operate mid-June through mid-October and during the winter ski season. The Panorama and Puflatsch lifts (both near Compatsch) run further into the off-season.

Three Easy Walks from Compatsch: Take a lift to Puflatsch for the two-hour loop north to Arnikahütte (has café) and back (elevation gain about 660 feet).

Or: Ride the lift to Panorama, then hike 90 minutes to Molignonhütte (6,725 feet) and back down to Compatsch; or continue 2.5 hours (fairly level) to Zallingerhütte (6,725 feet) and another 90 minutes to Saltria and the bus stop.

Or: Bus to Saltria and hike the 2.5-hour loop to Zallingerhütte (6,725 feet, 660-foot altitude gain).

Summit Hike of Schlern (Sciliar): For a challenging 12-mile, six-hour hike with a possible overnight in a traditional mountain refuge (generally open mid-June–mid-Oct), consider hiking to the summit of Schlern and spending a night in Rifugio Bolzano (Schlernhaus). Start at the Spitzbühl lift (5,659 feet, free parking lot, first bus stop in park). The Spitzbühl chairlift drops you at Spitzbühl (6,348 feet). Trail #5 takes you through a high meadow, down to the Saltner Schwaige dairy farm (6,004 feet), across a stream, and steeply up the Schlern mountain. You'll meet trail #1 and walk across the rocky tabletop plateau of Schlern to the mountain hotel, Rifugio Bolzano/Schlernhaus, three hours into your hike (8,038 feet, D-€36, dorm beds-€16, tel. 0471-612-024, call for reservation). From this dramatic setting, you get a great view of the Rosengarten range. Hike 20 more minutes up the nearby peak (Mount Pez, 8,399 feet) for a 360-degree alpine panorama. From the Schlernhaus, you can hike back the way you came or walk farther along the Schlern (7 miles, 2 hrs, past the Rifugio Alpe di Tires, €17 beds, €9.50 bunks, tel. 0471-727-958, 8,005 feet) and descend back into Alpe di Siusi and the road where the bus or funicular will return you to your starting point or hotel.

Loop around Sasso Lungo: Another dramatic but easy hike is the eight-hour walk around Sasso Lungo (Langkofel) group. You can ride the bus to Saltria (end of the line), take the chair-lift to Williamshütte, walk past the Zallingerhütte (overnight possible, Db-€31, D-€20, half-pension €6.50/person extra, tel. 0471-727-947), and circle the Sasso Lungo group.

MORE SIGHTS IN THE DOLOMITES

▲▲**Great Dolomite Road**—This is the definitive Dolomite drive: Belluno/Cortina/Pordoi Pass/Sella Pass/Val di Fassa/Bolzano. Connecting Venice with Bolzano this way (the Belluno–Venice autostrada is slick) takes two hours longer than the Bolzano–Verona–Venice autostrada. No public transit does this trip. In spring and early summer, passes labeled "closed" are often bare, dry, and, as far as local drivers are concerned, wide open.

▲▲**Abbreviated Dolomite Loop Drive**—See the biggies in half the miles (allow 3 hours, Bolzano/Castelrotto/Val Gardena/Sella Pass/Val di Fassa/Bolzano). Val Gardena (Grodner Tal) is famous for its skiing and hiking resorts, traditional Ladin culture, and wood-carvers (the wood-carver ANRI is from the Val Gardena town of St. Cristina). It's a bit overrated, but even if its culture has been suffocated by the big bucks of hedonistic European fun-seekers, it remains a good jumping-off point for trips into the mountains. Within an hour, you'll reach Sella Pass (7,349 feet). After a series of tight hairpin turns a half-mile or so over the pass, you'll see some benches and cars. Pull over and watch the rock climbers. Val di Fassa is Alberto Tomba country. The town of Canazei, at the head of the valley and the end of the bus line, has the most ambience and altitude (4,642 feet). From there, a lift takes you to Col dei Rossi Belvedere, where you can hike the Bindelweg trail past Rifugio Belvedere along an easy but breathtaking ridge to Rifugio Viel del Pan. This three-hour round-trip hike has views of the highest mountain in the Dolomites—the Marmolada—and the Dolo-mighty Sella range.

▲▲Reifenstein Castle—For one of Europe's most intimate looks at medieval castle life, let the friendly lady of Reifenstein (Frau Blanc) show you around her wonderfully preserved castle. She leads tours on the hour, in Italian and German, squeezing in whatever English she can (€3.50, open Easter–Oct, tours Sat–Thu at 9:30, 10:30, 14:00, and 15:00, closed Fri, picnic spot at drawbridge, tel. 0472-765-879).

To drive to the castle, exit the autostrada at Vipiteno (Sterzing) and follow signs toward Bolzano. The castle is just west of the freeway; park at the base of the castle's rock. Of the two castles here, Reifenstein is the one to the west. While this is easy by car, it's probably not worth the trouble by train (from Bolzano, 6/day, 70 min).

▲Glurns—Drivers connecting the Dolomites and Lake Como by the high road via Meran and Bormio should spend the night in the amazing little town of Glurns (45 min west of touristy Meran between Schluderns and Taufers). Glurns still lives within its square wall on the Adige River, with a church bell tower that has a thing about ringing, and real farms, rather than boutiques, filling the town courtyards. There are several small hotels in the town, but I'd stay in a private home (Family Hofer, 6 rooms, Db-€50 with breakfast, less for 3 nights, no CC, 100 yards from town square, near church, just outside wall on river, Via Adige 1, tel. 0473-831-597).

LAKE COMO

(Lago di Como)

Commune with nature where Italy is welded to the Alps, in the lovely Italian Lakes District. The million-euro question is: Which lake? For the best mix of accessibility, scenery, and off-beatness, Lake Como is my choice. You'll get a complete dose of Italian-lakes wonder and aristocratic-old-days romance. Bustling Milan, just an hour away, doesn't even exist. Now it's your turn to be *chiuso per ferie* (closed for vacation).

Lake Como, lined with elegant, 19th-century villas, crowned by snowcapped mountains, and busy with ferries, hydrofoils, and little passenger ships, is a good place to take a break from the intensity and obligatory-turnstile culture of central Italy. It seems half the travelers you'll meet have tossed their itineraries into the lake and are actually relaxing.

Today the hazy, lazy lake's only serious industry is tourism. Thousands of lakeside residents travel daily to nearby Lugano, in Switzerland, to find work. The lake's isolation and flat economy have left it pretty much the way the 19th-century Romantic poets described it.

Planning Your Time

If relaxation's not on your agenda, Lake Como shouldn't be either. Even though there are no essential activities, plan for at least two nights so you'll have an uninterrupted day to see how slow you can get your pulse.

Lake Como is Milan's quick getaway, and the sleepy mid-lake village of Varenna is the gateway and handiest base of operations. With good connections to Milan, Malpensa Airport, and midlake destinations, Varenna is my favorite home base.

Arrival in Varenna

I zip directly by train from Milan to Varenna, set up, and limit my activities to midlake (Varenna and Bellagio). From Milan's central station, catch a train heading for Sondrio or Tirano (often confused with Torino—wrong city). Be certain your train stops in Varenna; look at the

The Italian Lakes

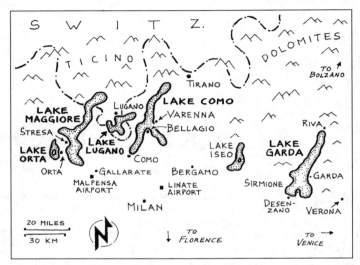

fine print on the *Partenze* (departures) schedule posted at Milan's train station to make sure Varenna is listed. Trains leave about hourly (usually at :15 past the hour). Sit on the left for maximum lake-view beauty. Get off at Varenna-Esino. Note that the name Varenna-Esino appears only at the train station, even though train schedules list simply Varenna. Same place. Know what time you are supposed to arrive in Varenna so you can be ready to disembark with luggage in hand; the train stops for only one minute (literally). Otherwise you'll be carried to the next town and have to backtrack (you may even have to pay a fine for not having the proper ticket).

You can also get to Varenna from Milan via the town of Como. Trains take you from Milan to Como (50-min rides usually leave at :25 past each hour), where you can catch a boat for the two-hour ride (about hourly, last departure at 19:00, €6.80–9.80) up the lake to Varenna.

Getting around Lake Como

By Boat: Lago di Como is well-served by boats and hydrofoils. The lake service is divided into three parts: south-north from Como to Colico; midlake between Varenna, Bellagio, Menaggio, and Cadenabbia (Villa Carlotta); and the southeastern arm to Lecco. Unless you're going through Como, you'll probably limit your cruising to the midlake service (boat info: tel. 031-579-211 or toll-free 800-551-801). Boats go about hourly between Varenna, Menaggio, and Bellagio (€2.60 per hop, 15 min, daily 7:00–21:00).

Lake Como

Passengers pay the same for car or passenger ferries, but 35 percent more for the enclosed, stuffy, speedy-but-less-scenic €4 hydrofoil. The free schedule (available at TIs, hotels, and boat docks) lists times and prices. Stopovers aren't allowed, and there's no break for round-trips, so buy a ticket for each ride. The one-day, €7.50 midlake pass saves you money if you make three rides.

By Car: With the parking problems, constant traffic jams, and expensive car ferries, this is no place to drive if you don't need to. While you can easily drive around the lake, the road is narrow, congested, and lined by privacy-seeking walls, hedges, and tall fences. It costs €8.80 including driver, plus €2.60 for every passenger, to take your car onto a ferry. To arrange a rental car for when you leave Varenna, contact the I Viaggi del Tivano travel agency in Varenna (see below).

Parking is rarely easy where you need it, especially in Bellagio. Park in Varenna and cruise. Parking is free Monday through Friday near

BOAT SCHEDULE LITERACY TIPS

Feriale = Monday–Saturday	*Autotraghetto* = Car ferry
Festivo = Sunday and holidays	*Aliscafo* = Hydrofoil
Partenze da = Departing from	*Battello* = Passenger-only ferry

Albergo Beretta (limited to 1 hour Sat–Sun, use the *discorario*—circular cardboard parking meter—usually in the glove compartment of the rental car) and at the train station (pay by the hour Sat–Sun 8:00–19:00—after that it's free—feed coins into meter at center of the lot and put the printed ticket on the dashboard). In town, white lines on the pavement indicate free parking (find spaces on road past Villa Monastero and a few near the harbor), yellow lines mean residents only, and blue lines mean you need to buy a ticket (€1/hr, 2 hours max). Buy tickets from the newsstand on the main square, the tobacco shop just south of the square, or Bar Cambusa near the ferry dock (scratch off the date and time you'll be parked and leave the ticket on your dashboard, 8:00–12:00 & 14:00–19:00, overnight plus 2 hours is OK).

Varenna

This town of 800 people offers the best of all lake worlds. Easily accessible by train, on the less-driven side of the lake, Varenna has a romantic promenade, a tiny harbor, narrow lanes, and its own villa. It's the right place to savor a lakeside cappuccino or *aperitivo*. There's wonderfully little to do here, and it's very quiet at night. The *passerella* (lakeside walk, unlit but safe after dark) is adorned with caryatid lovers pressing silently against each other in the shadows.

Tourist Information: Varenna's TI is on the main square to the right of the church (Pro Varenna, Tue–Sat 10:00–12:30 & 15:00–18:00, Sun 10:00–12:30, closed Mon, Nov–April Sat–Sun 10:00–12:30 & 15:00–18:00 only, tel. 0341-830-367, www.varennaitaly.com).

A bank, cash machine, and small post office are just off the main square (see town map). Accommodations are listed below.

Travel Agency: For bus and boat tours, consider Varenna's travel agency, I Viaggi del Tivano, next to Albergo Beretta below the train station. They book planes, trains, and automobiles and can offer half-day and day-long tours of the region and into Switzerland May–Sept; book tours by 18:00 the night before (Mon–Fri 8:30–12:30 & 15:00–19:00, Sat 9:00–12:00, closed Sun, CC accepted but there may be a nominal fee for small charges, Via per Esino 3, tel. 0341-814-009, www.tivanotours .com, helpful Silvia and Luana SE). They do town walks by appointment—arrange in advance—which usually depart around 17:00 or 18:00

and cost €5 for an hour-long introduction to Varenna (not including entrances to gardens).

Hello Varenna Walk

Since you came here to relax, this short walk gives you just the town basics.

Bridge near train station: This main road bridge, just below the train station, spans the tiny Esino River. The river divides two communities, Perledo (which sprawls up the hill—notice the church spire high above) and the old fishing town of Varenna (huddled around its harbor). While the towns were joined in fascist times, today they are separate and not without animosity. Perledo used to have a fine beach (where the river hits the lake) until recent storms washed it away. Varenna wanted to collaborate, by remaking and sharing an inviting public beach here. Perledo refused. The train station is called Varenna-Esino for a third community higher in the hills. Now, follow the river down to the lakeside promenade by the ferry dock.

Varenna ferry landing: Since the coming of the train, Varenna has been *the* convenient access point from "midlake" (the communities of Bellagio, Menaggio, and Varenna) to Milan. From this viewpoint, you can almost see how Lake Como is shaped like a man. The head is the north end (to the right, up by the Swiss Alps). Varenna is the left hip. Menaggio, across the lake, is the right hip. And Bellagio (hiding behind the wooded hill) is where the legs come together—you can see the point (Punta Spartivento—"where the wind is divided"). In a more colorful description, a local poem says "Lake Como is a man with Colico the head, Lecco and Como the feet, and Bellagio the testicles." In the local dialect, this rhymes. Ask a local to say it for you. The ridges high above the right hip are the border of Switzerland. The region's longtime poverty shapes the local character (much like the Great Depression shaped the outlook of a generation of Americans). Many still remember that this side of the lake was the poorest, because those on the other (Menaggio) side controlled the lucrative cigarette smuggling business over the Swiss border. Today, the entire region is thriving (with tourism and a booming—if mysterious—iron and steel industry...convenient to secret Swiss bank accounts). Walk past the Hotel Olivedo (Olivedo means the place where olive trees grow—Varenna is the only such place on this side of the lake) and past the ferry dock to the *passerella*, Varenna's elevated shoreline walk.

Passerella: A generation ago, a local eccentric (who won big-time on an Italian TV game show) and a determined town carpenter successfully promoted the idea to build Varenna's elegant lakeside walk, which connects the ferry dock with the old town center. Strolling this, you'll come to the tiny two-dinghy concrete breakwater of a local villa. Lake Como is lined with elegant 19th-century villas. Their front doors faced the lake to welcome boats. At this point, the modern *passerella* cuts between this villa's water gate and its private harbor. Around the next corner and over the hump look up at another typical old villa—with a veil of serious wisteria and a prime lakeview terrace. Many of these villas are owned by the region's "impoverished nobility." They were bred and raised not to work and, therefore, are now unable to cover the upkeep of their sprawling houses. From here, also enjoy a good Varenna town view. These buildings are stringently protected. You can't even change the color of your paint.

Varenna harborfront: Walk past the community harbor and under the old-time arcades to the fishermen's pastel homes, which face the harbor. Notice there are no streets in town...just characteristic stepped lanes called *contrada*. Varenna was originally a fishing community. Even today, old-timers enjoy Lago di Como's counterpart to lutefisk—air-dried and salted lake "sardines." Called *missoltino*, these sardines are served with this region's polenta (different from Venice's because buckwheat is mixed in with the corn). At the south end of the harbor (across from the gelato shop), belly up to the banister for another fine pastel town view. Another local ditty goes "If you love Lake Como, you know Bellagio is the pearl...but Varenna is the diamond." Continue straight, leaving the harbor. A lane leads around past Hotel du Lac (its fine lakeside terrace welcomes nonresidents for a drink) to the tiny and pebbly town beach (the only place for a swim). From here climb uphill to the town square.

Piazza San Giorgio: Four churches face Varenna's town square. The main church dates from the 14th century. Romantic Varenna is an understandably popular spot for a wedding—rice litters the church's front yard. Stepping inside, you'll find a few humble but centuries-old bits of carving and frescoes. The black marble floor was quarried right in town. Outside, past the WWI monument, is the TI. From this square you can head south to the gardens, or go north to go to the train station or up to the castle.

SIGHTS

Varenna

Castle—A steep trail leads to Varenna's ruined hilltop castle, Castello di Vezio. Start at the stairs to the left of Hotel Monte Codeno and figure on 20 minutes one-way. The castle is pretty barren, apart from a couple of medieval contraceptive devices and some spooky statuary on its grounds, though a new falconry training center has livened it up (€4, discounted ticket with this book, April–Oct daily from 10:00, closes one hour before sunset, off-season weekends only, closed Jan and when rainy, mobile 335-465-186). The castle, with a sleepy café at its entrance, is located in a peaceful, traffic-free, one-chapel town.

Varenna

(TRAIN STN. TO CHURCH IS A 10 MIN. WALK)

---- PASSERELLA (LAKESIDE WALK)
IIIII STEPPED STREETS

TRAIN STATION
TRAIN TUNNEL
TRAIL TO CASTLE VEZIO
TRAVEL AGENCY
TO TIRANO
MAIN ROAD
BANK
TRAIN TUNNEL
TO MILANO
TRAIL TO ❿ & FIUMELATTE
CHURCH
MAIN RD. TO LECCO
BANK
GARDENS
GROC.
PASSENGER BOAT DOCK + TICKETS
CAR FERRY DOCK
PIAZZA SAN GIORGIO
HARBOR
POST
L A K E
C O M O
TO MENAGGIO
TO BELLAGIO & COMO
DCH

❶ Albergo Olivedo
❷ Albergo Milano
❸ Hotel Monte Codeno
❹ Albergo Beretta
❺ Villa Elena Rooms
❻ Albergo Del Sole
❼ Villa Cipressi
❽ Hotel du Lac
❾ Hotel Victoria
❿ To Hotel Eremo Gaudio
⓫ Ristorante il Cavatappi
⓬ Vecchia Varenna Rest.
⓭ Nilus Bar & La Frulleria/Il Gelato

Gardens—Two manicured lakeside gardens—Villa Cipressi and the adjacent monastery—are tourable for a €4 combo-ticket available at Villa Cipressi or the monastery (€2.50 for one garden only, March–Oct daily 9:00–19:00).

Fiumelatte—This town, about half a mile south of Varenna, was named for its milky river. It's the shortest river in Italy at 800 feet and runs—like most of the local tourist industry—only April through September. The *"La Sorgente del Fiumelatte"* brochure, available at Varenna's TI, lays out a walk from Varenna to the Fiumelatte to the castle and back. It's a 30-minute hike to the source *(sorgente)* of the milky river (at Varenna's monastery, take high road, drop into peaceful and evocative cemetery, and climb steps to the wooded trail leading to peaceful and refreshing cave where the river sprouts). For a longer lakeside hike, ask the TI about the *Sentiero del Viandante* (hike one-way up the lake, about 90 min, much more level than the Castello hike, return by train).

Lake Como

▲▲**Bellagio**—The self-proclaimed "Pearl of the Lake" is a classy combination of tidiness and Old World elegance. If you don't mind that "tramp in a palace" feeling, it's a fine place to surround yourself with the more adventurous of the posh travelers and shop for ties and umbrellas. The heavy curtains between the arcades keep the visitors and their poodles from sweating. Thriving yet still cute, Bellagio is a much more substantial town than Varenna, which has almost no shops.

Steep-stepped lanes rise from the harborfront. While Johnny Walker and jewelry sell best at lake level, the locals shop up the hill. Piazza Chiesa, near the top of town, has a worth-a-look church.

The TI is right downtown at the passenger boat dock (Mon and Wed–Sat 9:00–12:00 & 15:00–18:00, Sun and Tue 10:00–12:30 & 15:00–17:30, Nov–March closed Sun and Tue, tel. 031-950-204, prombell@tin.it). If you need a destination, you can tour the Villa Serbelloni Park—overlooking the town—with a guide (€6, April–Oct 2 tours/day at 11:00 and 16:00 except Mon, 90 min, ask at TI).

The administrative capital of the midlake region, Bellagio is located where the two southern legs of the lake split off. For an easy break in a park with a great view, wander right on out to the crotch. Meander past the rich and famous Hotel Villa Serbelloni, and walk five minutes to Punta Spartivento, literally, "the point that divides the wind." You'll find a Renoir atmosphere complete with an inviting bar/restaurant, a tiny harbor, and a chance to sit on a park bench and gaze north past Menaggio, Varenna, and the end of the lake to the Swiss Alps.

For another stroll, head south from the car-ferry dock down the tree-shaded promenade. Ten minutes later, you'll hit Bellagio's beach. The Lido di Bellagio has a chilly pool, lounge chairs, and a diving board into the lake (€4, daily in summer 10:00–18:00, tel. 031-950-597).

Bikers would enjoy a downhill mountain-bike run. Cavalcalario Club shuttles you uphill, then lets you go (€20–25 includes bike rental, several itineraries, reservations necessary at least a day ahead, tel. & fax 031-964-814, mobile 339-530-8138, www.bellagio-mountains.it, cavalcalarioclub@tiscalinet.it). They also offer horseback riding, paragliding, canoeing, kayaking, sailboat rentals and trekking (see their Web site or call for details).

Bellagio has two docks a few minutes' walk apart: The northern dock is for the passenger-only ferry (*battello*) and the hydrofoil (*aliscafo*); the southern dock is for the car ferry (*autotraghetto*), which also takes foot passengers. To make sure you're waiting at the right dock for the boat you want to take, check the boat schedule carefully (posted near dock, free brochure from kiosk at dock). Its timetable is divided into

Bellagio

NOT TO SCALE
PASSENGER DOCK
TO CHURCH IS A
5 MINUTE WALK
UPHILL.

LAGO
DI
COMO

- ❶ Hotel du Lac
- ❷ Hotel Florence
- ❸ Hotel Metropole
- ❹ Grand Hotel Villa Serbelloni
- ❺ Albergo Europa
- ❻ Hotel Suisse
- ❼ Hotel Giardinetto
- ❽ Ristorante Bilicus
- ❾ Trattoria S. Giacomo
- ❿ Ristorante la Grotta
- ⓫ Art in Flower Café
- ⓬ To La Punta Ristorante
- ⓭ Gastronomia Mini Market

three different schedules: *battello* (passengers only), *aliscafo* (passengers in a hurry), and *autotraghetto* (passengers and cars). Confirm your intentions at the kiosk near either dock.

▲**Menaggio**—Menaggio has more urban bulk than its neighbors. Since Lake Como is too dirty for swimming, consider its fine public pool. This is the starting point for a few hikes. Only a few decades ago, these trails were used by cigarette smugglers, sneaking at night from Switzerland back into Italy with tax-free cigarettes. The hostel (see "Sleeping," below) has information about mountain biking and catching the bus to trailheads on nearby Mount Grona.

Villa Carlotta—This is the best of Lake Como's famed villas (€6.50, April–Sept daily 9:00–18:00, Oct daily 9:00–11:30 & 14:00–16:30, closed Nov–March, tel. 034-440-405). I see the lakes as a break from Italy's art, but, if you're in need of a place that charges admission, Villa Carlotta offers an elegant neoclassical interior, a famous Canova statue, and a garden (its highlight, best in spring). If you plan to tour one villa on the lake, this is the best. Nearby Tremezzo and Cadenabbia are pleasant lakeside resorts an easy walk away. Boats serve both places (5-min walk from either dock to the Villa).

Isola Comacina—This remote little island (just south of Bellagio) offers peace, ancient church foundations, goats, sheep, and a lovely view of Lago di Como. It takes 30 minutes to walk around the island, but longer to savor it. Bring a picnic or try the snack bar at the dock. Look for trips to Isola Comacina on the Colico–Como schedule (listed in Lago di Como boat timetable brochure, free at ticket booths at ferry docks). The *isola* is accessible from Varenna (1 hour), Menaggio (45 min), or Bellagio (30 min). Check return times carefully (Como–Colico direction) and don't miss your boat. Usually only one trip a day each way works out for a visit.

Como—On the southwest tip of the lake, Como has a good, traffic-free old town, an interesting Gothic/Renaissance cathedral, and a pleasant lakefront with a promenade (TI open Mon–Sat 9:00–13:00 & 14:30–18:00, closed Sun, tel. 031-269-712). It's an easy walk from the boat dock to the train station (from Milan in 30 min, usually leaving at :25 past each hour). Boats leave Como about hourly for midlake (ferries-€6.00–6.80, 2 hrs; hydrofoils-€8.70–9.80, 45 min; departures 7:00–19:00, tel. 031-579-211).

SLEEPING

The area is tight in August, snug in July, and wide open most of the rest of the year. Many places close in winter. All places listed (see map on page 151) are family-run and have lakeview rooms, and some English is spoken. If you're expecting friendliness, especially during peak season, you'll likely be disappointed. Enjoy the view. View rooms are given (sometimes for no extra cost) to those who telephone for reservations and request a *"camera con vista."* Prices get soft off-season (Nov–May). Varenna's TI, on the main square, can find private rooms (tel. 0341-830-367).

Varenna

$$$ **Albergo Milano**, located right in the old town and graciously run by Egidio and Bettina Mallone, has eight newly refurbished, well-plumbed rooms with balconies—rooms 1 and 2 have royal terraces—

SLEEP CODE

(€1 = about $1.10, country code: 39)
Sleep Code: **S** = Single, **D** = Double/Twin, **T** = Triple, **Q** = Quad, **b** = bathroom, **s** = shower only, **no CC** = Credit Cards not accepted, **SE** = Speaks English, **NSE** = No English. You can assume credit cards are accepted unless otherwise noted.

To help you sort easily through these listings, I've divided the rooms into three categories based on the price for a standard double room with bath:

$$$ **Higher Priced**—Most rooms €120 or more.
$$ **Moderately Priced**—Most rooms between €80-120.
$ **Lower Priced**—Most rooms €80 or less.

and views of the lake and gardens (Sb-€95–105, Db-€110–130, includes buffet breakfast; confirm arrival the day before; optional 3-course dinner specializing in seasonal produce and fresh lake fish-€25 per person, no dinner Sun or Tue; Via XX Settembre 29. from the station take main road to town and turn right at steep alley where sidewalk and guardrail break; tel. 0341-830-298, fax 0341-830-061, U.S. fax 781/634-0094, www.varenna.net, hotelmilano@varenna.net, SE, baby Carlotta and Sashimi NSE). This place whispers *luna di miele* (honeymoon) and offers a €250 three-night package including a welcome bottle of sparkling wine, candlelight dinner, breakfast in bed, and a picnic lunch basket.

$$$ **Hotel du Lac,** with 17 stylish and sleek rooms, overlooks the water (Db with view and balcony-€175, less without, suite Db-€210, includes breakfast, parking-€11, Via del Prestino 4, tel. 0341-830-238, fax 0341-831-081, www.albergodulac.com, albergodulac@tin.it, Ileana SE).

$$$ **Hotel Victoria,** on the main square, is a typical big hotel with a fine lakeview garden and a pool but no air-conditioning (43 rooms, Db-€120–160, add €35 for view, includes breakfast, Piazza San Giorgio 5, tel. 0341-815-111, fax 0341-830-722, www.royalvictoria.com, info@hotelroyalvictoria.com, SE).

$$ **Albergo Olivedo,** facing the ferry dock, is an Old World, elegant hotel with antique furniture and squeaky hardwood floors. Most of the newly remodeled rooms have glorious little lakeview balconies (except for those on the fourth floor, which also have small view windows). It's a fine place to hang out and watch the children, boats, and sun come and go (prices vary with season and views: Sb-€35–45, Db-€85–115, half-pension required in peak season—see below, includes

breakfast, no CC, air-con, closed mid-Nov–mid-Dec, tel. & fax 0341-830-115, www.olivedo.it, olivedo@tin.it, serious Laura SE). In May, June, July, and September, half-pension (dinner) is usually mandatory—and rarely regretted—with all rooms (€27 per person for dinner, which adds €54 to price of double room).

$$ Villa Cipressi, in a huge, quiet, lakeside garden, is a sprawling, centuries-old mansion with 32 plain, modern rooms and a terraced garden that people pay to see (Sb-€85–95, Db-€100, Db with view but no balcony-€115–130, Tb-€165, Qb-€205, rooms without views face the street and are noisier, includes breakfast, garden access, elevator, Internet access, Via IV Novembre 18, tel. 0341-830-113, fax 0341-830-401, www.hotelvillacipressi.it, villacipressi@libero.it, Elena and Davide SE).

$$ Eremo Gaudio, standing isolated halfway up the hill with a commanding lakeview high above Varenna, was once an orphanage (built by the Pirelli family—of tire fame), then a hermitage (run by the Church), and—since 2000—a hotel. Perfect for monks with champagne tastes, it's peaceful, with awe-inspiring view balconies and a breakfast terrace. There are 13 bright, comfortable rooms in the main building and 10 simpler, less expensive rooms below in a section that still feels like a priests' dorm (open April–Oct only; Sb-€90–95, Db-€105, Db with balcony-€120; lower rooms: Sb-€60–70, Db-€80; some rooms with air-con; taxi from station about €10, Via Roma 11, tel. 0341-815-301, fax 0341-815-314, www.eremogaudio.it, eremogaudio@yahoo.it, SE). From Varenna's main square, walk south about 650 feet. Across from Villa Monastero, veer left up the high road where you'll find the lower of two private funiculars that slide you up the mountainside to your perch.

$$ Hotel Monte Codeno, with 11 functional rooms and no views, is on the main road between the train station and lake (2 Sb-€70, Db-€93, includes breakfast buffet, extra bed-€16, 10 percent discount for 3 nights, attached restaurant serves fresh fish and a €22 "Rick Steves" *menu*—see below, Via della Croce 2, tel. 0341-830-123, fax 0341-815-227, ferrcas@tin.it, Marina Castelli SE). They rent a few apartments nearby (as low as €87 for 2 people, up to €195 for 6 people, minimum 2-night stay for apartments).

$ Albergo Beretta, on the main road a block below the station, has 10 decent rooms, several with balconies (D-€55–60, Db-€65–80, extra bed-€8, breakfast-€6, coffee shop on ground floor, Via per Esino 1, tel. & fax 0341-830-132, hotelberetta@iol.it, Signora Tosca NSE, Laura and daughter Julia SE).

$ Villa Elena, a grandmotherly, low-energy place on the main square, offers the best budget beds in town. English-speaking Signora Vitali rents her four rooms at the same price—room #1 has a bathroom and view terrace; the others don't even have sinks (Db-€42 with fine breakfast, €40 without, no CC; it's the vine-covered facade on Piazza San Giorgio #9 near Via San Giovanni; tel. 0341-830-575). **Albergo**

del Sole, a restaurant on the same square, may rent eight rooms in 2004 (Piazza San Giorgio 17, tel. 0341-815-218, NSE).

Bellagio
(€1 = about $1.10, country code: 39)
To locate hotels, see the map on page 153.

$$$ **Hotel du Lac**, a good waterfront splurge, comes with 48 rooms, a roof terrace, and old-time elegance with no loss of comfort (Sb-€95–105, Db-€160–190, plusher superior Db-€210, includes breakfast, and free access to the Bellagio Sporting Club's swimming pool outside town, parking-€8, air-con, TVs, minibars, closed Nov–March, Piazza Mazzini 32, tel. 031-950-320, fax 031-951-624, www.bellagiohoteldulac.com, dulac@tin.it, Leoni family SE).

$$$ **Hotel Florence**, a few doors away and 150 years old, is family-run, with hardwood, pastels, and a rich touch of Old World elegance (30 rooms, Sb-€105–125, Db-€140–200 depending on view and balcony, Db suite-€260, includes breakfast, closed Nov–March, elevator, handheld showers only, tel. 031-950-342, fax 031-951-722, www.bellagio .co.nz, hotflore@tin.it, Ketzlar family SE).

$$$ **Hotel Metropole**, a tired but grand old place, dominates Bellagio's waterfront with 42 spacious and reasonably comfortable rooms and plush public spaces (Db-€104–129, some rooms with view balconies, elevator, fridge, closed Nov–March, tel. 031-950-409, fax 031-951-534, Michela SE).

$$$ **Grand Hotel Villa Serbelloni**, a famous 19th-century palace, comes with history, doormen, two pools (inside and out), fitness center, a garden, an elite clientele, and sky-high prices. While the grounds and public spaces are fancy, their 81 rooms don't quite merit the high prices (standard Db-€240–350, deluxe Db-€328–460, executive double-€600, pricier rooms have views, air-con and all the comforts, closed Nov–April, tel. 031-950-216, fax 031-951-529, www.villaserbelloni.com, inforequest@villaserbelloni.com).

$$ **Albergo Europa**, run with low energy, is in a concrete annex behind a restaurant, away from the waterfront. Its 10 rooms have no charm but reasonable comfort (Db-€83–99, balconies lack views but overlook quiet courtyard, parking, Via Roma 21, tel. & fax 031-950-471, family Marchesi).

$ **Hotel Suisse**, the cheapest place on the waterfront, has 10 simple rooms, hardwood floors, dim lights, fine bathrooms, unpredictable beds, and some great views and balconies (Db-€77 with this book through 2004, breakfast-€10, 10 percent discount in hotel restaurant with this book, Piazza Mazzini 8/10, tel. 031-950-335, fax 031-951-755, hsuisse @tiscalinet.it, Guido SE).

$ **Hotel Giardinetto**, at the top of town near the TI, 100 steps above the waterfront, offers 14 squeaky-clean and quiet rooms. The rooms are stark, but the breezy, peaceful garden is a joy and available for picnics (S-€31, D-€46, Db-€54, Tb-€75, breakfast-€6, no CC but personal checks and traveler's checks OK, closed Nov–mid-March, Via Roncati 12, tel. 031-950-168, Eugene and Laura Ticozzi SE).

In or near Menaggio

$ **La Primula Youth Hostel** is a rare hostel. Run by Alberto, it caters to a quiet, savor-the-lakes crowd. Located about 300 yards south of the Menaggio dock, it has a view terrace; games galore; washing machine; bike, canoe, and kayak rentals (€10.50/day, €15 for non-hostelers); and easy parking (closed 10:00–17:00 and Nov–mid-March, €12.50 per night in a 4- to 6-bed room with sheets and breakfast, €13 per bed with private plumbing, no CC, hearty dinners for €10 including drinks, reserve dinner by 18:00). Show this book for a free half-hour Internet connection (Ostello La Primula, Via IV Novembre 106, Menaggio, tel. & fax 0344-32356, www.menaggiohostel.com, menaggiohostel@mclink.it). Alberto has plenty of ideas for hikes and bike rides in the area.

$ **La Marianna B&B** is run by a husband-and-wife team, Ty and Paola. They rent eight rooms and run a fine restaurant in Cadenabbia, about a mile south of Menaggio (Db with view-€68–72, attached restaurant with lakeside terrace, tel. 0344-43095, www.la-marianna.com, inn@la-marianna.com). The hourly Como–Menaggio bus C-10 and the Malpensa-Menaggio shuttle stops at its doorstep.

Buses run between Milan's Malpensa Airport and Menaggio (1/day year-round, 2 hrs, €13.20 one-way). These are the likely departure times (confirm on site): Menaggio to Malpensa departing from Piazza Garibaldi at 6:30; Malpensa Terminal 1 to Menaggio departing from exit 3/4 at 12:20, tel. 031-276-9934.

$*Other Hostels on Lago di Como:* The **Villa Olmo** hostel is at the south end of the lake in Como (€13/day including breakfast and sheets, membership required or pay €2.60 supplement, dinners from €8–10, bicycle rental and laundry service available, reception open 7:00–10:00 &16:00–23:30, lockout during the day, closed Dec–Feb, tel. & fax 031-573-800, ostellocomo@tin.it), and another hostel is in the north at Domaso (€11/day, includes breakfast and sheets, membership not required; open all day, midnight curfew during the week, 2:00 on weekends; closed Jan–Feb; tel. 0344-97449, fax 0344-97575, ostellolavespa @lombardiacom.it).

EATING

Varenna

On the Waterfront

Albergo Olivedo's restaurant serves fine food with no-nonsense service across from the ferry dock. Depending on the weather, meals are served either curbside under an awning with a lake view, or in a classy old dining hall. While Laura and her capable staff serve simple homemade pasta lunches, evening meals are a set two-course affair without an à la carte option. Sample regional specialty *pizzoccheri*, buckwheat noodles tossed with boiled potatoes, greens, and lots of local cheese (€25-35 dinner, daily 12:15–14:00 & 19:30–21:15, stop by the hotel and reserve dinner in advance, tel. 0341-830-115).

Vecchia Varenna, on the harbor, is respected, pricey, and the most romantic place in town. The menu features traditional cuisine and lake specialties (€25–45 meals, Tue–Sun 12:30–14:00 & 19:30–21:30, closed Mon, also closed Tue in winter, dressy indoors or on harborside deck, reservations smart, tel. 0341-830-793).

The **Nilus Bar**, with a stainless steel diner interior and the best harborfront seating in town, is *the* place for a light meal. The young wait-staff serves dinner crêpes, pizzas, salads, hot sandwiches, and cocktails with a smile (daily in summer 10:00–1:00, spring and fall 12:00–24:00, Dec–Feb Sat–Sun only, 0341-815-228, Fulvia and Giovanni SE).

The recommended hotel **Albergo Milano** serves up a fine fish dinner to guests and non-guests alike (€25 3-course *menu*, à la carte also available, closed Sun and Tue, reservations recommended, Via XX Settembre 29, tel. 0341-830-298; see "Sleeping in Varenna," page 154).

For cold, sweet, and fruity treats, check out the harborfront **La Frulleria/Il Gelato** (two doors down from Nilus Bar, daily May–Sept 10:00–2:00, Oct–April 10:00–17:00).

Off the Water, on or near Piazza San Giorgio
Ristorante del Sole, facing the town square, serves edible meals and Naples-style pizzas (€5–8). Making few concessions to the tourist crowds, this restaurant caters to locals, providing a fun ambience and a garden in back (daily 12:00–14:30 & 19:00–22:00, closed Wed in winter, Piazza San Giorgio 21, tel. 0341-815-218).

Victoria Grill, also on the square, is more modern, with a cheery, neon-and-red-checkered-tablecloth atmosphere. They serve good, well-priced meals and pizza (daily 12:00–14:00 & 19:00–22:00, closed Mon in winter, under fancy Hotel Victoria). In addition, Hotel Victoria has a tired upscale restaurant welcoming non-guests with a set €30 menu and lakeview terrace seating.

Ristorante il Cavatappi, a five-table place on a quiet lane 100 feet off the town square, is the new place in town. Helpful owner-chef Mario serves old-time specialties, such as *missoltino* (the air-dried lake fish that locals like more than tourists) as an antipasto. He's serious about his wine. Plan on spending €25 plus wine (daily 12:30–15:30 & 19:30–22:30, closed Wed off-season, reservations smart, tel. 0341-815-349).

Ristorante Monte Codeno, on the main road without a hint of lake ambience, serves a special "Rick Steves" menu designed to give visitors a sampler of lake cuisine. For €20, you get eight different fishy appetizers caught from Lake Como and a *secondo* with seasonal vegetables or a salad—all explained in a souvenir info sheet (daily 12:00–14:00 & 19:00–21:00, Via della Croce 2, tel. 0341-830-123).

Picnics: The three little grocery stores, on and just off the main square, have all you need for a classy balcony or breakwater picnic dinner (hours vary but are roughly daily 7:30–12:30 & 15:30–19:30, all are closed Mon afternoon).

Bellagio

Ristorante Bilicus, a busy and jolly place serving regional and lake cuisine with passion, is up a steep lane from the waterfront. While a little pricey, the restaurant is famous for value and quality cooking (Tue–Sun 11:45–14:00 & 19:00–22:00, closed Mon, indoor/outdoor seating, closed Nov–March, Salita Serbelloni, tel. 031-950-480).

Trattoria S. Giacomo, across the street, is less expensive and respected for its traditional cuisine, such as *riso e filetto di pesce*—rice and fish fillet (daily 12:00–14:30 & 19:00–21:30, closed Tue off-season, Salita Serbelloni 45, tel. 031-950-329).

Hotel Metropole Ristorante's terrace offers the best waterfront view, though a mediocre food value (see "Bellagio" in the sleeping section, page 157, tel. 031-950-409).

Try **La Grotta** for €5–8 pizzas and pastas (daily 12:00–14:30 & 19:00–24:00, closed Mon off-season, CC OK with minimum €25 purchase, Salita Cernaia 14, tel. 031-951-152).

Art in Flower serves up an assortment of quick and tasty pastas (€5–7), sandwiches, huge salads, and creative gelato sundaes (daily 9:00–24:00, closed Thu off-season, Via Garibaldi 21, tel. 031-950-875).

At Punto Spartivento, the dramatic park just north of town, you'll find **La Punta Ristorante** (daily 12:00–14:30, tel. 031-951-888) and a great setting for a picnic. Pick up picnic supplies at **Gastronomia Mini Market** (at Via Centrale and Via Marrafio, uphill from Hotel Florence) or from the grocery/deli on the corner of Via Garibaldi and Via Mella—they also have take-out roast chicken, ribs, focaccia, and sandwich fixings (Tue–Sun 7:30–13:00 & 15:30–19:00, closed Mon and Sun afternoons). You'll find picnic benches at the park, along the waterfront in town, and lining the promenade south of town.

TRANSPORTATION CONNECTIONS

From any destination covered in this book, you'll get to Lake Como via Milan. The quickest Milan connection to any point midlake (Bellagio, Menaggio, or Varenna) is via the train to Varenna. If leaving Varenna by train, note that the Varenna station doesn't sell tickets. Purchase a ticket either at the tobacco shop off the Main square or the helpful travel agency, I Viaggi del Tivano, next door to the Albergo Beretta. Stamp your ticket in the machine at the station before boarding. If both places are closed, win the sympathy of the conductor and buy your ticket on board (costs extra).

Milan to Varenna: Catch a train at Milano Centrale (€4.60; likely schedule: 8:15, 9:15, 12:15, 14:15, 16:15, 18:00, 19:10, 20:15, and 21:10; 60 min). In Milan, the large overhead departure schedules list Sondrio and Tirano rather than Varenna, a small stop en route (look at the fine print in the departure schedule posted at the station to make sure Varenna is listed). Some cars on long trains don't even get a platform. Ask for help so you don't miss the stop because the train stops for only a minute. You may have to open the door yourself.

Varenna to Milan: Trains leave Varenna for Milano Centrale at 6:16, 7:24, 8:23, 10:19, 12:22, 14:22, 16:22, 18:22, 20:20, and 22:30. (Confirm these times.) Varenna makes a comfy last stop before catching the shuttle from Milan's train station to the airport.

Malpensa Airport to Varenna: Two buses a day go direct to Varenna (€16.50, departs Terminal 1 at 11:00 and 21:30, 2 hrs) making stops in front of Albergo Beretta and at the main square, Piazza San Giorgio.

Varenna to Malpensa Airport: Two buses a day go direct to Malpensa Airport (€16.50, departs Varenna at Albergo Beretta and Piazza San Giorgio at 5:30 and 16:30, 2.25 hrs; must reserve and purchase tickets at least a day ahead at Varenna's travel agency—I Viaggi del Tivano, next to Albergo Beretta, Mon–Fri 8:30–12:30 & 15:00–19:00, Sat 9:00–12:00, closed Sun, Via per Esino 3, tel. 0341-814-009, www.tivanotours.com).

Varenna to St. Moritz in Switzerland: From Varenna, you have fantastic access to the Bernina Express and scenic train to St. Moritz. First take the train to Tirano and then transfer to St. Moritz (3/day, allow 6 hrs with transfer).

MILAN

(Milano)

For every church in Rome, there's a bank in Milan. Italy's second city and the capital of Lombardy, Milan is a hardworking, fashion-conscious, time-is-money city of 1.5 million. Milan is a melting pot of people and history. Its industriousness may come from the Teutonic blood of its original inhabitants, the Lombards, or from the region's Austrian heritage. Milan is Italy's industrial, banking, TV, publishing, and convention capital. The economic success of modern Italy can be blamed on this city of publicists and pasta power lunches.

As if to make up for its shaggy parks, blocky fascist architecture, and recently bombed-out feeling (World War II), its people are works of art. Milan is an international fashion capital with a refined taste. Window displays are gorgeous, cigarettes are chic, and even the cheese comes gift wrapped. Yet luckily, Milan is no more expensive for tourists than other Italian cities.

Three hundred years before Christ, the Romans called this place Mediolanum, or "the central place." By the fourth century A.D., it was the capital of the western half of the Roman Empire. It was from here that Emperor Constantine issued the Edict of Milan, legalizing Christianity. After some barbarian darkness, medieval Milan rose to regional prominence under the Visconti and Sforza families. By the time of the Renaissance, it was called "the New Athens" and was enough of a cultural center for Leonardo to call home. Then came 400 years of foreign domination (Spain, Austria, France, more Austria). Milan was a center of the 1848 revolution against Austria and helped lead Italy to unification in 1870.

Mussolini left a heavy fascist touch on the city's architecture (such as the central train station). His excesses also led to the WWII bombing of Milan. But Milan rose again. The 1959 Pirelli Tower (the skinny skyscraper in front of the station) was a trendsetter in its day. Today, Milan is people-friendly, with a great transit system and inviting pedestrian zones.

Many tourists come to Italy for the past. But Milan is today's Italy, and no Italian trip is complete without visiting it. While it's not big on the tourist circuit, Milan has plenty to see. And fortunately, seeing Milan—manageable and well-organized—is not difficult.

My coverage focuses on the old center. Nearly all the sights and hotels covered are within a 10-minute walk of the cathedral (Duomo), which is one straight eight-minute shot on the Metro from the train station.

For a pleasant day trip from Milan, consider Stresa on Lake Maggiore. This resort town has easy boat connections to lovely islands brimming with lush, exuberant gardens. Stresa, about an hour from Milan by train, is covered at the end of this chapter.

Planning Your Time

OK, it's a big city, so you probably won't linger. Compared to Rome and Florence, Milan's art is mediocre, but the city does have unique and note-worthy sights. To maximize your time, use the Metro and note which places stay open through the siesta.

With two nights and a full day, you can gain an appreciation for the town and see the major sights. (Note that about half of Milan's sights close on Monday.) With 36 hours, I'd sleep in Milan and focus on the center. Tour the Duomo, hit what art you like (Brera Gallery, Michelangelo's last *Pietà*, Leonardo's *Last Supper*—which requires a reservation), browse through the elegant shopping area and the Galleria, and try to see an opera. Technology buffs like the Science and Technology Museum, while medieval art buffs dig the city's early Christian churches. People-watchers and pigeon-feeders could spend their entire visit never leaving sight of the Duomo.

Since Milan is a cold Italian plunge, and most flights to the United States leave Milan early in the morning, you may want to start your Italian trip softly by going directly from Milan to Lake Como (1-hour train ride to Varenna), Lake Maggiore (about an hour by train to Stresa—see end of chapter), or the Cinque Terre (4 hrs to Vernazza). Then spend a night or two in Milan at the end of your trip before flying home.

Three-hour tour: If you're just changing trains in Milan (as sooner or later you will), consider this blitz tour: Check your bag at the station, pick up a city map at the station TI, ride the subway to the Duomo (in front of the train station, follow yellow line 3 direction per San Donato 4 stops to Duomo), peruse the square, explore the cathedral's rooftop and interior, have a scenic coffee in the Galleria, spin on the Taurus, see a museum or two (most are within a 10-minute walk of the main square), and return by subway to the station (yellow line 3, direction Zara). Art fans might make time for the Duomo's museum; *The Last Supper*, if they've made reservations (Metro: Cadorna or tram #24, direction Axum); or the Michelangelo Pietà in the fortress (no reservations nec-essary, Metro: Cairoli).

ORIENTATION

Tourist Information

Milan has two TIs. One is in the central train station (Mon–Fri 9:00–19:00, Sat 9:00–18:00, Sun 9:00–12:30 & 13:30–18:00, tel. 02-7252-4360). At track level (with your back to the tracks), look for the sign "APT Tourist Information" near the blinking orange-and-white T. The TI is tucked away down a corridor next to a Telecom telephone center (Internet access with phone card).

The other TI is on Piazza Duomo (Mon–Fri 8:45–13:00 & 14:00–18:00, Sat–Sun 9:00–13:00 & 14:00–17:00, Oct–April closes 1 hour earlier, tel. 02-7252-4301, www.milanoinfotourist.com). As you face the church, it's to your right in a skinny three-story building.

At either TI, confirm your sightseeing plans and pick up the free map and the classy *Museums in Milan* booklet (with latest museum hours). For events, concerts, films in English, expatriate groups, and cultural insights, ask for the free *Hello Milano* monthly newspaper (www.hellomilano.it) or the less-helpful *Milano Mese* (events are listed in Italian by category rather than date). The 130-page *Milano è Milano* booklet—useful, but overkill for most short visits—details several self-guided walking tours and provides a listing of sights, shopping ideas, bookstores, restaurants, nightlife, sports events, launderettes, Internet cafés, and much more (€3).

The TI sells a Welcome Card packet for €8, which includes a 24-hour transit pass (value: €3, good on Metro, trams, and buses); a coupon booklet good for discounts on their city bus tour (€4 off, includes Leonardo's *Last Supper,* offered Tue–Sun), Navigli boat cruise, classical music concerts, and several museums; a CD of opera music; and an unnecessary vinyl pouch. This is a decent value if you can manage to fit several of those activities into your day or want the CD.

While I've listed enough sights to keep you hectically busy for two days, there's much more to see in Milan. Its many thousand-year-old churches make it clear that Milan was an important beacon in the Dark Ages. The TI, the *Milano è Milano* booklet, and other local guidebooks can point you in the right direction if you have more time.

Arrival in Milan

By Train: The huge, sternly decorated, fascist-built (in 1931) train station is a city and a sight in itself. You'll get off the train and enter the lobby at track level; another floor is downstairs.

Orient from the track-level lobby with your back to the tracks. On your right: train information (daily 7:00–21:00, validate railpasses here at any window, tel. 89-20-21 for automated info in Italian), baggage check (€3/12 hrs, daily 6:00–1:00), and a 24-hour pharmacy *(farmacia,* look for green neon cross). At your back between the two clocks facing the tracks is Passaggi Travel Agency (daily 8:00–20:00, sells train tickets, supplements, and *cuccette* reservations without a commission, also domestic and international flights for €10–15 commission). On your left are cash machines (near track 14) and the TI (see above, look for blinking orange T). Out the side exit on the left (down the escalator under the "Gran Bar" sign), you'll find airport shuttle buses (to Malpensa and Linate, run by STAM) lined up. Past those buses is another Passaggi Travel Agency (daily 8:00–20:00, Piazza Luigi di Savoia 1, tel. 02-669-0531).

From the track level, go downstairs straight ahead to find train-ticket windows, Hertz/Avis/Europcar offices, and a great and huge supermarket/cafeteria that's hidden away (daily 7:30–23:00; after you descend stairs from track-level lobby, go right to the far end and enter Pellini bar, snake your way through the cafeteria to the Super Centrale market, also called Supermercato Sigma). Just outside the front of the station is the taxi stand (figure on €10 to Duomo) and escalators, which take you down into the Metro system.

Station change offices are a rip-off. Use a cash machine (from track 14, enter the lobby—you'll find a Bancomat cash machine to your left and another across the hall) or exit the station straight ahead and cross the square to Banca Commerciale Italiana (Mon–Fri 8:30–13:30 & 15:00–16:00, closed Sat–Sun).

For most quick visits, the giant city is one simple axis from the train station to the Duomo. To get to the Duomo, go straight into the Metro (look for red M) and buy a €1 ticket (from the underground ticket office at the Metro stop—with all prices listed in English over the window, or from a machine—push green button). Follow signs for line 3 (yellow), direction S. Donato, and in eight minutes you'll be facing the cathedral. To return to the station, take the yellow line 3, direction Zara. After one trip on the Metro, you'll dream up other excuses to use it.

By Car: Driving is bad enough in Milan to make the €20/day fee for a downtown garage a blessing. If you're driving, do Milan (and Lake Como) before or after you rent your car, not while you're renting it. If you have a car, use the well-marked suburban *parcheggi* (parking lots), which offer affordable and safe parking at city-edge subway stations.

By Plane: Frequent shuttle trains and buses connect the airports and train station. See "Transportation Connections," page 190.

Helpful Hints

Theft Alert: Be on guard. Milan's thieves target tourists. At the station and around the Duomo, thieves roam dressed as beggars, sometimes in gangs of several too-young-to-arrest children. Watch out for ragged people carrying newspaper and cardboard. If you're ripped off, ask the police to fill out a report; it's necessary if you plan to file a claim with your insurance company (Police Station,

"Questura," Via Fatebenefratelli 11, Metro: Turati, tel. 02-62261 or Piazza San Sepolcro 9 behind Pinacoteca Ambrosiana near Duomo, tel. 02-806-051). For police emergencies, call 113.

For lost or stolen credit cards or traveler's checks, contact Visa in Italy at 800-877-232 or 800-874-333; MasterCard at 800-870-866 (for credit cards); or American Express at 800-870-333 (for credit cards) or 800-872-000 (for traveler's checks).

U.S. Consulate: It's at Via Principe Amedeo 2/10 (Mon–Fri 8:30–12:30 & 13:30–17:30, Metro: Turati, tel. 02-290-351).

Scheduling: Monday is a terrible sightseeing day, since many museums are closed. August is rudely hot and muggy. Locals who can, vacate, leaving the city pretty quiet. Those visiting in August find the nightlife sleepy; many shops, restaurants, and some hotels closed; and the hotels that are open—empty and discounted. I've indicated which recommended hotels offer air-conditioning, worth the money for a summer visit.

Travel Agencies Selling Train Tickets: You can buy train tickets and reserve couchettes (cuccette in Italian) at Passaggi Travel Agency at the train station at no extra cost and without the lines (see their two offices listed in "Arrival in Milan by Train," above) or at a downtown travel agency. American Express is near the Duomo (Mon–Fri 9:00–17:50, pay cash or use AmEx credit card, at Via Larga 4, 2 blocks southeast of Duomo, tel. 02-721-041).

Bookstores: The handiest major bookstore is Libreria Feltrinelli, under the Galleria Vittorio Emanuele. The books in English—fiction and guidebooks—are at opposite ends of the store (Mon–Sat 10:00–23:00, Sun 10:00–20:00, shorter hours in Aug; store is huge but entrances are subtle: either enter at Ricordi Mediastore next to McDonald's in center of Galleria and go downstairs, or enter through Autogrill restaurant on Piazza Duomo, store is in the basement level; also sells maps; tel. 02-8699-6903). The American Bookstore is at Via Camperio 16, near the Sforza Castle (Mon 13:00–19:00, Tue–Sat 10:00–19:00, closed Sun, tel. 02-878-920). Internet Access: Major phone offices (e.g., at central train station and in Galleria) have phone card–operated computers online which work well (daily 8:00–21:30). The Leonardo da Vinci Science Museum has a wonderful room filled with computers for free Internet access on weekends (see page 181).

Street Markets: Milan's most popular flea market is Fiera di Senigallia, which spills down Viale d'Annunzio every Saturday from 8:30 to 17:00 (Metro: San Agostino, walk down Viale Papiniano—where market starts—to d'Annunzio, where it gets bigger). Small street markets are held every morning except Sunday in various neighborhoods; *Hello Milano* has a complete listing (free at TI). Be wary of pickpockets at any street market.

Medical Services: A 24-hour pharmacy is in Central Station; look for the neon green cross. Several international medical clinic/emergency care facilities are in Milan: at Via Cerva 25 (24-hr help, Metro: San Babila, tel. 02-7601-6047); at Via Durini 17 (in Galleria Strasburgo between Via Durini and Corso Europa, 3rd floor, Metro: San Babila, tel. 02-763-407-20), and at Via Mercalli 11 (Metro: Missori, call for appointments, tel. 02-5831-9808). Dial 118 for medical emergencies.

Getting around Milan

Use Milan's great subway system. The clean, spacious, fast, and easy four-line Metro zips you almost anywhere you may want to go, and trams and city buses fill in the gaps. A **ticket,** valid for 75 minutes, can be used for one subway, tram, or bus ride, plus a transfer (€1, sold at newsstands, many *tabacchi* shops, and at machines in subway station—push green *rete urbana di Milano* button; note that some machines sell only the €1 ticket—just feed in the money). Other options include: a *carnet* (€9.20 for 10 rides; you get 5 tickets that can be used twice—flip over to use a second time; these can be shared); the **24-hour pass** (€3, worthwhile if you take 4 rides; can usually cover a journey the following morning since

Milan's Metro

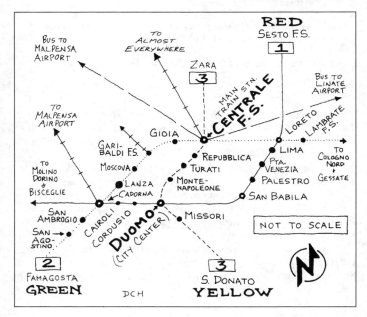

MILAN AT A GLANCE

▲▲**Duomo** Milan's showpiece cathedral on the main square. You can walk on its roof amid a forest of spires. **Hours**: Daily 7:00–19:00.

▲▲**Duomo Museum** Provides insight to the Duomo and a chance to see its original art. **Hours**: Daily 10:00–13:15 & 15:00–18:00.

▲▲**Galleria Vittorio Emanuele** Glass-domed arcade on the main square, perfect for window-shopping and people-watching. **Hours**: Always open.

▲▲**La Scala Opera House and Museum** The world's most prestigious opera house, under renovation until Dec 00. **Hours**: Museum—Daily 9:00–18:00 (temporarily at Palazzo Busca, across from church housing Leonardo's *Last Supper*). Opera performances held across town at Theater Arcimboldi.

▲**Brera Art Gallery** World-class collection of Italian paintings (13th–20th centuries), including Raphael, Caravaggio, Fabriano, Mantegna, and the Bellini brothers. **Hours**: Tue–Sun 8:30–19:15, maybe June–Sept Saturdays until 22:30, closed Mon.

▲**Risorgimento Museum** History of Italian unification. **Hours**: Tue–Sun 9:00–13:00 & 14:00–17:30, closed Mon.

▲**Sforza Castle and Branca Tower** Milan's castle containing

it's a 24-hour rather than a 1-day pass); and a **48-hour pass** (€5.50). Transit info: toll-free tel. 800-808-181 (underground ATM Point office at Duomo stop near exit Arengario or from topside, Metro entrance near TI, Mon–Sat 7:45–20:15).

I've keyed sightseeing to the subway system. While most sights are within a few blocks of each other, Milan is an exhausting city for walking. You'll rarely wait more than five minutes for a subway train, and the well-marked trams can be useful (especially for getting to the *Last Supper*, catch #24 1 block off Duomo in Via Mazzini in front of Hotel Rio, see "Sights," below).

Small groups go cheap and fast by **taxi** (metered, drop charge €3.10 and €0.70 per km, additional supplements for luggage, on Sundays and holidays, often easier to walk to a taxi stand than to flag down a cab).

a museum whose highlight is an unfinished Michelangelo *Pietà*. Also on the park grounds is the Branca Tower, offering great city views. **Hours**: Museum—Tue–Sun 9:00–17:30, closed Mon; Tower—Wed–Fri 10:30–12:30 & 15:30–18:30 & 21:30–24:00, Sat–Sun 10:00–18:00 & 21:30–24:00, closed Mon–Tue.

▲**The *Last Supper*** Leonardo da Vinci's masterpiece, viewable only with a reservation. **Hours**: Tue–Sun 8:15–18:45 (last visit), July–Sept maybe open Sat until 21:45 (last visit), always closed Mon.

▲**Leonardo da Vinci National Science and Technology Museum** Leonardo's designs illustrated in wooden models, plus a vast collection of historical, scientific bric-a-brac. **Hours**: Tue–Fri 9:30–16:50, Sat–Sun 9:30–18:30, closed Mon.

Church of Santa Maria presso San Satiro Pilgrim church with impressive 3-D paintings. **Hours**: Daily 7:30–11:30 & 15:30–18:00.

Pinacoteca Ambrosiana Oldest museum in Milan, with works by Raphael, Leonardo, Botticelli, Titian, and Caravaggio. **Hours**: Tue–Sun 10:00–17:30, closed Mon.

Poldi Pezzoli Museum Italian paintings (15th–18th centuries), weaponry, and decorative arts. **Hours**: Tue–Sun 10:00–18:00, closed Mon.

Bagatti Valsecchi Museum 19th-century Italian Renaissance furnishings. **Hours**: Tue–Sun 13:00–17:45, closed Mon.

TOURS

Bus Tours—The three-hour **Autostradale** city bus tour has a live guide, is a good value, and guarantees you'll see Leonardo's *Last Supper* (useful if you haven't booked ahead for this sight). The two different itineraries also include visits to the Duomo, Galleria, and Sforza Castle. Both tours cover entry fees to Last Supper, depart from Piazza Duomo next to TI in Via Marconi, and are €4 off with the TI's Welcome Card (€40 for morning tour offered at 9:30 Tue–Sun year-round; €43 for afternoon tour—which includes Brera Art Gallery—offered at 15:00 Tue–Sun April–July, Sat–Sun only Sept–Oct; book at TI on Piazza Duomo, tel. 02-3391-0794 or 02-725-243-01).

The **Ciao Milano** vintage tram, which does a figure-eight trip around the city with a taped spiel, isn't worth €20 for the transportation, because Milan's sights cluster in the center (3/day; multilingual tour; you

Milan

can hop on and off but what's the point; departs Piazza Duomo at roughly 11:00, 13:00, and 15:00; tel. 02-339-107-94).

Private Guide—Private guides in Milano work together and can be booked at centroguidemilano@tiscali.it (tel. 02-864-50433). Lorenza Scorti is a hardworking young woman who knows her local history and how to teach it. She can be booked well in advance (necessary in May and Sept) or with short notice (€100 for 3-hr tour, eves OK, €200/full day, price identical for individuals or groups, tel. 02-4801-7042, lorenza.scorti@libero.it).

SIGHTS

Milan's Cathedral and Museum

▲▲**Duomo (Cathedral)**—The city's centerpiece is the fourth-largest church in Europe—after the Vatican's, London's, and Sevilla's. Get the most out of your visit by starting with the adjacent Duomo Museum (see page 172), located just outside the church, around to the right, directly across from the south transept.

Back when Europe was fragmented into countless tiny kingdoms and dukedoms, the dukes of Milan wanted to impress their counterparts in Germany and France. Their goal was to earn Milan recognition and respect from both the Vatican and the kings and princes of northern Europe by building a massive, richly ornamented cathedral. Even after Renaissance domes were in vogue elsewhere in Italy, Milan's cathedral stayed on Gothic target. The dukes—thinking northerners would relate better to Gothic—loaded it with pointed arches and spires. For good measure, the cathedral was built not of ordinary stone but of marble—pink marble of Candoglia, from top to bottom—rafted across Lake Maggiore from a quarry about 50 miles away to a canal port at the cathedral. (Note: The glorious facade is covered with scaffolding through 2005.)

Dress Code: Modest dress is required. Don't wear shorts or sleeveless shirts (kids included), or you could be turned away at the door.

Interior: At 525 by 300 feet, with 52 100-foot-tall, sequoia-sized pillars inside and more than 2,000 statues, the place is immense. If you do two laps, you've done your daily walk.

Built from 1386 to 1810, this construction project originated the Italian phrase meaning "never-ending": "like building a cathedral." It started Gothic (best seen in the apse behind the altar) and was finished in the early 1800s under Napoleon (particularly the noteworthy west facade, which is wonderful—when not covered in scaffolding—late in the day, with the sun low in the sky).

While the church is a good example of the flamboyant, or "flame-like," overripe final stage of Gothic, architectural harmony is not its forte (church free, daily 7:00–19:00, Metro: Duomo, €3 for 45-min audio-guide, €5 for 2, available from kiosk located inside to right of entrance, ID required, kiosk open daily 9:30–17:30). The treasury, or *tesoro,* to the right under the altar, thrills pilgrims with reliquaries containing thorns from Jesus' crown and the "Tree of Apostles" with bones, fingernails and hair from each of the twelve apostles (€1, daily 10:00–12:00 & 14:30–18:00).

Standing inside (at the back rear), notice two tiny lights: The little red one above the altar marks where a nail from the cross of Jesus is kept. This relic was brought to Milan by St. Helen (Emperor Constantine's mother) in the fourth century, when Milan was the capital of the Western Roman Empire. It's on display for three days a year (in mid-September). Now look high to the right and find a tiny pinhole of white light. This is designed to shine a 10-inch sunbeam onto the bronze line running across the floor here at noon indicating where we are on the zodiac (but local guides claim they've never seen it work).

Wander deeper into the church up the right aisle. Notice the windows. Those on the right are 15th-century; these mosaics of colored glass are brilliant and expensive, bought by wealthy families seeking the Church's favor. Many on the left date from the time of Napoleon and are dimmer, cheaper painted glass.

Belly up to the bar facing the high altar. While the church is Gothic, the altar was made Baroque—the style of the Vatican in the 1570s (a Roman Catholic statement to counter the Protestant churches of the north that were mostly Gothic). Now look to the rear up at the ceiling and see the fancy carving (between the ribs)—nope, that's painted. It looks expensive, but, being painted, it was more affordable than carved stone.

Paleo-Christian Baptistery: In the rear of the church (buy €1.50 ticket at kiosk, daily 9:30–17:15), climb down into the church that stood here long before the present one. Milan was an important center of the early Christian Church. In Roman times, Mediolanum's street level was 10 feet below today's level. You'll see the scant remains of an eight-sided baptistery (where Saints Augustine and Ambrose were baptized) and a little church. Back then, since you couldn't enter the church until you were baptized—which didn't happen until the age of 18—churches had a little "holy zone" just outside for the unbaptized. This included a baptistery.

Cathedral Rooftop: This is the most memorable part of a Duomo visit. You'll wander through a fancy forest of spires with great views of the city, the square, and—on clear days—even the Swiss Alps. And, 330 feet above everything, overlooking everything is La Madonnina. This 15-foot-tall gilt Virgin Mary is a symbol of the city. (Climb stairs for €3.50 or ride elevator for €5; €7 combo-ticket includes elevator and Duomo Museum; daily mid-Feb–mid-Nov 9:00–17:30, mid-Nov–mid-Feb 9:00–16:15, enter outside from north transept, clue: in Europe old churches face roughly east, stair entrance is across from Rinascente department store and the elevator is further ahead towards the back of the church—be prepared to climb a few more stairs once you reach the lowest level of the roof by elevator).

▲▲**Duomo Museum (Museo del Duomo)**—To really understand Milan's cathedral and enjoy a chance to see its original art close up, visit the cathedral museum. While the admission is €6, they encourage attendance by selling cheaper, deeply discounted combo-tickets (€4 includes treasury—sold at treasury or the museum but only if you ask; €7 includes elevator to church rooftop; €12 covers Pinacoteca Ambrosiana and Museo Diocesano). The museum is open daily (10:00–13:15 & 15:00–18:00, in Ducal Palace next to south side of Duomo, Piazza Duomo 14, Metro: Duomo, tel. 02-860-358, free coat and bag lockers available for the asking). Here's a tour:

Room 1: After you buy your ticket, look up. Greeting you, as he did pilgrims 500 years ago, is God the Father, made of wood, wrapped in copper, and gilded. In 1425, this covered the keystone connecting the tallest arches directly above the high altar of the Duomo.

Room 2: Meet St. George. Among the oldest cathedral statues, it once stood on the front spire and shows nearly 600 years of pollution and aging. Some think this is the face of Duke Visconti—the man who started the cathedral. The museum is filled with originals like this. On the right, finger a raw piece of *marmo di Candoglia*—the material of the church, spires, and statues. The duke's family gave the entire Candoglia quarry (near Stresa) to the church for all the marble it would ever need.

Room 3: This room (which used to be the stable for the Duke's horses) shows how Gothic was an international style. Gothic craftsmen, engineers, and artists roamed across Europe to work on huge projects such as Milan's cathedral. The statues in this room show the national differences: Peter (near the door, showing off his big keys) is Italian. His expressive face is made even more expressive by his copper-button pupils. The smaller statues (which were models for the big ones) behind glass are German (showing inner strength) and French (more graceful). Pope Martino V, overlooking the room from his perch at the end (to the left as you enter), celebrated the first Mass in the cathedral in 1418. Study the 15th-century stained-glass windows close up. The grotesque gargoyles (originals), protruding over the door you entered, served two purposes: to scare away evil spirits and to spew rainwater away from the building. Leaving the room, you'll walk under a stylized sun—a symbol of both Jesus and the Visconti family.

Room 5: A lit panel shows how the church was built in stages from 1386 to 1774. Building resumed whenever the community had the money.

Room 6: The brick backdrop reminds us what the church would have looked like if not for the 15th-century dandy with the rolled-up contract in his hand. That's Galeazzo Sforza, making it official—the church now owns the marble quarry (and it makes money on it to this day). A photo of the contract is opposite.

Room 7: The Byzantine style crucifix (again, copper-sheet gilded with real gold nailed onto wood) is 900 years old. It hung in the church that stood here previously, as well as in today's cathedral. The two-sided miniature altar painting has been carried through the city on festival days for 500 years.

Room 8: These statues, from around 1500, are originals. Copies now fill their niches in the church. St. Paul the Hermit (in front of the blue curtain) got close to God by living in the desert. While wearing only a simple robe, he's filled with inner richness. The intent is for pilgrims to stare into his eyes and feel at peace. (But I couldn't stop thinking of the Cowardly Lion.)

Room 9: Five hundred years ago, this sumptuous Flanders-style tapestry—woven of silk, silver, and gold—hung from the high altar. In true Flemish style, it shows fun details of everyday life woven into the theology. It tells the story of the crucifixion by showing three scenes at once. Note the exquisite detail, down to the tears on Mary's cheeks. (A discreet WC hides behind the wooden door.)

Room 10: The sketchy red cartoons were designs for huge paintings (see an actual painting and photographs of others nearly opposite) that still hang between the cathedral pillars (Oct–Christmas). Notice the inlaid 16th-century marble floor. The black (from Lake Como) and red (from Verona) marble is harder. Go ahead, wear down the white a little more.

Room 12: Enter room 12 and turn around to see the artwork lining the wall. The terra-cotta was clay—worked in a creative frenzy and then baked. Study the quick design below the careful marble originals (flanking the doorway you entered). Notice what 300 years of acidic pigeon droppings do to marble.

The statues all around this room (c. 1600) were sculpted 100 years later than the statues in room 8, and therefore are more expressive.

Find the painting of Saint Carlo Borromeo in the black robe, to your right. The 16th-century saint carries a cross showing the holy nail (the church's top relic) as he leads the plague out of Milan. In the background, see the 13th-century original church's facade with today's church—before spires—behind it.

Circle the room clockwise. Crespi's monochrome painting of the *Creation of Eve (Creazione di Eva)* came first (1628). From that, the terra-cotta model was made (1629), and this served as the model for the marble statue that still stands above the center door on the church's west portal (1643). Three other sets line the wall.

Opposite *Eve,* see the swirling *Dance of Angels* and its terra-cotta model. This is the original, which decorated the ceiling over the door.

Room 20: This room (off room 20) displays vestments on loan from the treasury. Showing off rich red robes with lavish gold brocade, it's like a priestly fashion show from the 16th through 20th centuries.

Room 13: Standing like a Picasso is the original (1772) iron frame for the statue of the Virgin Mary that still crowns the cathedral's tallest spire. In 1967, a steel replacement was made for the 33 pieces of gilded copper bolted to the frame. The carved wood face of Mary (in the corner) is the original mold for Mary's cathedral-crowning copper face.

Room 15: From room 12, enter a tunnel-like hall. Along the left wall, diagrams show competition designs proposing possible facades for the cathedral. A photo of the actual west portal is at the end of the hall.

Room 16: This huge wooden model of the cathedral was the actual model—necessary in that pre-computer age—used in the 16th century by the architects and engineers to build the church. This version of the facade wasn't actually built. Climb around the back to see the spire-filled rooftop, which you'll explore later if you like.

Room 17: The art here seems a mix of old and new, but it's all 20th century. Notice the vibrant Pope Martin V popping out of the wall (bronze panel to the left as you enter; artist Lucio Fontana). On the opposite wall (between the windows), Fontana's *Ascension of Mary (Mary Assunta)* is making a jump shot into heaven. Her veil looks like flowing hair, like the wings of an angel.

The last rooms are technical, showing the recent restoration work and the stabilization and reinforcement of the main pylons. To exit, retrace your steps.

Near the Cathedral

▲**Piazza Duomo**—Milan's main square is a classic European scene and a popular local gathering point. Professionals scurry, label-conscious kids loiter, young thieves peruse. For that creepy-crawly, pigeons-all-over-you experience, buy a bag of feed.

Standing in the square (mid-way between the statue and the Galleria), you're surrounded by history. The statue is of Victor Emmanuel II, first king of Italy. He's looking at the grand Galleria named for him. The words above the entrance read: To Victor Emmanuel II from the people of Milan.

Behind the statue (opposite the cathedral) is the center of medieval Milan—Piazza Mercanti. The medieval city hall (look for its red brick arches), dating from 1220, marked the center of town back when the entire city stood within its immense fortified walls. The merchant's square is a strangely peaceful place today, with a fine smattering of old-time Milano architecture.

Opposite the Galleria are twin fascist buildings (one houses the TI). Mussolini made grandiose speeches from these balconies. Study its relief panels telling—with fascist drama—the history of Milan. Between the TI and the cathedral (set back a bit) is the historic ducal palace—reno-vated into the neoclassical style by Maria Theresa in the late 1700s—when Milan was ruled by the Austrian Hapsburgs. For a fine view of the Duomo and the piazza, climb the steps to the balcony above the TI.

The Duomo Center (to the right of the TI) is a modern mall with a Virgin Megastore, one-hour photo service, Spizzico pizzeria, and Ciao cafeteria. Behind the Duomo is a vibrant, pedestrian shopping zone along Vittorio Emanuele II.

▲▲**Galleria Vittorio Emanuele**—A symbol of Milan is its great four-story, glass-domed arcade on the cathedral square. Here you can turn an expensive cup of coffee into a good value by enjoying Europe's best peo-ple-watching (or get the same view for peanuts from the strategically placed McDonald's). The venerable Bar Zucca (at the entry), with a friendly staff and an art deco interior typical of the 1920s, is a fine place to enjoy a drink and people-watch (€2.80 per cup is a great deal if you relax and enjoy the view). Once called the Campari café, this is consid-ered the origin of the famous Campari bitter (€3.30 standing or €8 seated, Tue–Sat 7:30–20:30, Sun 9:00-20:30, closed Mon).

Wander around the gallery. Its art celebrates the establishment of Italy as an independent country. Around the central dome patriotic mosaics symbolize the four major continents. The mosaic floor is also patriotic. The white cross in the center is a symbol of the king. The she-wolf with Romulus and Remus (on the south side facing Rome) honors the city, which since 1870 has been the national capital. On the west side (facing Torino, the provisional capital of Italy from 1861–1865), you'll find that city's symbol: a *torino* (little bull). For good luck, locals step on his irresistible little testicles. Two local girls explained to me that it works better if you spin. Find the poor little bull and observe for a few minutes...it's a cute scene. With so much spinning, the mosaic is replaced every few years.

Piazza della Scala—This smart, little, traffic-free square, out the back between the Galleria and the opera house, is dominated by a statue of Leonardo da Vinci. The statue (from 1870) is a reminder that Leonardo spent many years in Milan working for the Sforza family (who dominated Milan as the Medici family dominated Florence). Under the great Renaissance genius stand four of his greatest "Leonardeschi." (He apprenticed a sizable group of followers.) The reliefs show his various contributions—painter, architect, and engineer. Leonardo, wearing his hydroengineer hat, re-engineered Milan's canal system complete with locks. (Until the 1920s, Milan was one of Italy's major ports, with canals connecting the city to the Po River and Lake Maggiore.)

▲▲**La Scala Opera House and Museum**—From the Galleria, you'll see a statue of Leonardo. He's looking at a plain but famous neoclassical building, possibly the world's most prestigious opera house: Milan's Teatrale alla Scala. La Scala opened in 1778 with an opera by Antonio Salieri (of *Amadeus* fame).

Milan's famous opera house and its adjacent museum are closed for renovation until December 2004. Until then, opera buffs can see the museum's extensive collection in Palazzo Busca at Collegio San Carlo immediately in front of Santa Maria della Grazie, which houses Leonardo's *Last Supper*. The collection features things that mean absolutely nothing to the MTV crowd: Verdi's top hat, Rossini's eyeglasses, Toscanini's baton, Fettuccini's pesto, and original scores, diorama stage sets, costumes, busts, portraits, and death masks of great composers and musicians (€5; daily 9:00–18:00, last entry 45 min before closing; Corso Magenta 71, Metro: Cadorna or Conciliazione, or tram #24 from near Duomo; tel. 02-469-1249).

Opera: While La Scala is being renovated, the show goes on at Theater Arcimboldi (shuttles run theater-goers to and from performances from Piazza del Duomo at the taxi rank starting at 18:45, every 5 minutes until 19:00; cost is €1 transit ticket each direction). Schedules vary, but the opera season is nearly year-round (show time 20:00), and ballet and classical concerts are held from October through June. No performances are held in August (for information and booking call Scala Infotel Service, daily 12:00–18:00, tel. 02-7200-3744—live; or tel. 02-860-775—automated booking, press 2 for English; or book online at La Scala's fine Web site: www.teatroallascala.org). On the opening night of an opera, a dress code is enforced for men (suit and tie).

Tickets generally go on sale two months before a performance. The expensive seats sell out quickly. At noon on the day of the show, any remaining seats (usually in the affordable, sky-high gallery) are sold at a 50 percent discount at the box office and on the Internet (Web sales cease 1 hour before show time).

▲Via Speronari—A block off Piazza Duomo, this is one of Milan's oldest streets and the most charming street in the old center. Via Speronari—named for the spurs once made and sold here—is worth a wander. Streets around here recall their medieval crafts: *speronari*—spurs, *spadari*—swords, *armorari*—armor. The weaponry made on these streets was high fashion among Europe's warrior class...like having an Armani dagger. While right in the city center, the neighborhood feels vital. That's because it's also a residential street. Banks of doorbells indicate that families live above the shops. Start at the recommended Hotel Speronari, formerly a dorm for monks from the church across the street. The classy Vino Vino wine shop next door welcomes tasters (about €2/glass—daily specials posted at the door, Tue–Sat 9:00–19:30, Mon 12:30–20:30, closed Sun). The sign next door—"*L'Ortolan Pusae Vecc de Milan*"—brags in the old Milanese language that this is the oldest fruit and veggie store in the city. The neighboring Princi bakery is understandably popular. Its brioches are rarely more than a few minutes old.

Where Via Speronari hits Via Torino, go 20 yards to the left to find the **Church of Santa Maria presso San Satiro** (Church of St. Mary at St. Satiro) hiding behind its Baroque facade (daily 7:30–11:30 & 15:30–18:00). It was the scene of a temper tantrum in 1242, when a losing gambler vented his anger by hitting the baby Jesus in the Madonna-and-Child altarpiece. Blood "miraculously" spurted out, and the beautiful little church has been on the pilgrimage trail ever since. While I've never seen any blood, I'd swear I've seen a 3-D background behind the basically flat altar (a trompe l'oeil illusion by Bramante). This church—squeezed between the earlier church of San Satiro and a street—had no room for a real apse, so, with the help of math, the Renaissance architect Bramante made what looks like an apse. In the north transept, you'll find that original ninth-century church of San Satiro (brother of St. Ambrogio, patron saint of Milan). This tiny church—with surviving bits of Byzantine fresco—predated the rest. From this chapel, look back at the main altar to see Bramante's 3-D work collapsed. On the opposite side (near entry)—with dimensions mirroring this old chapel—an eight-sided baptistery by Bramante from the 1480s shows the mathematically based values of the Renaissance. If you have a prayer in need of an extra boost, pop a coin into the box and "light" an electric candle.

Pinacoteca Ambrosiana—This oldest museum in Milan was inaugurated in 1618 to house Cardinal Federico Borromeo's painting collection. This prestigious collection includes Leonardo da Vinci's *Portrait of a Musician* and *Codex Atlanticus* (collection of his writings) and the impressive drawing Raphael used as a design for his *School of Athens* in the Vatican, plus minor works by Botticelli, Titian, and Caravaggio (€7.50, €12 combination ticket includes Museo del Duomo and Museo Diocesano, no English descriptions but small English guidebook for €6.20 covers museum's highlights nicely, Tue–Sun 10:00–17:30, last ticket sold at 16:30, closed Mon, a couple of blocks from Piazza Duomo at Piazza Pio XI 2, tel. 02-869-2225).

▲**Brera Art Gallery**—Milan's top collection of Italian paintings (13th–20th centuries) is world class, but it can't top Rome's or Florence's. Established in 1809 to house Napoleon's looted art, it fills the first floor above an art college. On the ground level, wander past the nude *Napoleon* (by Canova) in the courtyard and straight through the art school to a great, cheap cappuccino machine (with all the lingo).

Back in the courtyard, climb the stairway following signs to "Pinacoteca" (€5, more during special exhibits; open Tue–Sun 8:30–19:15, maybe June–Sept Saturdays until 22:30, closed Mon and May 1, last entry 45 min before closing; Via Brera 28, Metro: Lanza; tel. 02-722-631, www.brera.beniculturali.it).

The gallery's highlights include works by Gentile da Fabriano (room IV), the Bellini brothers and Mantegna (his textbook example of feet-first foreshortening, *The Dead Christ,* room VI), Crivelli (for someone new, in room XXI), Raphael (*Wedding of the Madonna,* room XXIV), and Michelangelo Merisi (a.k.a. Caravaggio, *Supper at Emmaus,* room XXIX). Since there are no English descriptions, consider the audio guide (€3.50, or €5.50 for 2 headsets).

▲**Risorgimento Museum**—With a quick 30-minute swing through this quiet, one-floor museum thoughtfully described in English, you'll learn the interesting story of Italy's rocky road to unity: from Napoleon (1796) to the victory in Rome (1870). It's just around the block from the Brera Art Gallery at Via Borgonuovo 23 (free, Tue–Sun 9:00–13:00 & 14:00–17:30, closed Mon, tel. 02-620-854-01, Metro: Montenapoleone).

Poldi Pezzoli Museum—This classy house of art features top Italian paintings of the 15th through the 18th centuries, old weaponry, and lots of interesting decorative arts, such as a roomful of old sundials and compasses (€6; Tue–Sun 10:00–18:00, closed Mon, Easter, Apr 25, May 1, Aug 15; not a word of English but free English audioguides, ID required; Via Manzoni 12, Metro: Montenapoleone; tel. 02-796-334).

Bagatti Valsecchi Museum—This unique 19th-century collection of Italian Renaissance furnishings was assembled by two aristocratic brothers who spent a wad turning their home into a Renaissance mansion.

Museum guards pack flashlights for closer examination of fine wood carvings (€6, half price on Wed; Tue–Sun 13:00–17:45; closed Mon, good English descriptions; Via Santo Spirito 10, Metro: Montenapoleone).

▲**Sforza Castle (Castello Sforzesco)**—The castle of Milan tells the story of the city in brick. Built in the late 1300s as a military fortress, it guarded the gate to the city wall (see the diagram on the flip side of the entry sign) and defended the city from enemies "within and without." It was beefed up by the Sforza duke in 1450 in anticipation of a Venetian attack. Later, it was the Renaissance palace of the Sforza family and even housed their in-house genius, Leonardo. During the centuries of foreign rule (16th–19th), it was a barracks for occupying soldiers. Today, it houses several museums.

This immense, much-bombed-and-rebuilt brick fortress—exhausting at first sight—can only be described as heavy. But its courtyard has a great lawn for picnics and siestas, and its free museum is filled with interesting medieval armor, furniture, early Lombard art, an Egyptian collection, and, most important, Michelangelo's unfinished *Rondanini Pietà*. Michelangelo died while still working on this piece, which hints at the elongation of the Mannerist style that would follow. This is a rare opportunity to enjoy a Michelangelo with no crowds (Tue–Sun 9:00–17:30, closed Mon, confirm location of museums at reception, English info fliers throughout, Metro: Cairoli, tel. 02-8846-3701).

For perhaps the best view in Milan, walk five minutes through the park from the castle to **Branca Tower**. For €3, a lift takes you as high as the Mary crowning the Cathedral (Sat–Sun 10:00–18:00 & 21:30–24:00, Wed–Fri 10:30–12:30, 15:30–18:30, & 21:30–24:00, closed Mon–Tue, trendy bar at ground level). At the far end of the park is the monumental Arco della Pace, a triumphal arch commemorating Napoleon's brief rule over "Italy" before Italy was unified.

Last Supper and Nearby
▲**Leonardo da Vinci's** *Last Supper (Cenacolo)*—You must have a reservation to see this Renaissance masterpiece in the church of Santa Maria delle Grazie. Because of Leonardo's experimental fresco technique, deterioration began within six years of its completion. The church was bombed in World War II, but—miraculously, it seems—the wall holding the *Last Supper* remained standing. The 21-year restoration project (completed in 1999) peeled 500 years of touch-ups away, leaving a faint but vibrant masterpiece. In a big, vacant, whitewashed room, you'll see faded pastels and not a crisp edge. The feet under the table look like negatives. But the composition is dreamy—Leonardo captures the psychological drama as the Lord says, "One of you will betray me," and the apostles huddle in stressed-out groups of three, wondering, "Lord, is it I?" Some are scandalized. Others want more information. Simon (on the

far right) gestures as if to ask a question that has no answer. In this agitated atmosphere, only Judas (fourth from left and the only one with his face in shadow)—clutching his 30 pieces of silver and looking pretty guilty—is not shocked.

The circle meant life and harmony to Leonardo. Deep into a study of how life emanates in circles—like ripples on a pool hit by a pebble—Leonardo positioned the 13 characters in a semicircle. Jesus is in the center, from whence the spiritual force of God emanates.

The room depicted in the painting seems like an architectural extension of the church. The disciples form an apse, with Jesus the altar—in keeping with the Eucharist. Jesus anticipates his sacrifice—his face sad, all-knowing, and accepting. His feet even foreshadowed his crucifixion. Had the door, which was cut out in 1652, not been added, you'd see how Leonardo placed Jesus' feet atop each other, ready for the nail.

The room was a refectory or dining room for the Dominican friars. Traditionally, they'd gather here to eat with a last supper scene on one wall facing a crucifixion scene on the opposite wall.

The perspective is mathematically correct. In fact, restorers found a tiny nail hole in Jesus' right ear, which anchored the strings Leonardo used to establish these lines. The table is cheated out to show the meal. Notice the exquisite lighting. The walls are lined with tapestries (as they would have been) and the one on the right is brighter—to fit the actual lighting in the refectory (with windows on the left). With the extremely natural effect of the light and the drama of the faces, Leonardo created an effective masterpiece.

Reservations are mandatory. To minimize the humidity problem—even though the damage has already been done—25 tourists are allowed in every 15 minutes for exactly 15 minutes. Prior to your appointment time, you wait in several rooms, while doors close behind you and open up slowly in front of you. The information posted on Leonardo is mainly in Italian. For a reservation, call 028-942-1146 (or from the U.S., call 011-39-028-942-1146, number is often busy, keep trying) a minimum of three days in advance for a weekday visit, and at least a week ahead for a weekend visit (booking office open Mon–Fri 9:00–18:00, Sat 9:00–14:00, closed Sun). It's a two-minute process, and you'll hang up with an appointed entry time and a number (€6.50 entry plus €1.50 reservation fee, cash only, pay upon arrival, visits scheduled at 9:30 and 15:30 cost €3.25 extra for guided visit in English.). Long-range planners can book up to three or four months in advance. While "reservations are required," if spots are available (more likely on weekdays and late) you can book one at the desk (even if "Sold Out" sign is posted). If fewer than 25 people show up for a particular time slot, you can get lucky. But those who show up without a reservation generally kill lots of time waiting around. Note that the city bus tour (see "Tours" page 169) includes entry to the *Last Supper*.

Hours of *Last Supper*: Tue–Sun 8:15–18:45 (last visit), July–Sept maybe open Sat until 21:45 (last visit), always closed Mon. You'll be asked to show up 15 minutes before your scheduled time (10 minutes should be enough but if you're a minute late, you get no supper). When an attendant calls your time, get up and move into the next room. Consider the fine €2.50 audioguide (€4.50 with 2 headphones). Its spiel is actually two minutes longer than your allotted visit—so try to start listening just before you enter. You might want to listen to it in the waiting room while studying the reproduction of the actual *Last Supper* there until you're let in. No photos are allowed.

Getting There: Take the Metro to Cadorna (plus a 5-min walk), or hop on tram #24 (catch it just off Piazza Duomo on Via Mazzini in front of Hotel Rio), which drops you off in front of the church. The Science Museum (see below) is two blocks away, and (until 2005) the temporary La Scala Opera House museum is across the street (for details, see "La Scala Opera House," page 176).

▲**Leonardo da Vinci National Science and Technology Museum (Museo Nazionale della Scienza e Tecnica "Leonardo da Vinci")**—The spirit of Leonardo lives here. Most tourists visit for the hall of Leonardo designs illustrated in wooden models, but Leonardo's mind is just as easy to appreciate by paging through a coffee-table edition of his notebooks in any bookstore. The rest of this immense collection of industrial cleverness is fascinating, with planes, trains and automobiles, ships, radios, old musical instruments, computers, batteries, telephones, chunks of the first transatlantic cable, interactive science workshops, and on and on. Some of the best exhibits (such as the Marconi radios) branch off the Leonardo hall. Pick up a museum map from the ticket desk—you'll need it (€6.20; Tue–Fri 9:30–16:50, Sat–Sun 9:30–18:30, closed Mon; Via San Vittore 21, bus #50 from Duomo, or Metro: Sant'Ambrogio; tel. 02-485-551). Complain politely about the lack of English descriptions. There's a great Internet access room off the Leonardo hall (free but available only on weekends).

Away from the Center

Leonardo's Horse—This largest equestrian monument in the world is a modern reconstruction of a model created in 1482 by Leonardo da Vinci for the Sforza family. The model was destroyed in 1499 by invading French forces, who used it for target practice. In 1999, American Renaissance art collector Charles Dent decided to build the statue from Leonardo's design. He presented it to the Italians in appreciation for their role in the Renaissance and in homage to Leonardo's genius. The exhibit, described in English, includes statue casts and photos of the construction (free; daily 9:30–18:30; located on outskirts near Meazza soccer stadium and San Siro racetrack, take tram #24 to Stratico Palatino stop—ask conductor when to get off, then head right on Via Palatino, and left on Piazzale dello Sport to #9).

Soccer—The Milanese claim that their soccer (*football* or *calcio* in Italian) team is the best in Europe. For a dose of Europe's soccer mania (which many believe provides a necessary testosterone vent to keep Europe out of a third big war), catch a match in Milan. Inter and A.C. Milan are the ferociously competitive home teams (tickets-€15–150, A.C. Milan tickets sold at Cariplo banks or through www.acmilan.com, Inter tickets at Banca Popolare di Milano, or visit www.ticketone.it). Games are held in the 85,000-seat Meazza stadium most Sunday afternoons from September to June (Metro: Lotto, or tram #24—just off Piazza del Duomo on Via Mazzini in front of Hotel Rio—directly to stadium, last stop, tel. 02-4870-7123).

WORLD-CLASS WINDOW-SHOPPING

The "Quadrilateral," an elegant, high-fashion shopping area around Via Montenapoleone, is fun for shoppers. Most places close Sunday and for much of August. On Mondays stores open only after 16:00. In this land where fur is still prized, the people-watching is as entertaining as the window-shopping. Notice also the exclusive penthouse apartments with roof gardens high above the scene. Via Montenapoleone and the pedestrianized Via Spiga are the best streets. From La Scala, walk up Via Manzoni to the Metro stop at Montenapoleone, browse down Montenapoleone to Piazza San Babila, then (for less expensive shopping thrills) walk down the pedestrian-only Corso Vittorio Emanuele II to the Duomo. Rinascente is a Nordstrom-type department store with reasonable prices (Mon–Sat 9:00–22:00, Sun 10:00–20:00; good toy selection; faces north side of Duomo on Piazza Duomo) and recommended restaurants (see "Eating," page 186).

NIGHTLIFE

For evening action, check out the arty, student-oriented Brera area in the old center and Milan's formerly bohemian, now gentrified "Little Venice," the Navigli neighborhood (Metro: Porta Genova). Specifics change quickly so it's best to rely on the entertainment information in periodicals from the TI.

SLEEPING

I have tried to minimize traffic noise problems in my listings. All are within a few minutes' walk of Milan's subway system. With Milan's fine Metro, you can get anywhere in town in a flash. Anytime in April, September, October, and November, the city can be completely jammed by conventions, and hotel prices increase by €5 to €60. Summer is usually wide open, though many hotels close in August for vacation. Hotels

SLEEP CODE

(€1 = about $1.10, country code: 39)

Sleep Code: **S** = Single, **D** = Double/Twin, **T** = Triple, **Q** = Quad, **b** = bathroom, **s** = shower only, **no CC** = Credit Cards not accepted, **SE** = Speaks English, **NSE** = No English. You can assume credit cards are accepted unless noted otherwise.

To help you sort easily through these listings, I've divided the rooms into three categories based on the price for a standard double room with bath:

    $$$ **Higher Priced**—Most rooms €150 or more.
     $$ **Moderately Priced**—Most rooms between €110-150
      $ **Lower Priced**—Most rooms €110 or less.

cater more to business travelers than to tourists. Everyone speaks at least some English.

Near the Duomo

The Duomo area is thick with people-watching, reasonable eateries, and the major sightseeing attractions. From the central train station to the Duomo, it's just four stops on a direct Metro line (yellow line 3, direction S. Donato) to Metro: Duomo.

$$$ Hotel Grand Duca di York, with 33 pleasant rooms and lavish public spaces, is oddly stuck in the middle of banks and big-city starkness three blocks southwest of Piazza Duomo (Sb-€102, Db-€160, Tb-€185, some rooms with balconies for no extra charge, includes breakfast; air-con, elevator, closed Aug; near Metro stops: Piazza Cordusio or Duomo, Via Moneta 1/A; tel. 02-874-863, fax 02-869-0344, SE).

$$$ Hotel Spadari is for art-lovers. Its Art Deco interior is designed by the Milanese artist Gio Pomodoro (Joe Tomato in English). The 40 rooms have billowing drapes, big paintings, and designer doors. It's next door to the recommended Peck deli (see below), and two blocks from the Duomo (standard Db-€217–281, no need for pricier suites, includes breakfast, Via Spadari 11, tel. 02-7200-2371, fax 02-861-184, www.spadarihotel.com, reservation@spadarihotel.com).

$$ Hotel Gritti, facing a peaceful square just off Via Torino, is a bright, classy, professionally run three-star hotel that comes with 48 comfortable rooms and a big, sleepy dog, Boris III. Run by a jolly trio of English-speaking gentlemen (Mario, Bruno, and Evandro), Hotel Gritti feels like home in a hurry (Sb-€99, Db-€142, Tb-€199, includes a sad little breakfast, same price all seasons, family deals, CC but 10 percent

Milan's Center

1 Hotel Grand
  Duca di York
2 Hotel Spadari & Peck Deli
3 Hotel Gritti
4 Hotel Santa Marta
5 Hotel Speronari & Princi Bakery
6 Hotel Nuovo
7 Hotel Star
8 London Hotel
9 Antica Locanda dei Mercanti
10 Trattoria Milanese
11 Ristorante Bruno
12 Ristorante al Mercante
13 Pizzeria Ristorante
   al 50 da Geggio
14 La Rinascente Bistrot & Brunch

15 Latteria Rest.
   & Pizzeria Calafuria Unione
16 Pastarito Pizzarito
17 Ristorante/Pizzeria Al Dollaro
18 Luini Panzerotti
19 Agnello Pizzeria
20 Ciao Cafeteria (2 locations)
21 Odeon Gelateria
22 Standa Supermarket
23 Bar Zucca, McDonald's,
   Taurus mosaic
24 Elevator to Duomo roof
25 Stairs to Duomo roof
26 Pinacoteca Ambrosiana (museum)

off with cash; open year-round, air-con, some smoky rooms, rooms off the square are quieter, elevator; 2 blocks southwest of Piazza Duomo, Piazza S. Maria Beltrade 4; tel. 02-801-056, fax 02-8901-0999, www .hotelgritti.com, hotel.gritti@iol.it).

$$ Hotel Santa Marta, a shiny little hotel on a small street, has 15 fresh, tranquil, and spacious rooms (Db-€135 most of year but €186 during conventions and as low as €100, includes breakfast, air-con, elevator, closed Aug, Via Santa Marta 4, tel. 02-804-567, fax 02-8645-2661, www.hotel-santamarta.it, info@hotel-santamarta.it).

$ Hotel Speronari is well located, with 32 bright, clean rooms on a great pedestrian street full of delis and food shops. Enjoy a free cappuccino upon arrival. For an elevator, air-conditioning, and more comfort, choose a more expensive hotel; this is a very simple, friendly, and cheap one-star hotel (S-€50, Ss-€62, D-€76, Db-€96, T-€88, Tb-€130, Qb-€145, these prices promised through 2004 with this book—mention it when you reserve, CC but €3 off per person per night if you pay cash; lots of stairs, no breakfast, ceiling fans; 200 yards off Piazza Duomo, Via Speronari 4; tel. 02-8646-1125, fax 02-7200-3178, hotelsperonari@inwind.it, run by the friendly Isoni family: father Paolo and Gianpaolo, Maurizio, Carla, and Adam). If you're flying out of Malpensa Airport, Maurizio drives you there, beating the €80 taxi fare (2 people-€60, 3 people-€65, 4 people-€70).

$ Hotel Nuovo, with 36 fine, smallish rooms and a lukewarm reception, is central on a noisy square east of the Duomo near a pedestrian street (S-€34, D-€52, Db-€83–105, Tb-€108–135, no breakfast, some air-con, request the third floor for less noise, no public space, Piazza Beccaria 6, tel. 02-8646-4444, fax 02-7200-1752).

Between La Scala and Sforza Castle

$$$ Hotel Star is a comfortable, modern, 30-room place with fancy plumbing and, more important, a helpful staff (Sb-€110, Db-€155, includes big breakfast, closed Aug, air-con, fridge, Via dei Bossi 5, tel. 02-801-501, fax 02-861-787, www.hotelstar.it, reception@hotelstar.it).

$$ London Hotel, a 30-room hotel with all the comforts, is warmly run by the friendly Gambino family (S-€80, Sb-€92, D-€120, Db-€140, Tb-€180, breakfast-€8, cheaper in July and maybe closed Aug, CC but 10 percent off with cash except during special events; air-con, elevator; near Metro: Cairoli at Via Rovello 3, on relatively quiet side street; tel. 02-7202-0166, fax 02-805-7037, www.traveleurope.it/hotellondon.htm, hotel.london@traveleurope.it, Tanya and Licia SE).

$$ Antica Locanda dei Mercanti feels like a library in heaven, well-located and seriously quiet (no TVs, lots of books). It lacks public spaces and a breakfast area but comes with fresh flowers in each of its 20 rooms, some with rare wall to wall carpeting, others with Venetian marble floors (standard Db-€130, master Db-€150–160, Db with air-con and garden terrace–€250, optional €9 breakfast served in room, no CC except to hold room; fans, elevator, no young children; Via San Tomaso 6, second floor, no sign—only a name on doorbell, Metro: Cordusio; tel. 02-805-4080, fax 02-805-4090, www.locanda.it, locanda@locanda.it).

Near the Train Station

If you like to drop your bag near the station, this is a handy, if dreary, area. The neighborhood between the train station and Corso Buenos Aires, in spite of its shady characters in the park and its 55-year-old prostitutes after dark, is reasonably safe. Many soulless business hotels have desperately discounted prices for those who drop in during slow times. Just walk down Via Scarlatti (leave the station's upper hall—with your back to the tracks—to the left).

Here are some decent options:

$ **"The Best" Hotel,** a five-minute walk from the station, rents 25 rooms (Sb–€75, Db–€110, includes breakfast, Via B. Marcello 83, tel. 02-2940-4757 fax 02-201-966, thebesthotel@tiscalinet.it, helpful Filippo and Riccardo SE).

$ **Hotel Andreola Central** is a four-star business hotel with occasional door-breaker prices (e.g., Db–€99 on weekends instead of mid-week €362 rate, Via Scarlatti 24, tel. 02-670-9141).

$ **Hotel Valley** is family-run, small, dark, and inexpensive (Db–€72–83, Via Soperga 19, tel. 02-669-2777, fax 02-6698-7252, hotelvalley@virgilio.it).

EATING

This is a fast-food city, but fast food in a fashion capital isn't a burger and fries. The bars, delis, *rosticcerie,* and self-service cafeterias cater to people with plenty of taste and more money than time. You'll find delightful eateries all over town (but many close in Aug for vacation).

I found the price between basic and classy restaurants was negligible (e.g., pastas–€7–10, *secondi*–€8–12, cover–€1–2), so it is worth springing for the places giving the best experience. To eat mediocre food on a famous street with great people-watching, choose an eatery on the pedestrian-only Via Mercanti or Via Dante. To eat with students in trendy little trattorias, explore the Brera neighborhood. To eat well near the Duomo, consider the recommended places below.

Locals like to precede a lunch or dinner with an aperitif (Campari made its debut in Milan). Bars fill their counters with inviting baskets of munchies, which are served free with these drinks. A cheap drink (if you're either likable or discreet) can become a light meal.

Breakfast is a bad value in hotels and fun in bars. It's OK to quasi-picnic. Bring in a banana (or whatever) and order a toasted ham-and-cheese sandwich (called and pronounced *tost*) or croissant (called *brioche*) with your cappuccino.

MILANESE SPECIALTIES

Milan's signature dishes (often served together as a *piatto unico* or single dish) are *risotto alla Milanese* and *ossobuco*. The risotto is flavored with saffron, which gives it its intense yellow color. It's said that a 16th-century Belgian glass worker first stumbled on the use of saffron as a spice. Initially, he used saffron to tint the glass mixture he used to complete the stained glass windows of the Duomo in 1574. His master joked that he'd end up adding the precious spice to his food as well. On the day of his master's daughter's wedding, the glassworker persuaded the chef to add saffron to the rice cooked for the reception. After the guests got over their initial surprise, the dish was a great success, and has been a staple on Milan's menus ever since. The subtle flavor of the saffron pairs nicely with the *ossobuco* (meaning 'hole in the bone' of the veal shank). The prized marrow is extracted with special little forks and considered the best part of the meal.

Eating Classy near the Duomo

Trattoria Milanese, a classy family-run place, is a splurge (€30 fixed-price *menu* at lunch, à la carte available). It has an enthusiastic and local clientele; the restaurant didn't even bother to get a phone until 1988. Expect a Milanese ambience and quality traditional cuisine (Wed–Mon 12:30–15:00 & 19:30–23:00, closed Tue and mid-July–Aug; air-con; Via Santa Marta 11, 5-min walk from Duomo, near Pinacoteca Ambrosiana; tel. 02-8645-1991).

Ristorante Bruno serves Tuscan cuisine with dressy waiters, hearty food, inexpensive desserts, and a fine antipasto buffet (a plate full of Tuscan specialties for €7). You can eat inside or on the sidewalk under fascist columns (Sun–Fri 12:00–14:45 & 19:00–22:45, closed Sat and Aug, moderate prices, air-con, Via M. Gonzaga 6, reservations wise, tel. 02-804-364).

Ristorante al Mercante is *the* place to dine elegantly inside or outside under historic arches in a peaceful square a block from the cathedral. It's pretty touristy and you'll pay extra for the location, but the food is very good. Make a meal out of their extensive antipasto buffet featuring fresh sliced prosciutto, *mozzarella di bufala*, grilled and marinated vegetables, and more for €6–13 (moderately expensive, €18 *secondi*; Mon–Sat 12:00–14:30 & 19:00–22:30, closed Sun; reservations wise; near Piazza Cordusio at Piazza Mercanti 17, follow Via Mercanti away from the Duomo and turn left just after passing the covered market square; tel. 02-805-2198).

Pizzeria Ristorante al 50 da Geggio is a friendly and bustling little favorite packed with locals eating delicious Tuscan food under fans (Wed–Mon 12:15–14:30 & 19:15–23:00, closed Tue and Aug, moderate prices, good daily specials, Via Torino 50, tel. 02-8645-2244).

The seventh floor of the big department store **La Rinascente,** alongside the Duomo, has three rooftop eateries (and a free WC, follow signs from the escalator to the left to *i servizi*), each with a terrace overlooking the ornate top of the cathedral (terrace dining only May–Sept): **Bistrot** is a dressy restaurant serving modern Mediterranean cuisine (5-course tasting menu-€62, Tue–Sat 12:00–14:30 & 19:30–22:00, Mon 19:30–22:00, closed Sun, tel. 02-877-120). The **Brunch** is a cafeteria with a much simpler, cheaper menu (Mon–Sat 12:00–15:30 full menu served at lunch, pizzas only from 18:00–22:00, Sun 12:00–15:30). Anyone can pop up to the **bar** for a look at the cathedral. While you can go through the department store taking escalators, a side entrance (on the Galleria Vittorio Emanuele side) has a direct elevator to the sixth floor, where you can ride the escalator to the seventh.

Eating Simple near the Duomo

See **La Rinascente**, above, for its Brunch cafeteria and bar with a view, next to the Duomo.

Latteria Cucina Vegetariana serves a good vegetarian Italian lunch. This busy joint is actually a tiny grocery store overrun with dining tables, where local workers enjoy soup, salads, pasta dishes, and affordable prices (€5–15 meals; Mon–Sat 11:30–16:30, closed Sun; just off Via Torino at Via dell' Unione 6, 2 blocks southwest of Duomo; tel. 02-874-401).

Pastarito Pizzarito is a pasta-and-pizza chain with a wonderful formula. In a bright atmosphere under literal walls of pasta, you can choose from 10 fresh pastas and lots of sauces to create a huge dish (€4.50–9.90); splitting is welcome. Pizzas run €5–10 (daily 12:00–14:30 & 19:30–23:30; air-con; 4 blocks from Duomo, a block behind opera house at Via Verdi 6; tel. 02-862-210).

Ristorante Pizzeria Calafuria Unione serves tasty €5–9 pizzas and €5–10 pastas in a non-smoking room (Mon–Sat 11:00–15:00 & 19:00–24:00, closed Sun and Aug; near where Via Falcone hits Via dell' Unione at Via dell' Unione 8, 2 blocks southwest of Duomo; tel. 02-866-103).

Ristorante/Pizzeria Al Dollaro is a mod, happy place with well-fed locals (Mon–Fri 12:00–16:00 & 18:00–23:00, closed Sat at lunch and all day Sun and Aug, air-con, smoke-free section, 4 blocks south of Duomo at Via Paolo da Cannobio 11, tel. 02-869-2432).

Luini Panzerotti serves up piping hot mini-calzones (called *panzerotti*) stuffed with mozzarella, tomatoes, ham, or whatever for €4–5. From the back of the Duomo, head north and look for the lines of hungry locals out front (Tue–Sat 10:00–20:00, Mon 10:00–15:00, closed Sun and Aug, Via S. Radegonda 16, tel. 02-8646-1917).

Agnello Pizzeria, less than a block off Piazza del Duomo, makes made-to-order pizzas and fresh pastas for reasonable prices (daily 12:00–14:30 & 19:00–23:00, Sun pizzas only, closed Aug, Via Agnello 8, tel. 02-8646-1654).

Ciao, a self-service cafeteria, offers a low-stress, affordable meal on Piazza Duomo (daily 11:30–23:00, next to TI, on second floor, inexpensive pasta and good salad bar, easy public WC). Bring your tray upstairs to the top terrace floor for views of the Duomo and Square.

Ristorante Rita, a block behind Ciao, is a classier budget option without the Italian fast food feel. While the downstairs has a take-out place, there's a sleek modern restaurant upstairs with a fine antipasti bar offering a small plate (with bread and water that come with the cover charge) for €5 (daily, Via Marconi between Piazza Duomo and Piazza Diaz, tel. 02-8699-7387).

Fast-food cheapskates enjoy the best people-watching in Milan inside the Galleria at **McDonald's** (salad/pasta plate and tall orange juice for €5).

Floodlit Mary gazes down from the top of the Duomo on the **Odeon Gelateria** for good reason (next to McDonald's on Piazza Duomo, on the far side of square opposite facade of the Duomo, open nightly until 2:00).

Picnics near the Duomo

For a fun adventure, assemble an elegant dinner **picnic** by hitting the colorful deli, cheese, and produce shops on Via Speronari. The **Princi bakery** is mobbed with locals vying for focaccia, olive breadsticks, and luscious pastries. At the small bar in the back, you get free, fresh munchies with your drink or you can try a cheap meal (about €5 per plate, 12:00–14:00 only, pay cashier first; bakery open Mon–Sat 7:00–20:00, closed Sun; on Via Speronari, off Via Torino, a block southwest of Piazza Duomo).

Peck is an aristocratic deli with a fancy coffee/pastry/gelato shop upstairs, a gourmet grocery and *rosticceria* on the main level, and an *enoteca* wine cellar in the basement (Mon 15:00–19:30, Tue–Sat 8:45–19:30, closed Sun, Via Spadari 9). The *rosticceria* serves fancy food to go for a superb picnic dinner in your hotel. It's delectable, beautiful, sold by weight (order by the *etto*—100-gram unit—about a quarter pound), and not cheap. Try the risotto.

The **Standa Superfresco supermarket** is within a few blocks of the Duomo (Mon–Sat 8:00–20:30, Sun 9:00–20:00; small deli on ground level, big supermarket in basement; on Via Torino, at intersection with San Maurilio).

Eating near Sforza Castle

Le Briciole Pizzeria draws a local crowd for its good prices, pizza, and varied meat dishes; it's packed by 21:00, go earlier (Tue–Fri and Sun 12:15–14:30 & 19:15–23:30, Sat 19:15–23:30, closed Mon and Aug; smoke-free dining room; Via Camperio 17, a block in front of castle, on small street at end of Via Dante; tel. 02-877-185).

Garbagnati is a tasty self-service cafeteria on Via Dante 13, a couple of blocks in front of the castle (daily 12:00–15:00 only, snacks otherwise, tel. 02-8646-0672; a smaller Garbagnati, with sweets and no seats, is near the Peck deli at Via Hugo 3, tel. 02-860-905).

Another **Ciao** Autogrill cafeteria is on Via Dante, just off Piazza Cordusio, with outdoor seating on the pedestrian-only street (daily 11:30–22:30).

Eating near the Brera Art Gallery

The Brera neighborhood surrounding the Church of St. Carmine is laced with narrow, inviting pedestrian streets. Find your own *ristorante* or consider **Al Pozzo**, which offers Tuscan cuisine (Tue–Fri and Sun 12:00–14:30 & 19:00–23:30, Sat 19:00–23:30, closed Mon, Via S. Carpoforo 7, tel. 02-877-775). **Bar Brera**, across the street from the Brera Art Gallery, creates dozens of made-to-order €4.70 sandwiches for throngs of art students (daily 6:00–2:00, Via Brera 23, tel. 02-877-091). **Caffè Vecchia Brera** serves up tempting sandwiches and savory and sweet crêpes from €4–7 (Mon–Sat 8:00–2:00, closed Sun, Via dell'Orso 20, tel. 02-8646-1695).

Eating Cheap near Montenapoleone

For inexpensive, healthy food near the classy shopping street, **Brek** cafeterias are good. One Brek is near one end of Montenapoleone (daily 11:30–15:00 & 18:30–22:30; Via dell' Annunciata 2, 2 blocks from Montenapoleone; tel. 02-653-619), and another is near the other end, a half block off Piazza San Babila (daily 11:30–15:00 & 18:30–22:30; Piazza Giordano 1: on Piazza Babila, with back to "egg monument" and facing fountain, Brek is through arch in building on right; tel. 02-7602-3379).

Eating near the Train Station

Again, it's **Brek**, for better food than you'll find at the station (Mon–Sat 11:30–15:00 & 18:30–22:30, closed Sun; with back to tracks, exit station to left, it's within a block; Via Lepetit 20, tel. 02-670-5149).

TRANSPORTATION CONNECTIONS

By train to: Venice (departures :05 after each hour, 3 hrs), **Florence** (hrly, 3 hrs, also check schedule for trains going to Rome and Naples—these stop in Florence), **Genoa** (hrly, 2 hrs), **Rome** (hrly, 4.5 hrs), **Brindisi** (3/day, 9–12 hrs), **Cinque Terre** (hrly, 2 hrs to Genoa, then hrly, 2 hrs to Monterosso, some direct trains to Monterosso; trains from La Spezia to the villages go nearly hourly), **Varenna** on Lake Como (small line to Lecco/Sondrio/Tirano leaves about every 2 hrs for the 1-hr trip to Varenna, roughly 8:15, 9:15, 12:15, 14:15, 16:15, 17:05, 18:00, 19:10, and 20:15), **Stresa** (hrly, 50–75 min, faster trains require reservations; trains going to Domodossola and some international destinations stop at Stresa), **Como** (around :25 after each hour, 30 min, ferries go from Como to Varenna until 19:00).

International destinations: Amsterdam (4/day, 14 hrs, changes required), **Barcelona** (1/day with no changes, 13 hours, or several with 2–5 changes, 12–17 hrs—before paying extra for Pablo Casals express, consider flying), **Bern** (7/day with change in Brig, 3–4 hrs), **Frankfurt** (5/day, 9 hrs), **London** (4/day, 12–18 hrs), **Munich** (5/day, 8 hrs), **Nice** (5/day, 6–10 hrs), **Paris** (4/day, 7 hrs), **Lyon** (3/day, 6 hrs), **Vienna** (4/day, 11–14 hrs).

Milan's Airports

To get flight information for either airport or the current phone number of your airline, call 02-74851 or 02-7485-2200.

Malpensa: Most international flights land at the manageable Malpensa Airport, 28 miles northwest of Milan. Customs guards fan you through, and even the sniffing dog seems friendly. You'll most likely land at Terminal 1 (international flights) rather than Terminal 2 (charter flights); buses connect the two. Both have cash machines (at Terminal 1, near exit 4 at Banca Nazionale del Lavoro), banks, and change offices. Terminal 1 has a pharmacy, eateries, and a hotel reservation service disguised as a TI (daily 8:00–21:00; when you exit the baggage-carousel area, go right to reach services and exit; tel. 02-5858-0080 or 02-5858-0230). At the *tabacchi* shop, buy a phone card and confirm your hotel reservation.

You have three easy ways to get to downtown Milan: by train, shuttle bus, or taxi.

The Malpensa Express **train** zips between Malpensa Airport and Milan's Cadorna station, which is both a Metro stop and a small train station, closer to the Duomo than the central train station (€9, sometimes discounted to €6 for Alitalia passengers; 40 min, 2/hr; departing airport at :15 and :45 past the hour from 6:00–1:30, departing Cadorna at :20 and :50 past the hour, runs 5:00–23:10, not covered by railpasses; tel. 02-27763 or 02-20222, www.ferrovienord.it/webmxp/). At the airport, follow signs (*Treni* and Malpensa Express) down the stairs; you'll go through a glass tunnel to the ticket office. After buying your ticket, take the ramp down to the tracks. If you're leaving Milan to go to the airport, take the Metro to the Cadorna stop, surface, and buy a ticket at the Malpensa Express office in the station or from ticket windows in front of track 8. Purchase your ticket before you board, or you'll pay €2.50 extra to buy it on the train. Note that some very early and late departures from Cadorna are by bus—ask when you buy your ticket. If your departure is by bus, the stop is outside the station; head left as you exit and the stop is 50 yards to the left on Via Paleocapa.

Two companies run **buses** between Malpensa Airport and Milan's central train station. The buses are virtually identical in everything except price, using the same departure points: in front of the airport (outside exit 5, stops 2 and 3) and from Piazza Luigi di Savoia at the east side of the train station. Buy your ticket from the driver for the 50-minute trip. Each company's buses depart every 20 to 30 minutes, but because the schedules are generally staggered, you'll find buses running every 10 to 15 minutes. The cheaper Malpensa Shuttle bus costs €4.50 (runs from station 4:30–22:30, from airport 6:40–0:15, at airport buy ticket on bus or at Airport 2000 office between exits 5 and 6, catch bus at exit 5, tel. 02-5858-3185, www.malpensa-shuttle.com). The Malpensa Bus Express costs €5 (from station 5:10–22:30, from airport 6:30–23:50, catch bus at exit 6, pay driver).

Taxis into Milan cost up to €80 (insist on meter, you'll pay supplements on Sun, holidays; avoid hustlers in airport halls; catch outside exit 6).

To **sleep** near Malpensa, consider **Hotel Cervo**, which offers newly renovated rooms and transport to and from the nearby airport for €3/person (Sb-€62, Db-€93; air-con, restaurant Mon–Fri, parking; Via de Pinedo 1, Somma Lombardo, Malpensa; tel. 0331-230-821, fax 0331-230-156, www.hotelcervo.it, hotelcervo@malpensa.it).

Linate: Most European flights fly into Linate, five miles east of Milan. The airport has a bank (just past customs, decent rates) and a TI (Mon–Sat 8:00–21:00, Sun 10:00–18:00, tel. 02-7020-0443). Linate is linked by STAM buses with the central train station. At the airport, catch the bus outside the arrivals hall; at the train station, catch it from Piazza Luigi di Savoia on the east side of the station (buy €2 tickets from driver, 2/hr; bus runs from station 5:35–21:35, from airport 4:30–21:35; in general buses leave at :05 and :35 after the hour in either direction; tel. 02-717-106). From the station, take the Metro or a taxi to your hotel. Taxis from Linate to the Duomo cost about €18.

Between Malpensa and Linate: The Malpensa Shuttle company runs a bus between the airports every 90 minutes (€7.75, runs 6:00–20:00, 75 min, catch bus outside exit 4, stops 20 and 21, buy tickets from Thomas Cooke or Airport 2000 offices).

Near Milan: Stresa, Borromeo Islands, and Lake Maggiore

Lake Maggiore is ringed by mountains, snow-capped in spring and fall, and lined with resort towns such as Stresa. While crassly touristic, the town of Stresa is a handy base from which to explore the exotic garden

Stresa and Borromeo Islands

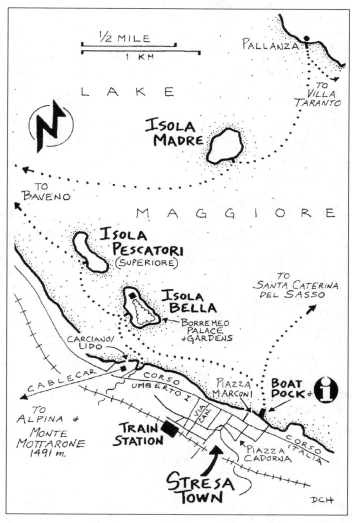

islands of Lake Maggiore. And many consider it a pleasant last stop before flying home from nearby Malpensa Airport near Milan.

A stop in this region is worth the trouble for its two islands—each with exotic gardens and Borromeo family villas. The Borromeo family—over many generations since 1630—lovingly turned their islands into magical retreats with elaborate villas and fragrant gardens. Isola Bella has the palace and terraced garden; Isola Madre has a villa and sprawling English-style (rougher) garden. A third island, Isola Pescatori, is simply small, serene, and residential. The Borromeos, who made their money from banking and trading, enjoyed the arts—from paintings (hung in lavish abundance throughout the palace and villa) to plays (performed in an open-air theater on Isola Bella) and marionette shows (you'll see the puppets that performed here).

Tourists flock to the lakes in May and June, when flowers are in bloom, and in September. Concerts held in scenic settings draw music-lovers, particularly during the Musical Weeks in August (concert schedule in English at www.stresa.net/settimanemusicali). For fewer crowds, visit in April, July, and August (when Italians prefer the Mediterranean beaches), and October. In winter, the snow-covered mountains (with resorts a 90-minute drive away) attract skiers.

Planning Your Time

This region is best visited on a sunny day, when the mountains are clear, the lake is calm, and the heat of the sun brings out the scent of the blossoms. The two top islands for sightseeing are Isola Bella and Isola Madre. Isola Pescatori has no sights but is a peaceful place for lunch.

Day trip from Milan: Catch an early train from Milan; there are two 50-min fast trains, leaving at 8:10 and 11:10, each requiring a seat reservation, which can be purchased when you buy your ticket. In Stresa, walk 10 minutes downhill to the boat dock, and catch a boat to Isola Madre first. Then work your way back to Isola Pescatori for a lazy lunch and Isola Bella for the afternoon before returning to the town of Stresa.

Overnight: Small, touristy Stresa makes a fine first or last stop in Italy, because its connections with Milan's airport, which is located about halfway between Stresa and Milan, don't involve a transfer in big Milan (see "Transportation Connections," page 200).

Stresa

Stresa—which means "thin stretch"—was named for the original strip of fishermen's huts that lined the shore. Today grand old hotels run along the shore. The old town—basically a traffic-free shopping mall—is just a few blocks deep, stretching inland from the main boat dock. A fine waterfront promenade leads past the venerable old hotels to the Lido (with the Carciano boat dock and a mountain cable car). Stresa's stately 19th-century lakeside hotels date back to the days when this town was on the "grand tour" circuit. In any grand-tour resort like Stresa, hotels had names designed to appeal to Victorian aristocrats...like Palace (rather than Palazzo), Astoria, Bristol, and Victoria.

Nineteen-year-old Ernest Hemingway first came here in 1918. Wounded as an ambulance driver for the Italian Red Cross, he was taken to the Grand Hotel des Lles Borromees. It was the first hotel on the shore (1862), and served—like its regal neighbors—as an infirmary during World War I. Hemingway returned to the same hotel in 1948, stayed in the same room (#205, now called the Hemingway suite, which rents for a couple of thousand dollars a night), and signed the guest book as "an old client." Another "old client" was Winston Churchill, who honeymooned here.

ORIENTATION

Arrival in Stresa: At the train station, ask for a free city map at the newsstand (marked *Libri Giornali Riviste*). To get downtown, exit right from the station and take your first left (on Viale Duchessa di Genova). This takes you straight down to the lake (the boat dock is about 4 blocks to your right; ask for a boat schedule at the ticket window). The TI is next door on the same dock. Taxis charge a fixed rate of €7 for even the shortest ride in town.

Tourist Information: The helpful TI, located to the right of the ticket window at the boat dock, gives out free maps and boat schedules (daily in summer 10:00–12:30 & 15:00–18:30, in winter Mon–Fri 10:00–12:30 & 15:00–18:30, Sat 10:00–12:30, closed Sun, Piazza Marconi 16, tel. 0323-30150, www.distrettolaghi.it).

Internet Access: The **New Data Internet Point** is a block off Piazza Cadorna in the old center (€3/30 min, Mon–Sat 9:00–12:30 & 15:00–19:00, Sun 15:00–19:00, Via de Vit 15A).

Getting around Lake Maggiore

Boats link the islands and Stresa, running about twice hourly. Allow roughly 10 minutes between stops. Short hops cost €3. It's simplest to get a day pass: €6 for two islands (Bella and Pescatori); €10 for all the islands, Pallanza (a town on the opposite shore), and Villa Taranto.

If you're planning to tour Isola Bella and Isola Madre, you'll save a couple euros if, when you buy your boat pass, you ask to include the admission fee *(ingresso)* to the sights. The ticket office might not display a sign advising you of this opportunity—you need to ask.

Boats run daily from March through October. The map in this chapter (on page 193) shows the route: Stresa, Carciano/Lido, Isola Bella, Isola Pescatori, Baveno (lakeside town), Isola Madre, Pallanza, and Villa Taranto. This route is part of a longer one. To follow the boat schedule (free, available at boat docks, TI, and maybe your hotel), look at the Arona–Locarno timetable for trips from Stresa to the islands, and the Locarno–Arona timetable for the return trip to Stresa.

Buy boat tickets directly from the dock ticket booth. Private taxi boat drivers and their little sales booths will try to talk you into paying way too much (boat info: tel. 800-551-801).

SIGHTS

Islands and Gardens

▲▲**Isola Bella**—This island, nearest Stresa, has the formal garden and the fanciest Baroque palace. The island was named by Charles Borromeo for his wife, Isabella. The island itself is touristy, with a gauntlet of souvenir stands and a corral of restaurants. A few back streets provide evidence that people actually live here. While the Borromeo family now lives in Milan, they spend a few weeks each summer here (when their blue-and-red family flag flies from the top of the garden).

Your visit is a one-way tour starting with the palace, finishing with the garden. (There's no way to see the garden without the palace.) In the lavishly decorated Baroque palace, stairs lead to stucco crests of Italy's top families (balls signify the Medici, bees mean the Barberini, and a unicorn the family motto: humility for the Borromeo). The next room shows a portrait of the first Borromeo. The richly stuccoed grand hall, with its 80-foot-high dome, features an 18th-century model of the villa, which includes a grand entry that never materialized. Next, the room with the musical instruments was the site of the 1935 Stresa Conference, in which Mussolini met with British and French diplomats in an attempt to scare Germany out of starting World War II. This "Stresa Front" soon fizzled when Mussolini attacked Ethiopia and joined forces with Hitler. A photocopy of the treaty with Mussolini's signature is on the wall. Napoleon's bedroom comes with an engraving showing his 1797 visit. (Napoleon is on a bench with his wife and sister enjoying festivities in his honor.) The last rooms display souvenirs and gifts that the Borromeo family picked up over the generations.

Downstairs, the 18th-century grotto, decorated from ceiling to floor with shell motifs and black-and-white stones, still serves its original function of providing a cool refuge from Italy's heat. Many of the famous Borromeo marionettes are on display here—with fine details, from beautiful to grotesque. (A larger collection is on Isola Madre.) The dreamy marble statues are by Gaetano Monti, a student of Canova. Climbing out of the basement, look up at the unique cantilevered stairs; they're from a 16th-century fortress that predates this building.

The ornate hall of 16th-century Flemish tapestries leads to the finale of this island visit, the garden, complete with Chinese white peacocks to give it all an exotic splash. Baroque—which is exactly what you see here—is all about controlling nature. The terraced gardens, which give the island the look of a stepped pyramid from the water, are crowned by the Borromeo family unicorn.

A fine €2.50 audioguide describes the villa (admission for the palace and garden €8.50, April–mid-Oct daily 9:00–12:30 & 13:30–18:30, last entry 1 hour before closing, English descriptions in palace, WC at entrance to garden, tel. 0323-30556). Note there are two docks on this island (one for each direction). Departure times are indicated by clocks at each dock. Picnicking is not allowed in the garden, but you can picnic at the point of the island (free and open to the public); take the mosaic sidewalk to the left of the palace entrance.

▲Isola Pescatori—This sleepy island—home to 35 families—is the smallest and most residential of the three. It has a couple of good seafood restaurants, picnic benches, views, and blissfully nothing to do—under arbors of wisteria. It's never really crowded and a delight for photographers and painters.

▲▲Isola Madre—Don't come here unless you intend to tour the sight, because that's all there is here: an interesting, furnished villa and a lovely garden filled with exotic birds and plants. Your visit is a one-way affair, starting with a long stroll through the garden and finishing with the villa. Eight gardeners with the help of water continually pumped from the lake keep this English-style garden paradise lush and a joy even for those bored by gardens. You'll see trees from around the world, a menagerie, and exotic silver pheasants. In front of the villa, a magnificent Himalayan cypress tree paints your world a streaky green. The 16th-century villa is the first of the Borromeo palaces. A century older than the other, it's dark, somber and Renaissance. The clever angled hinges keep the doors from flapping in the lake breeze. The family's huge collection of dolls, marionettes, and exquisite 17th-century marionette theater sets—painted by a famous La Scala opera set designer—fill several rooms. A corner room is painted to take you into an 18th-century Venetian Rococo sitting room under a floral green house. You'll see some of the garden's best flowers immediately after leaving the villa.

The sightseeing route is clearly signed for you, taking you through the gardens and villa, and ending at the chapel (€8, daily 9:00–18:30, no photos in villa, WC next to chapel, tel. 0323-31261). The €2.50 audioguide here is devoted almost entirely to the garden—a good investment to properly appreciate the plantings. While eating is best on Isola Pescatori, Isola Madre has one eatery: La Piratera Ristorante Bar (€18 tourist *menu*, daily 8:00–17:30, sit-down meals and simple sandwiches to go, picnic at rocky beach a minute's walk from restaurant).

▲Villa Taranto Botanical Gardens—Garden-lovers will enjoy this large landscaped park, located (across the lake from Stresa) on the mainland a 10-minute boat ride beyond Isola Madre. The gardens are a Scotsman's labor of love. Starting in the 1930s, Neil MacEacharn created this garden of delights—bringing in thousands of plants from all over the world—and here he stays, in the small mausoleum. The park's highlight is the terraced garden with a series of cascading pools. Villa Taranto is directly across the street from the boat dock (€7, April–Oct daily 8:30–19:30, ticket office closes at 18:30, tel. 0323-404-555).

Mountain Cable Car—From Stresa's Lido, a cable car takes you up—in two stages and a 20-minute ride—to the top of Mount Mottarone (about 5,000 feet). From here, you get great views of neighboring peaks and, by taking a short hike, a bird's-eye view of the small, neighboring Lake Orta. The cable-car runs April through October (daily 9:10–12:00 & 14:00–17:30, 3/hour, €11, one-way €7, tel. 0323-30295).

To visit the Alpine Gardens, get off at the midway Alpina stop, where a 10-minute walk leads to the gardens (€1.50, April–mid-Oct Tue–Sun 9:00–18:00, closed Mon, turn left as you leave). The gardens come with great lake views and picnic spots but can't compare to what you'll see on the islands.

If hiking down, bring a good map and allow 3.5 hours from the top of Mount Mottarone, or 1.5 hours from Alpine Gardens.

You can rent a bike at the base of the cable-car lift (full-suspension mountain bike-€26/day, €21/half day, regular bikes about €5 less, helmets, tel. 0323-30295) and bring it on the cable car with you (€5.50–9.20 extra). It's a treacherous ride, enjoyable only for serious bikers. While the ride is nice on top, you'll fight traffic on congested, rough, and windy roads for the rest of the trip.

Day Trips from Stresa

▲**Scenic Boat and Rail Trip to Locarno and Centovalli**—An enjoyable all-day excursion from Stresa involves three segments. Take the boat from Stresa to the end of Lake Maggiore past loads of small lakeside hamlets to Locarno, in the Italian-speaking Swiss canton of Ticino (bring your passport). Spend an hour or so exploring this lakeside town. Then catch the "Centovalli" train from Locarno for a 90-minute ride that links together remote mountain villages, as you return to Italy and the town of Domodossola. From here, frequent trains run to Stresa. Doing this train first gives you a more relaxing finish—cruising into your home port of Stresa. A special €27 ticket covers both the train and boat tickets.

▲**Lake Orta**—Just on the other side of Mount Mottarone is the small lake of Orta. The main town, Orta San Giulio, has a beautiful lakeside piazza ringed by picturesque buildings. The piazza faces the lake with a view of Isola San Giulio. Taxi boats (€2.60 round-trip) make the five-minute trip throughout the day. The island is worth a look for the church of San Giulio and the circular "path of silence" that takes about 10 minutes. In peak season, Orta is anything but silent, but off-season or early or late in the day, this place is full of peace and magic.

The train ride from Stresa to Orta-Miasino (a short walk from the lakeside piazza) takes two hours and requires a change in Domodossola.

SLEEPING

(€1 = about $1.10, country code: 39)

Because Stresa town is just a resort, I'd day-trip from Milan, but here are good options if you'd like to stay.

$$$ Hotel Milan Speranza is an impersonal, four-star, corporate-style hotel that caters mostly to tour groups, with 170 predictably comfortable rooms across from the boat dock (Db-€98–176 depending on season and view, €20–30 extra for lake views, air-con, elevator, tel. 0323-31178, fax 0323-32729, hotmispe@tin.it).

$$ Hotel Moderno offers 54 pastel rooms on a pedestrian street a block from the main square (Db-€80—125; closed mid-Oct–mid-March, air-con, elevator; Via Cavour 33, in Piazza Matteotti with your back to the lake, go right—up small street; tel. 0323-933-773, fax 0323-933-775, www.hms.it, moderno@hms.it).

$ Hotel Primavera, next door to Hotel Moderno, rents 34 decent rooms, many with terraces (Sb-€50–60, Db-€75–95, with breakfast, tel. 0323-31286, fax 0323-33458, www.stresahotels.net, hotelprimavera @stresa.it).

$ Hotel Saini Meuble is a cozy place located in a pedestrian zone in the old center. Its 14 rooms are big and modern, with hardwood floors (Sb-€50, Db-€90, lower prices off-season, ask for a 5 percent discount with this book, includes breakfast; elevator; Via Garibaldi 10, from Piazza Matteotti head up Via Mazzini and turn left on Via Garibaldi; tel. 0323-934-519, fax 0323-31169, www.hotelsaini.it, info@hotelsaini.it).

$ Albergo Luina is a cheap sleep with seven clean and basic rooms above a restaurant (S/Sb-€31–46, D/Db-€47–70, no breakfast and no CC, ask for a Rick Steves discount, Via Garibaldi, 2 blocks off Piazza Matteotti, with back to lake, go left up small street, tel. 0323-30285, luinastresa@yahoo.it).

$ Albergo Meuble Orsola di Gallia Cinzia is a humble and homey little place two blocks from the train station and just far enough off the tracks (only one train goes by in the middle of the night) with time-warp rooms—well-worn, not particularly clean…but the cheapest in town (S-€15, Sb-€20, D-€30, Db-€40 includes breakfast; 2-min walk from station at Via D di Genova 45; tel. 0323-31087, fax 0323-933-121, e-mail: what's that?).

EATING

Osteria degli Amici serves up tasty risotto, pastas, and pizzas with fast and friendly service under a canopy of grape and kiwi leaves (daily 12:00–14:30 & 19:00–24:00, deep in the old town past Piazza Cadorna at Via Bolongaro 33, tel. 0323-30453).

Osteria della Piazzetta, a fun little family-run place tucked away a block off the waterfront, is a world away from the tourist scene. Here fish, daily specials, and good pizzas are served at good prices (daily, indoor seating only, good yet inexpensive wines, a block south of the ferry dock and a block inland at Piazza San Michele 5, tel. 0323-31177).

Le Botte offers a variety of Piemonte's regional specialties in a casual atmosphere (daily 12:00–15:00 & 18:30–22:30, Via Mazzini 6/8, tel. 0323-30462).

La Rosa dei Venti is the locals' favorite pizzeria, located on the main drag, Corso Italia 50, two blocks south of the boat dock (Wed–Mon 12:00–14:00 & 19:00–22:00, closed Tue, tel. 0323-31431).

Piazza Cadorna (the main square) is a carnival of locals selling things to tourists. Still, at night it has a certain charm. It seems anyone who claims to be a musician can get a gig singing for eaters. The Pizzeria Centrale (on a platform in the center) is a good place to enjoy the ambience with decent pizzas, but don't order any serious food here.

TRANSPORTATION CONNECTIONS

By train to: Milan (hrly, 50 min fast train, 1.25-hr slow train), **Venice** (1/day, many more with changes in Milan, 4 hrs), **Domodossola**— French border (hrly, 35 min).

To Malpensa Airport: For a **train/bus combination**, take the train toward Milan (hrly), and get off at Gallarate (about 40 min from Stresa), where frequent, cheap shuttle buses run to Malpensa's Terminal 1 (€2.50, pay driver, 3/hr, 45 min; from Gallarate the bus departs from train station and runs 6:00–19:15; from Malpensa's Terminal 1 the bus runs 5:35–19:50).

Airport buses run between Stresa and Malpensa (€11, 50 min, leaves airport at 7:30, 10:30, 14:30, 17:30, and 20:30; leaves Stresa at 6:30, 9:30, 13:30, 16:30 and 19:30; confirm schedule, must reserve in advance if departing from Stresa, tel. 0322-844-862).

Taxis to the airport cost €80 (€100 for very early or very late service) and take about an hour; your hotel can arrange the taxi for you but may charge you for it. It's easy to arrange a taxi on your own at the taxi stand at the train station. Franco and Tiziano Ferrara's Taxi and Minibus Rental is reliable (tel. 0323-31000, mobile 335-644-5319, ferrara.t@libero.it).

THE
CINQUE TERRE

The Cinque Terre (CHINK-weh TAY-reh), a remote chunk of the Italian Riviera, is the traffic-free, lowbrow, underappreciated alternative to the French Riviera. There's not a museum in sight. Just sun, sea, sand (well, pebbles), wine, and pure unadulterated Italy. Enjoy the villages, swimming, hiking, and evening romance of one of God's great gifts to tourism. For a home base, choose among five villages, each of which fills a ravine with a lazy hive of human activity—calloused locals, sunburned travelers, and no Vespas. Vernazza is my favorite home base. While the Cinque Terre is now well-discovered (www.cinqueterre.it), I've never seen happier, more relaxed tourists.

The chunk of coast was first described in medieval times as "the five lands." Tiny communities grew up in the protective shadows of the castles (in feudal times, the land was the property of the castles), ready to run inside at the first hint of a Turkish "Saracen" pirate raid. Many locals were kidnapped and ransomed or sold into slavery somewhere far to the east. As the threat of pirates faded, the villages grew, with economies based on fish and grapes. Until the advent of tourism in this generation, the towns were remote. Even today, traditions survive, and each of the five villages comes with a distinct dialect and proud heritage. The region has become a national park, and its natural and cultural wonders will be carefully preserved.

Over the next decade, Italy has quiet plans for the Cinque Terre. For the sake of tranquility, a new train line will be built inland for the noisy fast trains, leaving the Cinque Terre tracks for just the pokey milk-run trains.

Sadly, a few ugly, noisy Americans are giving tourism a bad name here. Even hip young locals are put off by loud, drunken tourists. They say (and I agree) that the Cinque Terre is a special place. It deserves a special dignity. Party in Viareggio or Portofino, but be mellow in the Cinque Terre. Talk softly. Help keep it clean. In spite of the tourist

Cinque Terre

crowds, it's still a real community, and we are guests.

In this chapter, I cover Vernazza first (my favorite), then Riomaggiore (more of a workaday town), Manarola (picturesque), Corniglia (on a hilltop), and Monterosso (a resort).

Planning Your Time

The ideal minimum stay is two nights and a completely uninterrupted day. The Cinque Terre is served by the milk-run train from Genoa and La Spezia. Speed demons arrive in the morning, check their bags in La Spezia, take the five-hour hike through all five towns, laze away the afternoon on the beach or rock of their choice, and zoom away on the overnight train to somewhere back in the real world. But be warned: The Cinque Terre has a strange way of messing up your momentum.

2004 EVENTS ON THE CINQUE TERRE

late May	Monterosso: Lemon Festival
June 13	Monterosso: Corpus Domini (procession on carpet of flowers at 18:00)
June 24	Riomaggiore and Monterosso: Festival in honor of St. John the Baptist (procession and fireworks; big fire on old town beach the day before)
June 29	Corniglia: Festival of St. Peter and St. Paul
July 20	Vernazza: Festival for patron saint, St. Margaret
Aug 10	Manarola: Festival for patron saint, St. Lawrence
Aug 15	All towns: Ascension of Mary
Sept 8	Monterosso: Maria Nascente, or "Rising Mary" (fair with handicrafts)

The towns are each just a few minutes apart by hourly train or boat. There's no checklist of sights or experiences; just a hike, the towns themselves, and your fondest vacation desires. Study this chapter in advance and piece together your best day, mixing hiking, swimming, trains, and a boat ride. For the best light and coolest temperatures, start your hike early.

Market days perk up the towns from 8:00 to 13:00 on Tuesday in Vernazza, Wednesday in Levanto (see next chapter), Thursday in Monterosso, and Friday in La Spezia.

ORIENTATION

Cinque Terre Cards and Passes

Now that the Cinque Terre is a national park (www.parconazionale5terre .it), visitors hiking between the towns need to pay a **park entrance fee**. You have two options: the Hiking Pass or Cinque Terre Card. The **Hiking Pass** costs €3 (kids under 4 free, comes with map) and is valid for one day (until midnight). The Hiking Pass, which does not need to be validated, can be purchased at trailheads and usually at train stations. The pricier **Cinque Terre Card** covers the park entrance fee and your transportation on the local trains (from Levanto to La Spezia, including all Cinque Terre towns), plus the shuttle buses that run about twice an hour within each Cinque Terre town (€5.40/1 day, €13/3 days, €20.60/week, kids 4–12 half-price, under 4 free; includes map, brochure, and train schedule). A new **Cinque Terre Card Plus Boats** includes all of the above, plus unlimited passage on Cinque Terre boats (€13.60, valid for one day). Cinque Terre Cards, valid until midnight of the day they expire, are sold at train stations (but not at trailheads). Validate your Cinque Terre Card at a train station by punching it into the yellow machine.

Getting around the Cinque Terre

By Train: At La Spezia, the gateway to the Cinque Terre, you'll transfer to the milk-run Cinque Terre train. There might be a TI at the station in summer. But if not, skip the 20-minute hike to La Spezia's main TI at Viale Mazzini 47 near the waterfront (daily in summer 9:30–13:00 & 15:30–18:00; winter Mon–Sat 9:30–13:00 & 14:00–17:00, Sun 9:30–13:00; tel. 0187-718-997).

At the station, buy your train ticket (€1.05 weekdays, €1.10 weekends) or Cinque Terre Card, and take the half-hour train ride into the Cinque Terre town of your choice. Once in the Cinque Terre, you'll get around the villages more cheaply by train but more scenically by boat.

Cinque Terre Train Schedule: Since the train is the Cinque Terre lifeline, many shops and restaurants post the current schedule. Try to get a photocopied schedule—it'll come in handy (comes with Cinque Terre Card).

Trains leave La Spezia for the Cinque Terre villages at 7:12, 8:17, 10:08, 11:20, 12:23, 13:20, 14:27, 15:08, 16:20, 17:24, 18:25, 19:18, 20:25, 21:20, and 22:38 (last year's schedule, only daily trains listed—there are others that run only weekdays or only Sundays as well).

Trains leave Monterosso al Mare for La Spezia at 6:32, 8:12, 10:18, 12:11, 13:03, 14:12, 15:16, 16:17, 17:13, 18:40, 19:14, 20:28, 22:32, 23:24, and 0:02 (same trains depart Vernazza about 4 min later, last year's schedule).

Do not rely on these train times. Check the current posted schedule and then count on half the trains being 15 minutes or so late (unless you're late, in which case they are right on time).

To orient yourself, remember that directions are "*per* (to) Genova" or "*per* La Spezia." Note that many trains leaving La Spezia skip all of the towns or stop only in Monterosso. The five towns are just minutes apart by train. Know your stop. After the train leaves the town before your destination, go to the door to slip out before mobs pack in. Since the stations are small and the trains are long, you might get off the train deep in a tunnel, and you might need to flip open the handle of the door yourself.

The train stations should be staffed at all five Cinque Terre towns. Stations sell train tickets, the Cinque Terre Card, the Cinque Terre Card Plus Boats, and maybe the Hiking Pass. The Cinque Terre Card, which includes the national park entry fee, is convenient, but if you're on a tight budget, you can save a bit of money by buying a one-day Hiking Pass (€3) and paying separately for your train travel. For more on all of these passes, see "Cinque Terre Cards and Passes," above.

It's cheap to buy individual train tickets to travel between the towns. Since a one-town hop costs the same as a five-town hop (around

€1.10) and every ticket is good for six hours with stopovers, save money and explore the region in one direction on one ticket. Stamp the ticket at the station machine before you board.

If you have a Eurailpass, don't spend one of your valuable flexi-days on the cheap Cinque Terre.

By Boat: From Easter to late October (through Nov if weather is good), a daily boat service connects Monterosso, Vernazza, Manarola, Riomaggiore, and Portovenere (on Sat and Sun, a boat also makes an afternoon run to Portofino). Boats provide a scenic way to get from town to town and survey what you just hiked. It's also the only efficient way to visit the nearby resort of Portovenere (see next chapter); the alternative is a tedious train/bus connection via La Spezia. In peaceful weather, the boats are more reliable than the trains, but if sea is rough, they often don't run at all.

Boats go about hourly, from 10:30 until 18:00 from Monterosso and stop at the Cinque Terre towns (note that boats do not stop at Corniglia), ending in Portovenere. Boats coming from Portovenere to Monterosso run from 9:00 until 17:10. Single hops cost about €3. An all-day pass covering the Cinque Terre towns costs up to €22—less off-season and weekdays (you can save money by getting the €15 afternoon pass that kicks in at 14:30 and ends when boats quit for the evening). Also consider new Cinque Terre Card Plus Boats (see above). You can buy tickets at little stands at each town's harbor (tel. 0187-732-987 and 0187-818-440). Schedules are posted at docks, harbor bars, Cinque Terre Park offices, and hotels.

Hiking the Cinque Terre

All five towns are connected by good trails. You'll experience the area's best by hiking from one end to the other. The entire seven-mile hike can be done in about four hours, but allow five for dawdling. While you can detour to dramatic hilltop sanctuaries (one trail leads from Vernazza's cemetery uphill), I'd keep it simple by following the easy red-and-white-marked low trails between the villages. Good hiking maps (about €5–6, sold everywhere, not necessary for this described walk) cover the expanded version of this hike, from Portovenere through all five Cinque Terre towns to Levanto, and more serious hikes in the high country. Sometimes severe rains can wash out trails, especially in winter. Ask around whether the trails are open, particularly in spring. Remember that hikers need to pay a fee to enter the trails (see "Cinque Terre Cards and Passes," page 203).

Since I still get the names of the Cinque Terre towns mixed up, I think of the towns by number: Riomaggiore (town #1), Manarola (#2), Corniglia (#3), Vernazza (#4), and resorty Monterosso (#5).

Riomaggiore–Manarola (20 min): Facing the front of the train station in Riomaggiore (town #1), go up the stairs to the right, following signs for the Via dell' Amore. The film-gobbling promenade—wide enough for baby strollers—leads down the coast to Manarola. While there's no beach here, stairs lead down to sunbathing rocks.

Manarola–Corniglia (45 min): The walk from Manarola (#2) to Corniglia (#3) is a little longer and a little more rugged than that from #1 to #2.

Ask locally about the more difficult six-mile inland hike to Volastra (shuttle buses run hrly to Volastra from Manarola and Corniglia, €2.50 or free with Cinque Terre Card). This tiny village, perched between Manarola and Corniglia, hosts the Five-Terre wine co-op; stop by the Cantina Sociale. If you take this high road between Manarola and Corniglia, allow two hours; in return, you'll get sweeping views and a closer look at the vineyards.

Corniglia–Vernazza (90 min): The hike from Corniglia (#3) to Vernazza (#4)—the wildest and greenest of the coast—is most rewarding. From the Corniglia station and beach, zigzag up to the town (taking the steeper corkscrew stairs, the longer road, or the shuttle bus). Ten minutes past Corniglia toward Vernazza, you'll see the nude Guvano beach far beneath you (see "Corniglia," page 226). The trail leads past a bar and picnic tables, through lots of fragrant and flowery vegetation, and scenically into Vernazza.

Vernazza–Monterosso (90 min): The trail from Vernazza (#4) to Monterosso (#5) is a scenic up-and-down-a-lot trek. Trails are rough (and some readers report "very dangerous") and narrow but easy to follow. Camping at the picnic tables midway is frowned upon. The views just out of Vernazza are spectacular.

Swimming and Kayaking

Every town has a beach. Monterosso has the biggest and sandiest, with paddle boats, beach umbrellas, and beach-use fees (free where there are no umbrellas). Of Corniglia's two beaches, the Guvano beach is nude. Riomaggiore has a fine beach just outside town. Vernazza's is tiny—better for sunning than swimming. Manarola has the worst beach (no sand), but offers the best deep-water swimming.

Wear your walking shoes and pack your swim gear. Several of the beaches have showers (no shampoo, please) that may work better than your hotel's. Underwater sightseeing is full of fish—goggles are sold in local shops. Sea urchins can be a problem if you walk on the rocks; consider using Aquasocks or fins.

You can rent kayaks in Vernazza, Monterosso, and Riomaggiore (details listed below per town).

TOURS

Hiking Tour—For a guided tour, consider spending a day with a hard-working and likable American student, Sean Risatti, who liked the

Cinque Terre so much he moved in (€45, almost daily April–Oct, departing Monterosso at 10:00 or Vernazza at 10:45; book at cinqueterretrek@hotmail.com, tel. 320-047-6865, or ask for Sean in Monterosso at The Net or at Kate's Fishnet Travel Services). The day—which is a great way to meet other travelers—includes a hike from Vernazza to Manarola, lots of information, special glimpses of the area, and a dinner that evening.

Kayak Tour—An alternative to the often-crowded trails are Sean Risatti's kayak tours (half- and full-day itineraries, includes equipment, €40–80/person, also does boat tours, see contact information above).

Vernazza (Town #4)

With the closest thing to a natural harbor—overseen by a ruined castle and an old church—and only the occasional noisy slurping up of the train by the mountain to remind you of the modern world, Vernazza is my Cinque Terre home.

The action is at the harbor, where you'll find outdoor restaurants, a bar hanging on the edge of the castle (great for evening drinks), a breakwater with a promenade, and a tailgate-party street market every Tuesday morning. In the summer, the beach becomes a soccer field, where teams fielded by local bars and restaurants provide late-night entertainment. In the dark, locals fish off the promontory, using glowing bobs that shine in the waves.

The town's 500 residents, proud of their Vernazzan heritage, brag that "Vernazza is locally owned. Portofino has sold out." Fearing the change it would bring, keep-Vernazza-small proponents stopped the construction of a major road into the town and region. Families are tight and go back centuries; several generations stay together. Leisure time is devoted to the *passeggiata*—strolling lazily together up and down the main street. Sit on a bench and study the passersby. Then explore the characteristic alleys, called *carugi*. In October, the cantinas are draped with drying grapes. In the winter, the population shrinks as many people move to more comfortable big-city apartments.

A steep five-minute hike in either direction from Vernazza gives you a classic village photo op (for the best light, head toward Corniglia in the morning, toward Monterosso in the evening). Franco's Bar (a.k.a. Ristorante "La Torre"), with a panoramic terrace, is at the tower on the trail toward Corniglia.

The town has ATMs and two banks (in center and top of town). You can buy train tickets, Hiking Passes, and Cinque Terre Cards at the Vernazza train station/TI, staffed by helpful trio Eliano, Diego, and Francesco (daily in summer 6:30–22:00, in winter 8:00–20:00, tel.

0187-812-533, a little English spoken). Note that there is no luggage storage in Vernazza's train station.

Bus Service: A shuttle bus, generally with friendly English-speaking Beppe behind the wheel, runs twice hourly (free with Cinque Terre Card, otherwise €1.50) from the top of the main street to the non-resident parking lot (€11/24 hrs) about a half-mile above Vernazza. You can also catch the bus to the two sanctuaries in the hills above town (€2.50 each way or free with Cinque Terre Card, bus schedule posted in the train station).

Internet Access and Laundry: The slick Internet Point, run by Alberto and Isabella, is in the village center (daily 9:30–20:00, until 23:00 in summer, tel. 0187-812-949). The Blue Marlin bar (run by exuberant Massimo and Carmen, 7ish–24:00, open daily in Aug, otherwise closed Thu) also offers Internet access (€0.10/min) plus a self-service laundry (€4.50 wash, €4.50 dry, English instructions, buy tokens at Blue Marlin bar—note hours above, laundry open Fri–Wed 8:00–22:00, closed Thu, Via Roma 49, tel. 0187-821-149, 30 meters yards below train station).

Beach: The harbor's sandy cove has kayak rentals (June–Sept only, €7/hour for a 2-person kayak, €4 for single, also dinghy and taxi boat rentals, tel. 0187-920-011), sunning rocks, and showers by the breakwater. There's a ladder on the breakwater for deepwater access. The tiny *acque pendente* (waterfall) cove which locals call their *laguna blu,* between Vernazza and Monterosso, is accessible only by small hired boat.

Vernazza Top-Down Orientation Walk

Walk uphill until you hit the parking lot—with a bank, a post office, and a barrier that keeps all but service vehicles out. Vernazza's shuttle buses run from here to the parking lot and into the hills. The tidy new square is called Fontana Vecchia, after a long-gone fountain. Older locals remember the river filled with townswomen doing their washing. Begin your saunter downhill to the harbor.

Just before the Pension Sorriso sign, you'll see the ambulance barn (big brown wood doors) on your right. A group of volunteers is always on call for a dash to the hospital, 30 minutes away in La Spezia. Opposite that is a big empty lot next to Pension Sorriso. Like many landowners, the owner of the Sorriso had plans to expand, but the government said no. The old character of these towns is carefully protected.

Across from Pension Sorriso is the honorary clubhouse for the ANPI (members of the local WWII resistance). Only five ANPI old-timers survive. Cynics consider them less than heroes. After 1943, Hitler called up Italian boys over 15. Rather than die on the front for Hitler, they escaped to the hills. Only to remain free did they become "resistance fighters."

A few steps farther along, you'll see a monument (marble plaque in wall to your left) to those killed in World War II. Not a family was

Vernazza

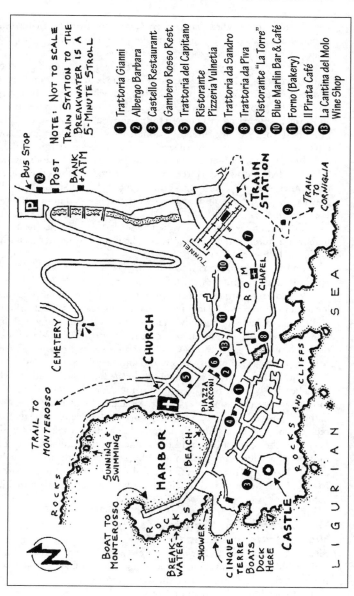

NOTE: Not to scale
TRAIN STATION TO THE
BREAKWATER IS A
5-MINUTE STROLL

1 Trattoria Gianni
2 Albergo Barbara
3 Castello Restaurant
4 Gambero Rosso Rest.
5 Trattoria del Capitano
6 Ristorante
  Pizzeria Vulnetia
7 Trattoria da Sandro
8 Trattoria da Piva
9 Ristorante "La Torre"
10 Blue Marlin Bar & Café
11 Forno (Bakery)
12 Il Pirata Café
13 La Cantina del Molo
   Wine Shop

BUS STOP
POST
BANK + ATM
P
CEMETERY
TUNNEL
TRAIN STATION
TRAIL TO CORNIGLIA
VIA ROMA
CHAPEL
CHURCH
PIAZZA MARCONI
TRAIL TO MONTEROSSO
BOAT TO MONTEROSSO
ROCKS
SUNNING + SWIMMING
HARBOR
BEACH
ROCKS
BREAK-WATER
SHOWER
CINQUE TERRE BOATS DOCK HERE
CASTLE
ROCKS AND CLIFFS
LIGURIAN SEA
N

spared. Study this: soldiers *"morti in combattimento"* fought for Mussolini, some were deported to *Germania*, and *Part* (stands for *partigiani* or "partisans") were killed later fighting against Mussolini.

The tiny monorail *trenino* (as you're facing plaque, look up on the wall on your right) is parked quietly here except in September and October, when it's busy helping locals bring down the grapes (sorry, not open to the public). The path to Corniglia leaves from here (it runs above plaque, starting at your left). Behind you is a tiny square playground, decorated with three millstones, which no longer grind local olives into oil. From here, Vernazza's tiny river goes underground.

In the tunnel under the railway tracks, you'll see a door marked "Croce Verde Vernazza" (Green Cross). Posted on the other side of the tunnel is the "P.A. Croce Verde Vernazza" (in a small green display case), the list of volunteers ready for ambulance duty each day of the month.

The train tracks are above you. The second set of tracks (nearer the harbor) was recently renovated to lessen the disruptive noise; locals say it made no difference.

Follow the road downhill. Until the 1950s, Vernazza's river ran open through the center of town from here to the *gelateria*.

Wandering through this main business center, you'll pass many locals doing their *vasca* (laps) past the entrepreneurial Blue Marlin bar and the tiny Chapel of Santa Marta (the small stone building with iron grillwork over the window, across from Il Baretto), where Mass is celebrated only on special Sundays. Next you'll see a grocery, *gelateria*, bakery, pharmacy, another grocery, and another *gelateria*.

On the left, in front of the second *gelateria*, an arch leads to what was a beach where the river used to flow out of town. Continue on down to the harbor square and breakwater. Vernazza, with the only natural harbor of the Cinque Terre, was established as the sole place boats could pick up the fine local wine. (The town is named for a kind of wine.) Peek into the tiny street behind the Vulnetia restaurant with the commotion of arches. Vernazza's most characteristic side streets, called *carugi*, lead up from here. The trail (above the church toward Monterosso) leads to the classic view of Vernazza (best photos just before sunset).

The Burned-Out Sightseer's Visual Tour of Vernazza

Sit at the end of the harbor breakwater (perhaps with a glass of local white wine or something more interesting from Bar Capitano—borrow the glass, they don't mind), face the town, and see...

The harbor: In a moderate storm, you'd be soaked, as waves routinely crash over the *molo* (breakwater, built in 1972). The train line (to your left), constructed 130 years ago to tie a newly united Italy together, linked Turin and Genoa with Rome. A second line (hidden in a tunnel at this point) was built in the 1960s. The yellow building alongside the tracks was Vernazza's first train station. You can see the four bricked-up alcoves where people once waited for trains. Vernazza's fishing fleet is down to three small fishing boats (with the net spools); the town's restaurants buy up everything they catch. Vernazzans are more likely to own a boat than a car. In the '70s, tiny Vernazza had one of the top water polo teams in Italy, and the harbor was their "pool." Later, when a real pool was required, Vernazza dropped out of the league.

The castle: On the far right, the castle, which is now a grassy park with great views, still guards the town (€1, daily 10:00–19:00, from harbor, take stairs by Trattoria Gianni and follow signs to Castello restaurant, tower is a few steps beyond, see the photo and painting gallery rooms). It's called *Belforte*, or "loud screams," for the warnings it made back in pirating days. The highest umbrellas mark the recommended Castello restaurant. The squat tower on the water is great for a glass of wine or a bite to eat (follow the rope to the Belforte Bar; open Wed–Mon 12:00–24:00, kitchen closes between 15:00–19:00 and at 22:30, closed Tue, tel. 0187-812-222; inside the submarine-strength door, a photo of a major storm shows the entire tower under a wave).

The town: Vernazza has two halves. *Sciuiu,* on the left (literally, "flowery"), is the sunny side, and *luvegu,* on the right (literally, "dank"), is the shady side. The houses below the castle were connected by an interior arcade—ideal for fleeing attacks. The pastel colors are regulated by a commissioner of good taste in the community government. The square before you is locally famous for some of the region's finest restaurants. The big, red, central house, the 12th-century site where Genoan warships were built, used to be a kind of guardhouse.

Above the town: The small, round tower above the guardhouse, another part of the city fortifications, reminds us of Vernazza's importance in the Middle Ages, when it was a key ally of Genoa (whose archenemies were the other maritime republics of Pisa, Amalfi, and Venice). Franco's Bar (also called Ristorante "La Torre"), just behind the tower, welcomes hikers finishing, starting, or simply contemplating the Corniglia–Vernazza hike, with great town views (12:00–21:30). Vineyards fill the mountainside beyond the town. Notice the many terraces. Someone calculated that the vineyard terraces of the Cinque Terre have the same amount of stonework as the Great Wall of China. Wine production is down nowadays, as the younger residents choose less physical work. But locals still work their plots and proudly serve their family wines. A single steel train line winds up the gully behind the tower. This is for the vintner's *trenino,* the tiny service train.

The church, school, and city hall: Vernazza's Ligurian Gothic church, built with black stones quarried from Punta Mesco (the distant point behind you), dates from 1318. The gray-and-red house above and

SLEEPING ON THE CINQUE TERRE

If you're trying to avoid my readers, stay away from Vernazza. Monterosso is a good choice for the younger crowd (more nightlife) and rich, sun-worshiping softies (who prefer firm reservations for hotels with private bathrooms). Wine-lovers and mountain goats like Corniglia. Sophisticated Italians and Germans choose Manarola. Travelers who show up without reservations enjoy Riomaggiore for its easy room-booking services.

While the Cinque Terre is too rugged for the mobs that ravage the Spanish and French coasts, it's popular with Italians, Germans, and Americans in the know. Hotels charge the most and are packed on Easter, in August, and on summer Fridays and Saturdays. August weekends are worst. But €65 doubles abound throughout the year.

If you'll be here in July or August, or on a weekend, it's smart to book ahead. To reserve ahead, call, fax, or e-mail. At other times, you can land a €65 double room on any day by just arriving in town (ideally by noon) and asking around at bars and restaurants, or simply by approaching locals on the street. This seems scary, but it's true.

Most prevalent in Vernazza, these private rooms—called *affitta camere*—are pleasant rooms in small apartment buildings or in homes (with separate entrances). Some are apartments with kitchens—cheap for families.

For the best value, visit three private rooms and snare the best. Going direct cuts out a middleman and softens prices. Plan on paying cash. Private rooms are generally bigger and more comfortable than those offered by the pensions and they offer the same privacy as a hotel room.

If you want the security of a reservation, make it at a hotel long in advance (small places generally don't take reservations made weeks ahead). If you don't get a reply to your faxed request for a room, assume the place is fully booked. If you do reserve, honor your reservation (or, if you must, cancel as early as possible). Since the owners of private rooms usually don't take deposits, they lose money if you don't show up. Cutthroat room hawkers at the stations might try to lure you away with offers of cheaper rates from a room that you've reserved. Don't do it. You owe it to your hosts to stick with your original reservation.

to the left of the spire is the local elementary school (which about 25 children attend). High school is in the "big city," La Spezia. The red building to the right of (and below) the schoolhouse is the former monastery and present city hall. Vernazza and Corniglia function as one community. Through most of the 1990s, the local government was communist. In 1999, they elected a coalition of many parties working to rise above ideologies and simply make Vernazza a better place. Finally, on the top of the hill, with the best view of all, is the town cemetery, where most locals plan to end up.

SLEEPING

Vernazza, the essence of the Cinque Terre, is my top choice for a home base. There are two recommended pensions and piles of private rooms for rent.

If you arrive without a reservation, you can call these places from the pay phone at the bottom of the stairs at the train station. Or drop by the nearest shop or bar; most locals know someone who rents rooms.

Anywhere you stay here will require some climbing. Night noises can be a problem if you're near the station, and rooms on the harbor come with church bells from 7:00–22:00.

A parking lot (€1.50/hr, €11/day, just over a half-mile out of town) and a hardworking shuttle service make driving to Vernazza a reasonable option for drivers with nerves of steel. The little shuttle bus makes the run from the lot to the top of town twice an hour.

Usually, when a price range is listed, the lower price is charged during winter (roughly Nov–March) and the higher price the rest of the year. See map on page 209 for location.

Pensions

$$ **Trattoria Gianni** rents 23 small rooms just under the castle. The funky ones are artfully decorated à la shipwreck and are up lots of tight, winding, spiral stairs; and most have tiny balconies and grand views. The new, comfy rooms lack views but have modern bathrooms and a super-scenic, cliff-hanging private garden. Marisa, who rarely smiles at anyone (not just you), requires a two-night minimum and check-in before 16:00 (S-€40, D-€60, or €65 with small balcony, sinks and bathrooms down the hall; Db-€77, Tb-€99, accepts credit cards but offers 10 percent discount for cash; Piazza Marconi 5, closed Jan–Feb, tel. & fax 0187-812-228, tel. 0187-821-003, www.giannifranzi .it, info@giannifranzi.it, a little English spoken). Pick up your keys at Trattoria Gianni's restaurant/reception on the harbor square and hike up dozens of stairs to #41 (funky, *con vista sul mare*) or #47 (new, *nuovo*) at the top. (Note: My tour company books this place 50 nights

SLEEP CODE

(€1 = about $1.10, country code: 39)

Sleep Code: **S** = Single, **D** = Double/Twin, **T** = Triple, **Q** = Quad, **b** = bathroom, **s** = shower only, **no CC** = Credit Cards not accepted, **SE** = Speaks English, **NSE** = No English. Breakfast is included only in real hotels. Unless otherwise noted, credit cards are accepted.

To help you sort easily through these listings, I've divided the rooms into three categories based on the price for a standard double room with bath:

$$$ **Higher Priced**—Most rooms €100 or more.
$$ **Moderately Priced**—Most rooms between €50-100
$ **Lower Priced**—Most rooms €50 or less.

of the season.) Telephone three days in advance and leave your first name and time of arrival. If you arrive on Wednesday, when the restaurant is closed, pick up your keys at the big *gelateria* by the grotto (they'll give you details when you reserve).

$ Albergo Barbara, on the harbor square, is run by kindly Giuseppe and his Swiss wife, Patricia. Their nine clean, modern rooms share three public showers and WCs (S-€45–€48 depending on season, D without view-€45, D with small view-€48, D with big view-€60, bunky family Q-€75, call to reserve, then fax with credit card information to hold room—but you'll have to pay cash, 2-night stay preferred, confirm before 17:00 on day of arrival or lose your room, loads of stairs, fans, closed Dec–Feb, Piazza Marconi 30 , tel. & fax 0187-812-398, mobile 338-793-3261, SE). The two big doubles on the main floor come with grand harbor views and are the best value (top-floor doubles have small windows and small views). The office is on the top floor of the big, red, vacant-looking building facing the harbor.

Private Rooms (Affitta Camere)

The town is honeycombed year-round with private rooms, offering the best values in Vernazza. The owners are usually reluctant to reserve rooms far in advance. It's easiest to call a day or two ahead or simply show up in the morning and look around. The rooms cost about €45–70 for a double, depending on the view, season, and plumbing. Most places accept only cash. Some have killer views, come with lots of stairs, and cost the same as a small dark place on a back lane over the train tracks. Little or no English is spoken at these places. Any main-street business has a line on rooms for rent. If you call to let them know your arrival time, they'll meet you at the train station.

$$ **Francamaria** rents four sharp, comfortable rooms overlooking the harbor square. One room sleeps 4–6 and comes with a kitchen and small terrace, another is just a few steps up from the harbor—a rarity in vertical Vernazza (Db-€60–100, Qb-€100–140, prices depend on season, rates soft Nov–Feb, Piazza Marconi 30, tel. 0187-812-002, fax 0187-812-956, www.francamaria.com, francamaria@francamaria.com). Son Giovanni has three rooms of his own to rent (same prices but no views, metalgearsolid@inwind.it).

$$ **Martina Callo** rents four fine, lofty rooms overlooking the square, up plenty of steps near the church tower (Db-€50–70, Qb-€103–110; room #1-Qb with harbor view, room #2-Qb huge family room with no view, room #3-Db with grand view terrace, room #4-roomy Db with no view; heating in winter; ring bell at Piazza Marconi 26, tel. & fax 0187-812-365, mobile 329-435-5344, roomartina@supereva.it).

$$ **Elisabetta's Villino Azzurro** rents an apartment and a comfy private room with a sea-view window. Both have big sun terraces overlooking the sea, castle, and town (Db-€45–60, Via Carattino 62, tel. 0187-458-437, mobile 347-451-1834, www.cinqueterreedintorni.it /elisabetta, carroelisabetta@hotmail.com

$$ **Mike and Franca Castiglione**, who speak New Yorkish (and have the attitude to prove it), rent a small double studio with kitchen, great sea view, and a private garden overlooking the sea and castle (Db-€65–75, prices guaranteed with this book through 2004; turn left at pharmacy, climb Via Carattino to #16; tel. 0187-812-374).

$$ **Tilde's** neat and tidy studio apartment has a superb sea view and comes with a kitchen (Db-€70, Via Mazzini 9, mobile 339-298-9323).

$$ **Affitta Camere da Annamaria** offers five pleasant rooms up spiral staircases (Db-€60–83 with sea or town views or terrace—the terrace rooms are best, turn left at pharmacy, climb Via Carattino to #64, tel. 0187-821-082).

$$ **Giuliano Basso** rents three fine rooms that share a large view balcony overlooking the whole town and his own terraced gardens below (Db-€65, €75 with breakfast; open year-round, fridge access; above train station, direction: Corniglia, take a right before Sorriso's, then take left fork, 5-min walk to harbor; mobile 333-341-4792, www.cdh.it/giuliano, giuliano@cdh.it).

$$ **Tonino Basso** rents four super, clean, modern rooms—each with its own computer for free Internet access—near the post office, in the only building in Vernazza with an elevator. Tranquil rooms come with a private bath and air-conditioning but no views (Sb-€60, Db-€80, Tb-€100, Qb-€130; when you arrive, call Tonino's mobile number from train station—phones at bottom of stairs—and he will meet you; or the Gambero Rosso restaurant at harbor can find him—but then you'll have to backtrack to get to his rooms; tel. 0187-821-264, mobile 335-269-436, fax 0187-821-260, toninobasso@libero.it).

$$ Nicolina rents four decent rooms: a large one with a view, two overlooking Vernazza's main drag (one comes with frescoed ceiling and a washing machine she'll let you use), and one without any view. Inquire at Pizzeria Vulnetia on the harbor square or reserve in advance by phone (Db–€65, Qb with terrace and view–€130, Piazza Marconi 29, tel. & fax 0187-821-193).

$$ Armanda rents a stylish, immaculate one-room apartment without a view near the Castello (€65, Piazza Marconi 15, tel. 0187-812-218, mobile 347-306-4760).

$$ Rosa Vitali rents two apartments overlooking the main street, one for three people (has terrace and fridge), the other (for 4 people) has windows and a full kitchen (€75–124/night, tel. 0187-821-181, mobile 340-267-5009, rosa.vitali@libero.it, SE).

$$ Egi Rooms, run by friendly Egidio Verduschi (SE), offers three rooms right in the center of the main drag. The common area includes a partial kitchen (no stove, but microwave, fridge, and sink), comfy living room, and shared bath (€30–45 per person depending on season, Via Visconti 9, call a day ahead to reserve, leave message at mobile 338-822-3202 or tel. 0187-703-905, egidioverduschi@libero.it).

$$ Memo Rooms offers three newly renovated, immaculate rooms overlooking the main street. This feels more like a hotel than any other private rooms in Vernazza (Db–€65, Via Roma 15, tel. 0187-812-360, mobile 338-285-2385).

$$ Camere Fontana Vecchia has four bright, spacious, quiet rooms near the post office (no view) and may be the only place in Vernazza with almost no stairs to climb (D–€50–60, Db–€60–70, T–€80, Tb–€100, closed Nov–March, Via Gavino 15, tel. 0187-821-130, mobile 333-454-9371, m.annamaria@libero.it, Annamaria SE).

$$ Moggia Manuela rents tranquil rooms at the top of town near the old fountain between the bank and the post office (Db–€70, Qb and kitchen–€110, cheaper Nov–mid-April, Via Gavino 22, tel. 0187-812-397, mobile 333-413-6374).

$$ L'Eremo sur Mare, perched high on the trail to Corniglia, has breathtaking views (literally—it's a hike to get here with your bags; heavy packers should look elsewhere). The three rooms share a garden and sun terrace (Db–€78 with breakfast, tel. 339-2685-617, www.eremosulmare.com).

$$ Mamma Rina was the first in Vernazza to rent out private rooms. Staying here is like staying at Grandma's. Rooms with terraces overlook the hills north of Vernazza (D–€60, D without terrace–€55, each room has a private bath but it's down the hall, Via Ettore 9, tel. 0187-812-025).

$$ Patrizia has a bright, cheery studio apartment with fishnet decor and views (across from grotto on main drag). Their other, smaller twin apartment, closer to the station, looks out onto the street (Db–

€65–70, tel. 0187-821-231, mobile 335-653-1563, fax 0187-812-907, bemili@libero.it).

$$ Renaldo Leonardini rents a three-bed room with loft and kitchen overlooking the grotto and lively main street of Vernazza. The full-length window opens to make a little balcony (Db–€60–75, Via Visconti 15, just a few stairs up from street level, tel. 0187-821-065 or leave message in English at tel. 0187-703-905, NSE).

$$ Villa Antonia has two remodeled rooms with a shared bath on the main drag (Db–€75, tel. 0187-821-143).

$ Giuseppina's Villa, a cozy apartment with a low-ceilinged loft and a mountainside forming one of the walls, has one window, no view, and a kitchen. The woman at the grocery store nearest the harbor (with *Salumi e Formaggi* on the awning) can check if it's available (€25 per person, Via S. Giovanni Battista 7, only a short climb from harbor, tel. 0187-812-026). Giuseppina also rents a double room up the street (no view, but has a garden, terrace, and kitchen).

EATING

If you enjoy Italian cuisine, Vernazza's restaurants are worth the splurge. All take pride in their cooking and have similar prices. Wander around at about 20:00 and compare the ambience.

Castello, run by gracious and English-speaking Monica, her husband Massimo, kind Mario, and the rest of her family, serves great seafood and regional specialties with great views, just under the castle (Thu–Tue 12:00–15:00 for lunch, 15:00–19:00 for drinks and snacks on cliff-hugging terrace, 19:30–22:00 for dinner, closed Wed and Nov–April, tel. 0187-812-296).

Four places fill the harborfront with happy eaters: **Gambero Rosso**, considered Vernazza's best restaurant, feels classy and costs only a few euros more than the others (Tue–Sun 12:00–15:00 & 19:00–22:00, closed Mon and Dec–Feb, Piazza Marconi 7, tel. 0187-812-265). **Trattoria del Capitano** might serve the best food for the money (Thu–Tue 12:00–15:00 & 19:00–22:00, closed Wed except in Aug, closed Dec–Jan, tel. 0187-812-201, Paolo and Barbara SE). **Trattoria Gianni** is an old standby for locals and tourists alike, especially for well-prepared seafood (daily 12:00–15:00 & 19:30–22:00 in July–Aug, otherwise closed Wed, tel. 0187-812-228). **Ristorante Pizzeria Vulnetia** serves regional specialties and pizza (Tue–Sun 12:00–15:00 & 18:30–22:00, closed Mon, Piazza Marconi 29, tel. 0187-821-193).

Trattoria da Sandro, on the main drag, mixes Genovese and Ligurian cuisine with friendly service, and can be a peaceful alternative to the harborside scene (Wed–Mon 12:00–15:00 & 19:00–22:00, closed Tue, just below train station, Via Roma 60, tel. 0187-812-223, Gabriella SE). The more offbeat and intimate **Trattoria da Piva** may come with

CINQUE TERRE CUISINE 101

Local Specialities: *Accuighe* (ah-CHOO-gay) are anchovies, a local specialty—always served the day they're caught. If you've always hated anchovies (the harsh, cured-in-salt American kind), try them fresh here. *Tegame alla Vernazza* is the most typical main course in Vernazza: anchovies, potatoes, tomatoes, white wine, oil, and herbs. *Pansotti* is ravioli with ricotta and spinach, often served with a hazelnut or walnut sauce...delightful and filling. While antipasto means cheese and salami in Tuscany, here you'll get *antipasti di mare,* a plate of mixed fruits of the sea and a fine way to start a meal. For many, splitting this and a pasta dish is plenty. Try the fun local dessert: *torta della nonna* (grandmother's cake), with a glass of *sciacchetrà* for dunking (see "Wine," below).

Pesto: This region is the birthplace of pesto. Basil, which loves the temperate Ligurian climate, is mixed with cheese (half *Parmigiano* cow cheese and half pecorino sheep cheese), garlic, olive oil, and pine nuts, and then poured over pasta. Try it on spaghetti, *trenette,* or *trofie* (made of flour with a bit of potato, designed specifically for pesto). Many also like pesto lasagna. If you become addicted, small jars of pesto are sold in the local grocery stores (you can take it home or spread it on focaccia here).

Focaccia: This tasty bread also originates from here in Liguria. Locals say the best focaccia is made between the Cinque Terre and Genoa. It's simply bread with olive oil and salt. The baker roughs up the dough with finger holes, then bakes it. Focaccia comes plain or with onions, sage, and olive bits, and is a local favorite for a snack on the beach. Bakeries sell it in rounds or slices by the weight (a portion is about 100 grams, or *un etto*).

Wine: The *vino delle Cinque Terre,* respected throughout Italy, flows cheap and easy throughout the region. It's white—great with the local seafood. *D.O.C.* is the mark of top quality. Red wine is better elsewhere. For a sweet dessert wine, the local *sciacchetrà* wine is worth the splurge (€2.60 per glass, often served with a cookie). While 10 kilos of grapes yield seven liters of local wine, *sciacchetrà* is made from near-raisins, and 10 kilos of grapes make only 1.5 liters of *sciacchetrà*. The word means "push and pull"...push in lots of grapes, pull out the best wine. If your room is up a lot of steps, be warned: *Sciacchetrà* is 18 percent alcohol, while regular wine is only 11 percent. In the cool, calm evening, sit on the Vernazza breakwater with a glass of wine and watch the phosphorescence in the waves.

late-night guitar strumming and Piva's songs in local dialect (Tue–Sun 12:00–14:30 & 19:00–22:00, closed Mon; Via Carattino 6, around corner from pharmacy; tel. 0187-812-194).

For basic grub, a grand view, and perfect peace, hike to Franco's **Ristorante "La Torre"** for a dinner at sunset (Wed–Mon 12:00–21:30, kitchen closes from 15:00–19:30 but drinks are served, sometimes closed Tue, on trail toward Corniglia, tel. 0187-821-082).

The main street is creatively determining tourists' needs and filling them. The **Blue Marlin** bar offers a good selection of sandwiches, salads, and *bruschetta*. The **Forno** bakery has good focaccia and veggie tarts, and several bars sell sandwiches and pizza by the slice. Grocery stores make inexpensive sandwiches to order (Mon–Sat 8:00–13:00 & 17:00–19:30, Sun 7:30–13:00). The town's two *gelaterias* are good.

At **Il Pirata delle Cinque Terre,** Sicilian twin brothers Gianluca and Massimo enthusiastically offer a great assortment of handcrafted authentic Sicilian pastries. Gianluca is a pastry artist and hand-paints fanciful sculptured marzipan. Their *granitas* (slushies) are made from fresh fruit garnished with thick whipped cream (daily 6:30–24:00; by the post office at the top of town, Via Gavino 36; tel. 0187-812-047).

La Cantina del Molo, the wine shop, will uncork the bottle you buy and supply cups to go (daily 10:30–20:00, until 22:00 in summer, owner makes 5 of the wines, tasting possible). Most harborside bars will let you take your glass on a breakwater stroll.

Breakfast: Locals take breakfast about as seriously as flossing. A cappuccino and a pastry or a piece of focaccia does it. The two harbor-front bars offer the most ambience (you can walk out with the cup, grab a view picnic bench, and return the cup when you're done). The bakery opens early, offering freshly-made focaccia. **Il Pirata delle Cinque Terre** (listed above) makes pastries every morning. The **Blue Marlin** serves a special €6.20 breakfast: ham and cheese focaccia, an assortment of fresh local pastries, juice, and cappuccino (Fri–Wed 7:00–24:00, closed Thu, open daily in Aug, just below station, tel. 0187-821-149).

Riomaggiore (Town #1)

The most substantial non-resort town of the group, Riomaggiore is a disappointment from the train station. But walk through the tunnel next to the train tracks (or ride the elevator through the hillside to the top of town), and you land in a fascinating tangle of pastel homes leaning on each other as if someone stole their crutches. There's homemade gelato at the Bar Central on main street, and, if Ivo is there, you'll feel right at home. When Ivo closes, the gang goes down to the harborside with a guitar.

Tourist Information: The TI is inside the train station (Mon–Fri 6:30–20:00 in winter, until 22:00 in summer, tel. 0187-920-633). Two Cinque Terre Park offices flank the TI; the one to the right of the TI with your back to the tracks has Internet access (9:00–23:00 daily in summer, until 22:00 in winter).

Bus Service: The bus shuttles locals and tourists up and down Riomaggiore's steep main street and continues to the parking lot outside of town (free with Cinque Terre Card, €1.50 without, 2/hr, just flag it down).

Hikes: Consider the cliff-hanging trail that leads from the beach to a hilltop botanical garden (free with Cinque Terre Card) and old WWII bunkers. Another climbs scenically to the Madonna di Montenero sanctuary high above the town.

Beach: The beach is rocky, but clean and peaceful. It's a two-minute walk from the harbor: face the harbor, then take the path to your left. At the La Conchiglia bar, go down the stairs to the right of the bar. Follow the path to the beach.

Mar Mar Rooms rents kayaks (€8/hr for 2-person kayak) and offers boat excursions (fishing or cruising €30/day per person for up to 8 people, Via Malborghetto 4, tel. & fax 0187-920-932, marmar@5terre.com). The town also has a diving center (scuba, snorkeling, boats, kayaks, Via San Giacomo, tel. 0187-920-011).

Introductory Riomaggiore Walk

Here's an easy loop trip that maximizes views and minimizes uphill walking. Start at the train station (if you arrive by boat, take the tunnel alongside the tracks to get to the station). From the station, walk past the colorful murals glorifying the nameless workers who constructed the nearly 300 million cubic feet of dry stone walls (without cement) throughout the Cinque Terre, giving the region its characteristic *mura secca* terracing for vineyards and olive groves.

At the entrance of the railway tunnel, take the elevator up to the top of town (€0.50, free with Cinque Terre Card). At the top, go right, following the walkway—with spectacular sea views—around the cliff. Ignore the steps marked *Marina Seacoast* (harbor). Instead, continue along the path; it's a five-minute, fairly level walk to the church. Continue past the church and then take a right down the stairs to Via Colombo, Riomaggiore's main street.

Stroll down Via Colombo. Just past the WC, you'll see flower boxes on the street, sometimes blocking it; these slide back electronically to let the shuttle bus get past. On your way down the hill, you'll pass colorful, small shops, including a bakery, a couple of grocery shops, and a self-service laundry (€3.50 wash, €3.50 dry, daily 8:00–22:00, next door to Edi Rooms). When Via Colombo dead-ends, on your left you'll find the stairs down to the harbor, boat dock, and a 200-yard trail to the

Riomaggiore

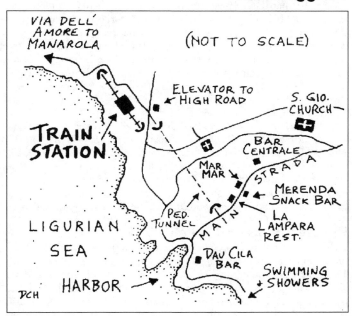

VIA DELL' AMORE TO MANAROLA

(NOT TO SCALE)

ELEVATOR TO HIGH ROAD

S. GIO. CHURCH

TRAIN STATION

BAR CENTRALE

MAR MAR

STRADA

MERENDA SNACK BAR

LA LAMPARA REST.

LIGURIAN SEA

PED. TUNNEL

MAIN

DAU CILA BAR

SWIMMING SHOWERS

HARBOR

DCH

beach *(spiaggia)*. To your right is the tunnel, running alongside the tracks, which takes you directly back to the station. Either take a train or hop a boat (from the harbor) to your next destination.

SLEEPING

Riomaggiore has organized its private room scene better than its neighbors. Several agencies within a few yards of each other on the main drag (with somewhat regular office hours, English-speaking staff, and e-mail addresses) manage a corral of local rooms for rent. Each of these offices can close unexpectedly; it's smart to settle up the day before you leave (in case they're closed when you have to depart). Expect lots of stairs.

Room-Finding Services
$$ Edi's Rooms rents five fine rooms and 12 apartments—half have views (Db-€52–80, Qb-€104 depending on view, season, and number of people, office open daily 9:00–20:00 in summer, otherwise 9:00–13:00 & 15:00–19:00, Via Colombo 111, tel. & fax 0187-920-325, tel. 0187-760-842, www.wel.it/vesignaedi, edi-vesigna@iol.it).

$$ **Mar Mar Rooms**, run by Mario Franceschetti, has 12 pleasant rooms, 10 apartments, and a mini-hostel (dorm bed-€21, Db apartments-€55–80, bunky family deals-€100–120 for 4 people, can request kitchen and balcony, parking €10/day but reserve in advance, unpredictable hours, Internet access in office, 30 yards above train tracks on main drag next to Lampara restaurant, Via Malborghetto 4, tel. & fax 0187-920-932, marmar@5terre.com). The same people run the recommended Albergo Caribana (below) using the same e-mail address; specify what you're interested in when you write. Mar Mar also rents kayaks and runs fishing trips (see page 220).

$$ **Luciano and Roberto Fazioli** loosely run three apartments, nine rooms, and a basic eight-bed mini-hostel (dorm bed-€20–25, D-€50–70, Db-€50–80, apartments-€30–70 per person, open daily 8:00–20:00, Via Colombo 94, tel. 0187-920-904, robertofazioli@libero.it).

$$ **La Dolce Vita,** across from Edi Rooms, offers five rooms and eight apartments (€20–30 per person; open daily 9:30–19:30, if they're closed, they're full; Via Colombo 120; tel. 0187-760-044, agonatal@tin.it).

Private Rooms and Hotels

$$$ **Villa Argentina** is worth considering if you want a real hotel. It's on the top ridge of town (15-min walk uphill from "downtown"), with 15 crisply clean, modern rooms, fine balconies (for 9 rooms), and sea views. While this is a good choice for drivers, the little bus that shuttles people (and their luggage) between the top and bottom of town also makes this hotel a possibility for train travelers (Db-€120, includes breakfast, no CC; Via de Gasperi 170, go through tunnel from station, wait for bus or walk 15 min uphill, then take a left at parking booth; tel. 0187-920-213, fax 0187-920-213, villaargentina@libero.it).

$$ **Michielini Anna** rents four clean, attractive apartments in the center with kitchens and no views (€52/2 people, €93/3 people, €104/4 people mid-April–Sept, less during low season, credit card to reserve but pay cash, cheaper for longer stays, 2 nights preferred June–Sept, across from Bar Centrale at Colombo 143, ring bell to open door; to call friendly Daniela, who speaks good English, dial 0187-920-950 or mobile 328-131-1032; for solo-Italiano-speaking mother, try tel. & fax 0187-920-411; anna.michielini@tin.it or michielinis@yahoo.it).

$$ **Albergo Caribana** has six modern rooms with views and shared terraces. At the edge of town, it's a five-minute walk to the center. The free, easy parking makes this especially appealing to drivers (Db-€64–90, depending on season, includes breakfast, Via Santuario 114, tel. 0187-920-773, tel. & fax 0187-920-932, marmar@5terre.com). The same people run Mar Mar Rooms, a room-finding service (see above), using the same e-mail address; specify what you want when you write.

EATING

Ristorante La Lampara serves a *frutti di mare* pizza, *trenette al pesto,* and the aromatic *spaghetti al cartoccio*—spaghetti with mixed seafood cooked in foil (€15 tourist *menu,* Wed–Mon 12:00–14:30 & 18:00–22:30, closed Tue in winter, on Via Malborghetto 10 just above tracks off Via Colombo, tel. 0187-920-120). Groceries and delis (such as Da Simone) on Via Colombo sell food to go, including pizza slices; have your picnic at the harbor.

    Bar Centrale, run by friendly Ivo and Alberto, is a good stop for breakfast, cheeseburgers, Internet access, and live music (sometimes in summer). Ivo lived in San Francisco, fills his bar with only the best San Franciscan rock, parties on the Fourth of July, speaks great English, and can even help you find a room. During the day, Bar Centrale is a shaded place to relax with other travelers. At night, it offers the only action in town (daily 7:30–1:00, closed Mon in winter only, confirm prices, Via Colombo 144, tel. 0187-920-208, barcentr@tin.it). There's prizewinning gelato next door.

    While the late-night fun is at Ivo's Bar Centrale, take a walk down to the harborside **Dau Cila** bar (10:30–24:30, closed Tue, tel. 0187-760-032) for jazz, nets, and mellow *limoncino*—a drink of lemon juice, sugar, and pure alcohol (a.k.a. *limoncello* elsewhere in Italy).

    For a snack or good takeout, try **Te Do Io La Merenda** ("I'll give you a snack"). Their counter is piled with an assortment of munchies, and they have pastas, roasted chicken, and focaccia to go (daily 8:30–21:30, tel. 0187-920-148, Via Colombo 171).

Manarola (Town #2)

Like Riomaggiore, Manarola is attached to its station by a 200-yard-long tunnel. The town is tiny and picturesque, a tumble of buildings bunny-hopping down its ravine to the fun-loving harbor. Notice how the I-beam crane launches the boats.

    Facing the harbor, look at the hillside to your right, dotted with a bar in the middle. It's Punta Bonfiglio, an entertaining park/game area/bar with the best view playground on the coast. The gate farther up the hillside is the entrance to the cemetery. From here you can get poster-perfect views of Manarola (2-min walk from the harbor on path to Corniglia).

    In the middle of town, across from the railway tunnel, you'll see Bar Aristide, which sometimes shows outdoor movies on weekends in August by hanging a screen over part of the tunnel entrance (closed Mon, Via Discovolo 290, tel. 0187-920-000). At the top of the town,

Manarola

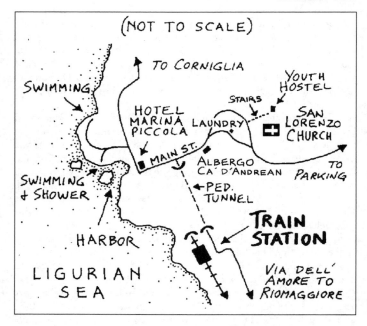

you'll find great views, the church, and a cluster of accommodations, including a super hostel.

The simple, wooden **religious scenes** that you'll likely see on the hillside are the work of local resident Mario Andreoli. Before his father died, Mario promised him he'd replace the old cross on the family's vineyard. Mario's been adding figures ever since. After recovering from a rare illness, he redoubled his efforts. The scenes, which do change occasionaly (a sheep here, an apostle there), are sometimes left up year-round. On religious holidays, everything's lit up: the Nativity, the Last Supper, the Crucifixion, the Resurrection, and more.

Services: You can store baggage in the Cinque Terre Park office in train station (€0.50/hr, up to 6 hours, then €6/up to 24 hrs, daily 7:00–22:00, 8:00–20:00 in winter). Within Manarola, the shuttle bus runs between main street and the parking lot (€1.50 one-way, €2.50 round-trip, free with Cinque Terre Card, 2/hr, just flag it down).

Beach: Manarola has no sand, but offers the best deepwater swimming of all of the Cinque Terre towns. The first "beach," with a shower, ladder, and wonderful rocks (with daredevil high-divers), is my favorite. The second has tougher access and no shower, but feels more remote and pristine (follow paved path around point).

SLEEPING

Manarola has plenty of private rooms. Ask in bars and restaurants. Otherwise, you'll find a modern three-star place halfway up the main drag, a cluster of great values around the church at the peaceful top of town (a 5-min hike above the train tracks), and a salty place on the harbor. The town's handy shuttle bus service makes getting to and from your car easier (€1.50 one-way, €2.50 round-trip, free with Cinque Terre Card).

$$ The utterly normal **Albergo ca' d'Andrean** is quiet, comfortable, modern, and very hotelesque, with 10 big, sunny rooms and a cool garden oasis complete with lemon trees (Sb-€60, Db-€80, breakfast-€6, closed Nov, up the hill at Via A. Discovolo 101, tel. 0187-920-040, fax 0187-920-452, www.cadandrean.it, cadandrean@libero.it, Simone SE).

$$ **Affitta Camere de Baranin** rents eight newly renovated, airy, refreshing rooms (Db-€63–80, Db with view and breakfast-€85, also have 5 apartments with kitchen for weekly rental, reserve with credit card but pay cash, Internet access; reception office open 7:30–13:30 & 15:30–19:30; climb stairway against wall beyond church square—with your back to the church, stairway is at 7:00, follow sign to Trattoria dal Billy, Via Rollandi 29; tel. & fax 0187-920-595, www.baranin.com, Sara, Silvia, and Andrea SE).

$$ **La Torretta** has four compact apartments with kitchens, five doubles, one quad, and a large, shared seaview terrace and sundeck with lounge chairs, all attractively designed by the young English-speaking architect/manager Gabriele Baldini (student Db-€26–38, standard Db-€52–72, Db apartment-€57–77, Qb-€83–124, prices vary with season, reserve with credit card but pay cash, $50 nonrefundable deposit is lost if you cancel, views, big garden; with your back to church, it's at 10:00—look left across the square toward the sea, Piazza della Chiesa, Vico Volto 14; tel. & fax 0187-920-327, www.cinqueterre.net/torretta, torretta@cdh.it, also rents a Tuscan villa).

$$ **Marina Piccola** offers 13 bright, modern rooms on the water—so they figure a warm welcome is unnecessary (Db-€80 for 1-night stays, discounts for longer stays, half-pension available at €72 per person but only for stays of 3 nights or longer, Via allo Scalo 16, tel. 0187-920-103, fax 0187-920-966, www.hotelmarinapiccola.com, info@hotelmarinapiccola.com).

$ **Casa Capellini** rents four fine rooms; one has a view balcony, another a 360-degree terrace (Db-€42; the *alta camera* on the top, with a kitchen, private terrace, and knockout view, costs €57; 2 doors down the hill from the church, with your back to the church, it's at 2:00, Via Ettore Cozzani 12, tel. 0187-920-823 or 0187-736-765, casa.capellini @tin.it, NSE).

$ **Ostello 5-Terre,** Manarola's modern and well-run hostel, stands like a Monopoly hotel behind the church square. It's smart to reserve at least two weeks in advance in high season (1 week in off-season). You book with your credit card number; if you cancel with less than three days' notice, you'll be charged for one night. This is not a party hostel; quiet is greatly appreciated (May–Sept: beds-€20, Qb-€80; off-season: beds-€17, Qb-€64; closed early Jan–mid-Feb; 48 beds in 4- to 6-bed rooms, not coed except for couples and families; office closed 13:00–17:00; rooms closed 10:00–17:00, curfew–1:00; off-season: office and rooms closed until 16:00 and curfew at 24:00; open to anyone of any age, laundry, safes, phone cards, Internet access, book exchange, elevator, optional €3.50 breakfast and €6 dinner, great roof terrace and sunset views, Via B. Riccobaldi 21, tel. 0187-920-215, fax 0187-920-218, www.hostel5terre.com, ostello@cdh.it). They also rent bikes, kayaks, and snorkeling gear.

Corniglia (Town #3)

From the station, a footpath zigzags up nearly 400 stairs to the only town of the five not on water. Take the bus (€1.50, free with Cinque Terre Card, 2/hr). Originally settled by a Roman farmer who named it for his mother, Cornelia (how Corniglia is pronounced), the town and its ancient residents produced a wine so famous that vases found at Pompeii touted its virtues. Today, wine is still its lifeblood. Follow the pungent smell of ripe grapes into an alley cellar and get a local to let you dip a straw into a keg. Remote and less visited, Corniglia has fewer tourists, cooler temperatures, a windy belvedere (on its promontory), a few restaurants, and plenty of private rooms for rent (ask at any bar or shop).

Beaches: This hilltop town has a rocky man-made beach below its station (toward Manarola). It's clean and uncrowded, and the beach bar has showers, drinks, and snacks.

The nude Guvano (GOO-vah-noh) beach is in the opposite direction (toward Vernazza). This beach made headlines in Italy in the 1970s, as clothed locals in a makeshift armada of dinghies and fishing boats retook their town beach. But big-city nudists still work on all-around tans in this remote setting. From the Corniglia train station, follow the road north, go over the tracks, then zigzag below the tracks, following signs to the tunnel in the cliff (walk past the *proprieta privata* sign). When you buzz the intercom, the hydraulic *Get Smart*–type door is opened from the other end. After a 15-minute hike through a cool, moist, and dimly lit unused old train tunnel, you'll emerge at the Guvano beach—and get charged €3. The beach has drinking water, but no WC. A steep (free) trail leads from the beach up to the Corniglia–Vernazza trail. The crowd is Italian counterculture: pierced nipples, tattooed punks, hippie drummers in dreads, and nude exhibitionist men.

Corniglia

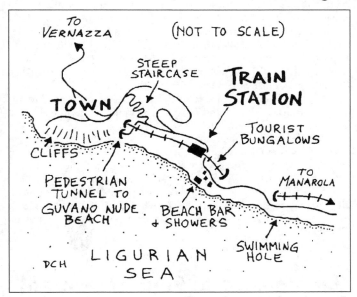

TO VERNAZZA

(NOT TO SCALE)

STEEP STAIRCASE

TRAIN STATION

TOWN

TOURIST BUNGALOWS

CLIFFS

PEDESTRIAN TUNNEL TO GUVANO NUDE BEACH

BEACH BAR + SHOWERS

TO MANAROLA

SWIMMING HOLE

DCH   LIGURIAN SEA

The ratio of men to women is about three to two. About half the people on the pebbly beach keep their swimsuits on.

SLEEPING

Perched high above the sea on a hilltop, Corniglia has plenty of private rooms (generally Db-€60). To get to the town from the station, catch the shuttle bus or take a 15-minute uphill hike. If you hike, choose between a long road or lots of stairs. At the top of the stairs, turn left to reach the town (if you've taken the road, just stay on the road). The main drag is Via Fieschi, stretching to the tip of the promontory and its viewpoint park.

$$ **Domenico Spora** has eight apartments scattered throughout town, all with views, terraces, and private bath (Db-€70, Qb-€100, Via alla Stazione 19, tel. 0187-812-293, NSE). Her place is about three-fourths of the way up the hill—if you're walking, take the road, rather than the stairs, up from the station.

$$ **La Lanterna** bar on the main square rents 12 sleepable rooms in town, some with a view (D-€53, Db-€65, also has 6 new rooms in Comeneco a 30-min walk away—better for drivers, tel. 0187-812-291, Via Fieschi 164, www.5terre.com).

$$ Louisa and Cristiana rent four rooms (2 with views) and a great apartment (with three doubles, big comfy living room/kitchen, and seaview terrace) on the tiny soccer court near the end of Via Fieschi (rooms are Db-€60, grand apartment for 2 people-€80, for 4 people-€100, for 6 people-€140, cheaper in winter, Via Fieschi 157, call English-speaking daughter Cristiana at tel. 0187-812-236—she works at Bar Matteo on Via Fieschi, below main square; also tel. & fax 0187-812-345; rents small apartment for €70 with no view).

$$ Villa Cecio, more like a hotel, has eight breezy, tranquil rooms on the outskirts of town (Db-€60, cash preferred, views, on main road 200 yards toward Vernazza, tel. 0187-812-043).

$ Pellegrini, on a quiet side street, offers three comfortable rooms (one with balcony) that share two baths and a terrace (D-€42 with view; going up Via Fieschi, take a left at Via Solferino, then go right, left, and left to find #34; tel. 0187-812-184 or 0187-821-176).

$ Villa Sandra has five good doubles (D-€55—2 have terraces, Db-€60) and seven apartments (Db-€62-70, Qb-€120, Via Fieschi 212, tel. & fax 0187-812-384, www.cinqueterre-laposada.com, la_posada @libero.it).

Monterosso al Mare (Town #5)

This is a resort with cars, hotels, rentable beach umbrellas, crowds, and a thriving nightlife. The town is split into the old and new (called Fegina), connected by a tunnel. The train station is in the new town, clustered with the TI and Cinque Terre park office. The statue named *Il Gigante*, which you'll see on the coast in the new town, is 45 feet tall, once held a trident, and looks as if it were hewn from the rocky cliff—but it's made of reinforced concrete and dates from the beginning of the 20th century.

Along the waterfront, whether in the new part of town or the breakwater of the old town, look for all the towns of the Cinque Terre strung out along the coast. Monterosso's old town contains Old World charm, small crooked streets, and Internet access.

Monterosso is 30 minutes off the freeway (exit: Carrodano). Parking is easy (except summer weekends and August) in the huge, beachfront guarded lot (€9/day).

Helpful Hints

Tourist Information: The TI Proloco is next to the train station (Mon–Sat 9:30–12:00 & 14:30–18:40, Sun 9:30–12:00, closed Nov–Easter, exit station and go left a few doors, tel. 0187-817-506). The Cinque Terre park office is in the station (Parco Nazionale delle Cinque Terre, daily 8:00–22:00, until 20:00 in winter, bag

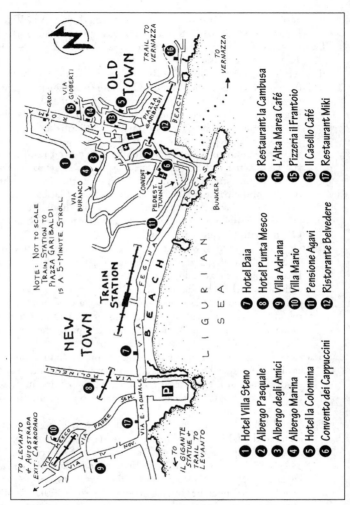

Monterosso

NOTE: NOT TO SCALE
TRAIN STATION TO
PIAZZA GARIBALDI
IS A 5-MINUTE STROLL

1 Hotel Villa Steno
2 Albergo Pasquale
3 Albergo degli Amici
4 Albergo Marina
5 Hotel la Colonnina
6 Convento dei Cappuccini
7 Hotel Baia
8 Hotel Punta Mesco
9 Villa Adriana
10 Villa Mario
11 Pensione Agavi
12 Ristorante Belvedere
13 Restaurant la Cambusa
14 L'Alta Marea Café
15 Pizzeria il Frantoio
16 Il Casello Café
17 Restaurant Miki

check (€0.50/hour up to 6 hrs, then €6/up to 24 hours; in the station, tel. 0187-817-059,www.parconazionale5terre.it, parconazionale5terre@libero.it).

Medical Help: The town's doctor is Dr. Vitone (mobile 338-853-0949).

Internet Access: The Net, a few steps off the main drag Via Roma on Via Vittorio Emanuele, offers 10 high-speed computers, classical music if Renato's on duty, and a free cuppa joe to patrons. Renato and Enzo happily provide information on the Cinque Terre and book accommodations, guides, and scuba diving (Via Vittorio Emanuele 55, tel. 0187-817-288, www.cinqueterrenet.com).

Laundry: A self-service launderette is at Via Mazzini 4 (daily 9:30–13:00 & 15:00–20:00).

Bus Service: There are two shuttle bus routes that run along the waterfront between the station, Piazza Garibaldi (main square in the old town just beyond the tunnel), the parking lot at the end of Via Fegina (stop is called Campo Sportivo), and the hills above Monterosso. Bus line #1 runs from Piazza Garibaldi to the train station (3 min, departs every hour at :30), then on to the parking lot and Colle di Gritta, where you can hike back down to Monterosso via the Sanctuary of Soviore (1 hr, easy), or to Levanto via Punta Mesco (2 hrs, strenuous). Bus line #2 runs in the opposite direction, from the parking lot to the station, Piazza Garibaldi, and up to Colle di Gritta (1/hr departing on the hour, runs daily 8:30–19:00, 10-min ride between old and new towns). Rides costs €1 (free with Cinque Terre Card).

Boats: From the old town harbor, boats run nearly hourly from 10:30–17:00 to Vernazza, Manarola, Riomaggiore and Portovenere. Boats also cruise twice daily to Levanto (June–Sept, otherwise weekends only). Schedules are posted in Cinque Terre park offices near every train station (€3 one-way to Vernazza or Levanto, €4.50 round-trip, €15 for a half-day pass beginning at 14:30, and up to €22 for a weekend all-day pass, pick up flier at any park office or at boat docks, tel. 0187-732-987 or 0187-818-440).

Beaches: The beaches, immediately in front of the train station, are easily the Cinque Terre's best and most crowded. Monterosso is a sandy resort with everything rentable...lounge chairs, umbrellas, paddleboats, and usually even beach access. Beaches are free only where you see no umbrellas.

Tours and Rentals: For hiking tours, boat excursions and rentals, chartered fishing, and other tourist services, check out American expat Kate Little's Fishnet Travel Services (tel. 328-842-6885, www.fishnet.it,kate@fishnet.it). Sean Risatti rents kayaks (€10/hour, €35/day) and offers kayak and hiking tours (see "Tours," near beginning of chapter, tel. 320-047-6865, cinqueterretrek@hotmail.com, or ask for Sean at The Net or Fishnet Travel Services).

Short Hike Connecting Old and New Towns

You can easily stroll the short tunnel between the new and old towns, but hikers prefer the trail. It's like a mini–Cinque Terre trail, combining scenery and greenery. Heading from the train station to the old town, take the path to the right of the tunnel entrance. The path leads to views of a German WWII bunker below on the rocks (worth seeing from afar, but not worth climbing down to).

Continuing on the path gets you into the old town. Or, at the point where you see the bunker, take the path up to the top of the hill (where you'll see a statue of St. Francis), and up farther still through the woods to reach a gate (marked Convento e Chiesa Cappuccini) leading to a church with a Van Dyck painting of the Crucifixion (accommodations next to church, see "Sleeping," below). You're a world away from the resort town below.

A trail to the right of the church leads up to the cemetery; appreciate its flowers, photos, and your beating heart. Backtrack to the St. Francis statue, and take the trail down into the old town. (Reversing this, if you're going from the old town to the new, take the trail to the right of the tunnel entrance; go right on Zii di Frati to see the church, or continue straight to get to the new town). Allow a total of 30 minutes if you include the church and cemetery.

NIGHTLIFE

Young travelers and night owls gather at Fast Bar on Via Roma in the old town to mix travel tales and beer (sandwiches and snacks served until midnight, closes 1:30, Oct–May closed Mon). For nightlife with a sea view, wander up to Il Casello by the *bocce* courts on the road toward Vernazza; its outdoor tables are sandwiched between the old town beaches (Wed–Mon 10:30–3:00, closed Oct–March, tel. 0187-818-330). Many of the little bars and *enotecas* (wine bars) in the old town stay open late during the summer months—wander the back streets until you find your favorite.

SLEEPING

Monterosso al Mare, the most beach-resorty of the five Cinque Terre towns, offers maximum comfort and ease. The TI (Pro Loco) just outside the train station can give you a list of €30–35-per-person double rooms (pricier for a single) or check with the Net Internet café in town.

Recommended hotels are listed for the old town and the new town (connected by a tunnel), with a convent-run place in between. To locate hotels, see the map on page 229. My favorite is the Hotel Villa Steno in the old town. To get to the old town from the station, exit left, walk along the waterfront, and go through the tunnel.

In the Old Town
$$$ The lovingly managed **Hotel Villa Steno** features great view balconies, private gardens off some rooms, air-conditioning, and the friendly help of English-speaking Matteo. Of his 16 rooms, 12 have view balconies (Sb-€90, Db-€135, Tb-€155, Qb-€175, includes hearty buffet breakfast, €10 discount per room per night if you pay cash and

show this book, Internet access, self-service laundry for guests only, 10-min hike from train station to top of old town at Via Roma 109, tel. 0187-817-028 or 0187-818-336, fax 0187-817-354, www.pasini.com, steno@pasini.com). Readers get a free Cinque Terre info packet and a glass of the local sweet wine, *sciacchetrà,* when they check in—ask. The Steno has a tiny parking lot (free, but call to reserve a spot).

   $$$ Albergo Pasquale is a modern, comfortable place, run by the same family who owns Hotel Villa Steno (see listing above). It's just a few steps from the beach, boat dock, tunnel entrance (to new town), and train tracks. The air-conditioning minimizes any train noise (Sb-€90, Db-€135, Tb-€155, Qb-€175, includes breakfast, €10 discount per room per night if you pay cash and show this book, readers get a free glass of the local sweet wine-*sciacchetrà*-at check-in, same-day laundry service, Via Fegina 4, tel. 0187-817-550 or 0187-817-477, fax 0187-817-056, pasquale@pasini.com, Felicita and Marco SE).

   $$$ The next two places, next door to each other on a quiet street, both require half-pension during peak season: the fancy **Albergo degli Amici** (40 modern rooms; Db-€98–130, breakfast included, Db with half-pension-€136—required July–Aug; no views from rooms, but peaceful above-it-all view garden with "sun beds"—lawn chairs with movable sun shades; Via Buranco 36, tel. 0187-817-544, fax 0187-817-424, www.cinqueterre.it/hotel_amici, amici@cinqueterre.it) and the less-fancy **Albergo Marina** (23 decent rooms, Db-€96–114, credit cards accepted but 5 percent discount with cash, elevator, air-con, garden with lemon trees, next door at Via Buranco 40, tel. & fax 0187-817-242 or 0187-817-613, www.hotelmarinacinqueterre.it, marina@cinqueterre.it). To get to the Amici and Marina from the old town harbor, go to the left of the arcaded building with the bell tower and turn left after a block; for the next listing go to the right of the arcaded building up Via Roma.

   $$ Hotel La Colonnina, a comfy, modern place on a sleepy side street, takes reservations in advance only for three-night stays. For a shorter stay, just call a day or two ahead to see if they have space (Db-€80–95, breakfast extra, elevator, garden, rooftop terrace, Via Zuecca 6, tel. 0187-817-439). In the old town by the train tracks, look for the playground and the square with a statue of Garibaldi; Via Zuecca is directly behind him (the hotel is one block up, to the right).

Between the Old and New Towns

$$ The religious **Convento dei Cappuccini** rents 16 spartan rooms on the hill above the tunnel connecting the old and new parts of town. The terrace, overlooking the garden and a long stretch of coastline, has a tremendous panoramic view (S-€35, D-€70, Db-€80, all twins, includes breakfast, dinner €15 and optional; reserve ahead, must send a deposit of 30 percent—personal check OK; €8 parking-reserve in advance; 19016 Monterosso; tel. 0187-817-531, monterosso.convento@libero.it, SE). To hike to the convent from the station (15 min), follow the recommended walk listed in Cinque Terre Towns/Monterosso, above. Or, instead of hiking, you can take a taxi (€8) or shuttle bus (€1) to the cemetery 200 yards away (go around or walk through cemetery to reach convent; its door is to left of church).

In the New Town

Turn right leaving the station for the following listings.

$$$ The central, waterfront **Hotel Baia** has appealing, high-ceilinged rooms, but impersonal staff (Db-€100–140, includes breakfast, slow elevator, some balconies, request view—same price, Via Fegina 88, tel. 0187-817-512, fax 0187-818-322, www.baiahotel.it).

$$$ **Hotel Punta Mesco** has 17 quiet, modern rooms (Db-€110, discount with cash, no views but some rooms have little terraces, free parking, exit right from station, take first right, Via Molinelli 35, tel. 0187-817-495, www.hotelpuntamesco.it, info@hotelpuntamesco.it, SE).

$$$ **Villa Adriana** has 55 decent, clean rooms divided between a 19th-century villa and an adjacent, modern annex. With a lofty setting (up off the street with a tropical garden as its front yard), and a religious, institutional atmosphere, it's peaceful (Sb-€65, Db-€130, half-pension available June–mid-Sept: Sb-€80, Db-€140, doubles and twins available; some views, some balconies, attached chapel, elevator, parking, private beach access-€6/day for umbrella and chair, €7/day for umbrella and lounge; exit right from station, walk along waterfront, turn right at Via IV Novembre, 300 yards off beach, Via IV Novembre 23, reception at back of building; tel. 0187-818-109, fax 0187-818-128, SE).

$$ **Villa Mario**, good for backpackers, has three basic rooms with a view terrace and a squawky bird (Db-€60–80, exit right from station, take second right, walk 5 min uphill, Via Padre Semeria 28, tel. & fax 0187-818-030, villamariomonte@libero.it).

$$ **Pensione Agavi** has 10 bright, airy rooms (Sb-€47, Db-€85, reserve with credit card but pay cash, refrigerators, turn left out of station to Fegina 30, tel. 0187-817-171, mobile 333-697-4071, fax 0187-818-264, www.paginegialle.it/hotelagavi, agavi@libero.it, spunky Hillary SE).

EATING

In the Old Town

Ristorante Belvedere is a good bet for good value. Their *amphora di pesce*—mixed seafood stew (€43/2 people minimum)—is inspiring (Wed–Mon 12:00–14:30 & 19:00–22:00, closed Tue, right on the harbor, across from Albergo Pasquale, tel. 0187-817-033).

La Cambusa serves up traditional Ligurian cuisine to hungry locals and tourists alike (Tue–Sun 12:00–14:30 & 18:45–22:00, closed Mon except July–Aug, Via Roma 6, tel. 0187-817-546).

Lots of shops and bakeries sell pizza and focaccia for an easy picnic at the beach. **L'Alta Marea** offers a specialty fish ravioli, the catch of the day, and huge crocks of fresh, steamed mussels (Thu–Tue 12:00–15:00 & 18:30–22:00, closed Wed, Via Roma 54, tel. 0187-817-170). **Il Frantoio** makes tasty pizza to go (Wed–Fri 9:00–14:00 & 16:00–20:00, closed Thu in winter, Via Gioberti 1, just off Via Roma, tel. 0187-818-333). For a quick salad or sandwich near the beach, try **Il Casello,** next to the *bocce* court on the trail to Vernazza (Wed–Mon 10:30–3:00 in morning, closed Tue Oct–March, tel. 0187-818-330).

In the New Town
Miki is packed with locals who know their seafood and don't want to spend a fortune (Wed–Mon 12:00–15:00 & 19:00–23:00, reservations wise, 100 yards north of train station at Via Fegina 104, tel. 0187-817-608).

TRANSPORTATION CONNECTIONS

Cinque Terre
The five towns of the Cinque Terre are on a milk-run train line described earlier in this chapter. Hourly trains connect each town with the others, La Spezia, and Genoa. While a few of the milk-run trains go to more distant points (Milan or Pisa), it's faster to change in La Spezia or Monterosso to a bigger train. Train info: Monterosso tel. 0187-817-458.

From La Spezia by train to: Rome (10/day, 4 hrs), Pisa (hrly, 1 hr, direction: Livorno, Rome, Salerno, Naples, etc.), Florence (nearly hrly, 2.5 hrs, change at Pisa), Milan (hrly, 3 hrs direct or 4 hrs with change in Genoa), Venice (2/day, 6 hrs, with change in Pisa and Florence or 2/day change in Milan, 1 direct/day in summer only).

From Monterosso by train to: Venice (2/day, 5.5 hrs with change in Florence and Pisa or 2/day 6 hrs with change in Milan), Milan (11/day with change in Genova, 3 hrs), Genoa (hrly, 1.25 hrs), Turin (7/day, 3 hrs), Pisa (8/day, 1.5 hrs), Sestri Levante (hrly, 15 min, most trains to Genova stop here), La Spezia (nearly hrly, 20 min), Levanto (nearly hrly, 6 min).

Driving in the Cinque Terre
Milan to the Cinque Terre (130 miles): Drivers speed south by autostrada A7 from Milan, skirt Genoa, and drive along some of Italy's most scenic and impressive freeways toward the port of La Spezia (A12). The road via Parma is faster, 30 miles longer, and less scenic.

All of the Cinque Terre towns have a parking lot and a shuttle bus to get you into town (except Corniglia—no lot, but parking is available). Monterosso's guarded beachfront lot fills only in August and on weekends (€9/day).

To drive to Monterosso (30 min from autostrada) or Vernazza (45 minutes from autostrada), exit the autostrada at Uscita Carrodano west of La Spezia. Note that the drive down to Vernazza is scenic, narrow, and treacherous. On busy weekends and in July and August, Vernazza fills up and police at the top of town will deny entry to anyone without a hotel reservation, so it's smart to have a confirmation in hand. If you don't, insist (politely) that they allow you to enter—but only if you actually have a room reserved (the police might call your hotel to check out your story). To drive to Riomaggiore, Corniglia, or Manarola, leave the freeway at La Spezia.

You can park your car near the train stations in La Spezia or Levanto (the first town past Monterosso). Confirm that parking is OK and leave nothing inside to steal. In La Spezia, the garage near the station can store your car for about €12 per day. Otherwise, free parking is a few blocks west of station at end of Via XV Giugno.

RIVIERA SIGHTS NEAR THE CINQUE TERRE

The Cinque Terre is tops, but several towns to the north have a breezy beauty and more beaches. Towns to the south offer a mix of marble, trains, and yachts.

Levanto, the northern gateway to the Cinque Terre, has a long beach and a scenic two-hour trail to Monterosso. Sestri Levante, on a narrow peninsula flanked by two beaches, is for sun-seekers. Santa Margherita Ligure is more of a real town, with actual sights, beaches, and easy connections with Portofino by trail, bus, or boat.

South of the Cinque Terre, you'll likely pass through (don't stay unless desperate) the work-a-day town of La Spezia, the southern gateway to the Cinque Terre. Carrara is a quickie for marble-lovers who are driving between Pisa and La Spezia. The picturesque village of Portovenere, near La Spezia, has scenic boat connections with Cinque Terre towns.

North of the Cinque Terre

Levanto

Graced with a long, sandy beach, Levanto is packed in summer. The rest of the year, it's just a small, sleepy town, with less colorful charm and fewer tourists than the Cinque Terre. With quick connections to Monterosso (6 min by train), Levanto makes a decent home base if you can't snare a room in the Cinque Terre.

Levanto has a new section (gridded street plan) and a twisty old town (bisected by a modern street), plus a few pedestrian streets, a castle (not open), and a scenic, no-wimps-allowed hike to Monterosso (2 hrs).

Tourist Information: From the Levanto train station to the **TI**,

Sights Near the Cinque Terre

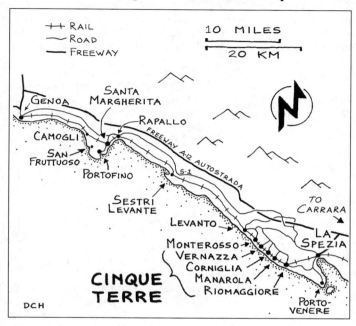

it's a 10-minute walk (head down the stairs in front of the station, cross the bridge, then follow Corso Roma to Piazza Mazzini). At the TI, pick up a map (Mon–Sat 9:00–13:00 & 15:00–18:00, Sun 9:00–13:00, shorter hours in winter, tel. 0187-808-125).

Drivers can park free at the train station (there's also a free lot north of Piazza Mazzini and the TI, but it's near a pay lot—confirm you're in the free one).

Internet Access: Try **Internet Buffet** (Mon–Sat 10:30–14:00 & 15:00–20:00, closed Sun, €3.60/30 min, Via Garibaldi 68, tel. 0187-804-025).

Launderette: A self-service laundry is at Piazza Staglieno 38 (daily 8:30–23:00, €5 wash, €5 dry, soap included).

SIGHTS

Beach—The beach is just two blocks away from the TI. During the summer, half the beach is free *(libero),* the other half is broken up into private sections that require an admission fee. Off-season, roughly October through May, when the sea is free, you can stroll the entire beach. Facing the harbor, the boat dock is to your far left and the diving center is at your far right (you can rent boats in summer at either place). **Old Town and Trailhead**—The old town, several blocks from the TI and beach, clusters around Piazza del Popolo. Until 10 years ago, the town market *(mercato)* was held at the 13th-century loggia in the square. Explore the back streets.

To get to the trailhead to Monterosso: from Piazza del Popolo, head uphill to the striped church, Chiesa di S. Andrea (with your back to the loggia, go straight ahead—across the square and up Via Don Emanuele Toso to the church). From the church courtyard, follow the sign to the *castello* (castle), go around the castle, and turn left. You'll see the sign for Punta Mesco, the rugged tip of the peninsula. From here you can hike up (2 hrs to Monterosso), or—if you have second thoughts—hike down, taking the stairs to the beach. You'll end up near the dock, where you can catch the boat for the Cinque Terre towns.

SLEEPING

(€1 = about $1.10, country code: 39)
In this popular beach town, a number of hotels want you to take half-pension (lunch or dinner) in summer.

$$ Ristorante la Loggia has four pleasant rooms perched above the old loggia on Piazza del Popolo (Db-€55–70, air-con, request balcony, quieter rooms in back, apartment available, attached restaurant, Piazza del Popolo 7, tel. & fax 0187-808-107, www.tigulliovino.it/ristorantelaloggia.htm).

$$ Villa Clelia B&B offers six peaceful rooms with fridge and terrace in a courtyard just 50 yards from the sea (Db €70–80, with loggia on your left it's straight ahead at Piazza da Passano 1, tel. & fax 0187-808-195, mobile 328-797-6403, villa_clelia@libero.it).

$$ Albergo Primavera has 17 comfortable rooms—10 with terraces but no views—just a half-block from the beach (Db-€100; buffet breakfast, closed Nov–Jan; Via Cairoli 5, about 100 yards from the beach; tel. 0187-808-023, fax 0187-801-588, www.primaverahotel.com, info@primaverahotel.com, friendly staff speaks a little English).

$$ Hotel Europa, is a good bet, with 22 decent, well-maintained rooms (Db-€65–90, Db with half-pension required Jun–Aug-€110–124, roof terrace, elevator, Via Dante Alighieri 41, tel. 0187-808-126, fax 0187-808-594, albeurop@tin.it).

$$ Villa Margherita B&B is 300 yards out of town, but the shady gardens, characteristic tiled rooms (some with terraces), and tranquility are worth the walk (Sb-€40–60, Db-€80–100, Tb-€85–100, apartment for up to 6 available by the week, free Internet, parking, 10-min walk to town, 5-min walk to train station, free shuttle service from station if you tell them when you'll arrive, Via Trentoe Trieste 31, tel. 0187-807-212, mobile 328-842-6934, www.villa margherita.net, info@villamargherita.net).

$ **Hostel:** The **Ostello Ospitalia del Mare** offers 67 beds, bright rooms, Internet access, and a terrace in a well-built building in the old town (beds-€19–28 in 2-, 4-, 6-, and 8-bed rooms with private bath, includes breakfast and sheets, anyone welcome but 10 percent discount with hostel card; not coed except for couples and families, no curfew; office hours daily April–Sept 8:00–13:00 & 14:30–23:00, Oct–March 10:00–12:00 & 16:00–18:00; Via San Nicolo 1, tel. 0187-802-562, fax 0187-803-696, www.ospitaliadelmare.it, ospitalia@libero.it, SE).

EATING

Totano Blu offers Ligurian specialties and pizzas at reasonable prices in the old town (Fri–Wed 12:00–16:00 & 19:00–22:00, Thu 19:00–22:00, Via Molinelli 10/12, tel. 0187-808-714). **Osteria Tumelin** is a bit spendier, but has great fresh seafood and ambience (Fri–Wed 12:00–16:00 & 19:00–23:30, closed Thu in winter, Via D. Grillo, across street from loggia, tel. 0187-808-379).

Taverna Garibaldi is an affordable, homey place on the most characteristic street in Levanto, serving focaccia with various toppings, made-to-order *farinata* (savory chickpea crêpe), salads, and light meals (daily in summer 19:30–23:00, closed Tue Sept–June, tel. 0187-808-098).

La Picea serves up wood-fired pizzas to go (Tue–Sun 11:30–14:30 & 16:30–21:30, Via della Concia 8, on the corner of Via Varego and Via della Concia behind the soccer field, tel. 0187-802-063).

Focaccerie, rosticcerie, and delis with take-out pasta abound on Via D. Alighieri. **Polleria** sells roasted chicken and potatoes to go (daily in summer 8:00–12:30 & 16:00–20:00, closed Mon off-season, Via Cairoli 3, tel. 0187-808-423). **Focacceria il Falcone** has a great selection of focaccia with different toppings (Tue–Sun 9:30–20:00, closed Mon, Via Cairoli 19, tel. 0187-807-370). For more picnic fare, try Levanto's modern, covered *mercato* (Mon–Sat 8:30–13:00, closed Sun; fish and produce market; between train station and TI: the street it's on—only a decade old—hasn't yet been officially named). On Wednesday morning, an open-air market fills the street in front of the *mercato*. Piazza C. Colombo, with its benches and sea view, makes an excellent picnic spot. For a shadier setting, lay out your spread on a bench near Piazza Staglieno.

For dessert, sample **Il Penguino Gelateria** on Piazza Staglieno 2 (Thu–Tue 8:00–late, closed Wed) or **Il Porticciolo Gelateria** at the end of Via Cairoli in Piazzeta Marina (closed Mon, tel. 0187-800-954).

TRANSPORTATION CONNECTIONS

To get to the Cinque Terre, take the **train** (nearly hrly, 6 min to Monterosso) or the **boat** (2/day Easter–Oct, none off-season, stops at every Cinque Terre town except Corniglia before heading to Portovenere; €3 one-way to Monterosso, or €15 for half-day pass to Portovenere—departing Levanto around 14:30, with 1-hr stop before return to Levanto; as much as €22 for all-day weekend pass to Portovenere; 1 return boat/day from Portovenere departing around 17:00; pick up boat schedule and price sheet from TI or boat dock, or call tel. 0187-732-987 or 0187-777-727).

Sestri Levante

This peninsular town is squeezed as skinny as a hot dog between its two beaches. The pedestrian-friendly Corso Colombo, which runs down the middle of the peninsula, is lined with shops selling take-away pizza, pastries, and beach paraphernalia.

Hans Christian Andersen enjoyed his visit here in the mid-1800s, writing, "What a fabulous evening I spent in Sestri Levante!" One of the bays—Baia delle Favole—is named in his honor (*favole* means fairy tale). The last week of May is a street festival, culminating in a ceremony for locals who write the best fairy tales (4 prizes for 4 age groups, from pre-kindergarten to adult). The "Oscar" awards are little mermaids. The small mermaid curled on the edge of the fountain (behind the TI) is another nod to the beloved Danish storyteller.

Tourist Information: From the train station (luggage storage- €3), it's a five-minute walk to the TI to get a map (May–Sept Mon–Sat 9:30–12:30 & 15:00–19:30, Sun 9:30–12:30 & 16:30–19:30, Oct–April closes at 17:30 and on Sun; go straight out of station on Via Roma, turn left at fountain in park, TI at next square—Piazza S. Antonio 10; tel. 0185-457-011). Market day is Saturday at Piazza Aldo Moro (8:00–17:00).

SIGHTS

Stroll the Town—From the TI, take Corso Colombo (to the left of Bermuda Bar), which runs up the peninsula. Follow this street—lively with shops and eateries—until nearly the end (about 5 min). Just before you get to the large white church at the end, turn off for either beach (free beach is on your left). Or head uphill behind the church. You'll pass the evocative arches of a ruined chapel (bombed during World War II, and left as a memorial). Continue a few minutes farther to the Hotel

Castelli and consider a drink at their view café (so-so view, reasonably priced drinks, café is at end of parking lot to your right). The rocky, forested bluff at the end of the town's peninsula is actually the huge, private backyard of this fancy hotel.

Beaches—These are named after the bays *(baias)* they border. The bigger beach, Baia delle Favole, is divided up much of the year (May–Sept) into sections that you pay to enter. The fees, which can soar up to €26 in August, generally include chairs, umbrellas, and fewer crowds. There are several small free sections: at the ends and in the middle (look for *libere* signs). For less-expensive sections of beach (where you can rent less than the works), ask for *spiaggia libera attrezzata.*

The town's other beach, Baia del Silenzio, is narrow, virtually all free, and packed, providing a good chance to see Italian families at play. There isn't much more to do than unroll a beach towel and join in.

SLEEPING

(€1 = about $1.10, country code: 39)

$$$ Hotel Due Mari, located in an old Genoese palazzo, has three stars, 49 fine rooms, and a rooftop terrace with a super view of both beaches. Ideally, reserve well in advance (Db-€110–140 depending on view, Db with half-pension required July–Aug-€156–188, buffet breakfast, some air-con, elevator, garden, swimming pool with heated seawater, take Corso Colombo to the end, hotel is behind church, parking €10/day, Vico del Coro 18, tel. 0185-42695, fax 0185-42698, www.duemarihotel.it, hotelduemari@inwind.it, SE).

$$$ Hotel Helvetia, overlooking Baia del Silenzio, is another good three-star bet, with 21 bright rooms, a large view terrace, and a peaceful atmosphere (Db-€140–155 depending on view/balcony, includes breakfast; parking-€10/day, air-con, elevator; from Corso Colombo turn left on Palestro and angle left at square, Via Cappuccini 43; tel. 0185-41175, fax 0185-457-216, www.hotelhelvetia.it, helvetia@hotelhelvetia.it, SE).

$$ Hotel Genova, run by the Bertoni family, is a shipshape hotel with shiny clean rooms, a rooftop sundeck, free loaner bikes, air-conditioning, and a good location just two blocks from Baia delle Favole (Sb-€45–90, Db-€68–106, Tb-€85–130 depending on season, includes buffet breakfast, free parking, elevator, Viale Mazzini 126, tel. 0185-41057, fax 0185-457-213, www.hotelristorantegenova.it, info@hotelristorantegenova.it).

$$ Hotel Elisabetta, less central, has 38 comfortable rooms on a busy street at the end of Baia delle Favole, a block from the beach (Db-€75–85 depending on season; half-pension available but not required, ask for quieter room in back; Via Novara 7, walk straight out of station, then turn right at park, 12-min walk; tel. 0185-41128, fax 0185-487-206, albergoelisabetta@libero.it, leetle English spoken).

$$ **Hotel Jolanda** is a homey, kid-friendly *pensione* with 17 simple rooms and a garden courtyard with a small swimming pool—perfect for families on a budget, located near Baia del Silenzio (Db-€70, Qb-€100, Via Pozzetto 15, tel. 0185-41354, www.villaiolanda.com, info @villaiolanda.com).

EATING

At **L'Osteria Mattana**, where everyone shares long tables, you can mix with locals while enjoying traditional cuisine (daily July–Aug, otherwise Tue–Sun 19:30–23:00, also Fri–Sun and in winter 12:30–14:30, closed Mon; take Corso Colombo from TI, turns into XXV Aprile, restaurant on right at #26; tel. 0185-457-633).

Polpo Mario is classier but affordable, with a fun people-watching location on the main drag (Tue–Sun 12:15–14:30 & 19:30–22:30, closed Mon, Via XXV Aprile 163, tel. 0185-480-203).

Ristorante Previna has good seafood and pizzas at fair prices (open Thu–Tue 12:00–14:30 & 19:00–22:00, closed Wed, Piazza della Repubblica 23, tel. 0185-42313).

For big salads, focaccia, and reasonably-priced pastas near Baia del Silenzio, try **Trattoria Mainolla** (Wed–Mon 12:00–15:00 & 19:00–22:00, closed Tue, Via XXV Aprile 187, tel. 0185-42556).

TRANSPORTATION CONNECTIONS

Sestri Levante is just 15 minutes away from Monterosso (hourly connections with Monterosso, nearly hourly with other Cinque Terre towns).

Santa Margherita Ligure

If you need the movie star's Riviera, park your yacht at Portofino. Or you can settle down in the nearby and more personable Santa Margherita Ligure (15 min by bus from Portofino and 1 hour by train from the Cinque Terre). While Portofino's velour allure is tarnished by snobby residents and a nonstop traffic jam in peak season, Santa Margherita tumbles easily downhill from its train station. The town has a fun resort character and a breezy promenade.

On a quick day trip, walk the beach promenade, see the small old town, and catch the bus (or boat) to Portofino to see what all the fuss is about. With more time, Santa Margherita makes a fine overnight stop.

Tourist Information: Pick up a map at the TI (daily 9:30–12:30 & 15:00–19:30, in winter Mon–Sat 9:30–12:30 & 14:30–17:30, closed

Sun, Via XXV Aprile 2b, tel. 0185-287-485, www.apttigullio.liguria.it).

Arrival by Train: To get to the city center from the station, take the stairs marked *Mare* (Sea) down to the harbor. The harborfront promenade is as wide as the skimpy beach. (The real beaches, which are pebbly, are a 10-min walk farther on, past the port.)

To get to the pedestrian-friendly old town and the TI, take a right at Piazza Veneto (with the roundabout, flags, and park) onto Largo Antonio Giusti. For the TI, angle left on Via XXV Aprile. For the old town (a block off Piazza Veneto), head toward the TI, but turn left on Via Torino, which opens almost immediately onto Piazza Caprera, a square with a church and morning fruit vendors in the midst of pedestrian streets.

Day-trippers arriving by train can store bags at the station's café/bar (€2.50/day per piece).

Internet Access: Internet Point gives readers with this book a free additional 30 minutes (€5.20/30 min; daily 9:00–21:00; Via Guinchetto 39, off Piazza Mazzini; tel. 0185-293-092, run by owners of recommended Hotel Fasce).

HISTORY OF
SANTA MARGHERITA LIGURE

This town, like the entire region (from the border of France to La Spezia), was ruled by the Republic of Genoa. In the 16th century, when Arab pirates from North Africa plagued the entire coastal area, Genoa had castles built in the towns and lookout towers in the neighboring hills.

Santa Margherita was actually two bickering towns—each with its own bay. In 1800, Napoleon came along, took over the Republic of Genoa, and made it one city—naming it Porto Napoleone. When Napoleon fell in 1815, the town stayed united and took the name of the patron saint of its leading church, Santa Margherita.

By 1850, residents set to work creating a Riviera resort. They imported palm trees from North Africa and paved a fine beach promenade. Santa Margherita and the area around it was studded with fancy villas built by the aristocracy of Genoa (which was controlled by just 35 families). English, Russian, and German aristocrats also discovered the town in the 19th century. Mass tourism only hit in the last generation. Even with the increased crowds, the town decided to stay chic and kept huge developments out. Its neighbor, Rapallo, chose the extreme opposite—giving Italian its word for uncontrolled growth ruining a once-cute town: *Rapallizzazione*.

Local Guide: Raffaella Cecconi communicates clearly in English and knows the region's history better than anyone I've met (half-day €100, full day €160, tel. 0185-41023, www.terra-mare.it, info @terra-mare.it).

Town Orientation Walk

Explore Santa Margherita Ligure on the following self-guided stroll. To begin, walk out to the tip of the **dock** (from Piazza Libertà). Find the statue of "Santa Margherita virgin martyr." Survey the town from here: the villas dotting the hills, the castle built in the 16th century (closed except for special exhibitions), the exclusive hotels.

Wander along the harborfront (down Via Marconi) past the castle to the marina and what's left of the town's fishing fleet. The fishing industry survives here (drag-netting octopus, shrimp, and miscellaneous "blue fish"—plus mountains of anchovies attracted to midnight lamps). The fish market (burgundy-colored stalls across the street) wiggles daily at 16:00—but don't be late. Residents complain it's easier to buy their locally-caught fresh fish in Milan than here.

Behind the fish market stands a small church, the **Oratory of San Erasmo.** St. Erasmus is the protector of the fishermen. Notice the fine and typically local black-and-white pebble mosaic (*riseu*) in front of the church (with maritime themes). The church is actually an "oratory," where a brotherhood of faithful men who did anonymous good deeds congregated and worshipped. It's decorated with ships and paintings of storms that—thanks to St. Erasmus—the local sailors survived. The huge crosses are carried through town on special religious holidays.

Next, climb the stairway (Via IV Novembre) to the church that stands overlooking the bay, the **Church of St. James** (Giacomo). Even though this is a secondary church in a secondary town, it's impressively lavish. The region's aristocrats amassed wealth from trade in the 11th to 15th centuries. When Constantinople fell to the Turks, free trade in the Mediterranean stopped and Genovese traders became bankers—making even more money. A popular saying of the day: "Silver is born in America, lives in Spain, and dies in Genoa." Bankers here served Spain's 17th-century royalty and aristocracy, and the accrued wealth paid for a golden age of art. Wander the church, noticing the inlaid marble floors and chapels.

Step out of the church and enjoy the sea view. Then turn left and step into **Durazzo Park** (Parco Comunale Villa Durazzo). This park was an abandoned shambles until 1973, when the city took it over (free, daily 9:00–19:00 in summer, until 17:00 in winter). Today it's a delight, with a breezy café enjoyed mostly by locals. The garden has two distinct parts: the carefully-coifed Italian garden (designed to complement the villa's architecture) and the calculatedly wild "English garden" below. The Italian garden is famous for its collection of palm trees—each one is different.

Santa Margherita Ligure

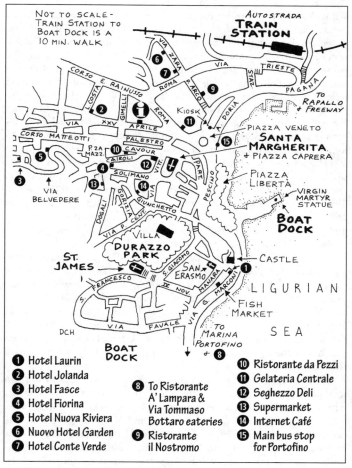

NOT TO SCALE—TRAIN STATION TO BOAT DOCK IS A 10 MIN. WALK

AUTOSTRADA
TRAIN STATION

TO RAPALLO + FREEWAY

PIAZZA VENETO
SANTA MARGHERITA
+ PIAZZA CAPRERA

PIAZZA LIBERTÀ

VIRGIN MARTYR STATUE

BOAT DOCK

CASTLE

LIGURIAN

FISH MARKET

SEA

BOAT DOCK

VILLA DURAZZO PARK

ST. JAMES

SAN ERASMO

KIOSK

VIA ZARA
VIA ROMA
CORSO E. RAINUSSO
COSTA
GIMELLI
ROMA
XXV APRILE
PALESTRO
CAVOUR
CAIROLI
SOLIMANO
GIUNCHETTO
GORINA
DOGALI
VIA P. CENT.
VIA P.
S. GIACOMO
IV NOV.
VIA FAVALE
S. FRANCESCO
VIA G. MARCONI
VIA MANARA
PESCINO
PART.
STAZ.
TRIESTE
PAGANA
DORIA
P. ARCO
VITT.
CORSO MATTEOTTI
P.ZA MAZZ.
VIA BELVEDERE

DCH

TO MARINA PORTOFINO

❶ Hotel Laurin
❷ Hotel Jolanda
❸ Hotel Fasce
❹ Hotel Fiorina
❺ Hotel Nuova Riviera
❻ Nuovo Hotel Garden
❼ Hotel Conte Verde

❽ To Ristorante A' Lampara & Via Tommaso Bottaro eateries
❾ Ristorante il Nostromo

❿ Ristorante da Pezzi
⓫ Gelateria Centrale
⓬ Seghezzo Deli
⓭ Supermarket
⓮ Internet Café
⓯ Main bus stop for Portofino

In the park, you'll see the **Villa Durazzo.** It's typical of the region, with some period furniture, several grand pianos, chandeliers, and paintings strewn with cupids on the walls and ceilings. It's not worth the entry fee for most (€5.50, summer Tue–Sun 9:30–18:30, winter Tue–Sun 9:30–16:30, closed Mon, WC in adjacent building, tel. 0185-205-449).

Your self-guided walk is over. Enjoy the park, then visit some other town sights.

SIGHTS

Church of Santa Margherita—The town's main church is textbook Italian Baroque. Its 18th-century facade hides a 17th-century interior. The chapels to the right of the high altar contain religious "floats" used in local festival parades. The wooden groups in the niches higher up used to be part of the processions, too. The altar is typical of 17th-century Ligurian altars—shaped like a boat, with lots of shelf space for candles, flowers, and relics. Remember, Baroque is like theater. After Vatican II in the 1960s, priests faced their flock, turning their back on the old altars rather than the people. For this reason, all over the Catholic world, modern tables serving as post-Vatican II altars stand in front of earlier altars that are no longer the center of attention during the Mass.

Via Palestro—This promenade (a.k.a. *caruggio*—"the big street" in local dialect) is *the* strolling street for window-shopping, people-watching, and studying the characteristic "liberty style" house painting from about 1900. Before 1900, people distinguished their buildings with pastel paint and distinctive door and window frames. Then they decided to get fancy and paint entire exteriors with false balconies, weapons, saints, beautiful women, and 3-D Gothic "concentrate."

As you wander from the Church of Santa Margherita inland, pop into the fanciest deli in town—Seghezzo (immediately to the right of the church on Via Cavour). Locals know they can find whatever odd ingredient the toughest recipe calls for in this venerable institution.

Farther up Via Palestro, you might drop into the traditional old Panificio (bakery) for a slice of fresh focaccia. Saying "*Vorrei un etto di focaccia*" will get you a greasy, 100-gram, €1 hunk of every kid's favorite beach munchie. Locals claim the best focaccia in Italy is made along this coast.

Markets—Around 16:00 on weekdays, fishing boats dock at the fish market to unload their catch, which is then sold to waiting customers. The market—Mercato del Pesce—is the rust-colored building with arches and columns on Via Marconi, on the harbor, just past the castle. The open-air market, a commotion of clothes and produce, is held every Friday morning on Corso Matteotti. Piazza Caprera (facing the main church) hosts a few farmers selling their produce from traditional stalls daily.

Beaches—The handiest Santa Margherita beaches are just below the train station. But the best are on the Portofino side of town ("Gio and Rino beach" just before Covo di Nordest is a favorite—not too expensive, fun and creative management). Paraggi (halfway to Portofino, easy bus connection) is by far the best, but it's very expensive (€25/day, you can't pay by the hour) and generally booked up by big shots from Portofino who have no beach.

Side-Trip to Portofino

Santa Margherita Ligure, with its aristocratic architecture, hints of old money, whereas Portofino, with its sleek shops, reeks of new money. Fortunately, a few pizzerias, bars, and grocery shops are mixed in with Portofino's jewelry shops, art galleries, and clothing boutiques, making the town affordable. The *piccolo* harbor, classic Italian architecture, and wooded peninsula can even turn glitzy Portofino into an appealing package. For an artsy park-like break, stroll around the Museo del Parco—a park just above the harbor littered with modern statues (€5, daily 10:00–13:30, 15:00–19:30).

Ever since the Romans founded Portofino for its safe harbor, it has had a strategic value (appreciated by everyone, from Napoleon to the Nazis). In the 1950s, *National Geographic* did a beautiful exposé on the idyllic port, and locals claim that's when Hollywood elite took note. Liz Taylor and Richard Burton came here annually. During one famous party, Rex Harrison dropped his Oscar into the bay. (It was recovered.) Ava Gardner came down from her villa each evening for a drink—sporting her famous fur coat. Greta Garbo loved to swim naked in the harbor, not knowing that half the town was watching. Truman Capote called Portofino home. But VIPs were here a century earlier. Nietzsche claimed he strolled with Zarathustra on the path between Portofino and Santa Margherita.

My favorite Portofino plan: Visit for the evening. Leave Santa Margherita on the bus around 17:00, hike the last 20 minutes from Paraggi beach, explore Portofino, splurge for a drink and then dinner on the harborfront, and return to Santa Margherita by bus (confirm late departures).

Portofino's **TI** is downhill from the bus stop, on your right (daily in summer 10:30–13:30 & 14:00–19:30, in winter Tue–Sun 10:30–13:30 & 14:30–17:30, closed Mon, Via Roma 35, tel. 0185-269-024). Pick up a free town map and a rudimentary hiking map.

For **hikers**, the best thing about Portofino is leaving it. Options include the well-trodden path that leads out to the lighthouse at the point (20 min, nonstop views, medieval castle en route); the pedestrian promenade to Paraggi (20 min, parallels main road, ends at ritzy beach where it's easy to catch the bus back to Santa Margherita Ligure); the trail to Santa Margherita Ligure (1 hr, 3 miles, leaving Santa Margherita start at Via Maragliano, several blocks past the castle); and the trail to San Fruttuoso Abbey (2.5 hrs, steep at beginning and end).

The 11th-century **San Fruttuoso Abbey,** accessible only by foot or boat (from Portofino or Santa Margherita) isn't the main attraction. The intriguing draw is a statue of Christ of the Abyss (Cristo degli Abissi), 60 feet underwater. Boats run from the abbey to the statue, where you can look down to see the arms of Jesus—outstretched, reaching upward.

Getting to Portofino from Santa Margherita: Portofino is an easy day trip by bus, boat, or foot.

Catch **bus** #82 from Santa Margherita's train station or at bus stops along the harbor (€1, 2–3/hr, 15 min, buy tickets at bar at station, at bus kiosk at Piazza Veneto—open daily 7:10–19:40, or at any shop that displays a *Biglietti Bus* sign). In Portofino, get tickets at the newsstand.

For a great 20-minute **hike** into Portofino, ride bus #82 only as far as the ritzy Paraggi beach. At the far end of the beach, cross the street and follow the paved trail marked "Pedonale per Portofino" high above the road. Twenty minutes later, you'll enter Portofino at a church labeled "Divo Martino"—which I figure means "the divine Martin" and has something to do with Dean Martin giving us all *Volare* (which I couldn't get out of my head for the rest of the day).

The **boat** makes the trip with more class and without the traffic jams (€3.50 one-way, €6 round-trip; hrly in summer 9:15–16:15, in spring and fall daily at 10:15 and 14:15, in winter only Sun at 10:15 and 14:15; dock is off Piazza Martiri della Libertà, a 2-min walk from Piazza Veneto; call to confirm or pick up schedule from TI, tel. 0185-284-670, www.traghettiportofino.it); the boats run between Rapallo and the San Fruttuoso Abbey, stopping in between at Santa Margherita Ligure and Portofino.

SLEEPING

(€1 = about $1.10, country code: 39)
To locate hotels, see map on page 245.

$$$ Hotel Laurin is a slick, air-conditioned, and modern place fixated on its harborfront views. All of its 43 rooms face the sea, most have terraces, and there's a heated pool and sundeck on the third floor. Though it's a Best Western, it's still family-run (Sb-€75–115, Db-€120–170 depending on season, request 10 percent discount with this book; air-con, double-paned windows, elevator; Lungomare G. Marconi 3, past the castle, 15-min walk from station; tel. 0185-289-971, fax 0185-285-709, www.laurinhotel.it, info@laurinhotel.it).

$$$ Hotel Jolanda is a solid, well-run, modern hotel with a revolving door, lavish public spaces, a friendly staff, and fine air-conditioned rooms (Db-€130, superior Db-€140, 10 percent discount with this book, about 20 percent less off season, 2 blocks from TI at Via Luisito Costa 6, tel. 0185-287-512, fax 0185-284-763, www.hoteljolanda.it, desk@hoteljolanda.it). They have 10 free loaner bikes parked at the front door.

$$ Hotel Fasce is a hardworking place with 16 bright rooms and a happy clientele (Sb-€85, Db-€95, Tb-€120, Qb-€140, includes breakfast, happy hour welcome drink, free round-trip train tickets to Cinque Terre for 3-night stays, free bikes, English newspapers, roof garden, parking-€16/day, laundry service-€16, 10-min walk from station at Via

Bozzo 3, taxi from station costs about €10, tel. 0185-286-435, fax 0185-283-580, www.hotelfasce.it, hotelfasce@hotelfasce.it, run enthusiastically by Englishwoman Jane Fasce and her husband, Aristide).

$$ Hotel Fiorina, with 55 airy rooms decorated in a light-and-dark color scheme, is on a busy square with quieter rooms in the back. It's family-run with pride and care (Db-€90–115 depending on season; fans in every room, sun terrace but no views; Piazza Mazzini 26, 2 blocks inland from pedestrian Piazza Caprera; tel. 0185-287-517, fax 0185-281-855, www.hotelfiorina.com, fiorinasml@libero.it, SE).

$$ At Hotel Nuova Riviera, a stately old villa, the Sabini family rents 12 non-smoking rooms (Db-€92, Tb-€120, Qb-€146, 5 percent discount with cash; fans in every room, some balconies, Internet access, free parking, peaceful garden; 10-min walk from station, walking or driving, follow signs to hospital, on Piazza Mazzini see hotel signs, Via Belvedere 10; tel. & fax 0185-287-403, www.nuovariviera.com, info@nuovariviera.com, pleasant daughter Cristina and son Giancarlo SE). Their annex is cheaper (3 nights preferred, D-€64, T-€90, Q-€104, 4 rooms share 2 bathrooms, cash only). Reserve carefully to avoid their strict cancellation penalties.

By the Train Station

Expect a little train noise at these places.

$$ Nuovo Hotel Garden is tucked away down a side street. From its 31 comfortable rooms to its restaurant, the hotel is high-quality (Db-€80–115 depending on season; terrace, bar, double-paned windows on train side, fans, free loaner bikes; Via Zara 13, a block from train station—instead of taking the stairs down to harbor, face stairs and go right; tel. 0185-285-398, fax 0185-290-439, www.nuovohotelgarden.com, info@nuovohotelgarden.com, SE).

$$ Hotel Conte Verde, on the same street, rents 33 rooms of varying quality and price. Ask if a room with a big terrace is available (Sb-€50–60, D-€50–80, Db-€70–80, price depends on season and size, includes breakfast, exercise room, garden, free loaner bikes, big public areas, parking-€11/day, Via Zara 1, tel. 0185-287-139, fax 0185-284-211, info@hotelconteverde.com, SE).

EATING

Ristorante "A' Lampara" is the locals' favorite for affordable Genovese cuisine cooked by an endearing family team. Try their specialty fish ravioli, *ravioli di pesce* (Fri–Wed 12:00–14:00 & 19:30–22:00, closed Thu, Via Maragliano 33, tel. 0185-288-926).

Ristorante il Nostromo, more central, also specializes in fish, offering a €20 *menu* plus à la carte options (daily in summer, closed Tue off-season; Via dell' Arco 6, a block off Piazza Veneto, take Via Gramsi and turn inland on Via dell' Arco; tel. 0185-281-390, Janet and Umberto).

Da Pezzi is a cheap and cheerful greasy spoon packed with locals munching *farinata* (thin pancake made from chickpeas) at the bar and enjoying pesto and fresh fish in the dining room (Sun–Fri 11:45–14:00 & 18:00–21:00, closed Sat, on Via Cavour, no reservations accepted).

Waterfront Dining: All along Via Tommaso Bottaro, you'll find restaurants, pizzerias, and bars serving food with a harbor view. The place above the fish market has the best views. The pizzeria next to Hotel Laurin is popular. Bar Giuli—the only place actually on the beach—serves forgettable salads and sandwiches for a reasonable price.

Gelato: The best *gelateria* I found (with *tartufo* and *riso*—that's rice) is Il Portico (under the castle, closest to the water on Piazza Liberta 48). Gelateria Centrale, just off Piazza Veneto near the cinema, serves up their specialty—*pinguino* (penguin), a cone with your chioce of gelato dipped in chocolate.

Groceries: Seghezzo (immediately to the right of the church on Via Cavour) is classiest. The Doro Centry supermarket, just off Piazza Mazzini, is much bigger, with better prices (Mon–Sat 8:30–12:30 & 15:30–19:30, Sun 8:30–12:30; Dogali 34, across from Hotel Fiorina).

TRANSPORTATION CONNECTIONS

By train to: Sestri Levante (hrly, 30 min), **Monterosso** (hrly, 1 hr), **La Spezia** (hrly, 1.5 hrs), **Pisa** (3/day, 2.25 hrs, more with transfer in La Spezia), **Genoa** (hrly, 45–60 min), **Milan** (4/day, 2 hrs, more with transfer in Genoa), **Ventimiglia** (2/day, 3.5 hrs, to French border, change in Genoa), **Venice** (2/day, 5.25 hrs). For **Florence**, you'll transfer in La Spezia, Pisa, or both (allow 3.5–4 hrs). If heading for the **Cinque Terre** (as most visitors who are home-basing in Santa Margherita are), the schedule is confusing. It's a 60-minute trip, with hourly departures, but beware—some trains are much slower, and the fastest trains stop only at Monterosso and Riomaggiore. Look for schedule on train station wall specifically listing Cinque Terre trains.

By boat to the Cinque Terre: Day-trip cruises from Santa Margherita to the Cinque Terre depart at 8:45, with lengthy stops in three Cinque Terre towns.

South of the Cinque Terre

La Spezia

While just a quick train ride away from the fanciful Cinque Terre (20–30 min), La Spezia feels like work-a-day Italy. The **TI** is a 20-minute walk from the station, near the waterfront (Mon–Sat 9:30–13:00 & 15:30–19:00, Sun 9:30–13:00, Viale Mazzini 47, tel. 0187-770-900). There's usually a kiosk branch at the station in summer. If not, skip it.

Sights are slim. On Fridays, a huge open-air market sprawls along Via Garibaldi (about 6 blocks from station). The pedestrian zone on Via del Prione to the gardens along the harbor makes a pleasant stroll. The **Museo Amedeo Lia** displays Italian paintings from the 13th to 18th centuries (€6, Tue–Sun 10:00–18:00, closed Mon, last entry 30 min before closing, no photos allowed, 10-min walk from station at Via Prione 234, tel. 0187-731-100, www.castagna.it/mal).

Stay on the Cinque Terre if you can, but if you're in a bind...

SLEEPING

(€1 = about $1.10, country code: 39)
The first five hotels are within a five-minute walk from the station. The last two are for drivers only.

$$$ The grand, old, but newly-restored **Hotel Firenze e Continentale** has 68 rooms with all the classy comforts (Sb-€69–80, Db-€115, maybe €83 in slow times, includes buffet breakfast, air-con, double-paned windows, some non-smoking rooms, elevator, parking-€13/day, Via Paleocapa 7, tel. 0187-713-200, fax 0187-714-930, www.hotelfirenzecontinentale.it, SE).

$$ **Hotel Venezia**, across the street from Hotel Firenze e Continentale, has a plain lobby, but its 19 rooms are modern (Db-€62–90, elevator, Via Paleocapa 10, tel. & fax 0187-733-465, SE).

$$ **Albergo Parma** is tight, bright, and bleachy clean, with 33 rooms (D-€46, Db-€63; double-paned windows; located just below station, down stairs to Via Fiume 143; tel. 0187-743-010, fax 0187-743-240, albergoparma@libero.it, some English spoken).

$$ **Hotel Mary**, just a few doors down from Albergo Parma, has 48 nondescript rooms with air-conditioning, double-paned windows, and an elevator (Sb-€48, Db-€87, Tb-€105, prices soft, breakfast extra, below station at Via Fiume 177, tel. 0187-743-254, fax 0187-743-375, hotelm@sp.itline.it).

$$ **Hotel Astoria**, with 56 decent rooms, has a combination lobby and breakfast room as large as a school cafeteria. It's a fine backup if the hotels nearer the station are full (Db-€75–110, includes breakfast; elevator; Via Roma 139, take Via Milano left of Albergo Parma, go 3 blocks and turn left on Via Roma; tel. 0187-714-655, fax 0187-714-425, hotelastoria@tiscali.it).

$$ Il Gelsomino, for drivers only, is a homey B&B in the hills above La Spezia overlooking the Gulf of Poets with three tranquil, tastefully decorated rooms: one with a bay-view terrace, another with hillside views, and a third that lacks views and a terrace. Hosts Carla and Walter Massi are gracious (D-€66, Db-€74, Tb-€85, Q-€132, please confirm arrival time 2 days in advance and cancel at least 24 hrs in advance, large breakfast, Via dei Viseggi 9, tel. & fax 0187-704-201, www.cinqueterreedintorni.it, ilgelsomino@)inwind.it).

$$ Santa Maria del Mare Monastery, a last resort for drivers, rents 15 comfortable rooms high above La Spezia in a scenic but institutional setting (Db-€60, dorm beds-€30/person, Castellazzo Stra, Via Montalbano, tel. 0187-711-332, mare@nse.it).

Carrara

Perhaps the world's most famous marble quarries are just east of La Spezia in Carrara. Michelangelo himself traveled to these valleys to pick out the marble that he would work into his masterpieces. The towns of the region are dominated by marble. The quarries higher up are vast digs that dwarf their hardworking trucks and machinery. The Carrara museum allows visitors to trace the story of marble-cutting here from pre-Roman times until today. For a guided visit, Sara Paolini is excellent (€80/half-day tour, tel. 0585-632-617, mobile 347-888-3833, casara00 @hotmail.com). She is accustomed to meeting and joining drivers at the Carrara freeway exit.

Portovenere

While the gritty port of La Spezia offers little in the way of redeeming touristic value, the nearby resort of Portovenere is enchanting. This Cinque Terre–esque village clings to a rocky promontory jutting into the sea, protecting the harbor from the crashing waves. On the harbor, next to colorful bobbing boats, a row of restaurants—perfect for alfresco dining—feature local specialties such as *trenette* pasta with pesto and spaghetti *frutti di mare*.

Local boats take you on excursions to nearby islands or over to Lerici, the town across the bay. Lord Byron swam to Lerici (not recommended). Hardy hikers enjoy the two-hour (or more) hike to Riomaggiore, the nearest Cinque Terre town.

Portovenere is an easy day trip from the Cinque Terre by boat (Easter–late Oct, nearly hrly 10:00–18:00), or take the bus from La Spezia (25 min). In peak season, buses shuttle drivers from the parking lot just outside Portovenere to the harborside square.

Sleeping: If you forgot your yacht, try **Albergo Il Genio**, in the building where the main street hits the piazza (Db-€85–93, Piazza Bastreri 8, tel. and fax 0187-790-611). If your *vita* is feeling *dolce*, consider **Grand Hotel Portovenere** (from €130 for viewless double off-season to €295 for view suite in summer with half-pension, tel. 0187-792-610, fax 0187-790-661, Via Garibaldi 5, ghp@village.it).

FLORENCE

(FIRENZE)

Florence, the home of the Renaissance and birthplace of our modern world, is a "supermarket sweep," and the groceries are the best Renaissance art in Europe.

Get your bearings with a Renaissance walk. Florentine art goes beyond paintings and statues—there's food, fashion, and handicrafts. You can lick Italy's best gelato while enjoying some of Europe's best people-watching.

Planning Your Time

If you're in Europe for three weeks, Florence deserves a well-organized day. Make reservations in advance for the Uffizi Gallery (best Italian paintings anywhere) and Accademia (Michelangelo's *David)*. For a day in Florence, see the Accademia, tour the Uffizi Gallery, visit the underrated Bargello (best statues), and do the Renaissance ramble (explained below).

Art-lovers will want to chisel out another day of their itinerary for the many other Florentine cultural treasures. Shoppers and ice cream–lovers may need to do the same.

Plan your sightseeing carefully. Some sights close Mondays and afternoons. While many spend several hours a day in lines, thoughtful travelers avoid this by making reservations or going late in the day. Places open at night are virtually empty.

Connoisseurs of smaller towns should consider taking the bus to Siena for a day or evening trip (75-min one-way, confirm when last bus returns). Siena is magic after dark. For more information, see the Siena chapter.

ORIENTATION

The Florence that we're interested in lies mostly on the north bank of the Arno River. The main historical sights cluster around the red-brick

Greater Florence

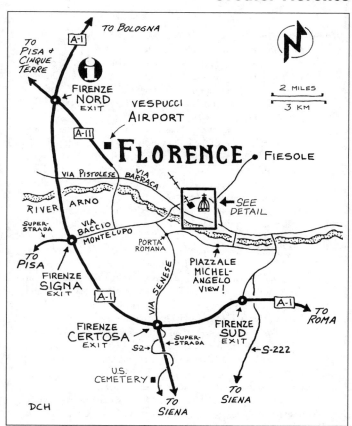

dome of the cathedral (Duomo). Everything is within a 20-minute walk of the train station, cathedral, or Ponte Vecchio (Old Bridge). The less impressive but more characteristic Oltrarno (south bank) area is just over the bridge. Though small, Florence is intense. Prepare for scorching summer heat, kamikaze Vespa moterscooters, slick pickpockets, few WCs, and erratic museum hours.

Tourist Information

There are three TIs in Florence: across from the train station, near Santa Croce Church, and on Via Cavour.

The **TI** across the square from the train station is most crowded—expect long lines (Mon–Sat 8:30–19:00, Sun 8:30–14:00; with your back

DAILY REMINDER

Sunday: Today the Duomo's dome, the Science Museum, and the Museum of Precious Stones are closed. These sights close early: the Duomo Museum (at 13:40) and the Baptistery's interior (at 14:00). A few sights are open only in the afternoon: Duomo (13:30–16:45), Santa Croce Church (15:00–17:30), and the Brancacci Chapel and Church of Santa Maria Novella (both 13:00–17:00).

    The Museum of San Marco, which is open on the second and fourth Sunday of the month until 19:00, closes entirely—as does the Bargello—on the first, third, and fifth Sunday. The Medici Chapels and the Modern Art Gallery (in the Pitti Palace) close on the second and fourth Sunday. (Need a calendar? Look in the appendix.)

Monday: The biggies are closed—Accademia (David) and Uffizi Gallery and the Palatine Gallery/Royal Apartments (in the Pitti Palace).

    The Medici Chapels and the Modern Art Gallery (in the Pitti Palace) close on the first, third, and fifth Monday of the month. The Museum of San Marco and the Bargello close on the second and fourth Monday. The Orsanmichele Church and Boboli Gardens close on the first and last Monday. The Palazzo Vecchio may stay open until 23:00 in summer.

    Target these sights on Mondays: Duomo Museum, Giotto's Tower, Brancacci Chapel, Michelangelo's House, Science Museum, Palazzo Vecchio, and churches. Or take a walking tour.

Tuesday: All sights are open except for Michelangelo's House and the Brancacci Chapel. The Science Museum closes early (13:00).

Wednesday: All sights are open except for the Medici Riccardi Palace.

Thursday: All sights are open. The Museum of Precious Stones stays open late (19:00) while these sights close early: Duomo (15:30) and Palazzo Vecchio (14:00).

Friday: All sights are open. The Church of Santa Maria Novella opens late (13:00–17:00) and Palazzo Vecchio closes late (maybe until 23:00 in summer).

Saturday: All sights are open, but the Science Museum closes at 13:00. These sights close early on the first Saturday of the month: Duomo (15:30) and the Duomo's dome (16:00). The Museum of San Marco stays open until 19:00. The Accademia, Uffizi, and Palatine Gallery/Royal Apartments may stay open until 22:00 in summer.

to tracks, exit the station—it's across the square in wall near corner of church, Piazza Stazione; tel. 055-212-245). Note: In the train station, avoid the Hotel Reservations "Tourist Information" window (marked *Informazioni Turistiche Alberghiere*) near the McDonald's; it's not a real TI but a hotel reservation business.

The TI near Santa Croce Church is pleasant, helpful, and uncrowded (Mon–Sat 9:00–19:00, Sun 9:00–14:00, shorter hours off-season, Borgo Santa Croce 29 red, tel. 055-234-0444).

Another winner is the TI three blocks north of the Duomo (Mon–Sat 8:15–19:15, Sun 8:30–13:30, closed Sun in winter, Via Cavour 1 red, tel. 055-290-832 or 055-290-833, international bookstore across street).

At any TI, pick up a map, a current museum-hours listing (extremely important, since no guidebook—including this one—has ever been able to accurately predict the hours of Florence's sights), and any information on entertainment. The free monthly *Florence Concierge Information* magazine lists museums, plus lots that I don't: concerts and events, markets, sporting events, church services, shopping ideas, bus and train connections, and an entire similar section on Siena. Get yours at the TI or from any expensive hotel (pick one up, as if you're staying there).

Arrival in Florence

By Train: The station soaks up time and generates dazed and sweaty crowds. If you arrive by train, there's no need to linger at the station. Extremely user-friendly, coin-operated gray-and-yellow machines can display schedules, issue tickets, and even make reservations for railpass holders. Otherwise, get onward tickets and train information at travel agencies away from the congested station (e.g., American Express, listed in "Helpful Hints," below). The fake "Tourist Information" office in the station (next to McDonald's) is actually a room-booking service funded by the hotels. The real TI is across the square from the station (see above).

With your back to the tracks, to your left are most of my recommended hotels, a 24-hour pharmacy (*Farmacia Comunale,* near McDonald's), city buses, and the entrance to the underground mall/passage that goes across the square to the Church of Santa Maria Novella. (Note: This tunnel is frequented by pickpockets, especially the surface point near the church.) Baggage check is near track 16. The taxi stand in front of the train station often has a line. To catch a cab without the line, wander deeper into the city.

By Car: If you're taking the autostrada (north or south) to Florence, get off at the Certosa exit and follow signs to *Centro;* at Porta Romana, go to the left of the arch and down Via Francesco Petrarca. After driving and trying to park in Florence, you'll understand why Leonardo never invented the car. Cars flatten the charm of

Florence. Don't drive in Florence and don't risk parking illegally (fines up to €150).

Non-residents are not allowed to park on the streets anywhere near or in the old center. The city has plenty of **parking lots.** For a short stay, park underground at the train station (€2/hr). The Fortezza da Basso is clearly marked in the center (€20/24 hrs). The least expensive lots are Parcheggio Parterre (Firenze Parcheggi, €16/24 hrs, perhaps cheaper with hotel reservation) and Parcheggio Oltrarno (near Porta Romana—pass through gate and on left, €15 per day). For parking information, ask at your hotel or call 055-500-1994.

By Plane: Florence has its own airport and Pisa's is nearby. See "Transportation Connections," on page 291, for details.

Helpful Hints

Theft Alert: Florence has particularly hardworking thief gangs. They specialize in tourists and hang out where you do: near the train station, the station's underpass (especially where the tunnel surfaces), and major sights. Also be on guard at two squares frequented by

TIPS ON SIGHTSEEING IN FLORENCE

Make Reservations to Avoid Lines: Florence has a great reservation system for its top five sights—Uffizi, Accademia, Bargello, Medici Chapels, and the Pitti Palace. Two of these sights nearly always have long lines: the Accademia (Michelangelo's *David*) and the Uffizi (Renaissance paintings). To avoid long waits—up to two hours at the Uffizi on busy days—simply make a reservation by phone. Frankly, it's stupid not to.

While you can generally make a reservation a day in advance (upon arrival in Florence), you'll have a wider selection of entry times by calling a few days ahead. You dial 055-294-883 (busy signals common—be persistent, Mon–Fri 8:30–18:30, Sat 8:30–12:30, closed Sun), an English-speaking operator walks you through the process, and two minutes later you say *grazie,* with appointments (15-minute entry window) and six-digit confirmation numbers for each of the top museums and galleries. The ticket phone number is often busy. If you call months in advance (during off-season) or request your hotel to make the appointment for you (when you confirm your hotel room), you may save some frustration. Some booking agencies offer reservations online for a fee (such as www.weekendafirenze.it).

drug pushers (Santa Maria Novella and Santo Spirito). American tourists—especially older ones—are considered easy targets.

Medical Help: To track down a doctor who speaks English, call 055-475-411 (reasonable hotel calls, cheaper if you go to the clinic at Via L. Magnifico 59) or get a list of English-speaking doctors from the TI. There are 24-hour pharmacies at the train station and near the Duomo on Borgo San Lorenzo.

Addresses: Street addresses list businesses in red and residences in black or blue (color-coded on the actual street number and indicated by a letter following the number in printed addresses: r = red, no indication = black). *Pensioni* are usually black but can be either. The red and black numbers each appear in roughly consecutive order on streets but bear no apparent connection with each other. I'm lazy and don't concern myself with the distinction (if one number's wrong, I look for the other) and find my way around fine.

American Express: American Express offers all the normal services, but is most helpful as an easy place to get your train tickets, reservations, supplements (all the same price as at the station), or even just

If you haven't booked ahead, you can make reservations for the top sights at the minor, less-crowded sights (such as the Museum of San Marco or Museum of Precious Stones). Clerks at the ticket booths at these sleepy sights can reserve and sell tickets to the major sights—often for admission the same day—allowing you to skip right past the dreary mob scene.

There is occasionally even a line at the Uffizi for those with reservations who are waiting to pick up tickets. If you have reservations, consider picking up your Uffizi ticket at a less-crowded sight (any ticket office can issue reserved tickets).

Hours of Sights Can Change Suddenly: Because of labor demands, hours of sights change without warning. Pick up the latest listing of museum hours at a TI, or you'll miss out on something you came to see. Don't put off seeing a must-see sight such as *David;* you never know when a place will close unexpectedly for a holiday, strike, or restoration.

More Tips: The biggies (Uffizi and Accademia) close on Monday. Several museums are closed alternating Sundays and Mondays (e.g., closed first, third, and fifth Sun and second and fourth Mon of each month); use the calendar in the appendix to figure out which day they're closed during your trip. Churches usually close from 12:30 to 15:00 or 16:00. Some museums close at 14:00 and stop selling tickets 30 minutes before that.

FLORENCE AT A GLANCE

▲▲▲**Uffizi Gallery** Greatest collection of Italian paintings anywhere—reserve ahead. **Hours:** Tue–Sun 8:15–18:50, 8:15–22:00 on holidays and maybe on summer Sat, closed Mon.

▲▲▲**Accademia** Michelangelo's *David* and powerful (unfinished) *Prisoners*—reserve ahead. **Hours:** Tue–Sun 8:15–18:50, 8:15–22:00 on holidays and maybe on summer Sat, closed Mon.

▲▲▲**Bargello** Underappreciated sculpture museum (Michelangelo, Donatello, Medici treasures). **Hours:** Daily 8:15–13:50; closed first, third, and fifth Sun and second and fourth Mon of each month.

▲▲**Museum of San Marco** Best collection anywhere of frescoes and paintings by the early Renaissance master Fra Angelico. **Hours:** Weekdays 8:15–13:50, Sat–Sun 8:15–19:00; closed first, third, and fifth Sun and second and fourth Mon of each month.

▲▲**Medici Chapels** Tombs of Florence's great ruling family, designed and carved by Michelangelo. **Hours:** Daily 8:15–17:00; closed the second and fourth Sun and the first, third, and fifth Mon of each month.

▲▲**Church of Santa Maria Novella** 13th-century Dominican church with Masaccio's famous 3-D painting. **Hours:** Mon–Thu and Sat 9:30–17:00, Fri and Sun 13:00–17:00.

▲▲**Santa Croce Church** 14th-century Franciscan church with precious art, tombs of famous Florentines, and Brunelleschi's Pazzi Chapel. **Hours:** Mon–Sat 9:30–17:30, Sun 15:00–17:30; off-season Mon–Sat 9:30–12:30 & 15:00–17:30, Sun 15:00–17:30.

▲▲**Science Museum** Fascinating collection of old clocks, telescopes, maps, and Galileo's finger. **Hours:** Mon and Wed–Fri 9:30–17:00, Tue and Sat 9:30–13:00, closed Sun.

▲▲**Pitti Palace** Three museums in lavish palace: Palatine Gallery (Raphael art), Modern Art Gallery, Grand Ducal Treasures (Medici treasure chest), plus sprawling Boboli Gardens. **Hours:** Palatine: Tue–Sun 8:15–18:50, closed Mon; Modern Art and Treasures: daily 8:15–13:50; closed second and fourth Sun and first, third, and fifth Mon; Boboli: daily 9:00–18:30, 9:00–19:30 June–Aug, 9:00–16:30 in winter, closed first and last Mon of month.

▲▲**Brancacci Chapel** Works of Masaccio, early Renaissance master who re-invented perspective. **Hours:** Mon and Wed–Sat 10:00–17:00, Sun 13:00–17:00, closed Tue.

▲▲**Duomo** Gothic cathedral with colorful facade, long nave, and the first dome built since ancient Roman times. **Hours:** Mon–Wed and Fri–Sat 10:00–17:00 except first Sat of month 10:00–15:30, Thu 10:00–15:30, Sun 13:30–16:45.

▲▲**Duomo Museum** Underrated cathedral museum with great sculpture. **Hours:** Mon–Sat 9:00–19:30, Sun 9:00–13:40, closed on holidays.

▲**Climbing Duomo's Dome** Grand view into the cathedral, close-up of dome architecture, and, after 463 steps, a glorious Florence vista. **Hours:** Mon–Fri 8:30–19:00, Sat 8:30–17:40 except first Sat of month 8:30–16:00, closed Sun.

▲**Giotto's Tower** Bell tower with views equaling Duomo's, 50 fewer steps, and fewer lines. **Hours:** Daily 8:30–19:30.

▲**Baptistery** Bronze doors fit to be the gates of Paradise. **Hours:** Doors always viewable; Baptistery open. Mon–Sat 12:00–19:00, Sun 8:30–14:00.

▲**Orsanmichele Church** Church made from walled-in loggia, with glorious tabernacle inside and niche statuary outside. **Hours:** Unreliably open 9:00–12:00 & 16:00–18:00, closed first and last Mon of month.

▲**Palazzo Vecchio** Fortified palace once the home of the Medici family, wallpapered with mediocre art. **Hours:** Fri–Wed 9:00–19:00, Thu 9:00–14:00, in summer maybe 9:00–23:00 on Mon and Fri.

▲**Ponte Vecchio** Famous bridge lined with gold and silver shops. **Hours:** Bridge always open.

▲**Mercato Nuovo** Bustling market in loggia. **Hours:** Open daily.

▲**Michelangelo's House** Museum featuring early, lesser-known works of the master. **Hours:** Wed–Mon 9:30–14:00, closed Tue.

▲**Piazzale Michelangelo** Hilltop square in south Florence offering stunning view of city and Duomo. **Hours:** Always open.

information on train schedules (Mon–Fri 9:00–17:30, Sat money exchange only 9:00–12:30, 3 short blocks north of Palazzo Vecchio on Via Dante Alighieri 22 red, tel. 055-50981).

Long-Distance Telephoning: Small newsstand kiosks sell PIN phone cards that give you cheap international rates (10 minutes/€1).

Books: Feltrinelli International, a fine bookstore that sells fiction and guidebooks in English, is a few blocks north of the Duomo and across the street from the TI on Via Cavour (Mon–Sat 9:00–19:30, closed Sun, Via Cavour 20 red, tel. 055-219-524). Edison Bookstore sells CDs and novels on the Renaissance (daily 9:00–24:00, facing Piazza della Repubblica, tel. 055-213-110). Paperback Exchange also sells fiction and guidebooks (cheaper but smaller selection; Mon–Fri 9:00–19:30, Sat 10:00–13:00 & 15:30–19:30, closed Sun, shorter hours in Aug; Via Fiesolana 31 red, at corner of Via Fiesolana and Via dei Pilastri, 6 blocks east of Duomo; tel. 055-247-8154).

Laundry: The Wash & Dry Lavarapido chain offers long hours and efficient, self-service launderettes at several locations (about €6.20 for wash and dry, daily 8:00–22:00, tel. 055-580-480). These are close to recommended hotels: Via dei Servi 105 (and a rival launderette at Via Guelfa 22 red, off Via Cavour; both near *David*), Via del Sole 29 red and Via della Scala 52 red (between train station and river), and Via dei Serragli 87 red (across the river in Oltrarno neighborhood).

Getting around Florence

I organize my sightseeing geographically and do it all on foot. A €1 ticket gives you one hour on the buses, €1.80 gives you three hours, and €4 gets you 24 hours (tickets not sold on bus—buy in *tabacchi* shops or newsstands before 21:00, validate on bus; after 21:00 buy tickets on bus, route map available at TI). Multi-day passes are also available.

The minimum cost for a taxi ride is €4, or, after 22:00, €5 (rides in the center of town should be charged as tariff #1). A taxi ride from the train station to Ponte Vecchio costs about €8. Taxi fares and supplements (e.g., €2 extra if you telephone a cab) are clearly explained on signs in each taxi.

TOURS

Walking Tours of Florence—This company offers a variety of tours (up to 4 per day Mon–Sat year-round plus summer Sundays) featuring downtown Florence, Uffizi highlights, or Tuscany (countryside, Siena, San Gimignano, Pisa, or the Cinque Terre), presented by informative, entertaining, native English–speaking guides. The "Original Florence" walk hits the main sights but gets off-beat to weave a picture of Florentine life in medieval and Renaissance times. You can expect lots of talking, which is great if you like history. Tours, offered throughout the year regardless of the weather, start at their office and are limited to a maximum of 22 but will go with as few as two participants. Extra guides are available if more people show up (€25 for 3-hr Original Florence walk; office open Mon–Sat 8:30–18:00, closed for lunch off-season; Piazza Santo Stefano 2 black, a short block north of Ponte Vecchio; go east on tiny Vicolo San Stefano, in Piazza Santo Stefano at #2, see map on page 265; booking necessary for Uffizi tour, private tours available; tel. 055-264-5033, mobile 329-613-2730, www.artviva.com). For all the schedule details, pick up their extensive brochure in your hotel lobby.

Florentia—These top-notch, historical walking tours of Florence and Tuscany are led by local scholars. The tours, ranging from introductory city walks to in-depth visits of museums and lesser-known destinations, are geared for thoughtful, well-heeled travelers with longer-than-normal attention spans (semi-private tours start at $45 per person, max 8 per group; private tours start at $180 for half-day tour, reserve in advance, tel. 055-225-535, U.S. tel. 510-549-1707, www.florentia.org, info@florentia.org).

Local Guide—**Paola Migliorini** offers museum tours, city walking tours, and Tuscan excursions by van. You (and your group) can tailor tours as you like. The van allows slow walkers to enjoy the city nearly sweat-free (€50/hr, or €65/hr with 8-seat van, Via S. Gallo 120, tel. 055-472-448, mobile 347-657-2611, www.florencetour.com, info@florencetour.com). Note that big bus companies offer tours of Florence but for most the city is really best on foot.

A Renaissance Walk through Florence

Even during the Dark Ages, people knew they were in a "middle time." It was especially obvious to the people of Italy—sitting on the rubble of Rome—that there was a brighter age before them. The long-awaited rebirth, or Renaissance, began in Florence for good reason. Wealthy because of its cloth industry, trade, and banking; powered by a fierce city-state pride (locals would pee into the Arno with gusto, knowing rival city-state Pisa was downstream); and fertile with more than its share of artistic genius (imagine guys like Michelangelo and Leonardo attending the same high school)—Florence was a natural home for this cultural explosion.

Take a walk through the core of Renaissance Florence by starting at the Accademia (home of Michelangelo's *David)* and cutting through the heart of the city to Ponte Vecchio on the Arno River. (A 13-page, self-guided tour of this walk is outlined in my museum guidebook, *Rick Steves' Mona Winks*, and in *Rick Steves' Florence;* otherwise, you'll find brief descriptions below.)

Florence Overview

At the Accademia, you'll look into the eyes of Renaissance man—humanism at its confident peak. Then walk to the cathedral (Duomo) to see the dome that kicked off the architectural Renaissance. Step inside the baptistery to view a ceiling covered with preachy, flat, 2-D, medieval mosaic art. Then, to learn what happened when art met math, check out the realistic 3-D reliefs on the doors. The painter, Giotto, also designed the bell tower—an early example of a Renaissance genius excelling in many areas. Continue toward the river on Florence's great pedestrian mall, Via de' Calzaiuoli (or "Via Calz")—part of the original grid plan given to the city by the ancient Romans. Down a few blocks, compare medieval and Renaissance statues on the exterior of the Orsanmichele Church. Via Calz connects the cathedral with the central square (Piazza della Signoria), the city palace (Palazzo Vecchio), and the Uffizi Gallery, which contains the greatest collection of Italian Renaissance paintings in captivity. Finally, walk through the Uffizi courtyard—a statuary think tank of Renaissance greats—to the Arno River and Ponte Vecchio.

Sights on a Renaissance Walk through Florence

▲▲▲**Accademia (Galleria dell' Accademia)**—This museum houses Michelangelo's *David* and powerful (unfinished) *Prisoners*. Eavesdrop as tour guides explain these masterpieces. More than with any other work of art, when you look into the eyes of *David*, you're looking into the eyes of Renaissance man. This was a radical break with the past. Hello, humanism. Man was now a confident individual, no longer a plaything of the supernatural. And life was now more than just a preparation for what happened after you died.

Florence Sights

The Renaissance was the merging of art, science, and humanism. In a humanist vein, *David* is looking at the crude giant of medieval darkness and thinking, "I can take this guy." (David was an apt mascot for a town surrounded by big bully city-states.) Back on a religious track, notice *David*'s large and overdeveloped right hand. This is symbolic of the hand of God that powered David to slay the giant...and enabled Florence to rise above its crude neighboring city-states.

Beyond the magic marble are two floors of interesting pre-Renaissance and Renaissance paintings, including a couple of lighter-than-air Botticellis.

Cost, Hours, Location: €6.50 (plus €3 reservation fee), Tue–Sun 8:15–18:50, until 22:00 on holidays and maybe on summer Sat, closed Mon (last entry 45 min before closing, Via Ricasoli 60, tel. 055-238-8609). No photos or videos are allowed. The museum is most crowded on Sun, Tue, and the first thing in the morning. It's easy to reserve ahead; see pages 258–259 for details.

Nearby: Piazza Santissima Annunziata, behind the Accademia, displays lovely Renaissance harmony. Facing the square are two fine buildings: the 15th-century Santissima Annunziata church (worth a peek) and Brunelleschi's Hospital of the Innocents (*Spedale degli Innocenti,* not worth going inside), with terra-cotta medallions by Luca della Robbia. Built in the 1420s, the hospital is considered the first Renaissance building.

▲▲**Duomo**—Florence's Gothic Santa Maria del Fiori cathedral has the third-longest nave in Christendom (free, Mon–Wed and Fri–Sat 10:00–17:00 except first Sat of month 10:00–15:30, Thu 10:00–15:30, Sun 13:30–16:45, modest dress code enforced, tel. 055-230-2885). Note: The massive crowds that overwhelm the entrance in the morning clear out by afternoon.

The church's noisy neo-Gothic facade from the 1870s is covered with pink, green, and white Tuscan marble. Since nearly all of its great art is stored in the Museo dell' Opera del Duomo (behind the church), the best thing about the interior is the shade. The inside of the dome is decorated by one of the largest paintings of the Renaissance, a huge (and newly restored) *Last Judgment* by Vasari and Zucarri.

Think of the confidence of the age: The Duomo was built with a hole awaiting a dome in its roof. This was before the technology to span it with a dome was available. No matter. They knew that someone soon could handle the challenge...and the local architect Brunelleschi did. The cathedral's claim to artistic fame is Brunelleschi's magnificent dome—the first Renaissance dome and the model for domes to follow.

▲**Climbing the Cathedral's Dome**—For a grand view into the cathedral from the base of the dome, a peek at some of the tools used in the dome's construction, a chance to see Brunelleschi's "dome-within-a-dome" construction, a glorious Florence view from the top, and the equivalent of 463 plunges on a Stairmaster, climb the dome. To avoid the long, dreadfully slow-moving line, arrive by 8:30 (€6, Mon–Fri 8:30–19:00, Sat 8:30–17:40 except first Sat of month 8:30–16:00, closed Sun, enter from outside church on south/river side, tel. 055-230-2885). When planning St. Peter's in Rome, Michelangelo rhymed (not in English), "I can build its sister—bigger, but not more beautiful, than the dome of Florence."

▲**Giotto's Tower (Campanile)**—If you're not interested in experiencing dome-within-a-dome architecture, you'll likely feel that climbing Giotto's 270-foot bell tower beats scaling the neighboring Duomo's dome because it's 50 fewer steps, faster, and offers the same view plus the dome (€6, daily 8:30–19:30, last entry 40 min before closing).

▲▲**Duomo Museum (Museo dell' Opera del Duomo)**—The underrated cathedral museum, behind the church at #9, is great if you like sculpture. It has masterpieces by Donatello (a gruesome wood carving of Mary Magdalene clothed in her matted hair, and the *cantoria,* a delightful choir loft bursting with happy children) and by Luca Della Robbia (another choir loft, lined with the dreamy faces of musicians praising the Lord). Look for a late Michelangelo *pietà* (Nicodemus, on top, is a self-portrait), Brunelleschi's models for his dome, and the original restored panels of Ghiberti's doors to the baptistery. This is one of the few museums in Florence open on Monday (€6, Mon–Sat 9:00–19:30, Sun 9:00–13:40, closed on holidays, tel. 055-230-2885). If you find all this church art intriguing, look through the open doorway of the Duomo art studio, which has been making and restoring church art since the days of Brunelleschi (a block toward the river from the Duomo at 23a Via dello Studio).

▲**Baptistery**—Michelangelo said its bronze doors were fit to be the gates of Paradise. Check out the gleaming copies of Ghiberti's bronze doors facing the Duomo. Making a breakthrough in perspective, Ghiberti used mathematical laws to create the illusion of receding distance on a basically flat surface. The earlier, famous competition doors are around to the right (north); Ghiberti, who beat Brunelleschi, got the job of designing these doors.

Inside, sit and savor the medieval mosaic ceiling where it's Judgment Day, and Jesus is giving the ultimate thumbs up and thumbs down (€3; interior open Mon–Sat 12:00–19:00, Sun 8:30–14:00, bronze doors are on the outside, so always "open"; original panels are in the Duomo Museum).

▲**Orsanmichele Church**—In the ninth century, this loggia (a covered courtyard) was a market used for selling grain (stored upstairs). Later, it was closed in to make a church. Notice the grain spouts on the pillars inside. The glorious tabernacle (1359) by Orcagna takes you back.

Study the sculpture in the niches outside. You can see man stepping out of the literal and figurative shadow of the Church in the great

Renaissance sculptor Donatello's *St. George*. Look into George's face; he's a sensitive new-age guy (SNAG). The predella (panels) at the base of this statue shows St. George slaying the dragon to protect the wispy, melodramatic maiden. This was groundbreaking Renaissance emotion and perspective (free; unreliably open 9:00–12:00 & 16:00–18:00, closed first and last Mon of month, often closed due to staffing problems; on Via Calzaiuoli, enter through back door). The iron bars spanning the vaults were the Italian Gothic answer to the French Gothic external buttresses.

The church's museum upstairs holds many of the church's precious originals. Someday tourists may be able to enjoy its fine statues by Ghiberti, Donatello, and company. (But don't hold your breath.)

A block away, you'll find the...

▲**Mercato Nuovo (a.k.a. the Straw Market)**—This market loggia is how Orsanmichele looked before it became a church. Originally a silk and straw market, Mercato Nuovo still functions as a rustic market today (at the intersection of Via Calimala and Via Porta Rossa). Prices are soft.

Notice the circled X in the center, marking the spot where people hit after being hoisted up to the top of the market and dropped as punishment for bankruptcy. You'll also find *Porcellino* (a statue of a wild boar nicknamed "little pig"), which people rub and give coins to in order to ensure their return to Florence. Nearby, a wagon sells tripe (cow innards) sandwiches.

▲**Palazzo Vecchio**—With its distinctive castle turret, this fortified palace, once the home of the Medici family, is a Florentine landmark. But if you're visiting only one palace interior in town, the Pitti Palace is better. The Palazzo Vecchio interior is wallpapered with mediocre magnificence, worthwhile only if you're a real Florentine art and history fan. The museum's most famous statues are Michelangelo's *Genius of Victory*, Donatello's static *Judith and Holerfernes*, and Verrocchio's *Winged Cherub* (a copy tops the fountain in the free courtyard at entrance, original inside).

Scattered throughout the museum are a dozen computer terminals with information in English on the Medici family, Palazzo Vecchio, and the building's architecture and art, including an animated clip showing how Michelangelo's *David* was moved from the square to the Accademia (€5.70, Fri–Wed 9:00–19:00, Thu 9:00–14:00, in summer maybe open until 23:00 on Mon and Fri, ticket office closes 1 hour earlier, tel. 055-276-8465).

Even if you don't go to the museum, do step into the free courtyard (behind the fake *David*) just to feel the essence of the Medicis. Until 1873, Michelangelo's *David* stood at the entrance, where the copy is today. While the huge statues in the square are important only as the whipping boys of art critics and rest stops for pigeons, the nearby Loggia dei Lanzi has several important statues. Look for Cellini's bronze statue of Perseus holding the head of Medusa. The plaque on the pavement in

Uffizi Gallery

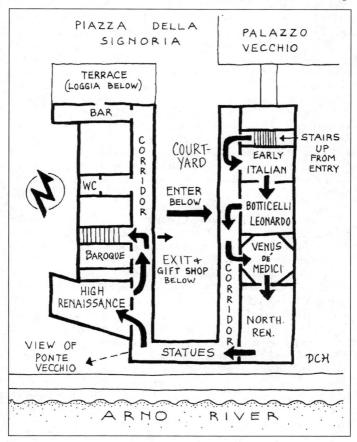

front of the fountain marks the spot where the monk Savonarola was burned in MCDXCVIII (for more on the monk, see "Museum of San Marco" listing, page 271).

▲▲▲Uffizi Gallery—The greatest collection of Italian paintings anywhere is a must, with plenty of works by Giotto, Leonardo, Raphael, Caravaggio, Rubens, Titian, and Michelangelo and a roomful of Botticellis, including his *Birth of Venus*. Make a reservation to avoid the long line (see pages 258–259). Because only 780 visitors are allowed inside the building at any one time, there's generally a very long wait during the day. The good news: No Louvre-style mob scenes. The museum is nowhere near as big as it is great: Few tourists spend more than two hours inside. The paintings are displayed on one comfortable floor in chronological order, from the 13th through 17th centuries.

Essential stops are (in this order): Gothic altarpieces (narrative, pre-Realism, no real concern for believable depth) including Giotto's altarpiece, which progressed beyond "totem-pole angels"; Uccello's *Battle of San Romano,* an early study in perspective (with a few obvious flubs); Fra Filippo Lippi's cuddly Madonnas; the Botticelli room, filled with masterpieces, including a pantheon of classical fleshiness and the small *La Calumnia,* showing the glasnost of Renaissance free-thinking being clubbed back into the darker age of Savonarola; two minor works by Leonardo; the octagonal classical sculpture room with an early painting of Bob Hope and a copy of Praxiteles' *Venus de Medici*—considered the epitome of beauty in Elizabethan Europe; a view through the window of Ponte Vecchio—dreamy at sunset; Michelangelo's only surviving easel painting, the round *Holy Family;* Raphael's noble *Madonna of the Goldfinch;* Titian's voluptuous *Venus of Urbino;* and Duomo views from the café terrace at the end (WC near café).

Cost, Hours, Reservations: €8.50, plus €3 for recommended reservation, Tue–Sun 8:15–18:50, until 22:00 on holidays and maybe on summer Sat, closed Mon, last entry 45 min before closing, after entering take elevator or climb 4 long flights of stairs.

Avoid the two-hour peak-season midday wait by making a telephone reservation. It's easy, slick, and costs only €3 (tel. 055-294-883, explained on pages 258–259). At the Uffizi, walk briskly past the 200-yard-long line—pondering the IQ of this gang—to the special entrance for those with reservations (labeled in English "Entrance for Reservations Only"), give your number, pay (cash only), and scoot right in.

If you haven't called ahead, there are other ways to make an Uffizi reservation—sometimes for the same day, depending on luck and availability: (1) buy Uffizi tickets with reservations at the Museum of San Marco, the Museum of Precious Stones, or another Florence sight; (2) try booking directly at the Uffizi (ask the clerk who stands at the reservations entrance if you can reserve in person—he may direct you to the ticket office); or (3) take a tour of the museum with Walking Tours of Florence (booking required, see "Tours" page 262).

In Courtyard of Uffizi: Enjoy the Uffizi's courtyard (free), full of artists and souvenir stalls. The surrounding statues honor earthshaking Florentines: artists (Michelangelo), philosophers (Machiavelli), scientists (Galileo), writers (Dante), and explorers (Amerigo Vespucci), and the great patron of so much Renaissance thinking, Lorenzo "the Magnificent" de Medici.

▲**Ponte Vecchio**—Florence's most famous bridge is lined with shops that have traditionally sold gold and silver. A statue of Cellini, the master goldsmith of the Renaissance, stands in the center, ignored by the flood of tacky tourism. This is a romantic spot late at night. In fact, hanging over the edge of the bridge (on either side of the Cellini bust) are piles of padlocks. Guys demonstrate the enduring quality of their love by ceremonially taking their girls here, locking a lock, and throwing the key into the Arno. (But what's with the combination lock?)

Notice the "prince's passageway" above the bridge. In less secure times, the city leaders had a fortified passageway connecting the Vecchio Palace and Uffizi with the mighty Pitti Palace, to which they could flee in times of attack. This passageway, called the **Vasari Corridor,** is technically open to the public, but good luck getting an appointment (tel. 055-265-4321).

OTHER SIGHTS

Near the Accademia

▲▲**Museum of San Marco (Museo di San Marco)**—One block north of the Accademia on Piazza San Marco, this museum houses the greatest collection anywhere of frescoes and paintings by the early Renaissance master Fra Angelico. You'll see why he thought of painting as a form of prayer, and couldn't paint a crucifix without shedding tears. Each of the monks' cells has a Fra Angelico fresco. Don't miss the cell of Savonarola, the charismatic monk who rode in from the Christian right, threw out the Medicis, turned Florence into a theocracy, sponsored "bonfires of the vanities" (burning books, paintings, and so on), and was finally burned himself when Florence decided to change channels (€6, daily 8:15–13:50, Sat–Sun 8:15–19:00, but closed first, third, and fifth Sun and second and fourth Mon of each month, tel. 055-238-8608). The ticket office can issue reserved tickets, and even sell tickets (often with immediate reservation) to the Uffizi and Accademia.

Museum of Precious Stones (Museo dell' Opificio delle Pietre Dure)—This unusual gem of a museum features mosaics of inlaid marble and semiprecious stones. You'll see remnants of the Medici workshop from 1588, including 500 different semiprecious stones, the tools used to cut and inlay them, and room after room of the sumptuous finished product. The fine loaner booklet describes it all in English (€2; Mon–Sat 8:15–14:00, Thu until 19:00, closed Sun; Via degli Alfani 78, around corner from Accademia). This ticket booth can also sell tickets with reservations (often for the same day) to the Uffizi and Accademia.

Heart of Florence

▲▲▲**Bargello (Museo Nazionale)**—This under-appreciated sculpture museum is in a former prison that looks like a mini–Palazzo Vecchio. It has Donatello's painfully beautiful *David* (the very influential first male nude to be sculpted in a thousand years), works by Michelangelo, and rooms of Medici treasures cruelly explained in Italian only—mention that English descriptions would be wonderful (€4, daily 8:15–13:50 but closed first, third, and fifth Sun and second and fourth Mon of each month, last entry 40 min before closing, Via del Proconsolo 4, tel. 055-238-8606).

▲▲Medici Chapels (Cappelle dei Medici)—The chapel, containing two Medici tombs, is drenched in lavish High Renaissance architecture and sculpture. The highlight is a chapel with interior decoration by Michelangelo, including the brooding Night, Day, Dawn, and Dusk statues (€6, daily 8:15–17:00 but closed the second and fourth Sun and the first, third, and fifth Mon of each month, tel. 055-238-8602).

Nearby: Behind the chapels on Piazza Madonna di degli Aldobrandini is a lively market scene that I find just as interesting. Take a stroll through the huge double-decker Mercato Centrale (central food market) one block north.

Medici Riccardi Palace (Palazzo Medici Riccardi)—Lorenzo the Magnificent's home is worth a look for its art. The tiny Chapel of the Magi contains colorful Renaissance gems—the *Procession of the Magi* frescoes by Benozzo Gozzoli. Another room has a High Baroque ceiling fresco by Luca Giordano, a prolific artist from Naples known as Fast Luke (*Luca fa presto*) for his ambidextrous painting abilities (€4, Thu–Tue 9:00–19:00, closed Wed, Via Cavour 3, kitty-corner from San Lorenzo Church, 1 long block north of Baptistery).

▲Piazza della Repubblica—This large square sits on the site of Florence's original Roman Forum. The lone column—nicknamed the belly-button of Florence—is the only remaining bit of Roman Florence except for its grid street plan. Look at the map (by the benches—where the old boys hang out to talk sports and politics) to see the ghost of Rome. Roman Florence was a garrison town—a rectangular fort with this square marking the intersection of the two main roads (Via Corso and Via Roma).

Today's piazza, framed by a triumphal arch, is really a nationalistic statement celebrating the unification of Italy. Florence, the capital of the country (1865–1870) until Rome was liberated, lacked a square worthy of this grand new country. So the neighborhood here was razed to open up a grand modern forum surrounded by grand circa-1890 buildings.

Between here and the river you'll find characteristic parts of the medieval city that give a sense of what this neighborhood felt like before it was bulldozed. Back then, writers described Florence as so densely built up that when it rained, pedestrians didn't get wet. Torches were used to light the lanes in midday. The city was prickly with noble family towers (like San Gimignano) and had Romeo-and-Juliet-type family feuds. But with the rise of the Medicis (c. 1300), no noble family was allowed to have an architectural ego trip taller then theirs, and nearly all other towers were taken down.

The fancy La Rinascente department store, facing the Piazza della

Repubblica, is one of the city's finest (WC on 4th floor, view terrace in small pricey bar above that).

▲▲Science Museum (Museo di Storia della Scienza)—This is a fascinating collection of Renaissance and later clocks, telescopes, maps, and ingenious gadgets. One of the most talked-about bottles in Florence is the one here containing Galileo's finger. Loaner English guidebooklets are available. It's friendly, comfortably cool, never crowded, and just a block east of the Uffizi on the Arno River (€6.50, Mon and Wed–Fri 9:30–17:00, Tue and Sat 9:30–13:00, closed Sun, Piazza dei Giudici 1, tel. 055-265-311).

▲▲Church of Santa Maria Novella—This 13th-century Dominican church, just south of the train station, is rich in art. Along with crucifixes by Giotto and Brunelleschi, there's every textbook's example of the early Renaissance mastery of perspective: *The Holy Trinity* by Masaccio; it's opposite the side entrance (€2.50, Mon–Thu and Sat 9:30–17:00, Fri and Sun 13:00–17:00)

Nearby: A palatial **perfumery** is around the corner 100 yards down Via della Scala at #16 (free but shopping encouraged, Mon–Sat 9:30–19:30, closed Sun, tel. 055-216-276). Thick with the lingering aroma of centuries of spritzes, it started as the herb garden of the Santa Maria Novella monks. Well-known even today for its top-quality products, it is extremely Florentine. Pick up the history sheet at the desk and wander deep into the shop. From the back room, you can peek at Santa Maria Novella's cloister with its dreamy frescoes and imagine a time before Vespas and tourists.

Dante's House (Casa di Dante)—Dante's house is closed indefinitely for restoration. It's actually a copy built near his house just a hundred years ago, consisting of five rooms in an old building with lots of documents and photos relating to his life and work. Well-described in English, it's interesting to literary buffs (across the street and around the corner from Bargello, at Via S. Margherita 1, tel. 055-219-416).

Santa Croce and Nearby

▲▲Santa Croce Church—This 14th-century Franciscan church, decorated with centuries of precious art, holds the tombs of great Florentines (€4, Mon–Sat 9:30–17:30, Sun 15:00–17:30, in winter Mon–Sat 9:30–12:30 & 15:00–17:30, Sun 15:00–17:30, modest dress code enforced, tel. 055-244-619). The loud 19th-century Victorian Gothic facade faces a huge square ringed with tempting shops and littered with tired tourists. Escape into the church.

On your right as you enter you'll see the tomb of Galileo (allowed in by the Church only long after his death). Directly opposite (across the back end of the nave) find the tomb of Michelangelo (with the allegorical figures of painting, architecture, and sculpture); a memorial to Dante (no body...he was banished by his hometown because of political differences); the tomb of Machiavelli (who wrote the book on hardball politics); a relief by Donatello of the Annunciation; and the tomb of the composer of the *William Tell* Overture (a.k.a. the *Lone Ranger* theme), Rossini.

To the right of the altar, step into the sacristy where you'll find a bit of St. Francis' cowl and old sheets of music. In the bookshop, notice the photos of the devastating flood of 1966 high on the wall. Beyond that is a touristy—but mildly interesting—"leather school." The chapels lining the front of the church are richly frescoed. The chapel to the right of the main altar is a masterpiece by Giotto featuring scenes from the life of St. Francis. Exit between the Rossini and Machiavelli tombs into the cloisters. On the left enter Brunelleschi's **Pazzi Chapel,** considered one of the finest pieces of Florentine Renaissance architecture.

▲**Michelangelo's House (Casa Buonarroti)**—Fans enjoy a house owned by Michelangelo that he gave to his nephew, who turned it into a little museum honoring his famous uncle. You'll see some of Michelangelo's early, much-less-monumental statues and sketches (€6.50, Wed–Mon 9:30–14:00, closed Tue, English descriptions, Via Ghibellina 70, tel. 055-241-752).

South of the Arno River

▲▲**Pitti Palace**—From the Uffizi, follow the course of the elevated passageway (closed to non-Medicis) across the Ponte Vecchio to the gargantuan Pitti Palace, which has several separate museums.

The **Palatine Gallery/Royal Apartments (Galleria Palatina)** is the biggie, featuring palatial room after chandeliered room, its walls sagging with masterpieces by minor artists and minor pieces by masters. Its Raphael collection is the biggest anywhere (first floor, €6.50, Tue–Sun 8:15–18:50, closed Mon, buy tickets on right-hand side of courtyard, tel. 055-238-8614).

The **Modern Art Gallery** features Romanticism, neoclassicism, and Impressionism by 19th- and 20th-century Tuscan painters (second floor, €5, daily 8:15–13:50 but closed second and fourth Sun and first, third, and fifth Mon).

The **Grand Ducal Treasures (Museo degli Argenti)** is the Medici treasure chest, with jeweled crucifixes, exotic porcelain, gilded ostrich eggs, and so on to entertain fans of applied arts (ground floor, €4, virtually the same hours as Modern Art Gallery).

Behind the palace, the huge landscaped **Boboli Gardens** offer a shady refuge from the city heat (€4, daily 9:00–18:30 in fall and spring, until 19:30 June–Aug, until 16:30 in winter, but closed first and last Mon of month).

▲▲**Brancacci Chapel**—For the best look at Masaccio's works (he's the early Renaissance master who re-invented perspective), see his restored frescoes here. Since only a few tourists are let in at a time, seeing the chapel often involves a wait (€3.10, Mon and Wed–Sat 10:00–17:00, Sun 13:00–17:00, closed Tue, cross Ponte Vecchio and turn right and hike to Piazza del Carmine).

The neighborhoods around the church are considered the last surviving bits of old Florence.

Santo Spirito Church—This has a classic Brunelleschi interior and a very early Michelangelo crucifix, painted on carved wood, given by the sculptor to the monastery in appreciation for the opportunity that they gave him to dissect and learn about bodies. Pop in here for a delightful Renaissance space and a chance to marvel at a Michelangelo all alone (free, most days 10:00–12:00 & 16:00–17:30, Sat–Sun only 16:00–17:30, closed Wed, Piazza Santo Spirito, tel. 055-210-030).

▲**Piazzale Michelangelo**—Overlooking the city from across the river (look for the huge statue of David), this square is worth the 30-minute hike, drive, or bus ride (either #12 or #13 from the train station) for the view of Florence and the stunning dome of the Duomo. After dark, it's packed with local schoolkids feeding their dates slices of watermelon and then licking them clean. Just beyond it is the stark and beautiful, crowd-free, Romanesque San Miniato Church.

EXPERIENCES

▲▲**Gelato**—Gelato is an edible art form. Italy's best ice cream is in Florence—one souvenir that can't break and won't clutter your luggage. But beware of scams at touristy joints on busy streets that turn a simple request for a cone into a €10 "tourist special." A key to gelato-appreciation is sampling liberally and choosing flavors that go well together. Ask, as the locals do, for "*Un assaggio, per favore?*" (A taste, please?) and "*Que si sposano bene?*" (What marries well?).

Gelateria Carrozze is very good (daily 11:00–24:00, closes at 21:00 in winter; on riverfront 30 yards from Ponte Vecchio toward the Uffizi, Via del Pesce 3; also has decent sandwiches to go). **Gelateria dei Neri** is another local favorite worth tracking down (daily in summer 12:00–23:00, closed Wed in winter, 2 blocks east of Palazzo Vecchio at Via Dei Neri 20 red).

Vivoli's, which serves "only today's production" is the most famous (Tue–Sun 8:00–1:00; closed Mon, the last 3 weeks in Aug, and winter; opposite the Church of Santa Croce, go down Via Torta a block, turn right on Via Stinche). Before ordering, try a free sample of their *riso* flavor—rice.

If you want an excuse to check out the little village-like neighborhood across the river from Santa Croce, enjoy a gelato at the tiny **no-name gelateria** at Via San Miniato 5 red (just before Porta San Miniato).

SHOPPING

Florence is a great shopping town. Busy street scenes and markets abound, especially near San Lorenzo, near Santa Croce, on Ponte Vecchio, and at Mercato Nuovo (a covered market square 3 blocks north of Ponte Vecchio, listed on page 268). Leather (often better quality for less than the U.S. price), gold, silver, art prints, and tacky plaster mini-*Davids* are most popular. Shops usually have promotional stalls in the market squares. Prices are soft in markets. Many visitors spend entire days shopping.

For ritzy Italian fashions, browse along Via de Tornabuoni, Via della Vigna Nuova, and Via Strozzi. Typical chain department stores are **Coin,** the local "Macy's" (Mon–Sat 9:30–20:00, Sun 11:00–20:00, on Via Calzaiuoli, near Orsanmichele Church); **Oviesse,** the local "Penny's," a discount clothing/grocery store (Mon–Sat 9:00–19:55, closed Sun; at intersection of Via Panzani and Via del Giglio, near train station); and **La Rinascente,** the local "Nordstroms" (Mon–Sat 9:00–21:00, Sun 10:30–20:00, on Piazza della Repubblica).

For shopping ideas, ads, and a list of markets, see the *Florence Concierge Information* magazine described under "Tourist Information," page 255 (free from TI and many hotels).

SLEEPING

The accommodations scene varies wildly with the season. Spring and fall are very tight and expensive, while mid-July through August is wide open and discounted. November through February is also generally empty. I've listed prices for peak season: April, May, June, September, and October. If a price range is listed, the lower end reflects off-season (Aug, Nov–March) and the higher end, peak season.

With good information and an e-mail or phone call beforehand, you can find a stark, clean, and comfortable double with breakfast and a shower down the hall for about €70 (for the room, not per person). A typical room with a private bath costs around €100 (less at the smaller places, such as the *soggiornos*). You get elegance in peak season for €150. Some places listed are old and rickety, and described as such. Virtually all of the accommodations are central, within minutes of the great sights. Few hotels escape Vespa noise at night.

Contact the hotels directly—not through a tourist agency. Tourist information room-finding services cannot give opinions on quality. If you're traveling off-season, you can show up without reservations and find huge discounts. Ask if you'll get a discount for paying in cash, for staying for three or more nights (or both), or for using this book. And ask if you can skip breakfast (the overpriced breakfasts are legally optional, though some hotels pretend otherwise).

SLEEP CODE

(€1 = about $1.10, country code: 39)

Sleep Code: **S** = Single, **D** = Double/Twin, **T** = Triple, **Q** = Quad, **b** = bathroom, **s** = shower only, **no CC** = Credit Cards not accepted, **SE** = Speaks English, **NSE** = No English. Unless otherwise noted, breakfast is included (but usually optional) and credit cards are accepted. English is generally spoken.

To help you sort easily through these listings, I've divided the rooms into three categories based on the price for a standard double room with bath:

$$$ **Higher Priced**—Most rooms €160 or more.
  $$ **Moderately Priced**—Most rooms between €110-160
    $ **Lower Priced**—Most rooms €110 or less.

Book ahead. I repeat, book ahead (by e-mail, fax, or phone). Places will hold a room until early afternoon. If they say they're full, mention that you're using this book.

Between the Station and Duomo

$$$ **Palazzo Castiglioni** offers 16 grand rooms with all the conveniences and a peaceful, *palazzo* decor. Most rooms are spacious, several have frescoes, and all make a fine splurge (Db-€170, Db suite-€200, Tb-€210, 5 percent discount with cash and this book in 2004, air-con, elevator, Via del Giglio 8, tel. 055-214-886, fax 055-274-0521, pal.cast@flashnet.it, Laura SE).

$$ **Hotel Accademia** is an elegant two-star place with marble stairs, parquet floors, attractive public areas, 21 pleasant rooms, and a floor plan that defies logic (Sb-€87, Db-€140, Tb-€170, prices promised through 2004 with this book, 5 percent additional discount with cash, air-con, tiny courtyard, Via Faenza 7, tel. 055-293-451, fax 055-219-771, www.accademiahotel.net, info@accademiahotel.net, Tea SE).

$$ **Hotel Bellettini** rents 30 bright, cool, well-cared-for rooms with inviting lounges (S-€78, Sb-€100, D-€105, Db-€135, Tb-€165, Qb-€210, 5 percent discount with this book if claimed upon arrival, air-con, Via de' Conti 7, tel. 055-213-561, fax 055-283-551, hotel .bellettini@dada.it, frisky Gina SE). Be warned, they rent much higher-priced rooms in a nearby annex.

$$ **Residenza dei Pucci,** a block north of the Duomo, has 12 tastefully decorated rooms—in soothing earth tones—with aristocratic furniture and tweed carpeting. It's fresh and bright (Sb-€130, Db-€145, Db in Aug and much of winter-€105, Tb-€165, suite with grand

Hotels in Florence

❶ Palazzo Castiglioni
   & Hotel Aldobrandini

❷ Hotel Accademia

❸ Hotel Bellettini

❹ Residenza dei Pucci

❺ Pensione Centrale

❻ Hotel Basilea

❼ Casa Rabatti

❽ Affitacamere Freda Lucia

❾ Soggiorno Magliani

❿ Hotel Loggiato dei Serviti

⓫ Hotel Morandi alla Crocetta

⓬ Hotel Le Due Fontane

⓭ Oblate Sisters of the Assumption

⓮ Hotel Pendini

⓯ Residenza Giotto

⓰ Pensione Maxim

⓱ Soggiorno Battistero

⓲ Albergo Firenze

⓳ Hotel Beatrice

⓴ Hotel Pensione Elite

㉑ Bellevue House

㉒ Hotel Sole

㉓ Hotel Torre Guelfa & Hotel
   Pensione Alessandra

㉔ In Piazza della Signoria B&B

㉕ Florence Walking Tours

Duomo view-€207 for 2 people, €233 for 4, claim a 10 percent discount through 2004 with cash and this book, breakfast served in room, Via dei Pucci 9, tel. 055-281-886, fax 055-264-314, http://residenzapucci .interfree.it, residenzapucci@interfree.it, SE).

$ **Hotel Aldobrandini,** a good budget choice, has 15 basic, clean rooms, with the San Lorenzo market at its doorstep and the entrance to the Medici Chapel a few steps away (Ss-€40, Sb-€50, D-€65, Db-€80 with this book, lots of night noise but has double-paned windows, fans, hiding behind market stalls and mopeds at Piazza Madonna Degli Aldobrandini 8, tel. 055-211-866, fax 055-267-6281, Ignazio SE).

$ **Pensione Centrale** is a traditional, yet institutional-feeling place with a creaky, elegant living room and 18 spacious rooms (D-€85, Db-€109, quiet, air-con, often filled with American students, elevator, Via de' Conti 3, tel. 055-215-761, fax 055-215-216, www.hotelcentralefirenze.it, info@hotelcentralefirenze.it).

Near the Central Market

$$ **Hotel Basilea** offers predictable three-star, air-conditioned comfort in its 38 modern rooms (Sb-€80–110, Db-€110–150, Tb-€150–210, low prices Aug and Nov–March, elevator, terrace, Via Guelfa 41, at intersection with Nazionale—a busy street, ask for a room in the back, tel. 055-214-587, fax 055-268-350, www.florenceitaly.net/basilea, basilea@dada.it, SE).

$ **Casa Rabatti** is the ultimate if you always wanted to be a part of a Florentine family. Its four simple, clean rooms are run with motherly warmth by Marcella and her husband Celestino, who speak minimal English. Seeing 10 years of my family Christmas cards on their walls, I'm reminded of how long they've been keeping budget travelers happy (D-€50, Db-€60, €25 per bed in shared quad or quint, prices good with this book, no CC; no breakfast, fans; no sign other than on doorbell, 5 blocks from station, Via San Zanobi 48 black; tel. 055-212-393, casarabatti@inwind.it).

$ **Affitacamere Freda Lucia** is basic, clean, and cheap. Its four ground floor-yet-quiet rooms share two bathrooms, a kitchenette, and a leafy garden terrace (S-€45, D-€55, T-€70, €5 less for 3 or more days, discounts in winter, cash only; no breakfast; Via San Zanobi 76, but ring at #31; tel. 055-487533, luciafreda@libero.it, kind Lucia and son Claudio).

$ **Soggiorno Magliani,** central and humble with seven rooms, feels and smells like a great-grandmother's place (S-€36, D-€46, T-€64, cash only but secure reservation with credit card, no breakfast, double-paned windows, near Via Guelfa at Via Reparata 1, tel. 055-287-378, hotel-magliani@libero.it, run by friendly family duo Vincenza and English-speaking daughter Cristina).

East of the Duomo

$$$ Hotel Loggiato dei Serviti, at the most prestigious address in Florence on the most Renaissance square in town, gives you Old World romance with hair dryers. Stone stairways lead you under open-beam ceilings through this 16th-century monastery's classy public rooms. The 34 cells, with air-conditioning, TVs, mini-bars, and telephones, wouldn't be recognized by their original inhabitants. The hotel staff is both professional and friendly (Sb-€146, Db-€210, family suites from €263, 30 percent discounts in Aug and late Nov–Feb, 5 elegant rooms in 17th-century annex, elevator, Piazza S.S. Annuziata 3, tel. 055-289-592, fax 055-289-595, www.loggiatodeiservitihotel.it, info@loggiatodeiservitihotel.it, Simonetta, Francesca, and Andrea SE). Ask for a backside room to avoid piazza night noise.

$$$ Hotel Morandi alla Crocetta, another former convent, envelops you in a 16th-century cocoon. Located on a quiet street, with period furnishings, parquet floors, and wood-beamed ceilings, it takes you back (10 rooms, Sb-€110, Db-€170, breakfast-€11, a block off Piazza S.S. Annunziata at Via Laura 50, tel. 055-234-4747, fax 055-248-0954, www.hotelmorandi.it, welcome@hotelmorandi.it, Claudio SE).

$$ Hotel Le Due Fontane faces the Renaissance Piazza S.S. Annunziata but fills its old building with a smoky, 1970s, business-class ambience. Its 57 air-conditioned rooms are big and comfortable (Sb-€110, Db-€160, Tb-€200, prices promised through 2004 only if you claim them upon reserving, elevator, Piazza S.S. Annunziata 14, tel. 055-210-185, fax 055-294-461, www.leduefontane.it, info @leduefontane.it, SE).

$ Oblate Sisters of the Assumption run an institutional 20-room hotel in a Renaissance building with a dreamy garden and a quiet, nice-place-to-relax-after-you-die feel. Not a hint of English spoken here (S-€35, Db-€70, elevator, no CC, Borgo Pinti 15, 50121 Firenze, tel. 055-248-0582, fax 055-234-6291).

Near Piazza Repubblica

These are the most central of my accommodations recommendations (and therefore a little overpriced). While worth the extra for many, given Florence's walkable core, nearly every hotel can be considered central.

$$ Hotel Pendini, a well-run and well-worn three-star hotel with Old World tiles, chandeliers, and 42 rooms, is popular and central, overlooking the grand Piazza Repubblica (Sb-€86–110, Db-€110–150 depending on season, elevator, fine lounge and breakfast room, air-con, Via Strozzi 2, tel. 055-211-170, fax 055-281-807, www.florenceitaly.net, pendini@dada.it, Barbara SE).

$$ Residenza Giotto has six bright and modern rooms, and a terrace so close to the Duomo you can almost touch it (Sb-€120, Db-

€130, Tb-€145, 10 percent discount for cash with this book if claimed at time of reservation; breakfast served in room, elevator; Via Roma 6, 4th floor; tel. 055-214-593, fax 055-264-8568, www.residenzagiotto.it, residenzagiotto@tin.it, SE).

$$ Pensione Maxim, right on Via dei Calzaiuoli, is a big, institutional-feeling place as close to the sights as possible. Its halls are narrow, but the 29 rooms are comfortable and well-maintained (Sb-€83, Db-€113, Tb-€148, Qb-€173, takes CC but pay first night in cash, air-con, elevator, Via dei Calzaiuoli 11, tel. 055-217-474, fax 055-283-729, www.hotelmaximfirenze.it, hotmaxim@tin.it, Paolo Maioli SE).

$ Soggiorno Battistero, next door to the Baptistery, has seven simple, airy rooms, most with great views, overlooking the Baptistery and square. You're in the heart of Florence (Sb-€73, Db-€95, Tb-€130, Qb-€140, these prices good with this book, 5 percent additional discount with cash; breakfast served in room, ceiling fans, double-paned windows, no elevator; Piazza San Giovanni 1, 3rd floor; tel. 055-295-143, fax 055-268-189, www.soggiornobattistero.it, battistero@dada.it, lovingly run by Italian Luca and his American wife, Kelly).

$ Albergo Firenze, a big, efficient place, offers 58 good, basic rooms in a wonderfully central, reasonably quiet locale two blocks behind the Duomo (Sb-€73, Db-€94, Tb-€132, Qb-€162, cash only, prepay first night with a bank draft or traveler's check, elevator, air-con, off Via del Corso at Piazza Donati 4, tel. 055-214-203, fax 055-212-370, www.hotelfirenze-fi.it, firenze.albergo@tiscali.it, Manuela SE).

Near Piazza della Signoria and Ponte Vecchio

$$$ Hotel Torre Guelfa is topped by a fun medieval tower with a panoramic rooftop terrace and a huge living room. Its 29 rooms vary wildly in size (Sb-€110, small Db-€145, standard Db-€180, Db junior suite-€220, family deals, 5 percent discount with cash and this book). Room #15, with a private terrace—€210—is worth reserving several months in advance (elevator, air-con; a couple blocks northwest of Ponte Vecchio, Borgo S.S. Apostoli 8; tel. 055-239-6338, fax 055-239-8577, www.hoteltorreguelfa.com, torreguelfa@flashnet.it, Sabina, Giancarlo, Carlo, and Sandro all SE).

$$$ In Piazza della Signoria B&B is peaceful, classy, and homey at the same time and overlooks Piazza della Signoria. It comes with all the special touches—much like a top-end American B&B. Each of its eight rooms has a huge and lavish bathroom (Sb-€130–190, Db-€190–240, Tb-€220–270, lower prices without view, family apartments, tiny elevator, air-con, Via dei Magazzini 2, tel. 055-239-9546, fax 055-267-6616, mobile 348-321-0565, www.inpiazzadellasignoria.it, info@inpiazzadellasignoria.it, Silka SE).

$$ Hotel Pensione Alessandra is a 16th-century, tranquil place with 27 big, modern rooms (S-€67, Sb-€108, D-€108, Db-€145,

T-€145, Tb-€191, Q-€160, Qb-€212, 5 percent discount with cash, air-con, Borgo S.S. Apostoli 17, tel. 055-283-438, fax 055-210-619, www.hotelalessandra.com, info@hotelalessandra.com, SE).

Near the Train Station

Note: As with any big Italian city, the area around the train station is a magnet for hardworking pickpockets on the alert for lost, vulnerable tourists with bulging moneybelts hanging out of their khakis.

$$ **Hotel Beatrice,** a three-star hotel popular with tour groups, is well-located—especially if you've packed heavy. It's a block north of the train and bus stations (20 rooms, Sb-€75–90, Db-€95–142, Tb-€120-190, 5 percent discount with cash and this book, most rooms air-con—request one as you reserve, elevator, Via Fiume 11, tel. 055-216-790, fax 055-280-711, www.hotelbeatrice.it, info@hotelbeatrice.it, Constantino SE).

$ **Hotel Pensione Elite,** run warmly by sunny Nadia, is a fine value. It has 10 comfortable—if plainly furnished—rooms and a charm rare in this price range (Ss-€60, Sb-€75, Ds-€75, Db-€90, breakfast-€6; air-con, fans; Via della Scala 12, 2nd floor; tel. & fax 055-215-395, easy reservations by phone, SE).

$ **Bellevue House** is a fourth-floor oasis (no elevator) with six spacious rooms flanking a long, mellow yellow lobby. It's a peaceful time-warp run by Suzanna and Antonio Di Grazia (Db-maximum €100 in May, June, Sept, and Oct, Db-maximum €80 off-season, prices promised through 2004, 5 percent cash discount, includes breakfast in a street level bar; over-sized modern bathrooms; Via della Scala 21, 50123 Florence; tel. 055-260-8932, fax 055-265-5315, mobile 333-612-5973, www.bellevuehouse.it, info@bellevuehouse.it).

$ **Hotel Sole,** a clean, cozy, family-run place with eight bright, modern rooms, is just off Santa Maria Novella square toward the river. Friendly Anna makes you feel like a guest of the family (Sb-€47, Db-€78, Tb-€105, no CC; no breakfast, air-con, elevator, 1:00 curfew; Via del Sole 8, 3rd floor; tel. & fax 055-239-6094, NSE).

Oltrarno, South of the River

Across the river in the Oltrarno area, between the Pitti Palace and Ponte Vecchio, you'll still find small traditional crafts shops, neighborly piazzas, and family eateries. The following places are an easy walk from the Ponte Vecchio.

$$$ **Hotel Lungarno** is *the* place to stay if money is no object. This deluxe, four-star hotel with 74 rooms strains anything stressful or rough out of Italy, and gives you only service with a salute, physical elegance everywhere you look, and fine views over the Arno and Ponte Vecchio (Sb-€225, Db-€385, Db facing river-€484, fancier suites, great riverside public spaces, air-con, elevator, 100 yards from Ponte

Hotels in Oltrarno

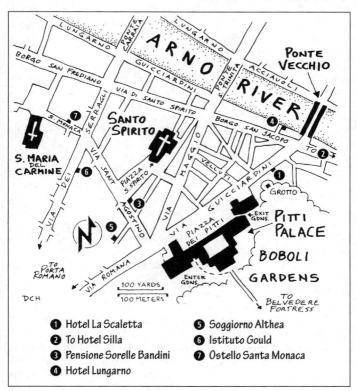

● Hotel La Scaletta
● To Hotel Silla
● Pensione Sorelle Bandini
● Hotel Lungarno

● Soggiorno Althea
● Istituto Gould
● Ostello Santa Monaca

Vecchio at Borgo San Jacopo 14, tel. 055-27261, fax 055-268-437, www.lungarnohotels.com, bookings@lungarnohotels.com, SE).

$$$ **Hotel Silla,** a classic three-star hotel with 36 cheery, spacious, pastel, and modern rooms, is a fine value. It faces the river and overlooks a park opposite the Santa Croce Church (Db-€170, Tb-€210, mention this book for a discount, elevator, air-con, Via dei Renai 5, tel. 055-234-2888, fax 055-234-1437, www.hotelsilla.it, hotelsilla@tin.it, Laura and Stefano SE).

$$ **Hotel La Scaletta,** ramshackle and reeking in character, is a dark, cool place with a labyrinthine floor plan, senseless stairs, loose tiles, lots of Old World lounges, and a romantic, panoramic roof terrace (16 rooms, S-€50, Sb-€95, D-€110, Db-€115–130, Tb-€130–150, Qb-€150–170, higher price is for quieter rooms in back, €5–10 discount for cash; mostly air-con, elevator, bar with fine wine at good prices; Via Guicciardini 13 black, 150 yards south of Ponte Vecchio; tel. 055-283-028, fax 055-289-562,

www.lascaletta.com, info@lascaletta.com, Barbara and her son Manfredo SE). Manfredo loves to cook and offers a fine family-style dinner. He also serves a €15 "Taste of Tuscany for Two" deal (plate of quality Tuscan meats and cheeses with bread and 4 glasses of robust Chianti)—ideal for a light lunch or dinner on the roof terrace.

$$ **Pensione Sorelle Bandini** is a rickety 500-year-old palace on a perfectly Florentine square, with cavernous rooms, museum-warehouse interiors, a musty youthfulness, cats, a balcony lounge-loggia with a view, and an ambience that, for romantic bohemians, can be a highlight of Florence. Mimmo or Sr. Romeo will hold a room until 16:00 with a phone call (D-€109, Db-€130, T-€148, Tb-€178, includes optional €9 breakfast, no CC, elevator, Piazza Santo Spirito 9, tel. 055-215-308, fax 055-282-761, pensionebandini@tiscali.it, SE). This square can attract drug pushers; just don't invite them to your room.

$ **Soggiorno Althea** is a small guesthouse run by Antonio deep in the Oltrarno. While it's on a noisy street, half its rooms are on the back (Db-€71, Tb-€80, prices special with this book; air-con, no breakfast, no reception desk, a couple blocks beyond Piazza San Spirito on corner of Via delle Caldaie and Via del Campuccio, at Via delle Caldaie 25; tel. 055-233-5341, mobile 388-233-5341, info@florencealthea.it).

$ **Istituto Gould** is a Protestant Church–run place with 41 clean but drab rooms with twin beds and modern facilities (S-€32, Sb-€38, D-€40, Db-€50, Tb-€66, €21 per person in quads, no breakfast, quieter rooms in back, Via dei Serragli 49, tel. 055-212-576, fax 055-280-274, gould.reception@dada.it). You must arrive when the office is open (Mon–Fri 9:00–13:00 & 15:00–19:00, Sat 9:00–13:00, no check-in Sun or holidays, SE).

$ **Ostello Santa Monaca,** a cheap hostel, is a few blocks south of Ponte Alla Carraia, one of the bridges over the Arno (€15.50 beds, 4- to 20-bed rooms, 1:00 curfew, Via Santa Monaca 6, tel. 055-268-338, fax 055-280-185, www.ostello.it, info@ostello.it).

Away from the Center

$$ **Hotel Ungherese** is good for drivers. It's northeast of the city center (near *stadio,* en route to Fiesole), with easy, free street parking and quick bus access (#11 and #17) into central Florence (Sb-€72, Db-€123, extra bed-€31, prices only with this book, additional 7 percent discount for cash, rooms are 20 percent less off-season, includes breakfast, most rooms air-con, Via G. B. Amici 8, tel. & fax 055-573-474, www.hotelungherese.it, info@hotelungherese.it, Giovanni and Francesca SE). It has great singles and a backyard garden terrace (ask for a room on the garden). They can recommend good eateries nearby.

$ **Villa Camerata,** classy for an IYHF hostel, is on the outskirts of Florence (€15.50 per bed with breakfast, 4- to 12-bed rooms, must have IYHF card, no CC; ride bus #17 to Salviatino stop, Via Righi 2; tel. 055-601-451).

EATING

To save money and time for sights, you can keep lunches fast and simple, eating in one of the countless self-service places and pizzerias or just picnicking (try juice, yogurt, cheese, and a roll for €5). For good sit-down meals, consider the following. Remember, restaurants like to serve what's fresh. If you're into flavor, go for the seasonal best bets—featured in the *Piatti del Giorno* ("special of the day") sections of the menus.

North of the River

Near Santa Maria Novella and the Train Station

Osteria Belledonne feels like eating dinner in a crowded terrarium. I loved the meal but had to correct the bill—read it carefully. They take only a few reservations; arrive early or wait (Mon–Fri 12:00–14:30 & 19:00–22:30, closed Sat–Sun, Via delle Belledonne 16 red, tel. 055-238-2609).

Ristorante La Spada is another fine local favorite serving typical Tuscan cuisine with less atmosphere and more menu. Order the €19 "Spada's Fantasy" for an unending parade of food (€11 lunch special, daily 12:00–15:00 & 19:00–22:30, air-con, near Via della Spada at Via del Moro 66 red, evening reservations smart, tel. 055-218-757). Their take-out *rosticcería* (at their Via della Spada entrance) serves the same food for picnic prices.

Trattoria Marione serves good home-cooked-style meals to a local crowd in a happy, food-loving, and steamy ambience (dinners run about €15 plus wine, open daily, Via della Spada 27 red, tel. 055-214-756).

Trattoria Sostanza-Troia is a characteristic and well-established place with shared tables and a loyal local following. Whirling ceiling fans and walls strewn with old photos create a time-warp ambience. They offer two seatings, requiring reservations: one at 19:30 and one at 21:00 (dinners for about €15 plus wine, great steaks, lunch 12:00–14:00, closed Sat, Via del Porcellana 25 red, tel. 055-212-691).

Ristorante il Latini is a hugely popular institution packed with Florentines and tourists munching cheap Tuscan cuisine noisily under pendulous hamhocks. Arrive right at 12:30 or 19:30 or you'll wait for a table (€6 pastas, €12 *secondis*, each table has a bottle of Chianti—you pay €1 per glass, closed Mon, off Via d. Vigna Nuova at Via Palchetti 6, tel. 055-210-916).

Near the Central and San Lorenzo Markets

For piles of picnic produce, people-watching, or just a rustic sandwich, try the huge Central Market—**Mercato Centrale** (Mon–Sat 7:00–14:00, a block north of San Lorenzo street market).

Trattoria la Burrasca is a Flintstone-chic, family-run place ideal for Tuscan home cooking. It's small—10 tables—and often filled with our readers. Anna and Antonio Genzano have cooked and served here with passion since 1982. If Andy Capp were Italian, he'd eat here for special nights out. Everything is homemade except the desserts. And if you want good wine cheap, order it here (Fri–Wed 12:00–15:00 & 19:00–22:00, closed Thu, Via Panicale 6b, at north corner of Central Market, tel. 055-215-827, NSE).

Osteria la Congrega brags it's "a Tuscan wine bar designed to help you lose track of time." In a fresh and romantic two-level setting, chef/owner Mahyar takes pride in his fun, easy menu featuring modern Tuscan cuisine, with top-notch meat and seasonal produce. He offers quality vegetarian dishes, creative salads, and an inexpensive but excellent house wine. With just 10 uncrowded tables, reservations are required for dinner (€5–6 pasta, €11 nightly specials, daily 12:00–15:00 & 19:00–23:00, Via Panicale 43 red, tel. 055-264-5027).

For a cheap lunch, try **Trattoria San Zanobi's** €5 Pasta Break Lunch (open daily, Via San Zanobi 33 red, a couple blocks northeast of Central Market, tel. 055-475-286).

Near the Accademia and Museum of San Marco

Gran Caffè San Marco, conveniently located on Piazza San Marco, churns out cheap but tired cafeteria fare to cheap but tired tourists (no cover charge, self-service and restaurant; door to cafeteria hides near Piazza San Marco 11 red, across square from Museum of San Marco entrance; tel. 055-215-833).

Near the Duomo (Cathedral)

Self-Service Ristorante Leonardo is fast, cheap, air-conditioned, and handy, just a block from the Duomo, southwest of the Baptistery (€3 pastas, €4 main courses, Sun–Fri 11:45–14:45 & 18:45–21:45, closed Sat, upstairs at Via Pecori 5, tel. 055-284-446). Luciano (like Pavarotti) runs the place with enthusiasm.

Antico Ristorante il Sasso di Dante serves standard Tuscan fare in a surprisingly pleasant indoor/outdoor setting in the shadow of the Duomo (€20 meals, always good vegetarian dishes and special menu of the day, daily 12:00–14:30 & 19:00–22:30, come early to snare the front-row view seats, Piazza delle Pallottole 6, tel. 055-282-113).

Cavernous **Ristorante il Ritrovo** offers a bright, dressy ambience and meaty Tuscan cuisine cooked with family pride. They serve a good two-course €10 lunch special for hurried office workers (€25 meals, 12 tables, air-con, Tue–Sun 12:30–15:00 & 19:00–23:00, closed Mon, a long block north of the Duomo at Via dei Pucci 4, tel. 055-281-688, Marco SE).

Near Palazzo Vecchio

Piazza della Signoria, the square facing Palazzo Vecchio, is ringed by

Restaurants in Florence

1. Osteria Belledonne
2. Ristorante La Spada
3. Trattoria Marione
4. Trattoria Sostanza-Troia
5. Ristorante il Latini
6. Mercato Centrale (Market)
7. Trattoria la Burrasca
   & Osteria la Congrega
8. Trattoria San Zanobi
9. Gran Caffè San Marco
10. Self-Service Ristorante Leonardo
11. Antico Ristorante il Sasso di Dante
12. Ristorante il Ritrovo
13. Ristorante il Cavallino
14. Osteria Vini e Vecchi Sapori
15. Cantinetta dei Verrazzano
    & Ristorante Paoli
16. I Fratellini Wine
    & Sandwich Shop
17. Trattoria Icche C'è C'è
18. Osteria del Porcellino
19. Trattoria Nella
20. Gelateria Carrozze
21. Gelateria dei Neri
22. Vivoli's Gelateria

beautifully situated yet touristic eateries. Any will do for a reasonably-priced pizza. Perhaps the least of these evils is **Ristorante il Cavallino** with its glum crowd of tourists, dumbed-down menu, and great outdoor seating in the shadow of the palace (€11 fixed-price lunch *menu*, €16 fixed-price dinner *menu*, open daily, tel. 055-215-818).

Osteria Vini e Vecchi Sapori, half a block north of Palazzo Vecchio, is a colorful hole-in-the-wall serving traditional food, including plates of mixed *crostini* (€1 each—step right up and choose at the bar) and €10 daily specials (Tue–Sun 11:00–22:00, closed Mon; Via dei Magazzini 3 red, facing the bronze equestrian statue in Piazza della Signoria, go behind its tail into the corner and to your left; gruff Giorgio SE).

Cantinetta dei Verrazzano is a long-established bakery/café/wine bar, serving delightful sandwich plates in an elegant old-time setting, and hot focaccia sandwiches to go. The *Specialita Verrazzano* is a fine plate of four little *crostini* (like mini *bruschetta*) featuring different local breads, cheeses, and meats (€7). The *Tagliere di Focacce,* a sampler plate of mini–focaccia sandwiches, is also fun. Either of these dishes with a glass of Chianti makes a fine light meal. Paolo describes things to make eating educational. As office workers pop in for a quick bite, it's traditional to share tables at lunchtime (Mon–Sat 12:30–21:00, closed Sun, just off Via Calzaiuoli on a side street across from Orsanmichele Church at Via dei Tavolini 18, tel. 055-268-590).

I Fratellini is a rustic little place where the "little brothers" have served peasants 27 different kinds of sandwiches and cheap glasses of Chianti wine (see list on wall) since 1875. Join the local crowd, then sit on a nearby curb or windowsill to munch, placing your glass on the wall rack before you leave (€4 for sandwich and wine, daily 8:00–20:00, 20 yards in front of Orsanmichele church on Via dei Cimatori).

Ristorante Paoli serves great local cuisine to piles of happy eaters under a richly frescoed Gothic vault. Because of its fame and central location, it's filled mostly with tourists, but for a dressy, traditional splurge meal, this is my choice (€20 tourist menu, à la carte is pricier, Wed–Mon 12:00–14:00 & 19:00–22:00, closed Tue, reserve for dinner, midway between old square and Duomo at Via de Tavolini 12 red, tel. 055-216-215). Salads are flamboyantly cut and mixed from a trolley right at your table.

Trattoria Icche C'è C'è (dialect for "whatever is, is"; ee-kay chay chay) is a small, family-style eatery where fun-loving Gino serves good traditional meals (3-course €11 meals, not too touristy, Tue–Sun 12:30–14:30 & 19:30–22:30, closed Mon, midway between Bargello and river at Via Magalotti 11 red, tel. 055-216-589).

Osteria del Porcellino is a rare place that serves late. This dark, dense, candlelit place is packed with a mix of locals and tourists and run with style and enthusiasm by friendly chef Enzo (daily 19:00–1:00, summer lunches; reserve for dinner, indoor/outdoor; Via Val di Lamona 7 red, half a block behind Mercato Nuovo; tel. 055-264-148).

Trattoria Nella serves good, typical Tuscan cuisine at affordable prices, including melt-in-your-mouth gnocchi. Arrive early or be disappointed—it's understandably popular (€20 meals, Mon–Sat 12:00–14:30 & 19:00–22:00, closed Sun; 3 blocks northwest of Ponte Vecchio, Via delle Terme 19 red; tel. 055-218-925).

Oltrarno, South of the River

Near Ponte Vecchio

Ristorante Bibo serves *"cucina tipica Fiorentina"* with a pink-tablecloth-and-black-bowties dressiness and a leafy, candlelit outdoor seating (good €15 three-course meal, leave this book face up on the table for a 15 percent discount, reserve for outdoor seating, Wed–Mon 12:00–14:30 & 19:00–22:30, closed Tue, Piazza Santa Felicita 6 red, tel. 055-239-8554, Tonino SE).

Trattoria Bordino, just up the street and actually built into the old town wall (c. 1170), serves tasty and beautifully presented Florentine cuisine in a brooding, candlelit atmosphere (Mon–Sat 12:00–14:30 & 19:30–22:30, closed Sun, Via Stracciatella 9 red, tel. 055-213-048).

Golden View Open Bar is a lively, trendy place good for a salad, pizza, or pasta with a view of Ponte Vecchio and the Arno River. Reservations for window tables are limited to 19:30 and 21:30 seatings (reasonable prices, daily 11:30–24:00, impressive wine bar, Internet access, 50 yards upstream from Ponte Vecchio at Via dei Bardi 58, tel. 055-214-502). They have live jazz Mondays and Wednesdays at 21:00.

Via Santo Spirito and Borgo San Jacopo

Several good and colorful restaurants line this multinamed street a block off the river in Oltrarno. I'd survey the scene before making a choice.

Cammillo Trattoria was formerly run by Cammillo, who is now is slurping spaghetti in heaven. But his granddaughter Chiara carries on the tradition, mixing traditional Tuscan and creative, modern cuisine. With a charcoal grill and a team of white-aproned waiters cranking out wonderful food in a fun, dressy-but-down-to-earth ambience, this place is a hit (full dinners about €36 plus wine, Thu–Tue 12:00–14:30 & 19:30–22:30, closed Wed, reservations smart, Borgo San Jacopo 57 red, tel. 055-212-427).

Trattoria Angiolino serves good, old-fashioned local cuisine. Sit in the main hall rather than the stuffy side rooms (€20 for dinner plus wine, Tue–Sun 12:00–14:30 & 19:30–22:30, closed Mon, Via di Santo Spirito 36 red, tel. 055-239-8976).

Trattoria Sabatino, farthest away and least touristy, is spacious and disturbingly cheap, with family character, red-checkered tablecloths, and

Florence's Oltrarno Neighborhood

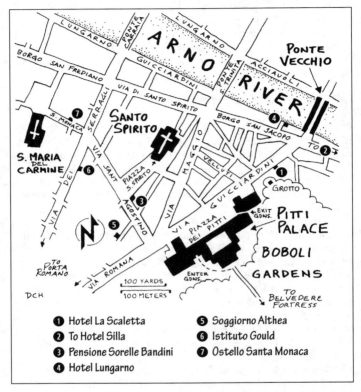

- **1** Hotel La Scaletta
- **2** To Hotel Silla
- **3** Pensione Sorelle Bandini
- **4** Hotel Lungarno
- **5** Soggiorno Althea
- **6** Istituto Gould
- **7** Ostello Santa Monaca

a simple menu. A wonderful place to watch locals munch, it's just out-side the Porta San Frediano (medieval gate), a 15-minute walk from Ponte Vecchio (Mon–Fri 12:00–14:30 & 19:20–22:00, closed Sat–Sun, Via Pisana 2 red, tel. 055-225-955, NSE).

Piazza Santo Spirito

This classic Florentine square (lately a hangout for drug pushers, there-fore a bit seedy-feeling and plagued by bag-snatchers on mopeds) has several popular little restaurants and bars that are open nightly. They offer good local cuisine, moderate prices, and impersonal service, with a choice of indoor or romantic on-the-square seating (reservations smart): lively **Borgo Antico** (Piazza Santo Spirito 6 red, tel. 055-210-437) and the quieter yet more bohemian **Osteria Santo Spirito** (entrée salads, Piazza Santo Spirito 16 red, tel. 055-238-2383).

Ricchi Caffè, next to Borgo Antico, has fine gelato and shaded outdoor tables. After noting the plain facade of the Brunelleschi church facing the square, step inside the café, and pick your favorite of the many ways it might be finished. **Café Cabiria,** next door, is a trendy local hangout with good light meals and a cozy Florentine funky room in back. If you're a scene crasher, try it here.

Trattoria Casalinga, an inexpensive standby, comes with aproned women bustling around the kitchen. You'll find more tourists than locals, but all seem to leave full, happy, and with euros to spare for gelato (Mon–Sat 12:00–14:30 & 19:00–21:45, after 20:00 reserve or wait, closed Sun and all of Aug; just off Piazza Santo Spirito, near the church at Via dei Michelozzi 9 red; tel. 055-218-624).

TRANSPORTATION CONNECTIONS

By train to: Pisa (2/hr, 1.25 hrs), **Lucca** (9/day, 1.5 hrs), **Siena** (9/day, 1.75 hrs, more with transfer in Empoli; bus is better), **La Spezia** (for the Cinque Terre, 2/day direct, 2 hrs, or change in Pisa), **Milan** (12/day, 3–5 hrs), **Venice** (7/day, 3 hrs), **Assisi** (3/day, 2 hrs, more frequent with transfers, direction: Foligno), **Orvieto** (6/day, 2 hrs), **Rome** (hrly, 2.5 hrs), **Naples** (10/day, 4 hrs), **Brindisi** (3/day, 11 hrs with change in Bologna), **Frankfurt** (3/day, 12 hrs), **Paris** (1/day, 12 hrs overnight), **Vienna** (4/day, 9–10 hrs).

Buses: The SITA bus station, a block west of the Florence train station, is user-friendly. Schedules are posted everywhere, with TV monitors indicating imminent departures. Bus service drops dramatically on Sunday. You'll find buses to: **San Gimignano** (€6, hrly, 1.75 hrs), **Siena** (€6.50, hrly, 75-min *corse rapide* fast buses are faster than the train, avoid the 2-hr *diretta* slow buses), and the **airport** (€4, hrly, 15 min). Bus info: tel. 800-373760 or 055-214-721 from 9:30 to 12:30; some schedules are in the *Florence Concierge Information* magazine.

Taxi to Siena: For around €100, you can arrange a ride directly from your Florence hotel to your Siena hotel. For a small group or for people with more money than time, this can be a good value.

Airports

The **Amerigo Vespucci Airport** (www.safnet.it), several miles northwest of Florence, has a TI, cash machines, car rental agencies, and easy connections by airport shuttle bus with Florence's bus station, a block west of the train station (€4, 2/hr, 30 min, from Florence runs 5:30–23:00, from airport 6:00–23:30). Airport info: 055-306-1300, flight info: 055-306-1700 (domestic), 055-306-1702 (international). Allow about €16–20 for a taxi.

International flights often land at Pisa's **Galileo Galilei Airport** (also has TI and car rental agencies, www.pisa-airport.com), an hour from Florence by train (runs hourly; if you're leaving Florence for this airport, catch the train at Florence's train station at platform #5). Flight info: 050-849-300.

Fiesole

Perched on a hill overlooking the Arno valley, Fiesole gives weary travelers a break in the action and, during the heat of summer, a breezy location from which to admire the city below. The ancient Etruscans knew a good spot when they saw one, and chose to settle here, establishing Fiesole about 400 years before the Romans founded Florence. Wealthy Renaissance families in pre-air-con days also chose Fiesole as a preferred vacation spot and built villas in the surrounding hillsides. Later, 19th-century romantics spent part of the Grand Tour admiring the vistas, much like the hordes of tourists do today. Most come here for the view—the actual sights pale in comparison to those in Florence.

Getting to Fiesole: From the Florence train station, take bus #7—enjoying a peek at gardens, vineyards, orchards, and villas—to the last stop, Piazza Mino (€1, 3/hr, fewer after 20:00, 30 min, departs Florence from Piazza Adua at northeast side of train station and also from south side of Piazza San Marco). Taxis from Florence cost about €15 (take taxi to highest point you want to visit—La Reggia Ristorante for view terrace, or Church of San Francesco—then explore downhill).

Tourist Information: To reach the TI from the bus stop, walk toward the bell tower and take the first right. Pick up a free map (Mon–Sat 9:00–18:00, Sun 10:00–13:00 & 14:00–18:00, closes 1 hour earlier in winter, Via Portigiani 3, tel. 055-598-720). **Market day** is Saturday, when a modest selection of food and household items fills Piazza Mino (early–13:00).

SIGHTS

▲▲**Terrace with a View**—Catch the sunset (and your breath) from the view terrace just below La Reggia Ristorante. It's a steep hike from the Fiesole bus stop (face bell tower, take Via San Francesco on left).

Church of San Francesco—For even more hill-climbing, continue up from the view terrace to this charming little church. Several colorful altar paintings and an intimate scale make this church more enjoyable than Fiesole's Duomo (free, Mon–Sat 10:00–12:00 & 15:00–19:00, Sun 15:00–19:00, Via San Francesco 13).

Duomo—While this church has a drab 19th-century exterior, the interior is worth a look, if only for the blue- and white-glazed Giovanni della Robbia statue of St. Romulus over the entry door (free, daily 7:30–12:00 & 15:00–18:00, across Piazza Mino from the bus stop).

Roman Theater and Archaeological Park—Occasionally used today for plays, this well-preserved theater held up to 2,000 people. The site's other ruins are…well…ruined and lacking in explanation. But the valley view and peaceful setting are lovely (€6.50 combo-ticket includes the Civic and Bandini Museums; daily 9:30–19:00, until 17:00 in winter; from the bus stop, cross Piazza Mino toward the back of the Duomo, entrance is on the right).

Civic Museum (Museo Civico)—As the mandatory exit to the Archaeological Park, the museum might seem like a funnel into the gift shop, but its decent collection of Roman artifacts is fairly interesting. Look for English explanations (€6.50 combo-ticket, daily 10:00–19:00).

Bandini Museum (Museo Bandini)—This teensy museum displays a modest morsel of quality Gothic and Renaissance art (€6.50 combo-ticket; daily 10:00–19:00; behind Duomo, Via Dupre 1).

Private Villas—Although most villas in the area are privately owned, many open their gardens to the public on a seriously limited, reservation-only basis. For the tenacious tourist, the TI can sort out schedules and entries (€4, not practical without a car, reservations and information in Italian, tel. 800-414-240).

SLEEPING

(€1 = about $1.10, country code: 39)

$$ Hotel Villa Bonelli is a three-star place with 23 rooms and a view from the breakfast room (Sb-€75, Db-€124, Tb-€160, Qb-€190, 10 percent less in winter; air-con; walk 8 min from bus stop up Via Gramsci, right on Via Poeti to #1; tel. 055-59513 or 055-598-941, fax 055-598-942, www.hotelvillabonelli.com, info@hotelvillabonelli.com).

EATING

The first two restaurants are on Piazza Mino, where the bus stops from Florence.

Ristorante Perseus serves authentic Tuscan dishes at a fair price. A local favorite with a rambling interior, its specials are scrawled on a scrap of paper (daily 12:30–14:30 & 19:30–23:30, Piazza Mino 9, tel. 055-59143, friendly Ago SE).

Ristorante Aurora is an upscale alternative, with a territorial view terrace (daily 12:30–14:30 & 19:30–22:30, next to bus stop on Piazza Mino).

Imagine eating in a Michaelangelo-designed Tuscan villa with a fabulous view—that's **Villa San Michele**. While the hotel may be unaffordable, the entrées at the restaurant, and a visit to the splendid gardens and public spaces, can be yours for €20–40. If the terrace is open, sit there (daily 12:00–14:45 & 19:30–22:00, closed Nov–March, reservations smart, Via Doccia 4, tel. 055-567-8200). From Piazza Mino, it's a five-minute taxi ride.

Fiesole is made to order for a scenic and breezy **picnic**. Pick up your goodies at the Co-Op supermarket on Via Gramsci and walk to the panoramic terrace (see "Sights," above). Or, for more convenience and less view, picnic at the shaded park across the way (walk up Via San Francesco about halfway to the terrace and climb the stairs to the right).

SIGHTS NEAR FLORENCE:
PISA AND LUCCA

Florence is within easy striking distance of a number of great cities—as their fortifications attest. Along with Siena (which merits solo coverage in another chapter), Pisa and Lucca show that Florence wasn't the only power and cultural star of the late Middle Ages and Renaissance.

Pisa is touristy, but worth visiting for its Field of Miracles (Leaning Tower, Cathedral, and Baptistery). Lucca, contained within its fine Renaissance wall, has a charm that causes many connoisseurs of Italy to claim it as a favorite stop. While Pisa is best as a short stop-over, to really enjoy Lucca it's best to spend the night. Each are a 90-minute train ride from Florence, 30 minutes from each other, and well-served by the excellent *autostrada*.

Pisa

In A.D. 1200, Pisa's power peaked. For nearly three centuries (1000–1300), Pisa rivaled Venice and Genoa as a sea-trading power, exchanging European goods for luxury items in Muslim lands. As a port near the mouth of the Arno River (6 miles from the coast), the city enjoyed easy access to the Mediterranean plus the protection of sitting a bit upstream. The Romans had made it a navy base, and by medieval times, it was a major player. Pisa controlled the islands of Corsica, Sardinia, and Sicily, with colonies and ports as far south as North Africa and as far east as Syria. The city used this wealth to build the grand monuments of the Field of Miracles, including the now-famous Tower.

But the Pisa fleet was routed in battle by Genoa (1284, at Meloria, off Livorno), their overseas outposts were taken away, the port silted up, and Pisa was left high and dry, with only its Field of Miracles and its university keeping it on the map.

Pisa and Lucca

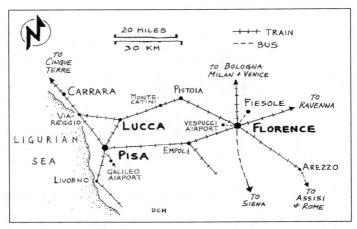

Pisa's three important sights (the cathedral, Baptistery, and bell tower) float regally on the best lawn in Italy. Even as the church was being built, the Piazza del Duomo was nicknamed the "Campo dei Miracoli," or Field of Miracles, for the grandness of the undertaking. The style throughout is Pisa's very own "Pisan Romanesque," surrounded by Italy's tackiest ring of souvenir stands. This spectacle is tourism at its most crass. Wear gloves.

The Tower recently reopened after a decade of restoration and topple prevention. To ascend, you'll have to make a reservation when you buy your €15 ticket (for details, see "Sights," page 299).

Planning Your Time

Seeing the Tower and the square and wandering through the church are 90 percent of the Pisan thrill. Pisa is a touristy quickie. By car, it's a headache. By train, it's a joy. Train travelers may need to change trains in Pisa anyway. Hop on the bus and see the Tower. If you want to climb it, go straight to the ticket booth to snare an appointment—usually for a couple of hours later (or for an extra €2, you can book a time online at www.opapisa.it). Sophisticated sightseers stop more for the Pisano carvings in the cathedral and baptistery than for a look at the tipsy Tower. There's nothing wrong with Pisa, but I'd stop only to see the Field of Miracles and get out of town. By car, it's a 45-minute detour from the freeway.

If you explore the rest of the city, its rather gutless heart stretches southeast of the Field of Miracles, framed by the Arno on the south, and bordered on the east and west by two streets, Borgo Stretto and Via Santa Maria.

ORIENTATION

Tourist Information: One TI is just outside the train station to the left as you exit (Mon–Sat 9:00–19:00, Sun 9:30–15:30; winter: Mon–Sat 9:00–17:00, Sun 9:30–15:30, tel. 050-560-464) and another is behind the Leaning Tower, next to the ticket office (daily 8:00–20:00; in winter Mon–Fri 9:00–18:00, Sat–Sun 10:30–16:30; tel. 050-560-464). There's one more at the airport (10:30–16:30 & 18:00–22:00, tel. 050-503-700).

Arrival in Pisa

By Train: To get to the Field of Miracles from the station, you can **walk** (25–30 min, get free map from TI at station, they'll mark the best route on your map), take a **taxi** (€8, at taxi stand at station or call 050-541-600), or catch a **bus.** The latest information on the bus route to the Field of Miracles is posted in the train information office in Pisa's station lobby (or ask at TI). Take bus #3 (3/hr) or Navette A (4/hr)— both leave across the street from the train station, in front of the Jolly Hotel. Buy an €0.80 ticket from the *tabacchi*/magazine kiosk in the station's main hall or at any *tabacchi* shop (good for 1 hr, round-trip OK, 10-minute ride one-way to Tower). Confirm the bus route number or risk taking a long tour of Pisa's suburbs. The correct bus will let you off at Piazza Manin, in front of the gate to the Field of Miracles. To return to the station, catch the bus across the street from where you got off (confirm the stop with a local or at the TI).

Drop your luggage at the baggage deposit, at the far end of plat-form #1, past the police office (€3/bag per 12 hours, daily 6:00–22:00, ignore non-functional lockers).

By Car: To get to the Leaning Tower, follow signs to the Duomo or Campo dei Miracoli, located on the north edge of town. If you're coming from the Pisa Nord autostrada exit, you won't have to mess with the city center, but you will have to endure some terrible traffic. There's no option better than the €1-per-hour pay lot just outside the town wall a block from the Tower.

By Plane: From Pisa's airport, take bus #3 into town (€0.80, 3/hr, 7 min) or a taxi (€6).

Prices

Pisa has a scheme to get you into its neglected secondary sights: the Baptistery, Cathedral Museum (Museo dell' Opera del Duomo), Camposanto Cemetery, and Fresco Museum (Museo delle Sinopie).

For any one monument, you'll pay €5; for two monuments the cost is €6; for four monuments it's €8.50; and for the works (including the cathedral) you'll pay €10.50. By comparison, the cathedral alone is a bargain (€2). You can buy any of these tickets at the usually crowded ticket office (behind Tower and cathedral entrance), or more easily at the

Pisa

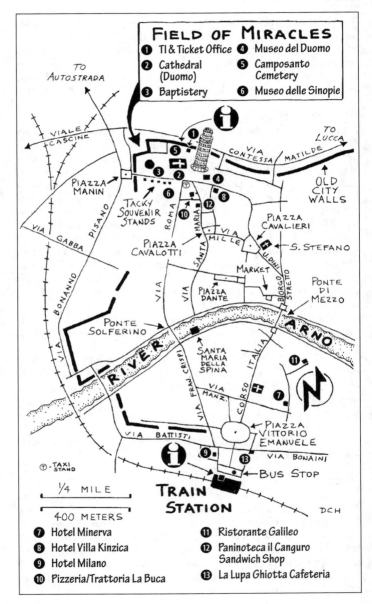

FIELD OF MIRACLES
- **1** TI & Ticket Office
- **2** Cathedral (Duomo)
- **3** Baptistery
- **4** Museo del Duomo
- **5** Camposanto Cemetery
- **6** Museo delle Sinopie

- **7** Hotel Minerva
- **8** Hotel Villa Kinzica
- **9** Hotel Milano
- **10** Pizzeria/Trattoria La Buca
- **11** Ristorante Galileo
- **12** Paninoteca il Canguro Sandwich Shop
- **13** La Lupa Ghiotta Cafeteria

T - TAXI STAND

¼ MILE

400 METERS

DCH

Camposanto Cemetery, Museo dell' Opera del Duomo, or Museo delle Sinopie (near the Baptistery, almost suffocated by souvenir stands); note that you can buy a ticket just for, say, the cathedral at any of these points.

For marathon sightseers there's a €13 Universalis ticket that covers all of the above sights, the Museo Nazionale di San Matteo, and many others, purchasable at the Tower of Santa Maria, behind the Baptistery, or at the Museo dell' Opera del Duomo.

No matter what ticket you get, you'll have to pay another €15 to climb the Leaning Tower. Tickets for the ascent are sold only at the crowded ticket office behind the Tower and Duomo or online at www.opapisa.it.

SIGHTS

Field of Miracles (Campo dei Miracoli)—Scattered across a golf-course-green lawn are four large white buildings that make up Pisa's religious center—the cathedral (or Duomo), its bell tower (the Leaning Tower), Baptistery, and Camposanto Cemetery. The four buildings share similar building materials, similar decoration, and a tendency towards circular designs—giving the Campo a pleasant unity. (They also share centuries-long construction schedules.)

The style is dubbed Pisan Romanesque. Where traditional Romanesque has a heavy fortress feel—thick walls, barrel arches, few windows—Pisan Romanesque is light and elegant. At ground level, most of the structures have a solid Romanesque base of simple pilasters and blind arches (columns and arches in relief). On the upper levels, you'll see a little of everything—tight rows of thin columns borrowed from the Lombards; pointed Gothic gables and prickly spires; Byzantine mosaics and horseshoe arches; and geometric designs (such as diamonds) and striped colored marbles inspired by mosques in Muslim lands.

▲▲**Leaning Tower**—The Tower is 200 feet tall, 55 feet wide, weighs 14,000 tons, and leans at an 85-degree angle (15 feet off the vertical axis). It started to lean almost immediately after construction began. There are eight stories—a simple base, plus six stories of columns (forming arcades), and a belfry on top. The inner, structural core is a hollow cylinder built of limestone bricks, faced with the arcaded spiral staircase. Near the entrance, find relief carvings of imaginary animals and of Pisa's navy.

The Tower was built over two centuries by (at least) three different architects. You can see how each successive architect tried to "correct" the problem of leaning—once half-way up (after the fourth story), once at the belfry on the top.

The first stones were laid in 1173, probably under the architect Bonanno Pisano (who also designed the Duomo's bronze back door). Five years later, just as they'd finished the base and the first arcade, someone turned to Bonanno and said, "Is it just me, or does that look crooked?" The heavy Tower was obviously sinking on the south side into the marshy, multi-layered, unstable soil. (Actually, all the Campo's buildings tilt somewhat.) They carried on anyway, until they'd finished four stories (the base plus three arcade floors) when construction was halted for a century.

Around 1272, the next architect continued, trying to correct the problem by angling the next three stories backward, in the opposite direction of the lean. The project then sat idle for several more decades. Finally, Tommaso Pisano put the belfry on the top (c. 1350–72), also kinking it backward.

After its completion, several projects were launched to stop the Tower's slow-motion fall. The architect/artist/writer Giorgio Vasari reinforced the base (1550), and it actually worked. But in 1838, well-intentioned engineers pumped out ground water, destabilizing the Tower, causing it to fall at a rate of a millimeter a year. It got so bad that, in 1990, it was closed for repairs. The formerly clean and tidy area around the Tower was turned into a construction zone as they spent $40 million to stabilize the Tower. Engineers dried the soil with steam pipes, anchored the Tower to the ground with steel cables, and placed lead bars on the north side as a counterweight (not visible). The Tower has actually been straightened by about six inches, turning the clock back 350 years on the still-leaning (and probably still falling) Tower.

Now 30 people every half-hour can clamber up the 294 tilting stairs to the top for €15 (daily 8:00–20:00, off-season 9:00–17:00, ticket office opens 30 minutes early).

If you want to make the necessary reservation in person (rather than online), go straight to the ticket office behind the Tower. You choose a time slot (30 min) for your visit at the time of purchase; it will likely be a couple of hours before you're able to go up (you could see the rest of the monuments and grab lunch while waiting), but the wait will probably be much shorter if you arrive at the beginning or end of the day. For an extra €2, you can book a time online at www.opapisa.it. Online bookings are accepted no more that 45 days in advance, but at least 14 days prior.

You must show up 10 minutes early and can't take any bags up the Tower (trust me, you don't want to), but teensy lockers are available in a room behind the TI desk to store daypacks (a guard opens the room every half-hour). Even though the ticket office sign says the visit is guided, that only means you'll be accompanied by a museum guard to make sure you don't stay up past your scheduled 30-minute appointment time. Not including the climb, you'll have about 15 minutes for vertigo on top.

▲▲**Cathedral**—The huge Pisan Romanesque church (known as the Duomo), with its carved pulpit by Giovanni Pisano, is artistically more important than its more famous bell tower (€2, summer: Mon–Sat 10:00–19:40, Sun 13:00–19:40; spring and fall: Mon–Sat 10:00–17:40,

Sun 13:00–17:40; winter: Mon–Sat 10:00–12:45 & 15:00–16:45, Sun 15:00–16:45). Shorts are OK as long as they're not short shorts, but shoulders should be covered (although it's not really enforced). Big backpacks are not allowed, nor is storage provided, but if you're climbing the Tower, you can leave a daypack in the Tower's locker room (see above).

The Duomo, or cathedral, is the centerpiece of the Field of Miracles' complex of religious buildings. Begun in 1063, it was largely financed by booty seized in Pisa's victory over the Saracens in Sicily (1069). Five decades later, the architect Rainaldo took over (1118), adding the impressive main entrance facade, the best example of Pisan Romanesque architecture anywhere. The lower half is simple Romanesque, with blind arches. The upper half is four rows of columns forming arcades. Different colored marble in stripes and inlay complete the decoration.

The bronze back door (the one at the Tower end) is by Bonanno Pisano (1186), who may have designed the Leaning Tower. Twenty-four different panels show scenes from Christ's life in a simple, minimal style influenced by Byzantine icons. Cast using the lost-wax technique, this door was an inspiration for Lorenzo Ghiberti's bronze doors in Florence. (The Duomo's front doors are by Giambologna, replacing an original, destroyed Bonanno Pisano set.)

The interior of the church matches the exterior—simple below, and decorative above, with striped marble, light from the windows, and galleries (where the women worshipped). Corinthian columns (68) divide the nave into five aisles. The Byzantine-style mosaic on the ceiling of the apse (c. 1300, partly done by Cimabue) shows Christ as the Ruler (Pantocrator) between Mary and John the Evangelist.

The pulpit by Giovanni Pisano (1301–11) is the most elaborate and Gothic of the three distinctive pulpits by the father-and-son Pisano sculpting team (Duomo, Baptistery, and Siena's Duomo). Christ's life unfolds in a series of panels crammed with figures. Giovanni learned classical realism from his father, then spiced it with the dramatic motion and sinuous lines of French-style Gothic.

The bronze incense burner that hangs from the ceiling (near the pulpit) is said to be the one—actually, this is a replacement for the original—that teenage Galileo watched to understand how pendulums work. The burner swings back and forth in the same amount of time regardless of how wide the arc. (This pendulum motion was a constant that allowed Galileo to measure this ever-changing universe.)

Pause at the tomb of Holy Roman Emperor Henry VII, the German king (c. 1275–1313) who invaded Italy and was welcomed by Pisans as a leader of unity and peace. Unfortunately, Henry took ill and died young, leaving Ghibelline Pisa at the mercy of its Guelph rivals.

▲Baptistery—The Baptistery, the biggest in Italy, is interesting for its great acoustics (open daily, summer: 8:00–19:40; spring and fall:

9:00–17:40; winter: 9:00–16:40; located in front of cathedral). If you ask nicely and leave a tip, the ticket-taker uses the place's echo power to sing haunting harmonies with himself.

The building is modeled on the circular, domed church of the Holy Sepulchre in Jerusalem seen by Pisan Crusaders who occupied Jerusalem in 1099.

The Baptistery is 180 feet tall (the tower is nearly 200), and notice that it leans nearly six feet (the Tower leans 15). From the outside, you see three distinct sections—simple Romanesque blind arches at the base (1152), ornate Gothic spires and pointed arches in the middle (1250), and a Renaissance dome (15th-century). Nicola Pisano did the mid-section, and his son Giovanni decorated it with sculpture. The east door (facing the Duomo) is the most interesting.

Inside, it's simple, spacious, and baptized with light. Tall arches encircle just a few pieces of religious furniture—particularly, the octagonal font (1246, topped by a statue of John the Baptist), the inlaid-marble altar, and the hexagonal pulpit by Nicola Pisano. This pulpit is the earliest (1260) and simplest of the Pisano father-and-son team. The speaker's platform stands on columns that rest on the backs of animals, representing Christianity's triumph over paganism. The relief panels, with scenes from the life of Christ, were patterned after carved Roman sarcophagi from the Camposanto. Some have called Nicola Pisano the "Giotto of sculpture," and hailed this classical-themed pulpit as the first seed of what would eventually blossom into the Renaissance.

The remarkable acoustics of the building are due to the 250-foot-wide dome. Recent computer analysis suggests that the 15th-century architects who built the dome intended this building to be not just a Baptistery but also a musical instrument.

Other Sights at the Field of Miracles—For Pisan art, see the **Museo dell' Opera del Duomo,** displaying treasures of the cathedral, including sculptures (12th–14th century, particularly by the Pisano dynasty), paintings, silverware, and ancient Egyptian, Etruscan, and Roman artifacts (same hours as Baptistery; housed behind Tower, Piazza Arcivescovado 18).

The **Camposanto** Cemetery (1277) borders the cathedral square on the north. This site has been a cemetery since ancient times, but I'd say skip it—even if its "Holy Land dirt" does turn a body into a skeleton in a day. Artillery fire during World War II set the lead roof ablaze, greatly damaging the building, and especially its frescoes. (Same hours as Baptistery.)

The **Museo delle Sinopie,** housed in a 13th-century hospital, features the sketchy frescoes that were preparatory work for the frescoes in the cemetery (€3, same hours as Baptistery, hidden behind souvenir stands, across street from Baptistery entrance).

The much-advertised **Panoramic Walk on the Wall,** which includes just a small section of the medieval wall, isn't worth your time or €2 (March–Dec daily 10:00–18:00, entrance near Baptistery, at Porta Leone).

More Sights—The **Museo Nazionale di San Matteo,** in a former convent, displays 12th- to 15th-century sculptures, illuminated manuscripts, and paintings by Martini, Ghirlandaio, Masaccio, and others (€4, Tue–Sat 8:30–19:30, Sun 9:30–13:30, closed Mon, on river near Piazza Mazzini at Lungarno Mediceo, tel. 050-541-865).

Walking between the station and Field of Miracles in the pedestrian zone from Via G. Oberdan to Piazza Vittorio Veneto shows you a student-filled, classy, Old World town with an Arno-scape much like its rival upstream. A little **fruit market** is pinched and squeezed into Piazza Vettovaglie (Mon–Sat 7:00–18:00, closed Sun; near river, between station and Tower). A **street market** attracts shoppers Wednesday and Saturday mornings between Via del Brennero and Via Paparrelle (just outside of wall, about 6 blocks east of Tower).

SLEEPING

$$ Hotel Minerva, a classy, peaceful place with all the comforts, is a seven-minute walk from the train station (Sb-€85, Db-€108, Tb-€128, air-con, garden terrace, Piazza Toniolo 20, tel. 050-501-081, fax 050-501-559, hotelminerva@csinfo.it, SE).

$$ Hotel Villa Kinzica, with 33 decent rooms, is just steps away from the Field of Miracles—ask for a room with a view of the Tower (Sb-€78, Db-€104, Tb-€124, elevator, air-con, attached restaurant, Piazza Arcivescovado 2, tel. 050-560-419, fax 050-551-204).

SLEEP CODE

(€1 = about $1.10, country code: 39)

Sleep Code: **S** = Single, **D** = Double/Twin, **T** = Triple, **Q** = Quad, **b** = bathroom, **s** = shower only, **no CC** = Credit Cards not accepted, **SE** = Speaks English, **NSE** = No English. Unless otherwise noted, credit cards are accepted and breakfast is included (but usually optional). English is generally spoken.

To help you sort easily through these listings, I've divided the rooms into three categories based on the price for a standard double room with bath:

$$$ **Higher Priced**—Most rooms €120 or more.
$$ **Moderately Priced**—Most rooms between €80-120.
$ **Lower Priced**—Most rooms €80 or less.

$ Hotel Milano, near the station, offers 10 spacious, tidy rooms (D-€52, Db-€70, breakfast-€3, air-con, Via Mascagni 14, tel. 050-23162, fax 050-44237, hotelmilano@pisaonline.it).

EATING

For a quick lunch or dinner, the pizzeria/trattoria **La Buca**—just a block from the Tower—has a good reputation among locals (Sat–Thu 12:00–15:30 & 19:00–23:00, closed Fri, at Via Santa Maria and Via G. Tassi, tel. 050-560-660).

Ristorante Galileo, south of the Arno, has excellent pizza and pasta (Wed–Mon 12:00–15:00 & 19:30–22:00, closed Tue, Via Silvestri 12, tel. 050-28-287).

Paninoteca il Canguro makes warm, hearty sandwiches to order. Try their popular *primavera* sandwich (Mon–Fri 12:00–22:00, closed Sat night and Sun, Via Santa Maria 151, tel. 050-561-942).

For a cheap, fast, and tasty meal a few steps from the train station, drop by cheery **La Lupa Ghiotta Tavola Calda.** It's got everything you'd want from a *ristorante* at half the price with faster service (build your own salad—5 ingredients for €4.50, Mon and Wed–Sat 12:15–15:30 & 19:15–24:00, Sun 19:00–24:00, closed Tue, Viale Bonaini 113, tel. 050-21018).

Bar Costa Gelateria has a good assortment of homemade gelato a block from the Museo dell' Opera del Duomo on Via Santa Maria 100 (daily 8:00–24:00, tel. 050-551-016).

TRANSPORTATION CONNECTIONS

By train to: Florence (hrly, 1.5 hrs), **Rome** (14/day, 3.25 hrs), **La Spezia,** gateway to Cinque Terre (hrly, 1 hr), **Siena** (change at Empoli: Pisa–Empoli, hrly, 30 min; Empoli–Siena, hrly, 1 hr), **Lucca** (hrly, 30 min). Even the fastest trains stop in Pisa, and you might be changing trains here whether you plan to stop or not.

By car: The drive between Pisa and Florence is that rare case where the non-autostrada highway (free, more direct, and at least as fast) is a better deal than the autostrada.

Lucca

Surrounded by well-preserved ramparts, layered with history, alternately quaint and urbane, Lucca charms its visitors. Romanesque churches seem to be around every corner, as do fun-loving and shady piazzas filled with soccer-playing children. Despite Lucca's appeal, few tourists seem to put it on their maps, and it remains a city for the Lucchese (loo-KAY-zee).

The city was a Roman settlement. In fact, the grid layout of the streets (and the shadow of an amphitheater) survives from Roman times. Trace the rectangular Roman wall—indicated by today's streets—on the map. As in typical Roman towns, two main roads quartered the fortified town, crossing at what was the forum (main market and religious/political center)—today's Piazza San Michele.

Christianity came early here; it's said that the first bishop of Lucca was a disciple of St. Peter. While churches were built here as early as the fourth century, the majority of Lucca's elegant Romanesque churches date to around the 12th century.

Feisty Lucca, though never a real power, enjoyed a long period of independence (maintained by clever diplomacy). While Pisa ruled the town for 30 years in the 14th century, Lucca was basically an independent city-state (until Napoleon came to town).

In the Middle Ages, wealthy Lucca's economy was built on the silk industry, dominated by the Guinigi (gwee-NEE-gee) family. Without silk, Lucca would have been little more than an Italian Barstow. In 1500, the town had 3,000 silk looms employing 25,000 workers. Banking was also big. Many pilgrims stopped here on their way to the Holy Land, deposited their money for safety...and never returned to pick it up.

In its heyday, Lucca packed 160 towers—one on nearly every corner—and 70 churches within its walls. Each tower was the home of a wealthy merchant family. Towers were many stories tall, with single rooms stacked atop each other: ground-floor shop, upstairs living room, and top-floor fire-safe kitchen, all connected by exterior wooden staircases. The rooftop was generally a vegetable garden with trees providing shade. Later, the wealthy city folk moved into the countryside—trading away life in their city palazzos to establish farm estates complete with fancy villas (popular to visit today).

In 1799, Napoleon stormed into Italy and took a liking to Lucca. He liked it so much, he gave it to his sister as a gift. It was later passed on to Napoleon's widow, Marie Louise. With a feminine sensitivity, Marie Louise was partially responsible for turning the city's imposing (but no longer particularly useful) fortified wall into a fine city park that is much enjoyed today.

ORIENTATION

Tourist Information: The TI is just inside the Porta Santa Maria gate, on Piazza Santa Maria (daily 9:00–20:00, Nov–March 9:00–13:00 & 15:00–19:00, Internet access, Piazza Santa Maria 35, tel. 0583-919-931, fax 0583-469-964, www.luccaturismo.it, info@luccaturismo.it, SE). There is also a glossy, privately-owned information office, marked with an "i," on Piazzale Verdi that offers information and a room- and

Lucca

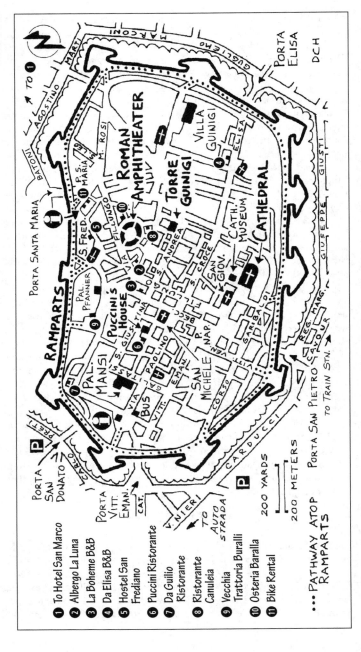

① To Hotel San Marco
② Albergo La Luna
③ La Boheme B&B
④ Da Elisa B&B
⑤ Hostel San Frediano
⑥ Puccini Ristorante
⑦ Da Giulio Ristorante
⑧ Ristorante Canuleia
⑨ Vecchia Trattoria Buralli
⑩ Osteria Baralla
⑪ Bike Rental

··· PATHWAY ATOP RAMPARTS

tour-booking service (daily 9:00–19:00, off-season 9:00–17:30, rents bikes, 80-min city walk audioguide-€9, tel. 0583-583150, SE).

Arrival in Lucca: To reach the city center from the train station, walk toward the walls and head left, to the entry at Porta San Pietro. Taxis are sparse at midday, but try calling 0583-333-434. There is no baggage check at the station.

Helpful Hints

Combo-Tickets: A €5.50 combo-ticket includes visits to Ilaria Guinigi memorial tomb in San Martino Cathedral (€2), the Cathedral Museum (€3.50), and Santi Giovanni Church (€2.50). A different €6.50 combo-ticket covers just Palazzo Mansi and Villa Guinigi.

Bike Rental: Several places with identical prices cluster around Piazza Santa Maria (€2.10/hour, €11/day, tandem bikes available, open daily, last rental around 19:00). **Antonio Poli** (Piazza Santa Maria 42, tel. & fax 0583-493-787, enthusiastic Christina SE) and **Cicli Bizzarri** (Piazza Santa Maria 32, tel. 0583-496-031) are each easy-going and rent good bikes. A one-hour rental gives you two leisurely loops around the ramparts.

Launderette: Lavanderia Self-Service Niagara is just off Piazza Santa Maria at Via Rosi 26 (daily 8:00–22:00).

Markets: Market days (8:00–13:00) are Wednesdays and Saturdays, along Via dei Bacchettoni.

Mondays: Shops close on Monday mornings. Many museums close on Monday as well.

SIGHTS

▲▲**Bike the Ramparts**—Lucca's most remarkable feature, its Renaissance wall, is also its most enjoyable attraction—especially when circled on a rental bike. Stretching for 2.5 miles, this is *the* place to come for a stroll, a bike ride, or an overview of the city.

Lucca has had a protective wall for 2,000 years. You can read three walls into today's map: the first rectangular Roman wall, the later medieval wall (nearly the size of today's), and the 16th-century Renaissance wall.

With the advent of cannons, thin medieval walls were suddenly vulnerable. A new design—the same one that stands today—was state-of-the-art when it was built (1550–1650). Much of the old medieval wall (look for the old stones) was incorporated into the Renaissance wall (with uniform bricks). The new wall was squat: a 100-foot-wide mound of dirt faced with bricks, engineered to absorb a cannonball pummeling. A wide no-man's-land was cleared around the town, exposing any attackers from a distance. Ten heart-shaped bastions (inviting picnic areas today) were designed to minimize exposure to cannonballs and maximize defense capabilities. The ramparts were armed with 130 cannons.

The town invested a third of its income for over a century to construct the wall, and—since it kept away the Florentines and nasty Pisans—it was considered a fine investment. In fact, nobody ever bothered to try to attack the wall. Locals say the only time it actually defended the city was during an 1812 flood, when the gates were sandbagged and its ramparts kept the high water out.

Today the ramparts seem made-to-order for a leisurely bike ride (20-min pedal, wonderfully smooth). You can rent bikes cheap and easy from one of several bike rental places in town (see "Helpful Hints," above).

Roman Amphitheater—Just off the main shopping street, the architectural ghost of a Roman amphitheater can be felt in the delightful Piazza Amfiteatro. With the fall of Rome, the theater (which seated 10,000) was gradually cannibalized for its stones and inhabited by a mish-mash of huts. These were cleared away in the last century to better appreciate the town's illustrious past, and today the square is a circle of touristy shops and mediocre restaurants that becomes a lively bar scene after dark. Today's street level is nine feet above the original arena floor. The only bits of surviving Roman stonework are a few arches on the northwest exterior (#42).

Via Fillungo—This main pedestrian drag, *the* street to stroll, takes you from the amphitheater almost all the way to the cathedral. Along the way you'll get a taste of this town's rich past, including many elegant century-old storefronts. Many of the original storefront paintings, reliefs, or mosaics survive—even if today's occupant of that shop sells something entirely different.

At #97 is a classic old **jewelry store** with a rare storefront that has kept its T-shaped arrangement (when closed, you see a wooden T, and during opening hours it unfolds with a fine old-time display). This arrangement dates from a time when the merchant sold his goods in front, did his work in the back, and lived upstairs.

Di Simo Caffè at #58 has long been the hangout of Lucca's artistic and intellectual elite. Composer and hometown boy Giacomo Puccini tapped his foot while sipping coffee here. Pop in to check out the 1880s ambience.

A surviving five-story **tower house** is at #67. Remember, there was a time when each corner sported its own tower. The stubby stones that still stick out once supported wooden staircases (there were no interior connections up or down). So many towers cast shadows over this part of town that the next street is called Via Buia (literally "dark street").

Opposite Via Buia a few yards off Via Fillungo is **Piazza Guidiccioni**. Filled with chairs, it serves as an outdoor theater each summer (pick up a program at the little office desk, nightly, €5).

At #45 and #43, you'll see two more good examples of **tower houses**. Across the street, the clock tower has a "hend"-wound Swiss clock that has clanged four times an hour since 1754 (€4 to climb up and see the mechanism flip into action on the quarter hour).

The intersection of Via Fillungo and Via Roma/Via Santa Croce marks the center of town (where the two original Roman roads crossed). Just down Via Santa Croce (past the Leonardo exhibit—€5 to see a room full of "don't touch" modern models of his sketches...not worth the money) is **Piazza St. Michael** (once the Roman Forum). Towering above the church's fancy Pisan Romanesque facade, the archangel Michael stands ready to flap his wings—which he actually did on special occasions. (See the stairs behind the facade, which church officials would climb to pull some strings and wow their gullible flock.) Piazza St. Michael is as fun a people center today as it has been since Roman times.

▲**San Martino Cathedral**—This church, begun in the 11th century, is an entertaining mix of architectural and artistic styles. Its elaborate Pisan-Romanesque **facade**—featuring Bible scenes, animals, and candy-cane-striped columns—dominates the piazza. The central figure of the facade is St. Martin, a Roman military officer from Hungary who, by offering his cloak to a beggar, more fully understood the beauty of Christian compassion. (The impressive original, a fine example of Romanesque sculpture, is just inside, hiding from the pollution.) Each of the columns on the facade is unique. On the lower right, the architect Guideo from Como holds a document declaring he finished the facade in 1204. On the right (at eye level), a labyrinth set into the wall relates the struggle and challenge our souls face in finding salvation. The Latin plaque just left of the main door is where moneychangers and spice traders met to seal deals (on the doorstep of the church—to underscore the reliability of their promise). Notice the date: An Dni MCXI (A.D. 1111).

The **interior** features Gothic arches, Renaissance paintings, and stained glass from the 19th century. On the left side of the nave, a small temple displays the wooden crucifix called Volto Santo. It's said to have been sculpted by Nicodemus in Jerusalem and set afloat in an unmanned boat that landed on the coast of Tuscany, from where wild oxen carried it to Lucca in 782. The sculpture (which is actually 12th-century Byzantine-style) has quite a jewelry collection, which you can see in the Cathedral Museum (see below). On the right side of the nave, the sacristy houses the enchantingly beautiful memorial tomb of Ilaria del Carretto by Jacopo della Quercia (1407). The young bride of silk baron Paolo Guinigi is decked out in the latest, most expensive fashions. She's so realistic that the statue was nicknamed "sleeping beauty." Her nose is partially rubbed off because of a long-standing tradition of lonely young ladies rubbing it for luck in finding a boyfriend (cathedral is free, Ilaria tomb-€2, included in €5.50 combo-ticket, Mon–Sat 7:00–18:00, Sun 13:00–18:00, Piazza San Martino).

Cathedral Museum (Museo della Cattedrale)—This beautifully-presented museum houses original paintings, sculptures, and vestments from the cathedral and other Lucca churches. The first room displays jewelry made to dress up the Volto Santo crucifix, including gigantic gold shoes. Nearby, notice the fine red silk—a reminder that this precious fabric is what brought riches and power to the city. The exhibits in this museum take on meaning only with the €1 audioguide—if you're not in the mood to listen to this, I'd skip the place altogether (€3.50; included in €5.50 combo-ticket, daily 10:00–18:00, off-season 10:00–14:00; Piazza Antelminelli, next to cathedral).

Santi Giovanni Church—This first cathedral of Lucca is interesting only for its excavations. The entire floor of the 12th-century church was excavated (1969–1992), revealing layers of Roman houses, early churches, and ancient hot tubs dating back to the time of Christ. Eager students can request an English translation of the floor plans to know what's what. As you climb under the church's present-day floor and wander the lanes of Roman Lucca, remember that the entire city sits on similar ruins (€2.50, included in €5.50 combo-ticket, daily 10:00–18:00, off-season 10:00–15:00, Piazza S. Giovanni, diagonal from cathedral).

Puccini's House—Opera enthusiasts (but nobody else) will want to visit the home where Giacomo Puccini (1858–1924) grew up. The museum has the great composer's piano and a small collection of his personal belongings (€3, daily 10:00–18:00, off-season Tue–Sun 10:00–13:00 & 15:00–18:00, closed Mon, Corte San Lorenzo 9, tel. 0583-584-028).

Guinigi Tower (Torre Guinigi)—Many Tuscan towns have towers, but none quite like the Guinigi family's. Up 227 steps is a small garden with fragrant trees (and a bar) surrounded by fantastic views (€4, daily mid-May–mid-Sept 9:00–24:00, March–mid-May and late Sept 9:00–19:00, Oct–Feb 10:00–18:00, Via S. Andrea, tel. 0583-316-846).

Palazzo Mansi—Minor paintings by Tintoretto, Pontormo, Veronese, and others vie for attention, but the palazzo itself, a furnished and decorated 17th-century confection, steals the show. This is your chance to appreciate the wealth of Lucca's silk merchants (€4, €6.50 combo-ticket includes Villa Guinigi, Tue–Sat 8:30–19:30, Sun 8:30–13:30, closed Mon, Via Galli Tassi 43, tel. 0583-55-570).

Villa Guinigi—Built by Paolo Guinigi in 1418, the family villa is now a museum displaying artifacts, sculptures, and paintings. Monumental paintings by multitalented Giorgio Vasari are the best reason to visit (€4, €6.50 combo-ticket includes Palazzo Mansi, Mon–Sat 9:00–19:00, Sun 9:00–14:00, Via della Quarquonia, tel. 0583-496-033).

SLEEPING

(€1 = about $1.10, country code: 39)

$$$ Hotel San Marco is a postmodern palace a seven-minute walk outside the Porta Santa Maria. Its 42 rooms are sleek, with all the comforts (Sb-€85, Db-€124, elevator, air-con, nice breakfast spread, free parking, taxi from station-€6, Via San Marco 368, tel. 0583-495-010, fax 0583-490-513).

$$ **Albergo la Luna** has 29 professional, spotless rooms in the heart of the city. Updated rooms are split between two adjacent buildings right off of the main shopping street. Frescoed top-floor suites are a palatial, romantic splurge (Sb-€78, Db-€90–110, suite-€175, elevator, air-con, parking-€10.50/day, breakfast-€10.50, Via Fillungo Corte Compagni 12, tel. 0583-493-634, fax 0583-490-021, www.hotellaluna.com, info@hotellaluna.com, Barbieri family).

$$ **La Boheme B&B** offers five spacious, chandeliered rooms, each painted a different color, a block from Piazza San Michele (Db-€100, less off-season, 5 percent discount with cash and this book, includes breakfast, Via del Moro 2, tel. & fax 0583-462-404, www.boheme.it, info@boheme.it).

$ **Da Elisa B&B** rents six basic, old-fashioned rooms sharing three worn-but-clean bathrooms (S-€47, D-€50, T-€67, Q-€80, breakfast-€5, common kitchen, Via Elisa 25, tel. 0583-494-539, fax 0583-471-609, www.daelisa.com, info@daelisa.com).

$ **Ostello San Frediano** is a cut above the average hostel. In a central palazzo with a peaceful garden, the rooms are bright and modern, some with fun lofts (Db-€39, Qb-€78, 6–8-person dorms-€16 per bed, €2.50/night extra for non-members, no CC, lock-out 10:00–15:30, cheap restaurant, Via della Cavallerizza 12, tel. 0583-469-957, fax 0583-461-007, www.ostellolucca.it, ostello.san.frediano@virgilio.it).

EATING

Puccini Ristorante is the place for a fancy €50 dinner. Fish and meat are featured here, with gourmet preparations and elegant presentation. Skip the basic sidewalk seats for the classy, modern art-strewn dining room (daily 12:30–14:30 & 19:30–22:30, closed Tue in winter, reserve on weekends, across the street from Puccini's House, Corte San Lorenzo 1, tel. 0583-316-116).

Da Giulio, dripping with character, attracts packs of happy diners to their cavernous dining room by feeding them typical, local dishes for a good price (pasta €4–5, meat €7–8, Tue–Sat 12:00–14:30 & 19:00–22:30, closed Sun–Mon, reservations smart, Via delle Conce 45, tel. 0583-55-948).

Ristorante Canuleia makes everything fresh in their small kitchen. While the portions aren't huge, the food is great. You can eat in their tiny dining room or garden courtyard (€18 tourist *menu*, daily 11:30–23:00, Via Canuleia 14, tel. 0583-467-470).

Vecchia Trattoria Buralli, on quiet Piazza S. Agostino, is a good bet with fun service, good traditional cooking, and fine indoor and piazza seating. They can throw together a *cucina Lucchese* extravaganza if you like—set the price in advance (€20–40 dinner, Thu–Tue 12:00–14:45 & 19:15–22:45, closed Wed, Piazza S. Agostino 10, tel. 0583-950-611).

Osteria Baralla, steps from the Roman amphitheater, is popular with locals for its quality meals. They have a breezy and spacious dining room under medieval vaults or a few quiet tables on the pedestrian street (Mon–Sat 12:30–15:00 & 19:30–22:00, closed Sun, Via Anfiteatro 7, tel. 0583-440-240).

Li per Li is a fun and fruity place serving crêpes (sweet and savory), *piadini* sandwiches, and fresh-squeezed fruit and veggie juices to go (daily, 12:00–14:30 & 17:00–23:00, via Fillungo 150, tel. 0583-496-479).

TRANSPORTATION CONNECTIONS

By train to: Florence (9/day, 90 min), **Pisa** (hrly, 30 min), **Milan** (5/day, 2 hrs), **Rome** (5/day 3 hrs).

Drivers: Lucca has a serious lack of public parking places. Try lots at Porta Santa Maria and Porta San Donato, or consider parking outside of the gates at the train station.

SIENA

Siena was medieval Florence's archrival. And while Florence ultimately won the battle, Siena still competes for the tourists. Sure, Florence has the most heavyweight sights. But Siena seems to be every Italy connoisseur's pet town. In my office, whenever Siena is mentioned, someone moans, "Siena? I looove Siena!"

Seven hundred years ago (from about 1260–1348), Siena was a major banking and trade center, and a military power in a class with Florence, Venice, and Genoa. With a population of 60,000, it was even bigger than Paris. Situated on the north-south road to Rome (the "Via Francigena"), Siena traded with all Europe. Then in 1348, the Black Plague that swept through Europe hit Siena and cut the population by a third. Siena never recovered. In the 1550s, her bitter rival, Florence, really "salted" her, forever making Siena a nonthreatening backwater. Siena's loss became our sightseeing gain, as its political and economic irrelevance pickled it purely medieval. Today, Siena's population is still 60,000, compared to Florence's 420,000.

Siena's thriving historic center, with red-brick lanes cascading every which way, offers Italy's best medieval city experience. Most people do Siena, just 30 miles south of Florence, as a day trip, but it's best experienced at twilight. While Florence has the blockbuster museums, Siena has an easy-to-enjoy soul: Courtyards sport flower-decked wells, alleys dead-end at rooftop views, and the sky is a rich blue dome. Right off the bat, Siena becomes an old friend.

For those who dream of a Fiat-free Italy, pedestrians rule in the old center of Siena. Sit at a café on the red-brick main square. Wander narrow streets lined with colorful flags and iron rings to tether horses. Take time to savor the first European city to eliminate automobile traffic from its main square (1966) and then, just to be silly, wonder what would happen if they did it in your city.

Planning Your Time

On a quick trip, consider spending three nights in Siena (with a whole-day side trip into Florence and a day to relax and enjoy Siena). Whatever you do, enjoy a sleepy medieval evening in Siena. After an evening in Siena, you can see its major sights in half a day.

ORIENTATION

Siena lounges atop a hill, stretching its three legs out from Il Campo. This main square, the historic meeting point of Siena's neighborhoods, is pedestrian-only. And most of those pedestrians are students from the local university.

Everything I mention is within a 15-minute walk of the square. Navigate by three major landmarks (Campo, Duomo, and church of San Domenico), following the excellent system of street-corner signs. The typical visitor sticks to the San Domenico–Il Campo axis.

Siena itself is one big sight. Its individual sights come in two little clusters: the square (Civic Museum and City Tower) and the cathedral (Baptistery and Duomo Museum with its surprise viewpoint). Check these sights off, and you're free to wander.

Tourist Information: Pick up a free town map from the main TI at #56 on Il Campo (Mon–Sat 8:30–19:30, tel. 0577-280-551, www.terresiena.it, info@terresiena.it). The helpful booklet *Terre di Siena* lists current hours and prices for sights in Siena and outlying towns. The little TI at San Domenico is for hotel promotion only and sells a Siena map for €0.50.

Arrival in Siena

By Train: The small train station, located on the edge of town, has a bar and bus office (baggage check and lockers closed indefinitely).

To get from the station to the city center, take a taxi or a city bus. The **taxi stand** is to your far right as you exit the station; allow about €8 to Il Campo, the main square (to call a taxi from the station, dial 0577-44504; for taxis at Piazza Matteotti in the center, call 0577-49222). For the **city bus,** buy a €0.75 ticket from the Bus Ticket Office in the station lobby (daily 6:15–19:30, ask for a city map—it's free and just a bus route map but helps get you started). You can also buy a bus ticket from the blue machine in the lobby (touch screen for English and select "urban" for type of ticket). Then cross the parking lot and the street to reach the sheltered bus stop. Catch orange city bus #3, #9 or #10 to get into town (punch ticket in machine on bus to validate it). You'll end up at one of three stops—Piazza Gramsci/Lizza, Piazza Sale, or Via Stufa Secca—all within several blocks of each other (buses run about every 15 min, fewer on Sun). If you get off at Via Stufa Secca's tiny square, you're soon faced with two uphill roads—take the one to the right for one block to reach the main drag, Banchi di Sopra.

To get to Siena's train station from the center of Siena, catch the city bus at Piazza Gramsci, Piazza del Sale, or Via Stufa Secca; note that bus stops are rarely marked with a "bus stop" sign but instead with a posted schedule and sometimes with yellow lines painted on the pavement, showing a bus-sized rectangle and the word "bus." Confirm with the driver that the bus is going to the *stazione* (stat-zee-OH-nay). Remember to purchase your ticket in advance from a *tabacchi* shop.

By Bus: Some buses arrive in Siena at the train station (see "Arrival by Train," above), others at Piazza Gramsci (a few blocks from city center), and some stop at both. The main bus companies are Sena and the confusingly named Tra-in (pronounced TRAAH-in). You can store baggage underneath Piazza Gramsci in Sotopassaggio la Lizza (€3.50, daily 7:00–19:45, no overnight).

By Car: Drivers coming from the autostrada take the Porta San Marco exit and follow signs for *Centro*, then *Stadio* (stadium, soccer ball). The soccer-ball signs take you to the stadium lot (Parcheggio Stadio, €1.50/hr, €12.50/day) at the huge, bare-brick San Domenico Church. The Fortezza lot nearby charges the same. Or park in the lot under the train station. You can drive into the pedestrian zone (a pretty ballsy thing to do) only to drop bags at your hotel. You can park free in the lot below the Albergo Lea, in white-striped spots behind Hotel Villa Liberty, behind the Fortezza, and overnight in most city lots from 20:00 to 8:00. (The signs showing a street cleaner and a day of the week indicate which day the street is cleaned; there's a €105 tow-fee incentive to learn the days of the week in Italian.)

Helpful Hints

Local Guide: Roberto Bechi, a hardworking Sienese guide, specializes in off-the-beaten-path tours of the city and the surrounding countryside. Married to an American (Patti) and having run restaurants in Siena and the United States, Roberto communicates well with Americans. His passions are Sienese culture, Tuscan history, and local cuisine. Book well in advance (full-day tours from €65–95 per person, half-day tours from €30–60 per person, mobile 328-727-3186 or 328-425-5648, www.toursbyroberto.com, tourrob@tin.it; for U.S. contact, fax Greg Evans at 540/434-4532).

Internet Access: In this university town, there are lots of places to get plugged in. **Internet Point** is just off Piazza Matteotti, on Via Paradiso (across street from McDonald's) and **Internet Train** is near Il Campo, at Via di Città 121 (tel. 0577-226-366).

Launderettes: Two modern, self-service places are Lavarapido Wash and Dry (daily 8:00–22:00; Via di Pantaneto 38, near Logge del Papa) and Onda Blu (daily 8:00–21:00; Via del Casato di Sotto 17, 50 yards from Il Campo).

SIENA AT A GLANCE

▲▲▲Il Campo Best square in Italy. **Hours:** Always open.

▲▲▲Duomo Art-packed cathedral with mosaic floors and statues by Michelangelo and Bernini. **Hours:** Mid-March–Oct daily 7:30–19:30, Sun 10:15–14:00 worship only, Nov–mid-March Mon–Sat 7:30–17:00, Sun 14:30–17:30.

▲▲Duomo Museum Displays cathedral art (Duccio's Maestà) and offers sweeping Tuscan view. **Hours:** Daily mid-March–Sept 9:00–19:30, Oct 9:00–18:00, Nov–mid-March 9:00–13:30.

▲Baptistery Cave-like building has baptismal font decorated by Ghiberti and Donatello. **Hours:** Daily mid-March–Sept 9:00–19:30, Oct 9:00–18:00, Nov–mid-March 10:00–13:00 & 14:00–17:00.

▲Civic Museum City museum in City Hall with Sienese frescoes of Good and Bad Government. **Hours:** Daily April–Oct 10:00–19:00, July–Sept until 23:00, Nov–March 10:00–16:00.

▲City Tower 330-foot tower climb. **Hours:** Same as Civic Museum.

▲Pinacoteca Fine Sienese paintings. **Hours:** Sun–Mon 8:30–13:15, Tue–Sat 8:15–19:15.

Santa Maria della Scala Museum with art, medieval hospital displays, and exhibitions. **Hours:** Daily 10:00–18:00, off-season 10:30–16:30.

Church of San Domenico Huge brick church with St. Catherine's head and finger. **Hours:** Daily March–Oct 7:00–13:00 & 14:30–18:30, Nov–Feb 9:00–13:00 & 15:00–18:00.

Sanctuary of St. Catherine Home of St. Catherine. **Hours:** Daily 9:00–12:30 & 15:00–18:30.

Markets: The produce market is held on Piazza del Marcato, behind Il Campo (Mon–Sat mornings). On Wednesday morning, the weekly market—consisting mainly of clothes and some food—sprawls between the Fortress and Piazza Gramsci along Viale Cesare Maccabi and the adjacent Viale XXV Aprile.

SIGHTS

Siena's Main Square

▲▲▲ **Il Campo**—Siena's great central piazza is urban harmony at its best. Like a people-friendly stage set, its gently tilted floor fans out from the tower and city hall backdrop. It's the perfect invitation to loiter. Think of it as a trip to the beach without sand or water.

Il Campo was located at the historic junction of Siena's various competing districts, or *contrade,* on the old marketplace. The brick surface is divided into nine sections, representing the council of nine merchants and city bigwigs who ruled medieval Siena.

The square is dominated by the City Hall (Palazzo Pubblico), with its 330-foot tower. In medieval Siena, this secular City Hall was the center of the city, and the whole focus of the Campo flows down to it. Its crenellated roofline and three-bay windows are echoed around the city.

At the square's high point, look for the *Fountain of Joy,* the two naked guys about to be tossed in, and the pigeons politely waiting their turn to gingerly tightrope down slippery spouts to slurp a drink. (You can see parts of the original fountain, of which this is a copy, in an interesting exhibit at Siena's Santa Maria della Scala museum, listed on page 322.) At the square's low point is the City Hall and tower. The chapel located at the base of the tower was built in 1348 as thanks to God for ending the Black Plague (after it killed more than a third of the population).

To say Siena and Florence have always been competitive is an understatement. In medieval times, a statue of Venus stood on Il Campo (where the *Fountain of Joy* is today). After the plague hit Siena, the monks blamed this pagan statue. The people cut it to pieces and buried it along the walls of Florence.

Picture the Campo at Palio time, when the famous horse races are held (July 2 and Aug 16). Ten horses and riders race hell-for-leather three times around the perimeter (the gray pavement), which is covered with dirt, with mattresses padding the sharpest turns. Spectators waving the banners of their neighborhoods cram (for free) into the center of the square or watch from temporary bleachers, or if they're lucky, from the balconies of their friends.

The market area behind the city hall, a wide-open expanse since the Middle Ages, originated as a farming area within the city walls to feed the citizens in times of siege. Now the morning produce market is held here Monday through Saturday. (The closest public WCs to Il Campo are each about a block away: at Via Beccheria—a few steps off Via de Città—and on Casato di Sotto; €0.60.)

▲ **Civic Museum (Museo Civico)**—At the base of the tower is Siena's City Hall (Palazzo Pubblico), the spot where secular government got its start in early Renaissance Europe. There, you'll find city government still at work, along with a sampling of local art.

Siena Sights

In the following order, you'll see: the Sala Risorgimento, with dramatic scenes of Victor Emmanuel's unification of Italy (surrounded by statues that don't seem to care); the chapel, with impressive inlaid wood chairs in the choir; and the Sala del Mappamondo, with Siena's first fresco, Simone Martini's *Maestà* (Enthroned Virgin—a groundbreaking, down-to-earth Madonna), facing the faded *Guidoriccio da Fogliano* (a mercenary providing a more concrete form of protection).

SIENA'S PALIO

In the Palio, the feisty spirit of Siena's 17 *contrade* (neighborhoods) lives on. These neighborhoods celebrate, worship, and compete together. Each even has its own historical museum. *Contrada* pride is evident any time of year in the colorful neighborhood banners and parades. (If you hear distant drumming, run to it for some medieval action, often featuring flag-throwers.) But *contrada* passion is most visible twice a year—on July 2 and August 16—when they have their world-famous horse race, the Palio di Siena. Ten of the 17 neighborhoods compete (chosen by lot), hurling themselves with medieval abandon into several days of trial races and traditional revelry. On the big day, jockeys and horses go into their *contrada*'s church to be blessed ("Go and win," says the priest). It's considered a sign of luck if a horse leaves droppings in the church.

On the evening of the big day, Il Campo is stuffed to the brim with locals and tourists, as the horses charge wildly around the square in this literally no-holds-barred race. A horse can win even if its rider has fallen off. Of course, the winning neighborhood is the scene of grand celebrations afterward. Winners receive a *palio* (banner), typically painted by a local artist and always featuring the Virgin Mary. But the true prize is simply proving your *contrada* is numero uno. All over town, sketches and posters depict the Palio. This is not some folkloristic event. It's a real medieval moment. If you're packed onto the square with 15,000 people who each really want to win, you won't see much, but you'll feel it. While the actual Palio packs the city, you could side-trip in from Florence to see horse-race trials each of the three days before the big day (usually at 9:00 and around 19:30).

▲**Palio al Cinema**—This 20-minute film, *Siena, the Palio, and its History,* helps recreate the craziness. See it at the Cinema Moderno in Piazza Tolomei, two blocks from Il Campo (€5.25, with this book pay €4.25, or €8 for 2; runs May–Oct only, Mon–Sat 9:30–17:30, English showings generally hourly at :30 past the hour, schedule posted on door, closed Sun; air-con, tel. 0577-289-201). Call or drop by to confirm when the next English showing is scheduled—there are usually nine a day. At the ticket desk, you can buy the same show on video or DVD (video-€10.50, DVD-€11.50, discount only with this book, video must be labeled "NTSC American System" or it'll be a doorstop at your home).

Next is the *Sala della Pace*—where the city's fat cats met. Looking down on the oligarchy during their meetings were two interesting frescoes showing the effects of good and bad government. Notice the whistle-while-you-work happiness of the utopian community ruled by the utopian government (in the better-preserved fresco) and the fate of a community ruled by politicians with more typical values (in a terrible state of repair). The message: Without justice, there can be no prosperity.

Take a moment to savor one of those to-sigh-for rural panoramas out the window of the *Sala della Pace*. The view out the window is essentially the same as that from the top of the big stairs (€6.50, €9.50 combo-ticket includes tower, daily March–Oct 10:00–19:00, July–Sept until 23:00, Nov–Feb 10:00–16:00, last entry 45 min before closing, audioguide €3.75 for 1 person, €5.25 for 2, tel. 0577-292-111).

▲**City Tower (Torre del Mangia)**—Siena gathers around its City Hall, not its church. It was a proud republic; its "declaration of independence" is the tallest secular medieval tower in Italy. The 330-foot-tall Torre del Mangia was named after a hedonistic watchman who consumed his earnings like a glutton consumes food (his chewed-up statue is in the courtyard, to the left as you enter). Its 300 steps get pretty skinny at the top, but the reward is one of Italy's best views (€5.50, €9.50 combo-ticket with Civic Museum, daily 10:00–19:00, mid-July–mid-Sept until 23:00, Nov–March 10:00–16:00, closed in rain, sometimes long lines, avoid midday crowd, limit of 30 tourists at a time, often sold out).

▲**National Picture Gallery (Pinacoteca)**—Siena was a power in Gothic art. But the average tourist, wrapped up in a love affair with the Renaissance, hardly notices. This museum takes you on a walk through Siena's art, chronologically from the 12th through the 15th centuries. For the casual sightseer, the Sienese art in the Civic and Duomo Museums is adequate. But art fans enjoy this opportunity to trace the evolution of Siena's delicate and elegant works, from stiff, gold-backed icon-like Madonnas to curvy, graceful Madonnas to Italian Renaissance. Concentrate on pieces by Duccio (artist of the *Maestà* in the Duomo Museum), Simone Martini (who did the *Maestà* in the Civic Museum), the brothers Ambrogio and Pietro Lorenzetti (Ambrogio did the *Allegory of Good and Bad Government* in the Civic Museum), Pinturicchio (who did the Piccolomini Library in the Duomo), and Domenico Beccafumi (who inlaid pavement in the Duomo). To reach the museum from Il Campo, walk out Via di Città and go left on Via San Pietro (€4, Sun–Mon 8:30–13:15, Tue–Sat 8:15–19:15, audioguide–€4, tel. 0577-281-161).

Siena's Cathedral Area

▲▲▲**Duomo**—Siena's 13th-century cathedral is as Baroque as Gothic gets. This cathedral, with its six-story striped bell tower—Siena's ultimate tribute to the Virgin Mary—is heaped with statues, plastered with frescoes, and paved with art. The striped facade is piled with statues and ornamentation, and the interior is decorated from top to bottom. The heads of 172 popes peer down from the ceiling, over the fine inlaid art on the floor. This is one busy interior. (Modest dress is required for entry.)

To orient yourself in this *panforte* of Italian churches, stand under the dome and think of the church floor as a big clock. You're the middle, and the altar is high noon: You'll find the *Slaughter of the Innocents* roped off on the floor at 10:00, Pisano's pulpit between two pillars at 11:00, Duccio's round stained glass window at high noon, Bernini's chapel at 3:00, two Michelangelo statues (next to doorway leading to a shop, snacks, and WC) at 7:00, the Piccolomini Library at 8:00, and a Donatello statue at 9:00.

Take some time with the floor mosaics in the front. Nicola Pisano's wonderful pulpit is crowded with delicate Gothic storytelling from 1268. To understand why Bernini is considered the greatest Baroque sculptor, step into his sumptuous *Cappella della Madonna del Voto*. This last work in the cathedral, from 1659, is enough to make a Lutheran light a candle. Move up to the altar and look back at the two Bernini statues: Mary Magdalene in a state of spiritual ecstasy, and St. Jerome playing the crucifix like a violinist lost in beautiful music.

The Piccolomini altar is most interesting for its two Michelangelo statues (the lower big ones). Paul, on the left, may be a self-portrait. Peter, on the right, resembles Michelangelo's more famous statue of Moses. Originally contracted to do 15 statues, Michelangelo left the project early (1504) to do his great *David* in Florence.

The Piccolomini Library—worth the €1.50 entry—is brilliantly frescoed with scenes glorifying the works of a pope from 500 years ago. It contains intricately decorated, illuminated music scores and a statue (a Roman copy of a Greek original) of the Three Graces. Donatello's bronze statue of St. John the Baptist, in his famous rags, is in a chapel to the right of the library.

Cost and Hours: Entrance is generally free, although you'll pay €3 to visit from September to mid-October (for *pavimento Cattedrale*, when much of the elaborate mosaic floor is uncovered for the annual viewing) and €1.50 to visit the Piccolomini Library. The church and library are open mid-March–Oct daily 7:30–19:30, worship only Sun 10:15–14:00; Nov–mid-March Mon–Sat 7:30–17:00, Sun 14:30–17:30. Modest dress is required to enter.

Audioguides: There's a daunting number of audioguides. An audioguide for just the church costs €3.50; to add the library, it's €4; and to add the Cathedral Museum (Museo dell' Opera de Panorama), it's €5.50. For the church and museum only, it's €4.50. Two headphones are available at a price break.

▲▲**Duomo Museum (Museo dell' Opera e Panorama)**—Siena's most enjoyable museum, on the Campo side of the church (look for the yellow signs), was built to house the cathedral's art. The ground floor is filled with the cathedral's original Gothic sculpture by Giovanni Pisano (who spent 10 years in the late 1200s carving and orchestrating the decoration of the cathedral) and a fine Donatello *Madonna and Child.* Upstairs to the left awaits a private audience with Duccio's *Maestà (Enthroned Virgin,* 1311*).* Pull up a chair and study one of the great pieces of medieval art. The flip side of the *Maestà* (displayed on the opposite wall), with 26 panels—the medieval equivalent of pages—shows scenes from the Passion of Christ.

Climb onto the "Panorama dal Facciatone." From the first landing, take the skinnier second spiral for Siena's surprise view. Look back over the Duomo and consider this: When rival republic Florence began its grand cathedral, proud Siena decided to build the biggest church in all Christendom. The existing cathedral would be used as a transept. You're atop what would have been the entry. The wall below you, connecting the Duomo with the museum of the cathedral, was as far as Siena got before a plague killed the city's ability to finish the project. Were it completed, you'd be looking straight down the nave—white stones mark where columns would have stood (€5.50, worthwhile 40-minute audioguide-€3, daily mid-March–Sept 9:00–19:30, Oct 9:00–18:00, Nov–mid-March 9:00–13:30, tel. 0577-283-048).

▲**Baptistery**—Siena is so hilly that there wasn't enough flat ground on which to build a big church. What to do? Build a big church and prop up the overhanging edge with the Baptistery. This dark and quietly tucked-away cave of art is worth a look (and €2.50) for its cool tranquility and the bronze panels and angels—by Ghiberti, Donatello, and others—adorning the pedestal of the baptismal font (daily mid-March–Sept 9:00–19:30, Oct 9:00–18:00, Nov–mid-March 10:00–13:00 & 14:00–17:00).

▲**Santa Maria della Scala**—This museum (opposite the Duomo entrance) was used as a hospital as recently as the 1980s. Now it displays a lavishly frescoed hall, a worthwhile exhibit on Quercia's *Fountain of Joy* (downstairs), and a so-so archaeological museum (subterranean, in labyrinthine tunnels). The entire museum is a maze, with various exhibitions and paintings plugged in to fill the gaps.

The frescoes in the **Pellegrinaio Hall** show medieval Siena's innovative health care and social welfare system in action (c. 1442, wonderfully described in English). The hospital was functioning as early as the 11th century, nursing the sick and caring for abandoned children (see frescoes). The good work paid off, as bequests and donations poured in, creating the wealth that's evident in the chapels elsewhere on this floor. The Old Sacristy was built to house precious relics, including a Holy Nail thought to be from Jesus' cross.

Downstairs, the engaging exhibit on Jacopo della Quercia's early 15th-century *Fountain of Joy* doesn't need much English description, fortunately, because there isn't much. In the 19th century, the *Fountain of Joy* in Il Campo was deteriorating. It was dismantled and plaster casts were made of the originals. The *Fountain of Joy* that stands in Il Campo today is a replica. In this exhibit, you'll see the plaster casts of the original, eroded panels paired with their restored twins, along with the statues that originally stood on the edges of the fountain. In general, the pieces at the beginning and end of the exhibit are original. If there's a piece in a dim room near the exit of the exhibit, it's likely an original chunk awaiting cleaning.

The **Archaeological Museum,** way downstairs, consists mainly of pottery fragments in cases lining tunnel after tunnel. It's like being lost in a wine cellar without the wine. Unless there's a special exhibit, it's not worth the trip.

Cost and Hours: €5.25, daily 10:00–18:00, off-season 10:30–16:30. The chapel just inside the door to your left is free (English description inside chapel entrance—also pick up a copy of *Il Giornale di Santa Maria della Scala* for a list of upcoming events, such as concerts and guided tours).

Siena's San Domenico Area

Church of San Domenico—This huge brick church is worth a quick look. The bland interior fits the austere philosophy of the Dominicans. Walk up the steps in the rear for a look at various paintings from the life of Saint Catherine, patron saint of Siena. Halfway up the church on the right, you'll see a metal bust of Saint Catherine and a small case containing her finger (sometimes loaned out to other churches). In the chapel surrounded with candles, you'll see her actual head (free, daily March–Oct 7:00–13:00 & 14:30–18:30, Nov–Feb 9:00–13:00 & 15:00–18:00; WC for €0.50 at far end of parking lot—facing church entrance, it's to your right).

Sanctuary of Saint Catherine—Step into Catherine's cool and peaceful home. Siena remembers its favorite hometown gal, a simple, unschooled, but mystically devout soul who, in the mid-1300s, helped convince the pope to return from France to Rome. Pilgrims have come here since 1464. Since then, architects and artists have greatly embellished what was probably a humble home (her family worked as wool-dyers). Enter through the courtyard and walk to the far end. The chapel on your right contains the wooden crucifix upon which Catherine was meditating when she received the stigmata in Pisa. The chapel on your left used to be the kitchen. Go down the stairs to the left of the chapel/kitchen to reach the saint's room. Catherine's bare cell is behind see-through doors. Much of the art throughout the sanctuary depicts scenes from her life (free, daily 9:00–12:30 & 15:00–18:30, Via Tiratoio). It's a few downhill blocks toward the center from San Domenico (follow signs to Santuario di Santa Caterina).

ST. CATHERINE OF SIENA
(1347–1380)

The youngest of 25 children born to a Sienese cloth dyer, Catherine began experiencing heavenly visions even in childhood. At 16, she became a Dominican nun, then locked herself away for three years in a room in her family's house, living the life of an ascetic, which culminated in a vision wherein she married Christ. Catherine emerged from solitude to join her Dominican sisters, sharing her experiences, caring for the sick, and gathering both disciples and enemies. At age 23, she lapsed into a spiritual coma, waking with the heavenly command to spread her message to the world. She wrote essays and letters to kings, dukes, bishops, and popes, imploring them to find peace for a war-ravaged Italy. While visiting Pisa during Lent of 1375, she had a vision in which she received the Stigmata, the wounds of Christ.

Still in her twenties, Catherine was invited to Avignon, France, where the pope had taken up residence. With her charm, sincerity, and reputation for holiness, she helped convince Pope Gregory XI to return the papacy to the city of Rome. Catherine also went to Rome, where she died young. She was canonized in the next generation (by a Sienese pope), and her relics were distributed to churches around Italy.

SHOPPING AND NIGHTLIFE

Shopping—Shops line Via Banchi di Sopra, the *passeggiata* route. For a budget department store, try Upim on Piazza Matteotti (Mon–Sat 9:30–19:50, closed Sun). The Feltrinelli bookstore closest to the Campo sells books and magazines in English (daily 9:00–19:30, Banchi di Sopra 52). The large, colorful scarves/flags, each depicting the symbol of one of Siena's 17 different neighborhoods (such as the wolf, the turtle, and the snail), are easy-to-pack souvenirs, fun for decorating your home (€7 apiece for large size, sold at souvenir stands).

Nightlife—Join the evening *passeggiata* (peak strolling time is 19:00) along Via Banchi di Sopra with gelato in hand. **Nannini's** at Piazza Salimbeni has fine gelato (daily 11:00–24:00).

The **Enoteca Italiana** is a good wine bar in a cellar in the Fortezza/Fortress (sample glasses in 3 different price ranges: €2, €3, €5.50; Mon 12:00–20:00, Tue–Sat 12:00–01:00, closed Sun; bottles and snacks available; cross bridge and enter fortress, go left down ramp, not to be confused with Enoteca Toscana—same location but not as nice; tel. 0577-288-497).

Museums are often open late on summer Fridays and Saturdays; check with the TI for current hours.

SLEEPING

Finding a room is tough during Easter or the Palio in early July and mid-August. Call ahead any time of year, as Siena's few budget places are listed in all the budget guidebooks. While day-tripping tour groups turn the town into a Gothic amusement park in midsummer, Siena is basically yours in the evenings and off-season.

Most of the listed hotels lie between Il Campo and the Church of San Domenico. Part of Siena's charm is its lively, festive character—this means that all hotels can be plagued with noise, even (and sometimes especially) the hotels in the pedestrian-only zone. If tranquility is important for your sanity, ask for a room that's off the street or consider staying at the recommended places outside the center.

Credit cards are accepted unless otherwise noted. A handful of the listings don't take credit cards, no matter how earnestly you ask. Cash machines are plentiful on the main streets.

Near Il Campo

Each of these listings is forgettable but inexpensive, and just a horse wreck away from one of Italy's most wonderful civic spaces.

$ **Piccolo Hotel Etruria,** a good bet for a hotel with 19 decent rooms but not much soul, is just off the square (S-€43, Sb-€48, Db-€78, Tb-€105, Qb-€127, breakfast-€5; curfew at 00:30; with your back to the tower, leave Il Campo to the right at 2:00, Via Donzelle 1—3; tel. 0577-288-088, fax 0577-288-461, hetruria@tin.it, Fattorini family SE).

$ **Albergo Tre Donzelle** has 28 plain, institutional rooms next door to Piccolo Hotel Etruria that make sense only if you think of Il Campo as your terrace (S-€36, D-€50, Db-€63, Via Donzelle 5, tel. 0577-280-358, fax 0577-223-933, Signora Iannini SE).

$ **Locanda Garibaldi** is a modest, very Sienese restaurant/*albergo*. Gentle Marcello wears two hats, as he runs a busy restaurant downstairs and seven pleasant rooms up a funky, artsy staircase (Db-€70, Tb-€89, family deals, no CC, takes reservations only a week in advance, half a block downhill off the square at Via Giovanni Dupre 18, tel. 0577-284-204, NSE).

$ **Hotel Cannon d'Oro,** a few blocks up Via Banchi di Sopra, is spacious, comfortable, and group-friendly (30 rooms, Sb-€69, Db-€86, Tb-€109, Qb-€128, these discounted prices promised through 2004 with this book, family deals, breakfast-€6, Via Montanini 28, tel. 0577-44321, fax 0577-280-868, cannondoro@libero.it, Maurizio and Debora SE).

Siena Hotels and Restaurants

1. Piccolo Hotel Etruria
2. Albergo Tre Donzelle
3. Locanda Garibaldi
4. Hotel Cannon d'Oro
5. To Hotel Duomo, Pen. Pal. Ravizza, & Ost. Nonna Gina
6. To Hotel Villa Liberty & Albergo Lea
7. Hotel Chiusarelli
8. Alma Domus
9. Albergo Bernini & Ost. la Chiacchera
10. To Casa Laura, Antica Torre, Hotel Sta. Caterina, & Palazzo di Valli
11. To Hostel
12. Antica Osteria Da Divo
13. Trattoria La Tellina
14. To Taverna San Giuseppe
15. Osteria il Tamburino
16. Ristorante Gallo Nero
17. Il Verrochio Rest.
18. Le Campane Rest.
19. Pizzeria Spadaforte
20. Gelateria Artigiana
21. Ciao Cafeteria & Spizzico
22. Consorzio Agrario Siena (grocery)
23. Lavarapido Launderette
24. Onda Blu Launderette

SLEEP CODE

(€1 = about $1.10, country code: 39)
Sleep Code: **S** = Single, **D** = Double/Twin, **T** = Triple, **Q** = Quad,
b = bathroom, **s** = shower only, **no CC** = Credit Cards not accepted,
SE = Speaks English, **NSE** = No English. Breakfast is generally not
included. Have breakfast on Il Campo or in a nearby bar.

To help you sort easily through these listings, I've divided the
rooms into three categories based on the price for a standard double room with bath:

$$$ **Higher Priced**—Most rooms €120 or more.
$$ **Moderately Priced**—Most rooms between €90-120.
$ **Lower Priced**—Most rooms €90 or less.

Sleeping Fancy, Southwest of Il Campo

These two places are a 10-minute walk from Il Campo.

$$$ **Hotel Duomo** is a classy place with 23 spacious rooms and a
bizarre floor plan (Sb-€110, Db-€150, Tb-€175, Qb-€200, includes
breakfast; air-con, elevator, picnic-friendly roof terrace, free parking;
follow Via di Città, which becomes Via Stalloreggi, to Via Stalloreggi
38; tel. 0577-289-088, fax 0577-43043, www.hotelduomo.it, booking
@hotelduomo.it, Stefania SE). If you arrive by train, take a taxi (€8); if
you drive, go to Porta San Marco and follow the signs to the hotel, drop
off your bags, and then park in nearby "Il Campo" lot.

$$$ **Pensione Palazzo Ravizza,** elegant and friendly, with an aris-
tocratic feel and a peaceful garden, is a worthwhile splurge (Sb-€130, Db-
€120–270, Tb-€220–310, suites available, includes breakfast, cheaper
mid-Nov–Feb, air-con, elevator, back rooms face open country, good
restaurant, free parking, Via Pian dei Mantellini 34, tel. 0577-280-462,
fax 0577-221-597, www.palazzoravizza.it, bureau@palazzoravizza.it, SE).

Near San Domenico Church

These hotels are within a 10-minute walk northeast of Il Campo.
Albergo Bernini and Alma Domus, which enjoy views of the old town
and cathedral, are the best values in town.

$$$ **Hotel Villa Liberty** has 18 big, bright, comfortable rooms (S-
€75, Db-€130, includes breakfast, only one room with twin beds; elevator,
bar, air-con, TVs, courtyard, facing fortress at Viale V. Veneto 11, tel. 0577-
44966, fax 0577-44770, www.villaliberty.it, info@villaliberty.it, SE).

$$ **Hotel Chiusarelli,** a proper hotel in a beautiful building with a
handy location, comes with traffic noise at night—ask for a quieter room

in the back (49 rooms, S-€63, Sb-€79, Db-€118, Tb-€160, includes buffet breakfast, suites available, air-con, pleasant garden terrace, across from San Domenico at Viale Curtatone 15, tel. 0577-280-562, fax 0577-271-177, www.chiusarelli.com, info@chiusarelli.com, SE).

$ **Alma Domus** is ideal—unless nuns make you nervous, you need a double bed, or you plan on staying out past the 23:30 curfew (no mercy given). This quasi-hotel (not a convent) is run with firm but angelic smiles by sisters who offer clean and quiet rooms for a steal and save the best views for foreigners. Bright lamps, quaint balconies, fine views, grand public rooms, top security, and a friendly atmosphere make this a great value. The checkout time is strictly 10:00, but they will store your luggage in their secure courtyard (Db-€60, Tb-€70, Qb-€90, no CC; ask for view room—*con vista*, elevator; from San Domenico walk downhill with the church on your right toward the view, turn left down Via Camporegio, make a U-turn at the little chapel down the brick steps to Via Camporegio 37; tel. 0577-44177 and 0577-44487, fax 0577-47601, NSE).

$ **Albergo Bernini** makes you part of a Sienese family in a modest, clean home with nine fine rooms. Friendly Nadia and Mauro welcome you to their spectacular view terrace for breakfast and picnic lunches and dinners. Outside of breakfast and checkout time, Mauro, an accomplished accordionist, might play a song for you if you ask (Sb-€77, D-€62, Db-€82, breakfast-€7, less in winter, no CC, midnight curfew, on the main San Domenico–Il Campo drag at Via Sapienza 15, tel. & fax 0577-289-047, www.albergobernini.com, hbernin@tin.it, son Alessandro SE).

$ **Albergo Lea** is a creaky, old-fashioned place in a residential neighborhood a few blocks away from the center (past San Domenico) with 11 rooms and easy parking (S-€50, Db-€87, Tb-€110, cheaper in winter, includes breakfast, yard and rooftop terrace, Viale XXIV Maggio 10, tel. & fax 0577-283-207, SE).

Southeast of Il Campo

These two places are near each other, in the direction of Porta Romana city gate.

$$$ **Antica Torre** rents eight rooms in an atmospheric medieval tower a 10-minute walk from Il Campo (Sb-€95, Db-€110, Tb-€115, breakfast-€7, Via Fieravecchia 7, tel. & fax 0577-222-255, anticatorre@email.it, SE).

$ **Casa Laura** has five clean, charming, well-maintained rooms, some of which have brick-and-beam ceilings (Db-€83 with breakfast, €73 without, cheaper for 3 nights or more; Via Roma 3, about a 10-min walk from Il Campo toward Porta Romana; tel. 0577-226-061, fax 0577-225-240, www.turismoverde.com/ospiti/casalaura, labenci@tin.it, NSE).

Farther from the Center

$$$ **Hotel Santa Caterina** is a three-star, 18th-century place, best for drivers who need air-conditioning. Professionally run with real attention to quality, it has 22 comfortable rooms with a delightful garden (Sb-€105, small Db-€105, Db-€140, Tb-€190, these prices only when you mention this book, includes buffet breakfast, elevator, garden side is quieter but street side—with multi-paned windows—isn't bad, fridge in room, parking-€15/day—request when you reserve, 100 yards outside Porta Romana at Via E.S. Piccolomini 7, tel. 0577-221-105, fax 0577-271-087, www.hscsiena.it, info@hscsiena.it, SE). A city bus runs frequently (Mon–Sat 4/hr, Sun 2/hr) to the town center. A taxi to/from the station runs around €8.

$$$ **Palazzo di Valli,** with 11 spacious rooms and a garden, is a seven-minute walk beyond Porta Romana (the Roman gate) and feels like it's in the country. Catch the city bus into town (Sb-€105, Db-€140, Tb-€170, includes breakfast; parking; Via E.S. Piccolomini 135, bus to center Mon–Sat 4/hr, Sun 2/hr; tel. 0577-226-102, fax 0577-222-255, Camarda family SE). From the autostrada, exit at Siena Sud in the direction of Porta Romana.

$$$ **Frances' Lodge** is a small farmhouse B&B a mile out of Siena. English-speaking Franca and Franco rent four modern rooms in a rustic yet elegant old place with a swimming pool, peaceful garden, eight acres of olive trees and vineyards, and great Siena views (Db-€150–180, Tb-€210; easy parking, great breakfast; near shuttle bus "B" into town, Strada di Valdipugna 2; tel. 0577-281-061, fax 0577-222-224, www.franceslodge.it, info@franceslodge.it).

$ Siena's **Guidoriccio Youth Hostel** has 100 cheap beds, but, given the hassle of the bus ride and the charm of downtown Siena at night, I'd skip it (€13 beds in doubles, triples, and dorms with sheets, no CC, cheap breakfast; office open 15:00–12:00, lock-out 9:30–15:00; bus #10 from train station or bus #15 from Piazza Gramsci, about 20 min, Via Fiorentina 89 in Stellino neighborhood; tel. 0577-52212, SE).

Outside of Siena

All within a 20-minute drive of Siena, the following accommodations are in the lush, peaceful countryside surrounding Siena.

$ **Poste Regie B&B** has three beautifully-furnished rooms run by spunky Beatrice. Owned by her family for generations, this farmhouse has a welcoming, genuine feel. She can recommend excellent hikes in the area (D-€65, includes breakfast; on a country road in Ancaiano, 20 min west of Siena, Via della Montagnola 68; mobile 349-475-4995, fax 0577-45387, www.posteregie.com, reservations @posteregie.com, SE).

$ **Agriturismo le Trappoline,** on I Sodi Farm in Chianti about a 20-minute drive east of Siena, is a renovated farmhouse with panoramic vistas and ample grounds for country walks. Lively Danilo and Gabriella Casini offer four apartments with fully-equipped kitchens and also produce their own Chianti Classico wine (4 person apartments-€100, 1-week stays required only in high season, discounts off-season, pool, Località Monti Gaiole, tel. 0577-747-012, www.agrisodi.com, info @agrisodi.com, some English spoken).

$ **Parri Nada Farmhouse,** a good choice for families, is tucked away in the vineyards in the hills of Chianti about a 20-minute drive northeast of Siena. Luca and Elena Masti rent two rooms in their comfortable home (D-€70, T-€85, Q—whole apartment-€105, 1-night rentals okay, kitchen, pool, private yard, Località Santa Chiara 4, tel. & fax 0577-359-072, mobile 333-840-8448, www.farm-house.it, info@farm-house.it).

EATING

Sienese restaurants are reasonable by Florentine and Venetian standards.

Antica Osteria Da Divo is the place for a fine €40 meal. The kitchen is creative, the ambience is candlelit, and the food is fresh and top-notch. The lamb goes baaa in your mouth. They offer a basket of exotic fresh breads and excellent seasonal dishes. And the chef is understandably proud of his desserts (daily 12:00–14:30 & 19:00–22:00, reserve for summer eves; Via Franciosa 29, facing baptistery door, take the far right and walk one long curving block; tel. 0577-286-054).

Trattoria La Tellina has patient waiters and great Mediterranean food, including excellent homemade tiramisu. Arrive early to get a seat (Sun–Fri 11:30–15:00 & 18:00–22:00, closed Sat; Via dell Terme 52, between St. Catherine's House and Piazza Tolomei—where Palio film is shown; tel. 0577-283-133).

Taverna San Giuseppe, a local favorite, offers modern Tuscan cuisine in a dressy grotto atmosphere. Check the posters tacked around the entry for daily specials. Reserve or arrive early to get a table (Mon–Sat 12:15–14:30 & 19:15–22:00, closed Sun; 7-min walk up street to the right of the City Hall, Via Giovanni Dupre 132; tel. 0577-42286).

Osteria il Tamburino is friendly, small, popular, and serves up tasty meals (Mon–Sat 12:00–14:30 & 19:00–21:30, closed Sun; follow Via di Città off Il Campo, becomes Stalloreggi, Via Stalloreggi 11; tel. 0577-280-306).

Ristorante Gallo Nero is a friendly "grotto" for Tuscan cuisine. Popular with groups, this "black rooster" serves *ribollita* (hearty Tuscan bean soup) and offers a €23 "medieval menu," as well as several Tuscan menus, starting at €16 (daily 12:00–15:30 & 19:00–24:00, 3 blocks down Via del Porrione from Il Campo at #65, tel. 0577-284-356).

Il Verrochio, a block away—tucked between a church and loggia—serves a decent €13 *menu* in a cozy, wood-beamed setting (daily

12:00–14:30 & 19:00–22:00, closed Wed in winter, Logge del Papa 1, tel. 0577-284-062).

Le Campane, two blocks off Il Campo, is classy. Run by the same family for 25 years, it features modern Tuscan fare (daily 12:15–14:30 & 19:15–22:00, closed Mon in winter, indoor/outdoor seating, a few steps off Via di Città at Via delle Campane 6, tel. 0577-284-035).

Osteria Nonna Gina wins praise from locals for its good quality and prices (Tue–Sun 12:30–14:30 & 19:30–22:30, closed Mon, Piano dei Mantellini 2, 10-min walk from Il Campo, near Hotel Duomo, tel. 0577-287-247).

Osteria la Chiacchera is an atmospheric, tasty, and affordable hole-in-the-brick-wall serving "peasant food" (daily 11:00–24:00, reservations wise, skip the *trippa*—tripe, 2 rooms, below Pension Bernini at Costa di San Antonio 4, tel. 0577-280-631).

For authentic Sienese dining at a fair price, eat at **Locanda Garibaldi,** down Via Giovanni Dupre at #18, within a block of Il Campo (€15 menu, Sun–Fri opens at 12:00–14:00 for lunch and 19:00–21:00 for dinner, arrive early to get a table, closed Sat). Marcello does a little *piatto misto dolce* for €4, featuring several local desserts with sweet wine.

Even with higher prices, lousy service, and lower-quality food, consider eating on Il Campo—a classic European experience. **Pizzeria Spadaforte,** at the edge of Il Campo, has a decent setting, mediocre pizza, and tables steeper than its prices (daily 12:00–16:00 & 19:30–22:30, to far right of city tower as you face it, tel. 0577-281-123).

Cheap Meals, Snacks, and Picnics

Snack with a view from a small balcony overlooking Il Campo. Survey these three places from Il Campo to see which has a free table. On Via di Città, you'll find **Gelateria Artigiana,** which has perhaps Siena's best ice cream, and **Barbero d'Oro,** which serves cappuccino and *panforte* (€1.75/100 grams, balcony with 2 tables, closed Sun). **Bar Paninoteca** is on Vicolo di S. Paolo, on the stairs leading down to Il Campo (sandwiches, has a row of chairs on balcony, closed Mon).

At the bottom of Il Campo, a **Ciao** cafeteria offers easy self-service meals, no ambience, and no views. The crowded **Spizzico,** a pizza counter in the front half of Ciao, serves huge, inexpensive quarter pizzas; on sunny days, people take the pizza, trays and all, out on Il Campo for a picnic (CC only in cafeteria, daily 11:00–22:00, non-smoking section—*non fumatori*—in back, to left of city tower as you face it).

Budget eaters look for *pizza al taglio* shops, scattered throughout Siena, selling pizza by the slice. Picnickers enjoy the market held mornings (except Sun) behind Il Campo, on Piazza del Mercato. Of the grocery shops scattered throughout town, the biggest is **Consorzio Agrario Siena;** it's one block off Piazza Matteotti, toward Il Campo. Their pesto is the besto (Mon–Sat 8:00–19:30, Via Pianigiani 5).

Sienese Sweets

All over town, **Prodotti Tipici** shops sell Sienese specialties. Siena's claim to caloric fame is its *panforte,* a rich, chewy concoction of nuts, honey, and candied fruits that impresses even fruitcake-haters. There are a few varieties to try: *margherita,* dusted in powdered sugar, is more fruity, *panepatto* has a spicy, peppery crust. Locals prefer a chewy white macaroon-and-almond cookie called *ricciarelli.* All this and more can be found at **Bini**, where women in aprons box your sweets like precious gifts (Tue–Sun 9:00–13:30 & 16:30–20:00, closed Mon, Via dei Fusari 13).

TRANSPORTATION CONNECTIONS

Siena has sparse trains connections, but is a great hub for buses to the hill towns.

By train to: Florence (9/day, 1.75 hrs, more with transfer in Empoli).

By bus to: Florence (2/hr, 1.25–2 hrs, by Tra-in bus, last bus at 20:45), **San Gimignano** (6/day, 1.25 hrs, by Tra-in bus, more frequent with transfer in Poggibonsi), **Assisi** (2/day, 2 hrs, by Sena bus; the morning bus goes direct to Assisi, the afternoon bus might terminate at Santa Maria degli Angeli, from here catch a local bus to Assisi, 2/hr, 20 min), **Rome** (7/day, 3 hrs, by Sena bus, arrives at Rome's Tiburtina station), **Milan** (4/day, 5 hr). Schedules get sparse on Sundays and holidays.

Buses depart Siena from Piazza Gramsci, the train station, or both; confirm when you purchase your ticket. You can get tickets for Tra-in buses or Sena buses at the train station (Tra-in bus office: Mon–Sat 5:50–20:00; for Sena, buy tickets at *tabacchi* shop unless they've opened a separate office in the station), or easier and more central, under Piazza Gramsci at Sottopassaggio La Lizza (Tra-in bus office: daily 5:50–20:00, tel. 0577-204-246, toll-free tel. 800-570-530, www.trainspa.it; Sena bus office: Mon–Sat 7:45–19:45, closed Sun, tel. 800-930-960, www.senabus.it).

Sottopassaggio La Lizza, under Piazza Gramsci, has a cash machine (neither bus office accepts credit cards), luggage storage (€3.50/day, daily 7:00–19:45, no overnight storage), posted bus schedules, TV monitors (listing imminent departures), an elevator, and expensive WCs (€0.55). If you decide to depart Siena after the bus offices close, you can buy the ticket directly from the driver (and get charged a supplement). You can also get tickets—and help sorting through schedules—from Palio Viaggi on Piazza Gramsci (La Lizza 12, tel. 0577-280-828, info@palioviaggi.it).

On schedules, the fastest buses are marked *corse rapide.* Note that if a schedule lists your departure point as Via Tozzi or La Lizza, you catch the bus at Piazza Gramsci (Via Tozzi is the street that runs alongside Piazza Gramsci and La Lizza is the name of the bus station).

ASSISI

Assisi is famous for its hometown boy, St. Francis, who made very good.

Around the year 1200, a simple friar from Assisi challenged the decadence of Church government and society in general with a powerful message of non-materialism, simplicity, and a "slow down and smell God's roses" lifestyle. Like Jesus, Francis taught by example. A huge monastic order grew out of his teachings, which were gradually embraced (some would say co-opted) by the Church. Clare, St. Francis' partner in poverty, founded the Order of the Poor Clares. Catholicism's purest example of simplicity is now glorified in beautiful churches. In 1939, Italy made Francis and Clare its patron saints.

Francis' message of love and sensitivity to the environment has a broad and timeless appeal. But any pilgrimage site will be commercialized, and the legacy of St. Francis is Assisi's basic industry. In summer, this Umbrian town bursts with flash-in-the-pan Francis fans and Franciscan knickknacks. Those able to see past the tacky friar mementos can actually have a "travel on purpose" experience.

Planning Your Time

Assisi is worth a day and a night. The town has a half-day of sightseeing and another half-day of wonder. The essential sight is the Basilica of St. Francis. For a good visit, take the Assisi Welcome Walk (below), ending at the basilica. Schedule time to linger on the main square. Hikers enjoy sunset at the castle.

Most visitors are day-trippers. While the town's a zoo by day, it's a delight at night. Assisi after dark is closer to a place Francis could call home.

ORIENTATION

Crowned by a ruined castle at the top, Assisi spills downhill to its famous Basilica of St. Francis. The town is beautifully preserved and rich in history. The 1997 earthquake did more damage to the tourist industry than to the local buildings. Fortunately, tourists have returned—whether art-lovers, pilgrims, or both—drawn by Assisi's powerful sights.

Tourist Information: The TI is in the center of town on Piazza del Comune (summer Mon–Sat 8:00–18:30, Sun 10:00–13:00 & 14:00–17:00; winter Mon–Sat 8:00–14:00 & 15:00–18:00, Sun 9:00–13:00; tel. 075-812-534, info@iat.assisi.pg.it; visit www.umbria2000.it for info on Umbria).

Also on (or just off) Piazza del Comune, you'll find the Roman temple of Minerva, a Romanesque tower, banks, a finely frescoed pharmacy, and an underground Roman Forum.

A combo-ticket *(biglietto cumulativo,* €5.25/1 day) covers three sights: Rocca Maggiore (castle), Pinacoteca (paintings), and the Roman Forum; you'd need to see all three to save money (sold at participating sights).

Market day is Saturday on Piazza Matteotti (which has a good parking garage). Your hotel may give you an Assisi Card, which offers discounts on parking and some affiliated restaurants and shops.

Arrival in Assisi

By Train and Bus: City buses connect Assisi's train station with the old town of Assisi on the hilltop (€0.80, 2/hr, about 15–20 min), stopping at Piazza Unita d'Italia (near Basilica of St. Francis), then Largo Properzio (near Basilica of St. Clare), and finally Piazza Matteotti (top of old town). Going to the old town, buses usually leave from the train station at :16 and :46 past the hour. Going to the train station from the old town, buses usually run from Piazza Matteotti at :10 and :40 past the hour, and from Piazza Unita d'Italia at :17 and :47 past the hour. At Piazza Unita d'Italia, there are two bus stops *(fermata bus):* one sign reads *"per f.s. S.M. Angeli"* (to the train station), and the other reads *"per P. Matteotti"* (to the top of the old town). Note that you can take this bus within Assisi to save a long walk uphill (e.g., visit basilica, walk down to bus stop, then catch bus up to the middle or top of town).

By Taxi: Taxis from the station to the old town run about €10–12. There are legitimate extra charges for luggage, night service, and each person above four passengers, but beware: Many taxis rip off tourists by using tariff #2 (Sunday and holiday fare); the meter should be set on tariff #1 (€2.85 drop). You can check bags at the train station (€2.60/12 hrs, daily 6:30–19:30), but not in the old town. When departing the old town of Assisi, you'll find taxi stands at Piazza Unita d'Italia, the Basilica of St. Clare, and Piazza del Comune (or have your hotel call for you, tel. 075-812-600).

By Car: Drivers just coming in for the day should follow the signs to Piazza Matteotti's wonderful underground parking garage at the top of the town (which comes with bits of ancient Rome in the walls,

€1.10/hr, €11/day with Assisi Card—offered by many hotels, €15.75 without, €0.05/hour and €2/day more on Sun and holidays; open 7:00–21:00, until 23:00 in summer).

Helpful Hints

Travel Agency: You can get train tickets and most bus tickets (but not for Siena) at Agenzia Viaggi Stoppini, between Piazza del Comune and the Basilica of St. Clare (Mon–Fri 9:00–12:30 & 15:30–18:30, Sat 9:00–12:30, closed Sun, Corso Mazzini 31, tel. 075-812-597). For Siena, you buy tickets on the bus (see "Transportation Connections," page 350).

Internet Access: Internet World has several computers at exorbitant rates (€2.50/10 min, non-smoking, Mon–Sat 11:00–13:00 & 15:00–21:00, Sun 16:00–21:00, Via San Gabriele 25, a long block off Piazza del Comune, tel. 347-528-2062).

Local Guide: Anne Robichaud, an American who has lived here since 1975, gives informative tours of the town and the countryside with the aim of connecting tourists to locals and their customs and culture. Set your own itinerary, or use one of her suggestions, including day trips to neighboring hill towns and tours during local festivals (half-day from €66 per person, full day from €99, cooking lessons, can combine small groups for price reduction, tel. 075-802-334, fax 075-813-698, www.annesitaly.com). Thanks to Anne for her help with the following self-guided walk.

Assisi Welcome Walk

There's much more to Assisi than St. Francis and what all the blitz tour groups see.

This walk, rated ▲▲, covers the town from Piazza Matteotti at the top, down to the Basilica of St. Francis at the bottom. To get to Piazza Matteotti, ride the bus from the train station (or from Piazza Unita d'Italia) to the last stop, or drive there (underground parking with Roman ruins).

The Roman Arena: Start 50 yards beyond Piazza Matteotti (at intersection at far end of parking lot, away from city center—see map). A lane named Via Anfiteatro Romano leads to a cozy circular neighborhood built around a Roman arena. Assisi was an important Roman town. Circle the arena counterclockwise (the chain stretched across the road is to keep cars out, not you). Imagine how colorful the town laundry must have been in the last generation, when the women of Assisi gathered here to do their wash. Adjacent to the laundry is a small rectangular pool filled with water; above it are the coats of arms of the town's leading families. A few steps farther, hike up the stairs to the top of the hill for an aerial view of the oval arena. The Roman stones have long been absorbed into the medieval architecture. It was Roman tradition

Assisi

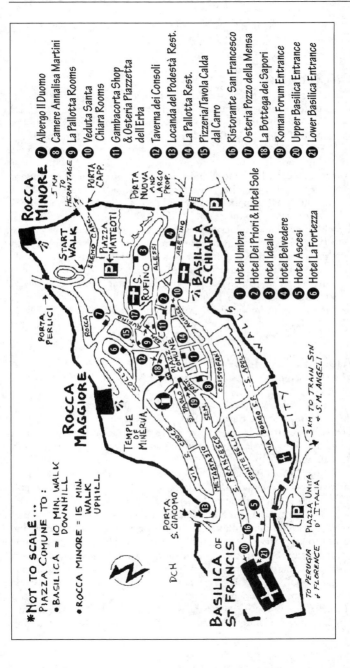

7 Albergo Il Duomo
8 Camere Annalisa Martini
9 La Pallotta Rooms
10 Veduta Santa
   Chiara Rooms
11 Gambacorta Shop
   & Osteria Piazzetta
   dell'Erba
12 Taverna dei Consoli
13 Locanda del Podestà Rest.
14 La Pallotta Rest.
15 Pizzeria/Tavola Calda
   dal Carro
16 Ristorante San Francesco
17 Osteria Pozzo della Mensa
18 La Bottega dei Sapori
19 Roman Forum Entrance
20 Upper Basilica Entrance
21 Lower Basilica Entrance

1 Hotel Umbra
2 Hotel Dei Priori & Hotel Sole
3 Hotel Ideale
4 Hotel Belvedere
5 Hotel Ascesi
6 Hotel La Fortezza

* NOT TO SCALE...
PIAZZA COMUNE TO:
• BASILICA = 10 MIN. WALK
  DOWNHILL
• ROCCA MINORE = 15 MIN.
  WALK
  UPHILL

to locate the arena outside of town...which this was. Continue on. The lane leads down to a city gate.

Umbrian view: Leave Assisi at the Porta Perlici for a commanding view. Umbria, called the "green heart of Italy," is the country's geographical center and only landlocked state. Enjoy the greens: silver green on the valley floor (olives), emerald green 10 yards below you (grapevines), and deep green on the hillsides (evergreen oak trees). Also notice Rocca Maggiore (big castle), a fortress providing townsfolk a refuge in times of attack, and, behind you atop the hill, Rocca Minore (little castle). Now walk back to Piazza Matteotti. Go to the opposite end of this piazza, to the corner with the blobby stone tower. As you walk down the lane next to this tower, you'll see the big dome of the Church of San Rufino. Walk to the courtyard of the church; its big bell tower is on your left.

Church of San Rufino: While Francis is Italy's patron saint, Rufino is Assisi's—the town's first bishop (martyred and buried here in the third century). The church is 12th-century Romanesque with a neo-classical interior. Enter the church (daily 7:00–13:00 & 15:00–19:00). To your right (in the back corner of the church with the black, iron grate) is the font where Francis and Clare were baptized. Traditionally, the children of Assisi are still baptized here.

The striking glass panels in the church floor reveal a recent discovery: ancient foundations dating from Roman times. You're walking on history. After the 1997 earthquake, the church was checked from ceiling to floor by structural inspectors. When they looked under the paving stones, they discovered bodies (it used to be a common practice to bury people in church, until Napoleon decreed otherwise) and underneath the graves, Roman foundations and some animal bones (suggesting the possibility of animal sacrifice). There might have been a Roman temple here; churches were often built on the sites of ruined Roman temples. Standing at the back of the church (facing the altar), look left to the Roman cistern (inside the great stone archway). This was once the town's water source when under attack.

Underneath the church, alongside the Roman ruins, are the foundations of an earlier Church of San Rufino, now the crypt. When it's open, you can go below to see the saint's sarcophagus (€3, mid-March–mid-Oct daily 10:00–13:00 & 15:00–18:00). With your back to the crypt entrance, you'll see the door to the museum of the church (entry included with crypt ticket, same hours as above except 10:00–18:00 in Aug). An archaeology museum may open here in 2004.

Medieval Architecture: When you leave the church, take a sharp left (on Via Dono Doni—say it fast three times), following the sign to Santa Chiara. Take the first right, down the stairway. At the bottom, notice the pink limestone pavement. The medieval town survives. The arches built over doorways indicate that the buildings date from the 12th through the 14th century. The vaults that turn lanes into tunnels are reminders of medieval urban expansion (mostly 15th century). While the population grew, people wanted to live within its protective walls, so Assisi became more dense. Medieval Assisi had five times the population density of today's Assisi.

Notice the floating gardens. Assisi has a flowering balcony competition each June. When you arrive at a street, turn left, going slightly uphill for a block, then jog right. Pause at Via Sermei 6b (on your left) to check out Signore Silvano Giombolini's display of mechanized figures petting sheep, sawing wood, and drawing well water. Look for the nativity scene, featuring an adoring baby Jesus captioned with scriptures and Franciscan-style admonitions to love one another and appreciate life's simple pleasures (free but donations appreciated). Continue ahead, following the "S. Chiara" sign down to the Basilica of St. Clare.

Basilica of St. Clare (Santa Chiara): For a description of this stark, impressive church built to honor St. Clare, see "More Sights," page 344.

Another Umbrian View: Belly up to the viewpoint in front of the basilica. On the left is the convent of St. Clare; below you, the olive grove of the Poor Clares since the 13th century; and, in the distance, a grand Umbrian view. Assisi overlooks the richest and biggest valley in otherwise hilly and mountainous Umbria. The municipality of Assisi has a population of 29,000, but only 1,000 people live in the old town. The lower town grew up with the coming of the railway in the 19th century. In the haze, the blue-domed church is St. Mary of the Angels (Santa Maria degli Angeli, see description below), the cradle of the Franciscan order, marking the place St. Francis lived and worked. This church, a popular pilgrimage sight today, is the first Los Angeles. Franciscans settled in California, naming L.A. (after this church), San Francisco, and even Santa Clara.

Arches and Artisans: From Via Santa Chiara, you can see two arches over the street. The arch at the back of the church dates from 1265. (Beyond it but out of view, the 1316 Porta Nuova marks the final expansion of Assisi.) Toward the city center (on Via Santa Chiara, the high road), an arch indicates the site of the Roman wall.

About 40 yards before this arch, pop into the souvenir shop at #1b. The plaque over the door explains that the old printing press (a national monument now, just inside the door) was used to make fake documents for Jews escaping the Nazis in 1943 and 1944. The shop is run by a couple of artisans: The man makes frames out of medieval Assisi timbers; the woman makes the traditional Assisi, or Franciscan, cross-stitch.

Just past the gate and on your left is the La Pasteria natural products shop (Corso Mazzini 18b, across from entrance of Hotel Sole). Cooks love to peruse Umbrian wines, herbs, pâtés, and truffles, and sample an aromatic "fruit infusion." The Lisa Assisi clothing shop (Corso Mazzini 25b, across the street and to your right) has a delightful basement, with surviving bits of a 2,000-year-old mortarless Roman wall. Ahead at Corso Mazzini 14d, the small shop (Poiesis) sells olive-wood carvings. Drop in. It's said that St. Francis made the first nativity scene to help teach the Christmas message, which is why you'll see so many in Assisi. Even today, nearby villages are enthusiastic about their "living" manger scenes. Ahead of you, the columns of the Temple of Minerva mark the Piazza del Comune (described below). Sit at the fountain on the square for a few minutes of people-watching—don't you love Italy? Within 200 yards of this square, on either side, were the medieval walls. Imagine a commotion of 5,000 people confined within these walls. No wonder St. Francis needed an escape for some peace and quiet. I'll meet you over at the temple on the square.

Roman Temple/Christian Church: Assisi has always been a spiritual center. The Romans went to great lengths to make this Temple of Minerva a centerpiece of their city. Notice the columns cutting into the stairway. It was a tight fit here on the hilltop. The stairs probably went down triple the distance you see today. The church of Santa Maria sopra (over) Minerva was added in the ninth century. The bell tower is 13th-century. Pop inside the temple/church (Mon–Sat 7:00–19:00, Sun 8:00–19:00, closes at sunset and midday in winter). Today's interior is 17th-century Baroque. Flanking the altar are the original Roman temple floor stones. You can even see the drains for the bloody sacrifices that took place here. Behind the statues of Peter and Paul, the original Roman embankment peeks through.

A few doors back toward the fountain, step into the 16th-century vaults from the old fish market. Notice the Italian flair for design. Even this smelly fish market was once finely decorated. The art style was "grotesque"—literally, a painting in a grotto. This was painted in the early 1500s, a few years after Columbus brought turkeys back from the New World. The turkeys painted here may have been that bird's European debut. (Public WCs are a few steps off Piazza del Comune; near the fountain, go through Via dell' Arco dei Priori, then down the street on the left.)

Church of Santo Stefano: From the main square, hike past the temple up the high road, Via San Paolo. After 200 yards, a sign directs you down a lane to Santo Stefano, which used to be outside the town walls in the days of St. Francis. Legend is that its bells miraculously rang on October 3, 1226, the day St. Francis died. Surrounded by cypress, fig, and walnut trees, it's a delightful bit of offbeat Assisi. Step inside. This is the typical rural Italian Romanesque church—no architect, just built by simple stonemasons who put together the most basic design (daily 8:30–21:30). The lane zigzags down to Via San Francesco. Turn right and walk under the arch toward the Basilica of St. Francis.

Via San Francesco: This was the main drag leading from the town to the basilica holding the body of St. Francis. Francis was a big deal even in his own day. He died in 1226 and was made a saint in 1228—the same year the basilica's foundations were laid—and his body was moved in by 1230. Assisi was a big-time pilgrimage center, and this street was a booming place. Notice the fine medieval balcony just below the arch. A few yards farther down (on the left), cool yourself at the fountain. The hospice next door was built in 1237 to house pilgrims. Notice the three surviving faces of its fresco: Jesus, Francis, and Clare.

SIGHTS

Basilica of St. Francis

A ▲▲▲ sight, the Basilica de San Francesco is one of the artistic and religious highlights of Europe. In 1226, St. Francis was buried (with the outcasts he had stood by) outside of his town on the "Hill of the Damned"—now called the "Hill of Paradise." The basilica is frescoed from top to bottom by the leading artists of the day: Cimabue, Giotto, Simone Martini, and Pietro Lorenzetti. A 13th-century historian wrote, "No more exquisite monument to the Lord has been built."

From a distance, you see the huge arcades "supporting" the basilica. These were 15th-century quarters for the monks. The arcades lining the square leading to the church housed medieval pilgrims.

Orientation: There are three parts to the church: the upper basilica, the lower basilica, and the saint's tomb (below the lower basilica). In the 1997 earthquake, the lower basilica—with walls nearly nine feet thick—was unscathed. The upper basilica, with bigger windows and walls only three feet thick, was damaged. After restoration was completed, the entire church was reopened to visitors in late 1999.

To get oriented, stand at the lower entrance in the courtyard. Opposite the entry to the lower basilica is the information center. You'll find two different WCs within a half-block (up the road in a squat building and halfway down the big piazza on the left).

Cost, Hours, and Information: Free entry, lower basilica daily 6:15–18:45, relic chapel in lower basilica supposedly 8:00–18:30 but often closed, upper basilica daily 8:30–18:30 (Tel. 075-819-0084, www.sanfrancescoassisi.org). Modest dress is required to enter the church—no sleeveless tops or shorts for men, women, or children. The info center sells an excellent guidebook, *The Basilica of Saint Francis—A Spiritual Pilgrimage* (€2.50, by Goulet, McInally, and Wood), which I used as a source for my self-guided tour (below).

Tours: At the info center, ask about tours in English—or better yet, call or e-mail in advance (tours Mon–Sat 9:00–12:30 & 14:30–17:30, no tours Sun, tel. 075-819-0084, assisisanfrancesco@libero.it). Tours are free, but a €25 donation per group is appropriate. The new 75-minute audioguide is also good (€5/person).

Self-Guided Tour: The Basilica of St. Francis, a theological work of genius, can be difficult for the 21st-century tourist/pilgrim to appreciate. Since the basilica is the reason most people visit Assisi, and the message of St. Francis has even the least devout blessing the town Vespas, I've designed this self-guided tour with an emphasis on the place's theology (rather than art history).

Enter through the grand doorway of the lower basilica. Just inside, decorating the top of the first arch, look up and see St. Francis, who greets you with a Latin inscription. Sounding a bit like John Wayne, he says the equivalent of "Slow down and be joyful, pilgrim. You've reached the Hill of Paradise, and this church will knock your spiritual socks off." Start with the tomb (turn left into the nave; midway down the nave to your right, follow signs and go downstairs to the tomb).

The message: Francis' message caused a stir. He traded a life of power and riches for one of obedience, poverty, and chastity. The Franciscan existence (Brother Sun, Sister Moon, and so on) is a space where God, man, and the natural world frolic harmoniously. Franciscan friars, known as the "Jugglers of God," were a joyful part of the community. In an Italy torn by fighting between towns and families, Francis promoted peace and the restoration of order. (He set an example by reconstructing a crumbled chapel.) While the Church was waging bloody Crusades, Francis pushed ecumenism and understanding. Even today the leaders of the world's great religions meet here for summits.

This rich building seems to contradict the teachings of the poor monk it honors, but it was built as an act of religious and civic pride to remember the hometown saint. It was also designed, and still functions, as a pilgrimage center and a splendid classroom.

The tomb: In medieval times, pilgrims came to Assisi because St. Francis was buried here. Holy relics were the "ruby slippers" of medieval Europe. They gave you power—got your prayers answered and helped you win wars—and ultimately helped you get back to your eternal Kansas. Assisi made no bones about promoting the saint's relics, but hid his tomb for obvious reasons of security. Not until 1818 was the tomb opened to the public. The saint's remains are above the altar in the stone box with the iron ties. His four closest friends and first followers are buried in the corners of the room. Opposite the altar, up four steps in between the entrance and exit, notice the small gold box behind the metal grill; this contains the remains of Francis' rich Roman patron, Jacopa dei Settesoli. Climb back to the lower nave.

Lower basilica nave: Appropriately Franciscan, subdued and Romanesque, its nave was frescoed with parallel scenes from the lives of Christ and Francis—connected by a ceiling of stars. Unfortunately, after the church was built and decorated, the popularity of the Franciscans meant side chapels needed to be built. Huge arches were cut out of some scenes, but others survive. In the fresco directly above the entry to the tomb, Christ is being taken down from the cross (just the bottom half of his body can be seen, to the left), and it looks like the story is over.

Defeat. But in the opposite fresco (above the tomb's exit), we see Francis preaching to the birds, reminding the faithful that the message of the Gospel survives.

These stories directed the attention of the medieval pilgrim to the altar, where he could meet God through the sacraments. The church was thought of as a community of believers sailing toward God. The prayers coming out of the nave (*navis*, or ship) fill the triangular sections of the ceiling—called *vele*, or sails—with spiritual wind. With a priest for a navigator and the altar for a helm, faith propels the ship.

Stand behind the altar (toes to the bottom step) and look up. The three scenes in front of you are, to the right, "Obedience" (Francis wearing a rope harness); to the left, "Chastity" (in a tower of purity held up by two angels); and straight ahead, "Poverty." Here Jesus blesses the marriage as Francis slips a ring on Lady Poverty. In the foreground, two "self-sufficient" merchants (the new rich of a thriving North Italy) are throwing sticks and stones at the bride. But Poverty, in her patched wedding dress, is fertile and strong, and even those brambles blossom into a rosebush crown.

Putting your heels to the altar and bending back like a drum major, look up at Francis on a heavenly throne, who traded a life of earthly simplicity for glory in heaven. Now, turn to the right and march to the corner, where steps lead down into the...

Relic chapel: This chapel is often unexpectedly closed, it's but worth a look if open. Circle the room clockwise. You'll see the silver chalice and plate that Francis used for the bread and wine of the Eucharist (in small, dark, windowed case set into wall, marked *Calice con Patena*). Francis believed that his personal possessions should be simple, but the items used for worship should be made of the finest materials. In the corner display case is a small section of the haircloth worn by Francis as penitence. In the next corner are the tunic and slippers that Francis wore during his last days. Next, find a prayer (in a fancy silver stand) that St. Francis wrote for Brother Leo, signed with his tau cross. Tav ("tau" in Greek), the last letter in the Hebrew alphabet, is symbolic of faithfulness to the end. Francis signed his name with this simple character. Next is a papal document (1223) legitimizing the Franciscan order and assuring his followers that they were not risking a (deadly) heresy charge. Finally, see the tunic lovingly patched and stitched by followers of the five-foot, four-inch-tall St. Francis.

Return up the stairs to the...

Lower basilica transept: This church brought together the greatest Sienese (Martini and Lorenzetti) and Florentine (Cimabue and Giotto) artists of the day. Look around at the painted scenes. In 1300, this was radical art—believable homespun scenes, landscapes, trees, real people.

Study the crucifix (by Giotto) with the eight sparrowlike angels. For the first time, holy people are expressing emotion: One angel turns her head sadly at the sight of Jesus, and another scratches her hands down her cheeks, drawing blood. Mary (lower left), previously in control, has fainted in despair. The Franciscans, with their goal of bringing God to the people, found a natural partner in Europe's first modern painter, Giotto.

To see the Renaissance leap, look at the painting to the right. This is by Cimabue—it's Gothic, without the 3-D architecture, natural backdrop, and slice-of-life reality of the Giotto work. Cimabue's St. Francis (far right with stigmata—the marks of the cross—for easy identification) is considered by some to be the earliest existing portrait of the saint. To the left, at eye level, enjoy the Martini saints and their exquisite halos.

Francis' friend, "Sister Death," was really not all that terrible. In fact, Francis would like to introduce you to her now (above and to the right of the door leading into the relic chapel). Go ahead, block the light and meet her. Then cross the transept to the other side of the altar for the staircase going up. By the way, monks in robes are not my idea of easy-to-approach people, but the Franciscans are still God's jugglers (and most of them speak English).

Courtyard: The treasury to the left of the bookstore is free (donation requested) and features ornately-decorated chalices, reliquaries, vestments, and altarpieces. There's a free, clean WC two-thirds of the way down the great hall on your right.

From the courtyard, climb the stairs to the...

Upper basilica: Built later than the lower, the upper basilica is brighter, Gothic (the first Gothic church in Italy, 1228), and practically wallpapered by Giotto. This gallery of frescoes by Giotto and his assistants shows 28 scenes from the life of St. Francis.

Look for these scenes:

• **A common man spreads his cape before Francis** (immediately to right of altar, as you face altar) out of honor and recognition to a man who will do great things. Symbolized by the rose window, God looks over the 20-year-old Francis, a dandy imprisoned in his selfishness. A medieval pilgrim fluent in symbolism would understand this because the Temple of Minerva (which you saw today on Assisi's Piazza del Comune) was a prison at that time. The rose window, which never existed, is symbolic of God's eye.

• **Francis offers his cape to a needy stranger** (next panel). Prior to this act of kindness, Francis had been captured in battle, held as a prisoner of war, and then released by his father's ransom.

• **Francis is visited by the Lord in a dream** (next panel) and told to leave the army and go home to wait for a non-military assignment: "Go and repair my house, which you see is in ruins." This marks the true beginning of Francis' conversion.

Francis prays to the crucifix in San Damiano church (next panel), which admonishes him to give up his life of wealth and privilege and follow Jesus.

• **Francis relinquishes his possessions** (next panel), giving his dad his clothes, his credit cards, and even his time-share condo on Capri. Naked Francis is covered by the bishop, symbolizing his transition from a man of the world to a man of the Church. Notice the disbelief and concern on the bishop's advisors' faces; subtle expressions like these wouldn't have made it into a medieval fresco of this scene.

• **The pope has a vision** (next panel) of a simple man propping up his teetering Church. This led to the papal acceptance of the Franciscan order.

• **Christ appears to Francis** being carried by a seraph—a six-winged angel (other side of church, fourth panel from the door). For the strength of his faith, Francis is given the marks of his master, the "battle scars of love"...the stigmata. Throughout his life, Francis was interested in chivalry; now he's joined the spiritual knighthood.

• **Francis preaches to the birds** (to the right of the exit). Francis was more than a nature-lover. The birds, of different species, represent the diverse flock of humanity and nature, all created and beloved by God and worthy of each other's love.

Before you leave, look at the ceiling above the altar and front entrance to see large tan patches; these careful repairs were made after the basilica was damaged in the 1997 earthquake. It's a blessing that so many of the frescoes remain.

Near the outside of the upper basilica are the Latin pax (peace) and the Franciscan tau cross in the grass. Tau and pax. For more pax, take the high lane back to town, up to the castle, or into the countryside.

More Sights

▲**Basilica of Saint Clare (Basilica di Santa Chiara)**—Dedicated to the founder of the order of the Poor Clares, this Umbrian Gothic church is simple, in keeping with the Poor Clares' dedication to a life of contemplation. The church was built in 1265, and the huge buttresses were added in the next century. The interior's fine frescoes were whitewashed in Baroque times. The Chapel of the Crucifix of San Damiano, on the right (actually an earlier church incorporated into this one), has the crucifix that supposedly spoke to St. Francis, leading to his conversion in 1206. Stairs lead from the nave down to the tomb of Saint Clare. Her tomb is at the far end. The walls depict scenes from Clare's life and death (1193–1253). The saint's robes, hair, and an enormous tunic she made—along with relics of Saint Francis (including a shoe that he was wearing when he received the stigmata)—are in a large case between the stairs. The attached cloistered community of the Poor Clares has flourished for 700 years (church open daily 6:30–12:00 & 14:00–19:00, until 18:00 in winter).

Roman Forum (Foro Romano)—For a look at Assisi's Roman roots, tour the Roman Forum, which is actually under Piazza del Comune. The floor plan is sparse, the odd bits and pieces obscure, but it's well-explained in English (a 10-page booklet is loaned to you when you enter) and you can actually walk on an ancient Roman road. For an orientation, look at the poster for sale at the entry to get an idea of the original setting of forum and temple (€2.50 entry, or included in €5.20 combo-ticket, daily 10:00–13:00 & 14:00–18:00, closes at 17:00 in winter; from Piazza del Comune, go one-half block down Via San Francesco—it's on your right).

Pinacoteca—This small museum attractively displays its 13th- to 17th-century art (mainly frescoes), with general English information in nearly every room. There's a damaged Giotto Madonna and a rare secular fresco (to right of Giotto), but it's mainly a peaceful walk through a pastel world, best for art-lovers (€2.20, or included in €5.20 combo-ticket: daily 10:00–13:00 & 14:00–18:00: Via San Francesco, no building number, look for banner above entryway, on main drag between Piazza del Comune and Basilica of St. Francis: tel. 075-812-033).

▲**Rocca Maggiore**—The "big castle" offers a good look at a 14th-century fortification and a fine view of Assisi and the Umbrian countryside (€2.20, or included in €5.20 combo-ticket, daily from 10:00 until an hour before sunset, opens at 9:00 July–Aug). If you're pinching your euros, the view is just as good from outside the castle, and the interior is pretty bare.

Commune with Nature—For a picnic with the same birdsong and views that inspired St. Francis, leave all the tourists and hike to the Rocca Minore (small private castle, not tourable) above Piazza Matteotti.

Santa Maria degli Angeli

This flat, modern part of Assisi has one major sight: The basilica that marks the spot where Francis lived, worked, and died.

▲▲**St. Mary of the Angels (Basilica di Santa Maria degli Angeli)**— This huge basilica, towering above the buildings below Assisi, was built around the tiny but historic Porziuncola Chapel (now directly under the dome). When the pope gave Francis his blessing, he was given this *porziuncola*, or "small portion"—a little land with a fixer-upper chapel. Francis lived here after he founded the Franciscan Order in 1208, and this was where he consecrated St. Clare as the Bride of Christ. A chapel called Cappella del Transito marks the place where Francis died (behind and to the right of the Porziuncola Chapel). Follow signs to the Roseta (Rose Garden). Francis, fighting off a temptation that he never named, threw himself onto roses. As the story goes, the thorns immediately dropped off the roses. Ever since, thornless roses have grown here. Look through the window at the rose garden (to the right of the statue of Francis petting a sheep). The Rose Chapel (Cappella delle Rose) is built over the place where Francis lived. The bookshop has some books in English and the free *museo* has a few monastic cells interesting to pilgrims (museum open April–Oct Mon–Fri 9:00–12:00 & 15:00–18:00, Sat–Sun 8:30–12:30 & 15:00–18:00, closed Wed and Nov–March).

Hours: The basilica is open daily 7:00–19:00. There's a little TI to your right as you face the church (supposedly open daily 9:00–12:00 & 15:00–18:00 but may be closed, tel. 075-812-534). A WC is 40 yards to the right of the TI, behind the hedge.

Getting There: To get to Basilica di Santa Maria degli Angeli from Assisi's train station, it's a five-minute **walk** (exit station left, take first left at McDonald's). When you're leaving the basilica, you can catch a bus directly to the station and on to the old town of Assisi (as you leave church, stop is to your right, next to basilica). The orange city buses run twice hourly (buses to the old town depart the basilica at :10 and :40 after the hour; tickets cost €0.80 if you buy at *tabacchi* or newsstand, €1.50 if you buy from driver; 20-min ride up to old town).

It's efficient to visit this basilica either on your way to the old town of Assisi or when you leave. You can easily walk to the basilica from the station (baggage check available, €2.60/12 hrs, access through shop). If you're heading to Siena next, visit the basilica right before you leave, because that's where you'll catch the bus to Siena (as you leave basilica, stop is to your right, across the street, buy ticket on bus); see "Transportation Connections," see page 350.

SLEEPING

The town accommodates large numbers of pilgrims on religious holidays. Finding a room at any other time should be easy. See the map on page 336 for hotel locations.

$$$ Hotel Umbra, the best splurge in the center, feels like a quiet villa in the middle of town (25 rooms, Sb-€77, Db-€95–120, Tb-€135, includes breakfast, air-con, peaceful garden and view sun terrace, most rooms have views, good restaurant, dinner only, go downhill in Piazza del Comune, take left fork towards Basilica of Saint Francis and turn immediately left under the arch at Via degli Archi 6, tel. 075-812-240, fax 075-813-653, www.hotelumbra.it, humbra@mail.caribusiness.it, family Laudenzi SE).

$$$ Hotel Dei Priori is a three-star palatial place in the old center, with big, quiet, posh rooms that have all the comforts (Db-€100–125, superior Db-€140–160, includes breakfast, elevator, air-con, Corso

SLEEP CODE

(€1 = about $1.10, country code: 39)
Sleep Code: **S** = Single, **D** = Double/Twin, **T** = Triple, **Q** =
Quad, **b** = bathroom, **s** = shower only, **no CC** = Credit Cards
not accepted, **SE** = Speaks English, **NSE** = No English. Unless
otherwise noted, credit cards are accepted.

To help you sort easily through these listings, I've divided
the rooms into three categories based on the price for a standard
double room with bath:

  $$$ **Higher Priced**—Most rooms €90 or more.
    $$ **Moderately Priced**—Most rooms between €55-90.
     $ **Lower Priced**—Most rooms €55 or less.

Mazzini 15, tel. 075-812-237, fax 075-816-804, www.assisi-hotel.com,
hpriori@tiscali.net, SE).

$$ Hotel Ideale, on the top edge of town overlooking the valley,
offers 12 bright, modern rooms (all with view, 10 with balconies), a
peaceful garden, free parking, and a warm welcome (Sb-€50, Db-€85,
includes big-for-Italy breakfast, confirm your arrival time, especially
if arriving after 17:00, Piazza Matteotti 1, tel. 075-813-570, fax 075-
813-020, www.hotelideale.it, info@hotelideale.it, sisters Lara and
Ilaria SE). This hotel, at the top of the old town, is close to the bus
stop (and parking lot) at Piazza Matteotti, easy to reach by public
transportation.

$$ Hotel Sole is well-located, with 35 spacious, comfortable rooms
in a 15th-century building (Sb-€42, Db-€64, Tb-€85, breakfast-€6; half
its rooms are in newer annex across the street, some rooms have views and
balconies, elevator in annex; Corso Mazzini 35, 100 yards before Basilica
of St. Clare; tel. 075-812-373, fax 075-813-706, www.assisihotelsole
.com, info@assisihotelsole.com, SE).

$$ Hotel Belvedere, which offers good views and 16 basic rooms
(9 with views), is run by Enrico and his American wife, Mary (Db-€75,
breakfast-€5, elevator, large communal view terrace, 2 blocks past
Basilica of St. Clare at Via Borgo Aretino 13, tel. 075-812-460, fax 075-
816-812, assisihotelbelvedere@hotmail.com, SE). Their attached restau-
rant is good (open by request and reservation only).

$ Hotel Ascesi has an inviting little lobby, nine pleasant rooms,
and a tiny terrace, all within a block of the Basilica of St. Francis. They
may close temporarily in 2004—if you get no response, try somewhere

else (Sb-€36, Db-€52, breakfast-€4; air-con; Via Frate Elia 5, walk up from Piazza Unita d'Italia, turn left at Piazzetta Ruggero Bonghi, see sign on right; tel. & fax 075-812-420, hotelascesi@libero.it). This hotel is near the bus stop and parking lot at the bottom of town (Piazza Unita d'Italia), handy if you're packing lots of luggage.

$ Hotel La Fortezza is a simple, modern, and quiet place with seven rooms (Db-€52, Tb-€70, Qb-€80, a short block above Piazza del Comune at Vicolo della Fortezza 19b, tel. 075-812-993, fax 075-819-8035, www.lafortezzahotel.com, lafortezza@lafortezzahotel.com, Lorenzo SE).

$ Albergo Il Duomo is tidy and *tranquillo*, with nine rooms on a stair-step lane one block up from San Rufino. Check in at Hotel Rufino, just before you head up the lane (Sb-€33, Db-€44, breakfast-€5; Vicolo S. Lorenzo 2, from Church of San Rufino follow sign, then turn left on stair-stepped alley; tel. & fax 075-812-742, www.hotelsanrufino.it, info@sanrufino.it, SE).

$ Camere Annalisa Martini is a cheery home swimming in vines and roses in the town's medieval core. Annalisa speaks English and enthusiastically accommodates her guests with a picnic garden, a washing machine (€5 per small load, including drying and ironing), a communal refrigerator, and six homey rooms (S-€23, Sb-€25, D-€32, Db-€36, Tb-€50, Qb-€60, no CC; 3 rooms share 2 bathrooms, no breakfast, you can use her computer to check your e-mail, €10/day parking nearby with her business card; 1 block from Piazza del Comune, go downhill toward basilica, turn left on Via S. Gregorio to #6; tel. & fax 075-813-536, cameremartini@libero.it).

$ La Pallotta, a recommended restaurant (see "Eating," below), offers seven clean, bright rooms (rooms and restaurant are in different locations). Rooms #12 and #18 have views (Db-€47; view terrace and view sitting room on top floor; Via San Rufino 6, go up short flight of stairs outside building to reach entrance, a block off Piazza del Comune; tel. & fax 075-812-307, www.pallottaassisi.it, pallotta@pallottaassisi.it, SE).

$ Veduta Santa Chiara offers 10 newly remodeled, comfortable rooms near the Basilica of Saint Clare. The two ground-floor rooms have part of the city's Roman foundations incorporated into their decor, and four rooms have basilica views (politely decline the cramped attic room). Staying here is like staying with family, Italian-style—Mamma Nadia and her daughter Annamaria take good care of their guests (Sb-€32, Db-€45, Tb-€65, Vicolo San Antonio 1, tel. & fax 075-815-220). At Piazza del Comune, face the fountain and go through the archway on your right. Jog left around the building and continue downhill past Ristorante Medioevo. At the bottom of that street, jog left again with the road and look for the sign at the bottom of the hill on your right.

The $ **Gambacorta** family rents several decent rooms and has a roof terrace on a quiet lane (Via Sermei 9) just above St. Chiara. There is no sign or reception desk, so you'll need to check in at their shop a half-block east of Piazza del Comune at San Gabriele 17; look for sign "Bottega del Buongustaio" on a raised piazzetta (S-€20 Db-€40, Tb-€50; 2-night stays preferred, no breakfast but has kitchen, bag transport available; store open Mon–Wed and Fri–Sat 8:00–13:00 & 16:30–20:00, Thu 8:00–13:00, closed Sun; if you can't arrive when store is open, call when you arrive, tel. 075-812-454, fax 075-813-186, www.ilbongustaio.com, geo@umbrars.com, SE a little). She also has two apartments for stays of at least four nights (3 rooms-€90/day, 5 rooms-€200/day, kitchen, no breakfast).

$ *Hostel:* Francis probably would have bunked with the peasants in Assisi's **Ostello della Pace** (€14 beds in 4- to 8-bed rooms, includes breakfast, dinner-€8; laundry; lockout 9:30–15:30, 23:30 curfew; get off bus at Piazza Unita d'Italia, then take 10-min walk to Via di Valecchie 177; tel. & fax 075-816-767, www.assisihostel.com, assisi.hostel@tiscalinet.it, Joseph SE).

Agriturismo near Assisi

$$ **Podere La Fornace** is a renovated farmhouse in the tiny village of Tordibetto, just a few miles outside Assisi. The four apartments (with 1–3 bedrooms) have full kitchens and a living room that can sleep an extra person. Local wine, olive oil, and pasta are available on-site; if you stay for a week, they'll include your breakfast ingredients (apartment-€75–240 depending on size and season, 3-night min, games for children, swimming pool, bikes, Via Ombrosa 3, tel. 075-801-9537, mobile 338-990-2903, fax 075-801-9630, www.lafornace.com, info @lafornace.com, SE).

EATING

For a fine Assisian perch, good regional cooking, and snappy service, relax on a terrace overlooking Piazza del Comune at the third-generation **Taverna dei Consoli** (€14 4-course *menu*, also à la carte, Thu–Tue 12:00–14:30 & 19:00–21:30, closed Wed and Jan, tel. 075-812-516). Friendly owner Moreno, who speaks a leetle English, recommends the *bruschetta, filet al tartufo, cinghiale* (boar), and *stringozzi* (noodles named for the cords that poor people used to strangle priests who extorted sky-high tithes).

At **Locanda del Podestà,** chef Selvio serves up tasty grilled Umbrian sausages, *gnocchi alla sacrantina* (cooked in local wine), and all manner of truffles while English-speaking Romina graciously serves happy diners. Try the tasty *scottadita* ("burn your fingers") lamb chops—as in "they're so good, you can't wait for them to cool before you dive in" (open Thu–Tue 12:00–15:00 & 19:00–22:00, closed Wed; 5-min walk uphill from St Francis' basilica, San Giacomo 6c; tel. 075-813-034).

La Pallotta, a local favorite run by a friendly, hardworking family, offers regional specialties, such as *piccione* (squab, a.k.a. pigeon), *coniglio* (rabbit), and several tasting *menus* of Umbrian cuisine (€15–€24, including vegetarian; Wed–Mon 12:15–14:30 & 19:15–21:30, closed Tue; also rents rooms—see listing above; a few steps off Piazza del Comune, through gate across from temple/church, Vicolo della Volta Pinta 2; tel. 075-812-649).

Osteria Piazzetta dell Erba is a fun, little, family-run place a block above Piazza del Comune, serving good, basic Umbrian specialties next to the Gambacorta grocery (Tue–Sun 12:00–14:00 & 19:00–21:45, closed Mon, Via San Gabriele 15b, tel. 075-815-352).

Pizzeria/Tavola Calda dal Carro is popular, affordable, and friendly (good pizzas and €13 *menu*; watch them grill up your steak or Umbrian sausages over the fire in their open kitchen; Thu–Tue 12:00–15:00 & 19:00–22:00, closed Wed; Vicolo di Nepis 2b, leave Piazza del Comune on Via San Gabriele, then take first right—down a stepped lane; tel. 075-815-249).

Ristorante San Francesco is the place to splurge for dinner (€12–14 *primi*) with a view on the Basilica of Saint Francis (Thu–Tue 12:00–14:30 & 19:30–22:00, closed Wed, facing Basilica at Via San Francesco 52, tel. 075-812-329).

Osteria Pozzo della Mensa offers up organic salads and lots of other typical Umbrian vegetarian choices, as well as locally-produced *salumi* and cheeses (Thu–Tue 12:00–15:00 & 19:00–22:00, closed Wed; Via del Pozzo della Mensa 11b; head up Via San Rufino from Piazza del Comune and take first right, then straight ahead 50 yards; tel. 347-344-0644).

For a picnic of Umbrian treats, try **La Bottega dei Sapori** for its good prosciutto sandwiches and specialty items, including truffle paste. Friendly Fabrizio may give you a taste (daily 9:00–20:00, closed Tue in winter, Piazza del Comune 34, tel. 075-812-294).

TRANSPORTATION CONNECTIONS

By train to: Rome (5/day, 1.75–2.5 hrs), **Florence** (5/day, 2–2.75 hrs, more with transfers at Terontola and Cortona), **Orvieto** (7/day, 2 hrs, transfer in Terontola), **Siena** (6/day, 3.25 hrs, transfers in Chiusi and Terontola; bus is more efficient). Train station: tel. 075-804-0272.

Several different bus companies offer service by **bus to: Rome** (3/day, 3 hrs, €16.50, pay driver, departs Assisi's Piazza Unita d'Italia, arrives at Rome's Tiburtina station), **Siena** (2/day, 2 hrs, €9, pay driver, departs from Basilica di Santa Maria degli Angeli near Assisi train station; to get from station to basilica, exit station left, take first left at McDonald's—as you face basilica, bus stop is to your left across street). Don't take the bus to **Florence** (1/day, departs Piazza Unita d'Italia at 6:45 a.m., 2.75 hrs); the train is better. From mid-June to mid-October, buses make daytrip runs to nearby hilltowns **Gubbio, Spello, Perugia, Todi, Lake Trasimeno**, and others. Pick up a schedule from the TI or call 075-812-534.

HILL TOWNS OF CENTRAL ITALY

Sun-dried tomatoes, homemade pasta, wispy cypress-lined driveways following desolate ridges to fortified 16th-century farmhouses, and dusty old-timers warming the same bench day after day while soccer balls buzz around them like innocuous flies. The sun-soaked hill towns of Central Italy offer what to many is the quintessential Italian experience.

Italy's hill towns retain their medieval charm, and are best enjoyed by adapting to the pace of the countryside. So...slow...down...and enjoy the delights that these villages offer. Spend the night if you can, as many hill towns are mobbed by day-trippers.

Planning Your Time

How in Dante's name does a traveler choose from the literally hundreds of Central Italy's hill towns? I cover some of the best towns in this chapter (listed roughly from north to south). The one(s) you visit will depend on your time, interests, and mode of transportation. There's no hard-and-fast best plan. Go where you want, stay as long as you want.

Multi-towered San Gimignano is a classic, but peak-season crowds can overwhelm the town's charms. Volterra and Chiusi rate highly on the Etruscan trail. Wine aficionados won't want to miss Montalcino or Montepulciano. Fans of architecture and urban design will appreciate Pienza's well-planned streets and squares. Art-lovers and those eager to trace Frances Mayes' footsteps under the Tuscan sun will make the pilgrimage to Cortona. The grand, classic town of Orvieto is famous for its wine, ceramics, and colorful Duomo. But my longtime favorite is the tiny, obscure, and (to be honest) dying hill town of Civita.

For a relaxing break from the intensity, traffic, and mandatory museums of big-city Italy, settle down in an *agriturismo*—a farmhouse that rents out rooms to travelers (usually for a minimum of a week in high season). These rural B&Bs—almost by definition in the middle of nowhere—provide a good home base from which to find the magic of

Hill Towns of Central Italy

Italy's hill towns. I've listed several good options throughout this chapter (for more information, see page 28 in the Introduction).

Getting around the Hill Towns

Bigger destinations (like Cortona, Orvieto, and Civita) are doable by public transportation. Smaller hill towns are easier to visit by car.

By Bus or Train: Traveling by public transportation is an economical way to see the countryside and rub elbows with the locals. While trains connect some of the smaller towns like Cortona and Chiusi, the train stations are likely to be in the valley several miles from the town center, usually connected by a local bus.

Buses are most often the better, if not the only, choice to connect destinations. Siena is a great hub of local bus lines. You can find schedules at local TIs and buy tickets at newsstands or tobacco shops (look for the black sign with a big white T on it). Confirm the departure point (*Dov'è la fermata?*). Some piazzas have more than one bus stop, so double-check that the posted schedule lists your destination and departure

Hill Towns: Public Transportation

time. In general, orange buses are local city buses and blue buses are for long distances.

Once the bus arrives, confirm the destination with the driver. You are expected to stow big packs underneath the bus (open the luggage compartment if it's closed). Sundays and holidays are problematic. Buses, even from large cities like Siena, have sparse schedules and the few departing ones are usually jam-packed. Bus ticket offices are often closed on Sundays, so make plans and buy your ticket ahead of time. If you must travel on a day when there are few choices (like Easter), drop into a travel agency and ask for help. Most agencies book bus and train tickets with little or no commission.

By Car: A car is the best way to maximize your time in Italy's hill towns. Since a car is a headache in big cities (such as Florence and Siena), pick up your car in the last big city you visit, then head to the countryside. Get a big, detailed regional road map at a newsstand. Although roads are numbered on the map, you will not find any numbers referenced on the actual road signs. Roads are indicated by blue signs with a city name on them (e.g., if you want to take route 146 out of Montepulciano to the west, look for signs leading to Pienza, the next town along this route to the west).

For two particularly scenic drives, from Siena to Montalcino, and from Montalcino to Montepulciano, see the Crete Senese Drives suggested below, under "More Hill Towns and Sights," page 393.

If you are staying overnight, ask your hotelier for parking suggestions. Keep all valuables out of sight and locked in the trunk of the car.

San Gimignano

The epitome of a Tuscan hill town, with 14 medieval towers still standing (out of an original 72!), San Gimignano is a perfectly preserved tourist trap, so easy to visit and visually pleasing that it's a good stop.

In the 13th century, back in the days of Romeo and Juliet, towns were run by feuding noble families. They'd periodically battle things out from the protection of their respective family towers. Pointy skylines were the norm in medieval Tuscany. But in San Gimignano, fabric was big business, and many of its towers were built simply to hang dyed fabric out to dry.

While the basic three-star sight here is the town of San Gimignano itself, there are a few worthwhile stops. From the town gate, shop straight up the traffic-free town's cobbled main drag to Piazza del Cisterna (with its 13th-century well). The town sights cluster around the adjoining Piazza del Duomo. Thursday is market day (on Piazza Duomo), but for local merchants, every day is a sales frenzy.

Tourist Information: The helpful TI is in the old center on Piazza Duomo (daily March–Oct 9:00–13:00 & 15:00–19:00, Nov–Feb 9:00–13:00 & 14:00–18:00, free maps, sells bus tickets, books rooms, tel. 0577-940-008, www.sangimignano.com, prolocsg@tin.it, SE). A public WC is just off Piazza della Cisterna (€.50).

SIGHTS

Collegiata—This Romanesque church, with round windows and wide steps, is filled with fine Renaissance frescoes, some painted by Domenico Ghirlandaio (€3.50, €5.50 combo-ticket includes mediocre Religious Art Museum, Mon–Fri 9:30–19:30, Sat 9:30–17:00, Sun 13:00–17:00).
Civic Museum (Museo Civico)—This is a small, fun museum inside the City Hall (Palazzo Comunale). As you enter, head right, into the room called Sala di Consiglio. It's *molto* medieval and covered in festive frescoes, including the *Maesta* by Lippo Memmi. This virtual copy of Simone Martini's *Maesta* in Siena proves that Memmi doesn't have quite

San Gimignano

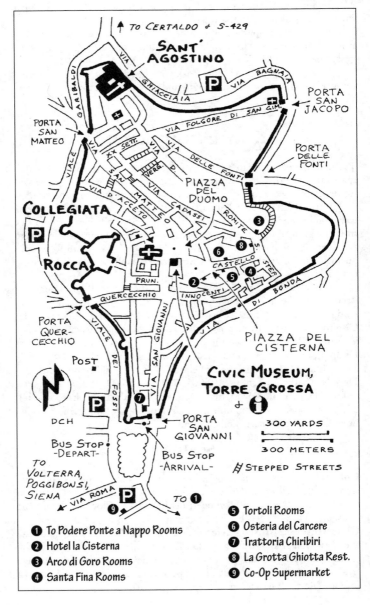

TO CERTALDO & S-429

SANT' AGOSTINO

VIA GHIACCIAIA

VIA BAGNAIA

VIA GARIBALDI

PORTA SAN JACOPO

VIA FOLGORE DI SAN GIM.

PORTA SAN MATTEO

PORTA DELLE FONTI

VIALE

VIA SETTI

XX SETT.

VIA D. VERG.

VIA DELLE FONTI

VIA SAN MATTEO

VIA D'ACCETO

VIA CADASSI

PIAZZA DEL DUOMO

ROMITE

S.

3

COLLEGIATA

8

6

ROCCA

PRUN.

QUERCECCHIO

CASTELLO

5

4

STEF.

DI BONDA

2

INNOCENTI

VIA

PORTA QUER-CECCHIO

VIALE DEI FOSSI

VIA SAN GIOVANNI

PIAZZA DEL CISTERNA

Post

CIVIC MUSEUM, TORRE GROSSA

7

& 🛈

DCH

PORTA SAN GIOVANNI

300 YARDS

Bus Stop -DEPART-

Bus Stop -ARRIVAL-

300 METERS

TO VOLTERRA, POGGIBONSI, SIENA

STEPPED STREETS

VIA ROMA

9

TO 1

❶ To Podere Ponte a Nappo Rooms
❷ Hotel la Cisterna
❸ Arco di Goro Rooms
❹ Santa Fina Rooms

❺ Tortoli Rooms
❻ Osteria del Carcere
❼ Trattoria Chiribiri
❽ La Grotta Ghiotta Rest.
❾ Co-Op Supermarket

the same talent as his famous brother-in-law. Upstairs the Pinacoteca displays a classy little painting collection, with a 1422 altarpiece by Taddeo di Bartolo honoring Saint Gimignano. You can see the saint with the town in his hands surrounded by events from his life. As you exit, be sure to stop by the Camera del Podesta to check out the medieval dating scene (€5, includes Torre Grossa, daily 9:30–19:30, Nov–Feb 10:00–17:00, includes Torre Grossa).

Torre Grossa—The city's tallest tower, at 200 feet, can be scaled (€5, includes Civic Museum, same hours as museum).

Sant' Agostino Church—This peaceful church, at the opposite end of town, has fewer crowds and more soul. Behind the altar, a lovely fresco cycle by Benozzo Gozzoli (who painted a chapel in the Medici-Riccardi Palace in Florence) tells of the life of Saint Augustine, a North African monk who preached simplicity. The kind, English-speaking friars are happy to tell you about their church and way of life, and also have Mass in English on Sundays. Pace the tranquil cloister before heading back into the tourist mobs (free, but €.50 lights the frescoes, daily 7:00–12:00 & 15:00–19:00).

Rocca—Formerly Florentine fortifications, these walls now enclose a park that's perfect for picnicking. Climb the steep stairs on the corner tower for a great (and free) view of the towers.

SLEEPING

Although the town is a zoo during the daytime, when evening comes, locals outnumber tourists and San Gimignano becomes peaceful and enjoyable.

$$$ **Podere Ponte a Nappo**, run by Carla Rossi, is a comfortable farmhouse just outside of the city gates. The tastefully decorated apartments and rooms are surrounded by vineyards and a view of San Gimignano (Db-€100, Tb-€115, Qb-€130, no CC, 15-min walk or 5-min drive from Porta San Giovanni, parking, air-con, tel. 0577-907-282, fax 0577-941-268, www.appartamentirossicarla.com, cabusini@tin.it).

$$ **Hotel la Cisterna**, right on Piazza Cisterna, offers 49 clean, predictable rooms, some with panoramic view terraces (Sb-€70, Db-€90, Db with view-€103, Db with terrace-€115, buffet breakfast, elevator, good restaurant with great view, discounts off-season, closed Jan–Feb, Piazza della Cisterna 24, tel. 0577-940-328, fax 0577-942-080, www.hotelcisterna.it, info@hotelcisterna.it, Alessio SE).

$$ Enterprising **Carla Rossi,** who runs Poldere Ponte a Nappo above, also rents rooms and apartments—most with views—throughout the town. You could rent rooms in the charming little houses of **Arco di Goro** and **Santa Fina**, while **Tortoli** has elegant rooms in a medieval tower overlooking Piazza Cisterna (Db-from €60, most around €100, Tb & Qb around €110–150, no CC, no breakfast, Via di Cellole 81, tel.

SLEEP CODE

(€1 = about $1.10, country code: 39)
Sleep Code: **S** = Single, **D** = Double/Twin, **T** = Triple, **Q** = Quad, **b** = bathroom, **s** = shower only, **no CC** = Credit Cards not accepted, **SE** = Speaks English, **NSE** = No English. Unless otherwise noted, credit cards are accepted.

To help you sort easily through these listings, I've divided the rooms into three categories based on the price for a standard double room with bath:

$$$ **Higher Priced**—Most rooms €100 or more.
$$ **Moderately Priced**—Most rooms between €70-100.
$ **Lower Priced**—Most rooms €70 or less.

& fax 0577-955-041, mobile 349-882-1565, www.appartamentirossi carla.com, cabusini@tin.it, son Francesco SE).

$ Associazione Strutture Extralberghiere is a clearinghouse for reasonably-priced private rooms around the city (Db-€60, no CC, no breakfast, Piazza della Cisterna, tel. 0577-943-190).

EATING

Osteria del Carcere has good food and prices (12:30–15:00 & 19:30–22:00, closed Wed and lunch Thu; Via del Castello 13, just off Piazza della Cisterna; tel. 0577-941-905).

The tiny **Trattoria Chiribiri,** just inside Porta San Giovanni, serves homemade pasta and desserts at a remarkably fair price (daily 11:00–23:00, Piazza della Madonna 1, tel. 0577-941-948).

La Grotta Ghiotta makes good soup and sandwiches that can be packed up *portare via*—to go (daily 10:00–20:00, Via Santo Stefano 10, tel. 0577-942-074)

Picnics: Co-Op sells all you need for a nice spread (Mon–Sat 8:30–20:00, closed Sun, at parking lot below Porta San Giovanni). Or browse the shops guarded by wild boar statues to buy boar by the gram. Pick up some boar (*cinghiale;* cheeng-gee-AH-lay), cheese, bread, and wine and enjoy a picnic in the garden at the Rocca or the park outside Porta San Giovanni.

TRANSPORTATION CONNECTIONS

By bus to: Florence (hrly, 75 min, change in Poggibonsi), **Siena** (5/day, 1.25 hrs, more with change in Poggibonsi), **Volterra** (4/day, 2 hrs, change in Colle di Val d'Elsa). Sunday buses are few, far between, and crowded. In San Gimignano, bus tickets are sold at the bar just inside the town gate or at the TI. The town has no baggage-check service.

Drivers: You can't drive within the walled town of San Gimignano, but a car park awaits just a few steps outside.

Volterra

Encircled by impressive walls and topped with a grand fortress, Volterra sits high above the rich farmland below. More than 2,000 years ago, Volterra was one of the most important Etruscan cities, an ancient cultural center much larger than the hill town we see today. Greek-trained Etruscan artists worked in the city and outlying areas, leaving a significant stash of art, particularly funerary urns. Eventually absorbed into the Roman Empire, the city bitterly fought against the Florentines in the Middle Ages, but like many Tuscan towns, lost in the end and was given a fortress atop the city to "protect" its citizens.

Compact and walkable, the city stretches out from the pleasant Piazza dei Priori to the old city gates. Time here is best spent in the Etruscan Museum or Roman Theater, but a couple of the city's other sights are worth a peek. With multiple connections and limited bus schedules, public transportation here is doable but tricky. Check bus schedules carefully for return trips.

Tourist Information: The information-packed TI is in Piazza dei Priori, next to the City Hall (daily 10:00–13:00 & 14:00–17:00, closed Nov, books rooms, tel. 058-886-099, www.volterratur.it, info@volterratur.it). Audioguides are rented here for use around the city and in the museums (€5, 40–90 min).

SIGHTS

Etruscan Museum (Museo Etrusco Guarnacci)—Filled top to bottom with rare Etruscan artifacts, this museum—even with few English explanations—makes it easy to appreciate how advanced this pre-Roman culture was. Don't miss the oddly modern figurine *Ombre della Sera* or the wrinkled, realistic faces on the funerary urn, *Urna degli Sposi* (€7, includes— like it or not—Pinacoteca and Sacred Art Museum; daily 9:00–19:00, Nov–March closes at 14:00; mildly interesting English pamphlet available, audioguide available at TI; Via Don Minzoni 15; tel. 058-886-347).

Pinacoteca—See this eerily-lit museum for the last room, two huge Luca Signorelli paintings and another by Rosso Fiorentino. You might as well; it's included in the Etruscan museum admission (€7 combo-ticket, daily 9:00–19:00, Via dei Sarti 1, tel. 058-887-580).

Roman Theater—This well-preserved theater is one of the few to have part of the stage remaining (€2, includes less-interesting Etruscan Acropolis in Parco Archeologico, or view it free from Via Lungo le Mure, daily 10:00–13:00 & 14:00–17:45, Nov–March weekends only).

Palazzo dei Priori—When not in use as the City Hall, the council chambers—lavishly painted and lit with fun dragon lamps—are open to visitors (€1, may be possible to scale tower, daily 10:00–13:00 & 14:00–18:00).

Duomo—This 13th-century church may not be as elaborate as its cousin in Pisa, but the simple facade and golden coffered ceiling are beautiful examples of the Pisan Romanesque style. The chapel to the left of the entry has unusual, large dioramas with painted terracotta figures (Mon–Sat 9:00–13:00 & 15:00–19:00, Sun 15:00–19:00).

SLEEPING

(€1 = about $1.10, country code: 39)

$$$ **Hotel la Locanda,** near the Roman Theater, is fancy, with nicely furnished rooms and huge bathrooms (Sb-€90, Db-from €115, elevator, air-con, Via Guarnacci 24, tel. 058-881-547 fax 058-881-541, www .hotel-lalocanda.com, staff@hotel-lalocanda.com, SE).

$ **Albergo Nazionale,** with 40 rooms, is clean, simple, and steps from the bus stop (Sb-€50, Db-€68, Tb-€80, less off-season, breakfast-€6, Via dei Marchesi 11, tel. 058-886-284, fax 058-884-097, www .albergonazionalevolterra.it, nazionalevolterra@tiscalinet.it).

$ Consider **Ostello della Gioventu** for budget beds a short walk from the Etruscan Museum (bed-€16, no CC, Via del Poggetto 3, tel. & fax 058-885-577).

EATING

Ristorante Etruria makes tasty ravioli, served in a frescoed dining room or on the piazza (€15 menu turistico, daily 12:00–15:00 & 19:00–22:00, closed Wed in winter, Piazza dei Priori 6, tel. 058-886-064).

For fresh sandwiches and wine, try friendly **Enoteca Scali** (daily 9:00–21:00, Via Guarnacci 13, tel. 058-881-170).

You can assemble a picnic at the few Alimentari around town (try Spar Market, Via Gramsci 12) and eat in the breezy Parco Archeologico.

TRANSPORTATION CONNECTIONS

To: Florence (4 buses/day, 2 hrs, change in Colle Val D'Elsa), **Siena** (4 buses/day, 2 hrs, change in Colle Val D'Elsa), **San Gimignano** (4 buses/day, 2 hrs, change in Colle Val D'Elsa), **Pisa** (9 buses/day, 2 hrs, change in Pontedera). Buses arrive in and depart from Volterra's Piazzi Martiri della Liberta (buy tickets at any tabacchi shop). For Siena, Florence, and San Gimignano, Tra-in bus tickets only get you as far as Colle Val D'Elsa; you must buy another ticket (for the other bus company) at the newsstand near the bus stop. There is virtually no bus service in or out of Volterra on Sundays and holidays.

Drivers: Easy parking lots are near the Roman Theater and underground, near Porta all'Arco (€1/hour or €10/24 hrs).

Montalcino

On a hill overlooking vineyards and valleys below, Montalcino—famous for its delicious and pricey Brunello di Montalcino red wines—is a must-sip for wine lovers.

In the Middle Ages, Montalcino (mohn-tahl-CHEE-noh) was considered Siena's biggest ally. Originally allied with Florence, the town switched sides after the Sienese beat up Florence in the battle of Monteaperti in 1260. The Sienese persuaded the Montalcini to their views by forcing them to sleep one night in the bloody, Florentine-strewn battlefield.

Montalcino prospered under Siena, but like its ally, waned after the Medici family took control of the region. The village regained fame when, in the late 19th century, the Biondi Santi family created a fine, dark red wine, calling it "the brunette."

Non–wine-lovers may find Montalcino a bit too focused on *vino*, but one sip of Brunello makes even wine skeptics believe that Bacchus was on to something. Note that the Rosso di Montalcino wine is also good at half the price. Those with sweet tooths will enjoy munching Ossi di Morta ("bones of the dead"), a crunchy cookie with almonds.

Tourist Information: The TI is just off Piazza Garibaldi, in the city hall (daily 10:00–13:00, 14:00–17:50, closed Mon in winter, tel. & fax 0577-849331, www.prolocomontalcino.it, info@prolocomontalcino .it, some English).

SIGHTS

Fortezza—The 14th-century fort, built under the rule of Siena, now houses an *enoteca* wine bar (see below). Climb the ramparts to enjoy a panoramic view of the Asso and Orcia valleys, or enjoy a picnic in the park surrounding the fort (€3.50 for rampart walk, daily 9:00–20:00, closed Monday off-season).

Museo Civico—Gothic art is the star of this museum, with works from Montalcino's heyday, the 13th- to 16th-centuries. Wooden sculptures and religious objects round out the collection (€4.50, €6 combo-ticket includes fort, Tue–Sun 10:00–13:00, 14:00–17:50, closed Mon, Via Ricasoli, tel. 0577-846-014).

Wineries—While there are plenty of *enotecas*, there are no real wineries inside the city. The countryside, however, is littered with them, and most wineries will give tastings, but require an appointment. Banfi is the most touristy and produces well-respected wines (tours Mon–Fri 16:00, 10 min south of Montalcino in Sant' Angelo Scalo, reserve in advance, tel. 0577-840111, www.castellobanfi.com, reservations@banfi.it). The TI can give you the list of more than 150 others to choose from (www.consorziobrunellodimontalcino.it, consbrun@tin.it).

SLEEPING

(€1 = about $1.10, country code: 39)

$$ **Albergo il Giglio**, although lacking in warmth, has 12 comfortable rooms, some with vaulted ceilings. Ask for a room with a view (Sb-€53, Db-€80, Tb-€85, breakfast-€6.50, Via Saloni 5, tel. & fax 0577-848-167, hotelgiglio@tin.it).

$ **Ristorante il Moro** rents four pleasant, modern rooms around the corner from their restaurant. The two upper rooms have views, the lower have terraces, and they all share a cozy common room with a kitchen (Db-€50, no breakfast, Via Mazzini 4, tel. 0577-849-384, Alessandro & Julia SE).

$ **Affittacamere Mariuccia** is basic and drab, but central and cheap (Sb-€35, Db-€44, no breakfast, air-con, check-in at Enoteca Pierangioli, Piazza del Popolo 16, tel. & fax 0577-849-113, www.enotecapierangioli.com, enotecapierangioli@hotmail.com, Stefania NSE).

$$ *Agriturismo*: **La Crociona,** a farm and working vineyard, rents seven fully-equipped apartments. Fiorella Vannoni and Roberto and Barbara Nannetti offer cooking classes and tastes of the Brunello wine grown and bottled on the premises (Db-€90, Qb-€130, lower weekly rates, pool, La Croce, 7-min drive from Montalcino, tel. 0577-847-133, tel. & fax 0577-848-007, www.lacrociona.com, lacrociona@tin.it, SE).

EATING

Taverna Il Grappolo Blu is dressy yet friendly, serving local specialties and vegetarian options (Sat–Thu 12:00–15:30 & 19:00–22:00, closed Fri, Scale di Via Moglio 1, tel. 0577-847-150, Luciano SE).

Trattoria Sciame, a family-run hole-in-the-wall, has nine small tables and homemade desserts (pasta-€7, meat-€8, Wed–Mon 12:00–14:30 & 19:00–21:30, closed Tue, Via Ricasoli 9, tel. 0577-848-017).

Gather ingredients for a picnic at the **Co-Op supermarket** on Via Ricasoli, then enjoy your feast in front of the Fortezza. **Market day** is Friday, in Viale della Liberta (7:00–13:00).

Wine Tasting

The medieval setting inside Montalcino's fort at **Enoteca La Fortezza** makes this a fun place for a glass or three of local wine. Spoil yourself with Brunello in the cozy enoteca or at outdoor tables (3 tastes for €12, snacks for two-€8, daily 9:00–20:00, closes at 18:00 and on Mon off-season, inside the Fortezza, tel. 0577-849-211, www.enotecalafortezza.it).

Ferruccio Biondi-Santi, the founder of the café, **Fiaschetteria Italiana**, was also the creator of the famous Brunello wine. The wine library in the back boasts many choices of local wine, including a prized bottle from 1955, a vintage year. A meeting place since 1888, this grand café also serves light lunches and espresso to tourists and locals alike (€8–10 for glass of Brunello and plate of snacks, daily 7:30–24:00, Piazza del Popolo 6, tel. 0577-849-043).

TRANSPORTATION CONNECTIONS

To: Siena (10 buses/day, 90 min), **Montepulciano/Pienza** (10 buses/day, change to line #114 in Torrenieri, 60 min plus transfer time). Bus tickets are sold at tobacco shops or on board. The town has no baggage-check service.

Montepulciano

Curving its way along a ridge, Montepulciano (mohn-tay-PULL-chee-ah-noh) delights visitors with *vino* and views. Alternately under Sienese and Florentine rule, the city still retains its medieval *contrade* districts, each with a mascot and flag. The neighborhoods compete the last Sunday of August in the *Bravio delle Botti*, where teams of men push large wine casks uphill from Piazza Marzocco to Piazza Grande, all hoping to win a banner and bragging rights.

The city is a collage of architectural styles, but the elegant San Biagio Church, at the base of the hill, is the most impressive Renaissance building. Most ignore the architecture and focus more on the city's other creative accomplishment, the tasty Vino Nobile di Montepulciano red wine.

The action in Montepulciano centers on two streets, the steep Via di Gracciano nel Corso, and Via Ricci, but the quiet back streets are well worth a visit.

Tourist Information: The TI is on Via Gracciano nel Corso 26, not to be confused with the more central and less helpful "Strada del Vino" office on Piazza Grande (daily March–Oct 9:30–13:00 & 15:00–18:30, closed Tue, tel. 0578-717-242, www.comune.montepulciano .si.it, prolocomp@bccmp.com).

Helpful Hints: Market day is Thursday, and a larger market takes place at the bus station on Saturday (8:00–14:00). Public WCs are located next to Palazzo del Comune and the church of St. Augustine.

SIGHTS

Piazza Grande—This pleasant, lively piazza is surrounded by an architectural grab-bag. The medieval Palazzo del Comune has a Florentine-style **clock tower;** you can climb to the top for a windy, panoramic view (€1.55, daily 10:00–18:00). The Palazzo de' Nobili-Tarugi is a Renaissance arcaded confection, while the unfinished Duomo glumly looks on, wishing the city hadn't run out of money for the facade. Dream up a way to finish it while you enjoy a cappuccino at the café on the square.

Civic Museum (Museo Civico)—Small and eclectic, this well-presented museum is worthwhile if only for its colorful Della Robbia ceramic altarpieces (€4.13, Tue–Sat 10:00–13:00 & 15:00–18:00, Sun 10:00–18:00, closed Mon, Via Ricci, tel. 0578-715-322).

San Biagio Church—Down a picturesque driveway lined with cypress, this church—designed by Antonio da Sangallo—is Renaissance perfection. The proportions of the Greek cross plan give the building a pleasing rhythmic quality. The lone tower was supposed to have a twin, but it was never built. The soaring interior is impressive, with a high dome and lantern (daily 9:00–13:00 & 15:00–19:00). The street Via di San Biagio, leading from the church up into town, makes for an enjoyable, if challenging walk.

Cantinas—Montepulciano's most popular attraction is its Vino Nobile. This robust red wine can be tasted in any of the cantinas lining Via Ricci and Via nel Corso, but **Contucci** is the most famous. Lively Adamo has been making wine since 1953 and welcomes tourists into his cellar with warmth and wisecracks (€5.50 for guided visit and 4 tastes, no reservation necessary, Piazza Grande 7, tel. 0578-717-484). The information office for the "Strada del Vino" on Piazza Grande may not give out much city information, but it does organize **wine tours** in the city (€13, Wed 17:30) and minibus winery tours farther afield (€21, Thu 13:30, call for current days and times, tel. 0578-717-484, www.stradavinonobile.it, info@stradavinonobile.it).

SLEEPING

(€1 = about $1.10, country code: 39)

$$ **Mueble il Riccio** (hedgehog in Italian) is medieval-elegant, with modern rooms, a view terrace, and friendly owners. When Giorgio isn't manning the desk, he's out giving country tours in one of his classic Italian cars (Sb-€75, Db-€85, Tb-€105, breakfast-€8, Via Talosa 21, tel. & fax 0578-757-713, www.ilriccio.net, info@ilriccio.net, *poco* English).

$ **Camere Bellavista** has simple rooms with views, and nicer rooms without. Room 6 has a view terrace worth reserving (standard Db-€55, nicer Db-€65, no CC, no breakfast, no elevator, Via Ricci 25, tel. 0347-823-2314, fax 0578-716-341, bellavista@bccmp.com, NSE).

EATING

Ai Quattro Venti is fresh, flavorful, fun, and right on Piazza Grande. Mushroom fans should try anything with the word *bosco* in it (pasta-€7, Fri–Wed 12:00–14:00 & 19:00–22:00, closed Thu, next to city hall on Piazza Grande, tel. 0578-717-231).

Osteria dell'Aquacheta serves pasta and salads at reasonable prices, with a mix of locals and tourists (€5 pasta and salads, Wed–Mon 12:30–15:00 & 19:30–22:30, closed Tue, Via del Teatro 22, tel. 0578-717-086).

TRANSPORTATION CONNECTIONS

To: Siena (8 buses/day, 1.25 hrs, few in afternoon, none on Sun), **Pienza** (8 buses/day, 30 min). The town has no baggage-check service.

Drivers: Route 146 to Montalcino is particularly scenic (see Crete Senese drive on page 395). It isn't wise to drive the tiny roads inside the city, so park outside the walls, either at the bus station or at the numerous lots on the edges of town.

Pienza

Set on a crest, surrounded by green, rolling hills, the small town of Pienza packs a lot of Renaissance punch. In the 1400s, locally-born pope Pius II of the Piccolomini family decided to remodel his hometown in the current Renaissance style. Propelled by papal clout, the town of Corsignano was transformed—in only five year's time—into a jewel of Renaissance architecture and renamed Pienza (after pope Pius). The plan was to remodel the whole town, but work ended in 1564 when both the pope and his architect, Bernardo Rossellino, died. The architectural focal point is the square Piazza Pio II, surrounded by the Duomo and pope's family residence, Palazzo Piccolomini. The culinary focal point is Pecorino cheese, a pungent sheep's cheese, which can be found at almost any shop and can be eaten fresh *(fresco)* or aged *(secco)*.

Tourist Information: The TI is on Piazza Pio II, across from the Duomo (Mon–Sat 9:30–13:00 & 15:00–18:30, closed Sun, tel. & fax 0578-749-071, www.comunedipienza.it, infopienza@quipo.it, little English). Audioguides are available for self-guided walking tours (€5.16, 50 min). **Market day** is Friday.

SIGHTS

Piazza Pio II—One of the classic piazzas in Italy, this square is famous for its elegance and artistic unity. The square and the surrounding buildings were all designed by Rossellino to form an "outdoor room." The well near the palazzo is also a work of art.

Duomo—Its classic, symmetrical Renaissance facade dominates Piazza Pio, but cannot disguise the fact that the altar is slowly sliding down the mountain. It began sagging only 10 years after construction and, despite attempts to shore it up, remains downwardly mobile. The interior is charming, with several Gothic altarpieces and painted arches. Windows feature the crest of Pius II, with five half-moons advertising the number of crusades his family funded. The left side of the church suffers the most from the faulty foundation. To measure the movement, bow-tie-shaped pieces of glass were recently set into the floor, bridging the cracks. Although it was thought that the foundation had been fixed, the glass pieces cracked. To the left of the altar, two slanty chapels might make you feel dizzy.

Palazzo Piccolomini—The home of Pius II and the Piccolomini family until 1962, the interior can be visited with a guided tour. Check out the well-preserved painted courtyard for free. In Renaissance times, most buildings were covered with elaborate paintings like these (€3, Tue–Sun 10:00–12:30 & 15:00–18:00, closed Mon).

Museo Diocesano—This museum contains religious paintings from local churches (€4.13, Wed–Mon 10:00–13:00 & 15:00–18:30, closed Tue).

View Terrace—Romantics walk up Via dell' Amore (street of love) or Via del Bacio (street of the kiss) to the panoramic promenade next to the Duomo. Views from the terrace include the Tuscan countryside and Monte Amiata, the largest mountain in southern Tuscany, in the distance.

SLEEPING

(€1 = about $1.10, country code: 39)
$ Oliviera Camere has five simple rooms in the center of town, run by

soft-spoken Nello (Db-€50, no CC, breakfast in room, Via Condotti 4, tel. 0578-748-205, NSE).

$$ *Agriturismo*: **Agriturismo Terrapille** sits just below Pienza, surrounded by dreamy scenery. Three country rooms with modern comforts, all within a mile of town make this a possibility for those without wheels (Db-€88, Qb-€190, breakfast-€6.50, dinner available, pool, take road #18 in direction of Monte Amiata, tel. & fax 0578-749-146, www.terrapille.it, terrapile@bccmp.com, SE).

EATING

Latte di Luna is a good, quality choice in a town of mediocre food (Wed–Mon 12:30–14:30 & 19:30–21:30, closed Tue, Via San Carlo 2, reservations suggested, tel. 0578-748-606).

La Taverna di Re Artu serves bruschetta and a variety of wines (daily 10:30–20:30, Via della Rosa 4).

Assemble a picnic at any of the numerous cheese and wine shops, and dine with a fantastic view along the walls of the view terrace.

TRANSPORTATION CONNECTIONS

To: Siena (6 buses/day, 90 min), **Montepulciano** (8 buses/day, 30 min). Bus tickets are sold at the bar just inside the town gate. The town has no baggage-check service.

Cortona

Cortona clings by its fingernails to the top of a mountain (1,700 feet), dangling above views of the Tuscan and Umbrian landscape below. Frances Mayes' books, such as *Under the Tuscan Sun,* have placed this town in the touristic limelight, just as Peter Mayle's books popularized (and populated) the Luberon region in France. But even before Mayes ever published a book, Cortona was considered one of the classic Tuscan hill towns.

The city began as one of the largest Etruscan settlements, the remains of which can be seen at the base of the city walls, as well as in the nearby tombs. It grew to its present size in the 13th to 15th centuries, when it was a colorful and crowded city, eventually allied with Florence.

The farmland that fills almost every view from the city was marshy and uninhabitable until about 300 years ago, when it was drained and turned into some of the most fertile land in Tuscany.

Bring good walking shoes; the streets here can be steep and unforgiving. Mercifully, most of Cortona's sights and shops cluster around the

Cortona

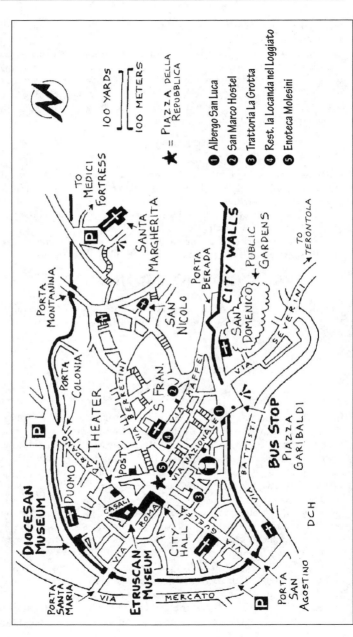

100 YARDS
100 METERS

★ = PIAZZA DELLA REPUBBLICA

1 Albergo San Luca
2 San Marco Hostel
3 Trattoria La Grotta
4 Rest. la Locanda nel Loggiato
5 Enoteca Molesini

TO MEDICI FORTRESS

SANTA MARGHERITA

PORTA BERADA

PORTA MONTANINA

PORTA COLONIA

SAN NICOLO

PUBLIC GARDENS

SAN DOMENICO

CITY WALLS

TO TERONTOLA

THEATER

S. FRAN.

VIA BERRETTINI

VIA MAFFEI

VIA NAZIONALE

VIA SEVERINI

VIA BATTISTI

BUS STOP

PIAZZA GARIBALDI

DIOCESAN MUSEUM

DUOMO

VIA CASALI

POST

VIA RUGA

VIA ROMA

VIA GUELFI

CITY HALL

ETRUSCAN MUSEUM

PORTA SANTA MARIA

VIA MERCATO

PORTA SAN AGOSTINO

DCH

level streets on the Piazza Garibaldi-to-Piazza del Duomo axis.

Art-lovers will know Cortona as the home of Renaissance painter Luca Signorelli, Baroque master Pietro della Cortona (Berretini), and the 20th-century Futurist artist Gino Severini. Cortona's museums and churches reveal many of the works of these native sons.

Tourist Information: The helpful TI is on the main drag, Via Nazionale 42 (daily March–Oct 9:00–13:00 & 15:00–19:00, cash machine, also sells train tickets, tel. 0575-630-352, info@cortonantiquaria.com, SE). **Market day** is Saturday (early–14:00, Piazza Signorelli).

Arrival in Cortona: You'll probably arrive at Piazza Garibaldi, where the bus stop is located outside the massive town walls. From here it is a level five-minute walk down bustling shop-lined Via Nazionale (stop by the TI) to Piazza della Reppublica, the heart of the town, dominated by the City Hall (Palazzo della Comune). From this square it's a five-minute level walk past the interesting Etruscan Museum and theater to Piazza Duomo, where you'll find the recommended Diocesan Museum. Steep streets, many of them stepped, lead from Piazza della Repubblica up to the San Nicolo and Santa Margherita churces and the Medici Fortress (30 min).

SIGHTS

Etruscan Museum (Museo della Accademia Etrusca)—Established in 1787, this was one of the first galleries dedicated to artifacts from the Etruscan civilization. The impressive display includes an intricate fifth-century B.C. chandelier and some fantastic gold and turquoise jewelry. This eclectic museum also has an Egyptian section and a room dedicated to modern works by Severini (€4.20, Tue–Sun 10:00–19:00, closed Mon, guided tour-€7, see ticket office for times, Palazzo Casali on Piazza Signorelli, tel. 0575-630-415, www.accademia-etrusca.net, info@accademia-etrusca.net).

Diocesan Museum (Museo Diocesano)—This collection, housed in the Gesu Church, has pieces by Beato Angelico and Duccio, but the highlights are the paintings by hometown hero and Renaissance master, Luca Signorelli (€5, daily 10:00–19:00, closed Mon Nov–March, Piazza del Duomo 1, tel. 0575-637-235).

San Nicolo Church—Signorelli fans will want to make the pilgimage up to this tiny church. Ring the bell and the caretaker will give you a short tour (in Italian) of this humble church including the highlight—an altarpiece by Signorelli that is painted on both sides. The caretaker will activate a tricky arm mechanism that moves the picture away from the wall to reveal the painting behind it. There's no admission fee, but you should tip the caretaker a euro or two.

From San Niccolo, a steep path leads uphill 10 minutes to the...

Santa Margherita Church—This church houses the remains of the town's patron saint. Saint Margaret was an unwed mother from Montepulciano who found her calling with the Franciscans in Cortona where she tended to the sick and poor. Her son eventually became a Franciscan monk.

Still need more altitude? Head uphill five minutes more to the Medici Fortress. It's usually closed, but the views are stunning, stretching all the way to distant Lake Trasimeno, where Hannibal defeated the Romans in the Punic Wars.

Near Cortona: Etruscan Tombs—Visits to nearby *melone* (melons, named for their shape) can easily be arranged with the Etruscan Museum. Just a couple miles out of town, the road is dotted with tombs dating as back as far as seventh-century B.C. (compulsory guided visit-€10.50, arrange through museum or Aioncultura, tel. 0575-630-415, meet at tomb site, www.aioncultura.org, aioncultura@aioncultura.org).

SLEEPING

(€1 = about $1.10, country code: 39)

$$$ Albergo San Luca, perched on a cliffside, has 54 modern, business-class, impersonal rooms, half with stunning views of Lago Trasimeno. Right at the bus stop, it's perfect if you want to avoid dragging your bags up the hill (Sb-€70, Db-€100, popular with Americans and groups, reserve view rooms ASAP, Piazza Garibaldi 1, tel. 0575-630-460, fax 0575-630-105, www.sanlucacortona.com, info@sanlucacortona.com, SE).

$ San Marco Hostel, at the top of town, housed in a remodeled 13th-century palace, is one of Italy's best (€10.50, in rooms with 2, 4 or 8 beds, lockout 11:00–17:00, Via Maffei 57, tel. 0575-601-392, SE).

Near Cortona

$$$ Casa San Martino, 12 miles east of Cortona near the isolated village of Lisciano Niccone, is a 250-year-old countryside farmhouse run as a B&B by American Italophile Lois Martin. While Lois reserves the summer (June–Aug) for one-week stays, she'll take guests staying a minimum of three nights for the rest of the year (Db-€160, 10 percent discount for my readers—mention this book when you reserve, includes breakfast, pool, washer/dryer, house rental available, Casa San Martino 19, Lisciano Niccone, tel. 075-844-288, fax 075-844-422). Lois' neighbors, Ernestine and Gisbert Schwanke, run the tidy **La Villetta di San Martino B&B** (Db-€110 includes breakfast, 2-night min, common kitchen and sitting room, San Martino 36, tel. & fax 075-844-309, erni@netemedia.net, SE).

$$ Castello di Montegualandro is a well-preserved castle on a hill opposite Cortona, overlooking the lake and countryside. Christina and dad, Claudio, rent four charming medieval apartments, formerly peasants' quarters, inside the peaceful castle walls. Each one is unique and named for its former use—the Fornaio's sunken living room used to be a kiln. The castle's chapel is a popular spot for weddings (3–4 person apartment-€100, 3-night min, mention this book for a 7 percent discount, discounts for longer stays, no CC; 10 min southeast of Cortona, Tuoro sul Trasimeno; tel. & fax 075-8230-267, montegualandro@iol.it, SE).

EATING

Trattoria la Grotta, just off Piazza Repubblica, is a traditional, cave-like place with daily specials and a fun outdoor seating area (pasta-€7, meat-€8, Wed–Mon 12:00–15:00 & 19:00–22:00, closed Tue, Piazza Baldelli 3, tel. 0575-630-271).

La Locanda nel Loggiato, run by Lara and Marco, serves up big portions of Tuscan cuisine (pasta-€7, meat-€7–15, Thu–Tue 12:00–15:00 & 19:00–23:00, closed Wed, Piazza Pescheria 3, tel. 0575-630-575).

Put together a **picnic** at the ultra-touristy Enoteca Molesini (Piazza della Repubblica 23) and munch with a million-euro view from Piazza Garibaldi or the public gardens behind San Domenico Church.

TRANSPORTATION CONNECTIONS

To: Rome (10 trains/day, 2.25 hrs), **Florence** (hrly, 1.5 hrs), **Montepulciano** (8/day, 1.25 hrs, change in Chiusi).

Most trains stop at Cortona's Camucia train station (tel. 0575-603-018), but fast trains from Rome and Florence stop at Terontola, 10 miles away (tel. 0575-670-034). From both Terontala and Camucia, orange buses depart for Piazza Garibaldi twice hourly (€1.60, buy tickets at newsstand).

Drivers: Some free parking is available inside the town walls—if you can find it. The best bets are Piazzale del Mercato and Piazzale di Santa Margherita.

Urbino

Urbino is famous as the hometown of the artist Raphael and architect Bramante, yet the town owes much of its fame to the Duke of Montefeltro. This mercenary general turned Urbino into an important Renaissance center, attracting artists such as Piero della Francesca, Paolo Uccello, and Raphael's papa, Giovanni Santi. Today Urbino is a small town of 24,000—the majority of which are students studying at the local university. Its primary economy is serving the students rather than tourists and, in spite of its historic and artistic importance, it feels far from the Italian mainstream. Since this was Vatican territory for over 200 years, you'll see lots of churches.

FEDERICO DA MONTEFELTRO
(1422–1482)

The Duke of Montefeltro is *the* man in Urbino history. A hired gun with a private army, he was expert at fighting other peoples' wars—and made a fortune doing it. The Duke lost an eye and a hunk of his nose in action and consequently is portrayed only in profile—with his...relatively...good side showing. He made his palace the "dwelling place of the Muses" and attracted the big names of his day to this remote cradle of Humanism high on a hill in the Marche region.

ORIENTATION

A classic hill town (500 meters above sea level), its medieval wall has four gates from which two main roads criss-cross at the town's main square, Piazza della Repubblica. Called simply "the Piazza," this main square is café central and a great place to nurse an *aperitivo* or coffee and feel the pulse of this town. There's barely a level road as ridged lanes fade into steep stairways, giving hardy locals traction as they climb about the village. While everything's a climb, it's a small town and the climbs are short.

Apart from Urbino's ambience, it can be "seen" in half a day. Ninety percent of the sightseeing thrills are in the Ducal Palace. The only other must-sees are the Oratory of San Giovanni and the town view from the fortress.

Tourist Information: The tiny **TI** is just across from the Ducal Palace (daily 9:00–13:00, sometimes also 15:00–18:00, Piazza Duca Federico 35, tel. 0722-2613).

Arrival in Urbino: The big entry square (Borgo Mercatale) is where buses stop and cars park (underground garage, about €1/hr). While it's a short hike through the old gate up Via Mazzini to the town center, a free elevator lifts you up fast and easy.

Helpful Hints

Internet: Students get online at 17 Via Mazzini (daily 10:00–24:00, just off Piazza della Repubblica).

Laundry: A self-service launderette is on Via C. Battisti.

Local Guide: Claudia Taglianetti is a good private guide (€70/3 hrs for small groups, tel. 0722-350-070, claudiataglianetti@libero.it).

Best Gelato: There are two places—each a few steps off the Piazza della

Urbino

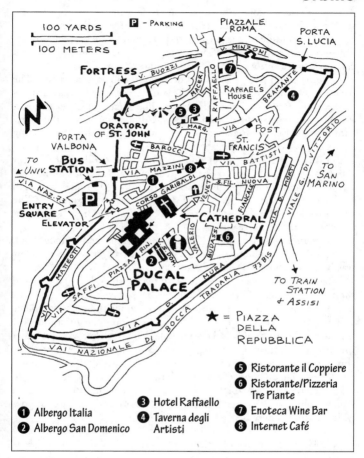

100 YARDS

100 METERS

P – PARKING

PIAZZALE ROMA

PORTA S. LUCIA

FORTRESS
V. BUOZZI

V. MINZONI

RAPHAEL'S HOUSE

BRAMANTE

ORATORY OF ST. JOHN

S. MARG.

POST

PORTA VALBONA

BAROCCI

VIA

ST. FRANCIS

TO UNIV.

BUS STATION

VIA MAZZINI

VIA BATTISTI

TO SAN MARINO

VIA NAZ. 73

VENETO

S. FIL. NUOVA

ENTRY SQUARE ELEVATOR

CORSO GARIBALDI

VALERIO

BUDASSI

CATHEDRAL

MATTEOTTI

PIAZZA RIN.

V. S. DOM.

DUCAL PALACE

MURA

D. BOCCA TRADARIA

73 BIS

TO TRAIN STATION & ASSISI

SAFFI

VIA

VAI NAZIONALE DI

★ = PIAZZA DELLA REPUBBLICA

5 Ristorante il Coppiere

6 Ristorante/Pizzeria Tre Piante

7 Enoteca Wine Bar

8 Internet Café

1 Albergo Italia

2 Albergo San Domenico

3 Hotel Raffaello

4 Taverna degli Artisti

Repubblica—where gelato is made on the premises: one is on Via Vittorio Veneto and the other is across from the church of St. Francis. **Public WC:** It's just below the main square on Via Mazzini.

SIGHTS

▲▲**The Ducal Palace**—The Ducal Palace is a sprawling and fascinating place. While the rooms are fairly bare, it holds a few very special paintings and exquisite inlaid wood decorations. The palace is a monument to how one man—the Duke of Montefeltro—motored the Renaissance in his small town (€4, Tue–Sun 8:30–19:15, Mon 8:30–14:00, tel. 0722-322-625).

Your visit is simple: the library and basement (off the main court-yard) and the first floor. The second floor was added a century after the rest of the building and is filled with porcelain and Mannerist paint-ings—you may skip it. There is precious little explained in English. You can buy a book, or follow this basic self-guided tour:

Courtyard: Just past the ticket desk, you'll enter the courtyard. The palace was built in the mid-1400s. As you can see by this courtyard, it's exuberantly Renaissance in its flavor. The Renaissance erupted in Florence and took about 50 years to reach Urbino. Notice how the court-yard bows up in good Renaissance style—it collected rainwater, helping power the palace's fancy plumbing system.

Library (Biblioteca del Duca): The duke's collection of over 2,000 books was taken to the Vatican when the Pope took over Urbino. Today it displays the travertine (soft marble) reliefs that used to decorate the palace exterior with scenes of work and war. The duke's eagle-in-the-sun emblem on the ceiling shows how he brought enlightenment to his realm.

Basement (Sotterranei): Wandering through the basement, look for bits of exposed plumbing, a huge cistern-like refrigerator (where snow was packed each winter), and a giant stable with a clever horse-pie dis-posal system. The palace is so big—with five levels and several hundred rooms—it was called "a city in the shape of a palace."

First Floor: Your route is a one-way system with numbered rooms and meager English descriptions. The first section—the guest rooms—is now filled with the Galleria Nazionale delle Marche, with the most important collection of paintings in the Marche region. At one time, this palace held many of the highlights of Florence's Uffizi collection (such as Titian's *Venus of Urbino*). As the Vatican army was about to take the city, the last duchess fled to Florence and later married a Medici. She took with her as much of her family's art treasures as pos-sible—quite a dowry.

Room 1: The fireplace—with an orgy of Greek-style decoration—is typical of the Renaissance, celebrating the rebirth of the cultural great-ness that Europe hadn't seen since the glory days of ancient Greece and Rome. Piero della Francesca's *Flagellation* is worth a close look. Pilate, dressed like a Turk, watches Jesus being whipped—an allegory of the Turks threatening Christendom. The three men on the right seem to discuss how Europe will handle this threat from the east. Notice how, in true Renaissance fashion, Jesus stands under a column capped with a classical statue. Together, Jesus and the pre-Christian god seem to illu-minate the ceiling. To a Renaissance thinker, there was no contradiction in celebrating Christian and pre-Christian ideals simultaneously.

The Duke's Study: The duke's richly-paneled study is the highlight of the palace. Take time to really study the exquisite inlaid images. Note the mastery of perspective (for example, the latticed cupboard doors look perfectly open). Let the duke share his passions: art, culture, religion, war, love, music, and caged birds. The period instruments include a delightful lute with a broken string. The duke considered himself an intellectual, inspired by the many great thinkers he portrayed on the walls higher up.

Room 20: In the duke's bedroom, the inlaid door shows a medieval fortress facing a Renaissance palazzo—a clear allegory of how war brings darkness, while the new enlightened thinking leads to a wide-open sea (in the background) of good and cultured living. The mercenary warlord put his initials—FEDVX (Federico Duke)—over the palazzo rather than the old-school fortress.

Room 21: This is called the "Angels' Room" for the fun-loving angels—with golden penises—decorating the fireplace mantle. The whole idea in these humanistic times was that life is good—angels can party, and people are invited, too. It's *dolce vita* time! Note the painting of the ideal city by Luciano Laurana—the primary architect of this complex and marvelous palace. While Laurana's city was never built, it shows the "divine proportions" of the day—balance, harmony, and light. The church is round, like a classical temple. Uninhabited, with black windows, it has a metaphysical feeling—a utopian city…is it possible? The only hints of real life: two tiny birds. The long skinny panel nearby by Uccello tells the sad story of a Christian woman who pawns some communion bread to a Jewish moneylender. He toasts it and it overflows with blood. She is executed and so is the Jew (with his entire family—children and all, burned at the stake). Because she asked for forgiveness, angels at the woman's deathbed wait to catch her soul the moment it vacates the body (normal exit path: through the mouth). The devils at her feet don't stand a chance.

Room 23: This room features the early-Renaissance paintings of Giovanni Santi, Raphael's father.

Room 25: You'll find the actual Raphaels here. The prize of the collection is Raphael's *Portrait of a Gentlewoman* (a.k.a. *La Muta*), a divinely beautiful portrait of a young woman some think is a hidden self-portrait of Raphael. Her hands are perfectly realistic. One possible interpretation of the scene is that the woman has accepted an offer of marriage (her necklace is knotted—heart tied up; she holds a letter—which told of the offer; and the portrait was sent to the nobleman who asked for her hand). Her melancholy but determined face seems to say, "This is a serious commitment that I am ready to undertake." Raphael painted this (like Leonardo painted the *Mona Lisa*) with oil on wood. Mussolini, thinking it only right that one great Raphael should reside in the hometown of the master, had this piece moved from Florence to Urbino. The tiny altar wing (to the right) was recently purchased from the Marcos estate in the Philippines.

Room 28: Look out the window for a fine view of the lower town. The cluster of houses below you was the ghetto (synagogue on lower left, with the two semi-circular windows). The fortress on the hilltop guarded the town. Today it offers a postcard view of Urbino—worth the climb (see below).

Leaving the Palace: The adjacent cathedral is considered an eyesore by locals for its towering neoclassical facade. In a town of fine Renaissance facades, this church (built after an earthquake destroyed the original around 1800) sticks out like a dog's balls. Next to the cathedral is the bishop's residence, and across the street from that is the city hall with its three flags: Europe, Italy, and UNESCO (the town is proud of its special World Heritage status).

▲**Oratory of St. John**—The Oratory of St. John (San Giovanni), the only other important interior in town, is worth a look for its remarkable frescoes. This was built by a brotherhood (dedicated to St. John the Baptist) who did random acts of kindness while wearing masks to be humble about their Christian charity. The interior tells the story of the life of St. John the Baptist, from the events leading up to his birth to his beheading at the request of Herod's dancing daughter Salomé (the actual scene where Herod presents his head to the *femme fatale* is missing).

Study the exuberant scene engulfing the Crucifixion. The two thieves crucified alongside Jesus meet their eternal fates—the soul of the man who repented is grabbed by an angel, the other's by the devil. The mischievous devil was given mirrors for eyes—sure to freak out the faithful 600 years ago. Above it all, a pelican pecks flesh from its own breast to feed its children—symbolic of the amazing power of Christian love.

This fresco was painted in 1400, before the Renaissance arrived in Urbino. It's a good example of the last stage of Gothic, called "International Gothic"—characterized by lots of color, jam-packed with detail and decor, and featuring a post-plague "we survived, let's enjoy life" outlook. Take a peek at Urbino circa 1400 in the people and slice-of-life corners of this art. Before leaving, check out the fine view of the Duke's Palace and the ghetto from the little room adjacent the chapel (€2, Mon–Sat 10:00–12:30 & 15:00–17:30, Sun 10:00–12:30; 5-min walk from main square—follow signs; if no one's there, find attendant at church a few steps away).

Fortress View—For the ultimate Urbino view, complete with its hilly countryside, climb up to the fortress (closed but surrounded by a grassy park). The Franciscan church spire on the left marks the main square. The hill behind that is the site of a huge kite festival (first Sunday of each September). In the distance on a ridge to the right is the duke's mausoleum, with the cypress trees next to it marking the community cemetery. The city gathers around the immense Ducal Palace. To the right of the palace, you can see today's parking lot, once the parade ground for the duke's army. The long front of its once-immense horse stables leads to a round tower, which provided a spiral ramp for horses to romp right up to the palace. While the fortress behind you is empty, the nearby bar is inviting.

SLEEPING

(€1 = about $1.10, country code: 39)
The TI has a line on lots of local families renting rooms. Otherwise, Urbino's accommodations scene is limited to a few comfortable, expensive hotels.

$$$ **Albergo San Domenico** is a four-star place across from the Ducal Palace with 31 spacious, air-conditioned rooms, offering all of the modern comforts and none of the traditional character (Db-€98–120, breakfast extra, parking right there-€8/day, Piazza Rinascimento 3, tel. 0722-2626, fax 0722-2727, www.viphotels.it, info@viphotels.it).

$$$ **Hotel Raffaello** is a more humble place buried in the back streets a two-minute walk from the main square (14 rooms, Db-€114 with breakfast, air-con, Vicolino S. Margherita 40, tel. 0722-4784, fax 0722-328540, info@albergoraffaello.com).

$$ **Albergo Italia** has 43 modern, business-class rooms in the old town (Db-€62–83 depending on size and view, breakfast extra, air-con, ride elevator from town entry and walk 100 yards down Corso Garibaldi arcade to Corso Garibaldi 32, tel. 0722-2701, fax 0722-322-664, www.albergo-italia-urbino.it, info@albergo-italia-urbino.com).

Near Urbino

$$ *Agriturismo:* At **Locanda della Valle Nuova,** a 185-acre organic farm eight miles outside Urbino, they raise cattle, pigs, and poultry; grow grapes for their wine; and harvest wheat for their homemade bread and pasta. The six rooms are tranquil and cozy (Db-€93, includes buffet breakfast, Db-€133 also includes 5-course evening meal, no CC, closed early Nov–late June, 3-night min, reserve 1 day in advance, swimming pool, horseback riding, 2 miles south of Fermingnano at La Cappella 14, Sagrata di Fermingnano, tel. & fax 0722-330-303, www.vallenuova.it, info@vallenuova.it, SE).

EATING

Taverna degli Artisti is a friendly place with a breezy terrace and good traditional cuisine (closed Tue, great pizzas, Via Bramante 52, tel. 0722-2676). At **Il Coppiere,** your entire meal, including the post-dinner *grappa*, can involve truffles (daily 12:00–14:00 & 19:00–22:30, Via Santa Margherita 1, tel. 0722-322-326). **Ristorante/Pizzeria Tre Piante** serves great food with a smile on a delightful terrace overlooking the Marche hills (Tue–Sun 12:00–24:00, closed Mon, Via Voltaccia della Vecchia 1, tel. 0722-4863). The *enoteca* at the top of Via Raphael (at #54)—which sells good locals wines by the glass—is a fun place to drop by. And the town action is at the bustling **Piazza della Repubblica**, with an endless parade of students and locals.

TRANSPORTATION CONNECTIONS

Buses connect Urbino with Pesaro, on the Ravenna–Pescara train line (buses run hourly, 60-min trip). The Pesaro bus stop is 100 yards from its train station. In Urbino, buses come and go from the Borgo Mercatale parking lot below the town, where an elevator lifts you up to the base of the Ducal Palace (or take a 5-min steep walk up Via Mazzini to Piazza della Repubblica).

Orvieto

Umbria's grand hill town, just off the freeway, is no secret, but worth a quick look. The town sits majestically on a big chunk of *tufa*, volcanic soil from Lake Bolsena. Locals will tell you that tufa is actually Swiss cheese because it's sturdy and riddled with holes (you can dig into it with bare hands). Since the Etruscan era, city dwellers have created a honeycomb of tunnels and catacombs underneath its streets.

Orvieto, which has three popular claims to fame (cathedral, Classico wine, and ceramics)—is loaded with tourists by day and quiet by night. Drinking a shot of wine in a ceramic cup as you gaze up at the cathedral lets you experience Orvieto all at once. (What I like best about Orvieto is its easy bus connection with my favorite hill town, Civita—covered below.)

Piazza Cahen is a key transportation hub at the entry to the hilltop town. As you exit the funicular, the town center and cathedral are straight ahead.

Tourist Information: The TI is at Piazza Duomo 24 on the cathedral square (Mon–Fri 8:15–13:30 & 16:00–19:00, Sat 10:00–13:00 & 15:00–19:00, Sun 10:00–12:00 & 16:00–18:00, tel. 0763-341-772). Pick up the free city map and ask about train and bus schedules. The TI sells a €3 admission ticket for the Chapel of St. Brizio (within the cathedral). For a longer visit, consider buying the €12.50 **Carta Unica** combo-ticket, which covers entry to the chapel, Archaeological Museum (Museo Claudio Faina e Museo Civico), Underground Orvieto Tours, and Torre del Moro (tower), plus your public transportation (bus and funicular) for one day or five hours of parking (at *parcheggio* Campo della Fiera).

Market Days: Drop by Piazza del Popolo with your cloth shopping bag on Tuesday and Saturday mornings.

Arrival in Orvieto

By Train: If you're day-tripping, you can check your bag at the station (€2.80/12 hrs, open daily 6:30–19:30, access from platform; if no one is around, ask at the newsstand in the station).

A handy funicular/bus shuttle will take you quickly from the train station and parking lot to the top of the town. Buy your ticket at the entrance to the *funiculare;* look for the *biglietteria* sign. The €0.90 ticket includes the funicular plus the minibus from Piazza Cahen to Piazza Duomo—where you'll find most everything that matters. Or you can pay €0.65 for the funicular only—the best choice if you're staying at the recommended Hotel Corso. The funicular runs every 10 minutes (Mon–Sat 7:20–20:30, Sun 8:00–20:30).

As you exit the funicular at the top, to your left is a ruined fortress with a garden, WC, and a commanding view, and to your right are St. Patrick's Well (described below), Etruscan ruins, and another sweeping view. Just in front of you is an orange bus waiting to shuttle you to the town center. It'll drop you off at the TI (last stop, in front of cathedral).

If you forgot to check at the station for the train schedule to your next destination (and now the station is far, far below), Orvieto is ready for you. The train schedule is posted at the top of the *funiculare* and also available if you ask at the TI.

By Car: Drivers park at the base of the hill at the huge, free lot behind the Orvieto train station (follow the P and *funiculare* signs), or also for free in Piazza Cahen, or on Via Roma; otherwise go to the pay lot to the right of Orvieto's cathedral (€0.80 for first hour, €0.60/hr thereafter).

SIGHTS

Orvieto's Piazza Duomo

▲▲**Duomo**—The cathedral has Italy's most striking facade (from 1330), thanks to architect Lorenzo Maitani and many others. Grab a gelato (to the left of the church) and study this fascinating, gleaming mass of mosaics and sculpture.

At the base of the cathedral, the broad marble pillars carved with biblical scenes tell the story of the world from left to right. The pillar on the far left shows the Creation (see the snake and Eve), next is the Tree of Jesse (father of King David), next the New Testament (look for Mary and a manger, etc.), and on the far right—the Last Judgment (with hell, of course, at the bottom). Each pillar is topped by a bronze symbol of one of the evangelists: angel (Matthew), lion (Mark), eagle (John), and bull (Luke). The bronze doors are modern, by the Sicilian sculptor Emilio Greco. (A museum devoted to Greco's work is to the right of the church; it's labeled simply *Museo*.) In the mosaic below the rose window, Mary is transported to heaven. In the uppermost mosaic, Mary is crowned.

Orvieto

400 METERS

400 YARDS

TO
BOLSENA
& VITERBO

PORTA
MAGGIORE

ETRUSCAN
TOMBS

P – PARKING

PORTO
ROMANO

PIAZZA
REPUB.

ARCHAEO
LOGICAL
MUSEUM

POPOLO

DCH

VIALE CARDUCCI

S-71

PARCO
DELLE
GROTTE

VIA DUOMO

WC

NEBBIA

DUOMO

PIAZZA
XXIX
MARZO

VIA ROMA

POSTIERLA

VIA CAVOUR

CORSO

VIALE CRISPI

ETRUSCAN
TEMPLE
RUINS

PIAZZA
CAHEN

**FORTRESS
RUINS** & WC

**ST.
PATRICK'S
WELL**

TO
FLOR.

FUNICULAR

**TRAIN
STN.**

P

TO
ROMA

TO AUTOSTRADA
& CIVITA

1. Hotel Duomo
2. Hotel Corso
3. Hotel Valentino
4. Hotel Virgilio, Gelateria & Enoteca Tozzi
5. Hotel Posta
6. Istituto SS Domenicane
7. Hotel Picchio
8. Valentina Rooms
9. Pergola Restaurant
10. La Palomba Restaurant
11. Antico Bucchero Restaurant
12. L'Antica Trattoria dell'Orso
13. Osteria San Patrizio
14. Museo Emilio Greco
15. Torre del Moro
16. Buy bus tickets to Civita

Why such an impressive church in a little *tufa* town? Because of a blood-stained cloth. In the 1260s, a Bohemian priest—who doubted that the bread used in Communion was really the body of Christ—went to Rome on a pilgrimage. On his return journey, he worshiped in Bolsena, near Orvieto. During Mass, the bread bled, staining a linen cloth. The cloth was brought to the pope, who was visiting Orvieto at the time. Such a miraculous relic required a magnificent church. You can see the actual cloth from the Miracle of Bolsena displayed in the chapel to the left of the altar.

Hours of Cathedral: April–Sept daily 7:30–12:45 & 14:30–19:15; March and Oct closes at 18:15, Nov–Feb at 17:15. Admission is free, but there is a charge for the Chapel of St. Brizio.

Cost and Hours of Chapel: Visitors' hours are Mon–Sat 10:00–12:45 & 14:30–19:15, Sun 14:30–17:45 (closes 1 hour earlier in winter). Buy the €3 ticket at the TI or the shop across the square from the facade of the church; it's included in the €12.50 Carta Unica combo-ticket. Only 25 people are allowed in the chapel at a time. The chapel is also open (and free, no ticket required) daily 7:30–10:00, but it's technically only for worshippers (keep a low profile and be respectful of those who are praying).

Chapel of St. Brizio: This chapel, to the right of the altar, features Luca Signorelli's brilliantly-lit frescoes of the Apocalypse (1449–1451). Step into the chapel and you're surrounded by vivid scenes, including the *Preaching of the Antichrist* (to your left as you enter—the figure standing on far left is a self-portrait of Signorelli, next to Fra Angelico, who worked on the ceiling); the *Calling of the Elect to Heaven* (left of altar—hear that celestial band); the *Damned in Hell* (right of altar—the scariest mosh pit ever); and the *Resurrection of the Bodies* (to your right as you enter; people dreamily climb out of the earth as skeletons chatter in the corner, wondering where to snare some skin). On the same wall is a gripping *pietà*. Fra Angelico started the ceiling and Signorelli finished it, turning the entire room into Orvieto's artistic, must-see sight.

After leaving the cathedral, if you want a break at a viewpoint park, exit left and pass the small parking lot. The nearest WCs are in the opposite direction (exit cathedral to the right), down the stairs from the left transept.

Archaeological Museum (Museo Claudio Faina e Museo Civico)—Across from the entrance to the cathedral is a fine Etruscan art museum (2 upper floors) combined with a miniscule city history museum on the ground floor that features a sarcophagus and temple bits. The Faina art—consisting largely of Etruscan vases, plates, and coins, with some jewelry and bronze dishes—was collected by Mauro Faina and his nephew starting in the late 19th century. They bought some of the art, and dug up the rest in haphazardly conducted excavations. Many of the vases came from the Etruscan necropolis (Crocifisso del Tufo) just outside Orvieto.

The English placards in most rooms offer some information, especially on the Faina family (€4.50, included in €12.50 Carta Unica combo-ticket, April–Sept Tue–Sun 9:30–18:00, Oct–March Tue–Sun 10:00–17:00, closed Mon, audioguide, WC after ticket desk and on top floor, tel. 0763-341-511). Look out the windows at the Duomo's glittering facade.

▲**Museo Emilo Greco**—This museum displays the work of Emilio Greco (1913–1995), the Sicilian artist who designed the doors of Orvieto's cathedral. His sketches and bronze statues show his absorption with gently twisting and turning nudes. In the back left corner of the museum, look for the sketchy outlines of women—simply beautiful. The artful installation of his work in this palazzo, with walkways and even a spiral staircase up to the ceiling, allows you to view his sculptures from different directions (€2.50, €4.50 includes St. Patrick's Well, April–Sept daily 10:30–13:00 & 14:30–18:30, Oct–March closes 1 hour earlier, no English but not essential, next to Duomo, marked *Museo*: tel. 0763-344-605).

Underground Orvieto Tours (Parco delle Grotte)—Guides weave a good archaeological history into an hour-long look at about 100 yards of caves (€5.50, included in €12.50 Carta Unica combo-ticket, 1-hr English tours daily at 12:15 and 17:15, confirm times by calling 335-733-2764 or checking with TI). Orvieto is honeycombed with Etruscan and medieval caves. You'll see the remains of an old olive press, two impressive 130-foot-deep Etruscan well shafts, and the remains of a primitive cement quarry. If you want underground Orvieto, this is the place to get it.

More Sights in Orvieto

Torre del Moro—For yet another viewpoint, this distinctive square tower comes with 250 steps and an elevator. The elevator goes only partway to the top, leaving you with a mere 173 steps to scurry up (€2.70, included in €12.50 Carta Unica combo-ticket, April–Oct daily 10:00–19:00, May–Aug until 20:00, Nov–March 10:30–13:00 & 14:30–17:00, terrace on top, at intersection of Corso Cavour and Via Duomo).

St. Patrick's Well (Posso de S. Patrizio)—Engineers are impressed by this deep well—175 feet deep and 45 feet wide—designed in the 16th century with a double-helix pattern. The two spiral stairways allow an efficient one-way traffic flow; intriguing now, but critical then. Imagine if donkeys and people, balancing jugs of water, had to go up and down the same stairway. At the bottom is a bridge that people could walk on to scoop up water.

The well was built because a pope got nervous. After Rome was sacked in 1527 by renegade troops of the Holy Roman Empire, the pope fled to Orvieto. He feared that even this little town (with no water source on top) would be besieged. He commissioned a well, which was started in 1527 and finished 10 years later. It was a huge project. Even today, when a local is faced with a difficult task, people say, "It's like digging St. Patrick's Well." The unusual name came from the well's supposed resemblance to the Irish saint's cave. It's not worth climbing up and down a total of 495 steps; a quick look is painless but pricey (€3.50, €4.50 includes Museo Emilio Greco, April–Sept daily 10:00–18:45, Oct–March 10:00–17:45; the well is to your right as you exit *funiculare*). Bring a sweater if you descend to the chilly depths.

View Walks—For short, pleasant walks, climb the medieval wall (access at western end of town, between Piazza S. Gionvenale and Via Garibaldi) or stroll the promenade park on the northern edge of town (along Viale Carducci, which becomes Gonfaloniera).

Sights near Orvieto

Wine-Tasting—Orvieto Classico wine is justly famous. For a short tour of a local winery with Etruscan cellars, visit Tenuta Le Velette, where English-speaking Corrado and Cecilia (cheh-CHEEL-yah) Bottai will welcome you—if you've called ahead to set up an appointment (€8 for tour and tasting, Mon–Fri 8:30–12:00 & 14:00–17:00, Sat 8:30–12:00, closed Sun, tel. 0763-29144, fax 0763-29114). From their sign (5 min past Orvieto at top of switchbacks just before Canale, on Bagnoregio road), cruise down a long, tree-lined drive, then park at the striped gate (must call ahead; no drop-ins).

SLEEPING

(€1 = about $1.10, country code: 39)
All of the recommended hotels are in the old town except Hotel Picchio, which is in a more modern neighborhood near the station.

$$$ **Hotel Duomo**, centrally located, is super-duper modern, with splashy art and 17 sleek rooms named after artists who worked on the Duomo (Sb-€70, Db-€100, Db suite-€120, Tb-€130, includes breakfast; elevator, air-con, double-paned windows keep out noise, sunny terrace out front; a block from Duomo, behind *gelateria* at Via di Maurizio 7; tel. 0763-341-887, fax 0763-394-973, www.orvietohotelduomo.com, hotelduomo@tiscalinet.it, SE).

$$ **Hotel Corso** is friendly and clean, with 18 comfy, modern rooms, some with balconies and views (Sb-€60, Db-€82, 10 percent discount with this book, buffet breakfast-€6.50, elevator, air-con, garage or free parking nearby, on main street up from funicular toward Duomo at Via Cavour 339, tel. & fax 0763-342-020, www.argoweb.it/hotel_corso, hotelcorso@libero.it, SE).

$$ **Hotel Valentino** offers 19 simple, quiet rooms in a modern hotel 200 yards off Corso Cavour (Db-€80, elevator, air-con, Via Angelo da Orvieto 30/32, tel. & fax 0763-342-464, hotelvalentino@libero.it).

$$ Hotel Virgilio has modern but faded and overpriced rooms shoehorned into an old building, ideally located on the main square facing the cathedral (Sb-€62, Db-€85, breakfast-€6, send personal or traveler's check for first night's deposit; elevator, noisy church bells every 15 min; Piazza Duomo 5, 05018 Orvieto; tel. 0763-341-882, fax 0763-343-797, www.hotelvirgilio.com, info@hotel.virgilio.com, SE). They also have a cheaper *dependencia*—a double and quad in a one-star hotel a few doors away (Db-€57, Qb-€103).

$ Hotel Posta is a five-minute walk from the cathedral into the medieval core. It's a big, old, formerly elegant but well-cared-for-in-its-decline building with a breezy garden, an elevator, and a grand old lobby. 20 spacious, clean, plain rooms hold vintage rickety furniture and good mattresses (S-€31, Sb-€37, D-€43, Db-€56, breakfast-€6, no CC, Via Luca Signorelli 18, tel. & fax 0763-341-909, NSE).

$ The sisters of the **Istituto SS Domenicane** rent 15 spotless twin rooms in their heavenly convent with a peaceful terrace (Sb-€41, Db-€52, 2-night min, breakfast-€3, no CC, elevator, parking, just off Piazza del Popolo at Via del Popolo 1, tel. & fax 0763-342-910, www.argoweb.it/istituto_sansalvatore/istituto.it.html, NSE).

$ Hotel Picchio, with 27 newly-remodeled rooms, is a wood-and-marble place, more comfortable but with less character than others in the area. It's in the lower, plain part of town, 300 yards from the train station (Sb-€36, Db-€48, Tb-€59, ask for the Rick Steves 5 percent discount; only some rooms are air-con and cost extra; Via G. Salvatori 17, tel. & fax 0763-301-144, dan_test@libero.it, family-run by Marco and Picchio, SE). A trail leads from here up to the old town.

$ Valentina rents six clean and airy, well-appointed rooms and a studio apartment (all with air-con) in the heart of Orvieto behind the grand staircase in Piazza del Popolo. Facing the stairs, head right around the Gothic palazzo and then left down Via Vivaria about 50 yards. She rents another 2-room apartment near the Duomo as well (Db-€60, Tb-€75, includes breakfast; also studio with kitchen-€80, apartment for up to 5-€130; Via Vivaria 7, tel. 0763-341-607, mobile 347-652-7779, valentina.z@tiscalinet.it, SE).

$ Franco Sala, who runs the Antico Forno restaurant and a B&B in Civita, also rents a comfortable, centrally-located one-bedroom apartment with a hand-carved stone spiral staircase and a curvy kitchen in a renovated 14th-century palazzo in Orvieto (€70–100, sleeps up to 5 people, 2-night min, tel. 0761-760-016).

Near Orvieto

$$$ Agriturismo Le Casette, outside the village of Baschi and seven miles southeast of Orvieto, is outstanding, with rooms in several restored stone farmhouses clustered around a grassy lawn and a swimming pool with a fabulous view of the green Umbrian landscape (Db-€100–120, includes breakfast and half-pension, minimum 1-week stays preferred, tel. 0744-957-645, fax 0744-950-500, www.pomurlovecchio-lecasette.it, pomurlovecchio@tiscalinet.it, run by charming Minghelli family, Daniela speaks "a leetle" English). The same family also owns **Pomurlo Vecchio**, a 12th-century tower house with three rooms a few miles away (Db-€65–75 with breakfast, half-pension not required, tel. 0744-950-190, fax 0744-950-500).

$$$ Agriturismo Sant' Angelo rents four apartments in an old stone farmhouse on a hillside near Monte Rufeno Natural Park Reserve, about 12 miles northwest of Orvieto. The apartments sleep up to four and have kitchenettes (2-night min stay, cost for 2 people/2 nights-€160–200 depending on season, weekly-€750–800 for up to 4 people, no CC, pool, spa, horseback riding, mountain bikes, S.S. Cassia Nord Km 136.300, Viterbo, tel. & fax 0763-734-738, mobile 338-727-1044, www.agriturismosantangelo.it, info@agriturismosantangelo.it, SE).

$ Agriturismo Pomonte Umbria, seven miles east of Orvieto, offers home-cooked meals, lovely vistas, and seven comfortable rooms in a newly-built guest house (€26 per person, includes breakfast, €42-half-pension, €52-full pension, Loc. Canino di Orvieto 1, Corbara, tel. 076-330-4041, fax 076-330-4080, www.pomonte.it, info@pomonte.it, SE).

EATING

Near the Duomo, consider **Pergola**—its affordable menu is popular with locals (Thu–Tue 12:30–15:00 & 19:15–22:00, closed Mon, Via dei Magoni 9, tel. 0763-343-065).

La Palomba, also a good bet, features game and truffle specialties (Thu–Tue 12:30–14:15 & 19:30–22:00, closed Wed; Via Cipriano Manente 16, just off Piazza della Repubblica; tel. 0763-343-395).

For a bit of a splurge, try **Antico Bucchero** for its classy candlelit ambience and fine food (Thu–Tue 12:00–15:00 & 19:00–24:00, closed Wed; indoor/outdoor seating; Via de Cartari 4, a half-block south of Corso Cavour, between Torre del Moro and Piazza della Repubblica; tel. 0763-341-725).

L'Antica Trattoria dell'Orso offers well-prepared Umbrian cuisine paired with fine wines in a cozy atmosphere. Ciro and chef Gabriele will steer you towards the freshest seasonal plates (Wed–Sun 12:30–14:00 & 19:30–22:00, closed Mon–Tue, Via della Misericordia 18–20, just off Piazza della Repubblica, tel. 0763-341-642).

Osteria San Patrizio, near the funicular, creatively presents traditional Umbrian specialties (12:00–15:00 & 19:00–23:00, closed Sun eve and Mon, Corso Cavour 312, tel. 0763-341-245).

For dessert, try the deservedly popular *gelateria* **Pasqualetti** (daily

Orvieto and Civita Area

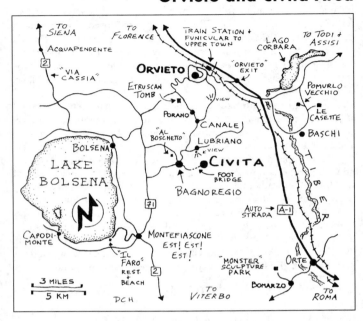

12:30–24:00, closed in winter; Piazza Duomo 14, next to left transept of church; another branch is at Corso Cavour 56, open until 20:30 during winter).

Enoteca Tozzi, to the left of the Duomo, serves up rustic *panini*—try the roast suckling pig (*porchetta*, por-KET-tah) if it's available (daily 8:30–21:00, 9:00–20:00 in winter, Piazza Duomo 13, tel. 0763-344-393).

TRANSPORTATION CONNECTIONS

By train to: Rome (19/day, 75 min, consider leaving your car at the large car park behind Orvieto station), **Florence** (14/day, 2.25 hrs), **Siena** (8/day, 2–3 hrs, change in Chiusi; all Florence-bound trains stop in Chiusi). The train station's Buffet della Stazione is surprisingly good if you need a quick focaccia sandwich or pizza picnic for the train ride.

By bus to Bagnoregio (near Civita): It's 70 minutes going, 40 minutes coming back (€2 round-trip). Departures in 2003 from Orvieto's Piazza Cahen on the blue Cotral bus, daily except Sunday: 6:20, 9:10, 12:45, 15:45, and 18:20 (buses stop at Orvieto's train station 5 min later). During the school year (roughly Sept–June), there are additional departures at 7:20, 7:50, and 13:55. Buy your ticket at the *tabacchi* stop on Corso Cavour (also confirm the schedule) a block up from the *funiculare* or from the train station bar. To find the bus stop, face the *funiculare;* the stop is at the far left end of Piazza Cahen where the blue buses are parked (no schedule posted; confirm departure and return times with driver). At the station, wait at the left of the funicular station as you're facing it. Once you're in Bagnoregio, you'll find the Bagnoregio–Orvieto bus schedule posted at the bus stop.

Civita di Bagnoregio

Perched on a pinnacle in a grand canyon, the traffic-free village of Civita is Italy's ultimate hill town. Curl your toes around its Etruscan roots.

Civita is terminally ill. Only 15 residents remain as, bit by bit, the town is being purchased by rich big-city Italians who come here to escape. The University of Washington architecture program that once brought American students here is a thing of the past.

Civita is connected to the world and the town of Bagnoregio by a long pedestrian bridge—and a Web site (www.civitadibagnoregio.it). While Bagnoregio lacks the pinnacle-town romance of Civita, it's actually a healthy, vibrant community (unlike Civita, the suburb that it calls "the dead city"). In Bagnoregio, get a haircut, sip a coffee on the square, and walk down to the old laundry (ask, *"Dov'è la lavanderia vecchia?"*). A Grand Spesa supermarket is 300 yards from the bus stop (Mon–Sat 8:30–13:00 & 17:00–20:00, closed Sun; take main drag from town gate—away from Civita, angle right at pyramid monument). A lively market fills the bus parking lot each Monday.

From Bagnoregio, yellow signs direct you along its long, skinny spine to its older neighbor, Civita. Enjoy the view as you walk up the bridge to Civita. Be prepared for the little old ladies of Civita, who can be aggressive at getting money out of visitors—tourists are their only source of support. Off-season, Civita, Bagnoregio, and Al Boschetto (see "Sleeping," page 391) are all deadly quiet—and cold. I'd side-trip in quickly from Orvieto or skip the area altogether.

Arrival in Bagnoregio, near Civita

If you're arriving by bus from Orvieto, you'll get off at the bus stop in Bagnoregio. Look at the posted bus schedule and write down the return times to Orvieto. (Drivers, see "Transportation Connections" page 386.)

Baggage Check: While there's no official baggage-check service in Bagnoregio, I've arranged with Mauro Laurenti, who runs the Bar/ Enoteca/Caffè Gianfu, to let you leave your bags there (€1/bag, daily

7:00–24:00 with a 13:00–13:30 lunch break, closed Thu Oct–March; to get to café from Orvieto bus stop where you got off, go back in the direction that the Orvieto bus just came from and go right around corner).

From Bagnoregio to Civita: From Bagnoregio, you can walk or take a little orange shuttle bus to the base of the bridge to Civita. From here, you have to walk the rest of the way. It's a 10-minute hike up a pedestrian bridge that gets steeper near the end. There's no bus—only you and your profound regret that you didn't get in better shape before your trip.

The little shuttle **bus** runs from Bagnoregio (catch bus across from gas station) to the base of the bridge (€1, pay driver, 10-min ride, first bus at 7:39, last at 18:20, 1–2/hr except during 13:00–15:30 siesta). If you'll want to return to Bagnoregio by bus, check the schedule posted near the bridge (at edge of car park, where bus let you off) before you head up to Civita.

To **walk** from Bagnoregio to the base of Civita's bridge (about 20 min, fairly level), take the road going uphill (overlooking the big parking lot), then take the first right and an immediate left onto the main drag, Via Roma. Follow this straight out to the belvedere for a superb viewpoint. From the viewpoint, backtrack a few steps (staircase at end of viewpoint is a dead end), and take the stairs down to the road leading to the bridge.

Civita Orientation Walk

Civita was once connected to Bagnoregio. The saddle between the separate towns eroded away. Photographs around town show the old donkey path, the original bridge. It was bombed in World War II and replaced in 1965 with the new **bridge** you're climbing today. The town's hearty old folks hang on the bridge's hand railing when fierce winter weather rolls through.

Entering the town, you'll pass through a cut in the rock (made by Etruscans 2,500 years ago) and under a 12th-century Romanesque **arch**. This was the main Etruscan road leading to the Tiber Valley and Rome.

Inside the town gate, on your left is the old **laundry** (in front of the WC). On your right, a fancy wooden door and windows (above the door) lead to thin air. This was the facade of a Renaissance palace—one of five that once graced Civita. It fell into the valley riding a chunk of the ever-eroding rock pinnacle. Today, the door leads to a remaining chunk of the palace—complete with Civita's first hot tub—owned by the "Marchesa," a countess who married into Italy's biggest industrialist family.

Peek into the museum next door if it's open (Wed and Sat–Sun 10:00–13:00, marked *Benvenuti a Civita*) and check out the **viewpoint** a few steps away. Nearby is the site of the long-gone home of Civita's one famous son, Saint Bonaventure, known as the "second founder of the Franciscans."

Civita

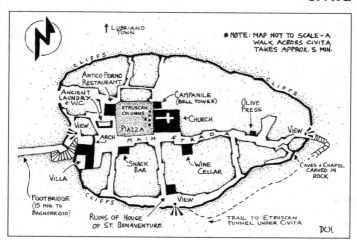

Now wander to the **town square** in front of the church, where you'll find Civita's only public phone, bar, and restaurant—and a wild donkey race on the first Sunday of June and the second Sunday of September. The church marks the spot where an Etruscan temple, and then a Roman temple, once stood. The pillars that stand like giants' bar stools are ancient—Roman or Etruscan.

Go into the **church**. You'll see frescoes and statues from "the school of Giotto" and "the school of Donatello," a portrait of the patron saint of your teeth (notice the scary-looking pincers), and an altar dedicated to Marlon Brando (or St. Ildebrando).

The basic grid street plan of the ancient town survives. Just around the corner from the church, on the main street, is Rossana and Antonio's cool and friendly **wine cellar** (their sign reads *bruschette con prodotti locali*). Pull up a stump and let them or their children, Arianna and Antonella, serve you *panini* (sandwiches), *bruschetta* (garlic toast with optional tomato topping), wine, and a local cake called *ciambella*. Climb down into the cellar and note the traditional wine-making gear and the provisions for rolling huge kegs up the stairs. Tap on the kegs in the cool bottom level to see which are full (April–Oct daily 10:00–21:00, even later in Aug, Nov–March Sat–Sun only, 10:00–18:00).

The rock below Civita is honeycombed with ancient cellars (for keeping wine at the same temperature all year) and cisterns (for collecting rainwater, since there was no well in town). Many of these date from Etruscan times.

Explore further down the street, but remember—nothing is abandoned. Everything is still privately owned. After passing an ancient Roman tombstone on your left, you'll come to Vittoria's **Antico Mulino**, an atmospheric collection of old olive presses. The huge press in the entry is about 1,500 years old and was in use as recently as the 1960s (donation requested, give about €1). Vittoria's sons, Sandro and Felice, and her grandson Fabrizio (with his American wife, Heather) run the local equivalent of a lemonade stand, toasting delicious *bruschetta* on weekends and holidays (roughly 10:00–20:00 in summer, winter Sat–Sun only, tel. 0176-793-179). Choose your topping (chopped tomato is super) and get a glass of wine for a fun, affordable snack.

Farther down the way and to your left, Maria (for a donation of about €1) will show you through her **garden** with a grand view (Maria's Giardino) and share historical misinformation (she says Civita and Lubriano were once connected). Maria's husband, Peppone, used to carry goods on a donkey back and forth on the path between the old town and Bagnoregio.

At the end of town, the main drag winds downhill past small **Etruscan caves** to your right. The first two were used as stables until last year. The third cave is an unusual chapel, cut deep into the rock, with a barred door—this is the **Chapel of the Incarcerated** (Cappella del Carcere). In Etruscan times, the chapel may have originally been a tomb, and in medieval times, it was used as a jail. When Civita's few residents have a religious procession, they come here, in honor of the Madonna of the Incarcerated.

After the chapel, the paving-stone path peters out into a dirt trail leading down and around to the right to a **tunnel**. Dating from the Etruscan era, the tunnel may have served as a shortcut to the river below. It was widened in the 1930s so farmers could get between their scattered fields more easily, and now the residents use it as a shortcut in fall to collect chestnuts from the trees that cover the hillside. Backtrack to the town square.

Evenings on the town square are a bite of Italy. The same people sit on the same church steps under the same moon, night after night, year after year. I love my cool, late evenings in Civita. If you visit in the morning, have cappuccino and rolls at the small café on the town square.

Whenever you visit, stop halfway up the donkey path and listen to the sounds of rural Italy. Reach out and touch one of the Monopoly houses. If you know how to turn the volume up on the crickets, do so.

SLEEPING

(€1 = about $1.10, country code: 39)

In Civita

$$$ **Carol Watts** rents a furnished two-bedroom Civita apartment with a terrace and cliffside garden ($900/week, 1-week minimum Sat to Sat, personal checks OK). Give her a call in Kansas (785/539-0815, evenings or weekends, http://homepage.mac.com/cmwatts/civita.html, cmwatts @mac.com).

$ **Civita B&B**, run by Franco Sala, who also owns the Antico Forno restaurant, has three comfortable rooms overlooking Civita's main square. Call a minimum of one day in advance to reserve (D-€62, Db-€68, €14 more for optional half-pension, Piazza del Duomo Vecchio, tel. 0761-760-016, mobile 347-611-5426, www.civitadibagnoregio.it, fsala@pelagus.it).

In Bagnoregio

$ **Romantica Pucci B&B** is a haven for city-weary travelers. Its five spacious rooms are indeed romantic with canopied beds and flowing veils, and Pucci and Lamberto take special care of their guests (Sb-€39, Db-€65, Piazza Cavour 1, tel. 0761-792-121, www.hotelromanticapucci.it, lacasadipucci@libero.it, SE). It's on the road to Civita from Bagnoregio at Piazza Cavour (from Civita bus stop, walk up stairs, turn left on the main street, continue 150 yards to square, B&B on left).

$ **Hotel Fidanza**, near the bus stop in Bagnoregio, is tired but decent and the only hotel in town. Of its 25 rooms, #206 and #207 have views of Civita (Sb-€52, Db-€62, breakfast-€5.50, no CC; attached restaurant; Via Fidanza 25, Bagnoregio/Viterbo; tel. & fax 0761-793-444).

Just outside Bagnoregio is $ **Al Boschetto.** The Catarcia family speaks no English, so have an English-speaking Italian call for you (Sb-€34, D-€40, Db-€50, breakfast-€3; Strada Monterado, Bagnoregio/Viterbo; tel. 0761-792-369). Most of the 12 rooms, while very basic, have private showers. The Catarcia family (Angelino, his wife Perina, sons Gianfranco and Domenico, daughter-in-law Giuseppina, and the grandchildren) offers a candid look at rural Italian life. Meals are uneven in quality, and the men are often tipsy (which can pose a problem for women). If the men invite you down deep into the gooey, fragrant bowels of the cantina, be warned: The theme song is *"Trinka Trinka Trinka,"* and there are no rules unless the female participants set them. The Orvieto bus drops you at the town gate (no bus on Sun). The hotel is a 15-minute walk out of town past the old arch (follow *Viterbo* signs); turn left at the pyramid monument and right at the first fork (follow *Montefiascone* sign). Civita is a pleasant 45-minute walk (back through Bagnoregio) from Al Boschetto.

EATING

In and near Civita

In Civita, try **Trattoria Antico Forno**, which serves up pasta at afford-able prices (daily for lunch 12:30–15:30 and sporadically for dinner 19:30–22:00, on main square, also rents rooms—see above, tel. 0761-760-016). At **Da Peppone**, the small café/bar on the square, you can get simple treats (daily 9:30–12:30 & 14:00–19:00, closed 17:00 and Mon or Tue in winter, tel. 0761-79320).

Hostaria del Ponte offers light, creative cuisine with a great view terrace at the parking lot at the base of the bridge to Civita (Tue–Sun 12:30–14:30 & 19:30–21:30, closed Mon; Nov–April closed Sun, tel. 0761-793-565).

In Bagnoregio, check out **Il Fumatore di Pizzo Ornelio** for tradi-tional Italian cuisine (Fri–Wed 12:30–15:00 & 19:00–22:00, closed Thu, on Piazza Marconi 5, 0761-792-642). At **Al Boschetto,** you'll get coun-try cooking, such as bunny (just outside Bagnoregio; see "Sleeping," above, daily 12:30–14:30 & 20:00–22:00).

TRANSPORTATION CONNECTIONS

To Orvieto: Public buses (7/day, 40 min, €2 round-trip) connect Bagnoregio to the rest of the world via Orvieto. Departures in 2003 from Bagnoregio, daily except Sunday: 5:30, 6:50, 9:50, 10:10, 13:00, 14:25, and 17:20. During the school year (roughly Sept–June), buses also run at 6:35, 13:35, and 16:40 (for info on Orvieto, see "Transportation Connections" for Orvieto, page 386).

Driving from Orvieto to Bagnoregio: Orvieto overlooks the autostrada (and has its own exit). The shortest way to Civita from the freeway exit is to turn left (below Orvieto) and follow the signs to Lubriano and Bagnoregio.

The more winding and scenic route takes 20 minutes longer: From the freeway, pass under hill-capping Orvieto (on your right, signs to Lago di Bolsena, on Viale I Maggio), then take the first left (direction: Bagnoregio), winding up past great Orvieto views through Canale, and through farms and fields of giant shredded wheat to Bagnoregio.

Either way, just before Bagnoregio, follow the signs left to Lubriano and pull into the first little square by the church on your right for a breathtaking view of Civita. Then return to the Bagnoregio road. Drive through Bagnoregio (following yellow Civita signs) and park at the base of the steep pedestrian bridge leading up to the traffic-free, 2,500-year-old, canyon-swamped pinnacle town of Civita di Bagnoregio.

More Hill Towns and Sights

If you haven't gotten your fill of hill towns, here are more to check out. I've also listed some worthwhile sights, plus a couple of recommended driving routes to connect the dots.

Hill Towns

▲**Gubbio**—This handsome town climbs Monte Ingino in northeast Umbria. Tuesday is market day, when Piazza 40 Martiri (named for 40 locals shot by the Nazis) bustles. Nearby, the ruins of the Roman amp-itheater are perfect for a picnic. Head up Via della Repubblica to reach the main square with the imposing Palazzo dei Consoli. Farther up, Via San Gerolamo leads to the funky lift that will carry you up the hill in two-person "baskets" for a stunning view from the top, where the basil-ica of St. Ubaldo is worth a look.

Buses run to Perugia, Rome, and Florence. The **TI** is at Piazza Oderisi (Mon–Fri 8:00–14:00 & 15:30–18:30, Sat 9:00–13:00 & 15:30–18:30, Sun 9:30–12:00 & 15:30–18:30, tel. 075-922-0693).

▲**Deruta**—Pottery-lovers the world over start to salivate when the name Deruta is mentioned. Colorful Deruta majolica pottery, considered to be Italy's best, features designs popular since Renaissance times. The high-quality local clay attracted artisans centuries ago, and today artists still practice their craft. Deruta is actually two towns: the upper hill town and the lower strip. The upper town, full of small shops run by local artisans, warrants a wander; prices and quality are higher up here. Ceramic fans drop by the Museo Regionale della Ceramica (closed Tue), in the upper town, next to the TI on the main square. Below, a commercial strip par-allel to the *superstrada* is lined with larger commercial outlets and facto-ries. Many offer demonstrations of their time-honored craft. Prices are about one-third cheaper than in the United States, and most will ship your purchases home with a guarantee of safe delivery.

Buses connect Deruta with Perugia.

▲**Bevagna**—This sleeper of a town south of Assisi has Roman ruins, interesting churches, and more. Locals offer their guiding services for free (usually Italian-speaking only) and are excited to show visitors their town. Get a map at the **TI** on Piazza Silvestri (daily 9:30–12:30 & 15:00–19:00, tel. 0742-361-667) and wander. Highlights are the Roman mosaics, remains of the arena that now houses a paper-making work-shop, the Romanesque church of San Silvestro, and a gem of a 19th-cen-tury theater. Bevagna has all the elements of a hill town except one—a hill. A couple of hours is plenty to see the main sights. For an overnight, consider the fancy Hotel Palazzo Brunamonti (Db-€65–86, more for superiore, Corso Matteotti 79, tel. 0742-361-932, fax 0742-361-948, www.brunamonti.com, hotel@brunamonti.com).

Buses connect Bevagna with Foligno (except on Sun).

Montefalco—Famous for its Sagrantino wine and its site (Montefalco means "Falcon's Mountain"), this village is dubbed the "Balcony of Umbria" for its expansive views. Intact medieval walls surround the town. The Museo Civico San Francesco displays frescoes by Benozzo Gozzoli (Fra Angelico's pupil) of the life of St. Francis. There is no TI, but the people at the museum can answer questions.

A few **buses** a day run to Bevagna.

▲**Spello**—Umbrian hill town aficionados always include Spello on their list. Just six miles south of Assisi, this town is much less touristy than its neighbor to the north. Spello will give your legs a workout. Via Consolare goes up, up, up to the top of town. Views from the terrace of the restaurant Il Trombone will have you singing a tune. The **TI** is on Piazza Matteotti 3 (daily 9:30–12:30 & 15:30–19:30, tel. 0742-301-009).

Spello is on the Perugia–Assisi–Foligno **train** line. **Buses** run to Assisi.

▲**Chiusi**—This small hill town (rated ▲▲ for Etruscan fans), which was once one of the most important Etruscan cities, is now a key train junction on the Florence–Rome line. The region's trains (to Siena, Orvieto, and Assisi) go through or change at this hub.

Highlights include the Archaeological Museum and the Etruscan tombs located just outside of town near Lago di Chiusi (€4, daily 9:00–19:30, Via Porsenna 93, tel. 0578-20177). One of the tombs is multi-chambered, with several sarcophagi; while another, the Tomba della Scimmia (Tomb of the Monkey) has some well-preserved frescoes. Visiting the tombs requires a guide, arranged through the TI or the Archaeological Museum (5 people allowed to view at a time).

Troglodyte alert! The Cathedral Museum on the main square has a dark, underground labyrinth of Etruscan tunnels (bring a flashlight). The mandatory guided tour ends in a large Roman cistern from which you can climb the church bell tower for an expansive view of the countryside (museum-€2, labyrinth-€3, combo-ticket-€4, daily 9:30–12:45 & 16:00–19:00, tours at 11:00 and 16:00, Piazza Duomo 1, 0578-226-490).

The **TI** is on the main square (daily in summer 9:00–12:30 & 15:30–19:00, off-season mornings only and closed Sun, tel. 0578-227-667, prolocochiusi@bcc.tin.it). **Trains** connect Chiusi with Rome, Florence, Siena, and more. Buses link the train station with the town center two miles away.

SIGHTS

▲**U.S. Cemetery**—Whatever one's feelings about war, the sight of endless rows of white marble crosses and Stars of David never fails to be moving. This particular cemetery is the final resting place of more than 4,000 Americans who died in the liberation of Italy during World War II. Their memory lives on in two Italian cemeteries, one in Nettuno near

Rome and this one just south of Tavernuzze, seven miles south of Florence. Climb the hill past the perfectly manicured grassy lawn, lined with grave markers, to the memorial, where maps and history of the Italian campaign detail the Allied advance (daily mid-April–Sept 9:00–18:00, Oct–mid-April 9:00–17:00, WC, just off Via Cassia road that parallels the *superstrada* between Florence and Siena, 2 miles south of Florence Certosa exit on A-1 autostrada). **Buses** from Florence stop just outside the cemetery.

San Galgano Monastery—Of southern Tuscany's several evocative monasteries, San Galgano is the best. San Galgano was a 12th-century saint who renounced his past as a knight by miraculously burying his sword up to its hilt into a stone. After his death, a large monastery complex grew up. Today, all you'll see is the roofless, ruined abbey and, on a nearby hill, the Chapel of San Galgano with its fascinating dome and sword in the stone. The adjacent gift shop sells a little bit of everything from wine to postcards to herbs, some of it made by religious orders (free, daily 8:00–sunset). Other more accessible Tuscan monasteries worth visiting include San Antimo (6 miles south of Montalcino) and Monte Oliveto Maggiore (15 miles south of Siena).

Although a bus reportedly comes here from Siena, this sight is realistically accessible only for drivers. It's just outside of Monticiano (not Montalcino), about an hour south of Siena. A warning to the queasy: these roads are curvy.

▲▲**Crete Senese Drives**—South of Siena, the area known as the "Clay Hills" is full of colorful fields and curvy, scenic roads. You'll see an endless parade of classic Tuscan scenes, rolling hills topped with medieval towns, olive groves, rustic stone farmhouses, and a skyline punctuated with cypress trees. You won't find many wineries here, since the clay soil is better for wheat and sunflowers—but you will find the pristine, panoramic Tuscan countryside that you see on calendars and postcards.

During the spring, the fields are painted in yellow and green with fava beans and broom, dotted by red poppies on the fringes. Sunflowers decorate the area during July and August, and expanses of wind-blown grass fill the landscape almost all year.

From Siena to Montalcino: Most roads to the southeast of Siena will give you a taste, but one of the most scenic stretches is the Laurentina road (Siena–Asciano–San Giovanni D'Asso, #438 on road maps, can easily continue to Montalcino). There are plenty of turn-outs on this road for panoramic photo opportunities, and a few roadside picnic areas.

For a break from the winding road, about 15 miles from Siena, you'll find the quaint and non-touristy village of **Asciano**. With a medieval town center and several interesting churches and museums, this is a great place for lunch (TI at Corso Matteotti 18, tel. 0577-719-510).

If you're in town on Saturday, gather a picnic at the outdoor market (Via Amendola, daily 8:00–14:00).

Five miles south of Asciano, the **Abbey of Monte Oliveto Maggiore** houses a famous fresco cycle of the life of St. Benedict, painted by Renaissance masters Sodoma and Luca Signorelli (free, daily 9:15–12:00 & 15:15–18:00). Once you reach the town of **San Giovanni d'Asso**, it's only another 12 miles southwest to Montalcino.

From Montalcino to Montepulciano: This lovely stretch, labeled #146 on road maps, alternates between the grassy hills of the Crete Senese and sun-bathed vineyards of the Orcia River valley. Stop by Pienza en route.

Sleeping in the Crete Senese: **Agriturismo il Molinello** rents four apartments, two built over a medieval mill. Hardworking Alessandro and Elisa share their organic produce and sometimes offer wine-tastings. With children, friendly dogs, toys, and a swimming pool, this is ideal for families (Qb-€70–100, apartment for up to 8-€130, 1-week stay required in summer, discounts and 2-night min off-season: mountain bike rentals; near Asciano, 30 min southeast of Siena; tel. 0577-704-791, mobile 335-692-5720, fax 0577-705-605, www.molinello.com, info@molinello.com, SE).

ROME

(Roma)

Rome is magnificent and brutal at the same time. Your ears will ring, if you're careless you'll be run down or pickpocketed, and you'll be frustrated by the kind of chaos that only an Italian can understand. You may even come to believe Mussolini was a necessary evil.

But Rome is required, and if your hotel provides a comfortable refuge, if you pace yourself and accept (and even partake in) the siesta plan, if you're well-organized for sightseeing, and if you protect yourself and your valuables with extra caution and discretion, you'll do fine. You'll see the sights and leave satisfied.

Rome at its peak meant civilization itself. Everything was either civilized (part of the Roman Empire, Latin- or Greek-speaking) or barbarian. Today, Rome is Italy's political capital, the capital of Catholicism, and a splendid..."junk pile" is not quite the right term...of Western civilization. As you peel through its fascinating and jumbled layers, you'll find its buildings, cats, laundry, traffic, and 2.6 million people endlessly entertaining. And then, of course, there are the magnificent sights.

Tour St. Peter's, the greatest church on earth, and scale Michelangelo's 330-foot-tall dome, the world's largest. Learn something about eternity by touring the huge Vatican Museum. You'll find the story of Creation, bright as the day it was painted, in the recently restored Sistine Chapel. Do the "Caesar Shuffle" through ancient Rome's Forum and Colosseum. Savor Europe's most sumptuous building—the Borghese Gallery—and take an early evening "Dolce Vita Stroll" down the Via del Corso with Rome's beautiful people. Enjoy an after-dark walk from Campo de' Fiori to the Spanish Steps, lacing together Rome's Baroque and bubbly nightspots.

Planning Your Time

For most travelers, Rome is best done quickly. It's a great city, but it's

Greater Rome

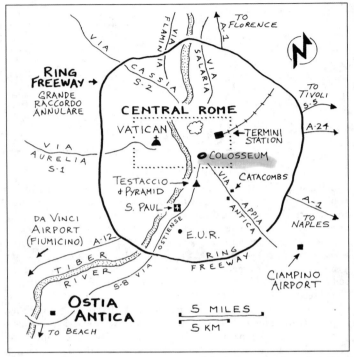

exhausting. Time is normally short, and Italy is more charming else-where. To "do" Rome in a day, consider it as a side trip from Orvieto or Florence, and maybe before the night train to Venice. Crazy as that sounds, if all you have is a day, it's a great one.

Rome in a day: Vatican (2 hours in the museum and Sistine Chapel and 1 hour in St. Peter's), taxi over the river to the Pantheon (picnic on its steps), then hike over Capitol Hill, through the Forum, and to the Colosseum. Have dinner on Campo de' Fiori and dessert on Piazza Navona.

Rome in two to three days: Day one, do the "Caesar Shuffle" from the Colosseum and Forum over Capitol Hill to the Pantheon. After a siesta, join the locals strolling from Piazza del Popolo to the Spanish Steps (see my recommended "Dolce Vita Stroll," page 453). Have dinner near your hotel.

On the second day, see the Vatican City (St. Peter's, climb the dome, and tour the Vatican Museum). Spend the evening walking from Campo de' Fiori—an atmospheric place for dinner—to the Trevi

Fountain and Spanish Steps (see "Night Walk Across Rome," page 455). With a third day, add the Borghese Gallery (reservations required) and the National Museum of Rome.

ORIENTATION

Sprawling Rome actually feels manageable once you get to know it. The old core, with most of the tourist sights, sits in a diamond formed by the train station (in the east), Vatican (west), the Borghese Gardens (north) and the Colosseum (south). The Tiber River runs through the diamond from north to south. To give an idea of scale, it takes about an hour-plus to walk from the train station to the Vatican.

Consider Rome in these layers:

The ancient city had a million people. The best of the classical sights stand in a line from the Colosseum to the Pantheon.

Medieval Rome was little more than a hobo camp of 50,000—thieves, mean dogs, and the pope, whose legitimacy required a Roman address. The medieval city, a colorful tangle of lanes, lies between the Pantheon and the river.

Window-shoppers' Rome twinkles with nightlife and ritzy shopping near Rome's main drag, Via del Corso—in the triangle formed by Piazza del Popolo, Piazza Venezia, and the Spanish Steps. **Vatican City** is a compact world of its own with two great, huge sights: St. Peter's Basilica and the Vatican Museum.

Trastevere, the seedy, colorful, wrong-side-of-the-river neighborhood/village, is Rome at its crustiest—and perhaps most "Roman."

Baroque Rome is an overleaf that embellishes great squares throughout the town with fountains and church facades.

Since no one is allowed to build taller than St. Peter's dome, the city has no modern skyline. And the Tiber River is ignored. After the last floods (1870), the banks were built up very high and Rome turned its back on its naughty, unnavigable river.

Tourist Information

While Rome has several main tourist information offices, the dozen or so TI kiosks scattered around the town at major tourist centers are handy and just as helpful. If all you need is a map, forget the TI and get one at your hotel.

You'll find helpful tourist offices—especially if they're not too busy—at the airport (daily 9:00–19:00, tel. 06-6595-6074) and at the train station (daily 8:00–21:00, near track 3, accessible from platforms or lobby, marked "Informazioni Turistiche/Tourist Info," crowded, combined with travel agency, tel. 06-4890-6300).

Smaller TIs (daily 9:00–18:00) include kiosks near the Forum (on Piazza del Tempio della Pace), at Via del Corso (on Largo Goldoni), in

Rome

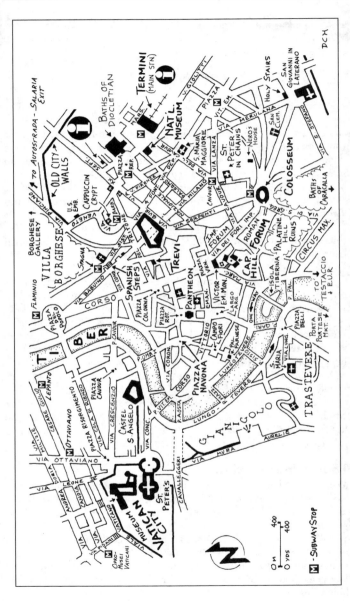

Trastevere (on Piazza Sonnino), on Via Nazionale (at Palazzo delle Esposizioni), at Castel Sant' Angelo, and at Santa Maria Maggiore. For more information, call 06-3600-4399 (daily 9:00–19:00).

At any TI, ask for a city map, a listing of sights and hours (in the free *Museums of Rome* booklet), and *Passepartout*, the free monthly entertainment guide for evening events and fun. Don't book rooms through a TI; you'll save money by booking direct.

The tourism promotion office, near Piazza della Repubblica's huge fountain, covers the city and the region. It's a five-minute walk out the front of the train station (Mon–Sat 9:00–19:00, Via Parigi 5, free Internet access to Rome tourism sites, www.romaturismo.com, tel. 06-360-64399). It's air-conditioned and less crowded than the TIs but more into promotion than information and therefore less helpful. It does have seats and a study table.

Roma c'è is a cheap little weekly entertainment guide with a helpful English section (at the back) on musical events and the pope's schedule for the week (new edition every Thu, sold at newsstands for €1, www.romace.it, Web site in Italian).

Arrival in Rome

Rome's main train station, **Termini**, is a minefield of tourist services: a TI (daily 8:00–21:00), train info office (daily 7:00–21:45), ATMs, late-hours banks, 24-hour thievery, luggage deposit (near track 24), the main city-bus hub (where you can catch the city orientation tour in front of train station), a subway stop, and the handy, cheery Food Village Chef Express Self-Service Ristorante (daily 11:00–22:30, WC at entrance, near east end of station). In the modern mall downstairs, under the station, you'll find a grocery (oddly named "Drug Store," daily 7:00–24:00) and pharmacy (daily 7:30–22:00, public showers). The station has some sleazy sharks with official-looking business cards. In general, avoid anybody selling anything at the station.

By Bus: Long-distance buses (e.g., from Siena and Assisi) arrive at Rome's small **Tiburtina** station, which is on Metro line B, with easy connections to the main train station (a straight shot 4 stops away) and the entire Metro system.

Most of my hotel listings are easily accessible by foot (those near the Termini train station) or by Metro (those in the Colosseum and Vatican neighborhoods). The train station has its own Metro stop (Termini).

By Plane: If you arrive at the airport, catch a train (hrly, 30 min, €9, credit card accepted) to Rome's train station or take (or share) a taxi to your hotel. For details, see "Transportation Connections" at the end of this chapter.

Dealing with (and Avoiding) Problems

Theft Alert: With sweet-talking con artists meeting you at the station, well-dressed pickpockets on buses, and thieving gangs of children at the ancient sites, Rome is a gauntlet of rip-offs. There's no great physical risk, but green or sloppy tourists will be scammed. Thieves strike when you're distracted. Don't trust kind strangers. Keep nothing important in your pockets. Assume you're being stalked. (Then relax and have fun.) Be most on guard while boarding and leaving buses and subways. Thieves crowd the door, then stop and turn while others crowd and push from behind. The sneakiest thieves are well-dressed businessmen (generally with something in their hands); lately many are posing as tourists with fanny packs and cameras. Scams abound: Don't give your wallet to self-proclaimed "police" who stop you on the street, warn you about counterfeit (or drug) money, and ask to see your wallet. If a bank machine eats your ATM card, see if there's a thin plastic insert with a tongue hanging out that thieves use to extract it.

If you know what to look out for, the gangs of children picking the pockets and handbags of naive tourists are no threat but an interesting, albeit sad, spectacle. Gangs of city-stained children (sometimes as young as 8–10 years old), too young to be prosecuted but old enough to rip you off, troll through the tourist crowds around the Colosseum, Forum, Piazza Repubblica, and train and Metro stations. Watch them target tourists who are overloaded with bags or distracted with a video camera. The kids look like beggars and hold up newspapers or cardboard signs to confuse their victims. They scram like stray cats if you're onto them. A fast-fingered mother with a baby is often nearby. The terrace above the bus stop near the Colosseum Metro stop is a fine place to watch the action and maybe even pick up a few moves of your own.

Reporting Losses: To report lost or stolen passports and documents or to file an insurance claim, you must file a police report (at the train station with Polizia at track 1 or with Carabinieri at track 20, also at Piazza Venezia). To replace a passport, file the police report, then go to your embassy (see below). The following phone numbers, beginning with 800, are Italian (dialed free in Italy). To report stolen or lost credit cards, call the company (Visa—tel. 800-877-232 or 800-819-014, MasterCard—tel. 800-870-866, American Express tel. 800-874-333), then file a police report. To report lost traveler's checks, call your bank (Visa—tel. 800-874-155, Thomas Cook/MasterCard—tel. 800-872-050, American Express—tel. 800-872-000), then file a police report.

Embassies: United States (Mon–Fri 8:30–13:00 & 14:00–17:30, Via Vittorio Veneto 119/A, tel. 06-46741, www.usembassy.it) and Canada (Via Zara 30, tel. 06-445-981, www.canada.it).

Emergency Numbers: Police—tel. 113. Ambulance—tel. 118.

Hit and Run: Walk with extreme caution. Scooters don't need to stop at red lights, and even cars exercise what drivers call the "logical option" of not stopping if they see no oncoming traffic. As noisy scooters are replaced by electric ones, they'll be quieter (hooray) but more dangerous for pedestrians. Follow locals like a shadow when you cross a street (or spend a good part of your visit stranded on curbs).

Staying/Getting Healthy: The siesta is a key to survival in summertime Rome. Lie down and contemplate the extraordinary power of gravity in the eternal city. I drink lots of cold, refreshing water from Rome's many drinking fountains (the Forum has 3). There's a pharmacy (marked by a green cross) in every neighborhood, including a handy one in the train station (daily 7:30–22:00, located downstairs, at west end), and a 24-hour pharmacy on Piazza dei Cinquecento 51 (next to train station on Via Cavour, tel. 06-488-0019). Embassies can recommend English-speaking doctors. Consider MEDline, a 24-hour home medical service (tel. 06-808-0995, doctors speak English). Anyone is entitled to free emergency treatment at public hospitals. The hospital closest to the train station is Policlinico Umberto 1 (entrance for emergency treatment on Via Lancisi, translators available, Metro: Policlinico). The American Hospital is a private hospital on the edge of town accustomed to helping Yankees (tel. 06-225-571).

Helpful Hints

In Rome, get train tickets and railpass-related reservations and supplements at travel agencies, rather than dealing with the congested train station. The cost is either the same or there's a minimal charge. Your hotel can direct you to the nearest travel agency. Quo Vadis, near the Vatican, is helpful (Via della Conciliazione, 22–24, tel. 06-6880-4941, fax 06-6880-3191, qv.viaggi@tiscalinet.it). Or purchase train tickets from the American Express office near the Spanish Steps (Mon–Fri 9:00–17:30, closed Sat–Sun, Piazza di Spagna 38, tel. 06-67641).

Bookstore: Try American Bookstore (Via Torino 136, Metro: Repubblica, tel. 06-474-6877).

Internet Access: The biggest is easyInternetcafe, centrally located on Piazza Barberini (access from €0.50, open 24/7, 350 terminals, www.easyinternetcafe.com). Your hotelier can direct you to an Internet access point near your hotel.

Laundry: Ask your hotelier for the nearest launderette (usually open daily 8:00–22:00, about €6 to wash and dry a 15-pound load). The Bolle Blu chain comes with Internet access (near train station at Via Milazzo 20, Via Palestro 59, and Via Principe Amedeo 70, tel. 06-446-5804).

Web Sites on Rome: www.romaturismo.com (music, exhibitions, and events, in English), www.wantedinrome.com (job openings and real estate, but also festivals and exhibitions, in English), and www.vatican.va (the pope's Web site, in English).

Getting around Rome

Sightsee on foot, by city bus, or by taxi. I've grouped your sightseeing into walkable neighborhoods.

Public transportation is efficient, cheap, and part of your Roman experience. It starts running around 5:30 and stops around 23:30, sometimes earlier. After midnight, there are a few very crowded night buses, and taxis become more expensive and hard to get. Don't try to hail one—go to a taxi stand.

Buses and subways use the same ticket. You can buy tickets at newsstands, tobacco shops (*tabacchi*, marked by a black-and-white "T" sign), or at major Metro stations or bus stops, but not on board. Since many Metro stations have no human ticket-sellers and the machines are either broken or require exact change (helps to put in smallest coin first), it's easier to buy a few tickets above ground at newsstands or *tabacchi* (€0.80, good for 75 min, valid for one Metro ride, including transfers, and unlimited buses) or an all-day bus/Metro pass (€3.25, for more info, visit www.atac.roma.it). One-week transit passes cost €12.50. Stamp your ticket before using it (machines are near subway turnstiles and on buses—watch others and imitate).

Buses (especially the touristic #64) and the subway are havens for thieves and pickpockets. Assume any commotion is a thief-created distraction. If one bus is packed, there's likely a second one on its tail with far fewer crowds and thieves.

By Metro: The Roman subway system (Metropolitana) is simple, with two clean, cheap, fast lines that intersect at Termini train station. While much of Rome is not served by its skimpy subway, these stops are helpful:

Termini—Train station, National Museum of Rome (at Palazzo Massimo), recommended hotels

Repubblica—Baths of Diocletian/Octagonal Hall, TI, recommended hotels

Barberini—Cappuccin Crypt, Trevi Fountain

Spagna—Spanish Steps, Villa Borghese, classy shopping area

Flaminio—Piazza del Popolo, start of recommended Dolce Vita Stroll down Via del Corso

Ottaviano—St. Peter's and Vatican City

Cipro-Musei Vaticani—Vatican Museum, recommended hotels

Colosseo—Colosseum, Roman Forum, recommended hotels

E.U.R.—Mussolini's futuristic suburb

First and last compartments are generally less crowded.

By Bus: Bus routes are clearly listed at the stops. Ask the TI for a bus map (bus info: tel. 06-4695-2027). Punch your ticket in the orange stamping machine as you board (even if you've already stamped it for the Metro)—or you are cheating. Riding without a stamped ticket on the bus, while relatively safe, is stressful. Inspectors fine even innocent-

Metropolitana: Rome's Subway

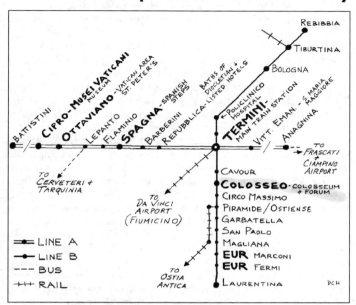

looking tourists €52. If the validation machine won't work, you can write the date, time, and bus number on the ticket. Ideally, buy a bunch of tickets from a tobacco shop or newsstand first thing so you can hop a bus without first having to search for a tobacco shop that's open.

Here are a few buses worth knowing about:

#64—Termini (train station), Piazza della Repubblica (sights), Via Nazionale (recommended hotels), Piazza Venezia (near Forum), Largo Argentina (near Pantheon), and St. Peter's Basilica. Ride it for a city overview and to watch pickpockets in action (can get horribly crowded).

#40—This express route is especially helpful—it's the same route as #64, but with fewer stops, crowds, and pickpockets.

#8—This tram connects Largo Argentina with Trastevere (get off at Piazza Mastai).

#H—Express connecting Termini train station and Trastevere, with a few stops on Via Nazionale (for Trastevere, get off at Piazza Belli, just over bridge).

#492—Stazione Tiburtina (bus station), Piazza Barberini, Piazza Venezia, Piazza Cavour (Castel Sant' Angelo), and Piazza Risorgimento (near Vatican Museum).

Rome has cute *"elettrico"* minibuses that wind through the narrow streets of old and interesting neighborhoods (daily except Sun). These are handy for sightseeing and fun for simply joyriding:

Elettrico #116: Through the medieval core of Rome from Ponte Vittorio Emanuele II (near Castel Sant' Angelo) to Campo de' Fiori to Piazza Barberini via the Pantheon and on to the Villa Borghese.

Elettrico #117: San Giovanni in Laterano, Colosseo, Via dei Serpenti, Trevi Fountain, Piazza di Spagna, and Piazza del Popolo.

By Taxi: I use taxis in Rome more often than in other cities. They're reasonable and useful for efficient sightseeing in a big, hot city. Taxis start at about €2.50 and charge about €1 per kilometer from there (surcharges of €1 on Sun, €2.75 for night hours of 22:00–7:00, €1 surcharge for luggage, €7.25 extra for airport, tip by rounding up to the nearest euro). Sample fares: Train station to Vatican–€9; train station to Colosseum–€6; Colosseum to Trastevere–€7. Three or four companions with more money than time should taxi almost everywhere. It's tough to wave down a taxi in Rome. Find the nearest taxi stand by asking a passerby or a clerk in a shop, *"Dov'è* (doh-vay) *una fermata dei tassi?"* (Some are listed on my maps.) Taxis listing their telephone number on the door have fair meters—use them. To save time and energy, have your hotel call a taxi; the meter starts when the call is received. To call a cab on your own, dial 06-3570, 06-4994, or 06-88177.

When you arrive at the train station or airport, beware of hustlers conning naïve visitors into unmarked rip-off "express taxis." Only use official taxis, with a "taxi" sign and phone number marked on the door. By law, they must display a multilingual official price chart.

By Boat: A new boat service makes stops up and down the Tiber (you'll see the docks, 2/hr, €1/ride, €2.50/day pass, daily 7:30–20:00, until 24:00 in summer). In 2004 they hope to extend the service all the way to Ostia Antica.

TOURS

Scala Reale—Tom Rankin (an American architect in love with Rome and his Roman wife) runs Scala Reale, a company committed to sorting out the rich layers of Rome for small groups with a longer-than-average attention span. Their excellent walking tours vary in length from two to four hours and start at €20 per person. Try to book in advance, since their groups are limited to six and fill up fast. Their fascinating "Rome Orientation" walks lace together lesser-known sights from antiquity to the present (tel. 06-474-5673, 888/467-1986 in the U.S., www.scalareale .org, info@scalareale.org).

If you're interested in weeklong classes on Rome, look into the Institute for Roman Culture, an innovative, educational organization run by Tom Rankin and his colleague, archaeologist Darius Arya (see www.romanculture.org for prices, details, and booking).

Through Eternity—This company, which gets mixed reviews from read-

DAILY REMINDER

Sunday: These sights are closed: Vatican Museum (except for the last Sunday of the month, when it's free and crowded) and the Catacombs of San Sebastian. The Pantheon and E.U.R.'s Museum of Roman Civilization close early in the afternoon. The old center is delightfully quiet.

Monday: Many sights are closed: National Museum of Rome, Borghese Gallery, Capitol Hill Museum, Octagonal Hall (at Baths of Diocletian), Etruscan Museum, Castel Sant' Angelo, Trajan's Market, Montemartini Museum, Protestant Cemetery, E.U.R.'s Museum of Roman Civilization, and Ostia Antica.

All of the ancient sights (e.g., Colosseum, Forum) and the Vatican Museum, among others, open. The Baths of Caracalla close early in the afternoon.

Tuesday: All sights are open in Rome except for Nero's Golden House. This isn't a good day to side-trip to Naples, because its Archaeological Museum is closed.

Wednesday: All sights are open except for the Catacombs of San Callisto.

Thursday: All sights are open except for the Cappuccin Crypt and Galleria Doria Pamphilj.

Friday: All sights are open in Rome.

ers, offers four walking tours, all led by native English speakers. The tours include St. Peter's and the Vatican Museum (€35, museum entry not included, 5 hrs, most days); the Colosseum and Roman Forum (€20, 2.5 hrs, daily); Rome at Twilight (€20, nightly); and a Wine Sampling Tour (€35, nightly, includes a glass at 4 or 5 wine bars and dinner). Call or visit their Web site to get the schedule and to book in advance (max of 20 people, tel. 06-700-9336, mobile 347-336-5298, private tours possible, www.througheternity.com, info@througheternity.com, Rob Allen).

Rome Walks—Students working for "Rome Walks" give tours in fluent English to small groups (2–8 people). Sample tours include Colosseum/Forum/Palatine Walk (€48, includes admission to Colosseum, 3 hrs), Scandal Tour (€30, 2 hrs to dig up the dirt on Roman emperors, royalty, and popes), Vatican City Walk (€55, includes admission to Vatican Museum, 4 hrs), and a Twilight Rome Evening Walk (all the famous squares that offer lively people scenes, €25, 2 hrs). See their Web site for the latest (www.romewalks.com) and book in advance by e-mail (info@romewalks.com) or phone (mobile 347-795-5175, private tours

ROME AT A GLANCE

▲▲▲**Vatican Museum** Four miles of the art of Western Civilization, culminating in the Sistine Chapel. **Hours:** March–Oct Mon–Fri 8:45–16:45, Sat 8:45–13:45; Nov–Feb Mon–Sat 8:45–13:45; closed many holidays and Sun except last Sun of the month.

▲▲▲**St. Peter's Basilica** Most impressive church on earth, with Michelangelo's *Pietà* and dome. **Hours:** Daily May–Sept 7:00–19:00, Oct–April 7:00–18:00. Dome: Daily May–Sept 8:30–18:00, Oct–April 8:30–17:00.

▲▲▲**Roman Forum** Ancient Rome's main square, with ruins and grand arches. **Hours:** Daily 9:00–19:00 or until an hour before dark.

▲▲▲**Colosseum** Huge stadium where gladiators fought. **Hours:** Daily 9:00–19:00 or until an hour before dark.

▲▲▲**Pantheon** The defining domed temple. **Hours:** Mon–Sat 8:30–19:30, Sun 9:00–18:00, holidays 9:00-13:00.

▲▲▲**National Museum of Rome** Greatest collection of Roman sculpture anywhere. **Hours:** Tue–Sun 9:00–19:45, closed Mon.

▲▲▲**Borghese Gallery Villa** Bernini sculptures and paintings by Caravaggio, Raphael, and Titian. **Hours:** Tue–Sun 9:00–19:30, Sat maybe until 23:00 June–Sept, closed Mon, reservations mandatory.

▲▲**Catacombs** Layers of tunnels with tombs, mainly Christian, outside the city. **Hours:** Open 8:30–12:00 & 14:30–17:30, until 17:00 in winter (San Callisto closed Wed and Feb, San Sebastian closed Sun and Nov).

▲▲**Capitol Hill Museum** Ancient statues, mosaics, and expansive view of Forum. **Hours:** Tue–Sun 9:00–20:00, closed Mon, Jan 1, May 1, and Dec 25.

▲▲**Capitol Hill** Hilltop square designed by Michelangelo with museum, grand stairway, and Forum overlooks. **Hours:** Always open.

▲**Trajan's Column** Tall column with narrative relief, on Piazza Venezia. **Hours:** Always viewable.

▲**Nero's Golden House** Sparse remains of Emperor Nero's sprawling home. **Hours:** Wed–Mon 9:00–19:45, last entry at 18:40, closed Tue.

▲**Mamertine Prison** Prison that held Saints Peter and Paul. **Hours:** Daily 9:00–12:30 & 14:30–18:00.

▲Arch of Constantine Honors Emperor Constantine, who legalized Christianity. **Hours:** Always open.

▲Palatine Hill Ruins of emperors' palaces, Circus Maximus view, and museum. **Hours:** Daily 9:00–19:00 or an hour before dark.

▲Castel Sant' Angelo Hadrian's Tomb turned castle, prison, papal refuge, now museum. **Hours:** Tue–Sun 9:00–19:00, plus June–Sept Sat 21:00–23:45, closed Mon.

▲Baths of Diocletian Once ancient Rome's immense public baths, now a Michelangelo church—Church of Santa Maria degli Angeli—and the Octagonal Hall, a room with minor ancient Roman Sculpture. **Hours:** Mon–Sat 7:00–18:30, Sun 8:00–19:30. Octagonal Hall: Tue–Sat 9:00–14:00, Sun 9:00–13:00, closed Mon.

▲Museum of Roman Civilization Lifeless museum, but has a 3-D model of ancient Rome. **Hours:** Tue–Sat 9:00–18:45, Sun 9:00–13:30, closed Mon.

▲Montemartini Museum 400 Roman statues in a 1932 electric power plant. **Hours:** Tue–Sun 9:30–19:00, closed Mon.

▲Galleria Doria Pamphilj Fancy palace packed with art. **Hours:** Fri–Wed 10:00–17:00, closed Thu.

▲Cappuccin Crypt Crypt decorated with the bones of 4,000 monks. **Hours:** Fri–Wed 9:00–12:00 & 15:00–18:00, closed Thu.

▲St. Peter-in-Chains Church with Michelangelo's *Moses*. **Hours:** Mon–Sat 7:00–12:30 & 15:30–19:00, Sun 7:30–12:30.

▲Santa Maria della Vittoria Church with Bernini's swooning *St. Teresa in Ecstasy*. **Hours:** Daily 7:00–12:00 & 15:30–19:00.

▲St. Paul's Outside the Walls Huge, Vatican-owned basilica in south Rome, rebuilt in 19th century. **Hours:** Daily 7:00–18:00, cloister closed 13:00–15:00.

▲Villa Borghese Central Park of Rome with lake, Borghese Gallery, and Etruscan Museum. **Hours:** Always open.

▲Trevi Fountain Baroque hotspot—bring coins. **Hours:** Always flowing.

also available, Annie). You'll need to give the name of your hotel and the phone number. Your guide will call or e-mail you to let you know the meeting place.

Roman Odyssey Tours—Another ex-pat tour company, Roman Odyssey, offers various 2-hour, €20 walks. To get folks on board, they often give free 40-minute tours of St. Peters' Square and Basilica (tel. 06-580-9902, mobile 328-912-3720, for a listing of tours see www.romanodyssey.com, Rahul and Jason).

Private Guides—Consider a personal tour. Any of the tour companies I list can provide a guide. I work with Francesca Caruso, a licensed guide who speaks excellent English and loves to teach and share her appreciation of her city (€100 for 2 hrs or more—she happily stretches the tour to half a day for eager students, individuals, and small groups; chris.fra@mclink.it).

Hop-on, Hop-off Bus Tour—The ATAC city bus tour offers a quick, cheap orientation tour of Rome. In under two hours, you'll have 80 sights pointed out to you (by a live guide in English and maybe one other language). If you've got a little more time and money, you can get out at any of the nine stops and catch a later bus (though stops are poorly marked and the included map is useless). The stops are: Piazza Barberini, Via Veneto, Villa Borghese, Piazza Cavour, St. Peter's Square, Corso Vittorio Emanuele (for Piazza Navona), Piazza Venezia, Colosseum, and Via Nazionale.

While the guide's spiel is limited to simple identification of the sights, this tour provides an efficient and economical orientation to Rome. I'd take the nonstop tour for €7.75; the hop-on, hop-off tour is €13. Bus #110 departs every 30 minutes—at the top and bottom of the hour—from in front of the Termini train station (near platform C, buy tickets at info kiosk there—marked "i bus"—or buy on the bus and pay about 10 percent more, runs March–Sept 9:00–20:00, Oct–Feb 10:00–18:00, tel. 06-4695-2252).

Archeobus—This handy hop-on, hop-off bus runs hourly from the west side of Piazza Venezia way out the Appian Way. By far the easiest way to see the sights down this ancient Roman road, it includes a basic, uninspired two-hour tour (longer if there's traffic) in Italian and English in an air-conditioned minibus (buy €7.75 tickets at green kiosk on Piazza Venezia, hourly departures from 9:00–17:00, tel. 06-4695-4695).

SIGHTS

From the Colosseum Area to Capitol Hill

Beware of gangs of young thieves, particularly between the Colosseum and the Forum; they're harmless if you know their tricks (see Theft Alert, page 402).

Colosseum Area

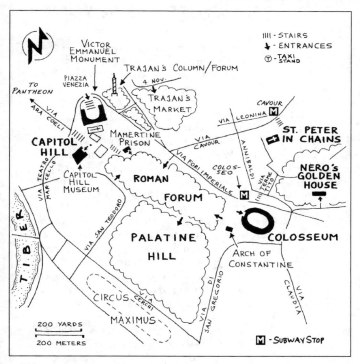

IIII - STAIRS
↓ - ENTRANCES
Ⓣ - TAXI STAND

200 YARDS
200 METERS

Ⓜ - SUBWAY STOP

▲**St. Peter-in-Chains Church (San Pietro in Vincoli)**—Built in the fifth century to house the chains that held St. Peter, this church is most famous for its Michelangelo statue. Check out the much-venerated chains under the high altar, then focus on Moses (free, Mon–Sat 7:00–12:30 & 15:30–19:00, Sun 7:30–12:30, modest dress required; the church is a short, uphill, zigzag walk from the Colosseum, or a shorter, simpler walk from the Cavour Metro stop—exiting the Metro stop, go up steep flight of steps, take a right at the top and walk a block to church).

Pope Julius II commissioned Michelangelo to build a massive tomb, with 48 huge statues, crowned by a grand statue of this egomaniacal pope. The pope had planned to have his tomb placed in the center of St. Peter's Basilica. When Julius died, the work had barely been started, and no one had the money or necessary commitment to Julius to finish the project. Michelangelo finished one statue—Moses—and left a few unfinished statues: Leah and Rachel flanking Moses in this church, the "prisoners" now in Florence's Accademia, and the "slaves" now in Paris' Louvre.

TIPS ON SIGHTSEEING IN ROME

Museums: Plan ahead. The marvelous Borghese Gallery and Nero's Golden House both require reservations. For the Borghese Gallery, it's safest to make reservations well in advance of your trip (for specifics, see page 425). You can wait until you're in Rome to call for a reservation time at Nero's Golden House, but it's wise to book ahead (see page 413).

A special **combo-ticket,** which costs €20, covers the National Museum of Rome, Colosseum, Palatine Hill, Baths of Caracalla, Crypt Balbi (medieval art), Museum of the Bath (Roman inscriptions), and Palazzo Altemps (so–so sculpture collection). The combo–ticket allows you to see seven sights for the price of three (purchase at participating sites, valid for 7 days). When you buy this, you can upgrade to a "Coupon Servizi" pass for an extra €5, giving you tours or audioguides at each site (normally about €4 each). The big plus of this ticket is that you avoid the long lines at the Colosseum (if you purchase it at a participating site other than the Colosseum).

Get a current listing of **museum hours** from one of Rome's TIs—ask for the booklet *Museums of Rome.* The opening hours of sights can vary in summer, in winter, on holidays, and just about anytime.

Churches: Churches generally open early (around 7:00), close for lunch (roughly 12:00–15:00), and close late (around 19:00). Kamikaze tourists maximize their sightseeing hours by visiting churches before 9:00 and seeing the major sights that stay open during the siesta (St. Peter's, Colosseum, Forum, Capitol Hill Museum, National Museum of Rome) while Romans are taking it cool and easy.

A modest dress code is strictly enforced at St. Peter's at the Vatican and St. Paul's Outside the Walls. That means no bare shoulders, miniskirts, or shorts—for men, women, or children. Elsewhere, you'll see many tourists in shorts touring many churches.

This powerful statue of Moses—mature Michelangelo—is worth studying. The artist worked on it in fits and starts for 30 years. Moses has received the Ten Commandments. As he holds the stone tablets, his eyes show a man determined to stop his tribe from worshiping the golden calf and idols...a man determined to win salvation for the people of Israel. Why the horns? Centuries ago, the Hebrew word for "rays" was mistranslated as "horns."

▲**Nero's Golden House (Domus Aurea)**—The barren remains of Emperor Nero's "Golden House" were reopened to the public in 1999. This massive house once sprawled across the valley (where the Colosseum now stands) and up the hill—the part you tour today. A colossal, 100-foot-tall bronze statue of Nero towered over everything. The house incorporated an artificial lake (where the Colosseum was later built) and a forest stocked with game.

Nero (ruled A.D. 54–68) was Rome's most notorious emperor. He killed his own mother, kicked his pregnant wife to death, crucified St. Peter, and—most galling to his subjects—was a bad actor. When Rome burned in A.D. 64, Nero was accused of torching it to clear land for an even bigger house. The Romans rebelled and Nero stabbed himself in the neck, crying, "What an artist dies in me!"

While only hints of the splendid, colorful frescoes survive, the towering vaults and the sheer immensity of the place are impressive. As you wander through rooms that are now underground (but originally were not), look up at the holes in the ceiling. Ponder how much of old Rome still hides underground...and why the subway is limited to two lines.

Visits are allowed only with an escort (30 people, about every 30 min) and a reservation (€6, Wed–Mon 9:00–19:45, last entry at 18:40, closed Tue, tour lasts 50 min, audioguide–€2, but listen to the intro before entering or you'll be forever behind, Metro: Colosseo, 200 yards northeast of Colosseum, through a park gate, up a hill, and on the left). If you show up without a reservation, you could luck out and be allowed in (chances are best on a late afternoon on a weekday). Guided tours in English are offered twice daily (€8.50); to reserve a place, call 06-3996-7700 (Mon–Sat 9:00–17:00).

▲▲▲**Colosseum**—This 2,000-year-old building is *the* great example of Roman engineering. Using concrete, brick, and their trademark round arches, Romans constructed much larger buildings than the Greeks. But in deference to the higher Greek culture, they finished their no-nonsense megastructure by pasting all three orders of Greek columns (Doric, Ionic, and Corinthian) as exterior decorations. The Flavian Amphitheater's popular name, "Colosseum," comes from the colossal statue of Nero that once stood in front of it.

Romans were into "big." By putting two theaters together, they created a circular amphitheater. They could fill and empty its 50,000 numbered seats as quickly and efficiently as we do our superstadiums. Teams of sailors hoisted canvas awnings over the stadium to give fans shade. This was where ancient Romans, whose taste for violence was the equal of modern America's, enjoyed their Dirty Harry and *Terminator*. Gladiators, criminals, and wild animals fought to the death in every conceivable scenario. The floor of the Colosseum is missing, exposing

Colosseum

underground passages. Animals were kept in cages here and then lifted up in elevators; they'd pop out from behind blinds into the arena. The gladiator didn't know where, when, or by what he'd be attacked.

Cost, Hours, Location: €8 (includes Palatine Hill visit within 24 hours; also covered by €20 combo-ticket). A dry-but-fact-filled audio-guide is available at the ticket office (€4 for 2 hours of use). Guided tours in English depart several times per day and last about one hour (€4). The Colosseum is open daily 9:00–19:00, or until an hour before sunset (tel. 06-3974-9907). Metro: Colosseo.

Outside the entrance of the Colosseum, vendors sell handy little *Rome: Past and Present* books with plastic overlays to un-ruin the ruins (marked €11, price soft). A WC is behind the Colosseum (facing ticket entrance, go right; WC is under stairway). Caution: For a fee, the incredibly crude modern-day gladiators snuff out their cigarettes and pose for photos. They take easy-to-swindle tourists for too much money. Watch out if you tangle with these guys (they're armed...and accustomed to getting as much as €100 from naïve Asian tourists). Also, be on guard as this is traditionally a happy-hunting ground for gangs of child pickpockets.

Avoid Long Lines: Instead of waiting in line (sometimes an hour long) at the Colosseum to purchase a ticket, you have several good alternatives:

1. Buy your ticket at either of the two rarely crowded Palatine Hill entrances near the Colosseum—there's one inside the Forum and another on Via di San Gregorio (facing Forum entry, with Colosseum at your back, go left on street). This €8 ticket includes entry to both the Colosseum and Palatine (valid for 24 hours).

2. Consider buying a €20 combo-ticket at a less-crowded sight. The combo-ticket—covering the Colosseum, Palatine Hill, National Museum of Rome, Museum of the Bath, Baths of Caracalla, and more—allows you to walk right past the Colosseum ticket line, through the turnstile, and into the Colosseum. Buy it at any of the included sights.

3. You can reserve your ticket in advance for an additional €1.50 fee by calling 06-3996-7700 (automated info in English, pay for ticket at side window of Colosseum's ticket office).

4. You can book a tour on the spot from hustlers who rescue individuals from the line by selling tours that include tickets they already have. This will cost you a few euros (€15 for the tour including the €8 ticket), but can save time and comes with a brief guided tour. Beware—American students working for the guides will tell you that there's a long line, when sometimes, there is none at all. (It can be hard for you to instantly judge the length of the line because it's tucked into the Colosseum arcade.)

▲**Arch of Constantine**—The arch, next to the Colosseum, marks one of the great turning points in history—the military coup that made Christianity mainstream. In A.D. 312, Emperor Constantine defeated his rival Maxentius in one crucial battle. The night before, he had seen a vision of a cross in the sky. Constantine became sole emperor and legalized Christianity. With this one battle, a once-obscure Jewish sect with a handful of followers was now the state religion of the entire Western world. In A.D. 300, you could be killed for being a Christian; later, you could be killed for not being one. Church enrollment boomed.

By the way, don't look too closely at the reliefs decorating this arch. By the fourth century, Rome was on its way down. Rather than struggle with original carvings, the makers of this arch plugged in bits and pieces scavenged from existing monuments. The arch is newly restored and looking great. But any meaning read into the stone will be very jumbled.

▲▲▲**Roman Forum (Foro Romano)**—This is ancient Rome's birthplace and civic center, and the common ground between Rome's famous seven hills (free, daily 9:00–19:00 or an hour before dark, Metro: Colosseo, tel. 06-3974-9907). A €4 audioguide helps decipher the rubble (rent at gift shop at entrance on Via dei Fori Imperiali). Guided tours in English are offered nearly hourly (€4); ask for information at the ticket booth at the Palatine Hill (near Arch of Titus). See "Roman Forum Walk," page 448.

▲**Palatine Hill**—The hill above the Forum contains scanty remains of the imperial palaces and the foundations of Rome, from Iron Age huts to the legendary house of Romulus (under corrugated tin roof in far corner). We get our word *palace* from this hill, where the emperors chose to live. The Palatine was once so filled with palaces that later emperors had to build out. (Looking up at it from the Forum, you see the substructure that supported these long-gone palaces.) The Palatine museum has sculptures and fresco fragments but is nothing special. From the pleasant garden, you'll get an overview of the Forum. On the far side, look down into an emperor's private stadium and then beyond at the dusty Circus Maximus, once a chariot course. Imagine the cheers, jeers, and furious betting. But considering how ruined the ruins are, the heat, the hill to climb, the €8 entry fee, and the relative difficulty in understanding what you're looking at, the Palatine Hill is a disappointment.

Cost and Hours: €8, includes Colosseum visit within 24 hours, also covered by €20 combo-ticket, daily 9:00–19:00, or one hour before sunset, Metro: Colosseo. The main entrance and ticket office—which also sells Colosseum tickets, enabling smart sightseers to avoid that long line—is near the Arch of Titus and Colosseum. Another Palatine entrance is on Via di San Gregorio.

Audioguides cost €4. Guided tours in English are offered once daily (€3.50); ask for information at the ticket booth.

▲**Mamertine Prison**—This 2,500-year-old, cistern-like prison, which once held Saints Peter and Paul, is worth a look (donation requested, daily 9:00–12:30 & 14:30–18:00, at the foot of Capitol Hill, near Forum's Arch of Septimius Severus). When you step into the room, you'll hit a modern floor. Ignore that and look up at the hole in the ceiling, from which prisoners were lowered. Then take the stairs down to the level of the actual prison floor. Downstairs, you'll see the column to which Peter was chained. It's said that a miraculous fountain sprang up in this room so Peter could convert and baptize his jailers, who were subsequently martyred themselves. The upside-down cross commemorates Peter's upside-down crucifixion.

Imagine humans, amid fat rats and rotting corpses, awaiting slow deaths. On the walls near the entry are lists of notable prisoners (Christian and non-Christian) and the ways they were executed: *strangolati*, *decapitato*, *morto di fame* (died of hunger)....

▲**Trajan's Column, Market, and Forum**—This offers the grandest column and best example of "continuous narration" from antiquity. Over 2,500 figures scroll around the 130-foot-high column, telling of Trajan's victorious Dacian campaign (circa A.D. 103, in present-day Romania), from the assembling of the army at the bottom to the victory sacrifice at the top. The ashes of Trajan and his wife were held in the mausoleum at the base while the sun once glinted off a polished bronze statue of Trajan at the top. Today, St. Peter is on top. Study the propaganda that winds up the column like a scroll, trumpeting Trajan's wonderful military exploits. You can see this close up for free (always open and viewable, just off Piazza Venezia, across the street from the Victor Emmanuel Monument). Viewing balconies once stood on either side, but it seems likely Trajan fans came away only with a feeling that the greatness of their emperor and empire was beyond comprehension (for a rolled-out version of the column's story, visit the Museum of Roman Civilization at E.U.R., below). This column marked **Trajan's Forum**, which was built to handle the shopping needs of a wealthy city of over a million. Commercial, political, religious, and social activities all mixed in the forum.

For a fee, you can go inside **Trajan's Market** (boring) and part of Trajan's Forum; the entrance is uphill from the column on Via IV Novembre. The market was once filled with shops selling goods from all over the Roman Empire (€6.20, summer Tue–Sun 9:00–18:30, winter 9:00–16:30, closed Mon, entrance is uphill from the column on Via IV Novembre, tel. 06-679-0048).

Time Elevator Roma—Equipped with headphones, you sit in a comfortable, air-conditioned theater as the history of Rome unfolds before you—from the founding of the city, through its rise and fall, to its impressive Renaissance rebound and up to the present—with special effects en route. Good if it's hot or you're tired (€11, daily 10:00–22:00, 45-min shows every 30 min, no kids under 5, Via dei S.S. Apostoli 20, just off Via del Corso, 3-min walk from Piazza Venezia, tel. 06-699-0053, wwww.time-elevator.it).

Capitol Hill Area

There are several ways to get to the top of Capitol Hill. If you're coming from the north (Piazza Venezia), take Michelangelo's impressive stairway to the right of the big, white Victor Emmanuel Monument (described below). Coming from the south (the Forum), take either the steep staircase or the winding road, which converge near the top of the hill at a great Forum overlook and a refreshing water fountain. Block the spout with your fingers; water spurts up for drinking. Romans, who call this *il nasone* (the big nose), joke that a cheap Roman boy takes his date out for a drink at *il nasone*. Near the *nasone* is a back-door entrance to the Victor Emmanuel Monument (see Monument listing, below).

▲▲**Capitol Hill (Campidoglio)**—This hill was the religious and political center of ancient Rome. It's still the home of the city's government. Michelangelo's Renaissance square is bordered by two fine museums and the mayoral palace. Its centerpiece is a copy of the famous equestrian statue of Marcus Aurelius (the original is behind glass in the adjacent museum).

Michelangelo intended that people approach the square from his grand stairway off Piazza Venezia. From the top of the stairway, you see the new Renaissance face of Rome with its back to the Forum. Notice how Michelangelo gave the buildings the "giant order"—huge pilasters make the existing two-story buildings feel one-storied and more harmonious with the new square. Notice also how the statues atop these buildings welcome you and then draw you in. The terraces just downhill (past either side of the mayor's palace) offer fine views of the Forum.

▲▲Capitol Hill Museum—This museum encompasses two buildings (Palazzo dei Conservatori and Palazzo Nuovo), connected by an underground passage that leads to the vacant Tabularium and a panoramic overlook of the Forum (€8, Tue–Sun 9:00–20:00, last entry 60 min before closing, closed Mon, audioguide-€4, tel. 06-3996-7800).

For an orientation to the museum's two buildings, face the equestrian statue on Capitol Hill Square (with your back to the grand stairway). The Palazzo Nuovo is on your left and the Palazzo dei Conservatori is on your right (closer to the river). Ahead is the mayor's palace (Palazzo Senatorio); below it and out of sight are the Tabularium and underground passage.

Buy your ticket (and rent the optional audioguide) at Palazzo dei Conservatori.

The **Palazzo dei Conservatori** is one of the world's oldest museums, at 500 years old. Outside the entrance, notice the marriage announcements and, possibly, wedding-party photo ops. Inside the courtyard, have a look at giant chunks of a statue of Emperor Constantine; when intact, this imposing statue held court in the Basilica of Constantine in the Forum. The museum is worthwhile, with lavish rooms and several great statues. Tops is the original (500 B.C.) Etruscan *Capitoline Wolf* (the little statues of Romulus and Remus were added in the Renaissance). Don't miss the *Boy Extracting a Thorn* or the enchanting *Commodus as Hercules*. The second-floor painting gallery—except for two Caravaggios—is forgettable. The café upstairs, with a splendid patio with city views, is lovely at sunset.

Connect the two museums with the underground passage that leads to the **Tabularium**. Built in the first century A.D., this once held the archives of ancient Rome. The word *Tabularium* comes from tablet, on which the Romans wrote their laws. You won't see any tablets, but you will see a superb head-on view of the Forum from the windows.

The **Palazzo Nuovo** houses mostly portrait busts of forgotten emperors. But it has three must-see statues: the *Dying Gaul*, the *Capitoline Venus* (both on the first floor up), and the original gilded bronze equestrian statue of Marcus Aurelius (behind glass in museum courtyard). This greatest surviving equestrian statue of antiquity was the original centerpiece of the square. While most such pagan statues were destroyed by Dark Age Christians, Marcus was mistaken for Constantine (the first Christian emperor) and therefore spared.

From Capitol Hill to Piazza Venezia—Leaving Capitol Hill, descend the stairs leading to Piazza Venezia. At the bottom of the stairs, look

Capitol Hill Museum

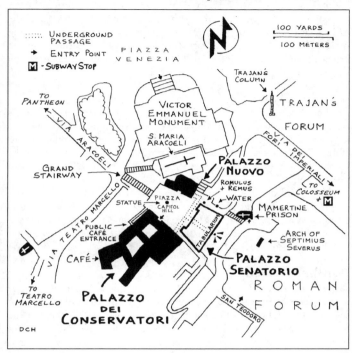

UNDERGROUND PASSAGE
ENTRY POINT
M - SUBWAY STOP

100 YARDS
100 METERS

PIAZZA VENEZIA

N

TRAJAN'S COLUMN

TO PANTHEON

VICTOR EMMANUEL MONUMENT

S. MARIA ARACOELI

VIA ARACOELI

TRAJAN'S FORUM

VIA DEI FORI IMPERIALI

GRAND STAIRWAY

PALAZZO NUOVO

ROMULUS + REMUS

WATER

TO COLOSSEUM + M

VIA TEATRO MARCELLO

STATUE

PIAZZA CAPITOL HILL

TABULARIUM

MAMERTINE PRISON

PUBLIC CAFÉ ENTRANCE

ARCH OF SEPTIMIUS SEVERUS

CAFÉ

PALAZZO SENATORIO

ROMAN FORUM

TO TEATRO MARCELLO

PALAZZO DEI CONSERVATORI

SAN TEODORO

DCH

left several blocks down the street to see a condominium actually built around surviving ancient pillars and arches of Teatro Marcello—perhaps the oldest inhabited building in Europe.

Still at the bottom of the stairs, look up the long stairway to your right (which pilgrims climb on their knees) for a good example of the earliest style of Christian church. While pilgrims find it worth the climb, sightseers can skip it. As you walk toward Piazza Venezia, look down into the ditch on your right to see the ruins of an ancient apartment building from the 1st century A.D.; part of it was transformed into a tiny church (faded frescoes and bell tower). Rome was built in layers—almost everywhere there is an earlier version beneath your feet.

Piazza Venezia—This vast square is the focal point of modern Rome. The Via del Corso, which starts here, is the city's axis, surrounded by Rome's classiest shopping district. In the 1930s, Mussolini whipped up Italy's nationalistic fervor here from a balcony above the square (to your left with your back to Victor Emmanuel Monument). Fascist masses filled the square screaming, "Four more years!"—or something like that.

Fifteen years later, they hung Mussolini from a meat hook in Milan.

Victor Emmanuel Monument—This oversized monument to Italy's first king—built to celebrate the 50th anniversary of the country's unification—was part of Italy's push to overcome the new country's strong regionalism and to create a national identity. Open to the public, it offers a grand view of the Eternal City (free, long hours, 242 punishing steps to the top).

Romans think of the 200-foot-high, 500-foot-wide monument not as an altar of the fatherland, but as "the wedding cake," "the typewriter," or "the dentures." It wouldn't be so bad if it weren't sitting on a priceless acre of ancient Rome and if they had chosen better marble (this is too in–your–face white and picks up the pollution horribly). Soldiers guard Italy's *Tomb of the Unknown Soldier* as the eternal flame flickers. At the tomb, stand with your back to the flame and see how Via del Corso bisects Rome.

Note: There is a clever little back door access from the top of Capitol Hill, leading directly to the top of the Victor Emmanuel Monument, saving you lots of hiking (go up wide steps in corner near *il nasone* and she-wolf statue, pass through iron gate at top of steps, enter small unmarked door on the right).

Pantheon Area

▲▲▲**Pantheon**—For the greatest look at the splendor of Rome, antiquity's best-preserved interior is a must (free, Mon–Sat 8:30–19:30, Sun 9:00–18:00, holidays 9:00–13:00, tel. 06-6830-0230). Because the Pantheon became a church dedicated to the martyrs just after the fall of Rome, the barbarians left it alone, and the locals didn't use it as a quarry. The portico is called Rome's umbrella—a fun local gathering in a rainstorm. Walk past its one-piece granite columns (biggest in Italy, shipped from Egypt) and through the original bronze doors. Sit inside under the glorious skylight and enjoy classical architecture at its best.

The dome, 142 feet high and wide, was Europe's biggest until the Renaissance. Michelangelo's dome at St. Peter's, while much higher, is about 3 feet smaller. The brilliance of this dome's construction astounded architects through the ages. During the Renaissance, Brunelleschi was given permission to cut into the dome (see the little square hole above and to the right of the entrance) to analyze the material. The concrete dome gets thinner and lighter with height—the highest part is volcanic pumice.

This wonderfully harmonious architecture greatly inspired Raphael and other artists of the Renaissance. Raphael, along with Italy's first two kings, chose to be buried here.

As you walk around the outside of the Pantheon, notice the "rise of Rome"—about 15 feet since it was built. Nearest WCs are at McDonald's and bars on the square. Great gelato is nearby at **Giolitti's** (Via Uffici del Vicario 40, see page 458).

Pantheon Area

▲▲**Churches near the Pantheon**—The **Church of San Luigi dei Francesi** has a magnificent chapel painted by Caravaggio (free, Fri–Wed 7:30–12:30 & 15:30–19:00, Thu 7:30–12:30, sightseers should avoid Mass at 7:30 and 19:00).

The only Gothic church in Rome is **Santa Maria sopra Minerva**, with a little-known Michelangelo statue, *Christ Bearing the Cross* (the church is on a little square behind the Pantheon, to the east). The **Church of St. Ignazio**, several blocks east of the Pantheon, is a riot of Baroque illusions with a false dome. (Both Sopra Minerva and St. Ignazio churches open early; take a siesta: Sopra Minerva closes at 12:00, St. Ignazio at 12:30; and reopen from around 16:00–19:00). A few blocks away, back across Corso Vittorio Emmanuele, is the rich and Baroque **Gesu Church**, headquarters of the Jesuits in Rome (free, daily 7:00–12:30 & 16:00–19:15). Modest dress is recommended at all churches.

▲**Galleria Doria Pamphilj**—This gallery, filling a palace on Piazza del Collegio Romano, offers a rare chance to wander through a noble family's lavish rooms with the prince who calls this downtown mansion home. Well, almost. Through an audioguide, the prince lovingly narrates his family's story, including how the Doria Pamphilj (pahm-FEEL-yee) family's cozy relationship with the pope inspired the word nepotism. Highlights include paintings by Caravaggio, Titian, and Raphael, and portraits of Pope Innocent X by Velázquez (on canvas) and Bernini (in marble). The fancy rooms of the palace are interesting, with a mini-Versailles-like hall of mirrors and paintings lining the walls to the ceiling in the style typical of 18th-century galleries (€7.30, includes fine audioguide, Fri–Wed 10:00–17:00, closed Thu, from Piazza Venezia walk 2 blocks up Via del Corso and take a left, tel. 06-679-7323, www.doriapamphilj.it).

▲**Trevi Fountain**—This bubbly Baroque fountain, worth ▲ by day and ▲▲ by night, is a minor sight to art scholars but a major nighttime gathering spot for teens on the make and tourists tossing coins. (For more information, see "Self-Guided Walks in Rome," page 446.)

East Rome, near the Train Station

These sights are within a 10-minute walk of the train station. By Metro, use the Termini stop for the National Museum and the Piazza Repubblica stop for the rest.

▲▲▲**National Museum of Rome in Palazzo Massimo**—This museum houses the greatest collection of ancient Roman art anywhere, and includes busts of emperors and a Roman copy of the *Greek Discus Thrower*. The ground floor is a historic yearbook of marble statues from the second century B.C. to the second century A.D., with rare Greek originals.

The first floor is peopled by statues from the first through fourth centuries A.D. To see the second-floor collection of frescoes and mosaics that once decorated Roman villas, you must reserve an entry time for a free, 45-minute tour led by an Italian- (and sometimes English-) speaking guide; if interested, book the next available tour when you buy your ticket. Finally, descend into the basement to see fine gold jewelry, dice, an abacus, and vault doors leading into the best coin collection in Europe, with fancy magnifying glasses maneuvering you through cases of coins from ancient Rome to modern times.

Cost and Hours: €6, covered by €20 combo-ticket, Tue–Sun 9:00–19:45, closed Mon, open some summer Saturdays until 23:00, last entry 45 min before closing. An audioguide costs €4 (buy ticket first, then get audioguide at bookshop). The museum is about 100 yards from the Termini train station. As you leave the station, it's the sandstone-brick building on your left. Enter at the far end, at Largo di Villa Peretti (Metro: Termini, tel. 06-481-4144).

Baths of Diocletian—Around A.D. 300, Emperor Diocletian built the

East Rome

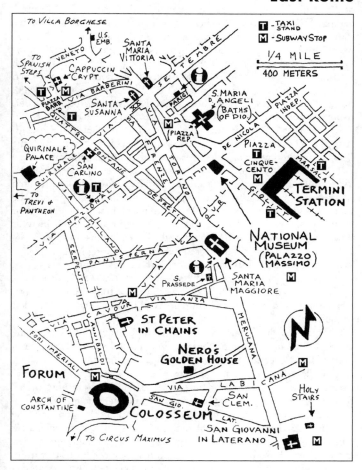

largest baths in Rome. This sprawling meeting place, with baths and schmoozing spaces to accommodate 3,000 bathers at a time, was a big deal in ancient Rome. While much of it is still closed, three sections are open: the Octagonal Hall, the Church of St. Mary of the Angels and Martyrs (both face Piazza della Repubblica), and the Museum of the Bath (skip it).

▲▲**Octagonal Hall**—The Aula Ottagona, or Rotunda of Diocletian, was a private gymnasium in the Baths of Diocletian. Built around A.D. 300, these functioned until 537, when the barbarians cut Rome's aqueducts. The floor would have been 23 feet lower (look down the window in the center of the room). The graceful iron grid supported the canopy of a 1928 planetarium. Today, the hall's a gallery, showing off fine bronze and marble statues—the kind that would have decorated the baths of imperial Rome. Most are Roman copies of Greek originals...gods, athletes, portrait busts. One merits a close look: the *Boxer at Rest* (first century B.C.). Textbook Hellenistic, this bronze statue is realistic and full of emotion. Slumped over, losing, and exhausted, the boxer gasps for air (free, Tue–Sat 9:00–14:00, Sun 9:00–13:00, closed Mon, borrow the English-description booklet, handy WC hidden in the back corner through an unmarked door).

▲**Church of St. Mary of the Angels and Martyrs (Santa Maria degli Angeli e dei Martiri)**—From Piazza della Repubblica, step through the Roman wall into what was the great central hall of the baths and is now a church (since the 16th century) that was designed by Michelangelo. When the church entrance was moved to Piazza Repubblica, the church was reoriented 90 degrees, turning the nave into long transepts and the transepts into a short nave. The 12 red granite columns still stand in their ancient positions. The classical floor was 15 feet lower. Project the walls down and imagine the soaring shape of the Roman vaults (free, Mon–Sat 7:00–18:30, Sun 8:00–19:30, closed to sightseers during Mass).

▲**Santa Maria della Vittoria**—This church houses Bernini's statue of a swooning *St. Teresa in Ecstasy* (free, daily 7:00–12:00 & 15:30–19:00, on Largo Susanna, about 5 blocks northwest of train station, Metro: Repubblica). Once inside the church, you'll find St. Teresa to the left of the altar.

Teresa has just been stabbed with God's arrow of fire. Now the angel pulls it out and watches her reaction. Teresa swoons, her eyes roll up, her hand goes limp, she parts her lips...and moans. The smiling, Cupid-like angel understands just how she feels. Teresa, a 16th-century Spanish nun, later talked of the "sweetness" of "this intense pain," describing her oneness with God in ecstatic, even erotic, terms.

Bernini, the master of multimedia, pulls out all the stops to make this mystical vision real. Actual sunlight pours through the alabaster windows; bronze sunbeams shine on a marble angel holding a golden arrow. Teresa leans back on a cloud and her robe ripples from within, charged with her spiritual arousal. Bernini has created a little stage setting of heaven. And watching from the "theater boxes" on either side are members of the family that commissioned the work.

Santa Susanna—The home of the American Catholic Church in Rome, Santa Susanna holds Mass in English daily at 18:00 and Sunday at 9:00 and 10:30. Their excellent Web site in English, www.santasusanna.org, contains tips for travelers (Via XX Settembre 15, near recommended Via Firenze hotels, Metro: Repubblica, tel. 06-4201-4554). They arrange papal audiences (see "Vatican City," below) and have an English library (with my Venice, Florence, and Rome guidebooks).

North Rome: Villa Borghese and nearby Via Veneto

▲Villa Borghese—Rome's scruffy "Central Park" is great for people-watching (plenty of modern-day Romeos and Juliets). Take a row on the lake or visit the park's fine museums.

▲▲▲Borghese Gallery—This private museum, filling a cardinal's mansion in the park, offers one of Europe's most sumptuous art experiences. Because of the gallery's slick mandatory reservation system, you'll enjoy its collection of world-class Baroque sculpture—including Bernini's *David* and his excited statue of Apollo chasing Daphne, as well as paintings by Caravaggio, Raphael, Titian, and Rubens—with manageable crowds.

The essence of the collection is the connection of the Renaissance with the classical world. Notice the second-century Roman reliefs with Michelangelo-designed panels above either end of the portico as you enter. The villa was built in the early 17th century by the great art collector Cardinal Borghese, who wanted to prove that the glories of ancient Rome were matched by the Renaissance.

In the main entry hall, opposite the door, notice the thrilling relief of the horse falling (first century A.D., Greek). Pietro Bernini, father of the famous Bernini, completed the scene by adding the rider.

Each room seems to feature a Baroque masterpiece. The best of all is in Room 3: Bernini's *Apollo Chasing Daphne.* It's the perfect Baroque subject—capturing a thrilling, action-filled moment. In the mythological story, Apollo races after Daphne. Just as he's about to reach her, she turns into a tree. As her toes turn to roots and branches spring from her fingers, Apollo is in for one rude surprise. Walk slowly around. It's more air than stone.

Cost and Hours: €8.50, Tue–Sun 9:00–19:30, sometimes on Sat. until 23:00 June–Sept, closed Mon. No photos are allowed.

Reservations: Reservations are mandatory and easy to get in English over the Internet (www.ticketeria.it) or by phone: call 06-32810 (if you get an Italian recording, press 2 for English; office hours: Mon–Fri 9:00–18:00, Sat 9:00–13:00, closed Sat in Aug and Sun year-round). Reserve a *minimum* of several days in advance for a weekday visit, at least a week ahead for weekends. When you reserve, request a day and time (which you'll be given if available), and you'll get a claim number. While you'll be advised to come 30 minutes before your appointed time, you can arrive a few minutes beforehand. But don't be late, as no-show tickets are sold to standbys.

Visits are strictly limited to two hours. Concentrate on the first floor, but leave yourself 30 minutes for the paintings of the Pinacoteca upstairs; highlights are marked by the audioguide icons. The fine bookshop and cafeteria are best visited outside your two-hour entry window.

North Rome

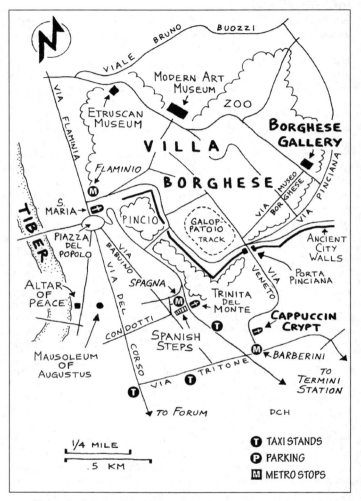

1/4 MILE

.5 KM

T TAXI STANDS
P PARKING
M METRO STOPS

If you don't have a reservation, just show up (or call first and ask if there are openings; a late afternoon on a weekday is usually your best bet). Reservations are tightest at 11:00 and on weekends. No-shows are released a few minutes after the top of the hour. Generally, out of 360 reservation-holders, a few will fail to show (but more than a few may be waiting to grab their slots).

Tours: Guided English tours are offered at 9:10 and 11:10 for €5;

reserve with entry reservation (or consider the excellent audioguide tour for €4).

Location: The museum is in the Villa Borghese park. A taxi (tell the cabbie your destination: gah-leh-REE-ah bor-GAY-zay) can get you within 330 feet of the museum. Otherwise, Metro to Spagna and take a 15-minute walk through the park.

Etruscan Museum (Villa Giulia Museo Nazionale Etrusco)—The Etruscan civilization thrived in this part of Italy around 600 B.C., when Rome was an Etruscan town. The Etruscan civilization is fascinating, but the Villa Giulia Museum is extremely low-tech and in a state of disarray. I don't like it, and fans will prefer the Vatican Museum's Etruscan section. Still, the Villa Giulia does have the famous "husband and wife sarcophagus" (a dead couple seeming to enjoy an everlasting banquet from atop their tomb—sixth century B.C. from Cerveteri); the *Apollo from Veii* statue (of textbook fame); and an impressive room filled with gold sheets of Etruscan printing and temple statuary from the Sanctuary of Pyrgi (€4.20, Tue–Sun 8:30–19:30, closes earlier off-season, closed Mon, Piazzale di Villa Giulia 9, tel. 06-322-6571).

▲**Cappuccin Crypt**—If you want bones, this is it. The crypt is below the church of Santa Maria della Immacolata Concezione on Via Veneto, just up from Piazza Barberini. The bones of more than 4,000 monks who died between 1528 and 1870 are in the basement, all artistically arranged for the delight—or disgust—of the always-wide-eyed visitor. The soil in the crypt was brought from Jerusalem 400 years ago, and the monastic message on the wall explains that this is more than just a macabre exercise. Pick up a few of Rome's most interesting postcards (donation, Fri–Wed 9:00–12:00 & 15:00–18:00, closed Thu, Metro: Barberini, tel. 06-487-1185). A painting of St. Francis by Caravaggio is upstairs. Just up the street you'll find the American Embassy, Federal Express, and fancy Via Veneto cafés filled with the poor and envious looking for the rich and famous.

Ara Pacis (Altar of Peace)—Now surrounded by a high fence, this may reopen in 2005 after restoration. In 9 B.C., after victories in Gaul and Spain, Emperor Augustus celebrated the beginning of the Pax Romana by building this altar of peace. Peace is almost worshiped here. The north and south walls show a procession with realistic portraits of the imperial family in Greek Hellenistic style. It's a fine combination of Roman grandeur and Greek elegance. Even during restoration, the altar can sometimes be seen through the windows (a long block west of Via del Corso on Via di Ara Pacis, on east bank of river near Ponte Cavour, nearest Metro: Spagna).

West Rome: Vatican City Area

▲▲▲**St. Peter's Basilica**—There is no doubt: This is the richest and most impressive church on earth. To call it vast is like calling God smart.

IS THE POPE CATHOLIC?

Rome's tour guides, who introduce tourists to the city's great art and Christian history, field a lot of interesting questions and comments from their groups. Here are a few of their favorites:

Is John Paul II the son of John Paul I?
Who's the guy on the cross?
Oh, to be here in Rome...where our Lord Jesus walked.
Is this where Christ fought the lions?
This guy who made so many nice things, Rene Sance, who
    is he? (Say it fast, and you'll get the gist.)
What's the Sistine Chapel worth in U.S. dollars?
How did Michelangelo get Moses to pose for him?
What's Michelangelo doing now?

Marks on the floor show where the next-largest churches would fit if they were put inside. The ornamental cherubs would dwarf a large man. Birds roost inside, and thousands of people wander about, heads craned heavenward, hardly noticing each other. Don't miss Michelangelo's *Pietà* (behind bulletproof glass) to the right of the entrance. Bernini's altar work and seven-story-tall bronze canopy *(baldacchino)* are brilliant.

For a quick walk through the basilica, follow these points (see map on page 431):

1. The atrium is larger than most churches. Notice the historic doors (the Holy Door, on the right, won't be opened until the next Jubilee Year, in 2025—see point 13 on page 430).

2. The purple, circular porphyry stone marks the site of Charlemagne's coronation in A.D. 800 (in the first St. Peter's church that stood on this site). From here, get a sense of the immensity of the church, which can accommodate 95,000 worshipers standing on its six acres.

3. Michelangelo planned a Greek-cross floor plan rather than the Latin-cross standard in medieval churches. A Greek cross, symbolizing the perfection of God, and by association the goodness of man, was important to the humanist Michelangelo. But accommodating large crowds was important to the Church in the fancy Baroque age, which followed Michelangelo, so the original nave length was doubled. Stand halfway up the nave and imagine the stubbier design Michelangelo had in mind.

4. View the magnificent dome from the statue of St. Andrew. See the vision of heaven above the windows: Jesus, Mary, a ring of saints,

Vatican City Overview

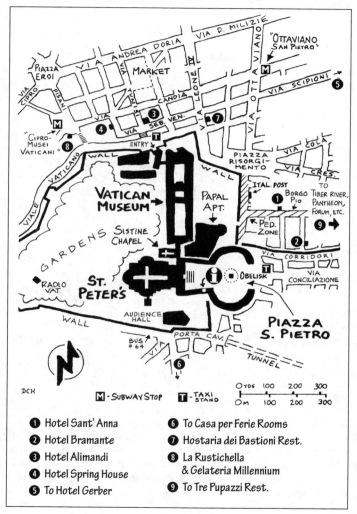

N = SUBWAY STOP   **T** = TAXI STAND

0 YDS 100 200 300
0 M 100 200 300

DCH

1 Hotel Sant' Anna
2 Hotel Bramante
3 Hotel Alimandi
4 Hotel Spring House
5 To Hotel Gerber

6 To Casa per Ferie Rooms
7 Hostaria dei Bastioni Rest.
8 La Rustichella
 & Gelateria Millennium
9 To Tre Pupazzi Rest.

rings of angels, and, on the very top, God the Father.

5. The main altar sits directly over St. Peter's tomb and under Bernini's 70-foot-tall bronze canopy.

6. The stairs lead down to the crypt to the foundation, chapels, and tombs of popes. (Do this last, since it leads you out of the church.)

7. The statue of St. Peter, with an irresistibly kissable toe, is one of the few pieces of art that predate this church. It adorned the first St. Peter's church.

8. St. Peter's throne and Bernini's starburst dove window is the site of a daily Mass (Mon–Sat at 17:00, Sun at 17:30).

9. St. Peter was crucified here when this location was simply "the Vatican Hill." The obelisk now standing in the center of St. Peter's square marked the center of a Roman racecourse long before a church stood here.

10. For most, the treasury (in the sacristy) is not worth the admission.

11. The church is filled with mosaics, not paintings. Notice the mosaic version of Raphael's *Transfiguration*.

12. Blessed Sacrament Chapel.

13. Michelangelo sculpted his *Pietà* when he was 24 years old. A *pietà* is a work showing Mary with the dead body of Christ taken down from the cross. Michelangelo's mastery of the body is obvious in this powerfully beautiful masterpiece. Jesus is believably dead, and Mary, the eternally youthful "handmaiden" of the Lord, still accepts God's will...even if it means giving up her son.

The Holy Door (just to the right of the *Pietà*) was bricked shut at the end of the Jubilee Year 2000 and won't be opened until 2025. Every 25 years, the Church celebrates an especially festive year derived from the Old Testament idea of the Jubilee Year (originally every 50 years), which encourages new beginnings and the forgiveness of sins and debts. In the Jubilee Year 2000, the pope tirelessly—and with significant success—promoted debt relief for the world's poorest countries.

14. An elevator leads to the roof and the stairway up the dome (€5, allow an hour to go up and down). The dome, Michelangelo's last work, is (you guessed it) the biggest anywhere. Taller than a football field is long, it's well worth the sweaty climb for a great view of Rome, the Vatican grounds, and the inside of the basilica—particularly heavenly while there is singing. Look around—Rome has no modern skyline. No building is allowed to exceed the height of St. Peter's. The elevator takes you to the rooftop of the nave. From there, a few steps take you to a balcony at the base of the dome looking down into the church interior. After that, the one-way, 300-step climb (for some people claustrophobic) to the cupola begins. The rooftop level (below the dome) has a gift shop, WC, drinking fountain, and a commanding view.

Dress Code: The church strictly enforces its dress code: no shorts or bare shoulders (men and women); no miniskirts. You might be required to check any bags at a free cloakroom near the entry.

Hours of Church: Daily May–Sept 7:00–19:00, Oct–April 7:00–18:00. All are welcome to join in the hour-long Mass at the front altar (Mon–Sat at 8:30, 10:00, 11:00, 12:00, & 17:00; Sun and holidays 9:00, 10:30, 12:10, 13:00, 16:00, & 17:30). The church is particularly

St. Peter's Basilica

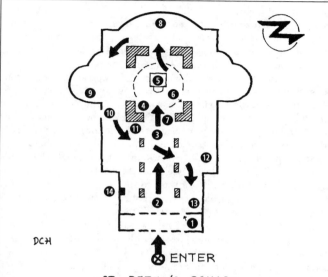

DCH

ENTER

ST. PETER'S SQUARE

❶ Holy Door

❷ Site of Charlemagne's coronation, 800 A.D.

❸ Extent of the original "Greek Cross" church plan

❹ St. Andrew statue (view the dome from here)

❺ Main altar directly over Peter's tomb

❻ Stairs down to the crypt — the foundation of old St. Peter's, chapels and tombs of popes (the entrance moves around)

❼ Statue of St. Peter with irresistibly kissable toe

❽ BERNINI — Dove window and "St. Peter's Throne"

❾ Site of Peter's — crucifixion

❿ Museum entrance

⓫ RAPHAEL — Transfiguration mosaic

⓬ Blessed Sacrament Chapel

⓭ MICHELANGELO — Pietà

⓮ Elevator to roof and dome climb (this entrance moves around, sometimes it is even outside)

moving at 7:00, while tourism is still sleeping. Volunteers who want you to understand and appreciate St. Peter's give free 90-minute tours (depart from TI daily at 14:15; also Mon, Wed, and Fri at 15:00; confirm schedule at TI, tel. 06-6988-1662); the tours are generally excellent but non-Christians can find them preachy. Seeing the *Pietà* is neat; understanding it is divine.

Cost and Hours of Dome: The view from the dome is worth the climb (€5 elevator plus 300-step climb, allow an hour to go up and down, May–Sept daily 8:30–18:00, Oct–April daily 8:30–17:00).

▲▲▲**Vatican Museum**—The four miles of displays in this immense museum—from ancient statues to Christian frescoes to modern paintings—are topped by the Raphael Rooms and Michelangelo's glorious Sistine Chapel. (If you have binoculars, bring them.)

Even without the Sistine, this is one of Europe's top three or four houses of art. It can be exhausting, so plan your visit carefully, focusing on a few themes. Allow two hours for a quick visit, three or four for time to enjoy it. The museum has a nearly impossible-not-to-follow, one-way system (although, for the rushed visitor, the museum does clearly mark out four color-coded visits of different lengths—A is shortest, D longest). Tip: The Sistine Chapel has an exit (optional) that leads directly to St. Peter's Basilica, saving you the 10-minute walk back to the Vatican Museum exit; if you want to squirt out at the Sistine, see the Pinacoteca painting gallery first (described below) and don't get an audioguide (which needs to be returned at the entry/exit).

Start, as civilization did, in Egypt and Mesopotamia. Next, the Pio Clementino collection features **Greek and Roman statues**. Decorating its courtyard are some of the best Greek and Roman statues in captivity, including the *Laocoön* group (first century B.C., Hellenistic) and the *Apollo Belvedere* (a second-century Roman copy of a Greek original). The centerpiece of the next hall is the *Belvedere Torso* (just a 2,000-year-old torso, but one that had a great impact on the art of Michelangelo). Finishing off the classical statuary are two fine fourth-century porphyry sarcophagi; these royal purple tombs were made (though not used) for the Roman emperor Constantine's mother and daughter. They were Christians—and therefore outlaws—until Constantine made Christianity legal (A.D. 312). The tombs, crafted in Egypt at a time when a declining Rome was unable to do such fine work, have details that are fun to study.

After long halls of tapestries, old maps, broken penises, and fig leaves, you'll come to what most people are looking for: The Raphael Rooms (or *stanza*) and Michelangelo's Sistine Chapel.

These outstanding works are frescoes. A fresco (meaning "fresh" in Italian) is technically not a painting. The color is mixed into wet plaster, and, when the plaster dries, the painting is actually part of the wall. This is a durable but difficult medium, requiring speed and accuracy, as the work is built slowly, one patch at a time.

After fancy rooms illustrating the "Immaculate Conception of Mary" (in the 19th century, the Vatican codified this hard-to-sell doctrine, making it a formal part of the Catholic faith) and the triumph of Constantine (with divine guidance, which led to his conversion to Christianity), you enter the first room completely done by **Raphael** and find the newly restored *School of Athens*. This is remarkable for its blatant pre-Christian classical orientation, especially since it originally wallpapered the apartments of Pope Julius II. Raphael honors the great pre-Christian thinkers—Aristotle, Plato, and company—who are portrayed as the leading artists of Raphael's day. The bearded figure of Plato is Leonardo da Vinci. Diogenes, history's first hippie, sprawls alone in bright blue on the stairs, while Michelangelo broods in the foreground—supposedly added late. Apparently, Raphael snuck a peek at the Sistine Chapel and decided that his arch-competitor was so good he had to put their personal differences aside and include him in this tribute to the artists of his generation. Today's St. Peter's was under construction as Raphael was working. In the *School of Athens*, he gives us a sneak preview of the unfinished church.

Next (unless you detour through the refreshingly modern Catholic art section) is the brilliantly restored **Sistine Chapel**. The Sistine Chapel, the pope's personal chapel, is where, upon the death of the ruling pope, a new pope is elected. The College of Cardinals meets here and votes four times a day until a two-thirds-plus-one majority is reached and a new pope is elected.

The Sistine is famous for Michelangelo's pictorial culmination of the Renaissance, showing the story of Creation, with a powerful God weaving in and out of each scene through that busy first week. This is an optimistic and positive expression of the High Renaissance and a stirring example of the artistic and theological maturity of the 33-year-old Michelangelo, who spent four years on this work.

Later, after the Reformation wars had begun and after the Catholic army of Spain had sacked the Vatican, the reeling Church began to fight back. As part of its Counter-Reformation, a much older Michelangelo was commissioned to paint the *Last Judgment* (behind the altar). Brilliantly restored, the message is as clear as the day Michelangelo finished it: Christ is returning, some will go to hell and some to heaven, and some will be saved by the power of the rosary.

In the recent and controversial restoration project, no paint was added. Centuries of dust, soot (from candles used for lighting and Mass), and glue (added to make the art shine) were removed, revealing the bright original colors of Michelangelo. Photos are allowed (without a flash) elsewhere in the museum, but as part of the deal with the company who did the restoration, no photos are allowed in the Sistine Chapel.

For a shortcut, a small door at the rear of the Sistine Chapel allows groups and individuals (without an audioguide) to escape directly to St. Peter's Basilica. If you exit here, you're done with the museum. The Pinacoteca is the only important part left. Consider doing it at the start. Otherwise it's a 10-minute, heel-to-toe slalom through tourists from the Sistine Chapel to the entry/exit.

After this long march, you'll find the **Pinacoteca** (the Vatican's small but fine collection of paintings, with Raphael's *Transfiguration*,

VATICAN CITY

This tiny independent country of just over 100 acres, contained entirely within Rome, has its own postal system, armed guards, helipad, mini–train station, and radio station (KPOP). Politically powerful, the Vatican is the religious capital of 800 million Roman Catholics. If you're not a Catholic, become one for your visit.

Small as it is, Vatican City has two huge sights: St. Peter's Basilica (with Michelangelo's *Pietà*) and the Vatican Museum (with the Sistine Chapel). A helpful TI is just to the left of St. Peter's Basilica (Mon–Sat 8:30–19:00, closed Sun, tel. 06-6988-1662; Vatican switchboard tel. 06-6982, www.vatican.va). The thief-infested bus #64 and the safer #40 express stop near the basilica. The nearest Metro stops are a 10-minute walk away from either sight: For St. Peter's, the closest stop is Ottaviano; for the Vatican Museum, it's Cipro-Musei Vaticani.

Post Office: The Vatican post, with offices on St. Peter's Square (next to TI) and in the Vatican Museum, is more reliable than Italy's mail service (Mon–Sat 8:30–19:00). The stamps are a collectible bonus. Vatican stamps are good throughout Rome, but to use the Vatican's mail service, you need to mail your cards from the Vatican; write your postcards ahead of time. (Note that the Vatican won't mail cards with Italian stamps.)

Tours: The Vatican TI conducts free 90-minute tours of St. Peter's (depart daily from TI at 14:15, also Mon, Wed, and Fri at 15:00, confirm schedule at TI, tel. 06-6988-1662). Tours are the only way to see the Vatican Gardens; book at least a day in advance by calling 06-6988-4466 (€9, Mon–Sat 10:00–12:00, tours start at Vatican Museum tour desk and finish on St. Peter's Square). To tour the necropolis of St. Peter's and the saint's tomb, call the Excavations Office at 06-6988-5318(€8, 2 hrs, office open Mon–Fri 9:00–17:00).

Seeing the Pope: Your best chances for a sighting are on Sunday and Wednesday. The pope usually gives a blessing at noon on Sunday from his apartment on St. Peter's Square (except summer, when he speaks at his summer residence at Castel Gandolfo 25 miles from Rome; train leaves Rome's Termini station). St. Peter's is easiest (just show up) and, for most, enough of a "visit."

CIPRO - MUSEI VATICANI METRO

VIA CANDIA

VIALE VATICANO

VATICAN MUSEUM →

SISTINE CHAPEL →

ST. PETER'S →

VATICAN BOUNDARY

BUS #64

DCH

OTTAVIANO METRO

TO TERMINI

VIA OTTAVIANO

VIALE GIULIO CESARE

PIAZZA RISORGIMENTO

TAXI STAND

VIA CONCILIAZIONE

ST. PETER'S SQUARE + OBELISK

☐ - TAXI STAND
M - SUBWAY STOP

NOT TO SCALE: VATICAN MUSEUM ENTRY TO OBELISK IS A 15 MINUTE WALK

Those interested in a more formal appearance (but not more intimate), can get a ticket for the Wednesday blessing (at 10:30) when the pope, arriving in his bulletproof Popemobile, greets and blesses the crowds at St. Peter's from a balcony or canopied platform on the square (except in winter, when he speaks at 10:30 in the 7,000-seat Aula Paola VI Auditorium, next to St. Peter's Basilica). This requires a ticket—arrange it in advance through your hotel or the Santa Susanna Church (they get it and you pick it up the day before at their church between 17:00 and 18:45; Via XX Settembre 15, near recommended Via Firenze hotels, Metro: Repubblica; tel. 06-4201-4554, www.santasusanna.org).

To find out the pope's schedule or to book a free spot for the Wednesday blessing (either for a seat on the square or in the auditorium), call 06-6988-4631. The weekly entertainment guide *Roma c'è* always has a "Seeing the Pope" section. If you only want to see the Vatican—but not the pope—minimize crowd problems by avoiding these times.

Leonardo's unfinished *St. Jerome*, and Caravaggio's *Deposition)*, a cafe-teria (long lines, mediocre food), and the underrated early-Christian art section, before you exit via the souvenir shop.

Cost and Hours: €10, March–Oct Mon–Fri 8:45–16:45, Sat 8:45–13:45; Nov–Feb Mon–Sat 8:45–13:45; closed Sun except last Sun of the month (when it's free, crowded, and open 8:45–13:45). Last entry is about 90 minutes before the closing time. The Sistine Chapel some-times shuts down 30 minutes early.

The museum is generally hot and crowded. Saturday, the last Sunday of the month, and Monday are the worst; afternoons are best.

The museum is closed on many holidays (mainly religious ones), including—for 2004: Jan 1 and 6, Feb 11, March 19, Easter and Easter Monday (April 11 and 12), May 1 and 20, June 10 and 29, Aug 14 and 15, Nov 1, and Dec 8 and 25–26.

Modest dress (no short shorts or bare shoulders for men or women) is appropriate and often required. Museum tel. 06-6988-4947.

Tours: A tour in English is offered once daily at 11:00 (€16.50, 2 hrs, call 06-6988-4466 to reserve). You can rent a €5 audioguide (but if you do, you lose the option of taking the shortcut from the Sistine Chapel to St. Peter's, because the audioguide must be returned at the Vatican Museum entrance).

▲**Castel Sant' Angelo**—Built as a tomb for the emperor; used through the Middle Ages as a castle, prison, and place of last refuge for popes under attack; and today, as a museum, this giant pile of ancient bricks is packed with history.

Ancient Rome allowed no tombs, not even the emperor's, within its walls. So Hadrian grabbed the most commanding position just out-side the walls and built a towering tomb (circa A.D. 139) well within view of the city. His mausoleum was a huge cylinder (210 by 70 feet) topped by a cypress grove and crowned by a huge statue of Hadrian himself riding a chariot. For nearly a hundred years, Roman emperors (from Hadrian to Caracalla in A.D. 217) were buried here.

In the year 590, the Archangel Michael—signaling the end of a plague by sheathing his sword—appeared above the mausoleum to Pope Gregory the Great. The mausoleum eventually became a fortified palace, renamed for the "holy angel."

In 1277, the pope built the elevated corridor connecting Castel Sant' Angelo with the Vatican. Since Rome was repeatedly plundered by invaders, Castel Sant' Angelo was a handy place of last refuge for threatened popes.

After you walk around the entire base of the castle, take the small staircase down to the original Roman floor. In the atrium, study the model of the castle in Roman times and imagine the niche in the wall filled with a towering "welcome to my tomb" statue of Hadrian. From here, a ramp leads to the right, spiraling 410 feet. At the end of the ramp, stairs climb to the room where the ashes of the emperors were kept. These stairs continue to the top, where you'll find the papal apartments. Don't miss the Sala del Tesoro (treasury), where the wealth of the Vatican was locked up in a huge chest. Do miss the 58 rooms of the military museum. The views from the top are great—pick out landmarks as you stroll around—and a restful coffee with a view of St. Peter's is worth the price.

Cost, Hours, Tours: €5, Tue–Sun 9:00–19:00, plus June–Sept Sat 21:00–23:45, closed Mon. You can take an English–language tour with an audioguide (€4) or live guide (€5, Tue–Fri at 15:00, Sat at 12:15 & 16:30, confirm tour times, tel. 06-3996-7600; Metro: Lepanto or bus #64, near Vatican City).

Ponte Sant' Angelo—The bridge leading to Castel Sant' Angelo was built by Hadrian for quick and regal access from downtown to his tomb. The three middle arches are actually Roman originals and a fine example of the empire's engineering expertise. The angels were designed by Bernini and finished by his students.

Southwest Rome: Trastevere

Trastevere is the colorful neighborhood across *(tras)* the Tiber *(tevere)* River. Trastevere (trahs-TAY-veh-ray) offers the best look at medieval-village Rome. The action unwinds to the chime of the church bells. Go there and wander. Wonder. Be a poet. This is Rome's Left Bank.

This proud neighborhood was long a working-class area. Now that it's becoming trendy, high rents are driving out the source of so much color. Still, it's a great people scene, especially at night. Stroll the back streets (for restaurant recommendations, see "Eating," page 471).

To get to Trastevere, taxi or ride the bus (from Vatican area—#23; or from Via Nazionale hotels—catch #64, #70, #115, or #640 to Largo Argentina, then transfer to tram #8 and get off at Piazza Mastai).

St. Maria in Trastevere Church—One of Rome's oldest churches, this was made a basilica in the fourth century, when Christianity was legalized (free, daily 7:30–13:00 & 15:00–19:00). It was the first church dedicated to the Virgin Mary. The portico (covered area just outside the door) is decorated with fascinating ancient fragments filled with early Christian symbolism. Most of what you see today dates from around the 12th century, but the granite columns come from an ancient Roman temple, and the ancient basilica floor plan (and ambience) survive. The 12th-century mosaics behind the altar are striking and notable for their portrayal of Mary—the first to show her at the throne with Jesus in Heaven. Look below the scenes from the life of Mary to see ahead-of-their-time mosaics (by Cavallini, from 1300), predating the Renaissance by 100 years.

The church is on Piazza di Santa Maria. While today's fountain is from the 17th century, there has been a fountain here since Roman times.

Trastevere

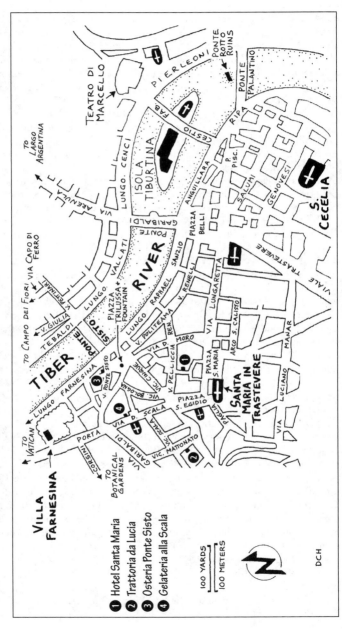

VILLA FARNESINA

TIBER RIVER

VENULA

TO LARGO ARGENTINA

TEATRO DI MARCELLO

PIER LEONI

PONTE ROTTO RUINS

PONTE PALANTINO

ISOLA TIBURTINA

FAB

CESTIO

RIPA

PONTE GARIBALDI

LUNGO. CENCI

LUNGO VALLATI

PIAZZA BELLI

ANGUILLARA

SANZIO

P. PISC.

SALUMI

GENOVESI

S. CECELIA

V. ARENULA

TO CAMPO DEI FIORI VIA CAPO DI FERRO

V. GIULIA

TEBALDI

LUNGO

PONTE SISTO

PIAZZA TRILUSSA + FOUNTAIN

LUNGO RAPHAEL

V. POLITEAMA

V. RENELLI

VIA LUNGARETTA

VIA S. CALISTO

VIALE TRASTEVERE

V. P. REN.

VIA D. MORO

V. PELLICCIA

ARCO S. CALISTO

VIA LUCIANO

MANAR

V. VERTINARI

LUNGO FARNESINA

3

V. PONTE SISTO

VIC. CINQUE

V. BOLOGNA

4

VIA D. SCALA

VIC. MATTONATO

1

PIAZZA S. MARIA

PIAZZA S. EGIDIO

PAGLIA

SANTA MARIA IN TRASTEVERE

2

TO VATICAN

PORTA

CORSINI

VIA GARIBALDI

TO BOTANICAL GARDENS

1 Hotel Santa Maria
2 Trattoria da Lucia
3 Osteria Ponte Sisto
4 Gelateria alla Scala

100 YARDS
100 METERS

N

DCH

Linking Trastevere with "Night Walk Across Rome"—You can easily walk from Trastevere to Campo de' Fiori to link up with the beginning of the Night Walk Across Rome (see page 455): From Trastevere's church square (Piazza di Santa Maria), take Via del Moro to the river and cross at Ponte Sisto, a pedestrian bridge with a good view of St. Peter's dome. Continue straight ahead for one block. Take the first left, which leads down Via di Capo di Ferro through the scary and narrow darkness to Piazza Farnese, with the imposing Palazzo Farnese. Michelangelo contributed to the facade of this palace, now the French Embassy. The fountains on the square feature huge, one-piece granite hot tubs from the ancient Roman Baths of Caracalla. One block from there (opposite the palace) is the atmospheric square of Campo de' Fiori.

South Rome

If you visit Ostia Antica (see page 446), you can maximize sightseeing efficiency by visiting any of the sights in south Rome on your return.

▲**St. Paul's Outside the Walls (Basilica San Paolo Fuori le Mura)**— One of the greatest churches in Christendom, St. Paul's was originally built in 324, then destroyed by fire in the 1820s. Today it's mammoth and pristine, rebuilt true to the ancient basilica plan. It feels sterile, but in a good way—like you're already in heaven. Along with St. Peter's Basilica, San Giovanni in Laterano, and Santa Maria Maggiore, this church is part of the Vatican rather than Italy. St. Paul is supposed to be buried under the altar (without his head, which San Giovanni in Laterano has). Alabaster windows light the vast interior, fifth-century mosaics decorate the triumphal arch leading to the altar, and mosaic portraits of all 264 popes, from St. Peter to John Paul II, ring the place—with blank spots ready for future popes. Find John Paul II (to right of the high altar: Jo Paulus II, no date) and John Paul I (to his right, with a reign of one month and three days). Wander the ornate yet peaceful cloister (closed 13:00–15:00). The courtyard leading up to the church is typical of early Christian churches; even the first St. Peter's had this kind of welcoming zone (free, daily 7:00–18:00, modest dress code enforced, Via Ostiense 186, Metro: San Paolo).

▲**Montemartini Museum (Musei Capitolini Centrale Montemartini)**—This museum houses a dreamy collection of 400 ancient statues, set evocatively in a classic 1932 electric power plant among generators and Metropolis-type cast-iron machinery. While the art is not as famous as the collections you'll see downtown, the effect is fun and memorable—and you'll encounter absolutely no tourists (€4.20, Tue–Sun 9:30–19:00, closed Mon, Via Ostiense 106, a short walk from Metro: Garbatella, tel. 06-574-8042).

Baths of Caracalla (Terme di Caracalla)—Today it's just a shell—a huge shell—with all of its sculptures and most of its mosaics moved to museums. Inaugurated by Emperor Caracalla in A.D. 216, this massive

South Rome

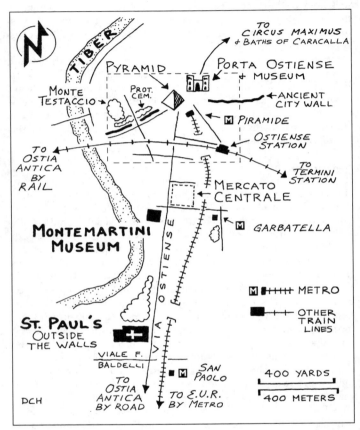

complex could accommodate 1,600 visitors at a time. Today you'll see a two-story, roofless brick building surrounded by a garden, bordered by ruined walls. The two large rooms at either end of the building were used for exercise. In between the exercise rooms was a pool flanked by two small mosaic-floored dressing rooms. Niches in the walls once held statues. In its day, this was a remarkable place to hang out. For ancient Romans, the baths were a social experience.

The Baths of Caracalla functioned until Goths severed the aqueducts in the sixth century. In modern times, operas were performed here from 1938 to 1993. To keep the ruins from becoming more ruined, the performances were discontinued (€5, covered by €20 combo-ticket, Mon 9:00–17:30, Tue–Sun 9:00–19:30, last entry 1 hour before closing,

Testaccio

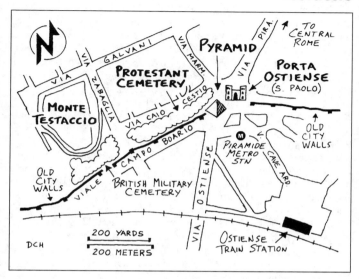

audioguide—€4, fine €8 guidebook—can read in shaded garden while sitting on a chunk of column, Metro: Circus Maximus, and a 5-min walk south along Via delle Terme di Caracalla, tel. 06-575-8628). Several of the baths' statues are now in Rome's Octagonal Hall; the immense *Toro Farnese* (a marble sculpture of a bull surrounded by people) snorts in Naples' Archaeological Museum.

Testaccio—Four fascinating but lesser sights cluster at the Piramide Metro stop between the Colosseum and E.U.R., in the gritty Testaccio neighborhood. (This is a quick and easy stop as you return from E.U.R. or when changing trains en route to Ostia Antica.)

Working-class since ancient times, Testaccio has recently gone trendy-bohemian, and visitors will wander through an awkward mix of yuppie and proletarian worlds, not noticing—but perhaps feeling—the "keep Testaccio for the Testaccians" graffiti.

Pyramid of Gaius Cestius: The Marc Antony/Cleopatra scandal (around the time of Christ) brought exotic Egyptian styles into vogue. A rich Roman magistrate, Gaius Cestius, had a pyramid built as his tomb. Made of brick covered in marble, it was completed in just 330 days (as stated in its Latin inscription) and fell far short of Egyptian pyramid standards. Later incorporated into the Aurelian Wall, it's now next to the Piramide Metro stop.

Porta Ostiense: This formidable gate (also next to Piramide Metro stop) is from the Aurelian Wall, begun in the third century under

Emperor Aurelius. The wall, which encircled the city, was 12 miles long and 26 feet high, with 14 main gates and 380 72-foot-tall towers. Most of what you'll see today is circa A.D. 400. The barbarians reconstructed this gate in the sixth century. (For more on the wall, visit the Museum of the Walls at Porta San Sebastian; see "Ancient Appian Way," below.)

Protestant Cemetery: The *Cimitero Acattolico per gli Stranieri al Testaccio* (cemetery for the burial of non-Catholic foreigners) is a Romantic tomb-filled park, running along the wall just beyond the pyramid. From the Piramide Metro stop, walk between the pyramid and the Roman gate on Via Persichetti, then go left on Caio Cestio to the gate of the cemetery. Ring the bell (donation box, Tue–Sun April–Sept 9:00–18:00, Oct–March 9:00–17:00, closed Mon).

Originally, none of the Protestant epitaphs were allowed to make any mention of heaven. Signs direct visitors to the graves of notable non-Catholics who died in Rome since 1738. Many of the buried were diplomats. And many, such as poets Shelley and Keats, were from the Romantic Age. They came on the Grand Tour and—"captivated by the fatal charms of Rome," as Shelley wrote—never left. Head left toward the pyramid to find Keats' tomb, in the far corner. At the pyramid, look down on Matilde Talli's cat hospice (flier at the gate). Volunteers use donations to care for these "Guardians of the Departed" who "provide loyal companionship to these dead."

Monte Testaccio: Just behind the Protestant Cemetery (as you leave, turn left and continue 2 blocks down Caio Cestio) is a 115-foot-tall ancient trash mountain. It's made of broken *testae*—earthenware jars used to haul mostly wine 2,000 years ago, when this was a gritty port warehouse district. After 500 years of sloppy dock work, Rome's lowly eighth hill was built. Because the caves dug into the hill stay cool, trendy bars, clubs, and restaurants compete with gritty car-repair places for a spot. The neighborhood was once known for a huge slaughterhouse and a Gypsy camp that squatted inside an old military base. Now it's home to the Villagio Globale, a site for concerts and techno-raves. The night scene at Monte Testaccio is lively and youthful, but the neighborhood can be rough (Metro: Piramide).

Ancient Appian Way (Via Appia Antica)

Since the fourth century B.C., this has been Rome's gateway to the East. The first section was perfectly straight. It was the largest, widest, fastest road ever, the wonder of its day, called the "Queen of Roads." Eventually, this most important of Roman roads stretched 430 miles to the port of Brindisi—where boats sailed for Greece and Egypt. Twenty-nine such roads fanned out from Rome. Just as Hitler built the autobahn system in anticipation of empire maintenance, the emperors realized the military and political value of a good road system. A central strip accommodated animal-powered vehicles, and elevated sidewalks served pedestrians. As it left Rome, the road was lined with tombs and funerary monuments. Imagine a funeral procession passing under the pines and cypress and past a long line of pyramids, private mini-temples, altars, and tombs.

Hollywood created the famous image of the Appian Way lined with Spartacus and his gang of defeated and crucified slave rebels. This image is only partially accurate. Spartacus was killed in battle.

Tourist's Appian Way: The road starts less than two miles south of the Colosseum at the massive San Sebastian Gate. The Museum of the Walls, located at the gate, offers an interesting look at Roman defense and (when open) a chance to scramble along a stretch of the ramparts (€2.60, Tue–Sun 9:00–19:00, closed Mon, tel. 06-7047-5284). Half a mile down the road are the two most historic and popular catacombs, those of San Callisto and San Sebastian (described below). Beyond that, the road becomes pristine and traffic-free, popular for biking and hiking.

To reach the Appian Way, take the Archeobus from Piazza Venezia (see "Archeobus," page 410) or take the Metro to the Colli Albani stop, then catch bus #660 to Via Appia Antica—its last stop and the start of an interesting stretch of the ancient road (the segment between the 3rd and 11th milestones is best). At the bus stop, you'll find Caffe dell' Appia Antica (Via Appia Antica 175), which serves light lunches and rents bikes (lots of fun). From here you can walk 15 minutes (or bike) to the Catacombs of San Callisto.

▲▲**Catacombs**—The catacombs are burial places for (mostly) Christians who died in ancient Roman times. By law, no one was allowed to be buried within the walls of Rome. While pagan Romans were into cremation, Christians preferred to be buried. But land was expensive and most Christians were poor. A few wealthy, landowning Christians allowed their property to be used as burial places.

The 40 or so known catacombs circle Rome about three miles from its center. From the first through the fifth centuries, Christians dug an estimated 375 miles of tomb-lined tunnels, with networks of galleries as many as five layers deep. The tufa—soft and easy to cut, but becoming very hard when exposed to air—was perfect for the job. The Christians burrowed many layers deep for two reasons: to get more mileage out of the donated land and to be near martyrs and saints already buried there. Bodies were wrapped in linen (like Christ's). Since they figured the Second Coming was imminent, there was no interest in embalming the body.

When Emperor Constantine legalized Christianity in 313, Christians had a new, interesting problem. There would be no more persecuted martyrs to bind them and inspire them. Thus the early martyrs and popes assumed more importance, and Christians began making pilgrimages to their burial places in the catacombs.

In the 800s, when barbarian invaders started ransacking the tombs, Christians moved the relics of saints and martyrs to the safety of churches in the city center. For a thousand years, the catacombs were forgotten. Around 1850, they were excavated and became part of the romantic Grand Tour of Europe.

Finding abandoned plates and utensils from ritual meals in the candlelit galleries led 18th- and 19th-century Romantics to guess that persecuted Christians hid out and lived in these catacombs. This Romantic legend grew. But catacombs were not used for hiding out. They are simply early Christian burial grounds. With a million people in Rome, the easiest way for the 10,000 or so early Christians to hide out was not to camp in the catacombs (which everyone, including the government, knew about), but to melt into the city.

The underground tunnels, while empty of bones, are rich in early Christian symbolism, which functioned as a secret language. The dove symbolized the soul. You'll see it quenching its thirst (worshiping), with an olive branch (at rest), or happily perched (in paradise). Peacocks, known for their "incorruptible flesh," symbolized immortality. The shepherd with a lamb on his shoulders was the "good shepherd," the first portrayal of Christ as a kindly leader of his flock. The fish was used because the first letters of these words—"Jesus Christ, Son of God, Savior"—spelled "fish" in Greek. And the anchor is a cross in disguise. A second-century bishop had written on his tomb: "All who understand these things, pray for me." You'll see pictures of people praying with their hands raised up—the custom at the time.

Catacomb tours are essentially the same. Which one you take is not important. The **Catacombs of San Callisto** (a.k.a. Callixtus), the official cemetery for the Christians of Rome and burial place of third-century popes, is the most historic. Sixteen bishops (early popes) were buried here. Buy your €5 ticket and wait for your language to be called. They move lots of people quickly. If one group seems ridiculously large (over 50 people), wait for the next tour in English (Thu–Tue 8:30–12:00 & 14:30–17:30, closed Wed and Feb, closes at 17:00 in winter, Via Appia Antica 110, tel. 06-5130-1580). Dig this: The catacombs have a Web site—www.catacombe.roma.it—that focuses mainly on San Callisto, featuring photos, site info, and a history.

The **Catacombs of San Sebastian** (Sebastiano) are 300 yards farther down the road (€5, Mon–Sat 8:30–12:00 & 14:30–17:30, closed Sun and Nov, closes at 17:00 in winter, Via Appia Antica 136, tel. 06-5130-1580).

E.U.R.

In the late 1930s, Italy's dictator, Benito Mussolini, planned an international exhibition to show off the wonders of his fascist society. But these wonders brought us World War II, and Il Duce's celebration never hap-

E.U.R.

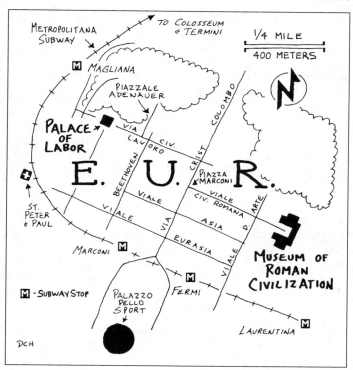

pened. The unfinished mega-project was completed in the 1950s and now houses government offices and big, obscure museums.

If Hitler and Mussolini won the war, our world might look like E.U.R. (ay-OOR). Hike down E.U.R.'s wide, pedestrian-mean boulevards. Patriotic murals, aren't-you-proud-to-be-an-extreme-right-winger pillars, and stern squares decorate the soulless, planned grid and stark office blocks. Boulevards named for Astronomy, Electronics, Social Security, and Beethoven are more exhausting than inspirational. Today E.U.R. is worth a trip for its Museum of Roman Civilization (described below).

The Metro skirts E.U.R. with three stops (10 min from the Colosseum). Use E.U.R. Magliana for the "Square Colosseum" and E.U.R. Fermi for the Museum of Roman Civilization (both described below). Consider walking 30 minutes from the palace to the museum through the center of E.U.R.

From the Magliana subway stop, stairs lead uphill to the **Palace of the Civilization of Labor (Palazzo della Civilta del Lavoro)**, the essence

of fascist architecture. With its giant, no-questions-asked, patriotic statues and its black-and-white simplicity, this is E.U.R.'s tallest building
and landmark. It's understandably nicknamed the "Square Colosseum."
Around the corner, Café Palombini is still decorated in a 1930s style and
is quite popular with young Romans (daily 7:00–24:00, good gelato, pastries, and snacks, Piazzale Adenauer 12, tel. 06-591-1700).

▲Museum of Roman Civilization (Museo della Civiltà Romana)—
With 59 rooms of plaster casts and models illustrating the greatness
of classical Rome, this vast and heavy museum gives a strangely lifeless, close-up look at Rome. Each room has a theme, from military
tricks to musical instruments. One long hall is filled with casts of the
reliefs of Trajan's Column. The highlight is the 1:250-scale model of
Constantine's Rome—circa A.D. 300 (€6.20; Tue–Sat 9:00–18:45,
Sun 9:00–13:30, closed Mon; Piazza G. Agnelli, from Metro: E.U.R.
Fermi, walk 10 min up Via dell' Arte, you'll see its colonnade on the
right; tel. 06-592-6041).

Near Rome

▲▲Ostia Antica—For an exciting day trip less than an hour from
downtown Rome, pop down to the ancient Roman port of Ostia Antica.
It's similar to Pompeii, but a lot closer and, in some ways, more interesting. Because Ostia was a working port town, it shows a more complete and gritty look at Roman life than does wealthy Pompeii.
Wandering around today, you'll see the remains of the docks, ware-
houses, apartment flats, mansions, shopping arcades, and baths that
served a once thriving port of 60,000 people. Later, Ostia became a
ghost town, and is now excavated. Start at the 2,000-year-old theater,
buy a map, explore the town, and finish with its fine little museum.

   Getting There: To get there, take the Metro's B Line to the
Piramide stop (consider popping out to see the ancient Roman pyramid
tomb, listed above in South Rome sights). From the Piramide stop,
catch the Lido train to Ostia Antica (2/hr, use a Metro ticket). From
the train station, cross the road via the blue sky-bridge and walk straight
down Via della Stazione di Ostia Antica, following signs to *Scavi di
Ostia Antica*, about 400 yards to the gate.

   Cost and Hours: €4, Tue–Sun 8:30–18:00 in summer, 9:00–16:00
in winter, closed Mon. The well-done audioguide costs €5 (tel. 06-
5635-8099).

SELF-GUIDED WALKS IN ROME

Here are three walks that give you a moving picture of Rome, an ancient
yet modern city. You'll walk through history (Roman Forum), take a
refreshing early evening stroll (Dolce Vita Stroll), and enjoy the thriving
night scene (Night Walk Across Rome).

Roman Forum (Foro Romano)

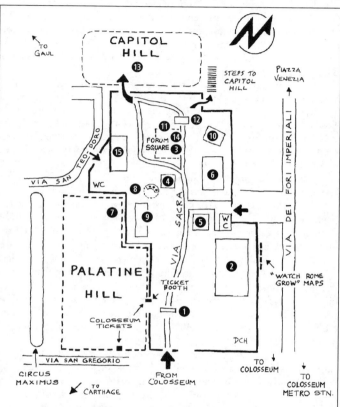

1. Arch of Titus
2. Basilica of Constantine
3. Forum's Main Square
4. Temple of Julius Caesar
5. Temple of Antoninus and Faustina
6. Basilica Aemilia
7. Caligula's Palace
8. Temple of Vesta
9. House of the Vestal Virgins
10. Curia (Senate House)
11. Rostrum
12. Arch of Septimius Severus
13. Temple of Saturn
14. Column of Phocas
15. Basilica Julia

Roman Forum Walk

The Forum was the political, religious, and commercial center of the city. Rome's most important temples and halls of justice were here. This was the place for religious processions, elections, political demonstrations, important speeches, and parades by conquering generals. As Rome's Empire expanded, these few acres of land became the center of the civilized world.

Cost, Hours, Location: Free, daily 9:00–19:00 or until an hour before dark, Metro: Colosseo, tel. 06-3974-9907. You can rent a €4 audioguide at the gift shop at the entrance on Via dei Fori Imperiali. Tours in English are offered almost hourly (€4); ask at the ticket booth at Palatine Hill (near Arch of Titus). Just like at the Colosseum, street vendors sell small *Rome: Past and Present* books with plastic overlays that restore the ruins (marked €11, offer less).

The Tour Begins: Walk through the entrance nearest the Colosseum, hiking up the ramp marked "Via Sacra." Stand next to the triumphal...

1. Arch of Titus *(Arco di Tito)*: The arch commemorated the Roman victory over the province of Judea (Israel) in A.D. 70. The Romans had a reputation as benevolent conquerors who tolerated the local customs and rulers. All they required was allegiance to the empire, which could be shown by worshiping the emperor as a god. No problem for most conquered people, who already had half a dozen gods on their prayer lists anyway. But the Israelites' god was jealous and refused to let his people worship the emperor. Israel revolted. After a short but bitter war, the Romans defeated the rebels, took Jerusalem, sacked their temple, and brought home 50,000 Jewish slaves...who were forced to build this arch.

Start down the Via Sacra into the Forum. After just a few yards, turn right and follow a path uphill to the three huge arches of the...

2. Basilica of Constantine *(a.k.a. Basilica Maxentius)*: These gigantic arches represent only one third of the original Basilica of Constantine, a mammoth hall of justice. The arches were matched by a similar set along the Via Sacra side (only a few squat brick piers remain). Between them ran the central hall, which was spanned by a roof 130 feet high—about 55 feet higher than the side arches you see. (The stub of brick you see sticking up began an arch that once spanned the central hall.) The hall itself was as long as a football field, lavishly furnished with colorful inlaid marble, a gilded bronze ceiling, fountains, and statues, and filled with strolling Romans. At the far (west) end was an enormous marble statue of Emperor Constantine on a throne. (Pieces of this statue, including a hand the size of a man, are on display in Rome's Capitol Hill Museum.)

This basilica was begun by the emperor Maxentius, but after he was trounced in battle, the victor—Constantine—completed the massive building.

Now stroll deeper into the Forum, down the Via Sacra. Many of the large basalt stones under your feet were walked on by Caesar Augustus 2,000 years ago. Pass the only original bronze door still swinging on its ancient hinges (green, on right) through the trees and between ruined buildings until the path opens up to a flat, grassy area.

3. The Forum's Main Square: The original Forum, or main square, was this flat patch about the size of a football field, stretching to the foot of Capitol Hill. Surrounding it were temples, law courts, government buildings, and triumphal arches.

Rome was born right here. According to legend, twin brothers Romulus (Rome) and Remus were orphaned in infancy and raised by a she-wolf on top of Palatine Hill. Growing up, they found it hard to get dates. So they and their cohorts attacked the nearby Sabine tribe and kidnapped their women. After they made peace, this marshy valley became the meeting place and then the trading center for the scattered tribes on the surrounding hillsides.

At the near (east) end of the main square (the Colosseum is to the east) find the foundations of a temple now capped with a peaked wood-and-metal roof. This is...

4. The Temple of Julius Caesar *(Tempio del Divo Giulio,* or *"Ara di Cesare"):* Julius Caesar's body was burned on this spot (under the metal roof) after his assassination.

Caesar (100–44 B.C.) changed Rome—and the Forum—dramatically. He cleared out many of the wooden market stalls and began to ring the square with even grander buildings. Caesar's house was located behind the temple, near that clump of trees. He walked right by here on the day he was assassinated ("Beware the Ides of March!" warned a street-corner Etruscan preacher).

Though popular with the masses, not everyone liked Caesar's urban design or his politics. When he assumed dictatorial powers, he was ambushed and stabbed to death by a conspiracy of senators, including his adopted son, Brutus *(Et tu, Brute?).*

The funeral was held here, facing the main square. The citizens gathered and speeches were made. Mark Antony stood up to say (in Shakespeare's words), "Friends, Romans, countrymen, lend me your ears. I come to bury Caesar, not to praise him." When Caesar's body was burned, the citizens who still loved him threw anything at hand on the fire, requiring the fire department to come put it out. Later, Emperor Augustus dedicated this temple in his name, making Caesar the first Roman to become a god.

Behind and to the left of the Temple of Julius Caesar are the eight tall columns of the...

5. Temple of Antoninus and Faustina: The respected Emperor Antoninus (A.D. 138–161) built this temple—originally called the Temple of Faustina—in honor of his late beloved wife. After the emperor's death, the temple became a monument to them both.

ROME—REPUBLIC AND EMPIRE
(500 B.C.–A.D. 500)

Ancient Rome spanned about a thousand years, from 500 B.C. to A.D. 500. During that time, Rome expanded from a small tribe of barbarians to a vast empire, then dwindled slowly to city size again. For the first 500 years, when Rome's armies made her ruler of the Italian peninsula and beyond, Rome was a republic governed by elected senators. Over the next 500 years, a time of world conquest and eventual decline, Rome was an empire ruled by a military-backed dictator.

Julius Caesar bridged the gap between republic and empire. This ambitious general and politician, popular with the people because of his military victories and charisma, suspended the Roman constitution and assumed dictatorial powers around 50 B.C., then he was assassinated by a conspiracy of senators. His adopted son, Augustus, succeeded him, and soon "Caesar" was not just a name but a title.

Emperor Augustus ushered in the Pax Romana, or Roman peace (from A.D. 1–200), a time when Rome reached her peak and controlled an empire that stretched even beyond Eurail— from Scotland to Egypt, from Turkey to Morocco.

The 56-foot-tall Corinthian (leafy) columns must have been awe-inspiring to out-of-towners who grew up in thatched huts. Although the temple has been reconstructed as a church, you can still see the basic layout—a staircase led to a shaded porch (the columns), which admitted you to the main building (now a church) where the statue of the god sat.

Picture the Forum covered with dirt as high as the green door—as it was until excavated in the 1800s.

There's a ramp next to the Temple of A. and F. Walk halfway up it and look to the left to view the...

6. Basilica Aemilia: A basilica was a Roman hall of justice. In a society that was as legal-minded as America is today, you needed a lot of lawyers and a big place to put them. Citizens came here to work out matters such as inheritances and building permits, or to sue somebody.

Notice the layout. It was a long, rectangular building. The stubby columns all in a row form one long, central hall flanked by two side aisles. Medieval Christians required a larger meeting hall for their worship services than Roman temples provided, so they used the spacious Roman basilica (hall of justice) as the model for their churches. Cathedrals from France to Spain to England, from Romanesque to Gothic to

Renaissance, all have the same basic floor plan as a Roman basilica.

Return again to the Temple of Julius Caesar. Notice the ruts in the stone street in front of the temple—carved by chariot wheels. To the right of the temple are the three tall Corinthian columns of the Temple of Castor and Pollux. Beyond that is Palatine Hill—the corner of which may be...

7. Caligula's Palace (a.k.a. the Palace of Tiberius): Emperor Caligula (ruled A.D. 37–41) had a huge palace on Palatine Hill overlooking the Forum. It actually sprawled down the hill into the Forum (some supporting arches remain in the hillside), with an entrance by the Temple of Castor and Pollux.

Caligula tortured enemies, stole senators' wives, and parked his chariot in handicap spaces. But Rome's luxury-loving emperors only added to the glory of the Forum, with each one trying to make his mark on history.

To the left of the Temple of Castor and Pollux, find the remains of a small white circular temple...

8. The Temple of Vesta: This was Rome's most sacred spot. Rome considered itself one big family, and this temple represented a circular hut, like the kind Rome's first families lived in. Inside, a fire burned, just as in a Roman home. And back in the days before lighters and matches, you never wanted your fire to go out. As long as the sacred flame burned, Rome would stand. The flame was tended by priestesses known as Vestal Virgins.

Around the back of the Temple of Vesta you'll find two rectangular brick pools. These stood in the courtyard of...

9. The House of the Vestal Virgins: The Vestal Virgins lived in a two-story building surrounding a central courtyard with these two pools at one end. Rows of statues to the left and right marked the long sides of the building. This place was the model—both architecturally and sexually—for medieval convents and monasteries.

The six Vestal Virgins, chosen from noble families before they reached the age of 10, served a 30-year term. Honored and revered by the Romans, the Vestals even had their own box opposite the emperor in the Colosseum.

As the name implies, a Vestal took a vow of chastity. If she served her term faithfully—abstaining for 30 years—she was given a huge dowry, honored with a statue (like the ones at left), and allowed to marry (life begins at 40?). But if the Romans found any Virgin who wasn't, she was strapped to a funeral car, paraded through the streets of the Forum, taken to a crypt, given a loaf of bread and a lamp...and buried alive. Many women suffered the latter fate.

Head to the Forum's west end (opposite the Colosseum). Stop at the big, reconstructed brick building (on right) with the triangular roof. If the door's open, look in.

10. The Curia: The Senate House (Curia) was the most important political building in the Forum. Though this current building is a 1930s reconstruction, this was the site of Rome's official center of government since the birth of the republic. Three hundred senators, elected by the citizens of Rome, met here to debate and create the laws of the land. Their wooden seats once circled the building in three tiers; the Senate president's podium sat at the far end. The marble floor is from ancient times. Listen to the echoes in this vast room—the acoustics are great.

(Note: Although Julius Caesar was assassinated in "the Senate," it wasn't here—the Senate was temporarily meeting across town.)

Go back down the Senate steps to the metal guardrail and look right to a 10-foot-high wall at the base of Capitol Hill marked...

11. Rostrum *(Rostri)*: Nowhere was Roman freedom more apparent than at this "Speaker's Corner." The Rostrum was a raised platform, 10 feet high and 80 feet long, decorated with statues, columns, and the prows of ships *(rostra)*.

Rome's orators, great and small, came here trying to draw a crowd and sway public opinion. Mark Antony rose to offer Caesar the laurel-leaf crown of kingship, which Caesar publicly (and hypocritically) refused while privately becoming a dictator. Men such as Cicero railed against the corruption and decadence that came with the city's newfound wealth. In later years, daring citizens even spoke out against the emperors, reminding them that Rome was once free.

The big arch to the right of the Rostrum is...

12. Arch of Septimius Severus: In imperial times, the Rostrum's voices of democracy would have been dwarfed by images of empire such as the huge, six-story-high Arch of Septimius Severus (A.D. 203). The reliefs commemorate the African-born emperor's battles in Mesopotamia. Near ground level, see curly haired Severus marching captured barbarians back to Rome for the victory parade. Despite Severus' efficient rule, Rome's empire was crumbling under the weight of its own corruption, disease, decaying infrastructure, and the constant attacks by foreign "barbarians."

Pass underneath the Arch of Septimius Severus and turn left. On the slope of Capitol Hill are the eight remaining columns of the..

13. Temple of Saturn: These columns framed the entrance to the Forum's oldest temple (497 B.C.). Inside was a humble, very old wooden statue of the god Saturn. But the statue's pedestal held the gold bars, coins, and jewels of Rome's state treasury, the booty collected by conquering generals.

Standing here, at one of the Forum's first buildings, look east at the lone, tall...

14. Column of Phocas: This is the Forum's last great monument (A.D. 608), a gift from the powerful Byzantine Empire to a fallen empire—Rome. After Rome's 1,000-year reign, the city was looted by Vandals, the population of a million-plus shrank to 10,000, and the

ROME FALLS

Again, Rome lasted 1,000 years—500 years of growth, 200 years of peak power, and 300 years of gradual decay. The fall had many causes, among them the barbarians who pecked away at Rome's borders. Christians blamed the fall on moral decay. Pagans blamed it on Christians. Socialists blamed it on a shallow economy based on spoils of war. (George W. Bush blamed it on the Democrats.) Whatever the reasons, the far-flung empire could no longer keep its grip on conquered lands, and it pulled back. Barbarian tribes from Germany and Asia attacked the Italian peninsula and even looted Rome itself in A.D. 410, leveling many of the buildings in the Forum. In 476, when the last emperor checked out and switched off the lights, Europe plunged into centuries of ignorance, poverty, and weak government—the Dark Ages.

But Rome lived on in the Catholic Church. Christianity was the state religion of Rome's last generations. Emperors became popes (both called themselves Pontifex Maximus), senators became bishops, orators became priests, and basilicas became churches. And remember that the goal for the greatest church building project ever—that of St. Peter's—was to "put the dome of the Pantheon atop the Basilica of Constantine." The glory of Rome remains eternal.

once-grand city center—the Forum—was abandoned, slowly covered up by centuries of silt and dirt. In the 1700s, an English historian named Edward Gibbon stood here. Hearing Christian monks singing at these pagan ruins, he looked out at the few columns poking up from the ground, pondered the "Decline and Fall of the Roman Empire," and thought, "Hmm, that's a catchy title...."

The Dolce Vita Stroll down Via del Corso

This is the city's chic and hip "cruise," from Piazza del Popolo (Metro: Flaminio) down a wonderfully traffic-free section of Via del Corso, and up Via Condotti to the Spanish Steps each evening around 18:00 (Sat and Sun are best). Strollers, shoppers, and flirts on the prowl fill this neighborhood of Rome's most fashionable stores (open after siesta 16:30–19:30). Throughout Italy, early evening is the time to stroll.

Start on **Piazza Popolo**. Historians: This area was once just inside medieval Rome's main entry. The delightfully car-free square is marked by an obelisk that was brought to Rome by Augustus after he conquered Egypt. (It once stood in the Circus Maximus.) The Baroque church of

Dolce Vita Stroll

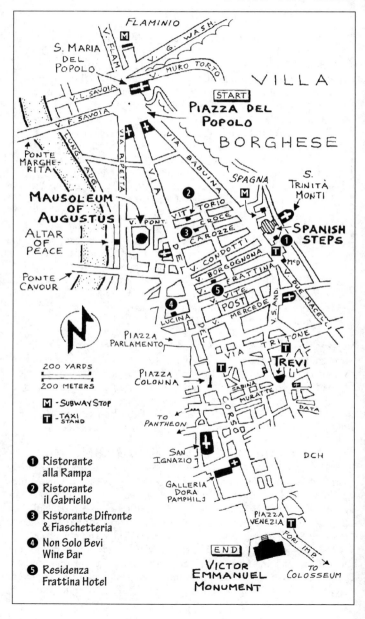

FLAMINIO

S. MARIA DEL POPOLO

V. G. WASH.
V. FLAM.
MURO TORTO

VILLA

START
PIAZZA DEL POPOLO

BORGHESE

V. L. SAVOIA
V. F. SAVOIA

LUNG. AUG.
V. RIPETTA
VIA BABUINA

SPAGNA

S. TRINITÀ MONTI

PONTE MARGHE-RITA

MAUSOLEUM OF AUGUSTUS

V. PONT.

VIT. ❷ TORIO
CROCE
❸ CAROZZE

M

SPANISH STEPS ❶
T
McD

ALTAR OF PEACE

V. CONDOTTI
V. BORGOGNONA
FRATTINA
❺ VITE
POST MERCEDE

V. S. AND.
DUE MACELLI

PONTE CAVOUR

❹ LUCINA

V.

PIAZZA PARLAMENTO

N

200 YARDS
200 METERS

PIAZZA COLONNA

T

VIA TRITONE

T
TREVI

SABINA
MURATTE
DATA

M - SUBWAY STOP
T - TAXI STAND

CORSU

TO PANTHEON

SAN IGNAZIO

GALLERIA DORA PAMPHILJ

DCH

PIAZZA VENEZIA
T
FORI IMP.

❶ Ristorante alla Rampa

❷ Ristorante il Gabriello

❸ Ristorante Difronte & Fiaschetteria

❹ Non Solo Bevi Wine Bar

❺ Residenza Frattina Hotel

END
VICTOR EMMANUEL MONUMENT

TO COLOSSEUM

Santa Maria del Popolo—with Raphael's Chigi Chapel (kee-gee, third chapel on left) and two Caravaggio paintings (side paintings in chapel left of altar)—is next to the gate in the old wall, on the far side of Piazza del Popolo, to the right as you face the gate (church open Mon–Sat 7:00–12:00 & 16:00–19:00, Sun 8:00–13:30 & 16:30–19:30).

From Piazza del Popolo, shop your way down **Via del Corso**. To rest your feet, join the locals sitting on the steps of various churches along the street.

At Via Pontefici, historians turn right and walk a block to see the massive, rotting, round brick **Mausoleum of Augustus**, topped with overgrown cypress trees. Beyond it, next to the river, is Augustus' Ara Pacis, or Altar of Peace (which should reopen in 2005).

From the mausoleum, return to Via del Corso and the 21st century, continuing straight until **Via Condotti**. Shoppers, take a left on Via Condotti to join the parade to the **Spanish Steps**. The streets that parallel Via Condotti to the south (Borgogno and Frattini) are just as popular. You can catch a taxi home at the taxi stand a block south of the Spanish Steps (at Piazza Mignonelli, near American Express and McDonald's).

Historians: Ignore Via Condotti. Continue three-quarters of a mile down Via del Corso—straight since Roman times—to the Victor Emmanuel Monument. Climb Michelangelo's stairway to his glorious (especially when floodlit) square atop Capitol Hill. From the balconies at either side of the mayor's palace, catch the lovely views of the Forum as the horizon reddens and cats prowl the unclaimed rubble of ancient Rome.

Night Walk Across Rome: Campo de' Fiori to the Spanish Steps

Rome can be grueling. But a fine way to enjoy this historian's rite of passage is an evening walk lacing together Rome's floodlit night spots and fine urban spaces with real-life theater vignettes.

Sitting so close to a Bernini fountain that traffic noises evaporate; jostling with local teenagers to see all the gelato flavors; enjoying lovers straddling more than the bench; jaywalking past flak-proof-vested *polizia;* and marveling at the ramshackle elegance that softens this brutal city for those who were born here and can imagine living nowhere else— these are the flavors of Rome best tasted after dark.

Start at the **Campo de' Fiori** (Field of Flowers), my favorite outdoor dining room after dark (see "Eating," page 471). The statue of Giordano Bruno, a heretic who was burned in 1600 for believing the world was round and not the center of the universe, marks the center of this great and colorful square. Bruno overlooks a busy produce market in the morning and strollers after sundown. This neighborhood is still known for its free spirit and occasional demonstrations. When the statue of Bruno was erected in 1889, local riots overcame Vatican protests

Night Walk Across Rome

against honoring a heretic. Bruno faces his executioner, the Vatican Chancellory (the big white building in the corner a bit to his right), while his pedestal reads: "And the flames rose up."

At the east end of the square (behind Bruno), the ramshackle apartments are built right into the old outer wall of ancient Rome's mammoth Theater of Pompey. This entertainment complex covered several city blocks, stretching from here to Largo Argentina. Julius Caesar was assassinated in the Theater of Pompey, where the Senate was renting space.

The square is lined with and surrounded by fun eateries. Bruno faces La Carbonara, the only real restaurant on the square. The Forno, next door to the left, is a popular place for hot and tasty take-out *pizza bianco* (plain pizza bread).

If Bruno did a hop, step, and jump forward, then turned right on Via dei Baullari and marched 200 yards, he'd cross the busy Corso Vittorio Emanuele and find **Piazza Navona.** Rome's most interesting night scene features street music, artists, fire-eaters, local Casanovas, ice cream, fountains by Bernini, and outdoor cafés (worthy of a splurge if you've got time to sit and enjoy the human river of Italy).

This oblong square retains the shape of the original racetrack that was built by the emperor Domitian. (If you want to see the ruins of the original entrance, exit the square at the north end, take an immediate left, and look down to the left 25 feet below the current street level.) Since ancient times, the square has been a center of Roman life. In the 1800s, the city would flood the square to cool off the neighborhood.

The **Four Rivers fountain** in the center is the most famous fountain by the man who remade Rome in Baroque style, Gian Lorenzo Bernini. Four burly river gods (representing four continents known in 1650) support an obelisk, while the water of the world gushes everywhere. The Nile has his head covered (since the headwaters were unknown then). The Ganges holds an oar. The Danube turns to admire the obelisk, which Bernini had moved here from a stadium on the Appian Way. And the Rio de la Plata from Uruguay tumbles backward in shock, wondering how he ever made the top four. Bernini enlivens the fountain with horses plunging through the rocks and exotic flora and fauna from these newly discovered lands. Homesick Texans may want to find the armadillo. (It's the big, weird armor-plated creature behind the Plata river statue.)

The Plata river god is gazing upward at the church of Saint Agnes, worked on by Bernini's former student turned rival, Borromini. Borromini's concave façade helps reveal the dome and epitomizes the curved symmetry of Baroque. Tour guides say that Bernini designed his river god to look horrified at Borromini's work. Or he may be shielding his eyes from St. Agnes' nakedness, as she was stripped before being martyred. But the fountain was completed two years before Borromini even started work on the church.

At the **Tre Scalini** café (near the fountain), sample some *tartufo* "death-by-chocolate" ice cream, world-famous among connoisseurs of ice cream and chocolate alike (€3.50 to go, €7 at a table, closed Wed). Seriously admire a painting by a struggling artist. Request "Country Roads" from an Italian guitar player, and don't be surprised when he knows it. Listen to the white noise of gushing water and exuberant humans.

Leave Piazza Navona directly across from Tre Scalini café, go east past rose peddlers and palm readers, jog left around the guarded building, and follow the brown sign to the Pantheon. The Pantheon is straight down Via del Salvatore (cheap pizza place on left just before the Pantheon, WC at McDonald's).

Sit for a while under the floodlit and moonlit **Pantheon's** portico. The 40-foot single-piece granite columns of the Pantheon's entrance show the scale the ancient Romans built on. The columns support a triangular, Greek-style roof with an inscription that says that "M. Agrippa" built it. In fact, it was built *("fecit")* by Emperor Hadrian (A.D. 120), who gave credit to the builder of an earlier structure. This impressive entranceway gives no clue that the greatest wonder of the building is inside—a domed room that inspired later domes, including Michelangelo's St. Peter's and Brunelleschi's Duomo (in Florence). Notice how the pavement slants down from McDonald's to the Pantheon, showing how high modern Rome has built on ancient rubble.

With your back to the Pantheon, veer to the right down Via Orfani. After passing Bar Pantheon, you'll see **Tazza d'Oro Casa del Caffè**, one of Rome's top coffee shops, dating back to the days when this area was licensed to roast coffee beans. Locals come here for its fine *granita di caffè con panna*. Look back at the fine view of the Pantheon from here. Then take Via Orfani to Piazza Capranica.

Piazza Capranica is home to the big, plain, Florentine Renaissance–style Palazzo Capranica. Big shots, like the Capranica family, built stubby towers on their palaces—not for any military use, but just to show off. Leave the piazza to the right of the palace, between the palace and the church. Via in Aquiro leads to a sixth-century B.C. **Egyptian obelisk** (taken as a trophy by Augustus after his victory in Egypt over Mark Antony and Cleopatra). Walk into the guarded square past the obelisk and face the huge parliament building.

A short detour to the left (past Albergo National) brings you to Rome's most famous gelateria. **Gelateria Caffè Pasticceria Giolitti** is cheap to go or elegant and splurge-worthy for a sit among classy locals (open daily until very late, Via Uffici del Vicario 40); get your gelato in a cone (*cono*) or cup (*coppetta*).

Piazza Colonna features a huge second-century column honoring Marcus Aurelius. The big, important-looking palace—headquarters of the deputies (or cabinet) of the prime minister. The **Via del Corso** is named for the Berber horse races—without riders—that took place here during Carnevale until the 1800s when a horse trampled a man to death in front of a horrified queen. Historically the street was filled with meat shops. When it became Rome's first gas lit street in the 1800s, "nastier" shops were banned and replaced by classier boutiques, jewelers, and antique dealers. Today, every evening most of Via del Corso is closed to traffic and it becomes a wonderful parade of Romans out for an evening stroll. Cross Via del Corso, Rome's noisy main drag, jog right (around the Y-shaped shopping gallery from 1928), and head down Via dei Sabini to the roar of the water, light, and people of the Trevi Fountain.

The **Trevi Fountain** shows how Rome took full advantage of the abundance of water brought into the city by its great aqueducts. This watery Baroque avalanche was built in 1762 by Nicola Salvi, hired by a pope celebrating the reopening of the ancient aqueduct that powers it. Salvi used the palace behind the fountain as a theatrical backdrop for the figure of "Ocean" who represents water in every form. The statue surfs through his wet kingdom—with water gushing from 24 spouts and tumbling over 30 different kinds of plants—while Tritone blows his conch shell. (From here, the water goes underground, then bubbles up again at Bernini's Four Rivers Fountain in Piazza Navona.)

The magic of the square is enhanced by the fact that no streets directly approach it. You can hear the excitement as you approach and then, bam, you're there. The scene is always lively, with lucky Romeos clutching dates while unlucky ones clutch beers. Romantics toss a coin over their shoulder, thinking it will give them a wish and assure their return to Rome. That may sound silly, but every year I go through this touristic ritual...and it actually seems to work.

Take some time to people-watch (whisper a few breathy *bellos* or *bellas*) before leaving. Face the fountain, then go past it on the right down Via delle Stamperia to Via del Triton. Cross the busy street and continue to the Spanish Steps (ask, *"Dov'è Piazza di Spagna?"*—Spagna rhymes with "lasagna,") a few blocks and thousands of dollars of shopping opportunities away.

The Piazza di Spagna, with the very popular **Spanish Steps**, is named for the Spanish Embassy to the Vatican, which has been here for 300 years. It's been the hangout of many Romantics over the years (Keats, Wagner, Openshaw, Goethe, and others). The British poet John Keats pondered his mortality, then died in the pink building on the right side of the steps. Fellow Romantic Lord Byron lived across the square at #66.

The Sinking Boat Fountain at the foot of the steps, which was done by Bernini or his father, Pietro, is powered by an aqueduct. All of Rome's fountains are aqueduct-powered; their spurts are determined by the water pressure provided by the various aqueducts. This one, for instance, is much weaker than Trevi's gush.

The piazza is a thriving night scene. Window-shop along Via Condotti, which stretches away from the steps. This is where Gucci and other big names cater to the trendsetting jet set. Facing the Spanish Steps, you can walk right about a block to tour one of the world's biggest and most lavish McDonald's (salad bar, WC). There's a taxi stand in the courtyard outside McDonald's; or, if you'd prefer, the Spagna Metro stop (usually open until 23:30) is just to the left of the Spanish Steps, ready to zip you home.

SLEEPING

The absolute cheapest beds (dorms or some cramped doubles) in Rome are €18 in small, backpacker-filled hostels. A nicer hotel (around €130 with a bathroom and air-con) provides an oasis and refuge, making it easier to enjoy this intense and grinding city. If you're going door to door, prices are soft—so bargain. Built into a hotel's official price list is a kickback for a room-finding service or agency; if you're coming direct, they pay no kickback and may lower the price for you. Many hotels have high-season (mid-March–June, Sept–Oct) and low-season prices. If traveling outside of peak times, ask about a discount. Room rates are lowest in sweltering August. Easter, September, and Christmas are most crowded and expensive. On Easter (April 11 in 2004), the entire city gets booked up.

English works in all but the cheapest places. Traffic in Rome roars. My challenge: To find friendly places on quiet streets. With the recent arrival of double-paned windows and air-conditioning, night noise is not the problem it was. Even so, light sleepers should always ask for a *tranquillo* room. Many prices here are promised only to people who show this book and reserve directly, without using a room-finding service. And many places prefer hard cash.

Bed-and-breakfasts are booming in Rome, offering comfy doubles in the old center for around €80. The Beehive hostel is a good contact for booking B&Bs in Rome (www.cross-pollinate.com, see "Sleeping Cheap, Northeast of the Train Station," page 464).

Most hotels are eager to connect you with a shuttle service to the airport. It's reasonable and easy for leaving, but upon arrival I think it's easiest to simply catch a cab or the shuttle train (covered in "Transportation Connections," page 479).

Almost no hotels have parking, but nearly all have a line on spots in a nearby garage (about €21/day).

On Via Firenze

I generally stay on Via Firenze because it's safe, handy, central, and relatively quiet. It's a 10-minute walk from the central train station and airport shuttle, and two blocks beyond Piazza della Repubblica and the TI. The Defense Ministry is nearby, and you've got heavily armed guards watching over you all night.

The neighorhood is well connected by public transportation (with the Repubblica Metro stop nearby). Virtually all the city buses that rumble down Via Nazionale (#64, #70, #115, #640, and the #40 express) take you to Piazza Venezia (Forum) and Largo Argentina (Pantheon).

SLEEP CODE

(€1 = about $1.10, country code: 39)
Sleep Code: **S** = Single, **D** = Double/Twin, **T** = Triple, **Q** = Quad, **b** = bathroom, **s** = shower only, **no CC** = Credit Cards not accepted, **SE** = Speaks English, **NSE** = No English. Breakfast is included in all but the cheapest places. You can assume a hotel takes credit cards unless you see "no CC" in the listing.

To help you sort easily through these listings, I've divided the rooms into three categories based on the price for a standard double room with bath:

$$$ **Higher Priced**—Most rooms €180 or more.
  $$ **Moderately Priced**—Most rooms between €115-180.
   $ **Lower Priced**—Most rooms €115 or less.

From Largo Argentina, electric trolley #8 goes to Trastevere (first stop after crossing the river) and #64 (jammed with people and thieves) and the #40 express continue to St. Peter's.

A 24-hour pharmacy near the recommended hotels is Farmacia Piram (Via Nazionale 228, tel. 06-488-4437). Neighborhood garages charge €24 per day.

$$$ Residenza Cellini is a gorgeous six-room place that feels like the guest wing of a neoclassical palace. It offers "ortho/anti-allergy beds" and four-star comforts and service (Db-€165, larger Db-€185, extra bed-€25, €30 discount in off-season—Aug plus mid-Nov–March, these prices good with this book and payment in cash through 2004, elevator, air-con, Via Modena 5, tel. 06-4782-5204, fax 06-4788-1806, www.residenzacellini.it, residenzacellini@tin.it, Barbara, Gaetano, and Donato SE).

$$ Hotel Oceania is a peaceful slice of air-conditioned heaven. This 15-room, manor house–type hotel is spacious and quiet, with spotless tastefully-decorated rooms, run by a pleasant father-and-son team. While Armando (the dad) serves world-famous coffee, Stefano (the son) works to give their hotel all the extra touches. He just added a plasma TV with surround sound to his lounge for guests to watch classic movies set in Rome...and Italy episodes from my TV series (Sb-€108, Db-€138, Tb-€168, Qb-€195, these prices promised through 2004 with this book and cash only, additional 25 percent off in Aug and winter; large roof terrace, family suite; Via Firenze 38, 3rd floor; tel. 06-482-4696, fax 06-488-5586, www.hoteloceania.it, info@hoteloceania.it, Anna and Stefano SE).

Hotels in East Rome

1. Residenza Cellini & Residence Adler
2. Hotels Oceania & Nardizzi
3. Hotel Aberdeen
4. Hotel Sonya
5. Hotel Pensione Italia
6. Hotel Montreal
7. YWCA Casa per Studentesse
8. Suore di Santa Elisabetta
9. Pensione per Pelligrini
10. Hotels Fenicia & Magic
11. Albergo Sileo
12. Hotel Duca d'Alba
13. Hotel Paba
14. Hotel Lancelot & Capo d' Africa
15. The Beehive Hostel
16. Gulliver's House Hostel
17. Casa Olmata Hostel

$$ **Hotel Aberdeen**, while a more formal place, offers a particularly great value, with minibars, phones, and showers in its 36 modern, air-conditioned, and smoke-free rooms. It's warmly run by Annamaria, with support from her cousins Sabrina, Laura, and Cinzia. Their inviting lounge, sleek business-class rooms, frescoed breakfast room, and cheery thoughtful staff make this place another winner (Sb-€82, Db-€125, Tb-€145, Qb-€160, these very special "dollar relief program" prices are promised through 2004 with this book only, 30 percent less in Aug and winter, Via Firenze 48, tel. 06-482-3920, fax 06-482-1092, check for deals online at www.travel.it/roma/aberdeen, hotel.aberdeen@travel.it, Fabio, Alessio and Sabrina SE).

$ **Residence Adler** offers breakfast on a garden patio, wide halls, and eight quiet, simple and air-conditioned rooms in a superb location. A fine value, it's run the old-fashioned way by a charming family (Db-€115, Tb-€150, Qb-€180, Quint/b-€195, prices through 2004 with this book only, additional 5 percent off with cash, 15 percent off in Aug and winter; elevator; Via Modena 5, 2nd floor; tel. 06-484-466, fax 06-488-0940, www.hoteladler-roma.com, info@hoteladler-roma.com, gracious Sr. Brando Massini NSE but tries).

$ **Hotel Nardizzi Americana** offers 18 simple, pleasant, air-conditioned rooms and a delightful rooftop terrace. While loosely run, it's a fine value (Sb-€90, Db-€110, Tb-€135, Qb-€150, prices through 2004 with this book only, 10 percent discounts for off-season and long stays, additional 10 percent off with cash; elevator; Via Firenze 38, 4th floor; tel. 06-488-0368, fax 06-488-0035, www.hotelnardizzi.it, info@hotelnardizzi.it, SE).

Between Via Nazionale and Basilica Santa Maria Maggiore

$$ **Hotel Sonya** is a small, family-run, but impersonal place with 23 comfortable, well-equipped rooms, a central location, and decent prices (Db-€119, Tb-€134, Qb-€155, Quint/b-€170, these special prices guaranteed through 2004 with this book; air-con, elevator; facing the opera at Via Viminale 58, Metro: Repubblica or Termini; tel. 06-481-9911, fax 06-488-5678, www.hotelsonya.it, hotelsonyaroma@katamail.com, Francesca SE).

$ **Hotel Pensione Italia**, in a busy, interesting, and handy locale, is placed safely on a quiet street next to the Ministry of the Interior. Thoughtfully run by Andrea, Nadine, and Francesca, it has 31 comfortable, airy, clean, and bright rooms (Sb-€75, Db-€100, Tb-€145, Qb-€165, prices through 2004 with this book and cash only, all rooms 30 percent off mid-July–Aug and Nov–March; air-con for €8 extra per day, most rooms have fans, elevator; Via Venezia 18, just off Via Nazionale, Metro: Repubblica or Termini; tel. 06-482-8355, fax 06-474-5550, www.hotelitaliaroma.com, hitalia@nettuno.it, SE). They have eight decent annex rooms across the street.

$ **Hotel Montreal**, run with care, is a bright, solid, business-class place on a big street a block southeast of Santa Maria Maggiore (soft prices, these are the max: Db-€115 but €90 in July–Aug, Tb-€140 but €120 in July–Aug, mention this book; air-con, elevator, good security; 1 block from Metro: Vittorio, 3 blocks west of train station, Via Carlo Alberto 4, Metro: Termini or Vittorio Emanuele; tel. 06-445-7797, fax 06-446-5522, www.hotelmontrealroma.com, info@hotelmontrealroma.com, SE).

YWCA and Convents

$ **YWCA Casa per Studentesse** accepts men and women. It's an institutional place, filled with white-uniformed maids, colorful Third-World travelers, and 75 single beds (€26 per person in 3- and 4-bed rooms, S-€37, Sb-€47, D-€62, Db-€74, includes breakfast except on Sun; elevator; Via C. Albo 4, Metro: Repubblica or Termini; tel. 06-488-0460, fax 06-487-1028, www.ywca-ucdg.it, segreteria@ywca-ucdg.it, a little reluctant English spoken). The YWCA faces a great little street market.

$ **Suore di Santa Elisabetta** is a heavenly Polish-run convent. While often booked long in advance and a challenge in communication, it's a super value (S-€34, Sb-€41, D-€55, Db-€71, Tb-€91, Qb-€110; 23:00 curfew, elevator, fine view roof terrace; a block southwest of Basilica Santa Maria Maggiore at Via dell' Omata 9, Metro: Termini or Vittorio Emanuele; tel. 06-488-8271, fax 06-488-4066, ist.it.s.elisabetta@libero.it, NSE).

$ **Pensione per Pelligrini**—which might close in 2004—is another nun-run place with 39 big, simple rooms and lots of twin beds. There's a language barrier, but the price is right (S-€35, Sb-€45, D-€65, Db-€84, Tb-€95, breakfast-€5; closed Aug, peaceful garden, elevator; just off Piazza Vittorio Emmanuele II, Istituto Buon Salvatore, Via Leopardi 17, no sign, from station take bus #714, #649, or #360 or Metro: Vittorio Emanuele; tel. 06-446-7147 or 06-446-7225, fax 06-446-1382, Sister Anna Maria SE).

Sleeping Cheap, Northeast of the Train Station

The cheapest hotels in town are northeast of the station (Metro: Termini). Some travelers feel this area is weird and spooky after dark, but these hotels feel plenty safe. With your back to the train tracks, turn right and walk two blocks out of the station.

$ **Hotel Fenicia** rents 13 decent rooms at a fine price (Sb-€53, Db-€80, Tb-€103, bigger and fancier Db-€93, prices through 2004 with this book only, air-con-€5/day, breakfast-€4, 5 percent off with cash, Via Milazzo 20, tel. & fax 06-490-342, www.hotelfenicia.it, info@hotelfenicia.it, Georgio and Anna SE).

$ **The Beehive** gives vagabonds—old and young—a cheap, clean, and comfy home in Rome. Its double rooms are a great value (D-€60, Db-€80, T-€90, Tb-€120, Q-€120, Qb-€160, no CC) and it has an 8-bed dorm (€18 beds). It's thoughtfully run by a friendly young American couple, Steve and Linda (2 blocks north of the train station at Via Marghera 8, tel. 06-447-04553, www.the-beehive.com). They also run a B&B booking service (private rooms in the old center of Rome, Florence, and Venice, offering comparable quality for €70–110—cheaper than the cost of a hotel, www.cross-pollinate.com).

$ **Hotel Magic** has 10 tidy, marbled rooms, up lots of stairs. It's family-run, though not with much warmth (Db-€85, Tb-€110, Qb-€120, air-con-€5/day, prices through 2004 with this book only, confirm rates, 25 percent cheaper in Aug and winter, no CC; thin walls, midnight curfew; Via Milazzo 20, 3rd floor, tel. 06-495-9880, www.hotel-magic-rome.com, info@hotel-magic-rome.com Carmela, Rosanna, and Caesarina NSE).

$ **Albergo Sileo** is a shiny-chandeliered, 10-room place. It has a contract to house train conductors who work the night shift, so its simple, pleasant rooms are rented from 19:00 to 9:00 only. If you can handle this, it's a wonderful value. During the day, they store your luggage, and though you won't have access to a room, you're welcome to shower or hang out in the lobby or bar (D-€45, Db-€55, Tb-€60, Db for 24 hours-€62 when available, elevator, Via Magenta 39, tel. & fax 06-445-0246, www.hotelsileo.com, info@hotelsileo.com, friendly Alessandro and Maria Savioli NSE, daughter Anna SE).

Near the Colosseum

These places are buried in a Roman world of exhaust-stained, medieval ambience. For Alba and Paba, take the subway one stop from the train station to the Cavour Metro stop. The *electrico* bus line #117 (San Giovanni in Laterano, Colosseo, Trevi Fountain, Piazza di Spagna, and Piazza del Popolo) connects you with the sights.

$$$ **Hotel Capo d'Africa** is a new (2002) sleek, business-class place next to recommended Hotel Lancelot and San Clemente Church. It offers 65 of the best rooms I list with plush and sprawling public spaces, top-end fine points, and all the extras (Db-€200–225 depending on season, promised with this book in 2004 by manager Angelo Battistini, air-con, elevator, sprawling roof terrace, smoke-free floor, gym, Via Capo d'Africa 54, tel. 06-772-801, fax 06-772-80801, www.hotelcapodafrica.com, info@hotelcapodafrica.com, SE).

$$ **Hotel Duca d'Alba**, a tight and modern pastel/marble/hardwood place, is more professional than homey (30 rooms, Sb-€134, Db-€120–160 but higher in Sept and Oct, extra bed-€20, air-con, elevator, Via Leonina 14, tel. 06-484-471, fax 06-488-4840, check Web site for deals, www.hotelducadalba.com, info@hotelducadalba.com, Angelo SE).

$$ **Hotel Paba** has six rooms, chocolate box–tidy and lovingly cared for by Alberta and Pasquale Castelli. While overlooking busy Via Cavour just two blocks from the Colosseum, it's quiet enough (Db-€125, extra bed-€35, show this book for 5 percent discount, breakfast

served in room, air-con, elevator, Via Cavour 266, tel. 06-4782-4902, fax 06-4788-1225, www.hotelpaba.com, info@hotelpaba.com, SE).

$$ **Hotel Lancelot**, a favorite among United Nations workers, is big, with 60 rooms, a shady courtyard, rooftop terrace, bar, and restaurant. It's quiet, safe, well-run by Faris and Lubna Khan, and popular with returning guests (Sb-€96–113, Db-€150, Tb-€170, Qb-€185, add €15 for balcony, air-con, elevator, parking-€11/day, behind Colosseum near San Clemente Church at Via Capo d'Africa 47, tel. 06-7045-0615, fax 06-7045-0640, www.lancelothotel.com, info@lancelothotel.com, Lubna S the queen's E).

$ **Hotel Casa Kolbe**, located in a former monastery, rents out 63 monkish, spartan rooms with no fans or air-conditioning. With vast public spaces and a peaceful garden, it's popular with groups. But the location is tranquil: it's on the river side of the Palatine ruins, on a quiet side street about a block from a little-used entrance to the Forum (Sb-€62, Db-€80, Tb-€100, Qb-€110, breakfast-€6, elevator, garden, courtyard, institutional and cheap meals served, not handy to public transit so taxi from the station, Via S. Teodoro 44, tel. 06-679-4974 or 06-679-8866, fax 06-6994-1550, Fortunato and Antonio SE).

Near Campo de' Fiori

While you pay a premium to stay in the old center (and endure a little extra night noise), each of these places is romantically set deep in the tangled back streets near the idyllic Campo de' Fiori and, for many, worth the extra money.

$$ **Casa di Santa Brigida** overlooks the elegant Piazza Farnese. With soft-spoken sisters gliding down polished hallways, and pearly gates instead of doors, this lavish 23-room convent makes exhaust-stained Roman tourists feel like they've died and gone to heaven. If you don't need a double bed, this is worth the splurge (Sb-€95, Db-€170, 3 percent extra with credit card, tasty €15 dinners, roof garden, plush library, air-con, Monserrato 54, tel. 06-6889-2596, fax 06-6889-1573, www.brigidine.org, brigida@mclink.it, many of the sisters are from India and speak English). If you get no response to your fax or e-mail within three days, consider that a "no." Groups are welcome here.

$$ **Hotel Smeraldo**, with 50 rooms, is well-run, clean and a great deal (Sb-€90, Db-€120—this special price through 2004 with this book, Tb-€140, breakfast-€7; flowery roof terrace, centrally-controlled air-con, elevator; Civolo dei Chiodaroli 9, midway between Campo de' Fiori and Largo Argentina; tel. 06-687-5929, fax 06-6880-5495, www.smeraldoroma.com, albergosmeraldoroma@tin.it, Massimo SE).

$$ **Hotel Arenula** is the only hotel in Rome's old Jewish quarter. While it has the ambience of a gym, it's a fine value in the thick of old Rome with 50 comfy rooms (Sb-€92, Db-€121, Tb-€134, €26 less in July, Aug, and winter, air-con, just off Via Arenula at Via Santa Maria de'

Calderari 47, tel. 06-687-9454, fax 06-689-6188, www.hotelarenula.com, hotel.arenula@flashnet.it, SE).

Near the Pantheon

These places are buried in the pedestrian-friendly heart of ancient Rome, each within a four-minute walk of the Pantheon. You'll pay more here—but you'll save time and money by being exactly where you want to be for your early and late wandering.

$$$ **Hotel Nazionale**, a four-star landmark, is a 16th-century palace sharing a well-policed square with the national Parliament. Its 90 rooms are served by lush public spaces, fancy bars, and a uniformed staff. It's a big hotel with a revolving front door, but it's a worthy splurge if you want security, comfort, and the heart of old Rome at your doorstep (Sb-€188, Db-€292—this special price guaranteed in 2004 with this book, extra person-€62, less in Aug and winter, air-con, elevator, Piazza Montecitorio 131, tel. 06-695-001, fax 06-678-6677, see Web site for discounts in summer and weekends, www.nazionaleroma.it, hotel @nazionaleroma.it, SE).

$$$ **Albergo Santa Chiara** is big, solid, and hotelesque, offering marbled elegance in the old center at an affordable price. Its ample public lounges are dressy and professional and its 100 rooms are quiet and spacious (Sb-€145, Db-€217, Tb-€250, elevator, all the big hotel services, behind the Pantheon at Via di Santa Chiara 21, tel. 06-687-2979, fax 06-687-3144, www.albergosantachiara.com, stchiara@tin.it).

$$$ **Hotel Due Torri,** hiding out on a tiny, quiet street, is a little over-priced but beautifully located. It feels professional yet homey, with an accommodating staff, generous public spaces, and 26 comfortable-if-tight rooms—four with balconies (Sb-€118, Db-€190, family apartment-€250 for 3 and €275 for 4; air-con; Vicolo del Leonetto 23, a block off Via della Scrofa; tel. 06-6880-6956, fax 06-686-5442, www.hotelduetorriroma.com, hotelduetorri@interfree.it, SE).

Between the Spanish Steps and Piazza Venezia

$$ **Residenza Frattina** is a pink palace—with 10 high-ceilinged rooms and a panforte-plush living room—in a posh locale. It has an old-fashioned feel and an unbeatable location on a main pedestrian shopping drag near Piazza di Spagna and the Spanish Steps (Db-€140–180, Tb-€160–220, prices change with season and are soft, 5 percent cash discount, air-con, Via Frattina 104, tel. 06-679-5509, fax 06-678-3701, www.residenzafrattinacorso.com, residenza.frattina@flashnet.it, owner Cesare SE; to locate hotel, see Dolce Vita Stroll map above).

$$ **Hotel Giardino,** thoughtfully run by Englishwoman Kate, offers 11 pleasant rooms in a central location three blocks northeast of Piazza Venezia (Easter–June and Sept–Oct: Sb-€80, Db-€120, other times: Sb-€60, Db-€90, these special prices are promised through 2004

Hotels in the Heart of Rome

① Casa di Santa Brigida   ⑤ Albergo Santa Chiara
② Hotel Smeraldo   ⑥ Hotel Due Torri
③ To Hotel Arenula   ⑦ To Residenza Frattina
④ Hotel Nazionale   ⑧ Hotel Giardino

with cash and this book; air-con, double-paned windows; busy street off
Piazza di Quirinale, Via XXIV Maggio 51; tel. 06-679-4584, fax 06-
679-5155, www.hotel-giardino-roma.com, hotel_giardino@libero.it).

Trastevere
To locate this hotel, see map on page 438.

$$ Hotel Santa Maria sits like a lazy hacienda in the midst of
Trastevere. Surrounded by a medieval skyline, you'll feel as if you're on
some romantic stage set. Its 19 small but well-equipped, air-conditioned
rooms—former cells in a cloister—are all on the ground floor, circling a
gravelly courtyard of orange trees and stay-awhile patio furniture.
Because this is the only hotel in Trastevere, it isn't cheap—but for well-

heeled poets, it's a deal (Db-€155, Tb-€191, Qb-€217, family room for 6-€270, for this 20–25 percent discount it's cash only and a 3-night min, good with this book through 2004, smaller discounts also available with this book for shorter stays and credit cards and off-season, a block north of Piazza Maria Trastevere at Vicolo del Piede 2, tel. 06-589-4626, fax 06-589-4815, www.htlsantamaria.com, hotelsantamaria@libero.it, Stefano SE).

Near the Vatican Museum
To locate these hotels, see map on page 429.

$$$ Hotel Sant' Anna is pricey, but located on a charming-for-Rome pedestrian street that fills up with restaurant tables at dinner-time. Its 20 comfy rooms, decorated with classical themes, are somewhere between tasteful and too much (Sb-€145, Db-€190, Db discounted to €145 July–Aug, winter, and slow times—any time of year, ask for a Rick Steves' discount; air-con, elevator, courtyard; Borgo Pio 133, near intersection with Mascherino, a couple blocks from entrance to St. Peter's; tel. 06-6880-1602, fax 06-6830-8717, www.hotelsantanna.com, santanna@travel.it, Viscardo SE).

$$$ Hotel Bramante sits like a grand medieval lodge in the shadow of the fortified escape wall that runs from the Vatican to Castel Sant' Angelo. The public spaces and the 16 thoughtfully-appointed rooms are generously sized, with rough wood beams and high ceilings (Sb-€133, Db-€190, Tb-€220, Qb-€230, these special prices promised with this book through 2004, air-con, no elevator, Vicolo delle Palline 24, tel. 06-6880-6426, fax 06-681-33339, www.hotelbramante.com, hotelbramante@libero.it, Maurizio and Loredana SE).

$$ Hotel Alimandi is a good value, run by the friendly and entrepreneurial Alimandi brothers—Paolo, Enrico, and Luigi—and the next generation, Marta, Irene, and Germano. Their 35 rooms are air-conditioned, modern, and marbled in white (Sb-€90, Db-€150, Tb-€175, 5 percent discount with this book and cash; closed Jan–mid Feb, elevator, grand buffet breakfast served in great roof garden, small gym, pool table, piano lounge, free parking; down stairs directly in front of Vatican Museum, Via Tunisi 8, near Metro: Cipro-Musei Vaticani; reserve by phone, no reply to fax means they are full; tel. 06-3972-6300, toll-free in Italy tel. 800-122-121, fax 06-3972-3943, www.alimandi.org, alimandi@tin.it, SE). They offer free airport pickup and drop-off, though you must reserve when you book your room and wait for a scheduled shuttle (every 2 hrs, see their Web site or lobby schedule).

$$ Hotel Spring House, with a hotelesque feel (it's a Best Western), offers 51 attractive rooms—some with balconies or terraces (standard Db-€135, superior Db-€180, Tb-€155–195, Qb-€175–210, mention this book for a 15 percent discount July–Aug and Jan–Feb; air-con, elevator, free loaner bikes; Metro: Cipro-Musei Vaticani, Via Mocenigo 7, 2 blocks from Vatican Museum; tel. 06-3972-0948, fax 06-3972-1047, www .hotelspringhouse.com, info@hotelspringhouse.com, Stefano Gabbani SE).

$$ **Hotel Gerber** is modern and air-conditioned, with 27 well-polished businesslike rooms, set in a quiet residential area (two S without air-con-€57, Sb-€100, Db-€130, Tb-€150, Qb-€170, 10 percent discount beyond their best price with this book in high season, 15 percent discount in low season, Via degli Scipioni 241, a block from Metro: Lepanto, at intersection with Ezio, tel. 06-321-6485, fax 06-321-7048, www.hotelgerber.it, info@hotelgerber.it, friendly dog Kira, Peter and Simonetta SE).

Sleeping Cheaply near the Vatican

$ **Casa per Ferie Santa Maria alle Fornaci dei Padri Trinitari** houses pilgrims and secular tourists with simple class just a short walk south of the Vatican in 54 stark utilitarian mostly twin-bedded rooms. This is the only user-friendly convent-type place I found (Sb-€60, Db-€80, Tb-€110; groups welcome, generally booked solid Easter, May, and Oct, fans, elevator; bus #64 from train station to St. Peters Station, then walk 100 yards to Piazza S. Maria alle Fornaci 27; tel. 06-393-67632, fax 06-393-66795, www.trinitaridematha.it, cffornaci@tin.it, SE).

Hostels and Dorms

For easy communication with young, friendly entrepreneurs, cheap dorm beds, and some inexpensive doubles—within a 10-minute hike of the train station—consider the following places:

$ **The Beehive,** listed above in "Sleeping Cheap, Northeast of the Train Station," offers €18 dorm beds (in an 8-bed room) in addition to affordable doubles.

$ **Gulliver's House Rome** is a fun little hostel in a safe and handy locale, run by helpful Simon and Sara. Its 24 beds in cramped quarters work fine for backpackers. They host English movie evenings (warm up with my TV shows on Rome) in their lounge nightly (€20 per bunk bed in 8-bed dorm, one D-€70, no CC, closed 12:00–16:00, 1:00 curfew, small kitchen, Via Palermo 36, tel. 06-481-7680, www.gullivershouse .com, stay@gullivershouse.com). Gulliver's also runs a five-room place a 10-minute walk north of the station offering simple, air-con doubles (D-€70, Db-€80, Tb-€100, Via Castro Pretorio 25).

$ **Casa Olmata** is a ramshackle, laid-back backpackers' place midway between the Termini train station and Colosseum (dorm beds-€20, S-€38, bunk bed D-€44, one queen-size D-€55; lots of stairs, laundry service, free Internet access, video rentals, games, rooftop terrace with views and nearly free dinner parties, dinners twice weekly, communal kitchen; a block southwest of Basilica Santa Maria Maggiore, Via dell' Omata 36, 3rd floor, Metro: Vittorio Emanuele; tel. 06-483-019, fax 06-486819, www.casaolmata.com, info@casaolmata.com, Mirella and Marco).

EATING

Romans spend their evenings eating rather than drinking, and the pre-ferred activity is simply to enjoy a fine, slow meal, buried deep in the old city. Rome's a fun and cheap place to eat, with countless little eater-ies serving memorable €20 meals.

Although I've listed a number of restaurants, I recommend that you just head for a scenic area and explore. Piazza Navona, the Pantheon area, Campo de' Fiori, and Trastevere are neighborhoods packed with characteristic eateries. Sitting with tourists on a famous square enjoying the scene works fine. But for places more out of the way, consider my recommendations.

For Rome's best gelato, see "Dining near the Pantheon," below.

Trastevere

Colorful Trastevere is now pretty touristy. Still, Romans join the tourists to eat on the rustic side of the Tiber River. Start at the central square (Piazza Santa Maria). Then choose: Eat with tourists enjoying the ambience of the famous square, or wander the back streets in search of a mom-and-pop place with barely a menu. Look over these two places (between Piazza Santa Maria Trastevere and Ponte Sisto) before making a choice. See map on page 438.

Trattoria da Lucia lets you enjoy simple traditional food at a good price in a great scene (Tue–Sun 12:30–15:30 & 19:30–24:00, closed Mon, homey indoor or evocative outdoor seating, Vicolo del Mattonato 2, tel. 06-580-3601, NSE).

Osteria Ponte Sisto, a rough-and-tumble little place, specializes in traditional Roman cuisine with a menu that changes often. Since it's just outside of the tourist zone, it offers the best value and caters mostly to Romans. It's also easy to find: Crossing Ponte Sisto (pedestrian bridge), continue across the little square (Piazza Trilussa) and you'll see it on the right (daily 12:30–15:00 & 19:30–24:00, Via Ponte Sisto 80, tel. 06-588-3411, SE).

The fine little **Gelateria alla Scala** (across from the church on Piazza della Scala) dishes up delightful cinnamon (*cannella*) and oh-wow pistachio (daily 12:30–24:00). Seek this place out.

On and near Campo de' Fiori

While it is touristy, Campo de' Fiori offers a classic and romantic square setting. And, since it is so close to the collective heart of Rome, it remains popular with locals. For greater atmosphere than food value, circle the square, considering each place. Bars and pizzerias seem to overwhelm the square. The **Taverna** and **Vineria** (#16 and #15) offer good perches from which to people-watch and nurse a glass of wine. The only real restaurant is **La Carbonara**. While famous and atmospheric with reasonable prices, it gets mixed reviews (closed Tue, Campo de' Fiori 23, tel. 06-686-4783). Although meals on small surrounding streets are a better value, they lack that Campo de' Fiori magic.

Ostaria da Giovanni ar Galletto—nearby, on the more elegant and peaceful Piazza Farnese—has a dressier local crowd, pleasant outdoor seating, and reasonable prices. Say hi to Angelo, who's committed to serving fine food (closed Sun, tucked in corner of Piazza Farnese at #102, tel. 06-686-1714). Of all my listings, this place offers perhaps the best alfresco dining experience.

Osteria Enoteca al Bric is a mod bistro-type place run by a man who loves to cook and serve good wine. Wine-case lids decorate the wall like happy memories. With candlelit grace and no tourists, it's perfect for the wine snob in the mood for pasta and fine cheese. Aficionados choose their bottle from the huge selection lining the walls as they enter. Beginners order wine with help from the waiter after they order their meal (open from 19:30, closed Mon, reserve after 20:30, 100 yards off Campo de' Fiori at Via del Pellegrino 51, tel. 06-687-9533). Al Bric offers my readers a special "Taste of Italy for Two" deal (fine plate of mixed cheese and meat with two glasses of full-bodied red wine and a pitcher of water) for €20 from 19:30, but you may need to finish by 20:30. This could be a light meal if you're kicking off an evening stroll, a substantial appetizer, or a way to check this place out for a serious meal later.

Filetti de Baccala, a tradition for many Romans, is basically a fish bar with paper tablecloths and cheap prices. Its grease-stained, hurried waiters serve old-time favorites—fried cod fillets, a strange bitter *puntarelle* salad, and their antipasto (delightful anchovies with butter)—to nostalgic locals (no CC; Mon–Sat 17:30–23:00, closed Sun; a block east of Campo de' Fiori tumbling onto a tiny and atmospheric square, Largo dei Librari 88; tel. 06-686-4018). Study what others are eating and order by pointing. Nothing is expensive (see the menu on wall). Urchins can get a cod stick to go and sit on the barnacle church doorsteps just outside.

Trattoria der Pallaro has no menu but plenty of return eaters. Paola Fazi—with a towel wrapped around her head turban-style—and her family serve up a five-course festival of typically Roman food for €19, including wine, coffee, and a wonderful mandarin liqueur. Their slogan: "Here, you'll eat what we want to feed you." Make like Oliver Twist asking for more soup and get seconds on the mandarin liqueur (Tue–Sun 12:00–15:00 & 19:00–24:00, closed Mon; indoor/outdoor seating on quiet square; a block south of Corso Vittorio Emmanuele, down Largo del Chiavari to Largo del Pallaro 15; tel. 06-6880-1488).

Ristorante Grotte del Teatro di Pompeo, sitting atop an ancient theater, serves good food at fair prices, perfect if you want to dine on a characteristic cobbled street busy with strolling people and musicians (closed Mon, Via del Biscione 73, tel. 06-6880-3686).

Between Campo de' Fiori and Piazza Navona: **Cul de Sac** is packed with happy locals cobbling together fun meals from the Italian dim sum-type menu of traditional dishes (often crowded, daily 12:00–16:00 & 19:00–24:00, a block southwest of Piazza Navona on Piazza Pasquino). **L'Insalata Ricca**, next door, is a popular chain that specializes in hearty and healthy €7 salads (daily 12:00–15:45 & 18:45–22:00, Piazza Pasquino 72, tel. 06-6830-7881). Another branch is nearby with more spacious outdoor seating (just off Corso Vittorio Emanuele on Largo del Chiavari).

Dining near the Pantheon

Ristorante da Fortunato is an Italian classic—with fresh flowers on the tables, and white-coated black-tie waiters politely serving good meat and fish to local politicians, foreign dignitaries, and tourists with good taste. Don't leave without perusing the photos of their famous visitors—everyone from Tariq Aziz to Bill Clinton. The outdoor seating is fine for watching the river of Rome flow by. The air-conditioned interior has a smoke-free room—but I prefer the ambience of the main room. For a dressy night out, this is my choice (surprisingly reasonable, plan to spend €30, Mon–Sat 12:30–15:30 & 19:30–23:30, closed Sun, a block in front of the Pantheon at Via del Pantheon 55, tel. 06-679-2788).

Ristorante Myosotis di Marsili, an elegant place with black-tie waiters and a coat check, is popular with local politicians and diners smart enough to look into the fish locker and make a knowledgeable choice. Secluded and private, it has a traditional yet imaginative menu with a good wine list. Everything here is made on the premises (€40 dinners, Mon–Sat 12:30–15:30 & 19:30–23:30, closed Sun, reservations wise, behind Osteria da Mario—see directions below—at Vicolo Della Vaccarella 3, tel. 06-686-5554).

Eating Cheap and Colorful near the Pantheon

Eating on the square facing the Pantheon is a temptation (there's even a McDonald's offering some of the best outdoor seating in town) and I'd consider it just to relax and enjoy the classic Roman scene. But if you walk a block or two away you'll get less view and better food. Here are some suggestions:

Miscellanea is run by much-loved Michelangelo, who's on a mission to keep foreign students well-fed. You'll find cheap pasta, hearty €3 sandwiches, and a long list of €5 salads. "Mikki" often tosses in a fun little extra (daily 11:00–24:00, indoor/outdoor seating, a block toward Via del Corso from the Pantheon at Via delle Paste 110).

Osteria da Mario, a homey little mom-and-pop joint with a no-stress menu, serves delicious traditional favorites. The pop (Mario), who passed away—you'll see his photo on the wall—would be happy with the way his wife and kids are carrying on (Mon–Sat 13:00–15:00 &

Restaurants in the Heart of Rome

1. Taverna, Vineria & La Carbonara Rest.
2. Ostaria da Giovanni ar Galletto
3. Osteria Enoteca al Bric
4. Filetti de Baccala & Trattoria der Pallaro
5. Ristorante Grotte del Teatro di Pompeo
6. Cul de Sac Bar & L'Insalata Ricca Rest.
7. Ristorante da Fortunato
8. Ost. da Mario, Rist. Myosotis di Marsili, & Tav. Le Coppele
9. Miscellanea Restaurant & Ristorante Due Colonne
10. Brek Cafeteria
11. To Non Solo Bevi & Vini e Buffet
12. Giolitti's Gelateria
13. To Rist. alla Rampa, Rist. il Gabriello, Rist. Difronte, & Fiaschetteria
14. Ristorante Pizzeria Sacro e Profano
15. Gelateria San Crispino

19:30–23:00, closed Sun; indoor/outdoor; from Pantheon walk 2 blocks up Via Pantheon, go left on Via della Coppelle, take first right to Piazza delle Coppelle 51; tel. 06-6880-6349).

Two other places within a block or so of the Pantheon to consider for inexpensive eating: **Taverna Le Coppele** is good—especially for pizza—with checkered table cloth ambience (closed Tue, Via delle Coppelle 39, tel. 06-688-06557). **Ristorante Due Colonne** serves daily homemade specials and great salads in a simple rustic setting (daily 11:30–15:30 & 18:30–23:30, air-con, indoors only, Via del Seminario 122, tel. 06-6781-449).

Cafeteria Brek, on Largo Argentina just south of the Pantheon, is an appealing, self-service restaurant with a modern, efficient atmosphere and really cheap prices (daily 12:00–15:30 & 19:00–22:15; skip the sandwiches and pizza slices downstairs and go to the cafeteria upstairs, northwest corner of square, Largo Argentina 1; tel. 06-6821-0353).

The classic **Antica Salumeria** is an old-time *alimentari* (grocery store, daily 9:00–19:00) on the Pantheon square. While they sell meager ready-made sandwiches, it's better and more fun to have one made to your specs—ideal for a temple-porch picnic. Sit at the base of a column in the shade and munch lunch.

Non Solo Bevi *enoteca* is a trendy bar several blocks north, tucked into a distant corner of the pedestrian square, Piazza San Lorenzo. Francesco and Lamberto serve fine wine and toothpick munchies free with a glass. Sit at a table (€5 for wine) and enjoy the scene or stand at the bar (€3.50 for wine) and be part of the commotion (open daily, Via in Lucina 15, tel. 06-687-1683; for location, see Dolce Vita Stroll map on page TK). A block off the square, at **Vini e Buffet**, Vittorio serves salads, *bruschette*, and wine by the glass (Mon–Sat 12:30–15:00 & 19:30–23:00, closed Sun, Piazza della Torretta 60, tel. 06-687-1445).

Gelato: Rome's most famous and venerable ice-cream joint is a minute's walk in front of the Pantheon. **Giolitti's** is good, with cheap take-away prices and elegant Old World seating (just off Piazza Colonna and Piazza Monte Citorio at Via Uffici del Vicario 40, tel. 06-699-1243).

Near the Spanish Steps

To locate these restaurants, see the Dolce Vita Stroll map on page 454.

Ristorante alla Rampa is a classic old restaurant just around the corner from the touristy crush of the Spanish Steps. You'll get quality Roman cooking here with appealing indoor/outdoor ambience for a moderate price. They take no reservations, so arrive by 19:30 or be prepared to wait. For a simple meal, go with the €9 *piatto misto all' ortolana*—a self-service trip to their magnificent antipasto spread with meat, fish, and veggies (closed Sun, 100 yards east of Spanish Steps at Piazza Mignanelli 18, tel. 06-678-2621).

Ristorante il Gabriello is inviting and small—mod under medieval arches—offering a peaceful and local-feeling respite from all the top-end fashion shops in the area. Claudio serves with charisma while his brother cooks creative Roman cuisine using fresh, organic products from his wife's farm. Simply close your eyes and point to anything on the menu (pastas-€7, *secondi*-€10; dinner only, Mon–Sat 19:00–24:00, closed Sun; air-con, reservations smart; Via Vittoria 51, 3 blocks from Spanish Steps; tel. 06-6994-0810).

Ristorante Difronte, with a fresh, stylish ambience, serves big fun salads (Tue–Sun 12:00–15:30 & 17:30–24:00, closed Mon, Via della Croce 38, tel. 06-678-0355). Stepping next door takes you back about 100 years to the bustling **Fiaschetteria,** serving quality traditional Italian cuisine (closed Sun, Via della Croce 39). Both places serve €7 plates and offer indoor and outdoor seating.

Near the Trevi Fountain

Ristorante Pizzeria Sacro e Profano fills an old church with spicy south Italian (Calabrian) cuisine and some pricey exotic dishes. Run by Pasquale and friends, this is just far enough away from the Trevi mobs. Their hearty €13 antipasto plate offers a fun montage of Calabrian taste treats—plenty of food for a light meal (daily 12:00–15:00 & 19:00–22:00, a block off Via del Tritone at Via dei Maroniti 29, tel. 06-6791-836).

Gelateria San Crispino, around the corner, serves particularly tasty gelato using creative ingredients such as balsamic vinegar, pear, and cinnamon (daily until 24:00, Via della Panetteria 42, tel. 06-679-3924).

Eating Cheap between the Colosseum and St. Peter-in-Chains Church

You'll find good views but poor value in the restaurants directly behind the Colosseum. To get your money's worth, eat at least a block away. Here are two handy eateries at the top of Terme Di Tito (a block uphill from the Colosseum, near St. Peter-in-Chains church—of Michelangelo's *Moses* fame) and a good mom-and-pop place beyond that.

Caffè dello Studente is a lively spot popular with local engineering students attending the nearby U of Rome. Pina, Mauro, and their daughter Simona (SE) serve typical *bar gastronomia* fare (pick a toasted sandwich at the bar, pizza, drinks). You can get your food to go; stand up and eat at the crowded bar; sit at an outdoor table and wait for a menu; or—if it's not busy—show this book when you order at the bar and sit without paying extra at a table (Mon–Sat 7:30–21:30, closed Sun, tel. 06-488-3240).

Ostaria da Nerone, next door, is less friendly and more aggressive, but still a good bet for a meal in the area—especially their €7 antipasti plate (Mon–Sat 12:00–15:00 & 19:00–23:00, closed Sun, indoor/outdoor seating, Via delle Terme di Tito 96, tel. 06-481-7952).

Ristorante al Cardello di Angelo e Lidia is a characteristic hole-in-the-wall on a scenic corner tucked in a colorful neighborhood (*secondi*-€7, full menu-€15, Mon–Sat from 12:30 and from 19:30, closed Sun, indoor/outdoor seating, near the Forum just off Via Cavour on the corner of Via Frangipani and Via del Cardello, tel. 06-474-5259).

Near Via Firenze and Via Nazionale Hotels

Munching on Via Firenze: You have plenty of eating options near my recommended hotels on Via Firenze.

Snack Bar Gastronomia is a local joint with one table and a booming take-out business—especially popular for its Greek-style yogurt with fruit and honey (€2–4, confirm price of various options; fresh meat or veggie sandwiches, freshly-squeezed juices, daily 7:00–24:00, Via Firenze 34). An old-fashioned *alimentari* (grocery) is across the street (7:00–19:30), just uphill from the McDonald's.

Pasticceria Dagnino, a block away, is popular for its top-quality Sicilian specialties, especially pastries and ice cream (daily 7:00–22:00, in Galleria Esedra off Via Torino, tel. 06-481-8660). Their *arancino*—a rice, cheese, and ham ball—is a greasy Sicilian favorite, and their cannoli is sweet. Direct the construction of your meal at the bar, pay for your trayful at the cashier, and climb upstairs where you'll find the dancing Sicilian girls (free).

Hostaria Romana is a great place for traditional Roman cuisine served by a fun-loving gang who seems to really enjoy their work. For an air-conditioned, classy, local favorite, eat here (closed Sun; reservations generally not needed; midway between Trevi Fountain and Piazza Barberini, Via del Boccaccio 1, at intersection with Via Rasella; tel. 06-474-5284). Go ahead and survey the antipasto bar in person (a plate costs €7.50). They're happy to serve an *antipasti misto della casa* and pasta dinner. Take a hard look at their *Specialita Romane* list.

Ristorante da Giovanni is a reasonable option feeding locals and hungry travelers now for 50 years (tired €13 *menu*, Mon–Sat 12:00–15:00 & 19:00–22:30, closed Sun and in Aug, just off Via XX Settembre at Via Antonio Salandra 1, tel. 06-485-950).

Cafeteria Nazionale, with woody elegance, offers light lunches—including salads—at fair prices. It's noisy with local office workers being served by frantic red-vested waitstaff (Mon–Sat 7:00–20:00, closed Sun; Via Nazionale 26–27, at intersection with Via Agostino de Pretis; tel. 06-4899-1716). Their lunch buffet is a delight but gets picked over early (€7.50, 12:00–15:00).

Restaurant Target is a soulless, modern, but handy place serving decent pizza and pasta near recommended hotels (inexpensive, open daily from 12:00 and 19:00, indoor/outdoor seating, don't expect great service, Via Torino 33, tel. 06-474-0066).

The **McDonald's** restaurants on Piazza della Repubblica (free

Restaurants in East Rome

1 Snack Bar Gastronomia
2 Pasticceria Dagnino
3 Hostaria Romana
4 Ristorante Giovanni
5 Cafeteria Nazionale
6 Restaurant Target
7 Flann O'Brien Irish Pub
8 Ost. da Nerone & Caffè dello Studente
9 Ristorante al Cardello

piazza seating outside), Piazza Barberini, and Via Firenze offer air-conditioned interiors and salad bars.

Flann O'Brien Irish Pub is an entertaining place for a light meal (of pasta or something *other* than pasta, such as grilled beef, served early or late when other places are closed), fine Irish beer, live sporting events on TV, and perhaps the most Italian crowd of all. Walk way back before choosing a table (daily 7:30–24:00; Via Nazionale 17, at intersection with Via Napoli; tel. 06-488-0418).

Near the Vatican Museum and St. Peter's

Avoid the restaurant pushers handing out fliers near the Vatican: bad food, expensive menu tricks. Try any of these instead (see map on page 429).

Antonio's Hostaria dei Bastioni is tasty and friendly. It's conveniently located midway on your hike from St. Peters' to the Vatican Museum, with noisy street-side seating and a quiet interior (pastas-€6, *secondi*-€8, no cover charge; Mon–Sat 12:00–15:00 & 19:00–23:30, closed Sun; at corner of Vatican wall, Via Leone IV 29; tel. 06-3972-3034). Antonio is your gracious host.

La Rustichella serves a sprawling antipasti buffet (€7 for a single meal-sized plate). Arrive when they open at 19:30 to avoid a line and have the pristine buffet to yourself (Tue–Sun 12:30–15:00 & 19:30–23:00, closed Mon; near Metro: Cipro-Musei Vaticani, opposite church at end of Via Candia, Via Angelo Emo 1; tel. 06-3972-0649). Consider the fun and fruity **Gelateria Millennium** next door.

Viale Giulio Cesare is lined with cheap **Pizza Rustica** shops, self-serve places, and fun eateries. Restaurants such as **Tre Pupazzi** (closed Sun, tel. 06-686-8371), which line the pedestrian-only Borgo Pio—a block from Piazza San Pietro—are worth a look.

Turn your nose loose in the wonderful **Via Andrea Doria** open-air market, three blocks north of the Vatican Museum (Mon–Sat roughly 7:00–13:30, until 16:30 Tue and Fri except summer, corner of Via Tunisi and Via Andrea Doria). If the market is closed, try the nearby **IN's supermarket** (Mon–Sat 8:30–13:30 & 16:00–20:00, closed Thu eve and Sun; a half block straight out from Via Tunisi entrance of open-air market, Via Francesco 18).

TRANSPORTATION CONNECTIONS

Termini is the central station (see "Arrival in Rome" near beginning of chapter; Metro: Termini). Tiburtina is the bus station (4 Metro stops away from train station; Metro: Tiburtina).

By train from Rome to: Venice (6/day, 5–8 hrs, overnight possible), **Florence** (12/day, 2 hrs, most stop at Orvieto en route), **Pisa** (8/day, 3–4 hrs), **Genoa** (7/day, 6 hrs, overnight option), **Milan** (12/day, 5 hrs, overnight possible), **Naples** (6/day, 2 hrs), **Brindisi** (2/day, 9 hrs, overnight available), **Amsterdam** (2/day, 20 hrs, overnight unavoidable), **Bern** (5/day, 10 hrs, overnight possible), **Frankfurt** (4/day, 14 hrs, overnight available), **Munich** (5/day, 12 hrs, overnight option), **Nice** (2/day, 10 hrs, overnight possible), **Paris** (5/day, 16 hrs, overnight available), **Vienna** (3/day, 13–15 hrs, overnight option).

By bus to: Assisi (3/day, 3 hrs), **Siena** (7/day, 3 hrs).

Rome's Airports

Rome's two airports—Fiumicino (a.k.a. Leonardo da Vinci) and the small Ciampino—share the same Web site (www.adr.it).

Fiumicino Airport: Rome's major airport has a TI (daily 8:00–19:00, tel. 06-6595-4471), ATMs, banks, luggage storage, shops, and bars.

A slick, direct **train** connects the airport and Rome's central Termini train station in 30 minutes. Trains run twice hourly in both directions from roughly 6:00 to 23:00. From the airport, trains depart at :07 and :37 past the hour. From the airport's arrival gate, follow signs to "Stazione/Railway Station." Buy your ticket from a machine or the Biglietteria office (€9, CC). Make sure the train you board is going to "Roma Termini," not "Roma Orte" or others.

Going from the Termini train station to the airport, trains depart at :20 and :50 past the hour, usually from track 25 or 26; to reach these tracks, take a 10-minute walk along track 24 to the end of the station (moving walkways are inside the building to the right on the lower level). Check the departure boards for "Fiumicino Aeroporto"—the local name for the airport—and confirm with an official or a local on the platform that the train is indeed going to the airport (€9, buy ticket from computerized yellow ticket machines, any *tabacchi* shop in station, or at the desk near entrance to track 26). Read your ticket: If it requires validation, stamp it in the yellow machine near the platform before boarding.

Your hotel can arrange a **taxi** to the airport at any hour for about €40. To get from the airport into town cheaply by taxi, try teaming up with any tourist also just arriving (most are heading for hotels near yours in the center). Be sure to wait at the taxi stand. Avoid unmarked, unmetered taxis; these guys will try to tempt you away from the taxi stand line-up by offering an immediate (rip-off) ride.

For **airport information**, call 06-65951. To inquire about flights, call 06-6595-3640 (Alitalia: tel. 06-65643, British Air: toll-free tel. 848-812-266, Delta: toll-free tel. 800-864-114, KLM/Northwest: tel. 06-6501-1441, Lufthansa: tel. 06-6595-4156, SAS: tel. 06-954-070, Swiss Air: tel. 06-847-0555, United: tel. 848-800-692, Air Europa: tel. 06-6595-5854).

Ciampino Airport: Rome's smaller airport (tel. 06-794-941) handles budget and charter flights. To get to downtown Rome from the airport, take the LILA/Cotral bus (2/hr) to the Anagnina Metro stop, where you can connect by Metro to the stop nearest your hotel.

Driving in Rome

The Grande Raccordo Anulare circles Greater Rome. This ring road has spokes that lead you into the center. Entering from the north, leave the autostrada at the Settebagni exit. Following the ancient Via Salaria (and the black-and-white *Centro* signs), work your way doggedly into the Roman thick of things. This will take you along the Villa Borghese park and dump you right on Via Veneto (where there's an Avis office). Avoid rush hour and drive defensively: Roman cars stay in their lanes like rocks in an avalanche. Parking in Rome is dangerous. Park near a police station or get advice at your hotel. The Villa Borghese underground garage is handy (€18/day, Metro: Spagna).

Consider this: Your car is a worthless headache in Rome. Avoid a pile of stress and save money by parking at the huge, easy, and relatively safe lot behind the Orvieto station (follow P signs from autostrada) and catching the train to Rome (every 2 hrs, 75 min).

NAPLES AND THE AMALFI COAST

If you like Italy as far south as Rome, go further south. It gets better. If Italy is getting on your nerves by the time you get to Rome, think twice about going further. Italy intensifies as you plunge deeper. Naples is Italy in the extreme—its best (birthplace of pizza and Sophia Loren) and its worst (home of the Camorra, Naples' "family" of organized crime).

Serene Sorrento, without a hint of big-city Naples and just an hour to the south, makes a great home base. It's the gateway to the much-loved Amalfi Coast. From the jet-setting island of Capri to the stunning scenery of the Amalfi Coast, from ancient Pompeii to even more ancient Paestum, this is Italy's coast with the most.

Planning Your Time

On a quick trip, give the area three days. With Sorrento as your sunny springboard, spend a day in Naples, a day exploring the Amalfi Coast, and a day split between Pompeii and the town of Sorrento. While Paestum, the crater of Vesuvius, Herculaneum, and the island of Capri are decent options, they are worthwhile only if you give the area more time. For a blitz tour, you could have breakfast on the early Rome–Naples express train (about 7:00–9:00), do Naples and Pompeii in a day, and be back in Rome in time for *Letterman*. That's exhausting but more memorable than a fourth day in Rome. Remember that in the afternoon, Naples' street life slows and many sights close as the temperature soars. The city comes back to life in the early evening.

For a small-town vacation from your vacation, spend a few more days on the Amalfi Coast, sleeping in Positano, Atrani, or Marina del Cantone.

For most, driving south of Rome is not only stressful, it's impractical. Take advantage of the wonderful public transportation: the slick two-hour Rome–Naples express trains (or direct 5-hour express connections with Florence); the handy Circumvesuviana commuter train

(lacing together Naples, Pompeii, and Sorrento); and the regular bus service between Sorrento and the Amalfi Coast (where parking and car
access are severely limited).

Regional Pass: The Campania ArteCard is a €25, three-day pass
that offers free entry to two sights of your choice in this area (Pompeii
and Herculaeum are the most expensive so you should choose these as
your freebies) and 50 percent off on all other sights covered by the card,
including Naples' Archaeological Museum and Royal Palace, Paestum,
and many more. The card also covers Naples' Metro, buses, and funiculars, as well as the regional Circumvesuviana trains (7-day version costs
€28, covers all sights but no transportation). For details, visit www.cam-
paniartecard.it. ArteCards are sold at participating sights, from Metro
and train stations, travel agencies, and at Naples' airport.

Naples (Napoli)

Italy's third-largest city (with 1.2 million people, 2 million in greater
Naples) has almost no open spaces or parks, which makes its position as
Europe's most densely populated city plenty evident. Watching the police
try to enforce traffic sanity is almost comical in Italy's grittiest, most pol-
luted, and most crime-ridden city.

But Naples surprises the observant traveler with its good humor,
decency, and impressive knack for living, eating, and raising children in
the streets. Overcome your fear of being run down or ripped off long
enough to talk with people—enjoy a few smiles and jokes with the man
running the neighborhood tripe shop or the woman taking her day-care
class on a walk through the traffic. (Ask a local about the New Year's Eve
tradition of tossing chipped dinner plates off of balconies into the
streets.)

Twenty-five hundred years ago, Neapolis ("new city") was a thriving Greek commercial center. It remains southern Italy's leading city,
offering a fascinating collection of museums, churches, and eclectic architecture. The pulse of Italy throbs in Naples. This tangled mess—the closest thing to "reality travel" you'll find in western Europe—still somehow
manages to breathe, laugh, and sing—with a captivating Italian accent.

Planning Your Time

For a quick visit, start with the archaeology museum, do the Slice-of-
Neapolitan-Life Walk (see "Sights," page 486), and celebrate your survival with pizza. Of course, Naples is huge. But even with limited time,
if you stick to the described route and grab a cab when you're lost or
tired, it's fun. Treat yourself well in Naples; the city is cheap by Italian
standards.

From Naples to Paestum

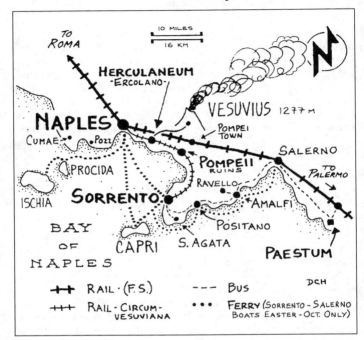

TO ROMA

HERCULANEUM
-ERCOLANO-

VESUVIUS 1277 M

NAPLES

CUMAE   POZZ

POMPEI TOWN

SALERNO

PROCIDA

POMPEII RUINS

TO PALERMO

RAVELLO

ISCHIA   SORRENTO

AMALFI

BAY OF NAPLES

CAPRI   S. AGATA

POSITANO

PAESTUM

10 MILES
16 KM

N

+-+ RAIL · (F.S.)   - - - BUS   DCH

+++ RAIL · CIRCUM-   • • • FERRY (SORRENTO - SALERNO
     VESUVIANA   BOATS EASTER - OCT. ONLY)

ORIENTATION

Tourist Information: The TI is in the central train station (Mon–Sat 9:00–19:00, Sun 9:00–13:00; with your back to the tracks, TI is in the lobby to your left—within the lobby, TI is to your right, look for *Ente Provinciale Turismo* sign; tel. 081-268-779). Pick up a map, and, even though the odds are against you, ask for the *Qui Napoli* booklet—when they say they're "finished," ask for an old one.

   Arrival in Naples: There are several Naples stations. You want Naples Centrale (facing Piazza Garibaldi), which has a TI, baggage check, and the Circumvesuviana stop for commuter trains to Sorrento and Pompeii. Centrale is a dead-end station, and through trains often stop at Piazza Garibaldi (actually a subway station just downstairs from Centrale), Campi Flegrei, or Napoli Mergellina across town before they arrive at Centrale. The stations of Campi Flegrei and Mergellina (which also has a TI) are connected to Centrale by a direct subway route; a railpass or train ticket to Napoli Centrale covers the ride (subway trains depart about every 10 min, less often on Sun). While on the train to

Naples, ask the conductor which Naples stations your train stops at. Get off at Mergellina or Campi Flegrei only if your train does not stop at Centrale or Garibaldi.

Helpful Hints

Local Guide: Aldo Sparice, a Naples native, offers tours of Naples' historic center (€100/3 hrs), Pompeii, Herculaneum and Paestum as well as many other destinations off the worn path (cost of tours vary according to itinerary, mobile 339-153-8009).

Traffic: In Naples, red lights are discretionary, and pedestrians need to be wary, particularly of the Vespa motorcycles.

Theft Alert: Lately, Naples, under an activist mayor, has been occupied by an army of police and feels much safer. Still, err on the side of caution. Don't venture into neighborhoods that make you uncomfortable. Walk with confidence, as if you know where you're going and what you're doing. Assume able-bodied beggars are thieves. Tighten your money belt and keep it completely hidden. Stick to busy streets and beware of gangs of hoodlums. A third of the city is unemployed, and past local governments set an example that the Mafia would be proud of. Assume con artists are more clever than you. Any jostle or commotion is probably a thief team smokescreen. Any bags are probably safest checked at the central train station (€3/12 hrs, open 6:00–24:00 daily, *deposito bagagli* near track #24, follow the corridor around to the left).

Perhaps your biggest risk of theft is catching or riding the Circumvesuviana commuter train. Remember, if you're connecting from a major train, you'll be stepping from a relatively secure compartment into a crowded Naples train sprinkled with thieves hunting disoriented American tourists. While I ride the Circumvesuviana comfortably and safely, each year I hear of many who get ripped off on this ride. You won't be mugged—just conned or pickpocketed. Con artists may say you need to "transfer" by taxi to catch the Circumvesuviana; you don't. There are no porters at the Centrale station or in the basement where the Circumvesuviana station is located; anyone offering to help you with your bags is likely a thief, despite displayed credentials. Wear your money belt, hang on to your bag, and don't display any valuables.

For €80–100, you can ride a **taxi** from Naples 30 miles directly to your Sorrento hotel; agree on a fixed price without the meter and pay upon arrival. As another option, consider the Naples–Sorrento **hydrofoil** (8/day, departing every other hour, 40 min, €7.50); it's faster, safer, and more scenic than the Circumvesuviana (taxi from the station about €8, supplement for bags, Sundays, and holidays). Naples' port (Beverello) is near Castel Nuovo at the low end of the walk described below and a quick taxi ride from the museum.

Naples Transportation

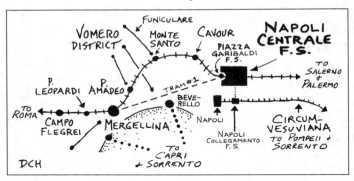

Getting around Naples

Naples' subway, the Servizio Metropolitano, runs from the Centrale station through the center of town (direction: Pozzuoli), stopping at Piazza Cavour (Archaeological Museum), Piazza Dante, and Montesanto (top of Spanish Quarter and Spaccanapoli). Tickets, which cost €0.75, are good for 90 minutes. All-day tickets cost €2.35. If you can afford a taxi, don't mess with the buses. A short taxi ride costs €3–5 (insist on the meter; supplement charged on Sun).

Getting to the Museum: From the Centrale train station, follow signs to *Metropolitano* (downstairs, buy tickets from yellow kiosk opposite Circumvesuviana ticket windows, ask which track—"*Binario?*" to Piazza Cavour—it's usually track 4, "*quattro*," direction Pozzuoli, go through a *solo metropolitano* turnstile and ride the subway one stop). As you leave the Metro, follow signs to *linea 1* through the underpass to the yellow Metro line. Take the elevator or escalators up. At the top, head left around the corner and follow signs to Museo. Go right at the top of the stairs and either surface to street level or continue to the new museum entrance down the corridor (to your left at 11 o'clock).

SIGHTS

▲▲▲**Archaeological Museum (Museo Archeologico)**—For lovers of antiquity, this museum alone makes Naples a worthwhile stop. It offers the only possible peek into the artistic jewelry boxes of Pompeii and Herculaneum. The actual sights are impressive but barren; the best art and all the artifacts ended up here.

Hours, Cost, and Information: €6.50 (extra for special exhibits), Wed–Mon 9:00–19:30, closed Tue. Tours in English are offered weekdays (except Tue, when museum is closed). There is no set schedule; they

Naples

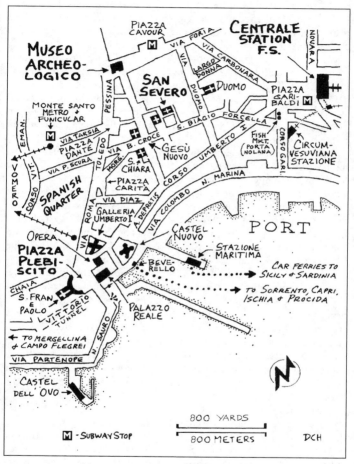

PIAZZA CAVOUR

CENTRALE STATION F.S.

VIA FORIA

NOVARA

MUSEO ARCHEO-LOGICO

VIA CARBONARA

LARGO DONNA

PIAZZA GARI-BALDI

MONTE SANTO METRO + FUNICULAR

SAN SEVERO

DUOMO

VIA TARSIA

PESSINA

S. BIAGIO

FORCELLA

PIAZZA DANTE

CORSO GARI.

EMAN.

VIA P. SCURA

VIA B. CROCE

Gesù Nuovo

UMBERTO I

FISH MKT. PORTA NOLANA

CIRCUM-VESUVIANA STAZIONE

VOMERO

CORSO VIT.

SPANISH QUARTER

TOLEDO

VIA ROMA

MORA

S. CHIARA

PIAZZA CARITÀ

CORSO

A. DEPRETIS

VIA DIAZ

VIA COLOMBO

N. MARINA

GALLERIA UMBERTO I

CASTEL NUOVO

P O R T

OPERA

PIAZZA PLEBI-SCITO

VIA

BEVE-RELLO

STAZIONE MARITIMA

CAR FERRIES TO SICILY & SARDINIA

CHAIA

S. FRAN E PAOLO

VITTORIO TUNNEL

PALAZZO REALE

TO SORRENTO, CAPRI, ISCHIA & PROCIDA

TO MERGELLINA & CAMPO FLEGREI

N. SAURO

VIA PARTENOPE

CASTEL DELL' OVO →

N

800 YARDS

800 METERS

M - SUBWAY STOP

DCH

wait until enough people request a tour and then depart from the entry (€3.50, 1.5 hrs, tel. 848-800-288). Audioguides cost €4 (at ticket desk, rentable for 3 hrs). Photos are allowed without a flash. The shop sells a worthwhile green guidebook, titled *National Archeological Museum of Naples* (€7.50). Bag check is obligatory and free.

Orientation: Look for signs for a free 20-minute tour of the Secret Room (containing erotic art from Pompeii and Herculaneum). You'll be given a tour time; meet at the Secret Room *(Gabinetto Segreto)* on the mezzanine on the other side of the partition from the *Battle of Alexander* mosaic. These short tours, generally offered at :15 and :45 past every hour, are usually given in Italian, but English tours are possible—ask.

The new entrance and frequent temporary exhibits means the floor plan of the museum and arrangement of the works often changes. If you can't find a particular work, ask a museum custodian, *"Dov'è?"* (Where?) To orient yourself, stand in front of the grand staircase. For the Farnese Collection of marble statues, turn right past the staircase. The Pompeii mosaics and the Secret Room are on the small mezzanine level (up the grand staircase and on your left). The huge first floor (top of the grand staircase) contains bronze statues from Herculaneum, frescoes from Pompeii, and vases from Paestum. Stairs behind the grand staircase lead to the basement WCs.

Statues, Frescoes, and Artifacts (top floor): Climb the stairs to the top floor. Before you enter the great hall, look right to locate the entrance to the bronze statues of Herculaneum. This large collection—including a dozen bronze statues, plus busts and marble statues—came from Villa Papiri (Papyrus) in Herculaneum. Look into the lifelike blue eyes of the two intense *atleta* (athletes); they are bent on doing their best. To the left of the staircase is Cardinal Borgia's collection of ancient coins from southern Italy when it was Magna Graecia (Greater Greece), the Etruscans, and Romans, all well explained in English.

Step inside the great hall. With your back to the entrance, the rooms on your left feature the Pompeii frescoes, paintings, artifacts, and an interesting model of the town of Pompeii (called *plastico di Pompeii*; near the glass objects). The rooms on your right feature ancient Greek art: a model of Paestum and ancient vases discovered on-site. (Paestum, a temple complex south of Naples, was part of a once-thriving region known as Greater Greece; for more info, see "Paestum," below.) If you contrast all of this ancient art with the darkness of medieval Europe, it becomes clear that classical art greatly inspired and enlightened the Renaissance greats.

Mosaics (mezzanine): On the mezzanine floor below (directly under the bronze statues from Herculaneum), you'll find a small, exquisite collection of Pompeian mosaics and the sexy Secret Room. Most of these mosaics were taken from the House of the Faun, which you'll see at Pompeii. Don't miss the house's delightful centerpiece: a bronze statue (20 inches high) of the *Dancing Faun*. A highlight of the mosaics is the grand *Battle of Alexander* (a first-century B.C. copy of a fourth-century B.C. Greek original). It decorated a floor in the House of the Faun.

The **Secret Room**, on the other side of the partition from the *Battle of Alexander* mosaic, contains a small assortment of frescoes, pottery, and statues that once decorated bedrooms, brothels, and even shops at Pompeii and Herculaneum. You can enter only with a guide; see "Orientation," above. If you didn't bother with making an appointment, you can still peek through the iron gate.

When this earthy art was unearthed in the mid-18th century, people were upset to find their view of the Romans as wise administrators and lawmakers upended. Actually, the meaning of an erect penis was more complex back then than today—dealing with abundance and good luck, as well as good sex.

Farnese Collection (ground floor): This floor has enough Egyptian, Greek, Roman, and Etruscan art to put any museum on the map. Its highlight is the Farnese Collection, a giant hall of huge, bright, and wonderfully restored statues excavated from Rome's Baths of Caracalla. The Toro Farnese—a tangled group with a woman being tied to a bull—is the largest intact statue from antiquity. Actually a third-century copy of a Hellenistic original, it was carved out of one piece of marble and restored by Michelangelo and others.

Once upon an ancient Greek time, King Lykos was bewitched by Dirce and abandoned his pregnant wife (standing regally in the background). The single mom gave birth to twin boys (shown here) who grew up to kill their deadbeat dad and tie Dirce to the horns of a bull to be bashed against a mountain.

You can almost hear the bull snorting. Read the worthwhile descriptions on the walls. At the far end of the hall (opposite the Toro, behind Hercules), a small room contains the sumptuous Farnese Cup, a large ancient cameo made of agates (well-described).

▲▲▲**The Slice-of-Neapolitan-Life Walk**—Walk from the museum through the heart of town and back to the station (allow at least 2 hours, plus lunch and sightseeing stops). Sights are listed in the order you'll see them on this walk.

Naples, a living medieval city, is its own best sight. Couples artfully make love on Vespas, surrounded by more fights and smiles per cobble here than anywhere else in Italy. Rather than seeing Naples as a list of sights, see the one great museum and then capture its essence by taking this walk through the core of the city. Should you become overwhelmed or lost, step into a store and ask for help: "*Dov'è la stazione centrale?*" (DOH-vay lah staht-zee-OH-nay chen-TRAH-lay?), or point to the next sight in this book.

Via Toledo and the Spanish Quarter (city walk, first half): Leaving the Archaeological Museum at the top of Piazza Cavour (Metro: Piazza Cavour), cross the street and walk through the ornate Galleria (the grand, arched gallery) on your way to Via Pessina to your right. (The walk ends near great pizzerias, but if you can't wait, try La Tana dell' Arte, just past the Galleria; see "Eating," page 496.)

The first part of this walk is a straight one-mile ramble down this boulevard to Galleria Umberto I near the Royal Palace.

Busy Via Pessina leads downhill to Piazza Dante—marked by a statue of Dante. Originally, a statue of a Spanish Bourbon king stood here. The grand red-and-gray building is typical of the Bourbon build-

Naples Walk

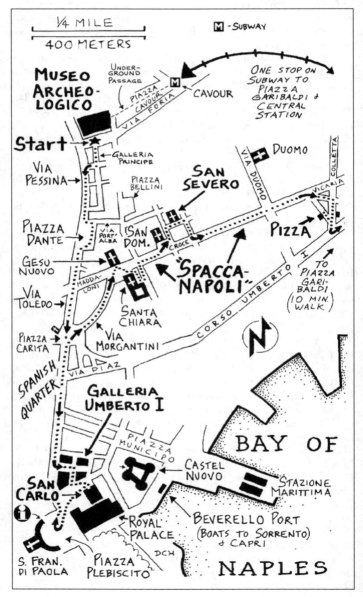

ings from that period. In 1861 with the unification of Italy, the king, symbolic of Italy's colonial subjugation, was replaced by Dante—considered the father of the Italian language and a strong symbol of Italian nationalism.

Poor old Dante looks out over the urban chaos with a hopeless gesture. The Alba Gate (with pizzeria), part of Naples' old wall and the entrance to a small street often lined with streetside book vendors, is to Dante's left. Via Pessina, the long, straight road that we're walking, originated as a military road built by Spain around 1600. It skirted the old town wall to connect the Spanish military headquarters (now the museum) with the Royal Palace (down by the bay).

A new subway station has recently been built here on Piazza Dante. Construction was slowed by the city's rich underground history: 13 feet down—Roman ruins, 23 feet down—Greek ruins.

Continue walking downhill, remembering that here in Naples, red lights are considered "decorations." Try to cross with a local. The people here are survivors; a long history of corrupt and greedy colonial overlords has taught Neapolitans to deal with authority creatively. Many credit this aspect of Naples' past for the advent of organized crime here.

Via Pessina becomes Via Toledo, Naples' principal shopping street. In 1860, from the white marble balcony (on the neoclassical building) overlooking Piazza Sette Settembre, the famous revolutionary Garibaldi declared Italy united and Victor Emmanuel its first king. A year later, the dream of Italian unity was actually realized.

Continue straight on Via Toledo (even though the arterial jogs left). At the next left (Via Maddaloni), about three blocks below Piazza Dante, you cross the long, straight street called **Spaccanapoli** (literally, "split Naples"). Look left. Look right. Since ancient times, this thin street (which changes names several times) has bisected the city. (We'll be coming back to this point later. If you want to abbreviate this walk, turn left here and skip down to the Spaccanapoli section.)

Via Toledo runs through Piazza Carità (also known by its new name, Piazza Salvo D'Acquisto), with fascist architecture (from 1938, stern, straight, obedient lines) overlooking the square. Wander down Via Toledo a few blocks, past more fascist architecture—the two banks on the left. Try robbing the second one (Banco di Napoli, Via Toledo 178).

Up the hill to your right is the **Spanish Quarter**, Naples at its rawest, poorest, and most historic. Thrill-seekers (or someone in need of a prostitute) can take a stroll up one of these streets and loop back to Via Toledo.

The only things predictable about this Neapolitan tide pool are the ancient grid plan of its streets (which survives from Greek times), the friendliness of its shopkeepers, and the boldness of its mopeds. Concerned locals will tug on their lower eyelids, warning you to be wary. Pop into a grocery shop and ask the man to make you his best ham and mozzarella sandwich. Trust him on the price—it should be around €3.

Continue down Via Toledo to Piazza Plebiscito. From here, you'll see the Church of San Francesco di Paola with its Pantheon-inspired dome and broad, arcing colonnades. A TI is in the colonnade to the right (Mon–Sat 9:00–19:30, Sun 9:00–15:00). Opposite is the **Royal Palace**, which has housed Spanish, French, and even Italian royalty. The lavish interior is open for tours (€4, Thu–Tue 9:00–20:00, closed Wed, shorter hours off-season, last entry 1 hour before closing, audioguide available, €4, or €6 for two people). Next door, peek inside the neoclassical Teatro San Carlo, Europe's oldest and Italy's second-most-respected opera house—after Milan's La Scala (guided visits €5, no set schedule for tours in English, tel. 081-400-300). The huge castle on the harborfront just beyond the palace houses government bureaucrats and the Civic Museum, featuring 14th- to 16th-century art (€5, Mon–Sat 9:00–19:00, closed Sun, tel. 081-795-2003).

Under the Victorian iron and glass of the 100-year-old **Galleria Umberto I**, enjoy a coffee break or sample a unique Neapolitan pastry called *sfogliatella* (crispy, scallop shell–shaped pastry filled with sweet ricotta cheese). To continue the walk, go through the tall yellow arch at the end of Via Toledo or across from the opera house (TI to left of entrance of Galleria opposite Teatro San Carlo, Mon–Sat 9:00–19:00, Sun 9:00–14:30). Gawk up.

Spaccanapoli back to the station (city walk, second half): To continue your walk, double back up Via Toledo to Piazza Carità, veering right on Via Morgantini to Via Maddaloni. You're back at the straight-as-a-Greek-arrow Spaccanapoli. Formerly the main thoroughfare of the Greek city of Neapolis, it starts up the hill near the Montesanto funicular.

The rest of this walk is basically a straight line down a series of streets that locals have nicknamed Spaccanapoli. Stop at Piazza Gesu Nuovo to visit the two bulky old churches. The square is marked by a towering monument to the Counter-Reformation (Baroque, early 18th century). Jesuits were powerful in Naples due to its Spanish heritage. But locals never attacked Protestants with the full fury of the Spanish Inquisition.

Check out the austere, fortress-like church of **Gesu Nuovo.** The unique pyramid grill facade was from a fortress (1470), which predated the church (1600s). Step inside for a brilliant Baroque interior. The second chapel on the right features a much-kissed statue of Giuseppe Moscati, a Christian doctor famous for helping the poor. Moscati was made a saint in 1987. Continue on to the third chapel and enter the Sale Moscati for a huge room filled with Ex Voto—tiny red-and-silver plaques of thanksgiving for miracles attributed to Saint Moscati. Each has a relief symbolic of the ailment cured. Naples' practice of "Ex Voto," while incorporated into its Catholic rituals, goes back to its pagan Greek roots. A glass case displays possessions and photos of the great doctor. As you leave, notice the big bomb casing hanging in the corner. It fell through the church's dome in 1943, but never exploded...yet another miracle.

Across the street, the simpler Gothic church of **Santa Chiara** dates from a period of French Angevin rule (14th century). Notice the stark Gothic/Baroque contrast between this church and the Gesù Nuovo. The faded Trinity (from the school of Giotto, left of entry) is an example of the fine frescoes that once covered the walls (most removed during Baroque times). The altar is adorned with the finely carved Gothic tomb of an Angevin king (both churches free, Mon–Sat 9:30–13:00 & 15:30–18:30, Sun 9:30–13:00).

Continue straight down traffic-free Via B. Croce. Since this is a university district, you'll see lots of students and bookstores. This neighborhood is also extremely superstitious. You may see incense-burning women with carts of good-luck charms for sale. At Via Santa Chiara, a detour to the left leads to shops of antique musical instruments.

The next square is Piazza S. Domenico Maggiore—marked by an ornate 17th-century plague monument. The well-loved **Scaturchio Pasticceria** is another good place to try Naples' *sfogliatella* pastry (€1.15 to go, costs double at a table in the square, daily 7:20–20:40, tel. 081-551-6944).

From this square, detour left along the right side of the castle-like church, then follow yellow signs and take first right for one block to **Cappella Sansevero** (€5, Mon and Wed–Sat 10:00–18:00, Nov–April 10:00–17:00, Sun year-round 10:00–13:30, last entry 20 minutes before closing, closed Tue, Via de Sanctis 19). No photos are allowed in the chapel (postcards available in gift shop).

This small chapel is a Baroque explosion mourning the body of Christ, who lies on a soft pillow under an incredibly realistic veil. It's also the personal chapel of Raimondo de Sangro, an eccentric Freemason. The monuments to his relatives have a second purpose: To share the Freemason philosophy of freedom through enlightenment. For example, the statue of *Despair* struggling with a marble rope net (carved out of a single piece of marble) shows how knowledge—in the guise of an angel—frees the human mind.

Study the incredible *Veiled Christ* in the center. It's all carved out of marble and is like no other statue I've seen (by Giuseppe "howdeedoo-dat" Sammartino, 1753). The Christian message (Jesus died for our salvation) is accompanied by a Freemason message (the veil represents how the body and ego are an obstacle to real spiritual freedom.) As you walk from Christ's feet to his head, notice how the expression of Jesus' face goes from suffering to peace. When you stand directly behind Him, the veil over the face and knees disappears.

To the right of *Despair* and the net, an inlaid Escher-esque maze on the floor leads to de Sangro's tomb. The maze is another Freemason reminder of how the quest for knowledge gets you out of the maze of life. Your Sansevero finale is downstairs: two mysterious...skeletons. Perhaps another of the mad inventor's fancies: Injecting a corpse with a fluid to fossilize the veins so they'll survive the body's decomposition.

Return to Via B. Croce, turn left, and continue your Spaccanapoli cultural scavenger hunt. At the intersection of Via Nilo, find the statue of *The Body of Naples* on your left, with the overflowing cornucopia symbolizing the abundance of Naples. (I asked a Neapolitan man to describe the local women, who are famous for their beauty. He replied simply, "Abundant.") This intersection is considered the center of old Naples.

At Via San Gregorio Armeno, a left leads you into a very colorful district (kitschy Baroque church on left with a Vesuvius lava shrine in its portico, lots of shops selling tiny components of fantastic manger scenes).

As Via B. Croce becomes Via S. Biagio dei Librai, notice the gold and silver shops. Some say stolen jewelry ends up here, is melted down immediately, and appears in a saleable form as soon as it cools. The wonderful Sr. Grassi runs the Ospedale delle Bambole (doll hospital) at #81.

Cross busy Via Duomo. The street and side-street scenes along Via Vicaria intensify. Paint a picture with these thoughts: Naples has the most intact street plan of any ancient Roman city. Imagine this city then (retain these images as you visit Pompeii), with street-side shopfronts that close up after dark to form private homes. Today, it's just one more page in a 2,000-year-old story of a city: all kinds of meetings, beatings, and cheatings; kisses, near misses, and little-boy pisses.

You name it, it occurs right on the streets today, as it has since ancient times. People ooze from crusty corners. Black-and-white death announcements add to the clutter on the walls. Widows sell cigarettes from buckets. For a peek behind the scenes in the shade of wet laundry, venture down a few side streets. Buy two carrots as a gift for the woman on the fifth floor if she'll lower her bucket to pick them up. The neighborhood action seems best around 18:00.

At the tiny fenced-in triangular park, veer right onto Via Forcella. Turning right on busy Via Pietro Colletta, walk 50 yards and step into the North Pole. Reward yourself for surviving this safari with a stop at the oldest *gelateria* (since 1923) in Naples, **Polo Nord Gelateria**. You'll have to elbow your way to the counter past the throngs of *Napolitani* who know where to get the best gelato (Mon–Sat 10:00–24:00, Sun 10:00–14:00 & 17:00–24:00, sample their *bacio* or "kiss" flavor before ordering, Via Pietro Colletta 41). Via Pietro Colletta leads past Napoli's two most competitive **pizzerias** (see "Eating," below) to Corso Umberto.

Turn left on the grand-boulevardian Corso Umberto. From here to the station, it's a 10-minute walk (if you're tired, hop on a bus; they all go to the station). To finish the walk, continue on Corso Umberto—past a gauntlet of purse/CD/sunglasses salesmen and shady characters hawk-ing stolen camcorders—to the vast, ugly Piazza Garibaldi. On the far side is the Centrale station.

Markets—Naples' **fish market** is fun for photos, with sawed-off sword-fish, wriggly eels in pans, and mussels taking a shower. It's at Piazza Nolana, a few blocks southwest of the train station (at the piazza, follow your nose and go through the old gate; market spills down small street, Vico Sopramuro). A bigger **general market** starts at the far corner of Piazza Capuana (several blocks northwest of the train station), filling the street Via Sant' Antonio Abate with a mix of clothes, olives, bags of gnocchi, hanging hams, shoes, produce, umbrellas, and shoppers on foot or on Vespas. These colorful markets are both open daily (Mon–Sat 7:00–16:00, Sun 8:00–13:00).

SLEEPING

With Sorrento just an hour away, I can't imagine why you'd sleep in Naples. But, if needed, here are several places, most within 200 yards of the station. The area can feel unnerving, especially after dark.

$$$ Grand Hotel Terminus, an American-style four-star chain hotel with worn carpeting across the street from the station (left side), feels perfectly safe, with 168 rooms and all the comforts (Db-€185 or so, less on weekends, includes breakfast, air-con 6:00–24:00, elevator, non-smoking rooms on second floor, gym, roof garden, bar, restaurants, Piazza Garibaldi 91, tel. 081-779-3111, fax 081-206-689, www.starhotels.it, terminus.na@starhotels.it, SE).

$ Hotel Ginevra, quiet and bright, has 21 rooms with comfortable beds and floral wallpaper and five new rooms with air-con. It's run by a

SLEEP CODE

(€1 = about $1.10, country code: 39)
Sleep Code: **S** = Single, **D** = Double/Twin, **T** = Triple, **Q** = Quad, **b** = bathroom, **s** = shower only, **no CC** = Credit Cards not accepted, **SE** = Speaks English, **NSE** = No English. Credit cards are accepted unless otherwise noted.

To help you sort easily through these listings, I've divided the rooms into three categories based on the price for a stan-dard double room with bath:

   $$$ Higher Priced—Most rooms more than €150.
    $$ Moderately Priced—Most rooms between €100–€150.
     $ Lower Priced—Most rooms €100 or less.

friendly family: Bruno and son Lello speak English, Anna speaks Italian (S-€30, Sb-€50, D-€50, Db-€60–75, T-€65, Tb-€80–100, Q-€80, Qb-€100, breakfast in room-€5, 10 percent discount with this book and cash, no CC, they keep your passport until you leave; Internet access, €5 laundry; turn right out of the station onto Corso Novara and walk 2 blocks, turn right on Via Genova to #116, 2nd floor; tel. & fax 081-283-210, www.hotelginevra.it, info@hotelginevra.it).

$ Hotel Siri is a peaceful oasis a 10-minute walk from the station, with 16 newly renovated, air-conditioned rooms (Sb-€43, Db-€80, Tb-€105, includes breakfast, Via Mignogna 15, tel. 081-554-3122, fax 081-554-3098, www.hotelsiri.com). Follow Piazza Garibaldi up the left side from the train station and take the second left after the square from Corso Umberto onto Via Mignogna; the hotel is ahead on the left at #15.

$ Hotel Guiren is a comfortable, safe place to call home, with 37 polished, quiet rooms two blocks from the station (Sb-€60–80, Db-€80–100, Tb-€120, includes breakfast, air-con, tel. 081-286-530, fax 081-200-893, http://guiren2.hotelsinnapoli.com, info@hotelguiren2.it). Exit the station and go to the far right, cross Via Novara and head up the right side of the square, turning right onto Via Bologna. Hotel Guiren is on the right on the next block.

EATING

Drop by one of the two most traditional pizzerias. Naples, baking just the right combination of fresh dough, mozzarella, and tomatoes in traditional wood-burning ovens, is the birthplace of pizza. **Antica Pizzeria da Michele**, a few blocks from the train station, is for purists (Mon–Sat 11:00–24:00, closed Sun, cheap, filled with locals; head left off Piazza Garibaldi from the station, turn left onto Corso Umberto (juts off Piazza Baribaldi at 11 o'clock as you're facing away from the station, then turn right on Via Cesare Sersale, look for vertical red "Antica Pizzeria" sign, tel. 081-553-9204). It serves two kinds: *margherita* (tomato sauce and mozzarella) or *marinara* (tomato sauce, oregano, and garlic, no cheese). A pizza with beer costs €6. Some locals prefer **Pizzeria Trianon** across the street. Da Michele's archrival offers more choices, higher prices (€3.50–7), air-conditioning, and a cozier atmosphere. Here you can survey the evolution of a humble wad of dough into a smoldering, bubbly feast in their entryway pizza kitchen (daily 10:00–15:30 & 18:30–23:00, Via Pietro Colletta 42, tel. 081-553-9426).

La Tana dell'Arte is a handy pizzeria with outdoor seating on a quiet pedestrian square just past the Galleria near the Archaeological Museum (daily 12:00–17:00 & 19:00–24:00, Via Bellini 29, tel. 081-549-1844).

Iris' cadre of bowtied waiters sling good, reasonably priced seafood, pastas, and pizzas near the station in a comfortable *ristorante* and outdoor patio (Sun–Fri 12:00–16:00 & 17:00–24:00, closed Sat; Piazza

Garibaldi 121–125, from the station head halfway up the left side of Piazza Garibaldi; tel. 081-269-988).

TRANSPORTATION CONNECTIONS

By boat to: Sorrento (8/day, 40 min, €7.50), **Capri** (11 hydrofoils/day, 45 min, €12).

By train to: Rome (hrly, 2–3 hrs), **Florence** (12/day, 3.5–5 hrs, more with change in Rome), **Brindisi** (8/day, 5–7 hrs, overnight possible; from Brindisi, ferries sail to Greece), **Milan** (hrly, 6.5–9 hrs, overnight possible, more with a change in Rome), **Venice** (about hrly with change in Rome or Bologna, 6–10 hrs), **Nice** (2/day, 12 hrs with change in Genoa), **Paris** (3/day, 14–18 hrs with change in Rome or Milan, **Palermo** (2/day, 10 hrs).

The Circumvesuviana: This useful commuter train links Naples, Herculaneum, Pompeii, and Sorrento. At Naples' Centrale Station, signs direct you downstairs to the Circumvesuviana. In the long corridor in

CIRCUMVESUVIANA STOPS BETWEEN NAPLES AND SORRENTO

I list these so you can look at the scenery rather than your watch.

Napoli
Napoli Collegamento FS
    (a.k.a. Piazza Garibaldi;
    below Centrale station)
Gianturco
S. Giovanni
Barra
S. Maria d. Pozzo
S. Giorgio
Cavalli di Bronzo
Bellavista
V. Liberta
Ercolano Scavi
    (Herculaneum site)
Ercolano Miglio d'Oro
Torre del Greco
V.S. Antonio
V. del Monte
V. Monaci
Villa della Ginestra

Leopardi
V. Viuli
Trecase
Torre Annunziata
Pompei Scavi (Pompeii site)
Moregine
Ponte Persica
Pioppaino
V. Nocera
C. Mare Stabia
C. Mare Terme
Pozzano
Scraio
Vico Equense
Seiano
Meta
Piano di Sorrento
S. Agnello
Sorrento

the basement, the ticket windows—marked Circumvesuviana—are on your left. Schedules are posted on the wall. When you buy your ticket, ask which track your train will depart from (*"Che binario?"*; kay bee-NAH-ree-oh). Don't go through the turnstiles opposite the ticket windows. Instead, continue down the corridor and jog right when it does, down another long corridor that has turnstiles at the end (insert your ticket). The platforms are just beyond. (The Circumvesuviana also has its own terminal, 1 stop or a 10-min walk beyond the Centrale Station, but there's no reason to use it.) Two trains per hour, marked Sorrento, take you to Herculaneum (Ercolano) in 15 minutes, Pompeii in 40 minutes, and Sorrento, the end of the line, in 70 minutes (€3.10 one-way, not covered by railpass, not all of the trains go as far as Sorrento—look at the schedule carefully or confirm with a local before boarding to make sure the train is going where you want to). Express trains marked DD (12/day) get you to Sorrento 30 minutes quicker. When returning to Naples' Centrale station on the Circumvesuviana, get off at the second-to-the-last station, the Collegamento FS or Garibaldi stop (Centrale station is just up the escalator).

Note: Many readers report being ripped off on this train (see theft alert in "Helpful Hints," on page 485).

Sorrento

Wedged on a ledge under the mountains and over the Mediterranean, spritzed by lemon and olive groves, Sorrento is an attractive resort of 20,000 residents and—in the summer—as many tourists. It's as well-located for regional sightseeing as it is a fine place to stay and stroll. The Sorrentines have gone out of their way to create a completely safe and relaxed place for tourists to come and spend money. (None of its 40 banks has ever been robbed.) Everyone seems to speak fluent English and work for the Chamber of Commerce. This gateway to the Amalfi Coast has an unspoiled old quarter, a lively main shopping street, and a spectacular cliffside setting. Skip the port and its poor excuse for a beach unless you're taking a ferry. Locals are proud of the many world-class romantics who've vacationed here. In 1921, the famed tenor Enrico Caruso chose Sorrento as his place to die.

ORIENTATION

Sorrento is long and narrow. The main drag, Corso Italia (50 yards in front of the Circumvesuviana train station), runs parallel to the sea from the station through the town center and out to the cape, where it's renamed Via Capo. Everything mentioned (except the hotels on Via

Capo) is within a 10-minute walk of the station. Sorrento hibernates in January and February when many places close down.

Tourist Information: The TI, located inside the Foreigner's Club, hands out a free *Surrentum* magazine with a great city map and schedules of boats, buses, and events (Mon–Sat 8:45–18:15, closed Sun, shorter hours off-season, tel. 081-807-4033, www.sorrentotourism.com, info@sorrentotourism.com). To reach the TI *(Soggiorno e Turismo)* from the train station, go left on Corso Italia and walk five minutes to Piazza Tasso; turn right at the end of the square, then head down Via L. de Maio through Piazza Sant Antonino to the Foreigners' Club mansion at #35. You'll pass fake "tourist offices" (travel agencies selling bus and boat tours). If you arrive after the TI closes, look for key TI handouts in the lobby of the Foreigners' Club (open until midnight).

The **Foreigners' Club** provides reasonably priced snacks and drinks, relaxation, views, and a handy place for visitors to meet locals (behind TI, public WC). It's lively with concerts or dancing every summer evening (starting at 21:00, tel. 081-877-3263; see "Nightlife" and "Eating," below). Drop in for an orientation view of the harbor and a commanding view of the Bay of Naples.

Laundry: A handy coin-op laundry is at Corso Italia 30; turn right down the alley for the side entrance (€8/load, includes soap, daily 8:00–21:00, tel. 081-078-1185).

Getting around Sorrento

Orange city buses all stop in the main square (Tasso). Bus A runs to the Meta beach and Via Capo hotels, Bus B and C to the port (Marina Piccola), and Bus D to the fishing village (Marina Grande). Tickets cost €1 within the center (sold at *tabacchi* shops and newsstands, purchase before boarding and stamp upon entering).

Rental Wheels: For mopeds and Vespas (about €29/3 hrs), consider Sorrento Rent-A-Car (daily 8:30–13:00 & 16:00–21:00, Corso Italia 210, tel. 081-878-1386) and across the street, Happy Rent (daily 9:00–19:00, located in Hotel Nice). In summer, forget renting a car unless you enjoy traffic jams. You can rent bikes, tandems, and *risciò* (four-wheeled, 2 seats side by side, canopied bikes) at Bicilandia in the old town (daily 10:00–13:30 & 17:00–22:00, shorter hours in winter, Via B. Donnorso 8, mobile 339-169-2304).

Taxis: Taxis are expensive, charging at least €10 for the short ride from the station to hotels.

SIGHTS

▲**Strolling**—Take time to explore the surprisingly pleasant old city between Corso Italia and the sea. Views from the public park next to Imperial Hotel Tramontano are worth the detour. Duck into the Church of England. The evening *passeggiata* (along Corso Italia and Via San Cesareo) peaks around 22:00. Check out the old-boys' club playing cards, oblivious to the tourism, under their portico (with great 3-D frescoes) at Via San Cesareo and Via Tasso.

Lemon Grove Garden (L'Agruminato)—This small park consists of an inviting lemon and orange grove lined with paths. The owners of the grove are seasoned greenthumbs, working the orchard through generations since the 1800s, and have even grafted orange tree branches onto a lemon tree so that both fruits now grow on the same tree. The garden is dotted with benches, tables, and a little stand offering free tastes of *limoncello*, a local specialty made of lemons, sugar, and pure alcohol, and various other homemade liquors made from basil, mandarins, or fennel (March–Sept 9:30–20:30, Oct–Feb 10:00–16:00, samples free, glass of liquor €1, shop selling all their organic, homemade products is outside the Corso Italia entrance). Enter the garden on Corso Italia (100 yards to the north of the train station on Corso Italia #165, see door flanked by tiles, marked "*L'Agruminato, il giardino della città*") or at intersection of Via Capasso and Via Rota (next to Hotel La Meridiana Sorrento).

ACTIVITIES

Tennis—The Sorrento Sport Snack Bar has fine courts open to the public (daily 9:00–23:00, 20:00 in winter, €10/hr, €12/hr after dark for 2, includes use of rackets and balls, call for reservation, across from recommended Ambasciatori Hotel at Via Califano 5, tel. 081-807-1616).

Swimming near Sorrento—If you need immediate tanning, you can rent a chair on the pier by the port. There are no great beaches near Sorrento. The best sandy, family-friendly beach is less than two miles east at Meta (easy Orange bus connection from Sorrento—take bus A from Piazza Tasso). Tarzan might take Jane to the wild and stony beach at **Punta del Capo**, a 15-minute bus ride west of town (2/hr from Piazza Tasso to American Bar, then walk 10 min past ruined Roman Villa di Pollio). Beyond that, **Marina di Poulo** is a tiny fishing town popular in the summer for its sandy beach, surfside restaurants, and beachfront disco.

NIGHTLIFE

This town is filled with Brit-friendly pubs. These two are most popular and within a few blocks of each other: The **Merry Monk Irish Pub** offers good draft beer, hamburgers, fries, darts, live dance music nightly, noisy Internet access (€3/30 min), and a free transfer back to your hotel if necessary. And you haven't heard "Mustang Sally" until you've heard it in Italian (from 11:30–2:00, at the west end of town at Via Capo 4, tel. 081-877-2409). **The English Inn** is another place designed to make English guests feel right at home. Its rough-feeling pub serves baked

Sorrento

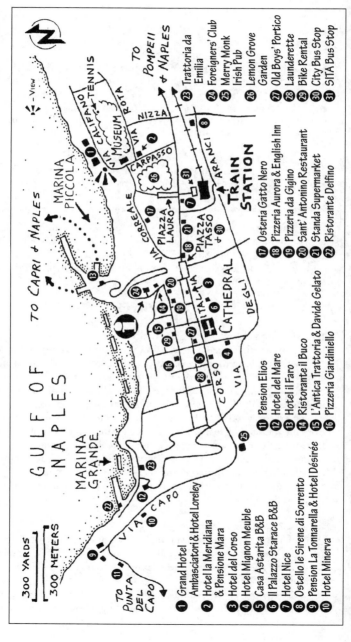

300 YARDS
300 METERS

GULF OF NAPLES

TO CAPRI & NAPLES

MARINA GRANDE

MARINA PICCOLA

TO PUNTA DEL CAPO

VIA CAPO

CORSO ITALIA

VIA CORREALE

PIAZZA LAURO

PIAZZA TASSO

VIA CALIFANO

MUSEUM

TENNIS

VIA ROTA

VIA NIZZA

CARPASSO

VIA DEGLI ARANCI

CATHEDRAL

TRAIN STATION

TO POMPEII & NAPLES

◆ View

1 Grand Hotel Ambasciatori & Hotel Loreley
2 Hotel la Meridiana & Pensione Mara
3 Hotel del Corso
4 Hotel Mignon Meuble
5 Casa Astarita B&B
6 Il Palazzo Starace B&B
7 Hotel Nice
8 Ostello le Sirene di Sorrento
9 Pension La Tonnarella & Hotel Désirée
10 Hotel Minerva
11 Pension Elios
12 Hotel del Mare
13 Hotel il Faro
14 Ristorante il Buco
15 L'Antica Trattoria & Davide Gelato
16 Pizzeria Giardiniello
17 Osteria Gatto Nero
18 Pizzeria Aurora & English Inn
19 Pizzeria da Gigino
20 Sant' Antonino Restaurant
21 Standa Supermarket
22 Ristorante Delfino
23 Trattoria da Emilia
24 Foreigners' Club
25 Merry Monk Irish Pub
26 Lemon Grove Garden
27 Old Boys' Portico
28 Launderette
29 Bike Rental
30 City Bus Stop
31 SITA Bus Stop

SLEEP CODE

(€1 = about $1.10, country code: 39)

Sleep Code: **S** = Single, **D** = Double/Twin, **T** = Triple, **Q** = Quad, **b** = bathroom, **s** = shower only, **no CC** = Credit Cards not accepted, **SE** = Speaks English, **NSE** = No English.

To help you sort easily through these listings, I've divided the rooms into three categories based on the price for a standard double room with bath:

$$$ **Higher Priced**—Most rooms more than €150.
$$ **Moderately Priced**—Most rooms between €100-150.
$ **Lower Priced**—Most rooms €100 or less.

beans on toast, fish and chips, and draft beer with fun music, Internet access, and a more refined-feeling garden out back (daily 8:00–2:00, Corso Italia 53, tel. 081-807-4357). The **Foreigners' Club** has live music nightly at 21:00 and is just right for old-timers feeling frisky (in the center, see "Tourist Information," page 499).

SLEEPING

Sorrento offers the whole range of rooms. Hotels often charge the same for a room whether it has a view, balcony, or neither. At hotels that offer sea views, ask for a room "*con balcone, con vista sul mare*"—with a balcony, with a sea view. "*Tranquillo*" is taken as a request for a room off the street. Every place includes breakfast and takes credit cards unless otherwise noted. Hotels listed are either near the station and city center or along the way to Punta del Capo, a 20-minute walk (or short bus ride) from the station. While many hotels close for the winter, you should have no trouble finding a room any time outside of August, when the place is jammed and many hotel prices go way up. Spring for a hotel with air-conditioning if you wilt in the heat. Note: The spindly, more exotic, and more tranquil Amalfi Coast town of Positano (below) is also a good place to spend the night.

East of the Center

A block in front of the train station, turn right onto Corso Italia, then left down Via Capasso, which winds right and becomes Via Califano. At the Loreley and Ambasciatori, the "private beach" is actually a sundeck built out over the water.

$$$ **Grand Hotel Ambasciatori** is a sumptuous four-star hotel with 108 rooms, cliffside setting, sprawling garden, and pool. This is

Humphrey Bogart–land, with plush public spaces, a stay-awhile relaxing ambience, and a free elevator to its beach (Db-€254, occasionally less, closed Jan–Feb, air-con, some balconies, parking, Via Califano 18, tel. 081-878-2025, fax 081-807-1021, www.manniellohotels.it, ambasciatori @manniellohotels.it).

$$ **Hotel la Meridiana Sorrento**, a fine three-star place with everything but character, offers business-class public spaces and 45 modern rooms. You'll pay €10 per day for air-conditioning that's only on from 13:00–5:00 (Db-€108, Tb-€145, half-pension at Db-€146 and Tb-€210 required Aug, add €10/night for air-con, prices soft when slow; big rooftop terrace with grand views; next door to public Lemon Grove Garden, Via Rota 1; tel. 081-807-3535, fax 081-807-3484, lameridiana .sorrento@tiscalinet.it, SE).

$ **Hotel Loreley**, a rambling, spacious, colorful, old Sorrentine villa next door to the Grand Hotel Ambasciatori, feels a bit like a sanitorium. It's ideal for those wishing to sit on the bluff and stare at the sea. Of its 27 rooms, 19 are quiet and have seaview balconies. The noisy, streetside rooms lack views but are air-conditioned, which helps drown out the traffic noise. A €3 elevator takes you to the hotel's beach (Db-€93; from July–mid-Sept half-pension at Db-€118 is required but the dinner's good; unpredictable management cannot guarantee view rooms but promises these prices through 2004 with this book, some free parking, Via Califano 2, tel. 081-807-3187, fax 081-532-9001, SE).

$ **Pensione Mara** is a dirty ashtray kind of place, with 6 simple ground floor rooms in a dull building with a good location (Db-€45–50, Tb-€70, cheap quads and family room, prices promised through 2004, no CC; closed in March, no breakfast; from Via Capasso, turn right at Hotel La Meridiana to Via Rota 5; tel. & fax 081-878-3665, Adelle speaks a little English).

In the Town Center

$$ **Hotel del Corso**, a funky, Old World, three-star hotel, is central, family-run, and comfortable, with 26 clean and spacious rooms (Db-€110, Tb-€150, Qb-€170, ask for Rick Steves discount when you reserve; air-con, cheap Internet access, rooftop sun terrace; Corso Italia 134, near Piazza Tasso, tel. 081-807-1016; tel. & fax 081-807-3157, www.hoteldelcorso.com, helpful Luca SE).

$ **Hotel Mignon Meuble**, with 23 big, clean, and pleasant rooms, is on a quiet street off Corso Italia. A 10-minute walk from the station, this is the best hotel value in the town center (Sb-€70, Db-€83, Tb-€96; some balconies, no views, air-con, owned by Hotel Loreley; Via Sersale 9, from station turn left on Via del Corso; tel. 081-807-3824, fax 081-877-4348, Anna and Magda SE).

$ **Casa Astarita B&B** is a shining gem in the middle of town, with a crazy-quilt tiled entryway, six bright, tranquil, air-conditioned rooms

(3 with little balconies), and a fully-stocked fridge and sideboard for help-yourself breakfasts (Db-€90, Tb-€100, Internet access, elevator, double-paned windows, just past Ristorante Parrucchiano as you're coming from the station on Corso Italia at #67, tel. 081-877-4906, fax 081-807-1146, www.casastarita.com, casastarita@tiscali.it, SE)

$ **Il Palazzo Starace B&B** offers seven peaceful, tidy rooms in a little alley off Corso Italia, one block from Piazza Tasso (Sb-€54–62, Db-€73—88; no elevator but a luggage dumbwaiter; ring bell at Via S.M. della Pietà #9, then climb 3 floors; tel. 081-878-4031, fax 081-532-9344, palazzostarace@tiscali.it).

$ **Hotel Nice** rents 24 basic rooms 100 yards in front of the station on the noisy main drag. Ask for a room off the street (Sb-€50, Db-€75, Tb-€95, Qb-€110, prices increase about €5 July–Aug, rooftop terrace, elevator, air-con, Corso Italia 257, tel. 081-878-1650, fax 081-878-3086, albergo.nice@katamail.com, SE).

$ **Ostello le Sirene di Sorrento**, a tiny hostel four blocks from the train station, offers the cheapest beds in town (50 beds in quads and rooms of 6—€18 with bath, breakfast included, no CC, membership not required, Internet access, Via degli Aranci 160, tel. & fax 081-877-1371, info@hostel.it, SE).

Sleeping with a View on Via Capo

These hotels are outside of town, near the cape (straight out Corso Italia, which turns into Via Capo; from the city center, it's a 15-min walk, a €15 taxi ride, or a cheap bus ride). The bus situation is goofy because there are two competing companies. To get from the train station to Via Capo, you can catch a blue SITA bus (any except those heading for Positano/Amalfi) or an orange Circumvesuviana bus (Bus A). Tickets for both (€1) are sold at the station newsstand and tobacco shops but not on the bus. Orange is more frequent (3/hr). If you're in Sorrento to stay put and luxuriate, these accommodations are ideal (although I'd rather luxuriate on the Amalfi Coast).

$$ **Pension La Tonnarella** is a freshly renovated Sorrentine villa with several terraces, stylish tiles, sea views, a dreamy chandeliered dining room, and uninterested owners. Fifteen of its 21 rooms have a sea view (viewless Db-€140, Db with view-€145, Db with view balcony-€150, Db with view terrace-€160, view suite-€190, obligatory €20 extra per person for half-pension (dinner) in Aug, rooms near the kitchen come with clanging pots and pans, air-con, small beach with free elevator access, Via Capo 31, tel. 081-878-1153, fax 081-878-2169, www.latonnarella.com, latonnarella@libero.it, SE).

$$ **Hotel Minerva** is like a sun worshiper's temple. Catch the elevator at Via Capo 32. Getting off at the fifth floor, you'll step into a spectacular terrace with outrageous Mediterranean views and a small, cliff-hanging swimming pool and jacuzzi *con vista* complementing 60

large, tiled *limoncello* rooms. Looking for the room numbers, you'll wonder if you're on Candid Camera (Db-€140, Tb-€155, Qb-€170, plus €10 for a balcony and €20 for junior suite, these discounted prices promised with this book through 2004 only if claimed at time of inquiry—otherwise pay €30 more, no summer half-pension requirement, air-con 7:00–2:00 mid-June–Sept only, Internet access, parking €10/day, Via Capo 30, tel. 081-878-1011, fax 081-878-1949, www.acampora.it, minerva@acampora.it, SE).

$ **Hotel Désirée**, run by friendly Corinna, is a simpler affair with humbler views but no traffic noise. Half of the 22 rooms have views or balconies or both, fans in most rooms, a fine roof sunning terrace, free beach access, lovable cats, and no half-pension requirements (maximum prices: Sb-€58, small Db-€72, Db-€88, Tb-€103, Qb-€119, price promised through 2004 with this book, no CC, laundry-€8, shares La Tonnarella's driveway and beach, Via Capo 31, tel. & fax 081-878-1563). Corinna is hugely helpful with tips on exploring the peninsula, SE.

$ The humble **Pension Elios**, run by Luigi, Maria, and daughter Gianna, offers 14 simple but spacious rooms, most with balconies and views, and a panoramic sun terrace (Db-€50–55, Tb-€75, family rooms, cheaper off-season but closed from Nov or Dec until Easter, free parking, Via Capo 33, tel. 081-878-1812, a little English spoken).

Via del Mare
$$ **Hotel del Mare**, with 31 modern rooms (views from 3rd floor rooms), is located a 15-minute walk from the center, 100 yards from the Marina Grande beach, from which buses run to the center every 30 minutes (Sb-€83, Db-€135, Qb-€185, prices soft, air-con, Via del Mare 30, near Via Capo hotels, tel. 081-878-3310, fax 081-807-1244, www.hoteldelmare.com, info@hoteldelmare.com).

Near the Port
$$ **Hotel il Faro**, located near Marina Piccola, is handy to travelers arriving by hydrofoil from Naples or visiting Capri, and to buses into the center. All of its 50 rooms have balconies, many with views, and all the comforts (Sb-€90, Db-€120–130, Tb-€150–170 depending on sea or garden view, July–Aug add €10/person, 15 percent discount on room and 10 percent discount at its Ristorante Pizzeria Vela Bianca through 2004 with this book, air-con, tel. 081-878-1390, fax 081-807-3144, www.hotelilfaro.com, info@hotelilfaro.com).

EATING

Downtown Splurges
In a town proud to have no McDonald's, consider eating well for a few extra bucks. Each of these places is a worthwhile splurge in the old center.

Ristorante il Buco, once the cellar of an old monastery, is now a small, dressy restaurant serving delightfully presented, top-quality food, showcasing good wine from Campania (but also has wines from other regions) and offering snappy service. The owner, Peppe, designs his menu around whatever's fresh and travels in the winter to assemble a wine list sure to offer connoisseurs something new and memorable (dinners run about €45–50 plus wine, several tasting menus available or order à la carte, Thu–Tue 12:00–15:00 & 19:00–23:00, closed Wed and Jan, reservations smart, just off Piazza Sant Antonino at II Rampa Marina Piccola 5, tel. 081-878-2354).

L'Antica Trattoria serves hearty portions of more traditional cuisine in a *romantico* candlelit ambience, full of contagiously fun waiters and enthusiastic eaters (€40 fixed price seafood menu includes 4 courses). Its wine list is more predictable, featuring well-known domestic wines. Walk around before you select a place to sit (daily 12:00–15:00 & 19:00–23:30, closed Mon off-season, air-con, shady terrace, non-smoking sections, reservations smart for eves, no shorts please, Via P.R. Giuliani 33, tel. 081-807-1082, Aldo will take good care of you).

Eating Well and Cheaply Downtown

Pizzeria Giardiniello is a family show offering good food, good prices, friendly smiles, and a peaceful, tropical garden setting (mid-July–Sept daily 12:00–24:00, off-season closed Thu, Via Accademia 7, tel. 081-878-4616). Like an old sailor checking the lines, Franco makes sure you're well fed.

Osteria Gatto Nero is a fresh, modern place catering to trendy young locals out for good traditional cooking, especially pasta and seafood. Chagall would eat here (Tue–Sun 12:00–15:00 & 19:00–24:00, closed Mon except July–Aug, eat indoors or out back in the garden, a few minutes' walk east of old center at Via Correale 19, tel. 081-877-3686, Gaetano SE).

Pizzeria Aurora makes 50 different kinds of prizewinning pizzas and calzones from €6–9 on Piazza Tasso. Sit inside to watch the *pizzaiolo* create your dinner, or outside for optimum people-watching (daily 12:00–16:00 & 18:30–24:00, closed Mon in winter, Piazza Tasso 10/11, east of taxi stand, tel. 081-878-1248).

Pizzeria da Gigino is lively, small, and makes huge tasty pizzas (Wed–Mon 12:00–15:00 & 18:30–24:00, closed Tue except daily July–Aug; just off Piazza Sant Antonino, take first road to the left of Sant' Antonino as you face him, pass under the archway and take the first left; tel. 081-878-1927).

Nearby, **Sant' Antonino's** offers friendly service, red-checkered tablecloths, an outdoor patio, decent prices, and edible food (daily 12:00–16:00 & 19:00–24:00, Oct–March closed Mon, just off Piazza Sant Antonino on Santa Maria delle Grazie 6, tel. 081-877-1200).

If you fancy a picnic dinner on your balcony, on the hotel terrace, or in the public garden, you'll find many markets and take-out pizzerias in the old town. The **Standa supermarket** at Corso Italia 223 has it all (Mon–Wed and Fri–Sat 8:30–13:20 & 17:00–20:55, Sat eve until 21:30, closed Sun).

Gelato: A few doors downhill from L'Antica Trattoria, **Davide Gelato** has many repeat customers—so many flavors, so little time. Walk the most enticing chorus line in Italy before ordering (mid-June–mid-Sept daily 9:30–24:00, otherwise closed Mon; Via P.R. Giuliani 39, 2 blocks off Corso Italia).

Dinners with Sea Views

For a decent dinner, the following places come with great view terraces.

Ristorante Delfino gets their seafood right off the fishermen's boats at Marina Grande and serves it up in big portions to hungry locals in a quiet pier restaurant. It's lovingly run by English-speaking Luisa, her brother Andrea, and Luisa's husband Antonio (singing in the kitchen), who take good care of their guests and won't let you leave until you're stuffed (daily 11:30–15:30 &18:30–23:30, closed Nov—Feb; Marina Grande, facing the water, go all the way to the left and follow signs; tel. 081-878-2038).

Trattoria da Emilia is where locals go for straightforward, typical Sorrentine homecooking including *maccheroni, gnocchi di mamma,* and fresh fish (Wed–Mon 12:00–15:00 & 19:30–22:00, closed Tue except July—Aug; on the Marina Grandewaterfront—walk to the right as you face the sea, Via Marina Grande 62; tel. 081-807-2720).

The **Foreigners' Club Restaurant** is a place where the English Patient could recuperate. It has the best sea views in town (under breezy palms), live music nightly at 21:00, and passable meals (March–Nov daily, bar opens at 9:30, snacks served 11:30–15:00, dinner 19:00–23:00, closed in winter, Via L. De Maio 35, tel. 081-877-3263).

Hotel Loreley's restaurant serves reasonably priced, so-so meals with a spectacular sea view (daily 12:00–14:30 & 19:00–21:30; if it's busy, non-guests may be turned away; 10-min walk east of town center, Via Califano 2; listed in "Sleeping," page 503).

TRANSPORTATION CONNECTIONS

It's impressively fast to zip by boat from point to point during the summer, when there are many more departures. In fact, many locals get around quicker by fast boat than by car or train.

By boat to: Naples (8/day, 40 min, €7.50), **Positano** (4/day daily mid-June–mid-Oct only, otherwise only weekends, pick up schedule from TI, 40 min, €6), **Amalfi** (4/day daily mid-June–mid-Oct only, weekends only off season, pick up schedule from TI, 1 hr, €6) **Capri** (at least hrly by 3 different means: slow boat, 40 min, €7; fast ferry, 25 min,

€5.70; and fastest and priciest, hydrofoil, 20 min, €9.50). For an untouristy alternative to Capri, consider the nearby island of **Ischia**, where part of *The Talented Mr. Ripley* was filmed (1/day, Easter–Nov only, departure usually around 9:30, otherwise from Naples).

To get from Sorrento's Piazza Tasso to the port, walk down the stairs near the statue's left side or take the orange shuttle bus B or C (3/hr). Tickets are sold only at the port. Several lines compete, using boats and hydrofoils. Buy one-way tickets only (there's no round-trip discount) for schedule flexibility, so you can take any company's boat back. Prices are the same among the companies. Check times for the last return crossing upon arrival (pick up a schedule from the Capri TI on the dock or check at boat ticket kiosks—around the corner to the right as you leave the dock, behind the bus and funicular ticket kiosk). The first boats leaving Sorrento can be jammed (arrive early—by 9:30 at the latest to minimize crowds).

To the Amalfi Coast: See "Amalfi Coast," below.

To Pompeii, Herculaneum, and Naples by Circumvesuviana train: This commuter train runs about every 30 minutes between Naples and Sorrento. From Sorrento, it's 30 minutes to Pompeii, 45 minutes to Herculaneum (€1.80 one way for either trip), and 70 minutes to Naples (€3.10 one-way). See Naples' "Transportation Connections," page 497, for more information on the Circumvesuviana and theft precautions. Note: The risk of theft is limited mostly to suburban Naples. Sorrento to Herculaneum is much safer.

SORRENTO PENINSULA

Marina del Cantone, a tiny fishing village near Nerano, on a Sorrento Peninsula dead end, is the place to establish a sleepy, fun-in-the-sun residency (8 buses/day from Sorrento Circumvesuviana station to Marina del Cantone, €1, weekends-€1.60, €2 all-day pass, 60 min, or a 40-min, €50 taxi ride). There are some good hikes from here: Punto Penna is a four-hour loop with great views. A more strenuous hike leads along the coast, past the stunning Gulf of Salerno to Torca, where buses go to Sant Agata (and from there, back to Sorrento). Along the trail, you might detour down to the cliff-hugging fishing village of—no kidding—Crapolla. Bring water and a good map.

Sleeping in Marina del Cantone: For a peaceful place to call home, sleep literally on the beach at the friendly **Pensione La Certosa**. This family-run place offers 16 basic, air-conditioned rooms (air-con from 10:30–7:00), six with partial sea views, a great beachfront restaurant, boat excursions, and information on a number of peaceful little beaches nearby (June–Sept Db-€90, otherwise Db-€73, half-pension required in Aug-€63/person, family rooms, tel. 081-808-1209, fax 081-808-1245, www.hotelcertosa.com, run by smart aleck Alfonso, SE).

The Amalfi Coast

The bus trip from Sorrento to Salerno along the Amalfi Coast is a ▲▲▲ sight and one of the world's great bus rides. It will leave your mouth open and your film exposed. You'll gain respect for the Italian engineers who built the road—and even more respect for the bus drivers who drive it. As you hyperventilate, notice that the Mediterranean, a sheer 500-foot drop below, really twinkles.

Cantilevered garages, hotels, and villas cling to the vertical terrain, and beautiful sandy coves tease from far below and out of reach. If you know where to look, you'll see the villa of Sophia Loren. Gasp from the right side of the bus as you go out and from the left on the way back. Those on the wrong side really miss out. Traffic is so heavy that private tour buses are only allowed to go east—summer traffic is infuriating. Even if you have a car, you may want to take the bus or hire a taxi. Some enjoy doing the coast by motorbike (rented in Sorrento).

Amalfi Coast towns are pretty but generally touristy, congested, overpriced, and a long hike above tiny beaches. The real thrill is the scenic drive. Catch a blue or green and white SITA bus from the Sorrento train station (see "Traveling along the Amalfi Coast," below).

If you're thinking of taking a round-trip bus ride from Sorrento along the Amalfi Coast to Salerno and back, consider these options instead: Get off at a prettier town (such as Cetera) near Salerno and return from there by bus rather than go into the big, plain town of Salerno. Or take the bus to Salerno, then catch the ferry back (Salerno's dock is conveniently located at the bus stop; see Salerno's "Transportation Connections" at the end of this chapter) to Amalfi or Positano, and from either town, hop a ferry to Sorrento.

This is perhaps the simplest option: Take the bus to Positano and boat from there back to Sorrento (or vice versa). Note that ferry service for this trip decreases off-season (mid Oct–early June) to weekends only. It's wise any time of year to pick up ferry schedules from the TI to figure out the best plan.

Traveling along the Amalfi Coast

From Sorrento to the Amalfi Coast by Bus: The big tourist activity from Sorrento is riding the bus along the Amalfi Coast. Blue SITA buses depart from Sorrento's train station nearly hourly (in peak season, 20/day) and stop at all Amalfi Coast towns (Positano in 35 min, €1.30; Amalfi in another 50 min, €2.30, tickets valid for 2 hrs), ending up in Salerno at the far end of the coast in just under three hours (one easy transfer in Amalfi). Buses start running as early as 6:30 and run as late as 20:00 (22:00 in summer). Buy tickets at the tobacco shop nearest any bus stop before boarding. (There's a *tabacchi*/newsstand at street level at the

Amalfi Coast

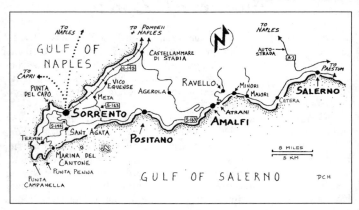

Sorrento station.) Line up under the "Riservato SITA" sign (where a schedule is posted on the wall) in front of the station (10 steps down). Leaving Sorrento, grab a seat on the right for the best views. Returning, it's fun to sit directly behind the driver for a box seat over the hairpin twisting action.

Avoiding Crowds on the Amalfi Bus: Buses are routinely unable to handle the demand during summer months. Occasionally an extra bus is added to handle the overflow but, generally, if you don't get on, you're well-positioned to catch the next bus (bring a book). In the morning, arrive early (buses start running as early as 6:30 and go about every 30 min after 8:30, crowds start forming after 9:00). Count the line: buses pull in empty and seat 49. The congestion can be so bad in the summer that return buses don't even stop in Positano (they were filled in Amalfi), and those trying to get back to Sorrento have no option but extortionist taxis or, if stranded in Positano, to take a boat. From Easter to mid-Oct boats run sporadically—daily around Easter, then just on weekends until the first week in June, when they run daily again (4/day, 45 min, €6, buy ticket on dock). Consider taking a boat anyway—it's faster, scenic, cooler, and you can take photos of the wild coastline that you cannot get from the bus.

If crowds are horrendous, you could gather a small group and share a taxi from Sorrento (4 by car one-way to Positano for around €50, or 6 by minibus taxi for €70, 50 percent more to Amalfi; while taxis must use meter within city, a fixed rate is okay otherwise—negotiate; ask about a round-trip).

Amalfi Coast Tours by Taxi: Given the hairy driving, impossible parking, congested buses, and potential fun, you might consider splurging to hire your own car and driver for the Amalfi day. Fun-loving

Carmine Monetti (a jolly, singing, in-love-with-life, grandfatherly type who speaks "inventive English") and his son Raffaele (much better English, fewer smiles, more information) have long taken excellent care of my readers' transportation needs from Sorrento.

Sample trips and rates for the taxi (to get these special prices, mention this book): Amalfi Coast Day (Positano–Amalfi–lunch in Ravello), seven hours, €170; Amalfi Coast and Paestum, 10 hours, €250; Pompeii and Vesuvius, seven hours, €170; transfer to Naples airport or train station, one hour, €85.

The Monettis can take six passengers—at a higher rate schedule—in their air-conditioned minivan. Payment is cash only (Raffaele's mobile 335-602-9158, Carmine's mobile 338-946-2860, "office" run by Raffaele's English-speaking wife, Susanna: fax 081-878-4795, www.monettitaxi17.it, monettitaxi17@libero.it). Their reservation system is simple, easygoing, and reliable. Be careful: many cabbies are claiming to be the Monettis. The Monettis drive Mercedes station wagon taxi #17, usually found in Piazza Tasso. Couples wanting to reduce their costs can tell Susanna they're open to sharing (but be sure to agree on your itinerary with the other party first), allowing her to try to fill the minivan. Carmine's specialty is helping Italo-Americans find their families in southern Italy. E-mail him in advance if you want to find your long-lost relatives, and he can put together a meeting and transportation package. If in any kind of a jam, call Raffaele's mobile phone for information.

Umberto Benvenuto offers transport and narrated excursions throughout the Amalfi Coast as well as to Rome, Naples, Pompeii, and more (Via Roma 54, tel. 089-874-024, mobile 330-353-294, www.taxibenvenuto.com, info@taxibenvenuto.com).

Amalfi Coast by Boat: From the first week in June to mid-October, boats run from Marina Piccola in Sorrento to Positano and then Amalfi, offering a handy and cooler alternative to the throngs of bus riders (4/day, 1 hr, €6, buy tickets at dock, pick up schedule at TI or call 199-446-644, www.metrodelmare.com).

Positano

Specializing in scenery and sand, Positano hangs halfway between Sorrento and Amalfi on the most spectacular stretch of the coast. The village, a three-star sight from a distance, is a pleasant gathering of cafés and expensive women's clothing stores, with a good but pebbly beach. Squished into a ravine, the center of town has no main square, unless you count the beach. There's little to do here but eat, window-shop, and enjoy the beach and views (hence the town's popularity). Consider seeing Positano as a day trip from Sorrento: take the bus out and the afternoon ferry home. If you stay the night, save the day for the beach and the cooler morning and evening for hiking up and down this hilly town. The town has a local flavor at night, when the grown-ups stroll and the kids play soccer on the church porch.

Tourist Information: The TI is a half block from the beach, in a small building at the bottom of the church steps (daily 8:30–14:00 & 14:45–20:00; Oct–March shorter hours and closed Sun, tel. 089-875-067).

Arrival in Positano: The town has only two scheduled bus stops: Chiesa (at Bar Internazionale, nearer Sorrento) and Sponda (nearer Amalfi Town). To minimize your descent, take the Sponda stop (the second Positano stop if you're coming from Sorrento). It's a 20-minute stroll/shop/munch from here to the beach (and TI).

If you're catching the bus back to Sorrento, remember it may leave from Sponda five minutes before the printed departure. There's no place for the bus to wait, so in case the driver is early, you should be, too. If the walk up is too tough, take the little orange bus (marked Interno Positano) which does a loop from the center of Positano (at Via Columbo and Via del Mulini, across from Bar Mulino Verde) up to the main highway and the SITA bus stops (€0.93, 2/hr, buy tickets for the orange bus on board; buy tickets for SITA from Bar Mulino Verde or Positour Agency—both are on Via Columbo).

Drivers must go with the one-way flow entering the town only at the Chiesa bus stop (closest to Sorrento) and exiting at Sponda.

SIGHTS

Beach—Positano's wide beach, colorful with beach umbrellas, is mostly public (free) but also has a private section (April–Oct, €10–15/person, includes use of sun beds and umbrellas). At the harbor, the nearest WC is behind the waterfront Bucca di Bacco bar.

Boat Trips—At the right side of the beach (as you face the sea), you'll see a series of booths selling boat tickets. Boats to Fornillo make three-minute, free journeys to Fornillo Beach—a quieter beach nearby (or an easy 10-min walk, take trail near ticket booths).

You could catch a boat to Amalfi (8/day, 30 min, mid-June–Aug only, €5), Capri (hydrofoil 3/day, 30 min, €13, or slow boat, 1 hr, €10.50), Sorrento (3/day 3 of which depart in afternoon, 50 min), or Naples (2/day, 50 min on hydrofoil, 2 hrs on slow boat €10); there may be boats off-season but don't count on it. Consider renting a rowboat or taking various boat tours of a nearby cave (La Grotta dello Smeraldo—Emerald Cave), fishing village (Nerano), and small islands.

Positano

200 YARDS
200 METERS

P – PARKING
— ROADS FOR CARS
- - PEDESTRIAN STREETS

N-163

VIALE CRISTOFORO

VIA MARCONI N-163

TO SORRENTO

VIA MARCONI N-163

CHIESA ←BUS STOP

VIA MULINI

VIA COLOMBO

SPONDA BUS STOP

VIALE PASITEA

CHURCH

TO AMALFI

VIA FORNILLO

VIA T. GEMOINO

VIA POSITANESI

SPIAGGIA GRANDE

FORNILLO BEACH

MEDITERRANEAN SEA

TO CAPRI, SORRENTO & NAPLES

TO AMALFI & SALERNO

1. Hotel Marincanto
2. Albergo California
3. Residence la Tavolozza
4. Hotel Savoia
5. Hotel Bougainville
6. Brikette Hostel
7. La Tre Sorrelle Rest.
8. Da Vincenzo Rest.

SLEEPING

(€1 = about $1.10, country code: 39, zip code: 84017)
These hotels (but not the hostel) are all on Via Colombo, which leads from the Sponda SITA bus stop down into the village.

$$$ **Hotel Marincanto** is a newly restored four-star hotel (Db-€195, superior Db-€220, suites-€270–375, includes breakfast, private stairs to beach, large sundeck, Via Colombo 50, tel. 089-875-130, fax 089-875-595, www.marincanto.it, SE).

$$$ **Hotel Savoia** rents 39 three-star, air-conditioned (10:00–2:00) rooms (prices vary with season: Db-€135–170, deluxe Db-€140–230, mention this book and ask for discount, some sea views, elevator, Via Colombo 73, tel. 089-875-003, fax 089-811-844, www.savoiapositano .it/com, info@savoiapositano.it, SE).

$$ **Albergo California** has great views, spacious rooms (15 of 20 with

sea views), and a grand terrace draped with vines (Db-€140–150 depending on season and amenities, viewless Db-€100–120, includes breakfast, air-con, free parking, can arrange tours, Via Colombo 141, tel. 089-875-382, fax 089-812-154, www.hotelcaliforniapositano.it, albergocalifornia @tiscalinet.it, Maria and Antonio and sons, Frank and John SE).

$ **Residence la Tavolozza** is an attractive eight-room hotel, warmly run by Celeste (cheh-LES-tay). Flawlessly restored, each room comes with a view, a balcony, fine tile, and silence (Db-€85 through 2004 with this book, breakfast extra, no CC, requires $100 travelers check as deposit, also has a small apartment and royal family apartment with 6 beds, Via Colombo 10, 84017 Positano, tel. & fax 089-875-040, celeste .dileva@tiscali.it, a little English spoken).

$ **Hotel Bougainville** is spotless, with eager-to-please owners and 14 basic rooms (Db-€85–105 with view balcony, Db without view-€62–78, includes breakfast only with this book, air-con, some traffic noise and fumes, Via Colombo 25, tel. 089-875-047, fax 089-811-150, www.bougainville.it, hotel@bougainville.it, Carlo, Luisa, and son Cristiano SE).

$ **Brikette Hostel** offers your best cheap, dorm-bed option in this otherwise ritzy town. It's bright and clean with the normal hostel rules: 10:00–16:00 lockout, midnight curfew, and check out by 9:00. You can't store luggage here, but the Internet café across the street stores bags for a small fee (late March–Nov only; dorm bed-€23, Db-€75, includes breakfast, no CC; Via G. Marconi 358, leave bus at Chiesa/Bar Internazionale stop and backtrack uphill 500 feet; tel. 089-812-2814, www.brikette.com, info@brikette.com).

EATING

The pizzerias on the beach, while overpriced, are pleasant and convenient. At the waterfront, I like **Le Tre Sorrelle** (daily 12:30–15:30 & 19:00–23:30, tel. 089-875-452) but the neighboring places also leave people fat and happy.

A 10-minute uphill hike rewards you with the very Italian **Da Vincenzo.** This is a jolly festival of food with tasty surprises, prepared by Gisue and Marcella Porpora (Tue 19:00–23:30, Wed–Mon 13:00–14:45 & 19:15–23:30, Viale Pasitea 178, tel. 089-875-128).

The family-run **Da Costantino**, so high on the hill that the restaurant sends a van to pick you up and take you home, offers reasonably priced, simple, filling meals (Thu–Tue 13:00–15:30 & 19:00–24:00, closed Wed for lunch, in winter all day, Via Corvo 107, ask your hotel to call for the van, tel. 089-875-738).

If a picnic dinner on your balcony or the beach sounds good, Emilia at **Enogastromia Delikatessen** can supply the ingredients (daily in summer 7:00–14:00 & 16:00–22:00, in winter and on Sun closes at 20:00, just below car park at Via del Mulini 5, tel. 089-875-489). **Vini e Panini**, another small grocery, is a block from the beach and TI (Mon–Sat 8:00–14:00 & 16:30–21:30, Sun 8:00–14:00, tel. 089-875-175, just off church steps).

Amalfi and Atrani

Amalfi Town was once a powerful maritime republic. Today, the waterfront of this most famous of the Amalfi Coast villages is dominated by a bus station, a parking lot, and two gas stations. But step into the town, and you find its once rich and formidable medieval shell filled with trendy shops and capped by an impressive cathedral. The main street through the village—hard for pedestrians to avoid—is packed with cars and bully mopeds.

Amalfi's **cathedral** is the only sight marginally worth visiting. Climb the imposing stairway. The 1,000-year-old bronze door was given to Amalfi by a wealthy local merchant, who had it made in Constantinople. Head left to tour the "Cloister of Paradise," the Basilica of the Crucifix (the original ninth-century church, now a museum filled with the art treasures of the cathedral), and the Crypt of St. Andrew. Andrew was the apostle who left his nets to become the original "fisher of men"; his remains were brought here in 1206 during the Crusades—an indication of the wealth and importance of Amalfi then. As you exit the crypt, you'll go through the church (€2.50, daily in summer 9:00–21:00, winter 10:00–17:00, closed Jan–Feb, pick up the English flier, tel. 089-871-324).

Atrani, just a 15-minute stroll away, is a world apart. Amazingly, it has none of the trendy resort feel of Amalfi, relatively few tourists, a delightful town square, and a free, sandy beach. For a classic Amalfi hike, walk from Atrani to Ravello (a venerable cliff-hanging resort town) and then to Amalfi.

SLEEPING

If you're marooned in Amalfi, stay at the 40-room **$$ Hotel Amalfi** (Db-€62–114, July–Aug obligatory half-pension is €78 per person; roof-terrace restaurant, no sea views, on a garden; 50 yards from cathedral, head up the pedestrian street and take the staircase to the left before the underpass, Via dei Pastai 3; tel. 089-872-440, fax 089-872-250, www .starnet.it/hamalfi, hamalfi@starnet.it, SE).

$$ Hotel la Conchiglia, a 10-minute walk north along the harbor, offers 11 rooms, some with balconies and most with views (Db-€110, no CC, breakfast extra, free parking, packed July–Aug, Piazzale dei Protontini, tel. and fax 089-871-856, SE).

In Atrani: $ A'Scalinatella is an informal hostel—with a honey-comb of cramped two- to five-bed dorms, private rooms, family apart-ments, a washer (€5.50/load), Internet access, communal kitchen, no membership required. It's a small-town Amalfi hideaway, without the glitz and hill-climbing of Positano. The English-speaking owners, Filippo and Gabriele, are friendly and helpful (€10–21 per bed in 4–6 bed rooms, D-€36–47, Db-€47–73, breakfast available, prices soft, no CC; 100 yards from the main square, hike up the ravine and look for signs, Scalinatella Piazza Umberto I #5; tel. 089-871-492, www .hostelscalinatella.com, scalinatella@amalficoast.it).

Capri

Made famous as the vacation hideaway of Roman emperors Augustus and Tiberius, Capri these days is a world-class tourist trap packed with gawky visitors searching for the rich and famous, and finding only their prices. The four-by-two-mile "Island of Dreams" is a zoo in July and August—tacky low-grade group tourism at its worst. Other times of year, it provides a relaxing and scenic break from the cultural gauntlet of Italy. While Capri has some Roman ruins and an interesting 14th-century Carthusian monastery, its chief attraction is its famous Blue Grotto, and its best activity is a scenic hike.

Tourist Information: The TI at the ferry dock offers a room-find-ing service (April–Oct daily 8:30–20:30; Nov–March Mon–Sat 9:00–13:00 & 15:30–18:30, closed Sun, tel. 081-837-0634). Baggage storage service is in front of the dock in the shop to the left of the Salumeria (€1.50/day per bag, open daily 8:30–17:45). As you exit the pier, the bus and funicular ticket kiosk is around the end of the pier to the right, return boat ticket kiosks are behind that, public WCs are on the opposite side of the street, and the funicular is across the street to your left. Bar Augusto, a few doors down to the left of the funicular, has Internet access (daily 9:00–19:00).

Getting around Capri: The buses and funicular are covered by the same ticket options: €1.30 per ride on the bus or funicular, €2.20 for 60 minutes of unlimited use (this is the best option if you plan to go straight to the Blue Grotto by public transportation), or €6.70 for an all-day pass. You can hire a convertible taxi for about €45 an hour—negotiate. From the ferry dock at Marina Grande, the funicular lifts you 500 feet to the town of Capri (5 min, 4/hr), or if the funicular is jammed, take the bus from the station that is 50 yards uphill to the right of the pier as you exit it. From Capri, cliff-hanging buses run to Anacapri (7 min, 4/hr, note that buses can be packed returning from Anacapri to Capri; if so, guarantee a seat by catching the bus at the end

Capri

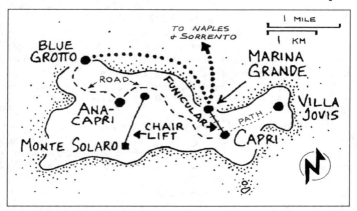

of the line—a 5-min walk to your left as you're facing away from the square-stop is just in front of the telephone on left side of the street). From Anacapri, you can take yet another bus to the Blue Grotto from the end of the line in Piazza del Cimitero (don't get off yet when the driver announces "Anacapri," but ride one more stop, then transfer to *Grotta Azzurra* buses which are well signed).

SIGHTS

Capri Town—This is a cute but touristy shopping town. The TI is in a closet on the main square (immediately to the left as you enter the square from the funicular), same hours as ferry dock TI—listed above, tel. 081-837-0700, WC down stairs behind TI). For a view restaurant with good seafood, try **Da Gemma**, serving movie stars and famous writers since Capri's jetsetting days (Tue–Sun 12:00–15:00 & 19:15–24:00, closed Mon; Via Madre Serafina 6, from town square go up stairs near church and follow the sign; tel. 081-837-0461). Overall, Capri Town is most useful as a place to catch the bus to Anacapri (from funicular exit, jog right onto shop-lined street; the bus station is about 100 yards ahead on your right).

Anacapri—This is the island's second town. From the busy square where the bus drops you, head down the pedestrian street with the curvy pavement to reach the TI (Mon–Sat 9:00–15:00, closed Sun, often closed in winter, tel. 081-837-1524) and eventually the footpath to the Blue Grotto. Oddly, there are no sea views from the town, but there are hikes worth taking and one sight worth seeing. **St. Michael's Church** has a remarkable majolica tile floor showing paradise on earth (€1, daily 9:30–18:15, off-season 10:30–17:00, 150 yards after the TI). **Ristorante Materita,** on the same pedestrian street, offers 30 types of wood-oven pizza, seafood, and a variety of regional wines (daily 12:00–15:00 & 18:50–23:00, Oct–March closed Tue, Via G. Orlandi 140, tel. 081-837-3375).

Sleeping in Anacapri: **$ Villa Eva**, a 10-minute walk from town on the Blue Grotto road, is a family-run place with 20 rooms, a lush tropical garden setting, and a swimming pool. If you call in advance and let them know what time you're coming, they can pick you up at the port or from Anacapri (Db–€80–100 depending on season, Via la Fabbrica 8, tel. 081-837-1549, fax 081-837-2040, www.villaeva.com, villa.eva @capri.it, SE).

$ Alla Bussola di Hermes draws students, backpackers, and budget travelers (dorm bed–€21, €25-28 in 4-bed rooms, Db–€60–90, some rooms with air-con, pool and solarium, laundry services, Internet access, can pick you up from port or from Anacapri if you call in advance, Via Traversa la Vigna 14, tel. 081-838-2010, bus.hermes@libero.it, run by lovely Rita and her brother Cristiano, SE).

Hike down Monte Solaro—From Anacapri, ride the €4 chairlift to the 1,900-foot summit of Monte Solaro for a commanding view of the Bay of Naples and a pleasant 40 minute downhill hike through lush vegetation and ever-changing views, past the 14th-century Chapel of Santa Maria Cetrella, and back into Anacapri (€5.50 roundtrip, daily 9:30–17:00, last run down at 17:30, Nov–March last run 15:30, 12 min each way).

Blue Grotto—To most, a visit to Capri's Blue Grotto is an overrated and overpriced "must." The roundtrip boat from Marina Grande costs €7. Once you reach the grotto, you pay €4.30 for a rowboat to take you in for three minutes' row around the inside of the grotto (after your rowman jockeys for position for at least 20 minutes), plus €4 to cover the admission to the grotto (total €15.30, but your rowman will expect a tip—€1 is enough). You can lop off €7 if you catch the bus to Anacapri, and hike briskly for one hour to the grotto and back instead of taking the boat from Marina Grande. Or you can save about €2.20 if you take the bus to Anacapri, then catch the local bus that runs to the grotto (every 20 min from Piazza del Cimitero, a 5-min walk from Piazza Diaz; 60 min ticket is enough time to visit the grotto and take the bus back to town). Anyone can dive in for free after 18:00, when the boats stop running.

Touristy as this is, the grotto, with its eerily beautiful blue sunlight reflecting through the water, is impressive (daily 9:00 until an hour before sunset, boats don't run in stormy weather or during high tides-check this out *before* you purchase €7 boat ticket).

Villa Jovis—Emperor Tiberius' now-ruined villa is a scenic 45-minute hike from Capri Town. Tiberius ruled Rome from here for a decade in about A.D. 30 (€2, daily 9:00 until an hour before sunset).

TRANSPORTATION CONNECTIONS

By boat to: Sorrento (nearly hrly, €7 for 40-min ride, €5.70 for fast ferry, €9.50 for 20-min hydrofoil), **Naples** (11 hydrofoils/day, 40 min, €12). Confirm the schedule carefully—the last boat leaves between 18:00–20:10.

Pompeii, Herculaneum, and Vesuvius

▲▲▲**Pompeii**—Stopped in its tracks by the eruption of Mount Vesuvius in A.D. 79, Pompeii offers the best look anywhere at what life in Rome must have been like 2,000 years ago. An entire city of well-preserved ruins is yours to explore. A thriving commercial port of 20,000, Pompeii grew from Greek and Etruscan roots to become an important Roman city. Then, it was buried under 30 feet of hot mud and volcanic ash. For archaeologists, this was a shake-and-bake windfall, teaching them almost all they know about daily Roman life. Pompeii was rediscovered in the 1600s; excavations began in 1748.

Cost, Hours, Information: €10; or €18 combo-ticket includes Herculaneum and three lesser sites (valid 3 days); or free or 50 percent off with Campania ArteCard (see page 483); April–Oct daily 8:30–19:30, Nov–March daily 8:30–17:00. The ticket office closes 1.5 hours before closing time. A good map is included with admission (pick up at TI window to left of WCs; for more information, check www.pompeiisites .org). A free baggage check is near the site entrance turnstiles (retrieve bags by 19:20).

Stop by the bookshop. A guidebook on Pompeii makes this site more meaningful. (Books are also on sale in Sorrento.) The small Pompeii and Herculaneum "past and present" book has a helpful text and allows you to re-create the ruins with plastic overlays—with the "present" actually being 1964 (available for €11 in bookstore unless they're "finished"; if you buy from a street vendor, pay no more than €11). Good audioguides are available at the ticket booth for €6, 2 for €9 (ID required).

Live guides cluster near the ticket booth. If you gather 10 people, the price is reasonable when split (around €10 apiece, total cost about €105, 2 hrs). For a local guide, consider Gaetano Manfredi (tel. 081-863-9816, mobile 338-725-5620).

Background: Pompeii was a booming Roman trading city. Most streets would have been lined with stalls and jammed with customers from sunup to sundown. Chariots vied with shoppers for street space, and many streets were off-limits to chariots during shopping hours (see street signs with pictures of men carrying vases—this meant pedestrians only).

Fountains overflowed into the streets, flushing the gutters into the

Pompeii

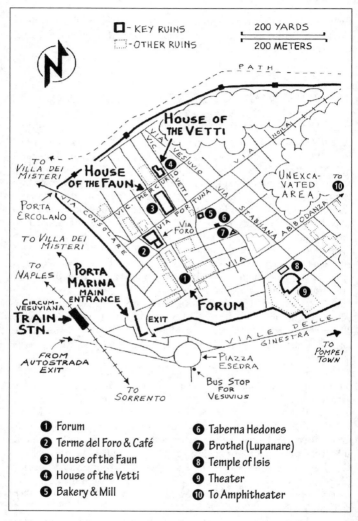

1 Forum
2 Terme del Foro & Café
3 House of the Faun
4 House of the Vetti
5 Bakery & Mill
6 Taberna Hedones
7 Brothel (Lupanare)
8 Temple of Isis
9 Theater
10 To Amphitheater

sea (thereby cleaning the streets). The stones you see at intersections allowed pedestrians to cross the constantly gushing streets. A single stone designated a one-way street (just enough room for one chariot, stone straddled by its two oxen), and two stones meant a two-way chariot street. There were no posh neighborhoods. Rich and poor mixed it up, as elegant homes existed side by side with simple homes throughout Pompeii. While nearby Herculaneum would have been a classier place to live (traffic-free streets, more elegant homes, far better drainage), Pompeii was the place for action and shopping. It served its estimated 20,000 residents with more than 40 bakeries, 30 brothels, and 130 bars, restaurants, and hotels. Rome controlled the entire Mediterranean 2,000 years ago—making it a kind of free-trade zone—and Pompeii was a central and booming port town. With most buildings covered by brilliant, white ground-marble stucco, Pompeii in A.D. 79 was an impressive town. Remember, Pompeii's best art is in the Naples Archaeological Museum, described above.

Tour of Pompeii: Allow at least three hours to tour the site. Consider the following route, starting at the Porta Marina (town gate) after the ticket booth. Before Vesuvius blew, the sea came nearly to this gate. As you approach the Porta Marina, notice the two openings—big for chariots, small for pedestrians.

From the Porta Marina, Via Marina leads straight to Pompeii's main square, the forum.

The **forum** *(foro)*, Pompeii's commercial, religious, and political center, stands at the intersection of the city's two main streets. While the most ruined part of Pompeii, it's grand nonetheless—with temples, lots of pedestals that once sported statues (now in the museum in Naples), and the basilica (Pompeii's largest building, the ancient equivalent of law courts and stock market—on the right as you enter). The Curia (home of the government) stands at the end of the forum. It's built of brick and mortar, a Roman invention. While brick now, it was once faced with marble. Note that while Pompeii was destroyed by the eruption of A.D. 79, it was also devastated by an earthquake in A.D. 62. It's safe to assume any brick you see dates from between A.D. 62 and A.D. 79—restoration work done by Pompeians after the quake.

Walk (away from the Curia) along the fenced, roofed area that runs alongside the forum. Behind the iron fence are piles of pottery and, at the end, some eerie casts of volcano victims. With the unification of Italy in the 1860s, national spirit fueled efforts to excavate Pompeii. During this period, archaeologists made these molds (during excavations, when they detected hollows underfoot—left by decomposed bodies—they'd pour liquid plaster into the cavities, let it dry, and dig up the casts).

Such a busy square needed a public toilet. Just past the warehouse, turn left into an ancient public WC. Notice the ditch that led to the sewer (marked by an arch in the corner). The stone supports once held wooden benches with the appropriate holes. Even back then, this area had pay toilets.

Continue on, leaving the forum through the gate at the end. Take an immediate right, then a left. You're on Via del Foro, passing a convenient

21st-century cafeteria (decent value, gelato, books, WCs upstairs; a fancier restaurant in a more elegant ancient gymnasium setting is adjacent).

Head down Via del Foro and enter the impressive baths, **Terme del Foro** (on the left, past the cafeteria). You'll enter through the gymnasium. After working out, clients would find four rooms: a waiting room, warm bath *(tepidarium)*, hot bath *(caldarium)*, and cold-plunge bath *(frigidarium)*.

The *tepidarium* is ringed by mini-statues or *telamones* (male caryatids, figures used as supporting pillars), which divided clients' lockers. They'd undress and warm up here, perhaps stretching out on one of the benches near the bronze heater for a massage. Notice the ceiling: half crushed by the eruption and half surviving with its fine blue-and-white stucco work.

Next, in the *caldarium*, you'd get hot. Notice the engineering. The double floor was heated from below—so nice with bare feet (look into the grate to see the brick support towers). The double walls with brown terra-cotta tiles held the heat. Romans soaked in the big tub, which was filled with hot water. To keep condensation from dripping annoyingly from the ceiling, the fluting (ribbing) was added to carry the drips down the walls.

Next came the cold plunge in the *frigidarium*—a circular marble basin with the spout spewing frigid water, opposite the entry.

Exit the baths. Notice the oxcart wheel grooves and stepping stones in the street. During ancient rainstorms, streets would turn into filthy rivers. Do as the ancient Romans did. Keep your feet dry by using the stepping stones to cross the street. Directly in front of you is an ancient fast-food stand (notice the holes in the counters for pots). To your left, a few doors down, is the **House of the Tragic Poet** (Casa de Poeta Tragico), with its famous "Beware of Dog" (Cave Canum) mosaic in the entryway. On either side, grooves in the doorway indicate a shop with sliding doors.

Face the House of the Tragic Poet, then walk to your right two blocks to the House of the Faun (Casa del Fauno, Danzante). Notice the holes drilled into the curbs—to hitch your animal or perhaps to support an awning from your storefront.

Pompeii's largest home (with 40 rooms), the **House of the Faun** provided Naples' Archaeological Museum with many of its top treasures, including the original dancing faun (you'll see a copy here) and the famous mosaic of the "Battle of Alexander." Wander past the welcome mosaic (*HAVE*, or "hail to you") and through its courtyards. The back courtyard leads to the exit. It's lined by pillars rebuilt after the A.D. 62 earthquake. Take a close look at the brick, mortar, and fake marble stucco veneer.

Back on the street, turn right and look for the exposed 2,000-year-old lead pipes in the wire cage (ahead and down on the ground to your right). The lead was imported from Roman Britannia. A huge water tank—fed by an aqueduct—stood at the high end of town. Three independent pipe systems supplied water to the city from here: one each for baths, private homes, and public water fountains. In case of a water shortage, supply could be limited. Democratic priorities prevailed: first the baths were cut, then the private homes. The last water to be cut was that which fed the public fountains (where people got their water for drinking and cooking).

Take your first left on Vicolo dei Vetti. Enter Pompeii's best-preserved home, the House of the Vetti (Casa dei Vetti).

The **House of the Vetti**, (may still be under restoration in 2004) which has retained its mosaics and frescoes, was the bachelor pad of two wealthy merchant brothers. In the entryway, see if you can spot the erection. This is not pornography. There's a meaning here: The penis and the sack of money balance each other on the goldsmith scale above a fine bowl of fruit. The meaning: Only with a balance of fertility and money can you have abundance.

Step into the atrium, its ceiling open to the sky to collect light and rainwater. The pool, while decorative, was a functional water-supply tank. It's flanked by large money boxes anchored to the floor. The brothers were certainly successful merchants, and possibly moneylenders, too.

Exit on the right, passing the tight servant quarters, and go into the kitchen, with its bronze cooking pots (and a touchable lead pipe on the back wall). The passage dead-ends in the little Venus Room with its erotic frescoes behind glass.

Return to the atrium and pass into the big colonnaded garden. It was planted according to the plan indicated by traces of roots excavated in the volcanic ash. This courtyard is ringed by richly frescoed entertainment rooms. Circle counterclockwise. The dining room is finely decorated in "Pompeian red" (from iron rust) and black. Study the detail. Notice the lead humidity seal between the wall and the floor designed to keep the moisture-sensitive frescoes dry. (Had Leonardo taken this clever step, his *Last Supper* in Milan might be in better shape today.) Continuing around, notice the square white stones inlaid in the floor. Imagine them reflecting like cat eyes as the brothers and their friends wandered around by oil lamp late at night. Frescoes in the Yellow Room (near the exit) show off the ancient mastery of perspective, which was not matched elsewhere in Europe for nearly 1,500 years.

Leaving the House of the Vetti, go left past the pipes again. Then turn right, following Vicolo dei Vetti to Via della Fortuna. Intersections like this, with public fountains, were busy neighborhood centers, where rent was high and people gathered.

Turn left on Via della Fortuna and take a quick right on Vicolo Storto, which leads down a curving street to the **bakery and mill** *(forno e mulini)*. The ovens look like a modern-day pizza oven. The stubby stone towers are flour grinders: After grain was poured into the top, donkeys pushed wooden bars that turned the stones, and eventually powdered grain dropped out the bottom as flour—flavored with tiny bits of rock. Perhaps this is why sifters were invented.

Take the first left after the bakery onto Via degli Augustali, and check out the mosaics on the left at the Taberna Hedones. This must be the tavern of hedonism; see the cute welcome mosaic—like the one we saw earlier at the House of the Faun—reading *HAVE* ("hail to you"), with the bear licking its wounds.

Next turn right, over the street dam, and follow the signs to the **brothel** *(lupanare)*, at #18. Prostitutes were nicknamed *lupe* (she-wolves). Wander into the brothel, a simple place with stone beds and pillows. The ancient graffiti includes stroke tallies and exotic names of the girls, indicating they came from all corners of the Mediterranean. The faded frescoes above the cells may have served as a kind of menu for services offered. Note the idealized portrayal of women (white, considered beautiful) and man (dark, considered horny). Outside at #17 is a laundry—likely to boil the sheets (thought to guard against venereal disease).

Leaving the brothel, go down the hill to Pompeii's main drag, Via Abbondanza. The forum (and exit) is to the right. (The huge amphitheater—which you can skip—is 10 minutes to your left.) Go straight down Via dei Teatri, then left before the columns, downhill to the **Temple of Isis** (on the right). This Egyptian temple served Pompeii's Egyptian community. The little shrine with the plastic roof housed holy water from the Nile. Pompeii must have had a synagogue, but it has yet to be excavated.

Exit the temple where you entered and take an immediate right down an alleyway to our last stop, the **theater**. Originally a Greek theater (Greeks built theirs with the help of a hillside), this marks the spot of the birthplace of the Greek port here in 470 B.C. During Roman times, the theater sat 5,000 in three price ranges: the five marble terraces up close (filled with romantic wooden seats for two), the main section, and the cheap nosebleed section (surviving only on the right). The square stones above the cheap seats used to support a canvas rooftop. Notice the high-profile boxes, flanking the stage, for guests of honor. From this perch, you can see the gladiator barracks—the colonnaded courtyard beyond the theater. They lived in tiny rooms, trained in the courtyard, and fought in the nearby amphitheater.

There's much more to see; 75 percent of Pompeii's 164 acres has been excavated. But this tour's over. When you're ready to leave, the exit is to the left of the steep hill at the entrance to the Foro. When it forks, head right to get back to the site entrance to pick up bags or revisit the bookshop. *Ciao!*

Getting to Pompeii: Pompeii is halfway between Naples and Sorrento, about 30 minutes from either by direct Circumvesuviana train (runs at least hrly). Get off at the Pompei Scavi, Villa dei Misteri stop on the Naples–Sorrento train line. A different Circumvesuviana line, which does *not* go to Sorrento, has a Pompeii stop that leaves you far from the excavation site entrance. Check your bag at the Pompei Scavi train station (at the bar, €1.50, pick up by 19:00, 18:00 Oct–Feb) or, better yet, at the Pompeii ruins for free. From the train station, turn right and walk down the road about a block to the entrance (first left turn). The TI is further down the street, but not a necessary stop for your visit.

▲▲**Herculaneum (Ercolano)**—Smaller, less ruined, and less crowded than its famous big sister, Herculaneum offers a closer peek into ancient Roman life but with none of the grandeur of Pompeii (there's barely a colonnade). Informative and interesting audioguides shed light on the ruins and life in Herculaeum in the 1st century A.D. (€6 for one, €9 for two, ID required, turn in half hour before closing).

Caked and baked by the same A.D. 79 eruption, Herculaneum is a small community of intact buildings with plenty of surviving detail. Unlike Pompeii, which was buried in ash and pumice, Herculaneum was buried under 35 feet of boiling mud, which hardened into baked tufa, perfectly preserving the city until excavations began in 1738.

As you enter the site from the tunnel and make your way to the arches, you are walking across what was formerly Herculaneum's beach. The arches you see were boat storage areas. During excavations in 1981, hundreds of bodies were found here, between the wall of volcanic stone behind you and the city in front of you. Herculaneum's 4,000 citizens had a little more time than the people of Pompeii to flee the eruption. They tried to escape to the sea but were forced back to shore by a violent tidal wave. The baths nearest the entrance illustrate the city's devastation. After you descend into the baths, look back at the steps. You'll see the original wood charred in the disaster, pretected by the wooden planks you just walked on. At the bottom of the stairs, in the waiting room to the right, you'll see where the floor collapsed under the sheer weight of the volcanic mud. (The sunken pavement reveals the baths' heating system; hot air generated by wood-burning furnaces circulated between different levels of the floor.) A doorway in the room in front of the stairs is still filled with rock-hard mud. Despite the damage, elements of refinement remain intact, such as the delicate stuccoes in the *caldarium* (warm, steamy bath).

Stroll the city and find the House of Deer (*Casa dei Cervi*), named for the statues of deer being attacked by dogs in the garden courtyard (these are copies, originals are in Archaeological Museum in Naples). The Seat of the Augustali (*Sede degli Augustali*), decorated with frescoes of Hercules (for whom this city was named), was a forum for freed slaves climbing their way up the ladder of Roman society. The *Bottega ad Cucumas* wine shop still has its drink list frescoed on the wall. Don't miss the gymnasium complex with its Hydra of Lerna, a sculpted bronze fountain featuring the seven-headed monster defeated by Hercules as one of his twelve labors.

Herculaneum is 15 minutes from Naples and 45 minutes from Sorrento on the same Circumvesuviana train that goes to Pompeii. To get to the ruins, leave the Ercolano station and turn right, then left following yellow signs; go eight blocks straight downhill from station to the end of the road. The site entrance is 200 yards beyond and on your left as you curve around its perimeter (€10, €18 combo-ticket includes Pompeii and three lesser sites—valid 3 days, can be free or 50 percent off with Campania ArteCard—see page 483, daily April–Oct 8:30–19:30, Nov–March 8:30–17:00, ticket office closes 90 min earlier, free baggage storage before turnstiles—pick up half hour before closing, WCs to the left of the audioguide kiosk, tel. 081-739-0963, www.pompeiisites.org).

▲Vesuvius—The 4,000-foot summit of Vesuvius, mainland Europe's only active volcano (sleeping restlessly since 1944), is accessible year-round by car, taxi (€40 round-trip), or by the blue Transporti Vesuviani bus (often 5/day but irregular, roughly hourly departures 9:00–14:00 from Herculaneum station or near the Autostrada toll booths 100 yards downhill from Pompeii site entrance; 60 min up with stop at bar, 40 min down, call tel. 081-559-2582 for exact departure times). The round-trip bus ride costs €3.10 from Herculaneum, €5.20 from Pompeii, site entry with mandatory guide is €6. Be prepared for a long wait for the return trip. Beware of expensive pit stops: the bus may make a bathroom stop at a tourist shack along the way—if you use the WC, you may be expected to purchase a candy bar or some other item at a premium.

From the bus and car park, it's a steep, often cold and windy (bring a sweater or coat, especially if Oct–Apr) 30-minute hike to the top for a sweeping view of the Bay of Naples. Up here, it's desolate and lunar-like. The rocks are hot. Walk the entire crater lip for the most interesting views; the far end overlooks Pompeii. Be still and alone to hear the wind and tumbling rocks in the crater. Any steam? Closed when erupting.

Paestum

Paestum (PASTE-oom) is one of the best collections of Greek temples anywhere—and certainly the most accessible to western Europe. Serenely situated, it's surrounded by fields and wildflowers and has only a modest commercial strip.

This town was founded as Poseidonia by Greeks in the sixth century B.C. and became a key stop on an important trade route. In the fifth century B.C., the Lucans, a barbarous inland tribe, conquered Poseidonia, changed its name to Paistom, and tried to adopt the cultured ways of the Greeks. The Romans, who took over in the third cen-

Paestum

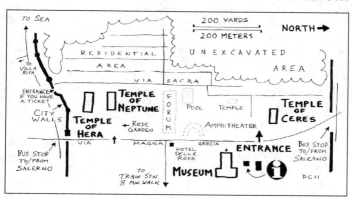

tury B.C., gave Paestum the name it bears today. The final conquerors of Paestum, malaria-carrying mosquitoes, kept the site wonderfully deserted for nearly a thousand years. Rediscovered in the 18th century, Paestum today offers the only well-preserved Greek ruins north of Sicily (TI: July–Aug Mon–Sat 9:00–19:00, Sun 9:00–13:00, off-season Mon–Sat 9:00–16:00, Sun 9:00–13:00, hours may vary, tel. 082-881-1016, info@infopaestum.it).

Arrival at Paestum: Buses from Salerno (see "Transportation Connections," below) stop near a corner of the ruins (at a little bar/café). Arriving by train, exit the station and walk through the old city gate; the ruins are an eight-minute walk straight ahead. Stop by the TI (next to museum) to pick up a free map of the site. If you ask politely, you might be able to store luggage at the TI, site, or museum.

Cost, Hours, Information: €4 for the museum, €4 for the site, €6.50 for a combo-ticket. Both the museum and site open daily at 9:00 (except the first and third Mon of month, when museum is closed, though the site is open). Year-round, the museum closes at 19:00 (last ticket sold at 18:30). The site closes one hour before sunset (as late as 19:30 June–Aug, as early as 15:45 in Dec, last ticket sold an hour before closing). Several mediocre guidebooks are offered at the museum's book-shop, including a €13 past-and-present guide. Dull €4 audioguides are rented at museum and site entrance and cover both (ID required). The site and museum have separate entrances. The museum, just outside the ruins, is in a cluster with the TI and a small paleo-Christian basilica.

Planning Your Time: Allow two hours, including the museum. Depending on your interest and the heat of the day, start with either the museum or the site.

Museum: This offers you the rare opportunity to see artifacts—dating from prehistoric to Greek to Roman times—at the site where they were discovered. These beautifully crafted works help bring Paestum to life. There are good English descriptions throughout. On weekends *Paestum: the Polis in History* video is shown at noon and also at 18:00 Friday and Saturday.

The large ground floor (the most impressive part) contains Greek artifacts. The upstairs, after remodeling is completed, may still contain the prehistory exhibits (displays of pottery, blades, and arrowheads) as well as the Roman Room (contains statues, busts, and inscriptions dating from the time of the Roman occupation). No matter where you start, you'll feel like you've come in on the middle of something, but much of the work is described in English, and the art speaks for itself.

On the ground floor, the large carvings overhead—wrapping around the first room you see as you enter the museum—once adorned a sanctuary of the goddess Hera (wife of Zeus) outside the city. Some of the carvings show scenes from the life of Hercules. In the various ground-floor rooms, you'll see startlingly well-preserved Greek vases, crumbling armor, and paintings. The highlight of the museum is a rare example of Greek painting, known as the Diver's Tomb (480 B.C.). These slabs—showing a diver and four scenes of banqueting—originally were the sides of a tomb. The simple painting of a diver arcing down into a pool was the top of the tomb (painting faced inward). Though the deceased might have been a diver, it's thought the art more likely represents our dive from life to death. It's rare to see a real Greek statue (most are Roman copies), even rarer to see a Greek painting. The many other painted slabs in the museum date from a later time under Lucan rule. The barbarous people who conquered the Greeks tried to appropriate their art and style, but lacked the Greeks' distinct, light touch. Regardless, the Lucan paintings, as well as the crisply drawn pictures on dozens of Greek vases, are instructive and enjoyable—consider them ancient snapshots.

Site: The key ruins are the impossible-to-miss Temples of Neptune, Hera, and Ceres, but the scattered village ruins are also interesting. Lonely Ceres, in an evocative setting, is about a 10-minute walk from Neptune and Hera, which stand together. Entries to the site are in front of the Temple of Ceres, on the south side near the Temple of Hera, and if you already have a ticket you can also enter near the Temple of Neptune.

The misnamed Temple of Neptune is a textbook example of the Doric style. Constructed in 450 B.C. and actually dedicated to Hera, the Temple of Neptune is simply overwhelming. Better preserved than the Parthenon in Athens, this huge structure is a tribute to Greek engineering and aesthetics. Contemplate the word "renaissance"—the rebirth of this grand Greek style of architecture. Notice how the columns angle out and the base bows up (scan the short ends of the temple). This was a trick ancient architects used to create the illusion of a perfectly straight building. All important Greek buildings were built using this technique. Now imagine it richly and colorfully decorated with marble and statues.

Adjacent to the Temple of Neptune is the almost-delicate Temple of Hera, dedicated to the Greek goddess of marriage in 550 B.C.

Sleeping near Paestum: Paestum at night, with views of the floodlit ruins, is magic.

$ **Hotel delle Rose**, which has 12 small, fine rooms and a respectable restaurant, is near the Neptune entrance, on the street bordering the ruins (Db-€55, includes breakfast, Via Magna Grecia 193, tel. 082-881-1070, www.hoteldellerose.com, NSE).

$ The **Agriturismo Seliano** offers spacious, spotless rooms on a farm, complete with horses, a pool, and great cooking using produce from the garden (Db-€80 with breakfast, €100 in July–Aug, run by an English-speaking baroness, serves a fine €20 dinner, near beach, 2 miles from ruins, best for drivers, tel. 082-872-4544, fax 082-872-3634).

$ **Hotel Villa Rita** is a tidy, quiet, country hotel set on two acres within walking distance of the beach with 14 clean rooms, a swimming pool, and free parking (Db-€73, half-pension required in Aug at €56/person; 5 min walk west of Hera entrance, Via Principe di Piedmonte—a.k.a. Via Nettuno—9; tel. 0828-811-081, fax 0828-722-555, www.hotelvillarita.it,).

TRANSPORTATION CONNECTIONS

Salerno and Paestum

Salerno, the big city just north of Paestum, is the nearest transportation hub. From Naples or Sorrento, you'll change buses or trains in Salerno to get to Paestum. Salerno's TI has bus, ferry, and train schedules (Mon–Sat 9:00–14:00 & 15:30–19:30, closed Sun, shorter hours off-season, on Piazza Veneto, just outside train station, tel. 089-231-432, toll-free 800-213-289).

Salerno to Paestum by bus: Four companies (CSTP, SCAT, Giuliano, and Lettieri) offer a Salerno–Paestum bus service, all conveniently leaving from the same stop at Piazza Concordia on the waterfront (2–3/hr, 70 min, schedules extremely sparse on Sun). Buy the €3 round trip ticket on the bus, except on CSTP buses (CSTP prefers you buy a ticket at their office, next to TI at Piazza Veneto/train station, but driver will grumpily sell you a ticket on bus if necessary). No clear schedule is posted at the Salerno stop. Simply ask a local or a bus rep at the stop for the next bus to Paestum; otherwise, get a schedule at the TI (more impartial, since they don't represent a particular company and their schedule shows all companies and times). Note that orange city buses use the same stop; ignore these.

When leaving Paestum, catch a northbound bus from either of the intersections that flank the ruins (see map on page 527). Flag down any

Salerno Connections

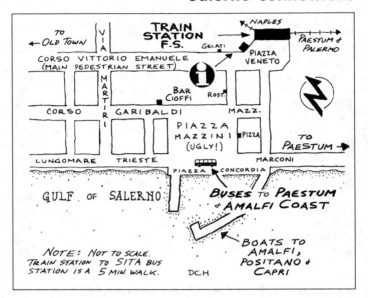

bus, ask "Salerno?", and buy the ticket on board (except for CSTP buses—try to buy ticket at bar closest to stop).

Salerno to Paestum by train: The train from Salerno to Paestum (hrly, 40 min, direction: Paola or Sapri) runs far less frequently than the buses, though it's a quicker ride because it's immune from traffic jams; check schedules at Salerno's TI or train station. Paestum's train station is an eight-minute walk from the ruins (from station, go through old city wall, ruins are straight ahead). If you plan to leave Paestum by train, buy your train ticket at the bar/café near the TI because the station is unstaffed (train schedules at TI). Leaving Paestum, trains bound for Salerno (direction: Battipaglia) usually continue to Naples.

Naples to Salerno by train: 2/hr, 45min trip (some trains stop at Pompeii).

Sorrento to Salerno by bus: The scenic three-hour Amalfi Coast drive (blue SITA bus, 12/day, 3 hrs, easy transfer in Amalfi) drops you in Salerno, on the waterfront at Piazza Concordia, at the same place where the buses to Paestum depart. Salerno's train station and TI are two blocks inland.

If you plan to take a bus from Salerno to Sorrento (or points in between), buy your bus ticket at Salerno's Bar Ciofi (CHOH-fee), across the square from Piazza Concordia (see map above). Ticket vendors change periodically; if Bar Ciofi no longer sells tickets, ask anyone or a clerk at a *tabacchi* shop, "Who sells bus tickets to ____?" by saying, *"Chi vendi i biglietti dell'autobus per* ___*?"* (kee VEHN-dee ee beel-YET-tee del-OW-toh-boos pehr ___).

Salerno by ferry to Amalfi towns: If you take the bus to Salerno, consider returning by boat. Catch the ferry from Salerno's Piazza Concordia (where the SITA bus drops you off) to **Amalfi** (12/day, 35 min, €4) or **Positano** (12/day, 70 min, €6; tickets and info at TravelMar, Piazza Concordia, tel. 089-873-190).

Sorrento to Salerno by train: Ride the Circumvesuviana to Naples Centrale station (hrly, 70 min) and catch the Salerno train (2/hr, 45 min). Or ask about connecting in Pompeii.

Drivers: While the Amalfi Coast is a thrill to drive off-season, summer traffic is miserable. From Sorrento, Paestum is 60 miles and three hours via the coast and a much smoother two hours by autostrada. To reach Paestum from Sorrento via the autostrada, drive toward Naples, catch the autostrada (direction: Salerno), skirt Salerno (direction: Reggio), exit at Eboli, and drive straight through the modern town of Paestum. You'll hit the ruins just about the time you start to worry you missed the turnoff. Along the way, you'll see many signs for "*mozzarella di bufala,*" the cheese made from the milk of water buffalo that graze here. Try it here—it can't be any fresher.

ITALIAN HISTORY

Italy has a lot of history, so let's get started.

Origins

When Rome was founded by farmers and shepherds of the Latin tribe (traditionally in 753 B.C.), it was just one crude settlement among the many "Italic" tribes in the center of the peninsula. To Rome's south was "Magna Grecia" (greater Greece), prosperous Greek-speaking cities founded by Greek colonists. To the north, the sophisticated Etruscans—whose origins and language are still a mystery to historians—built a wealthy trading confederation of twelve cities that dominated Rome.

But Rome's convenient location near the mouth of the Tiber was perfect for a future trading power dealing in salt and wine, and the city soon controlled central Italy. When an Etruscan king raped a Roman (509 B.C.), her husband led a revolt that drove out the monarchy. Power was divided between landowners (patricians) and workers (plebeians, or plebs in Latin) in an arrangement later codified in the bronze-carved Laws of the Twelve Tables (450 B.C.). The Roman Republic was born.

Roman Republic—c. 500 B.C.–A.D. 1

The energetic Romans expanded by trade and conquest through the Italian peninsula. They defeated invading Gauls in the north (390 B.C.) and their Samnite rivals (343–283 B.C.). Both wars caught the Etruscans in the crossfire, weakening that rich civilization, and Rome slowly swallowed up its northern neighbor, militarily and culturally.

Next came "Magna Grecia." Through a series of costly battles ("Pyrrhic victories"), Rome defeated the Greek general Pyrrhus and occupied the south of the peninsula (c. 275 B.C.). Rome now ruled a united federation stretching from Tuscany to the toe, with a standard currency, a system of roads (including the Via Appia), and a standing army of a half million soldiers ready for the next challenge.

When Rome crossed over to Sicily—a possession of Carthage (modern-day Tunisia)—it sparked three Punic Wars for control of the Mediterranean (264–201 B.C. and 146 B.C.; "Punic", from the Latin *Poeni*, means Phoenician, the founders of Carthage). In the Second Punic War (218–201 B.C.), Hannibal of Carthage crossed the sea to Spain with a huge army of men and elephants, then marched 1,200 miles overland, crossing the Alps to boldly penetrate Italy from the rear, almost reaching the gates of Rome before being turned back. Rome prevailed and, in the mismatched Third Punic War, burned Carthage to the ground (146 B.C.).

The Mediterranean's most cultured civilization, Greece, was a pushover for the well-tuned Roman legions (three Macedonian Wars (215–146 B.C.). Rome conquered Greece, but Greek culture dominated the Romans. From hairstyles to statues to temples to the evening's entertainment, Rome was forever "Hellenized," becoming the curators of Greek culture, passing it down to future generations.

Rome was master of the Mediterranean. Booty, cheap grain, and thousands of captured slaves poured in, turning the economy from small-farmers to unemployed city dwellers living off tribute from conquered lands. The Republic had changed.

1st Century B.C.—Civil Wars and the Transition to Empire

With wealth pouring in and traditional roles obsolete, Romans bickered among themselves over their slice of the pie. Wealthy landowners (patricians, the ruling Senate) wrangled with the middle- and working classes (plebeians) who demanded greater say-so in government (the "Social Wars" 90–88 B.C.). When the patrician-backed general Lucius Sulla's troops occupied the city of Rome itself to confirm his election (88 B.C.), it was clear that money and brute force had become more powerful than the traditional rule of law.

In 73 B.C., Spartacus—a Greek-born soldier turned Roman slave and forced to fight as a gladiator—escaped to the slopes of Mount Vesuvius, where he gathered an army of 70,000 slaves against Rome. After two years of fighting, the revolt was crushed, Spartacus died (presumably in battle) and 6,000 rebels were crucified along the Via Appia as a warning.

Amid the chaos of class war and civil war, charismatic generals who provided wealth and security became dictators—men such as Sulla, Crassus, Pompey...and Julius Caesar. Caesar (100–44 B.C.) was a cunning politician, riveting speaker, conqueror of Gaul, author of *The Gallic Wars*, and lover of Cleopatra, Queen of Egypt. In his four-year reign, he reformed and centralized the government around himself, until some feared he would be king. Disgruntled Republicans stabbed Caesar to death on the "Ides of March" (March 15, 44 B.C.).

Roman Empire

HADRIAN'S WALL · CALEDONIA · SCANDIA · HIBERNIA · BRITANNIA · BARBARIANS · RHINE RIVER · DANUBE RIVER · GER-MANIA · GAUL · ITALIA · ILLYRICUM · DACIA · ROMA · THRACE · HISPANIA · MEDI-TERRANNEAN · ASIA · CAPPADOCIA · ARMENIA · MEDIA · MAURITANIA · AFRICA · SIRIA · MESOPOTAMIA · EGYPT

THE ROMAN EMPIRE AT ITS PEAK: PAX ROMANA 100 A.D.

DCH

Julius Caesar died, but the concept of strong, one-man rule lived on. Caesar's adopted son Octavian defeated his rival Marc Antony (another lover of Cleopatra, 31 B.C.) and was proclaimed Emperor Augustus (27 B.C.). Ruling under the humble title of "first citizen," Augustus outwardly followed the traditions of the Republic while in practice acting as a dictator with the backing of Rome's legions and the rubber-stamp approval of the Senate. He established his family to succeed him (making the family name "Caesar" a title), and set the pattern of rule for the next 500 years.

Roman Empire—c. A.D. 1–500

In his forty-year reign, Augustus ended Rome's civil wars and ushered in 200 years of prosperity and relative peace (called the Pax Romana) that even survived the often turbulent and naughty behavior of Augustus' successors, emperors like Caligula and Nero. The empire reached its peak of power in the 2nd century under the emperors Trajan (98–117), Hadrian (117–138), and Marcus Aurelius (161–180).

Rome ruled an empire of 54 million people, stretching from Scotland to Africa, from Spain to the Cradle of Civilization (modern-day Iraq). Conquered peoples were welcomed into the fold of prosperity, linked by roads, common laws, common gods, education, and the Latin language. The city of Rome, with over a million inhabitants, was decorated with Greek-style statues and monumental structures faced with marble...it was the marvel of the known world.

The empire prospered on a (false) economy of booty, slaves, and cheap imports. On the Italian peninsula, traditional small farms were swallowed up by large farming and herding estates. In this "global economy," the Italian peninsula became just one province of many in a worldwide, Latin-speaking empire, ruled by an emperor who was likely born elsewhere.

Decline and Fall

After its peak (c. A.D. 120), the Roman Empire declined for the next three centuries, shrinking in size and wealth, a victim of corruption, disease, an overextended army, and the constant pressure of "barbarian" tribes pecking away at the borders. By the 3rd century, the army had become the real power, hand-picking figurehead emperors to do its bidding—in a 40-year span, 15 emperors were saluted then assassinated by fickle generals.

Trying to stall the disintegration, Emperor Diocletian (284–305) split the empire into two administrative halves under two equal emperors. Constantine (306–337) legalized Christianity (313), and soon, the once-persecuted cult became virtually the state religion, the backbone of Rome's fading hierarchy. Constantine moved the capital of the empire from decaying Rome to the new city of Constantinople (330, present-day Istanbul), turning the city of Rome and the Italian peninsula into minor players in imperial affairs.

By 410, "Rome" had shrunk to the city itself, surrounded by a protective wall. Huns, Vandals, and Visigoths from the north and east poured in to loot and plunder. The city was sacked (410) and the pope had to plead with Attila the Hun for mercy (451). The peninsula's population fell to 6 million, trade and agriculture were disrupted, schools closed, and the infrastructure collapsed. Peasants huddled near powerful lords for protection from bandits, planting the seeds of medieval feudalism.

In 476, the last emperor sold his title for a comfy pension, and Rome fell like a huge column, kicking up dust that would plunge Europe into a thousand years of darkness. For the next thirteen centuries, there would be no "Italy," just a patchwork of rural dukedoms and towns, victimized by foreign powers. Italy lay helpless.

Invasions—A.D. 500–1000

In 500 years, Italy suffered through the following three paragraphs of invasions:

Justinian (r. 527–565)—the emperor of the eastern half of the former Roman Empire —invaded Italy (536), briefly re-uniting East and West, and establishing the Byzantine influence in coastal cities (Venice), with his capital at Ravenna. The Lombard tribe from Germany invaded north Italy (568), occupying the interior for two centuries.

Charlemagne, King of the Franks (a Germanic tribe), allied with the pope in Rome to defeat the Lombards. On Christmas, A.D. 800, Charlemagne knelt in St. Peter's in Rome and was crowned "Holy Roman Emperor," a title meant to resurrect the glory of ancient Rome united with medieval Christianity. When another German king invaded and was crowned with the same title (Otto I, 962), it started a thousand-year tradition of Italians pledging nominal allegiance to a weak, distant German king as their "Holy Roman Emperor."

In the south, Saracens (a Muslim people from Tunisia) took Sicily (827) and made sea-pirate raids on the Italian coast, even damaging Rome (846). Later, they were driven out by Norman (French) warriors (1061), who established two centuries of peace and prosperity, making their Kingdom of Sicily a cultural powerhouse with profitable sea-trade to eastern lands.

Through all of the invasions and chaos, the glory of ancient Rome was preserved in the pomp, knowledge, hierarchy, and wealth of the Christian Church. Monasteries—inspired by the model of Italy's St. Benedict (480–543)—were Italy's centers of religion, commerce, and culture. Strong popes (Leo I, 440–461 and Gregory the Great, 590–604) took on the governing role vacated by the emperors, ruling territories around Rome called (after 1278) the Papal States.

A.D. 1000–1300

Italy survived Y1K, and the economy picked up. Coastal cities—Venice, Genoa, Pisa, Naples, Amalfi—became wealthy through sea-trading. As northern Europeans passed through Italy on their way east on the Crusades (First Crusade 1097–1130), Italian ships carried soldiers and supplies, returning with spices and high-mark-up luxury goods from the Orient. Trade spawned banking, and these cities became budding centers of capitalism, loaning money at interest to Europe's royalty.

In fact, even through the chaos of the so-called "Dark Ages," Italy's cities had remained fairly profitable and independent—an urban phenomenon almost unique in Europe. Cities (*comuni*) were self-governing city-states, not bound by traditional allegiance to local feudal lords, foreign powers, or popes. The medieval prosperity of the cities laid the foundation of the future Renaissance.

The peninsula's two greatest powers—the pope in Rome and the German "Holy Roman Emperor" with holdings in the north— competed for territory and power. In 1077, Pope Gregory VII excommunicated and humbled Emperor Henry IV, confirming the pope's right to appoint bishops, and forcing Henry to stand barefoot in the Alpine snow at Canossa in repentence.

When Emperor Frederick I, Barbarossa (r. 1152–1190) crossed

the Alps from Germany to grab land (1154), the pope organized a united "Lombard League" of Italian states to oppose him. For the next century, supporters of the popes, called Guelfs (centered in urban areas), squared off against supporters of the German emperors (Ghibellines, popular with the rural nobility), dividing the populace and causing civil wars, riots, and disputes in every political arena. Only when the last German emperor died without an heir (1268) and their armies retreated across the Alps did the confusing strife between Guelfs and Ghibellines die down.

The Unlucky 1300s

No sooner had the emperors returned to Germany than the popes—enticed by Europe's fast-rising power, the French monarchy—moved from Rome to Avignon, France (1309–1377, with a Great Schism when two popes reigned, one in Avignon and the other in Rome, until 1417). In Italy, central authority broke down, exacerbated by an outbreak of bubonic plague (Black Death, 1347–1348) that killed a third of Italy.

In the power vacuum, new powers emerged—Venice, Florence, Milan, and Naples, under the protection and leadership of local noble families (*signoria*) such as the Scaligeri in Verona, and the Medici in Florence. Florence, in particular, thrived in the wool and dyeing trade, which led to international banking, with branches in all Europe's capitals. A positive side-effect of the terrible Black Death was that the smaller population got a bigger share of the land, jobs, and infrastructure. Italy bounced back and prepared to enter its most glorious era since antiquity.

The Renaissance—1400s

The Renaissance (Rinascimento)—the "rebirth" of ancient Greek and Roman art styles, knowledge, and humanism—began in Italy (c. 1400), and spread throughout Europe over the next two centuries. Many of Europe's most famous painters, sculptors, and thinkers—Michelangelo, Leonardo, Raphael, etc.—were Italian.

It was a cultural boom that changed people's thinking about every aspect of life. In politics, it meant democracy. In religion, it meant a move away from Church dominance and toward the assertion of man (humanism) and a more personal faith. Science and secular learning were revived after centuries of superstition and ignorance. In architecture, it was a return to the balanced columns and domes of Greece and Rome. In painting, the Renaissance meant 3-D realism.

Italians dotted their cities with public-financed art—Greek gods, Roman-style domed buildings. They preached Greek-style democracy, and explored the natural world.

The cultural boom was financed by Italian cities' energetic trade (acting as middleman between Europe and the Orient) and banking industry (loaning money to Europe's aristocracy). Thanks to a four-decade lull in fighting between Italy's oft-warring city-states (Peace of Lodi, 1454), the peninsula once again became the cultural center of Europe.

End of the Renaissance, France and Spain Invade—1500s

France, Spain, England, Holland, Portugal—these nation-states under strong central rule began to overtake decentralized Italy. Portugal discovered a new trade route around Africa to Asia (c. 1490s), breaking Italy's monopoly in trade with the East. Spain exploited the New World market, and England, Holland, and France plied the Atlantic and Baltic. Italy's once-great maritime cities now traded in an economic backwater, just as Italy's bankers (such as the Medici in Florence) were going bankrupt. While the Italian Renaissance was all the rage throughout Europe, it declined in its birthplace. Italy—culturally sophisticated but weak and decentralized—was ripe for the picking by Europe's rising powers.

France and Spain invaded (1494 and 1495)—initially invited by Italian lords to attack their rivals—and began claiming territory for their noble families. After Martin Luther challenged the pope with a rising Protestant movement (1517), Italy became a battleground in religious conflicts. In the chaos, the city of Rome was brutally sacked by foreign mercenary warriors (1527).

Spain and France divvied Italy up (the Peace of Cateau-Cambresis, 1559), with Spain getting the vast majority. Only the Papal States and Venice remained independent.

For the next two centuries, most of Italy's states were ruled by Spanish noble families, and Italy ceased to be a major player in Europe, politically or economically.

Foreign Rule—1600–1800

Spain was Europe's most Catholic and conservative country. They brought peace and stability to Italy, but Italian intellectual life was often cropped short by the Counter Reformation. Galileo, for example, was forced by the Inquisition to renounce his belief that the earth orbited the sun (1633). But Italy did export Baroque art (Gian Lorenzo Bernini) and the budding new medium of opera.

In the 1700s, Italy's scattered states became a prize awarded to the winners of Europe's dynastic wars. The War of the Spanish Succession (1713)—a war in which Italy did not participate—turned much of northern Italy over to Austria's ruling family, the Hapsburgs (who now wore the crown of "Holy Roman Emperor"). Austria's rulers, following the model of "enlightened despots" elsewhere, promoted gradual liberal reforms and brought some economic progress—silk production, wool, flax, boats, metal-working, Carrara marble.

In the south, Spain's Bourbon family ruled the Kingdom of Naples, making it one of Europe's most culturally sophisticated but economically backward areas, preserving a medieval, feudal caste system.

A minor war (the War of Austrian Succession, 1720) had major consequences for Italy's future. The peace treaty created a new state at the foot of the Alps, called the Kingdom of Sardinia (a.k.a. the Kingdom of Piedmont or Savoy). Ruled by the Savoy family from their capital in Turin, this was the only major state on the peninsula actually ruled by Italians.

Italy Unites (the Risorgimento)—1800s

In the wake of the French Revolution, Napoleon Bonaparte swept through Italy to outflank Austria (1796), and his Italian campaign changed everything. He overthrew conservative Spanish dukes, created republics where there were feudal states, confiscated Church lands, and united Italy's scattered states under central rule.

When Napoleon was crowned "King of Italy" (1805), he planted a seed: What if Italy could unite like Europe's other modern nations? Napoleon himself proved a dictator, and after his defeat (1815), Italy's old ruling order (namely, Austria and Spain) was restored. But the idea of an Italy free of foreign rule and united under a single, Italian government would not die.

The 50-year movement to unite Italy was called the Risorgimento, a word that means "rebirth" (it's a synonym for Renaissance), meaning a revival of Italy's glory. It started as a revolutionary, liberal movement punishable by death. Members of a secret society called the Carbonari exchanged secret handshakes, printed flyers, planted bombs, and assassinated conservative rulers to spark small revolutions (1820–1821, 1831) that were easily and brutally slapped down.

One of the Carbonari, a professional revolutionary named Giuseppe Mazzini, was exiled to France where he founded the "Young Italy" movement. Under the slogan "God and the People" he led a takeover of the city of Rome during the Europe-wide revolutions of 1848. It ultimately failed and the old order returned, but the cause grew.

Gradually, Italians of all stripes warmed to the idea of unification. Whether it was a united dictatorship, a united papal state, a united kingdom, or a united democracy, most Italians could agree that it was time for Spain, Austria, and France to leave. In Italy's opera houses, people watched stories set in ancient Egypt or Babylon, but they knew that the rousing chorus numbers that rang the curtain down were coded messages expressing Italians' desire to rise again.

In 1859, the prime minister of the Italian-ruled Kingdom of Sardinia, Camillo Cavour, cleverly engineered France and Austria into a war fought on Italian soil. The French and Italians defeated Austria, rallying Italian-speakers everywhere, and scaring nobles into fleeing the country. Austria was forced to hand over its possessions in north Italy to the Kingdom of Sardinia. The following year, a plebescite (vote) was held, and several other central Italian states (including some of the pope's) rejected their feudal lords and chose to join the Kingdom of Sardinia. The Kingdom of Sardinia was now a united, Italian-run state comprising nearly the whole northern third of the peninsula.

After victory in the north, Italy's most renowned Carbonari general, Giuseppe Garibaldi (1807–1882), steamed south, landing in Sicily (April 1860) with a Thousand *(I Mille)* of his best soldiers. They bivouacked in the mountains, padding their army with 3,000 locals, then crossed to Italy's toe and marched on Naples. The old order simply collapsed. In two short months, Garibaldi achieved a seemingly impossible victory against a far superior army. Italy went ape.

Garibaldi sent a one-word telegram to the King of Sardinia: "*Obbedisco*" (I obey). King Victor Emmanuel II, the man around whom the Risorgimento movement rallied, headed south and marched triumphantly through the streets of Naples, annexing that kingdom to his own. (Garibaldi marched at the king's right hand, then quietly retired from public life without any payment for his services.) In 1861, an assembly of deputies from throughout Italy met in Turin and crowned Victor Emmanuel "King of Italy."

But the pope in Rome held out, protected by French troops. When France was defeated in a war with Prussia, the city finally fell easily to the unification forces, and on September 20, 1870, the Risorgimento was complete.

The Risorgimento was the work of four men: Garibaldi (the sword), Mazzini (the spark), Cavour (the diplomat), and Victor Emmanuel (the rallying point). Today, street signs throughout Italy honor them.

Mussolini and War—1900–1950

Italy—now an actual nation-state, not just a language—entered the twentieth century with a progressive government (a constitutional monarchy), a collection of colonies (Eritrea, Somalia, and Libya), and a flourishing northern half of the country. However, the south (the Mezzogiorno) remained feudal in its mentality but its feudal structure. (Rich, industrial north vs. poor, rural south persists today.) At the turn of the century, millions of (mostly) poor peasants emigrated to the Americas.

During World War I, 650,000 Italians died (1915–1918). Italy was on the winning Allied side, gaining possession of the alpine regions. In the post-War cynicism and anarchy, many radical political parties rose up—communist, socialist, popular, and fascist. Benito Mussolini (1883–1945), a popular writer for socialist and labor-union newspapers, led the Fascists. ("Fascism" comes from Latin *fasci*, the bundles of rods that symbolized unity in ancient Rome. Fascists "bundled" together discontents from the right and left.)

THE MARCH ON ROME

In October 1922, Benito Mussolini, head of the newly-formed Fascist Party boldly proposed a coup d'etat, saying: "Either the government will be given to us, or we will take it by marching on Rome." Throughout Italy, black-shirted fascists occupied government buildings in their hometowns. Others grabbed guns, farming hoes, and kitchen knives and set off to converge on the outskirts of Rome. (Estimates of the size of the fascist band range from 300 to the 300,000 of fascist legend.) Mussolini sent the government an ultimatum to surrender. Though the fascists were easily outmanned and outgunned by government forces, the show of force intimidated the king into avoiding a nasty confrontation. He invited Mussolini to Rome. Mussolini arrived the next day (by first-class train), was made prime minister, then marched his black-shirted troops triumphantly through the streets of Rome.

In 1921, the Fascist Party (Partito Nazionale Fascista) won 32 of 529 seats (6 percent) in the parliament. But amid the nation's anarchy, six percent combined with organized violence by black-shirted Fascist gangs meant something. In 1922, Mussolini called for fascists to March on Rome and seize the government (see sidebar). Mussolini ruled for the next two decades (23 years).

In 1924, the fascists gained a majority in parliament and by 1926 they could lawfully ban all opposition parties, establishing Mussolini as a dictator. Mussolini solidified his reign among Catholics by striking an agreement with the pope (Concordato, 1929), giving Vatican City to the pope while Mussolini ruled Italy, with the implied blessing of the Catholic Church.

Mussolini responded to the great worldwide Depression (1930s) with big public works projects and government investment in industry. His corporate state controlled the nation's capital, resources, and labor pool to use for the common good. Italy's expanded army invaded and took Ethiopia as a colony (1935) and supported the fascist forces of Franco in the Spanish Civil War (1936).

Mussolini—a kinder, gentler Hitler—allied his country with Hitler's Nazi regime in Germany. Their Pact of Steel (1939) drew an unprepared Italy into World War II on Germany's side (1940). Italy's lame army was never a factor in the war, and when Allied forces landed in Sicily (1943), Italians welcomed them as liberators. They toppled Mussolini's government, but Nazi Germany sent troops to continue the war and rescue Mussolini, installing him as ruler of the north. The war raged on Italian soil as the Allies inched their way north against German resistance. Italians were reduced to dire poverty. In the last days of the war (April, 1945) Mussolini was captured by the Italian resistance. They shot him and his girlfriend and hung their bodies upside down in a public square in Milan.

Post-War Italy

Under agreements with the War's winning side, Italy's constitutional monarchy ended and a republic began (1946). Italy was physically ruined and extremely poor. In the 1950s and 60s, the nation rebuilt (the "economic miracle") with Marshall Plan aid from America. Many Italian men moved to northern Europe to find work, many others left the farm and flocked to cities. Italy regained its standing among nations, joining the United Nations, NATO, and, eventually, the European Union.

However, the government remained weak, changing on average once a year, shifting from right to left to centrist coalitions (59 governments in 56 years). All Italians acknowledged that the real power lay in the hands of backroom politicians and organized crime—a phenomenon called *Tangentopoli*, or "Bribe City."

Italian society changed greatly in the 1960s and 70s, spurred by the liberal reforms of the Catholic Church at the Vatican II conference (1962–1965). The once-conservative Catholic country legalized divorce and contraception, and the birth rate plummeted. In the 1970s, the economy slowed thanks to inflation, strikes, and the worldwide energy crisis. Italy suffered a wave of violence from left- and right-wing domestic terrorists and organized crime, punctuated with the assassination of the prime minister Aldo Moro (1978).

A series of coalition governments in the 1980s brought some agreement between warring political parties, stabilizing the economy. In the early 1990s, the judiciary launched a campaign to rid politics of corruption and Mafia ties. Though still ongoing, the investigation sent a message that Italy would no longer tolerate evils that were considered necessary just a generation earlier. In 2001, billionaire Silvio Berlusconi, the owner of many of Italy's media outlets, financed his own political party (Forza Italia), won 30 percent of the popular vote, and became prime minister, heading a center-right coalition.

As you travel through Italy today, you'll encounter a thriving country with a rich history and a per capita income rivaling its neighbors to the north. Italy is enthusiastically part of Europe...yet it's as wonderfully Italian as ever.

APPENDIX

Let's Talk Telephones

This is a primer on telephoning in Europe. For specifics on Italy, see "Telephones" in the Introduction.

Making Calls within a European Country: What you dial depends on the phone system of the country you're in. About half of all European countries have phone systems that use area codes; the other half uses a direct-dial system without area codes.

If you're calling within a country that uses a direct-dial system (Italy, Belgium, the Czech Republic, Denmark, France, Norway, Portugal, Spain, and Switzerland), you dial the same number whether you're calling across the street or across the country.

In countries that use area codes (such as Austria, Britain, Finland, Germany, Ireland, the Netherlands, and Sweden), you dial the local number when calling within a city, and you add the area code if calling long-distance within the country. Example: The phone number of a hotel in Munich is 089-264-349. To call it in Munich, dial 264-349; to call it from Frankfurt, dial 089-264-349.

Making International Calls: You always start with the international access code (011 if you're calling from America or Canada, 00 from Europe), then dial the country code of the country you're calling (see list of country codes, below).

What you dial next depends on the particular phone system of the country you're calling. If the country uses area codes, you drop the initial zero of the area code, then dial the rest of the area code and the local number. Example: To call the Munich hotel (mentioned above) from Spain, dial 00, 49 (Germany's country code), then 89-264-349.

Countries that use direct-dial systems (no area codes) differ in how they're accessed internationally by phone. For instance, if you're making an international call to Italy, the Czech Republic, Denmark, Norway,

European Calling Chart

Just smile and dial, using this key:
AC = Area Code, LN = Local Number.

European Country	Calling long distance within ...	Calling from the U.S.A./ Canada to ...	Calling from a European country to ...
Austria	AC + LN	011 + 43 + AC (without the initial zero) + LN	00 + 43 + AC (without the initial zero) + LN
Belgium	LN	011 + 32 + LN (without initial zero)	00 + 32 + LN (without initial zero)
Britain	AC + LN	011 + 44 + AC (without initial zero) + LN	00 + 44 + AC (without initial zero) + LN
Czech Republic	LN	011 + 420 + LN	00 + 420 + LN
Denmark	LN	011 + 45 + LN	00 + 45 + LN
Estonia	LN	011 + 372 + LN	00 + 372 + LN
Finland	AC + LN	011 + 358 + AC (without initial zero) + LN	00 + 358 + AC (without initial zero) + LN
France	LN	011 + 33 + LN (without initial zero)	00 + 33 + LN (without initial zero)
Germany	AC + LN	011 + 49 + AC (without initial zero) + LN	00 + 49 + AC (without initial zero) + LN
Gibraltar	LN	011 + 350 + LN	00 + 350 + LN From Spain: 9567 + LN
Greece	LN	011 + 30 + LN	00 + 30 + LN

European Country	Calling long distance within...	Calling from the U.S.A./ Canada to...	Calling from a European country to...
Ireland	AC + LN	011 + 353 + AC (without initial zero) + LN	00 + 353 + AC (without initial zero) + LN
Italy	LN	011 + 39 + LN	00 + 39 + LN
Morocco	LN	011 + 212 + LN (without initial zero)	00 + 212 + LN (without initial zero)
Netherlands	AC + LN	011 + 31 + AC (without initial zero) + LN	00 + 31 + AC (without initial zero) + LN
Norway	LN	011 + 47 + LN	00 + 47 + LN
Portugal	LN	011 + 351 + LN	00 + 351 + LN
Spain	LN	011 + 34 + LN	00 + 34 + LN
Sweden	AC + LN	011 + 46 + AC (without initial zero) + LN	00 + 46 + AC (without initial zero) + LN
Switzerland	LN	011 + 41 + LN (without initial zero)	00 + 41 + LN (without initial zero)
Turkey	AC (if no initial zero is included, add one) + LN	011 + 90 + AC (without initial zero) + LN	00 + 90 + AC (without initial zero) + LN

- The instructions above apply whether you're calling a fixed phone or mobile phone.

- The international access codes (the first numbers you dial when making an international call) are 011 if you're calling from the U.S.A./Canada, or 00 if you're calling from anywhere in Europe.

- To call the U.S.A. or Canada from Europe, dial 00, then 1 (the country code for the U.S.A. and Canada), then the area code and number. In short, 00 + 1 + AC + LN = Hi, Mom!

Portugal, or Spain, you simply dial the international access code, country code, and the phone number in full. But if you're calling Belgium,
France, or Switzerland, you drop the initial zero of the phone number.
Example: The phone number of a Paris hotel is 01 47 05 49 15. To call
it from Rome, dial 00, 33 (France's country code), then 1 47 05 49 15
(the phone number without the initial zero).

Calling America or Canada from Europe: Dial the international
access code (00 for Europe), then dial 1, the area code, and local phone
number. Example: My number here at Europe Through the Back Door
(in Edmonds, WA) is 425/771-8303. To call me from Europe, dial 00-
1-425-771-8303.

International Access Codes
When dialing direct, first dial the international access code. For the
United States and Canada, it's 011. For Europe, it's 00.

Country Codes
After you've dialed the international access code, dial the code of the
country you're calling.

Austria—43	Ireland—353
Belgium—32	Italy—39
Britain—44	Morocco—212
Canada—1	Netherlands—31
Croatia—385	Norway—47
Czech Rep—420	Poland—48
Denmark—45	Portugal—351
Estonia—372	Slovenia—386
Finland—358	Spain—34
France—33	Sweden—46
Germany—49	Switzerland—41
Gibraltar—350	Turkey—90
Greece—30	U.S.A.—1
Hungary—36	

Useful Italian Phone Numbers
Emergency (English-speaking police help): 113
Emergency (military police): 112
Road Service: 116
Directory Assistance (for €0.50, an Italian-speaking robot gives the
number twice, very clearly): 12
Telephone help (in English; free directory assistance): 170

U.S. Embassies
In Rome: American Embassy at Via Veneto 119, tel. 06-46741;

Canadian Embassy at Via Zara 30, tel. 06-445-981.
In Milan: U.S. Consulate at Via Principe Amedeo 2, tel. 02-290-351.

Public Holidays and Festivals

Italy (including most major sights) closes down on these national holidays: January 1, January 6 (Epiphany), Easter Sunday and Monday (April 11 and 12 in 2004), April 25 (Liberation Day), May 1 (Labor Day), May 20 (Ascension Day), June 2 (Republic Day), August 15 (Assumption of Mary), November 1 (All Saints' Day), December 8 (Immaculate Conception of Mary), and December 25 and 26.

Each town has a local festival honoring its patron saint. For more information on Italian festivals, check out www.italiantourism.com, www.hostetler.net, and www.whatsonwhen.com. Here's a partial list of events:

January	Epiphany Fair (religious festival)—Jan 6, Rome
February	Carnevale (Mardi Gras, www.carnivalofvenice.com)— Feb 14–24 in 2004, Venice
April	Vinitaly (wine festival)—early April, Verona; Holy Week and Good Friday (processions), All Italy; Scoppio del Carro (fireworks)—Easter, Florence
May	Florence May Music Festival—early May– mid-June, Florence
June	Battle of the Bridge (medieval festival)—last Sunday in June, Pisa
June	Regatta of the Great Maritime Republics (rowing competition, parade)—first week of June, Geona in 2004; Calcio Fiorentino (costumed soccer game, fireworks)—late June, Florence
July	Feast of the Redeemer (parade, fireworks)—third weekend in July, Venice; Festa de'Noantri neighborhood fair)—mid- to late July, Rome; Il Palio (horse race)—July 2, Siena; Verona Arena Outdoor Opera, Verona
August	Il Palio (horse race)—Aug 16, Siena; Siena Music Week—late Aug, Siena
September	Historical Regatta (boat parade)—first weekend in September, Venice; Chestnut Festivals (festival, chestnut roasts), Most towns, mainly north of Rome; Festival of San Genarro (religious festival)— Sept 19, Naples
December	Christmas Market, Rome, Piazza Navona

2004

JANUARY
S	M	T	W	T	F	S
				1	2	3
4	5	6	7	8	9	10
11	12	13	14	15	16	17
18	19	20	21	22	23	24
25	26	27	28	29	30	31

FEBRUARY
S	M	T	W	T	F	S
1	2	3	4	5	6	7
8	9	10	11	12	13	14
15	16	17	18	19	20	21
22	23	24	25	26	27	28
29						

MARCH
S	M	T	W	T	F	S
	1	2	3	4	5	6
7	8	9	10	11	12	13
14	15	16	17	18	19	20
21	22	23	24	25	26	27
28	29	30	31			

APRIL
S	M	T	W	T	F	S
				1	2	3
4	5	6	7	8	9	10
11	12	13	14	15	16	17
18	19	20	21	22	23	24
25	26	27	28	29	30	

MAY
S	M	T	W	T	F	S
						1
2	3	4	5	6	7	8
9	10	11	12	13	14	15
16	17	18	19	20	21	22
23/30	24/31	25	26	27	28	29

JUNE
S	M	T	W	T	F	S
		1	2	3	4	5
6	7	8	9	10	11	12
13	14	15	16	17	18	19
20	21	22	23	24	25	26
27	28	29	30			

JULY
S	M	T	W	T	F	S
				1	2	3
4	5	6	7	8	9	10
11	12	13	14	15	16	17
18	19	20	21	22	23	24
25	26	27	28	29	30	31

AUGUST
S	M	T	W	T	F	S
1	2	3	4	5	6	7
8	9	10	11	12	13	14
15	16	17	18	19	20	21
22	23	24	25	26	27	28
29	30	31				

SEPTEMBER
S	M	T	W	T	F	S
			1	2	3	4
5	6	7	8	9	10	11
12	13	14	15	16	17	18
19	20	21	22	23	24	25
26	27	28	29	30		

OCTOBER
S	M	T	W	T	F	S
					1	2
3	4	5	6	7	8	9
10	11	12	13	14	15	16
17	18	19	20	21	22	23
24/31	25	26	27	28	29	30

NOVEMBER
S	M	T	W	T	F	S
	1	2	3	4	5	6
7	8	9	10	11	12	13
14	15	16	17	18	19	20
21	22	23	24	25	26	27
28	29	30				

DECEMBER
S	M	T	W	T	F	S
		1	2	3	4	
5	6	7	8	9	10	11
12	13	14	15	16	17	18
19	20	21	22	23	24	25
26	27	28	29	30	31	

Numbers and Stumblers

• Europeans write a few of their numbers differently than we do. 1 = 1, 4 = 4, 7 = 7. Learn the difference or miss your train.

• In Europe, dates appear as day/month/year, so Christmas is 25/12/04.

• Commas are decimal points and decimals commas. A dollar and a half is 1,50, and there are 5.280 feet in a mile.

• When pointing, use your whole hand, palm down.

• When counting with fingers, start with your thumb. If you hold up your first finger to request one item, you'll probably get two.

• What Americans call the second floor of a building is the first floor in Europe.

• Europeans keep the left "lane" open for passing on escalators and moving sidewalks. Keep to the right.

Metric Conversion (approximate)

1 inch = 25 millimeters
32 degrees F = 0 degrees C
1 foot = 0.3 meter
82 degrees F = about 28 degrees C
1 yard = 0.9 meter
1 ounce = 28 grams
1 mile = 1.6 kilometers

1 kilogram = 2.2 pounds
1 centimeter = 0.4 inch
1 quart = 0.95 liter
1 meter = 39.4 inches
1 square yard = 0.8 square meter
1 kilometer = .62 mile
1 acre = 0.4 hectare

Climate Chart

First line, average daily low; second line, average daily high; third line, days of no rain.

J	F	M	A	M	J	J	A	S	O	N	D

Rome

40°	42°	45°	50°	56°	63°	67°	67°	62°	55°	49°	44°
52°	55°	59°	66°	74°	82°	87°	86°	79°	71°	61°	55°
13	19	23	24	26	26	30	29	25	23	19	21

Milan

32°	35°	43°	49°	57°	63°	67°	66°	61°	52°	43°	35°
40°	46°	56°	65°	74°	80°	84°	82°	75°	63°	51°	43°
25	21	24	22	23	21	25	24	25	23	20	24

Converting Temperatures: Fahrenheit and Celsius

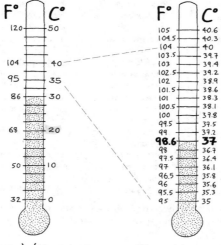

FOR WEATHER   FOR HEALTH

Basic Italian Survival Phrases

Good day.	**Buon giorno.**	bwohn JOR-noh
Do you speak English?	**Parla inglese?**	PAR-lah een-GLAY-zay
Yes. / No.	**Sì. / No.**	see / noh
I (don't) understand.	**(Non) capito.**	(nohn) kah-PEE-toh
Please.	**Per favore.**	pehr fah-VOH-ray
Thank you.	**Grazie.**	GRAHT-seeay
I'm sorry.	**Mi dispiace.**	mee dee-speeAH-chay
Excuse me.	**Mi scusi.**	mee SKOO-zee
(No) problem.	**(Non) c'è un problema.**	(nohn) cheh oon proh-BLAY-mah
Good.	**Va bene.**	vah BEHN-ay
Goodbye.	**Arrivederci.**	ah-ree-vay-DEHR-chee
one / two	**uno / due**	OO-noh / DOO-ay
three / four	**tre / quattro**	tray / KWAH-troh
five / six	**cinque / sei**	CHHENG-kway / SEHee
seven / eight	**sette / otto**	SEHT-tay / OT-toh
nine / ten	**nove / dieci**	NOV-ay / deeAY-chee
How much is it?	**Quanto costa?**	KWAHN-toh KOS-tah
Write it?	**Me lo scrive?**	may loh SKREE-vay
Is it free?	**È gratis?**	eh GRAH-tees
Included?	**È incluso?**	eh een-KLOO-zoh
Where can I buy / find...?	**Dove posso comprare /trovare...?**	DOH-vay POS-soh kohm-PRAH-ray / troh-VAH-ray
I'd like / We'd like...	**Vorrei / Vorremo...**	vor-REHee /vor-RAY-moh
...a room.	**...una camera.**	OO-nah KAH-meh-rah
...the bill.	**...il conto.**	eel KOHN-toh
...a ticket to ___.	**...un biglietto per___.**	oon beel-YEHT-toh pehr
Is it possible?	**È possibile?**	eh poh-SEE-bee-lay
Where is...?	**Dov'è...?**	DOH-veh
...the train station	**...la stazione**	lah staht-seeOH-nay
...the bus station	**...la stazione degli autobus**	lah staht-seeOH-nay DAYL-yee OW-toh-boos
...tourist information	**...informazioni per turisti**	een-for-maht-seeOH-nee pehr too-REE-stee
...the toilet	**...la toilette**	lah twah-LEHT-tay
men	**uomini, signori**	WOH-mee-nee, seen-YOH-ree
women	**donne, signore**	DON-nay, seen-YOH-ray
left / right	**sinistra / destra**	see-NEE-strah / DEHS-trah
straight	**sempre diritto**	SEHM-pray dee-REE-toh
When do you open / close?	**A che ora aprite / chiudete?**	ah kay oh-rah ah-PREE-tay / keeoo-DAY-tay
At what time?	**A che ora?**	ah kay OH-rah
Just a moment.	**Un momento.**	oon moh-MAYN-toh
now / soon / later	**adesso / presto / tardi**	ah-DEHS-soh / PREHS-toh TAR-dee
today / tomorrow	**oggi / domani**	OH-jee / doh-MAH-nee

For more user-friendly Italian phrases, check out *Rick Steves' Italian Phrase Book and Dictionary* or *Rick Steves' French, Italian & German Phrase Book and Dictionary*.

Faxing Your Hotel Reservation

Use this handy form for your fax or find it online at
www.ricksteves.com/reservation. Photocopy and fax away.

One-Page Fax

To: _____ @ _____
             hotel   fax

From: _____ @ _____
             name   fax

Today's date: ____ / ____ / ____
                  day   month   year

Dear Hotel _____,

Please make this reservation for me:

Name: _____

Total # of people: _____   # of rooms: _____   # of nights: _____

Arriving: ____ / ____ / ____   My time of arrival (24-hr clock): _____
               day   month   year   (I will telephone if I will be late)

Departing: ____ / ____ / ____
                 day   month   year

Room(s): Single___ Double___ Twin___ Triple___ Quad___

With: Toilet___ Shower___ Bath___ Sink only___

Special needs: View___ Quiet___ Cheapest___ Ground Floor___

Credit card: Visa___ MasterCard___ American Express___

Card #: _____

Expiration date:_____

Name on card: _____

You may charge me for the first night as a deposit. Please fax, e-mail, or mail
me confirmation of my reservation, along with the type of room
reserved, the price, and whether the price includes breakfast. Please also
inform me of your cancellation policy. Thank you.

_____
Signature

_____
Name

_____
Address

_____
City   State   Zip Code   Country

_____
E-mail Address

Road Scholar Feedback for ITALY 2004

We're all in the same travelers' school of hard knocks. Your feedback helps us improve this guidebook for future travelers. Please fill this out (or use the online version at www.ricksteves.com/feedback), attach more info or any tips/favorite discoveries if you like, and send it to us. As thanks for your help, we'll send you our quarterly travel newsletter free for one year. Thanks! **Rick**

Of the recommended accommodations/restaurants used, which was:

Best _____

     Why? _____

Worst _____

     Why? _____

Of the sights/experiences/destinations recommended by this book, which was:

Most overrated _____

     Why? _____

Most underrated _____

     Why? _____

Best ways to improve this book:

_____

_____

I'd like a free newsletter subscription:

_____ Yes   _____ No   _____ Already on list

_____
Name

_____
Address

_____
City, State, Zip

_____
E-mail Address

Please send to: ETBD, Box 2009, Edmonds, WA 98020

INDEX

Accademia (Florence): 260, 264, 266; reservations, 258

Accademia (Venice): 55, 56, 62, 63

Accademia Bridge (Venice): 55, 63, 78

Accommodations: See Sleeping; and specific destinations

Agritourism: overview of, 28–29, 352–353. See also specific destinations

Airfares: 2–3

Airports: Florence, 258, 291–292; Milan, 165, 191–192; Rome, 401, 480; sleeping near, 27–28; Venice, 44

Alpe di Siusi (Seiser Alm): 137, 140–143; map, 141

Altar of Peace (Rome): 427, 455

Amalfi Coast: 509–531; map, 510; planning tips, 482–483

Amalfi Town: 515

American Bookstore (Rome): 403

American Catholic Church (Rome): 424, 435

American Express: 5, 25; Florence, 259, 262; Milan, 166; Rome, 403; Venice, 46–47

Amerigo Vespucci Airport: 291

Amphitheater (Arena): Assisi, 335, 337; Lucca, 308; Pompeii, 524; Verona, 114. See also Colosseum

Anacapri: 516, 517–518

Anthony, Saint: 96, 98

Apartments rentals: 28

Appian Way (Rome): 442–444

Ara Pacis (Rome): 427, 455

Arch of Constantine (Rome): 409, 415

Arch of Septimius Severus (Rome): 452

Arch of Titus (Rome): 448

Arco dei Gavi (Verona): 119

Art: Venice Biennale: 57, 69. See also Renaissance; and specific artists

Art museums: general tips, 10–11. See also specific art museums

Asciano: 395–396

Assisi: 333–351; eating, 349–350; map, 336; shopping, 338–339; sights, 335, 337–346; sleeping, 346–349; tourist information, 334; transportation, 334–335, 350–351

ATM machines: 5

Atrani: 515–516

Augustus: 427, 449, 450, 453, 455, 516, 534

Back Door travel philosophy: 37

Bagatti Valsecchi Museum (Milan): 169, 178–179

Bagnoregio: 352, 387–392

Baia delle Favole: 240, 241

Bandini Museum (Fiesole): 293

Banks: 5, 7. See also Money

Baptistery: Florence, 261, 267; Milan, 172; Pisa, 296, 301–302; Siena, 316, 322

Bargello (Florence): 260, 271–272

Baschi: sleeping, 384–385

Basilica Aemilia (Rome): 450–451

Basilica of Constantine (Rome): 448

Basilica Palladiana (Vicenza): 108–109

Basilicas: See Churches and cathedrals

Baths of Caracalla (Rome): 439–441
Baths of Diocletian (Rome): 409, 422–424
Beaches: Atrani, 515; Bellagio, 152; Cinque Terre, 206, 208, 220, 224, 226, 230; Levanto, 236, 237–238; Portofino, 247; Positano, 511, 512; Rimini, 127; Santa Margherita, 246; Sestri Levante, 240, 241; Sorrento, 500; Stresa, 194; Varenna, 149, 150; Venice, 57, 66
Bellagio: 152–153; eating, 160; map, 153; sleeping, 157–158
Bellini family: 63, 64–65, 108, 178
Bell Towers: See Campaniles
Bernini, Gian Lorenzo: 321, 422, 424, 425, 428, 437, 455, 457, 459
Bevagna: 393–394
Biking: Alpe di Siusi, 142; Bellagio, 152; Lucca, 307–308; Mount Mottarone, 198; Ravenna, 123; Sorrento, 499; Verona, 114
Blue Grotto (Capri): 518
Boat travel: Amalfi Coast, 511, 531; Cinque Terre, 203, 205, 230; Lake Como, 146–147, 149, 152–153; Lake Maggiore, 195–196, 198; Portofino, 248; Positano, 512; Rome, 406; Salerno, 531; Sorrento, 507–508. See also Gondolas; Regattas; Vaporetto
Boboli Gardens (Florence): 260, 274
Bolzano (Bozen): 131–137; map, 133
Borghese Gallery (Rome): 408, 425–427
Borromeo Islands: 192–194, 196–198; map, 193
Botticelli, Sandro: 178, 269–270
Brancacci Chapel (Florence): 261, 274–275
Branca Tower (Milan): 168–169, 179
Brera Art Gallery (Milan): 168, 178
Bridge of Sighs (Venice): 56, 62
Brunelleschi, Filippo: 266–267, 273, 274, 275, 291, 420
Brunello di Montalcino: 361, 362, 363
Budgeting: 2–3

Burano: 66–69
Business hours: 3–4, 5
Bus travel: Amalfi Coast, 509–510; Assisi, 334, 350–351; Central Italy hill towns, 353–354; Florence, 291; Rome, 401, 404–406; Siena, 314–315, 331–332; Venice, 44; Verona, 113; Vicenza, 106

Cable cars: Alpe di Siusi, 140, 142–143; Mount Mottarone, 198; Oberbozen, 132, 134
Cadenabbia: 154
Ca' d'Oro (Venice): 53–54
Caffè Florian (Venice): 71
Caffè Pedrocchi (Padua): 99
Caligula: 451, 534
Campaniles: Florence, 261, 267; Venice, 56, 63
Campo de' Fiori (Rome): 455–457; eating, 471–473
Campo dei Miracoli (Pisa): 296, 299–303
Camposanto Cemetery (Pisa): 302
Canals of Venice: gondolas, 52–53, 68, 70; Grand Canal, 51–55, 57; vaporetto, 43, 48–49, 66
Canazei: 144
Capitol Hill (Rome): 408, 417–419, 455
Capitol Hill Museum (Rome): 408, 418; map, 419
Cappuccin Crypt (Rome): 409, 427
Capri: 482, 516–519; map, 517
Caravaggio: 178, 269–270, 418, 421, 422, 425, 436, 455
Ca' Rezzonico (Venice): 55, 56, 64
Carnevale (Venice): 68–69
Carrara: 236, 252
Car rentals: 3, 20
Car travel: 15, 21–23; Amalfi Coast, 531; Assisi, 334–335; best three-week trip, 6, 7; Central Italy hill towns, 354–355; Cinque Terre, 234–235; Crete Senese Drives, 395–396; distance and time, 22; Florence, 257–258; Great Dolomite Road, 131, 143; Lake Como region, 147–148; Milan,

165; road signs, 21; Rome, 481; Siena, 315; Venice, 43

Casa Buonarroti (Florence): 261, 274

Casino, in Venice: 53

Castello Sforzesco (Milan): 168–169, 179

Castelrotto (Kastelruth): 129, 137–140, 141; map, 138

Castel Sant' Angelo (Rome): 409, 436–437

Castelvecchio (Verona): 119

Catacombs of Rome: 408, 443–444

Cathedrals: See Churches and cathedrals

Catherine of Siena, Saint: 323, 324

Cell phones: 24–25

Cemetery, U.S. (Tavernuzze): 394–395

Centovalli: 198

Chapel of the Reliquaries (Padua): 96, 98

Chianti: sleeping, 328–329

Chiusi: 352, 394

Churches and cathedrals: sightseeing tips, 10, 39, 62, 412; Domenican Church (Bolzano), 132; Eremitani Church (Padua), 103; Fiesole Duomo, 292; Florence Duomo, 261, 266–267; Frari Church (Venice), 45, 56, 64–65; Gesu Church (Rome), 421; Gesu Nuovo (Naples), 492–493; La Salute (Venice), 55, 56, 64, 69; Milan Duomo, 168, 170–172; Orsanmichele (Florence), 261, 267–268; Orvieto Duomo, 379, 381; Pienza Duomo, 366; Pisa Duomo, 296, 300–301; St. Anthony Basilica (Padua), 96, 98; Saint Clare Basilica (Assisi), 344; St. Francis Basilica (Assisi), 340–344; St. Ignazio (Rome), 421; St. Maria in Trastevere (Rome), 437; St. Mark's Basilica (Venice), 45, 56, 59–61, 62; St. Mary of the Angels and Martyrs (Rome), 424; St. Paul's Outside the Walls (Rome), 409, 439; St. Peter-in-Chains (Rome), 409, 411–413; St.

Peter's Basilica (Vatican City), 408, 427–432; San Biagio (Montepulciano), 363, 364; San Domenico (Siena), 316, 323; San Francesco (Fiesole), 292; San Francesco Basilica (Ravenna), 126–127; San Giorgio Maggiore (Venice), 45, 47, 56, 57, 66; San Luigi dei Francesi (Rome), 421; San Martino (Lucca), 309–310; San Nicolo (Cortona), 369; San Rufino (Assisi), 337; Santa Corona (Vicenza), 108; Santa Croce (Florence), 260, 273–274; Santa Elena (Venice), 56, 66; Sant' Agostino (San Gimignano), 357; Santa Margherita (Cortona), 369–370; Santa Margherita Church, 246; Santa Maria degli Angeli (Assisi), 345–346; Santa Maria della Immacolata Concezione (Rome), 427; Santa Maria della Vittoria (Rome), 409, 424; Santa Maria delle Grazie (Milan), 169, 179–181; Santa Maria del Popolo (Rome), 455; Santa Maria Novella (Florence), 260, 273; Santa Maria presso San Satiro (Milan), 169, 177–178; Santa Maria sopra Minerva (Assisi), 339; Santa Maria sopra Minerva (Rome), 421; Sant' Anastasia (Verona), 117–118; Sant' Apollinare Nuovo (Ravenna), 126; Santa Susanna (Rome), 424, 435; Santi Giovanni (Lucca), 310; Santo Spirito (Florence), 275; Santo Stefano (Assisi), 339; San Vitale Basilica (Ravenna), 125; San Zeno Maggiore (Verona), 112, 113, 119; Siena Duomo, 316, 320–321; Vernazza Church, 211, 213; Verona Duomo, 118; Volterra Duomo, 360

Ciampino Airport: 480

Cimabue, Giovanni: 301, 340, 342–343, 343

Cinque Terre: 201–235; cards and

passes, 203–204; cuisine, 218; festivals, 203; hiking, 202, 205–206, 220, 230–231; passes, 203–204; tours, 206–207; map, 202; planning tips, 202–203; sleeping, 212; transportation, 204–205, 234–235

Circumvesuviana: 482–483, 485, 497–498, 508

Civic Museum: *See* Museo Civico

Civita: 352, 387–392; map, 389

Clare, Saint: 333, 338, 345–346; Basilica of (Assisi), 344

"Clay Hills": 395–396

Climate: 4, 549

Colosseum (Rome): 408, 413–415; map, 414

Column of Phocas (Rome): 452–453

Como (town): 154

Como, Lake: 145, 149–150, 154; boat travel, 146–147, 149, 152–153; map, 147. *See also* Lake Como region

Compatsch: 142–143

Constantine: 162, 418, 432, 443, 535; Arch of (Rome), 409, 415; Basilica of (Rome), 448

Consulates, in Milan: 166

Corniglia: 202, 226–228; beaches, 206, 226–227; hiking, 206; map, 227; sleeping, 227–228

Correr Museum (Venice): 56, 63

Corso Palladio (Vicenza): 108–109

Cortona: 352, 367–371; map, 368

Crapolla: 508

Crete Senese Drives: 395–396

Cuisine: 30; Cinque Terre, 218; Milanese, 187; seasonal produce, 32

Culture shock: 35

Curia (Rome): 452

Customs regulations: 8

Dalmatian School (Venice): 56, 66

Dante Alighieri: 117, 273–274; House (Florence), 273; Tomb (Ravenna), 127

David (Michelangelo): 260, 264, 266

Da Vinci, Leonardo: 162, 176, 178, 179, 269–270, 309, 436; Horse

(Milan), 181; *Last Supper,* 169, 179–181; National Science and Technology Museum (Milan), 169, 181

Deruta: 393

Dining: *See* Eating; *and specific destinations*

Diocesan Museum (Cortona): 369

Discounts: 4, 16–17; Venice, 44–45

Doge's Palace (Venice): 56, 61–63

Dolomites (Dolomiti): 129–144; map, 130

Domenican Church (Bolzano): 132

Domus Aurea (Rome): 408, 413

Donatello: 64, 96, 98, 267–268, 271, 274, 321, 322

Doria Pamphilj Gallery (Rome): 409, 422

Driving: *See* Car travel

Ducal Palace (Urbino): 373–377

Duccio di Buoninsegna: 320, 321, 322, 369

Duomos: *See* Churches and cathedrals

Durazzo Park (Santa Margherita): 244–245

Eating: 30–35; budgeting, 3. *See also* Cuisine; Gelato; Markets; *and specific destinations*

Electricity: 5

E-mail: 25. *See also specific destinations*

Embassies, in Rome: 402, 546–547

Ercolano: 519, 525–526

Eremitani Church (Padua): 103

Etruscans: 292, 359, 367, 378, 382, 388, 389, 390, 394, 519, 532; Museum (Chiusi), 394; Museum (Cortona), 369; Museum (Orvieto), 381–382; Museum (Rome), 427; Museum (Volterra), 359; Tombs (Chiusi), 394; Tombs (near Cortona), 370

E.U.R. (Rome): 444–446; map, 445

Eurailpasses: 15, 17, 18, 20

Exchange rate: 3

Farm accommodations: *See* Agritourism

Feedback: 35–36; form, 552
Festivals: 547; Cinque Terre, 203; Venice, 68–69
Field of Miracles (Pisa): 296, 299–303
Fiesole: 292–294
Fiesole Duomo: 292
Fiumelatte: 151–152
Fiumicino Airport: 480
Florence (Firenze): 254–292; arrival in, 257–258; eating, 275, 285–291; helpful hints, 258–259, 262; layout of, 254–255, 259; planning tips, 254; shopping, 276; sights, 256, 258–261, 263–275; sleeping, 276–284; tourist information, 255, 257; tours, 262–263; transportation, 257–258, 262, 291–292
Florence Duomo: 261, 266–267; eating near, 286; Museum, 261, 267
Food: See Cuisine; Eating; Gelato; Markets
Foro Romano: See Roman Forum
Fra Angelico: 271, 381
Francesca, Piero della: 374
Francis, Saint: 333, 338, 339–340, 345–346; Basilica of (Assisi), 340–344
Frari Church (Venice): 45, 56, 64–65

Galileo: 100, 273, 301, 538
Galileo Galilei Airport: 291–292
Galla Placidia Mausoleum (Ravenna): 125–126
Galleria dell' Accademia: See Accademia
Galleria Doria Pamphilj (Rome): 409, 422
Galleria Vittorio Emanuele (Milan): 168, 175–176
Gelato: Florence, 275; Milan, 189; Naples, 494; Orvieto, 385–386; Padua, 105; Rome, 420, 458, 475; Sorrento, 507; Urbino, 372–373; Venice, 92
Gesu Church (Rome): 421
Gesu Nuovo (Naples): 492–493
Ghiberti, Lorenzo: 267, 268, 301, 322
Ghirlandaio, Domenico: 303, 355

Giardino Giusti (Verona): 116
Giorgione: 63, 102
Giotto di Bondone: 269–270, 273; St. Francis Basilica (Assisi), 340, 342–344, 345; Scrovegni Chapel (Padua), 95, 100–102; Tower (Florence), 261, 267
Glass: 67, 69–70; museum (Murano), 67
Glurns: 144
Gondolas of Venice: 52–53, 68, 70
Gozzoli, Benozzo: 272, 357, 394
Grand Canal (Venice): 51–55, 57; map, 52
Great Dolomite Road: 131, 143
Greco, Emilio, Museum (Orvieto): 379, 382
Gubbio: 393
Guggenheim (Peggy) Museum (Venice): 55, 56, 64
Guidebooks: 13–14; Rick Steves', 11–13

Hadrian: 436, 437, 458, 534
Harry's Bar (Venice): 57
Herculaneum: 519, 525–526
Hiking: Assisi, 345; Capri, 517, 518; Cinque Terre, 202, 205–206, 220, 230–231; passes, 203–204; tours, 206–207; Civita, 388–390; Dolomites, 131, 137–138, 142–143, 144; Lake Como, 151–152, 153–154; Levanto, 238; Marina del Cantone, 508; Mount Mottarone, 198; Portofino, 247, 248
Hill towns: 352–396; map, 353
History: 532–542
Holidays: 547
Horseback riding, in Bellagio: 152
Hotels: overview of, 25–28; reservations, 29, 551. See also specific destinations
House of Juliet (Verona): 112, 114, 116
House of the Vestal Virgins (Rome): 451

Ice Man: 132
Il Campo (Siena): 316, 317, 319;

eating, 330
Information sources: 9–10. *See also specific destinations*
Internet access: 25. *See also specific destinations*
Isola Bella: 194, 195, 196–197; map, 193
Isola Comacina: 154
Isola Madre: 194, 195, 197; map, 193
Isola Pescatori: 194, 195, 197; map, 193
Isola San Giulio: 198
Italian Lakes District: 145–161; map, 146
Italian Riviera: *See* Riviera
Italy Rail Card: 6, 15, 18

Jewish Ghetto (Venice): 53, 56, 65
Jewish Museum (Venice): 65
Juliet's House (Verona): 112, 114, 116
Julius Caesar: 449–452, 457, 533–534

Kayaking, Cinque Terre: 206, 207, 208, 220, 230

Lace: 67–68, 69; museum (Burano), 67–68
Lake Como region: 145–161; map, 146; transportation, 146–148, 160–161
Lakes: *See specific lakes*
Language: 8, 39; basic survival phrases, 550
La Rinascente: 182, 188, 272–273, 276
La Salute Church (Venice): 55, 56, 64, 69
La Scala Opera House (Milan): 168, 176–177
La Spezia: 204, 251–252
Last Supper (Da Vinci): 169, 179–181
Leaning Tower of Pisa: 296, 299–300
Lemon Grove Garden (Sorrento): 500
Lerici: 252–253
Levanto: 236–240

Lido of Venice: 57, 66
Limoncello: 223, 500
Linate Airport: 192
Locarno (Switzerland): 198
Lorenzetti, Ambrogio and Pietro: 320, 340, 342
Lucca: 304–312; map, 306

Maggiore, Lake: 192–198; boat travel, 195–196, 198; map, 193
Mail: 25. *See also specific destinations*
Malpensa Airport: 161, 191–192, 200
Mamertine Prison (Rome): 408, 416
Manarola: 202, 223–226; beaches, 206, 224; hiking, 205–206; map, 224; sleeping, 225–226
Mantegna, Andrea: 103, 119, 178
Maps: 14. *See also specific destinations*
Marco Polo Airport (Venice): 44
Marina del Cantone: 508–509
Marina di Poulo: 500
Markets: 35; seasonal produce, 32; Asciano, 396; Bagnoregio, 387; Bolzano, 134, 136; Castelrotto, 137; Cortona, 369; Florence, 261, 268, 272, 276, 285; Gubbio, 393; La Spezia, 251; Milan, 166; Montalcino, 363; Montepulciano, 364; Naples, 495; Orvieto, 378; Padua, 98–99; Pienza, 366; Pisa, 303; Ravenna, 124–125; Rome, 455, 479; San Gimignano, 355; Santa Margherita, 244, 246; Siena, 316; Venice, 45, 54, 92; Vernazza, 207; Verona, 112; Vicenza, 106
Martini, Simone: 303, 318, 320, 340, 342–343
Masaccio: 273, 274–275, 303
Mayes, Frances: 352, 367
Medici Chapels (Florence): 260, 272
Medici Riccardi Palace (Florence): 272
Menaggio: 153–154; sleeping, 158
Metro: Milan, 167–168; Rome, 404, 405
Michelangelo: 179, 252, 267–273, 275, 321, 417–418, 421, 424, 425, 428, 430, 439; *David,* 260, 264, 266; House (Florence), 261,

274; *Moses,* 409, 411–413; Sistine
    Chapel (Rome), 432, 433, 436
Milan: 162–192; arrival in, 164–165;
    eating, 186–190; helpful hints,
    165–167; nightlife, 182; planning
    tips, 163; shopping, 182; sights,
    170–182; sleeping, 182–186;
    tourist information, 164; tours,
    169–170; transportation,
    164–165, 167–168, 190–192
Milan Duomo: 168, 170–172; eating
    near, 187–189; Museum, 168,
    172–175; picnics near, 189; sleep-
    ing near, 183, 185
Money: 5, 7; budgeting, 2–3;
    exchange rate, 3
Money-saving tips: *See* Discounts
Montalcino: 352, 361–363
Montefalco: 394
Monte Ingino: 393
Montemartini Museum (Rome):
    409, 439
Monte Oliveto Maggiore Abbey: 396
Montepulciano: 352, 363–365
Monterosso al Mare: 202, 228–234;
    beaches, 206, 230; eating,
    233–234; hiking, 206, 230–231;
    map, 229; nightlife, 231; sleeping,
    231–233
Monte Rufeno Natural Park
    Reserve: 385
Monte Solaro (Capri): 518
Monte Testaccio (Rome): 442
Mosaics: 59, 60, 68, 176, 488;
    Ravenna, 122, 125–127
Moses (Michelangelo): 409, 411–413
Mount Mottarone: 198
Mount Vesuvius: 519, 526, 533
Murano: 66, 67, 69, 70
Musei Capitolini Centrale
    Montemartini (Rome): 409, 439
Museo Amedeo Lia (La Spezia): 251
Museo Archeologico (Naples):
    486–489
Museo Archeologico dell'Alto Adige
    (Bolzano): 132
Museo Bandini (Fiesole): 293
Museo Civico: Fiesole, 293;
    Montalcino, 362; Montefalco,

394; Montepulciano, 364;
    Orvieto, 381–382; Padua, 102;
    San Gimignano, 355, 357; Siena,
    316, 317–318, 320; Venice, 56,
    63
Museo Claudio Faina (Orvieto):
    381–382
Museo del Duomo (Milan): 168,
    172–175
Museo della Accademia Etrusca
    (Cortona): 369
Museo della Civilta Romana
    (Rome): 409, 446
Museo delle Sinopie (Pisa): 302
Museo dell' Opera del Duomo
    (Florence): 261, 267
Museo dell' Opera del Duomo
    (Pisa): 302
Museo dell' Opera e Panorama
    (Siena): 316, 321–322
Museo dell' Opificio delle Pietre
    Dure (Florence): 271
Museo Diocesano (Cortona): 369
Museo Diocesano (Pienza): 366
Museo di San Marco (Florence):
    260, 271
Museo di Storia della Scienza
    (Florence): 260, 273
Museo Emilo Greco (Orvieto): 379,
    382
Museo Etrusco Guarnacci
    (Volterra): 359
Museo Nazionale (Florence): 260,
    271–272
Museo Nazionale della Scienza e
    Tecnica "Leonardo da Vinci"
    (Milan): 169, 181
Museo Nazionale di San Matteo
    (Pisa): 303
Music: *See* Opera

Naples (Napoli): 482, 483–498;
    eating, 496–497; helpful hints,
    485; sights, 486–495; sleeping,
    495–496; tourist information,
    484; transportation, 484–485,
    486, 497–498
Naples Archaeological Museum:
    486–489

National Museum of Rome: 408, 422
National Picture Gallery (Siena): 316, 320
National Science and Technology Museum (Milan): 169, 181
Nero: 60, 534; Golden House (Rome), 408, 413
Nightlife: Milan, 182; Monterosso, 231; Siena, 324–325; Sorrento, 500, 502; Venice, 70

Oberbozen: 132, 134
Octagonal Hall (Rome): 409, 423–424
Olympic Theater (Vicenza): 106–108
Opera: Milan, 176–177; Naples, 492; Verona, 112, 113–114, 547
Oratory of St. John (Urbino): 376
Orsanmichele Church (Florence): 261, 267–268
Orta, Lake: 198
Orto Botanico (Padua): 100
Orvieto: 352, 378–387; map, 380
Orvieto Duomo: 379, 381
Ostia Antica: 446

Padua (Padova): 94–105; eating, 104–105; map, 97; sights, 96, 98–103; sleeping, 103–104; transportation, 95–96, 105
Paestum: 526–529; map, 527
Palatine Hill (Rome): 409, 416, 451
Palazzo Busca (Milan): 168, 176
Palazzo dei Conservatori (Rome): 408, 418
Palazzo dei Priori (Volterra): 360
Palazzo della Ragione (Padua): 98
Palazzo della Ragione (Verona): 117
Palazzo Ducale (Venice): 56, 61–63
Palazzo Mansi (Lucca): 310
Palazzo Massimo (Rome): 408, 422
Palazzo Medici Riccardi (Florence): 272
Palazzo Nuovo (Rome): 408, 418
Palazzo Piccolomini (Pienza): 366
Palazzo Pitti (Florence): 260, 274
Palazzo Vecchio (Florence): 261, 268–269

Palio (Siena): 317, 319
Palladio, Andrea: 105–110
Pallanza: 195
Pantheon (Rome): 408, 420, 458; eating near, 473, 475; map, 421
Papal audiences: 424, 434–435
Paragliding, in Bellagio: 152
Parco delle Grotte (Orvieto): 382
Pazzi Chapel (Florence): 260, 274
Peggy Guggenheim Museum (Venice): 55, 56, 64
Perledo: 149
Peter, Saint: 413, 416; Basilica of (Vatican City), 408, 427–432
Phone cards: 8–9, 23–24
Piazza Colonna (Rome): 458–459
Piazza dei Signori (Verona): 117
Piazza del Duomo (Pisa): 296, 299–303
Piazza della Repubblica (Florence): 272
Piazza della Scala (Milan): 176
Piazza della Signoria (Florence): 264, 286, 288–289
Piazza del Popolo (Rome): 399, 453, 455
Piazza di Spagna (Rome): 455, 459–460
Piazza Duomo (Milan): 175
Piazza Duomo (Orvieto): 378, 379, 381
Piazza Erbe (Padua): 98–99, 104
Piazza Erbe (Verona): 114, 116, 117
Piazza Frutta (Padua): 98–99, 104
Piazzale Michelangelo (Florence): 261, 275
Piazza Navona (Rome): 457–458
Piazza San Giorgio (Varenna): 150, 159–160
Piazza San Marco (Venice): 56, 57, 59–63, 70; eating, 59, 71, 90–92; map, 58; sleeping near, 72–76
Piazza Santissima Annunziata (Florence): 266
Piazza Santo Spirito (Florence): 290–291
Piazza Venezia (Rome): 408, 418–420
Piccolomini Library (Siena): 321
Picnics: 35. See also Markets; and

specific destinations
Pienza: 352, 365–367
Pienza Duomo: 366
Pinacoteca: Assisi, 345; Siena, 316, 320; Vatican City, 433, 436; Volterra, 360
Pinacoteca Ambrosiana (Milan): 169, 178
Pisa: 295–304; eating, 304; map, 298; sights, 299–303; sleeping, 303–304; transportation, 297, 304
Pisa Duomo: 296, 300–301; Museum, 302
Pisano, Giovanni: 102, 296, 300–301, 301, 322
Pisano, Nicola: 302, 321
Pitti Palace (Florence): 260, 274
Pizza: 32–33. *See also specific destinations*
Poldi Pezzoli Museum (Milan): 169, 178
Pompeii: 519–525; map, 520
Ponte Sant' Angelo (Rome): 437
Ponte Vecchio (Florence): 261, 270–271
Porta Borsari (Verona): 118–119
Porta Ostiense (Rome): 441–442
Portofino: 236, 242, 247–248
Portovenere: 236, 252–253
Positano: 509, 511–515; map, 513
Post offices: 25. *See also specific destinations*
Protestant Cemetery (Rome): 442
Puccini, Giacomo: 308; House (Lucca), 310
Punta del Capo: 500
Punta Mesco: 230, 238
Pyramid of Gaius Cestius (Rome): 441

Quercia, Jacopo della: 309, 322–323

Railpasses: 15, 17, 18, 20
Rapallo: 243, 248
Raphael: 178, 269–270, 375, 420, 422, 425, 433, 436, 455; Rooms (Vatican City), 432–433
Ravenna: 122–128; map, 124
Regattas: 69, 547

Reifenstein Castle: 144
Renaissance: 100–102, 162, 178–179, 365–366, 373–376, 537–538; Florence, 254, 263–271, 275; Venice, 64–65, 66; Vicenza, 105–110
Reservations, hotel: 29; form for, 551
Restaurants: *See* Eating; *and specific destinations*
Rialto Bridge (Venice): 54, 76
Rimini: 127
Rinascente: 182, 188, 272–273, 276
Riomaggiore: 202, 219–223; beaches, 206, 220; eating, 223; hiking, 205–206, 220–221; map, 221; sleeping, 221–222
Risorgimento Museum (Milan): 168, 178
Riva di Biasio (Venice): 53
Riviera: 236–253; map, 237. *See also* Cinque Terre
Robbia, Luca della: 266, 267, 364
Rocca Maggiore (Assisi): 345
Roman Amphitheater: See Amphitheater
Roman Forum (Assisi): 345
Roman Forum (Rome): 408, 415, 448; map, 447; walking tour, 448–453
Roman Theater: *See* Teatro Romano
Rome: 397–481; arrival in, 401; eating, 471–479; helpful hints, 402–403; layout of, 399; planning tips, 397–399; sights, 408–409, 410–460; sleeping, 460–470; tourist information, 399, 401; tours, 406–407, 410; transportation, 401, 404–406, 479–481; walking tours, self-guided, 446–460. *See also specific neighborhoods*
Romeo and Juliet, in Verona: 112, 114, 116, 117
Royal Palace (Naples): 492

St. Anthony Basilica (Padua): 96, 98
St. Brizio Chapel (Orvieto): 381
Saint Catherine Sanctuary (Siena): 316, 324

Saint Clare Basilica (Assisi): 344
St. Cristina: 143–144
St. Francis Basilica (Assisi): 340–344
St. Ignazio (Rome): 421
St. James Church (Santa
    Margherita): 244
St. Maria in Trastevere Church
    (Rome): 437
St. Mark's Basilica (Venice): 45, 56,
    59–61, 62
St. Mark's Square (Venice): 56, 57,
    59–63, 70; eating, 59, 71, 90–92;
    map, 58; sleeping near, 72–76
St. Mary of the Angels (Assisi):
    345–346
St. Mary of the Angels and Martyrs
    (Rome): 424
St. Moritz (Switzerland): transporta-
    tion, 161
St. Patrick's Well (Orvieto):
    382–383
St. Paul's Outside the Walls
    (Rome): 409, 439
St. Peter-in-Chains Church (Rome):
    409, 411–413
St. Peter's Basilica (Vatican City):
    408, 427–432; map, 431
St. Teresa in Ecstasy (Bernini): 409,
    424
Salerno: 529–531; map, 530
Saltria: 140, 142, 143
San Biagio Church
    (Montepulciano): 363, 364
San Domenico Church (Siena): 316,
    323
San Erasmo (Santa Margherita): 244
San Francesco Basilica (Ravenna):
    126–127
San Francesco Church (Fiesole): 292
San Fruttuoso Abbey: 247, 248
San Galgano Monastery: 395
San Gimignano: 352, 355–359;
    map, 356
San Giorgio Maggiore (Venice): 45,
    47, 56, 57, 66
San Giovanni d'Asso: 396
San Luigi dei Francesi (Rome): 421
San Martino Cathedral (Lucca):
    309–310

San Nicolo Church (Cortona): 369
San Pietro in Vincoli (Rome): 409,
    411–413
San Rocco School (Venice): 56, 65, 70
San Rufino Church (Assisi): 337
Sansevero Chapel (Naples): 493–492
San Silvestro (Venice): 54–55
San Simeone Piccolo (Venice): 53
Santa Corona Church (Vicenza): 108
Santa Croce Church (Florence):
    260, 273–274
Santa Elena (Venice): 56, 66
Sant' Agostino Church (San
    Gimignano): 357
Santa Margherita Church: 246
Santa Margherita Church
    (Cortona): 369–370
Santa Margherita Ligure: 236,
    242–250; eating, 249–250; history
    of, 243; map, 245; sights,
    244–247; sleeping, 248–249;
    transportation, 243, 250
Santa Maria degli Angeli (Assisi):
    345–346
Santa Maria degli Angeli e dei
    Martiri (Rome): 424
Santa Maria del Fiori (Florence):
    261, 266–267
Santa Maria della Immacolata
    Concezione (Rome): 427
Santa Maria della Scala (Siena): 316,
    322–323
Santa Maria della Vittoria (Rome):
    409, 424
Santa Maria delle Grazie (Milan):
    169, 179–181
Santa Maria delle Salute (Venice):
    55, 56, 64, 69
Santa Maria del Popolo (Rome): 455
Santa Maria Novella Church
    (Florence): 260, 273
Santa Maria presso San Satiro
    (Milan): 169, 177–178
Santa Maria sopra Minerva (Assisi):
    339
Santa Maria sopra Minerva (Rome):
    421
Sant' Anastasia Church (Verona):
    117–118

Index 563

Sant' Angelo (Venice): 55
Sant' Apollinare in Classe (Ravenna): 126
Sant' Apollinare Nuovo (Ravenna): 126
Santa Susanna (Rome): 424, 435
Santi Giovanni Church (Lucca): 310
San Tomà (Venice): 55
Santo Spirito Church (Florence): 275
Santo Stefano Church (Assisi): 339
San Vitale Basilica (Ravenna): 125
San Zeno Maggiore (Verona): 112, 113, 119
San Zulian Church (Venice): 47
Sasso Lungo: 140–141, 143
Schlern, the: 140–141, 143
Science and Technology Museum (Milan): 169, 181
Science Museum (Florence): 260, 273
Scrovegni Chapel (Padua): 95, 100–102
Scuola Dalmata dei San Giorgio (Venice): 56, 66
Scuola Grande di San Rocco (Venice): 56, 65, 70
Seasons: 4
Sestri Levante: 236, 240–242
Sforza Castle (Milan): 168–169, 179
Shakespeare, William: 112, 449; theater productions, 108, 116
Shopping: 39; Assisi, 338–339; budgeting, 3; Florence, 276; Milan, 182; Siena, 324; VAT refunds, 7–8; Venice, 69–70
Siena: 313–332; eating, 330–332; maps, 318, 326; nightlife, 324–325; shopping, 324; sights, 316–323; sleeping, 325–330; tourist information, 314; transportation, 314–315, 332
Siena Duomo: 316, 320–321; Museum, 316, 321–322
Siena Tower: 316, 320
Sightseeing: best three-week trip, 6, 7; budgeting, 3; general tips, 10–11; opening hours, 3–4, 5, 10; priorities, 4–5. See also specific sights and destinations
Signorelli, Luca: 360, 369, 381, 396
Sistine Chapel (Vatican City): 432,

433, 436
Siusi: 140
Skiing, in the Dolomites: 131, 143–144
Sleeping: 25–29; air-conditioning, 4, 26–27; budgeting, 3; reservations, 29; reservations form, 551. See also specific destinations
Soccer, in Milan: 182
Sorrento: 482, 498–508; eating, 505–507; map, 501; nightlife, 500, 502; sights, 499–500; sleeping, 502–505; transportation, 499, 507–508
South Tirol Museum of Archaeology (Bolzano): 132
Spanish Quarter (Naples): 489, 491–492
Spanish Steps (Rome): 455, 459; eating near, 475–476
Special events: 547; Cinque Terre, 203; Venice, 68–69
Spello: 394
Straw Market (Florence): 261, 268, 276
Stresa: 192–198; eating, 199–200; map, 193; sleeping, 199
Subway: Milan, 167–168; Rome, 404, 405
Suisi: 142
Swimming: See Beaches

Tabularium (Rome): 418
Tavernuzze: 394–395
Tavola caldas: overview of, 33, 34
Taxes: VAT refunds, 7–8
Taxis: tipping, 31. See also specific destinations
Teatrale alla Scala (Milan): 168, 176–177
Teatro Olimpico (Vicenza): 106–108
Teatro Romano: Fiesole, 292–293; Verona, 116, 118; Volterra, 360
Telephones: 23–25, 543–546
Temple of Antoninus and Faustina (Rome): 449–450
Temple of Julius Caesar (Rome): 449, 451
Temple of Saturn (Rome): 452
Temple of Vesta (Rome): 451

Tennis, in Sorrento: 500
Testaccio (Rome): 441–442; map, 441
Tiepolo, Giovanni Battista: 63, 64, 102, 109–110
Tintoretto: 61, 62, 63, 65, 66, 102, 310
Tipping: 31
Titian: 63, 64, 65, 102, 118, 178, 269, 270, 422, 425
Torcello: 66, 68
Tordibetto: sleeping, 349
Torre dei Lamberti (Verona): 117
Torre del Mangia (Siena): 316, 320
Torre del Moro (Orvieto): 382
Torre Grossa (San Gimignano): 357
Torre Guinigi (Lucca): 310
Tourist information: 9–10. See also specific destinations
Tours: Florence, 262–263; of Italy, 14–15; Milan, 169–170; Rome, 406–407, 410; Venice, 49, 51, 66
Train travel: 15–20; Assisi, 334, 350; best three-week trip, 6, 7; Bolzano, 137; Central Italy hill towns, 353–354; Cinque Terre, 204, 234; Circumvesuviana, 482–483, 485, 497–498, 508; cost and distance, 17; Florence, 257, 291; Lake Como region, 146–148, 160–161; map, 19; Milan, 164–165, 186, 190–191; Naples, 484–485; Padua, 95–96, 105; Ravenna, 128; Rome, 401, 479–480; schedules, 16; Siena, 314–315, 331; Sorrento, 508; Varenna, 145–146; Venice, 43, 53, 92, 93; Verona, 113, 122; Vicenza, 106, 111
Trajan's Column, Market, and Forum (Rome): 408, 416–417
Transportation: 15–23; budgeting, 3; map, 19. See also Boat travel; Bus travel; Car travel; Train travel
Trastevere (Rome): 399, 437, 439, 471; eating, 471; map, 438; sleeping, 468–469
Tremezzo: 154
Trevi Fountain (Rome): 409, 422, 459; eating, 476

Turkish Exchange (Venice): 53
Tuscany: hill towns, 352–378, 395–396. See also Fiesole; Florence; Lucca; Pisa; Siena

Uccello, Paolo: 270, 375
Uffizi Gallery (Florence): 260, 269–270; map, 269; reservations, 258, 270
Umbria: 337, 338. See also Assisi
University of Padua: 94, 99–100
Urbino: 371–378; map, 373

Val Gardena: 143–144
Vaporetto (Venice): 43, 48–49, 66; Grand Canal tour, 51–55, 57
Varenna: 145–146, 147–152, 160–161; eating, 158–160; map, 151; sleeping, 154–157
Varenna Castle: 150
Vasari, Giorgio: 266, 271, 300, 310
Vatican City: 397, 398–399, 434–435; eating, 479; maps, 429, 435; papal audiences, 424, 434–435; post office, 434; sights, 427–437; sleeping near, 469–470; tours, 406–407, 434. See also Rome
Vatican Museum (Vatican City): 408, 432–433, 436
VAT refunds: 7–8
Venetian glass: 67, 69–70
Venice: 40–93; arrival in, 43–44; eating, 82–92; festivals, 68–69; helpful hints, 45–48; layout of, 42; nightlife, 70; passes, 44–45; planning tips, 40, 42; shopping, 69–70; sights, 51–68; sleeping, 71–82; tourist information, 42–43; tours, 49, 51, 66; transportation, 43–44, 48–49, 92, 93. See also specific neighborhoods
Venice Biennale: 57, 69
Venice canals: See Canals of Venice
Venice lagoon: 40, 57, 66–68; map, 67
Vernazza: 202, 207–219; beaches, 206, 208; eating, 217, 219; hiking, 206; map, 209; sights, 208, 210–211, 213; sleeping, 212, 213–217

Vernazza Castle: 211
Vernazza Church: 211, 213
Verona: 112–122; eating, 121–122; map, 115; sights, 114, 116–119; sleeping, 119–121; transportation, 122
Verona Duomo: 118
Veronese, Paolo: 61, 63, 102, 310
Verrocchio, Andrea del: 268
Vesuvius: 519, 526, 533
Via Appia Antica (Rome): 442–444
Via Condotti (Rome): 453, 455, 459
Via del Corso (Rome): 399, 419, 453, 455, 458–459; map, 454
Via Fillungo (Lucca): 308–309
Via Montenapoleone (Milan): 182
Via Palestro (Santa Margherita): 246
Via Speronari (Milan): 177–178
Via Spiga (Milan): 182
Via Toledo (Naples): 489, 491
Vicenza: 105–111; map, 107
Victor Emmanuel Monument (Rome): 420
Villa Borghese (Rome): 409, 425–427
Villa Carlotta (Lake Como): 154
Villa Cipressi (Varenna): 151
Villa Durazzo (Santa Margherita): 245
Villa Giulia Museo Nazionale Etrusco (Rome): 409, 427

Villa Guinigi (Lucca): 310
Villa Jovis (Capri): 518
Villa la Rotonda (Vicenza): 109
Villa Serbelloni (Bellagio): 152, 157
Villa Taranto Botanical Gardens: 195, 197–198
Villa Valmarana Ai Nani (Vicenza): 109–110
Vino Nobile di Montepulciano: 363, 364
Vittorio Emanuele Gallery (Milan): 168, 175–176
Volastra: 206
Volterra: 352, 359–361
Volterra Duomo: 360

Water taxis, in Venice: 44, 49
Weather: 4, 549
Wine and vineyards: 34; Cinque Terre, 211, 218, 226; Montalcino, 361, 362, 363; Montefalco, 394; Montepulciano, 363, 364; Orvieto, 378, 383
Wood carvings: 143–144, 339
World War II: 103, 118, 162, 179, 196, 208, 210, 230–231, 302, 338, 444–445, 541–542; U.S. Cemetery (Tavernuzze), 394–395

ABOUT THE AUTHOR

RICK STEVES

RICK STEVES is on a mission: to help make European travel accessible and meaningful for Americans. Rick has spent 100 days every year since 1973 exploring Europe. He's researched and written 24 travel guidebooks. He writes and hosts the public television series *Rick Steves Europe*, now in its seventh season. With the help of his hardworking staff of 60 at Europe through the Back Door, Rick organizes and leads tours of Europe and offers an information-packed Web site (www.ricksteves.com). Rick, his wife (and favorite travel partner) Anne, and their two teenage children, Andy and Jackie, call Edmonds, just north of Seattle, home.

Free, fresh travel tips, all year long.

Visit **www.ricksteves.com**
to get Rick's free
64-page newsletter... and more!

Rick Steves

COUNTRY GUIDES 2004

Best of Europe
Best of Eastern Europe
France
Germany, Austria & Switzerland
Great Britain
Ireland
Italy
Scandinavia
Spain & Portugal

CITY GUIDES 2004

Amsterdam, Bruges & Brussels
Florence & Tuscany
London
Paris
Provence & The French Riviera
Rome
Venice

MORE EUROPE FROM RICK STEVES

Europe 101
Europe Through the Back Door 2004
Mona Winks
Postcards from Europe

More Savvy. More Surprising. More Fun.

PHRASE BOOKS & DICTIONARIES

French, Italian & German
French
German
Italian
Portuguese
Spanish

VHS RICK STEVES' EUROPE

The Best of Ireland
Bulgaria, Eastern Turkey, Slovenia
    & Croatia
The Heart of Italy
London & Paris
Prague, Amsterdam & the Swiss Alps
Romantic Germany & Berlin
Rome, Caesar's Rome, Sicily
South England, Heart of England & Scotland
Southwest Germany & Portugal
Travel Skills Special
Venice & Veneto 2003

DVD RICK STEVES' EUROPE

Rick Steves' Europe
    All Thirty Shows 2000-2003
Britain & Ireland
Exotic Europe
Germany, the Swiss Alps
    & Travel Skills
Italy